RIGHTS, DUTIES AND THE BODY

Rights, Duties and the Body

Law and Ethics of the Maternal–Fetal Conflict

ROSAMUND SCOTT
King's College London

·HART·
PUBLISHING
OXFORD – PORTLAND OREGON

Published in North America (US and Canada) by
Hart Publishing
c/o International Specialized Book Services
5804 NE Hassalo Street
Portland, Oregon
97213-3644
USA

Distributed in the Netherlands, Belgium and Luxembourg by
Intersentia, Churchillaan 108
B2900 Schoten
Antwerpen
Belgium

First published 2002, reprinted with corrections 2004

Hart Publishing is a specialist legal publisher based in Oxford, England.
To order further copies of this book or to request a list of other
publications please write to:

Hart Publishing, Salter's Boatyard, Folly Bridge,
Abingdon Road, Oxford OX1 4LB
Telephone: +44 (0)1865 245533 or Fax: +44 (0)1865 794882
e-mail: mail@hartpub.co.uk
WEBSITE: http//www.hartpub.co.uk

British Library Cataloguing in Publication Data
Data Available
ISBN 1–84113–134–2 (hardback)

Typeset by Hope Services (Abingdon) Ltd.
Printed and bound in Great Britain by
TJ International Ltd, Padstow, Cornwall

To Riccardo
and my parents

Acknowledgements

Since a much earlier incarnation of this book was a doctoral thesis, my greatest debt is to my supervisor, Professor Andrew Grubb. How difficult was the task of supervising a student with a background in philosophy and law in the production of a thesis that would be satisfactory in both respects, only he can say. For my part, I can report that he always received my work with interest and enthusiasm, offered invaluable criticism (without which the work would have been much the poorer) and, not least, great encouragement. I thank him for the opportunity to work with him and learn from his abundant and astute knowledge of medical law (and much else besides) and for the skilful blend of help and freedom he gave me in this process.

I am also deeply grateful to my publisher, Richard Hart, for his decision to accept my book proposal.

The philosophical sections of the book greatly benefited from the guidance and criticism of Ms Pat Walsh and Dr Roger Crisp. Pat Walsh read drafts of Part I, providing careful and imaginative criticism in the process. I thank her for the generosity of her assistance. For similar generosity I am also indebted to Roger Crisp, who helped with Part I, and a section in chapter seven. For his thoughtful comments, judicious criticism and encouragement I am very grateful. I would also like to thank Dr Robert Wintemute for helpful comments on a section of chapter four and Dr John Stanton-Ife for advising on a point in the General Introduction. Needless to say, the responsibility for the final content and its shortcomings rests with me.

Additionally, Professors Ian Kennedy and Alexander McCall Smith I thank for their great encouragement. Professor Jonathan Glover expressed both interest and faith in the book as it took shape; for this I am very grateful.

I would also like to thank various friends for their interest in and enthusiasm about the work at different times: Brigid Ballard, John Ballard, Donatella Cifali, Valerie Duvivier, Daniel Hallgarten, Stephen Jones, Tuija Kauppinen, Nieves La Casta, Ermanno Mattio, Liz McCarty, Catherine Paxton, Paul Robinson (who also kindly read material) and Rachel Short. John Curran has been a particular source of advice.

Turning to my family, my parents have been both loving and visionary in their support, for which I will always be grateful. My brother and his wife, godfather and his wife and parents-in-law always showed great faith in the project. But I owe most to my husband, Riccardo, for his belief, love and support.

Rosamund Scott

An adapted section of chapter two was previously published as "The Pregnant Woman and the Good Samaritan: Can a Woman have a Duty to Undergo a Caesarean Section?", (2000) 20(3) *Oxford Journal of Legal Studies* 407–36 and a version of chapter six appeared as "Maternal Duties Toward the Unborn? Soundings from the Law of Tort", (2000) 8(1) *Medical Law Review* 1–68. These are reproduced herein by kind permission of Oxford University Press.

Contents

PART III: THE LEGAL ARGUMENTS FROM DUTY

Table of Cases

Table of Legislation

United States

General Introduction:
The Problem and the Issues Raised

THE ISSUES explored in this book relate to part of a cluster of problems which have come to be known as instances of "maternal–fetal conflict". This is an unfortunate term, since pregnant women are generally renowned for putting the interests of the fetus they are carrying before their own, for worrying enormously about the potential impact of their choices and actions on the fetus and for doing all they can to enhance its wellbeing. Indeed, one obstetrician strikingly observed that the majority of women he sees "would cut off their heads to save their babies".[1] On occasion, however, a pregnant woman may make a treatment choice (perhaps for religious reasons) or conduct a part of her daily life in a way which risks or causes harm to her unborn child. Assuming she has chosen to carry this fetus, or not to abort in the case of an unplanned pregnancy (not necessarily a straightforward matter in itself),[2] the question arises as to the degree of her moral and legal responsibilities in pregnancy. How minimal or how great are her duties and how far do her rights extend as regards the unborn other which is, for nine months, inside her? The answer to this question has typically been driven by either one of two views which together reflect a great deal of what has been written in the (mostly legal) debate on the subject: that a pregnant woman "must have legal rights" or that she "must have legal duties", answers accompanied by attendant acceptance or criticism of the state of the law under discussion. In essence, however, the answer is not that she has rights but not duties, nor duties but not rights. But understanding this entails consideration of a complex web of moral and legal arguments.

In an attempt to move beyond the impasse in much of what has been said about this topic, this book explores the moral and legal issues in the following three ways. First, it examines the ethics of the "conflict" primarily as it occurs within the medical treatment context and secondarily as an aspect of a pregnant woman's daily life. Second, it explores and analyses the relevant English, American and, to some extent, Canadian law. Third and overall, given the book's joint philosophical and legal approach, it seeks to justify the existence of a pregnant woman's legal right to

---

[1] Statement of Dr M Golbus, Professor of Obstetrics, Gynecology and Reproductive Science, and Director of Reproductive Genetics Unit, Univ. of Cal. Medical Center, San Francisco, made at Planned Parenthood Conference on "Human Fertility Regulation: Technological Frontiers and their Implications", New York (14 Dec. 1984), as cited in N Rhoden, "The Judge in the Delivery Room: The Emergence of Court-Ordered Cesareans", (1986) 74 *Cal L Rev* 1951, 1959.

[2] Abortion may be problematic for the pregnant woman for religious reasons or there may be difficulties with access to abortion, for instance for financial reasons in the United States. These issues are touched on in due course. Questions of a pregnant woman's rights and obligations also arise, of course, in relation to abortion itself.

refuse medical treatment required by the fetus she carries where this does exist, for instance in England and in some US states, and to promote it where it does not, for instance in all those US states which have yet to decide the issue or to decide it in her favour. Since the granting of such a right is really a conclusion, not an argument in itself, such a justification—which the debate so far has barely touched on—is clearly required. The book also explores and rejects the idea of a maternal legal duty of care toward the fetus, with one exception.

I. WHAT IS THE "MATERNAL–FETAL CONFLICT"?

The term "maternal–fetal conflict" concerns two main senses in which a pregnant woman may cause prenatal harm. First, she may refuse medical treatment, caesarean or other surgery, forceps delivery or a therapy that is estimated to enhance fetal well-being or preserve fetal life typically,[3] but not necessarily, for religious reasons. (She might also refuse prenatal screening or indicated treatment resulting therefrom. These issues are not discussed directly here, but some of my arguments would have application to them.[4]) Second, aspects of her daily life could be detrimental to the well-being of her unborn child, such as smoking, the consumption of alcohol and drug-taking or, for that matter, her failure to take care in crossing a road. The latter issue, encompassing the question of a pregnant woman's prenatal obligations in the course of her general conduct is briefly touched on by way of counterpoint since consideration of this issue may illuminate our understanding of my primary concern—the nature and extent of maternal duties within the treatment context. Although there are relatively few instances of maternal refusal of medical treatment during pregnancy compared with the incidence of general maternal conduct which may cause prenatal harm, the former is an issue of acute moral interest and considerable legal significance, raising—in particular—important issues of principle. The latter, by contrast is a comparatively diffuse social issue which tends to call more for a broad-based policy analysis.

Regarding the treatment context, the classic maternal refusal is of delivery of the fetus by caesarean section. The legal cases have largely concerned this issue and, given that a caesarean section is major invasive surgery which also carries a risk of death estimated to be four times that of natural delivery, a woman's refusal thereof may present us with a particularly acute instance of potential maternal-fetal conflict.[5] A pregnant woman's refusal of medical treatment needed by the fetus

---

[3] For some indication of the possibilities see the notes to ch. 1, s. II.

[4] For thoughts on this issue, see e.g. I Feitshans, "Legislating to Preserve Women's Autonomy during Pregnancy", (1995) 14 *Med and Law* 397 and D Heyd, "Prenatal diagnosis: whose right?", (1995) 21 *JME* 292.

[5] The *Baby Boy Doe* decision, which I discuss in various chapters, described the risk of death from caesarean birth as 1 in 10,000, compared with 1 in 20,000 to 50,000 in normal birth. 632 NE 2d 326, 328 (Ill App 1 Dist 1994).

may well be even more complex than the issue of abortion (sometimes described as an instance of "maternal–fetal conflict"). It is certainly more complex than the situation of a non-pregnant competent adult patient refusing treatment, who clearly has a moral and legal right to refuse even life-sustaining medical treatment for herself:[6] in such a case the patient—the right-holder—is the only person whose life is at stake. By contrast, a pregnant woman's exercise of a right to refuse medical treatment clearly has implications for another being—the fetus. Further, we are generally concerned with a woman who has chosen to carry her unborn child to term and who may, for this reason, be thought to owe it extensive moral duties. Hence, regardless of whether or not the fetus has any moral rights, given a woman's share in the moral responsibility for its continued existence, she may well have some moral obligation to accept treatment for the fetus in at least some circumstances. The difficulty is to determine which. Does she have the duty to submit to any treatment the fetus might require, including that which goes against the tenets of her religious faith, or that regarding which the physical burdens are very great?

Further, moral and legal analysis is made more complex by the fact that occasionally a fetus will die as a result of a treatment refusal, whilst on other occasions a child will subsequently be born harmed as a result of its mother's decision to decline certain intervention: sometimes the result of a refused caesarean may be a brain-damaged child; or the treatment refused—such as corrective rather than life-saving surgery—will by definition result in harm rather than death. Hence there is a need to provide an analysis which covers not only fetal death, but also the prospect of harm to the "future child" (who is not yet but will be born)[7] who is sometimes the subject in these cases. It is the future child who may be harmed particularly where a woman's general conduct is in issue.

I now explain why a joint ethical and legal approach to the problem is important and helpful and how I bring these aspects together here.

II. THE RELATIONSHIP BETWEEN THE ETHICS AND THE LAW OF THE MATERNAL–FETAL CONFLICT

I shall first outline the current legal position and some of the anomalies and concerns relating to it.

Following a wave of compelled obstetric interventions in the United States in the 1980s which reached England in the early 1990s, the legal position in England is now relatively clear. The decision of the Court of Appeal in *Re MB (Cesarean Section)*[8] (affirmed by the Court of Appeal in 1998 in *St George's Healthcare NHS Trust* v. *S, R* v. *Collins and Others, ex parte S*)[9] held that a pregnant woman has the legal right "for religious reasons, other reasons, or for no reasons at all" to choose

---

[6] Subject to exceptions touched upon in the body of the book.
[7] See discussion in ch. 1.
[8] [1997] 8 Med LR 217.
[9] [1998] 3 All ER 673.

to decline *any* medical intervention for the fetus's sake, essentially because the fetus has no legal personality of its own.[10] In the United States, the position is only clear in some states. The caesarean decision of the Appellate Court of Illinois in *Baby Boy Doe*[11] (following the somewhat uncertain lead provided by the District of Columbia Court of Appeals' 1990 decision in *Re AC*)[12] held that a pregnant woman has the right to refuse treatment as invasive as a caesarean, although it left open the question of less invasive interventions. In 1997 the same court held in *Re Fetus Brown* that a pregnant woman has the right to refuse a blood transfusion, deeming transfusions to be invasive treatment.[13] In some US states therefore, the legal position regarding invasive treatment is settled, although the position in relation to *non*-invasive treatment appears to remain open and the position in those states which have yet to decide the issue is distinctly unclear. (Some states only have relatively early cases in their law reports which reject the idea of a pregnant woman's legal rights in the treatment context.[14] Given the general developments in patients' rights since these cases were decided, they would now be very dubious precedents.)

Importantly, notwithstanding the upholding of maternal rights in the cases mentioned, there was clearly judicial concern both in *Re MB* and *Re Fetus Brown* regarding the question of the alignment of the law and ethics of the maternal–fetal conflict, a question the court in *Re MB*—which was "not one of morals"—considered beyond its scope. Likewise in the latest English caesarean case of *St George's* the potential gap between a woman's moral and legal obligations to her fetus was noted. Moreover, the Court of Appeal in *Re MB* considered it anomalous that a woman is not permitted to abort after viability (unless her life or health are at serious risk or the fetus is at risk of serious disability), but can refuse treatment resulting in fetal death for any or no reason even at the point of birth. In other words, notwithstanding the fetus's lack of legal personality, the case itself can be said to acknowledge that it leaves unanswered the question of *why* a pregnant woman should be able to harm the fetus in this way. Indeed, given that the fetus is not deemed a legal person essentially because such personhood would conflict with a pregnant woman's legal rights, then the fetus's lack of such personhood cannot of its own accord explain and justify such rights.

Another issue concerns the question of a woman's competence to decide treatment questions. Although *Re MB* holds that a pregnant woman can refuse treatment needed by the fetus "for religious reasons, other reasons, or for no reasons at all", most importantly her presumed competence, as an adult, must not be rebutted if she is to be able to exercise this right. In this regard, although the decision gave detailed guidance as to the issue of a pregnant woman's competence to make treatment decisions, even on

---

[10] [1997] 8 Med LR at 227.

[11] 632 NE 2d 326 (Ill App 1 Dist 1994).

[12] 573 A 2d (DC App 1990).

[13] 294 Ill App 3d 159 (Ill App 1 Dist 1997).

[14] *Jefferson* v. *Griffin Spalding County Hospital Authority*, Ga 274 SE 2d 457 (1981); *Raleigh Fitkin-Paul Morgan Memorial Hospital* v. *Anderson* 201 A 2d 537 (1964), cert denied, 12 LE 2d 1032.

judgment it is apparent that the determination of a pregnant woman's competence will sometimes be a highly complex and difficult matter. Moreover, certain unforeseen issues may well have a bearing upon the operation of the law. In essence, given that the test for competence in English medical law includes a requirement that the patient be able to balance risks and needs—which in this context often translates, I point out, as the morally charged issue of risks to the woman versus fetal medical needs—there is scope for the moral concerns and judgments of others regarding a woman's decision to exercise her right to refuse treatment needed by the fetus to *permeate the determination of her competence* to decide treatment questions herself. The result may be that she is, in effect, illegitimately deemed *in*competent. In this way, her legal right would thus be removed through the "back door", raising serious concerns both at common law and under the Human Rights Act 1998.

Further, no doubt with a view to the way in which a woman's decision to refuse treatment may be viewed by others, the court in *Re MB* legitimised the option of attempting to *persuade* a pregnant woman to accept treatment for the fetus's sake, but gave no direction on this issue. That is, the court did not consider what degree and form of persuasion would be *consistent with a woman's right*, questions which (as I shall explore) have been closely considered in related contexts in the United States and which should be considered in England under the Human Rights Act 1998 given the concern, under the European Convention on Human Rights, that rights should be guaranteed in practice, not just in theory.[15]

In the light of these points about some of the leading decisions, an *ethical justification* of the idea of a pregnant woman's legal right to refuse medical treatment is essential to the understanding and acceptance of such rights where these exist and to their promotion where they do not. Thus, in part such an analysis may offer some indication of what the law should be in the United States regarding treatment which cannot be characterised as invasive, or in those states yet to decide the issue either in any form or in favour of the pregnant woman. Of the various questions which have been identified about the relationship between law and morality, the project of morally defending the idea of a pregnant woman's treatment rights entails subjecting the idea of a pregnant woman's legal right to refuse medical treatment to moral appraisal.[16] The intention at one point is also to offer *practical*

---

[15] "The Convention is intended to guarantee not rights that are theoretical or illusory but rights that are practical and effective." *Airey* v. *Ireland* (1979–80) 2 EHRR 305, para. 24. See further ch. 4.

[16] HLA Hart identified essentially four questions about the relationship between law and morality: "The first is . . . Has the development of the law been influenced by morals?. . .The second [is] . . . Must some reference to morality enter into an adequate definition of law or legal system? Or is it just a contingent fact that law and morals often overlap . . . and that they share a common vocabulary of rights, obligations, and duties? . . . A third question [is] . . . Is law open to moral criticism? Or does the admission that a rule is a valid legal rule preclude moral criticism or condemnation of it by reference to moral standards or principles? Few perhaps . . . would find any contradiction or paradox in the assertion that a rule of law was valid and yet conflicted with some binding moral principle requiring behaviour contrary to that demanded by the legal rule. . . .The fourth question is . . . Is the fact that certain conduct is by common standards immoral sufficient to justify making that conduct punishable by law?". Thus, it is with the third question that I am concerned. HLA Hart, *Law, Liberty and Morality* (Oxford: Oxford University Press, 1963) 1–4. Regarding the debate between positivism and natural law I can thus remain neutral.

guidance in the situation of maternal treatment refusals, in particular upon issues relating to competence and the ideas of persuasion, discussion and counselling.

Turning to address the links between the ethics and the law, it is my view that the maternal–fetal conflict is not so much a problem inhering in the legal enforcement of presumed moral obligations, as there has been a tendency to suppose. Rather, the difficulty is to understand why a supposedly voluntarily pregnant woman, *in theory* at least, justifiably has moral and legal rights in self-determination and bodily integrity throughout pregnancy which support her legal right to refuse treatment even though this may lead to fetal harm or death. (This is not to deny that *in practice* on some occasions a moral duty may clearly exist about which questions as to the appropriateness of legal enforcement would then arise.) Against the backdrop of liberalism in front of which medical law plays out, at least part of the reason we grant rights in relation to the individual's very personal interests lies in the difficulty of judging the "reasonableness" of matters which such rights protect and, concomitantly, the "reasonableness" of the decision to exercise a right in such contexts, at least where such rights are exercised—as they likely are—for what I call "serious" reasons. The example of the religious reason is here in point. In turn, this foreshadows the problem of trying to determine when an area of interest which is protected by a *prima facie* right should "give way to" a duty. Thus, if the medical treatment context generally invokes a patient's interests and rights in self-determination and bodily integrity, then how would we determine when, if ever, a woman has the duty—moral or legal—to accept medical treatment for the fetus? This *is* the problem, in effect, of the maternal–fetal conflict within the medical treatment context and it lies at the heart, not only of an ethical analysis of the conflict, but also of the relevant law. In effect, the maternal–fetal conflict is thus a problem which lies at the interface between rights and duties, both moral and legal. On this analysis, therefore, there are important *conceptual links* between the ethics and the law which underpin my suggestion that the problem is not primarily one inhering in the legal enforcement of moral obligations.[17]

Located at the heart of this rights–duty interface, the conflict is riddled with *tensions* about the idea of a moral and legal right to make choices which may result in harm to the fetus. Reflecting on this, it will become apparent that while there may be no *legal* objection to a pregnant woman's exercise of her legal right to refuse medical treatment—in the narrow sense, for instance, that the fetus is not a legal person—*morally* her choice to exercise that right could well be the subject of criticism: for instance, for the sake of argument, in the purely hypothetical case of a woman declining a caesarean section in order to avoid an abdominal scar, a clearly "trivial" reason. Ethical and legal examination of the maternal–fetal conflict therefore raises questions not only about *why we grant such rights*, but also about the *moral quality of the decision to exercise them*. We may ask, for instance, whether a pregnant

---

[17] Given the conceptual links to which I draw attention, there will inevitably be a small element of repetition as I refer back, within the legal discussion in the latter two-thirds of the book, to the first philosophical part. This is an unavoidable aspect of this approach. But if the arguments are truly brought home by this means, my purposes will have been achieved.

woman's legal right to refuse medical treatment required by the fetus is being exercised in a "morally appropriate" manner, given the likely adverse consequences for the fetus. In effect, given the scope for reasonable disagreement surrounding such decisions, this is to ask whether she is exercising her legal right in a manner consistent with its theoretical justification. Where she has "serious reasons" relating to her moral and legal interests in self-determination and bodily integrity this is likely the case. It might be noted that I focus on these particular moral and legal interests because they are uncontroversially at the core of the right to refuse medical treatment. Whilst, for instance, the right to privacy may also be implicated, there is a great deal of unresolved debate as to its meaning and scope.[18]

Overall, my purpose is to analyse the issue in a way which reconciles the individual's and what we might deem the "public interest" in this area. In the light of the increasing scope for *in utero* interventions for the benefit of the fetus, this is crucial. Indeed, as in some ways with the issue of abortion and as evidenced in the literature about and publicity surrounding the legal cases of maternal–fetal conflict, the denial of a tension regarding a pregnant woman's legal right to refuse medical treatment needed by the fetus is inclined, on the one hand, to provoke dogmatic and ultimately question-begging assertions about a *woman's rights* and, on the other, possible consequent backlash against these, including overly rigid assertions of *fetal rights* which do not attend sufficiently to a woman's interests and difficulties in pregnancy or to the context of the conflict in question. In fact, these two rather polarised approaches might be said to dominate much of the literature to date.

The key to the project of reconciliation lies in attention to a woman's *reasons* for exercising her right, the ways these relate to her *underlying interests* in bodily integrity and in self-determination, to the *moral claims of the fetus* and to the *values* inherent in the right to refuse medical treatment on the one hand and to abort on the other. These points are developed in different ways throughout the book. Although it may seem that the term "maternal–fetal *conflict*" becomes inappropriate as a result of this approach, the reality of possible harm to the unborn child can never be extinguished.

III. THE STRUCTURE OF THE BOOK

Turning now to give an indication of the structure of the book, *Part I* begins with some brief but important theoretical groundwork on the nature of rights and duties and their place within moral theory as well as a brief exploration of the idea of autonomy. I then proceed to a moral analysis of the maternal–fetal relationship with particular reference to the treatment context. This entails reflection, in part, upon the moral status of the fetus. Since it is clear that the fetus is not a legal person in either English or US law, it might be considered either inappropriate or pointless to reflect upon the fetus's moral status. But such reflection is essential in

---

[18] See ch. 4.

the light of my overall purpose of explaining and justifying a pregnant woman's moral and legal right to refuse medical treatment and reconciling this with the prospect of prenatal harm or death. Thus, I am concerned to formulate an argument which addresses the *justification* of harm to the fetus. When we turn to the law, this is an analysis which pays attention to the *de facto*, rather than the *de jure* interests of the fetus. In this regard, the key to the "gradualist" understanding of the maternal–fetal relationship which I endorse at the level of moral theory is that the more advanced the fetus's development, the more serious the reason a woman will need to justify harm to it, an argument which I refine to apply also to the "future child" (who will be but is not yet born) who may instead be in issue in some cases.

The critical issue of the justification of harm to the fetus is developed from the woman's perspective by analysing her relationship to the fetus in two ways: first, in terms of her *rights* and second, in terms of her *duties*. Regarding her rights, I focus upon her interest in self-determination and the question of religious reasons for refusing medical treatment, noting the difficulties of judging such reasons in their own terms and the attention that must therefore be paid to the place of religion within such a woman's life. A pregnant woman's relationship to the fetus is discussed in terms of the idea of her *duties* by seeking to analyse the idea of a duty being owed *through the body*. Here we encounter difficulties in determining the existence and extent—the reasonableness—of a very bodily (indeed extraordinary) duty, to aid another. Such a duty is contrasted with both negative and positive duties not to cause physical harm to others within the realm of what I dub "general conduct". Reflection upon the social context of pregnancy and the treatment refusal scenario within this is also instructive.

Thus, the philosophical work in Part I grounds the two subsequent discussions of a pregnant woman's legal rights and the idea of her legal duties which generally fall into Parts II and III respectively. The intention in Part I, therefore, is to give a moral account of the relationship which then infuses our understanding of the idea of a pregnant woman's legal right to refuse medical treatment and the moral and social acceptability of this.

Turning to the essentially legal parts of the book, in Part II I consider the maternal–fetal conflict cases within the framework of arguments from legal rights. Following exploration of the early cases of maternal–fetal conflict, in which US courts ordered obstetric interventions in the face of maternal refusals, I highlight the extent to which these precedents developed along a parallel but distinct line from the principal body of the law of treatment refusal. Whilst the later cases of maternal–fetal conflict are now broadly in line with the law as it relates to any competent adult, a pregnant woman is clearly not identical to a non-pregnant patient, as refusal of treatment in her case affects an unborn other. In turn, this begs questions about why—given that it is her choice (usually in these cases) to have a child—she should have the same rights as the non-pregnant patient, notwithstanding her strong interests in self-determination and bodily integrity.

In essence, the task of justifying her rights within the law hinges upon an exploration of the values underlying the right of any patient to refuse medical treatment on the one hand (through exploration of the development of the ordinary patient's right to refuse treatment) and the abortion right on the other. I argue that we can understand the State interests invoked in relation to these rights—in the preservation of life and in the potential life of the fetus—in a way which theoretically *supports* a woman's right to refuse treatment during pregnancy. (These interests are explicitly present within US law and largely implicitly so in the English setting.) In effect, I argue that the public interest these State interests represent amounts to a concern that a woman's reasons for refusing medical treatment are serious—hence truly founded in her moral and legal interests in self-determination and bodily integrity—so that she exercises her rights with meaning and care. Whether this interest is satisfied in practice will depend upon a pregnant woman's reasons for refusing medical treatment: in the unlikely event that these are not serious and considered, there may be limited scope for the involvement of others in her treatment choice. Importantly, the fact that the existing cases have concerned women with serious reasons for refusing medical treatment needed by the fetus may enable us to recognise the extent to which the maternal–fetal conflict usually involves serious maternal reasons and thus to feel that, where she has the legal right to refuse medical treatment, this is correct. Here I build upon arguments first formulated in purely moral terms in Part I.

The implication of the position that a pregnant woman does and should have the legal right to refuse treatment needed by the fetus is that she does not and should not have the legal duty to submit to treatment on its behalf. Yet this conclusion is not just the inverse of the argument from rights, as the idea of duty is analysed in its own terms. Part III, which addresses the issue primarily in this way, discusses the relevance of certain arguments from the law of abortion, tort and rescue (an aspect of the law of tort) relevant to arguments from legal duty. Importantly, some of the arguments from Parts I and II are thus teased out in related but distinct and significantly different ways.

As regards abortion, for example, various "technical" arguments are addressed, such as whether restrictions on abortion following fetal viability could be construed as mandating the imposition not just of a negative duty not to abort, but also of affirmative obligations to accept medical treatment for the fetus.

Turning to the relevance of arguments from tort, ethical analysis in Part I of the difficulties of subjecting the domain of the religious reason to a duty (at least when a pregnant woman's own body is in issue as compared, say, with the situation of a parent and a born child) and of determining the reasonableness—hence the existence and extent—of a duty seriously to aid another through one's body (as in the caesarean cases), in turn grounds aspects of the reasoning relating to the difficulties of determining a "standard of care" in pregnancy. In Part III we also find legal recognition of my arguments, first formulated in Part I, relating to the social context of pregnancy. Further, important differences—of principle and policy—between the ideas of maternal and third-party liability for prenatal harm or death are identified. These build upon distinctions formulated in Part I between maternal choices within the treatment context and those which are part of a woman's general conduct: in the latter cases she may harm the fetus or future child in a manner more akin to that of a "detached" third party. In this way, since it is unlikely that specific rights of hers are implicated, a determination of moral duty may be forthcoming. Policy considerations, however, tend to weigh against the imposition of a tortious duty of care.

A particular contribution of the final chapter on aspects of rescue law is to identify, especially, certain moral but also legal and policy problems in coerced, especially surgical, medical treatment of pregnant women. The chapter also addresses the hypothetical question of what we should do when faced with maternal refusals which appear trivial. Lastly, consideration of the protection afforded to incompetents in relation to organ and tissue donations is salutary as regards the earliest maternal–fetal cases in the United States and England.

From the above outline, it will be apparent that the book analyses the maternal–fetal conflict in both philosophical and legal terms and that the discussion of the latter encompasses, mostly, American and English law. I have indicated that my concern is to explain and justify a pregnant woman's legal right to refuse medical treatment where and to the extent that this exists and to promote it where it does not. Our understanding of this complex and relatively new topic and hence of the development of the law in general can be enriched by considering relevant legal arguments from England and the United States, as well as (on occasion) Canada and Australia. Overall, this approach is generally supported by the important links between English and American (and in turn Canadian and Australian) medical law. Although I turn to the law in Canada and Australia where this is helpful in elucidating certain arguments or where one jurisdiction has taken the lead on a certain aspect, no attempt is made comprehensively to cover, say, relevant Canadian and Australian law, although leading Canadian decisions on the issue of maternal conduct which may cause prenatal harm are discussed in depth. My analysis does, however, cover the English and key US law.[19]

Note that an issue which I do not have the scope to address here is the question of *paternal* links to and potential responsibility for prenatal harm. It is important to acknowledge this possibility, lest it be thought that only pregnant women can cause such harm.[20]

---

[19] Whilst my analysis might to some extent apply to issues of post-conception genetic interventions, these issues are not directly addressed and are highly complex in different ways. See e.g. A Buchanan *et al*, *From Chance to Choice: Genetics and Justice* (Cambridge: Cambridge University Press, 2000).

[20] Cynthia R Daniels has done much important work in this area. See e.g., most recently, her "Between Fathers and Fetuses: The Social Construction of Male Reproduction and the Politics of Fetal Harm", in DL Dickenson (ed.), *Ethical Issues in Maternal–Fetal Medicine* (Cambridge: Cambridge University Press, 2002) 113–129. "Since at least the 1980s, and in some cases far earlier, studies have shown a clear link between paternal exposures to drugs, alcohol, smoking, environmental and occupational toxins, and fetal health prolems. Yet men have been spared the retribution aimed at women." (At 113.) Of course, a father might also harm the fetus through such conduct as negligent driving.

Overall, and importantly, although framed by the concepts of (a woman's) "rights" and "duties", since the heart of my analysis lies at the interface between them, the discussion highlights, amongst other things, the inadequacies of purely rights-based reasoning, notwithstanding my attempt ultimately to uphold and promote a woman's rights in pregnancy.

PART I

The Moral Relationship between a Pregnant Woman and her Fetus:

Exploring a Woman's Moral Rights and Duties

Introduction

THIS PART explores the moral relationship between a pregnant woman and her fetus with specific reference to the context of maternal refusal of medical treatment needed by the latter. There is an underlying assumption in the literature on this subject that the problems of the maternal–fetal conflict begin with the legal enforcement of moral duties.[1] But the problems start prior to this, not only with the obvious complexity of exploring the moral status of the fetus, but particularly with previously unrecognised difficulties inherent in the question of determining when, if ever, a pregnant woman's *prima facie* moral rights should "give way" to the interests of the fetus. Put another way, when does she have a moral duty to the fetus to submit to certain medical treatment on its behalf?

Part I is divided into two chapters. In chapter one, I recognise that the maternal–fetal conflict may be between a woman's interests and either those of the fetus *qua* fetus or those of the child who will be, but is not yet, born. Regarding the latter possibility, however, the truly difficult question is to determine the moral weight of the interests of the child who will be born *when in conflict with those of the mother in whom it is currently situated, as opposed to a "detached" third party*. Although the term "child who will be but is not yet born" is more precise, for ease of exposition, hereafter I adopt the shorter "future child", which is also the term most common to the literature. For the purposes of this discussion, then, a "future child" is one who *will* be born (rather than die *in utero*) but is currently (because not yet born) inside the body of a woman, as discussed in chapter one.[2] Where it is not important to distinguish between the two, sometimes I use the term "unborn child" to denote either the fetus or the future child.

---

[1] Consider, for instance, the following passage in the work of John Robertson: "Moral rights and duties are, of course, distinct from legal rights and duties. Finding that there are moral duties to avoid harmful prenatal conduct does not mean that those duties should always have legal standing." *Children of Choice: Freedom and the New Reproductive Technologies* (Princeton, NJ: Princeton University Press, 1994) 177. Note also N Rhoden's statement: "[I]n this very private and bodily sphere, the issue of moral obligations, even very compelling ones, must be kept distinct from the issue of legal coercion of individuals to meet their moral obligations." "The Judge in the Delivery Room: The Emergence of Court-Ordered Cesareans", (1986) 74 *Cal L Rev* 1951, 1980. Robertson and Rhoden are correct in distinguishing moral and legal duties. My point, however, is that the determination of the moral duty may in itself be a complex issue. Sometimes, however, clear moral duties do exist, about which the only residual problem is indeed the appropriateness of legal compulsion. For a recent endorsement of Robertson's position by authors who nevertheless uphold the idea of a pregnant woman's legal right to refuse medical treatment, see S Fovargue and J Miola, "Policing Pregnancy: Implications of the *Attorney-General's Reference (No.3 of 1994)*", (1998) 6 *Med L Rev* 265, 288.

[2] The term is used similarly by various scholars. See e.g. JC Callahan and JW Knight, "Women, Fetuses, Medicine and the Law", in HB Holmes and L Purdy (eds.), *Feminist Perspectives in Medical Ethics* (Indianapolis, IN: Indiana University Press, 1992) 224–39, 227.

Whilst on terminology, for the purposes of the issues under discussion here it is unnecessary to distinguish between the differing stages of the unborn child's development, that is, from zygote to embryo to fetus. Since two zygotes sometimes merge to form one embryo, however, some have concluded that before fourteen days post-conception there is no individuated human organism. At fourteen days the "primitive streak" which will become the spinal cord begins to form.[3]

Chapter one examines four key arguments about the moral status of the fetus, considering their implications for the maternal–fetal conflict and piecing together, over the course of the chapter, an understanding of this relationship. An important dimension of this understanding lies in the recognition that the interests of either the fetus or the future child cannot be viewed in abstract terms, but rather are linked with and to some extent affected by the interests of the pregnant woman.[4] Ultimately, I adopt a "gradualist" approach, the essence of which consists in the suggestion that the justification of harm to the fetus requires, as the fetus develops, an increasingly strong reason upon a woman's part, a point which is refined to apply also to the future child. Such an approach may be applied to our understanding of a woman's rights, telling us that a woman justifiably asserts a *right* to refuse treatment needed by the fetus/future child when she has a *serious reason* for so doing.

The second chapter addresses the relationship from the perspective of the pregnant woman. Having suggested that the maternal–fetal conflict is in some ways a problem located at the interface between a woman's rights and duties, chapter two considers the relationship first in terms of a woman's rights and second her duties. Whilst the gradualist approach to the relationship suggested in chapter one may enable us to say that a woman is justified in exercising a right to refuse treatment where she has a serious reason to do so, in chapter two we encounter the difficulty of judging whether, in any given case of a *non-trivial* reason, that reason is in fact *sufficiently serious* to outweigh the fetus's/future child's claims. The problem arises because very *personal* moral interests—essentially in self-determination and bodily integrity—are implicated in the treatment context. (The meaning of "self-determination" and "bodily integrity" are touched on below when I discuss the idea of autonomy.)

Such very personal interests are generally not raised *outside* the maternal–fetal relationship, about which four points should be noted regarding the prospect of one individual physically harming another. First, a very personal interest in self-determination does not tend to be at stake regarding what I shall dub the individual's "general conduct", by which I mean specifically those aspects of day-to-day

---

[3] MA Warren, *Moral Status: Obligations to Persons and Other Living Things* (Oxford: Oxford University Press, 1997) 204, citing N Ford, *When Did I Begin? Conception of the Human Individual in History, Philosophy and Science* (Cambridge: Cambridge University Press, 1988).

[4] Note one writer's observation that scholarly or judicial opinion which favours the fetus tends to depict it as an "*independent entity, abstracted from the reality of the woman's body,* much as though commentators had encountered it upon the street." J Gallagher, "Fetus as Patient", in N Taub and S Cohen (eds.), *Reproductive Laws for the 1990s* (Clifton, NJ: Humana Press, 1989) 185–235, 187, my emphasis.

conduct (acts or omissions) which we might have cause to limit in the interests of preventing *physical harm* to third parties. Second, although in the term "general conduct" I include acts and omissions, in reality most of us refrain from physically harming others by not acting in certain ways, rather than by assisting, for instance, injured others (unless, for example, we are doctors or others with special duties to save lives). Third, the individual's general conduct—that which she or he lacks very personal and particular reasons for engaging (or not engaging) in—does not tend to be protected by specific rights: concomitantly, it appears easier to judge the reasonableness or otherwise of such conduct insofar as it causes physical harm to others. Fourth, and perhaps most strikingly, the individual's *bodily integrity* is not in issue when we review his or her general conduct in terms of its possible physically harmful effects on others: the opportunity positively[5] to assist another by *using one's body* in the serious sense with which I am concerned—by donating a kidney or bone marrow, for instance—is very rare. Further, one can only harm others through one's body by breaching a negative duty in quite contrived (and hence not day-to-day) ways.[6] Regarding the question of physical harm to others, the distinction I draw between the very personal interests of the pregnant woman in the treatment context, including those in the body, and the general conduct of the individual (including that of the pregnant woman in at least some other contexts) is of considerable importance to the book overall.

This distinction between physical harm to others occurring through general conduct and harm occurring as the result of choices pertaining to moral interests in self-determination and bodily integrity underpins aspects of the discussion both of a woman's rights and duties. The argument from *rights* focuses upon a woman's interest in self-determination, with particular reference to the issue of religious reasons for refusing medical treatment and the difficulties of judging the reasonableness thereof. The argument from *duty* focuses upon a woman's interest in bodily integrity, contrasting this with the determination of duty in the domain of general conduct.

Thus, in turning to consider the relationship in terms of a woman's *duties*, I focus upon an important argument which attempts to analyse the idea of a duty being owed by means of the body, specifically in the abortion context. Consideration of this argument reveals a number of significant and helpful distinctions. Yet, given that it works by analogy with the domain of "general conduct"—as illustrated by the actions of the Good Samaritan—in fact it fails to acknowledge or bring out

---

[5] On positive and negative duties, see ch. 2.

[6] It may be relevant that John Stuart Mill seems to refer in his "harm principle" to the *actions* of individuals harming others: "[T]he sole end for which mankind are warranted, individually or collectively, in interfering with the *liberty of action* of any of their number, is self-protection. . . . the only purpose for which power can be rightfully exercised over any member of a civilized community, against his will, is to prevent harm to others." "On Liberty", (1859) in Mill, *Utilitarianism*, M Warnock (ed.), (Fontana: London, 1962) 135. (My emphasis.) In alluding to Mill at this point, I mean to imply that the idea of harming another through one's body was probably not one he considered and hence that he would not have made the distinction that I suggest and introduce here. The comment should not be taken to imply that the "harm principle" is restricted to physical harm.

important differences between the idea of duties attaching to the domain of general conduct on the one hand and that of duties owed by means of the body on the other, especially in the particular context of pregnancy. In considering the application of this argument to our determination of the nature or extent of maternal duties arising in the maternal–fetal conflict, I draw attention to the *social context* of pregnancy and to the particular situation of maternal treatment refusal within this. At the end of the chapter, I seek to bring together the argument from rights with that from duties, building on the important "gradualist" conclusions about the maternal–fetal relationship formulated in the first chapter.

An important idea to emerge from this discussion will be touched upon as the book progresses: in the light of the scope for reasonable disagreement which tends to surround the intensely personal interests which are invoked in the treatment context—which in turn are protected by at least *prima facie* rights—it may be important in such arenas to allow for a domain of individual responsibility. Ideally, through this the individual can be responsible to the interests both of herself and others.

Before beginning a study of the moral relationship between a pregnant woman and her fetus it will be helpful to consider briefly the idea of autonomy, which is centrally implicated in the maternal–fetal conflict, the meaning and basis of rights and duties and to touch upon their place in moral thinking. This important groundwork will facilitate discussion both in ethical and legal parts of the book of the critical issue of the extent of a woman's rights in pregnancy, or, put another way, when—if ever—her *prima facie* rights "give way" to her duties.

1

The Relation of the Fetus to the Pregnant Woman

I. AUTONOMY, RIGHTS AND DUTIES—SOME BRIEF THEORETICAL GROUNDWORK

A. The Idea of Autonomy—Self and Other

THE IDEA and value of autonomy is so prevalent in medical law and ethics that it barely needs an introduction, underpinning as it does a patient's moral interests in self-determination and bodily integrity. Nevertheless, some words are in order here. One of the most obvious connections is with the philosophy of Kant, who associated autonomy with the concept of the will and gave to the latter—which he attributed to human beings by virtue of their rationality—the pivotal status of value in his moral theory. For Kant, reason has particular qualities, most notably necessity and universality. The "pure practical reason" which is concerned with the moral domain must originate in *a priori* reason if it is to ground moral principles of universal validity for rational beings. The will is thus intrinsically connected with the idea of reason and is defined in opposition, particularly, to what is conceived as contingent, empirical desire. In Kant's thought, just as the autonomous moral agent is the source of moral value (and to be valued in him- or herself) so autonomy becomes an important moral value in itself.[1] To some extent these ideas are reflected in contemporary accounts of autonomy, such as those of John Rawls and Susan Wolf.[2]

Just as the contemporary literature on autonomy is vast so the conceptions of autonomy are various. Consider the following passage from the work of Gerald Dworkin, which is meant to illustrate the sense in which autonomy is a "term of art".[3]

"It is used sometimes as an equivalent of liberty. . . to self-rule or sovereignty, . . . as identical with freedom of the will. It is equated with dignity, integrity, individuality,

---

[1] I Kant, *Groundwork of the Metaphysic of Morals*, trans. by HJ Paton in *The Moral Law* (London: Hutchinson, 1948).

[2] See e.g. J Rawls, "Kantian Constructivism in Moral Theory: The Dewey Lectures 1980", (1980) 77 *J of Phil* 515; S Wolf, *Freedom within Reason* (New York, NY: Oxford University Press, 1994).

[3] G Dworkin, *The Theory and Practice of Autonomy* (New York, NY: Cambridge University Press, 1988) 6.

independence, responsibility, and self-knowledge. It is identified with qualities of self-assertion, with critical reflection, with freedom from obligation, with absence of external causation, with knowledge of one's own interests. . . It is related to actions, to beliefs, to reasons for acting, to rules, to the will of other persons, to thoughts, and to principles."

Dworkin suggests that almost the only recurrent feature here is that autonomy is associated with persons and perceived as something valuable.

Much of the work on autonomy is associated with the very much larger liberalism–communitarianism and feminist debates. I cannot explore these debates here, but I can make a few points about the idea of autonomy by touching on the idea of the self, her ends and her relationship to society, particularly within liberalism, in order to indicate the complexity of some of the positions and issues.[4] Indeed, this is a convenient point to make a few introductory remarks about liberalism as a foundation for discussion generally. It is also important that I clarify what I mean by autonomy, so that we have some idea of when a pregnant woman may be said to be acting autonomously. In this section I also introduce the notion of "bodily integrity".

Starting with the idea of the self in liberal theory, Rawls' theory of justice and the conception of the person it seemed to suppose has been the target of a well-known communitarian critique by Michael Sandel.[5] In particular, criticism has focused on Rawls' use of the "original position" in which, for the purposes of theorising about justice and reaching agreement on just or fair principles, people are behind a "veil of ignorance" such that they do not know certain facts about themselves. Sandel charges that Rawls, who holds that "the self is prior to the ends which are affirmed by it"[6] (meaning that we can step back from our projects and evaluate whether we wish to continue them)[7], presents an atomised view of moral and political subjects which does not sufficiently attend to the way in which our ends and attachments and the communities in which we live partly define us.[8] Rawls has, however, defended his use of the "original position", arguing that his picture of the individualist self is purely a device of representation for the purposes of building a theory of justice which could be supported by members of a society with very differing views of the good.[9] Further, he clearly considers his recent work, which is intended as a theory of purely political liberalism, shows that he is not committed

---

[4] For an excellent and comprehensive introduction to the issues to which I am here indebted, see A Swift and S Mulhall, *Liberals and Communitarians*, 2nd edn. (Oxford: Blackwell, 1996).

[5] J Rawls, *A Theory of Justice* (Cambridge, MA: Belknap Press of Harvard University Press, 1971).

[6] *Ibid.*, 560.

[7] As interpreted by W Kymlicka, *Contemporary Political Philosophy: An Introduction* (Oxford: Oxford University Press, 1990) 207. Kymlicka notes that this is often described as the "Kantian" view of the self, since Kant endorsed a view of the self as prior to its social roles and relationships, whose freedom requires a distanced and rational appraisal of these aspects.

[8] See e.g. M Sandel, "Introduction", in M Sandel (ed.), *Liberalism and its Critics* (Oxford: Blackwell, 1984) 5–6.

[9] See J Rawls, "Justice as Fairness: Political not Metaphysical", in S Avineri and A de-Shalit (eds.), *Communitarianism and Individualism* (Oxford: Oxford University Press, 1992) 186, 199*ff.*

to any of the ethical, metaphysical or philosophical doctrines that communitarians have laid at his door.[10]

Another important focus of communitarian criticism of liberal thought has centred on the relationship between the self and society, in particular the social conditions necessary for the fulfillment of the interests of the self.[11] Charles Taylor argues that:[12]

> "[T]he identity of the autonomous, self-determining individual requires a social matrix, one, for instance, which through a series of practices recognizes the right to autonomous decision and which calls for the individual having a voice in deliberation about public action."

This is his "social thesis"[13] and it shows that communitarians are not necessarily committed to a view in which the social dominates the self, thereby recognising a place for reflection and critical scrutiny.[14] Indeed, the communitarian concern to emphasise the senses in which a person should not be seen as autonomous of her community does not necessarily imply a rejection of autonomy; rather, suggest Stephen Mulhall and Adam Swift, the purpose is to query the "absoluteness of the priority and the universality of the scope" which liberals tend to give this value.[15] But the idea that we cannot exercise the capacity for self-determination "alone" is not denied by liberals such as Rawls, Ronald Dworkin and Isaiah Berlin,[16] who recognise the role of society in providing meaningful choices and fostering the growth of the ability to choose between them.[17]

Since Dworkin does not use any device such as the original position in developing his theory of liberal equality, he has not been the target of the criticisms that have been levelled at Rawls, such as those exemplified by Sandel's critique. Indeed, he readily acknowledges the influence of the social on people's attachments to particular communities, the conditions of their existence and their conceptions of the good.[18] An important difference between Rawls and Dworkin is that Dworkin's

---

[10] A Swift and S Mulhall, *Liberals and Communitarians*, 296.

[11] W Kymlicka, *Contemporary Political Philosophy*, 216.

[12] C Taylor, "Atomism", in S Avineri and A de-Shalit (eds.), *Communitarianism and Individualism*, 29–50, 49, excerpted from *Philosophy and the Human Sciences: Philosophical Papers* ii (1985) 187–210.

[13] Yet, as W Kymlicka notes, for Taylor this means that we should reject liberal neutrality on the basis that a neutral state is unable adequately to protect the social environment required by self-determination; rather, there must be some limits on self-determination in order to preserve the social conditions which enable it. W Kymlicka, *Contemporary Political Philosophy*, 216. (See also M Walzer, *Interpretations and Social Criticism* (Cambridge, MA: Harvard University Press, 1987) for a defence of the idea of criticism from within one's society.)

[14] As noted by N Lacey, *Unspeakable Subjects: Feminist Essays in Legal and Social Theory* (Oxford: Hart Publishing, 1998) 55.

[15] A Swift and S Mulhall, *Liberals and Communitarians*, 163–4.

[16] See e.g. I Berlin, "Two Concepts of Liberty", in his *Four Essays on Liberty* (Oxford: Oxford University Press 1969) 156.

[17] W Kymlicka, *Contemporary Political Philosophy*, 216, citing J Rawls, *A Theory of Justice* and R Dworkin, *A Matter of Principle* (Oxford: Oxford University Press, 1985).

[18] See his "Liberal Community", (1989) 77 *Calif L Rev* 479. Whilst rejecting the idea of community as a need in general, he acknowledges that "the value or goodness of any individual citizen's life is only a reflection and function of the value of the life of the community in which he lives" (at 480). On

liberalism is comprehensive, in that he is committed to a continuity between ethics and politics.[19] This further shields him from communitarian attack insofar as the latter criticises the split between the individual's personal convictions and the political demands of purely political liberalism. At the same time, contrary to the communitarian position, of course, Dworkin adheres to a position of State neutrality between its citizens' first-person ethics[20] or conceptions of the good, since liberalism is "a theory of equality that requires official neutrality amongst theories of what is valuable in life".[21] This does not mean that he holds that people choose their ethical beliefs from scratch but "[i]t does suppose that they *reflect* on their ethical beliefs and that they choose how to behave on the basis of those reflections".[22] The importance to the liberal of self-determination lies not so much in the idea of fully respecting individuals as human beings but in acknowledging the important place for reflection about ends as well as means, recognising that the resulting judgments might well be mistaken but rejecting paternalism on the basis that lives go better when led from the inside, according to the individual's beliefs about value.[23]

A strong defence of liberalism centred on the notion of autonomy and described as transcending the debate between liberalism and communitarianism can be found in the work of Joseph Raz.[24] Autonomy is not rights-based in Raz's work,[25] but rather is an ultimate value central to well-being (a view I find helpful), making

the question of identity, he writes: "Citizens identify with their political community when they recognize that the community has a communal life, and that the success or failure of their own lives is ethically dependent on the success or failure of that communal life." (At 499.) I cannot discuss the complexities of his argument here. For a discussion of Dworkin's views of Sandel's arguments on self-identity and community, see S Guest, *Ronald Dworkin*, 2nd edn. (Edinburgh: Edinburgh University Press, 1997) 73–5. W Kymlicka suggests that although liberals are understood to think that a coercive state is needed to hold society together, in fact liberals think that people readily form social relations and groups in which they appreciate and follow the good, whereas it is actually communitarians who apparently think that, without the state bringing them together to appraise and follow the good, individuals will become detached and isolated. W Kymlicka, "Liberal Individualism and Liberal Neutrality", in S Avineri and A de-Shalit (eds.), *Communitarianism and Individualism*, 165–85, 185, excerpted from (1989) 99 *Ethics* 883–905.

[19] Dworkin says "ethics shapes justice". "The Foundations of Liberal Equality", in S Darwall (ed.), *Equal Freedom* (Ann Arbor, MI: University of Michigan Press, 1996) 214. I cannot explore this here. See discussion in A Swift and S Mulhall, *Liberals and Communitarians*, 277ff.

[20] "First-person ethics", as defined by Mulhall and Swift, concern people's "views about what kinds of life are valuable for themselves (except in those cases where a person's conception of what is good for her involves her treating others unjustly)". A Swift and S Mulhall, *Liberals and Communitarians*, 301.

[21] R Dworkin, "Liberalism", in his *A Matter of Principle*, 203. Thus, "government must be neutral in ethics in the following sense. It must not forbid or reward any private activity on the ground that one substantive set of ethical values, one set of opinions about the best way to lead a life, is superior or inferior to others". "The Foundations of Liberal Equality", 228.

[22] *Ibid.*, 295, emphasis in original.

[23] W Kymlicka, *Contemporary Political Philosophy*, 203–4.

[24] J Raz, *The Morality of Freedom* (Oxford: Clarendon Press, 1986) as described by A Swift and S Mulhall, *Liberals and Communitarians*, 345.

[25] "A right to autonomy can be had only if the interest of the right-holder justifies holding individual members of the society at large to be duty-bound to him to provide him with the social environment necessary to give him a chance to have an autonomous life. Assuming that the interest of one person cannot justify holding so many to be subject to potentially burdensome duties . . . it follows that there is no right to personal autonomy". J Raz, *The Morality of Freedom* (Oxford: Clarendon Press, 1986) 247. He also argues that some liberal rights are valuable for their defence and promotion of "a certain

his conception of autonomy a rich or "thick" conception. To be able to lead an autonomous life one must be able to choose from an "adequate" range of options.[26] For Raz, this means that the State can promote its citizens' well-being by judging the value of certain ways of life, making his liberalism perfectionist.[27] Since Raz's conception of autonomy is embedded within a theory of well-being, he is unlikely to be a target of, for instance, Alexander McCall Smith's questioning of the supremacy of autonomy as an end itself within medical law and ethics.[28]

Whilst I shall explore such aspects of Raz's and Dworkin's work as are relevant to my arguments, as indicated I cannot explore either the liberalism–communitarianism debate in its own terms or the complex positions of the liberal theorists alluded to here. Rather, since autonomy is clearly central to medical law and ethics in general and to the maternal–fetal conflict in particular, I would like further to touch upon the richer account of autonomy which is emerging as a result of the liberal–communitarian and feminist debates.[29]

In particular, some recent feminist work reconceives and re-evaluates autonomy in a way which both acknowledges the socially situated nature of individuals and hence the contribution that socialisation makes to the development and realisation of autonomy and, importantly, rejects critiques of liberalism which underplay the possibility and value of autonomy.[30] This work typically construes autonomy in "social, relational, interpersonal, or intersubjective terms".[31] Feminist work in particular gives greater and more detailed attention to the notion of agency in critiques which highlight autonomy as a feature "of agents who are emotional, embodied, desiring, creative, and feeling as well as rational, creatures".[32] As indicated, however,

---

public culture" and hence that the liberal tradition is not "unequivocally individualistic" (at 245). See further ch. 2 in this volume.

[26] *Ibid.*, 373 and following discussion.

[27] "[T]he autonomy principle is a perfectionist principle. Autonomous life is valuable only if it is spent in the pursuit of acceptable and valuable projects and relationships. The autonomy principle permits and even requires governments to create morally valuable opportunities, and to eliminate repugnant ones." *Ibid.*, 417.

[28] A McCall Smith, "Beyond Autonomy", (1997) 14 *J Contemp HL & Policy* 23. McCall Smith argues "that autonomy should be . . . seen as a means of facilitating the good rather than constituting the good itself". (At 31.)

[29] M Charlesworth notes that "[n]o doubt a complete ethics cannot be generated from the idea of autonomy: nonetheless a great deal of ethical capital can be extracted from it." M Charlesworth, *Bioethics in a Liberal Society* (Cambridge: Cambridge University Press, 1993) 6.

[30] See in particular the collection of essays in C MacKenzie and N Stoljar (eds.), *Relational Autonomy: Feminist Perspectives on Autonomy, Agency and the Social Self* (New York, NY: Oxford University Press, 2000). See also N Lacey, *Unspeakable Subjects*, 67, suggesting that whilst it is important to see ourselves as "distinct and autonomous", greater attention should be paid to "social context, social institutions, communities and cultures".

[31] M Friedman, "Autonomy, Social Disruption and Women", in C MacKenzie and N Stoljar (eds.), *Relational Autonomy*, 35, 40 and see references to mainstream and feminist work in her n. 33.

[32] "Introduction: Autonomy Refigured", in C MacKenzie and N Stoljar (eds.), *Relational Autonomy*, 3, 21. Additionally, the work "highlight[s] the ways in which agents are both psychically internally differentiated and socially differentiated from others" (*ibid.*). The complexities of the feminist debate should be noted. Thus, Susan Dodds has criticised liberal feminist work for its assumption that patient decision-making occurs in a "social vacuum", such that the social factors affecting the range of alternatives are neutral and that everyone is equally capable of making such decisions since no

at the same time the work highlights the value of autonomy[33] to a greater extent than communitarianism may do. For instance, whilst communitarians value such notions as tradition and community, generally believing that the State should protect shared values and ways of living over and above individual autonomy, feminist recognition of the role played by social determinism is not a prelude to the celebration of existing social roles but rather a first step toward questioning the necessity of arrangements which may well be seen as oppressive.[34]

The debate on autonomy also divides into procedural and substantive theories. On a procedural conception, personal autonomy is achieved when a person is able to reflect on his or her motivations and actions in an appropriate way.[35] By contrast, substantive accounts maintain that the content-neutral procedural conditions may be necessary but are not sufficient in the light of the role played by socialisation. These accounts propose either that the autonomous preferences of agents include specific contents or that autonomy requires further necessary conditions which constrain the contents of the desires or preferences which autonomous agents are capable of holding.[36]

These debates are enormously complex and cannot be pursued here. For this reason I cannot choose between procedural or substantive theories in any generally defensible way. I can, however, focus and reflect on those elements which are helpful for our understanding of a pregnant woman's autonomy in the medical treatment context. Here, it seems that what is important is that, to be acting autonomously, a woman chooses what treatment she will accept or reject by what Marilyn Friedman has described as "the right sort of reflective self-understanding or internal coherence along with an absence of undue coercion or manipulation by others".[37] Friedman has also observed:[38]

> "Unity, coherence and self-consciousness . . . are matters of degree. A subject need not be absolutely unified, coherent, or transparently and incorrigibly self-aware in order to exercise autonomy; she need merely have those traits to a sufficient degree. Nothing about feminism in itself necessitates rejection of the idea that selves have some minimal degree of unity, coherence, reliable self-awareness, or differentiation from others."

competent person is unduly limited by such aspects as oppressive social conditioning. S Dodds, "Choice and Control in Feminist Bioethics", in C MacKenzie and N Stoljar (eds.), *Relational Autonomy*, 213–35, 219.

[33] For instance in understanding oppressive socialisation.

[34] L Barclay, "Autonomy and the Social Self", in C MacKenzie and N Stoljar (eds.), *Relational Autonomy*, 52, esp. 66–7. And see W Kymlicka on the uncertainties regarding the extent to which communitarianism endorses a review of the socially embedded self and its attachments. W Kymlicka, *Contemporary Political Philosophy*, 215.

[35] "Introduction: Autonomy Refigured", in C MacKenzie and N Stoljar (eds.), *Relational Autonomy*, 13–14.

[36] *Ibid.*, 19.

[37] M Friedman, "Autonomy, Social Disruption and Women", 40. Friedman is of course a communitarian.

[38] M Friedman, "Feminism in Ethics: Conceptions of Autonomy", in M Fricker and J Hornsby (eds.), *The Cambridge Companion to Feminism in Philosophy* (Cambridge: Cambridge University Press, 2000), 205–24, 220.

In this picture it also seems important that, apart from being able to reflect on one's motivational structure, as Gerald Dworkin has emphasised, one can also change one's preferences and give effect to them in action.[39] Further, in this conception reflective or critical understanding covers not only the strictly rational but also the emotional.[40]

As a matter of terminology, recognition of the relational or interpersonal nature of autonomy might be thought to require some re-evaluation of terms associated with the language of autonomy. In the medical treatment context, one of the key interests and rights with which autonomy is associated is, as traditionally conceived, that of "self-determination". To the extent that this term may obscure the role of social upbringing and continued interaction with others in fostering autonomy, it might be thought more appropriate to use another, perhaps less ambitious term, to convey the nature of the interest and right at stake here. I do not, for instance, feel comfortable with Charles Fried's understanding of self-determination as requiring a "determinate domain. . . free of the claims of others".[41] It is hard, however, to find an alternative that carries the appropriate meaning without sounding precious. The idea of "self-choice" is a possible candidate. Whilst far from ideal, it leaves behind the notion, perhaps conveyed by "self-determination", that the individual is not just capable of, but has an interest in, determining herself or her life *on her own*, so to speak, but at the same time captures the importance (and this is critical) of the (competent) individual, rather than others, reflectively making decisions herself in the medical treatment context.[42] However, in the literature of medical ethics and law the right in question is clearly known as the right to "self-determination". So I continue to use "self-determination", to be understood as concerning a person's interest and right, derived from the value of autonomy, in reflectively making significant personal choices. In general, I think it preferable to enrich our understanding of existing terms rather than invent new ones.

---

[39] G Dworkin, *The Theory and Practice of Autonomy*, 108.

[40] M Friedman, "Autonomy, Social Disruption and Women", 37. Elsewhere, Friedman has suggested that since current mainstream views of autonomy acknowledge the social relationships in which personal autonomy is grounded, feminist theories have "[p]erhaps" been wrong to criticise them, suggesting, however, that the true target of such critiques is an ideal of *masculine* autonomy typified by notions of self-sufficiency, substantive independence and freedom from emotional and financial dependence on others. M Friedman, "Feminism in Ethics: Conceptions of Autonomy", 218.

[41] C Fried, "Distributive Justice", (1983) 1(1) *Social Philosophy and Policy* 45, 55.

[42] Another term might be that of "personal determination", which Nicola Lacey appears to use at some points. N Lacey, *Unspeakable Subjects*, 68–9. This perhaps has the benefit of not necessarily seeming to exclude others from the domain of the individual. S Dodds is critical of what she dubs the "voluntary choice model" which identifies autonomy with informed consent. S Dodds, "Choice and Control in Feminist Bioethics", 225. This is an important issue which I touch upon in chs. 3 and 4. At the end of the day, however, the notion of *choice*, remains important if the pregnant woman is to have the final say. Dodds does acknowledge the risk of women being seen as generally incompetent if the identification of autonomy with informed consent is rejected, rather than retaining some "imperfect" control if this move is not made (at 218). In this light, she argues that in moving away from a narrow focus on informed consent we can consider the ways in which "health-care institutions, policies and professionals" can influence "the development, promotion, and exercise of autonomy competency" (at 232).

Whilst on terminology associated with autonomy, this is an appropriate point to identify what is significant about one's interest in bodily integrity or "bodily autonomy" (as this interest is sometimes described) since this interest will be prominent in the discussion throughout. At its heart, it concerns an interest in being able to decide what happens in and to one's body. This is important because one's body is a central part of oneself. Sometimes the right is construed as a property right, but I shall not follow this line here.[43] Rather, the interest in deciding matters involving one's body, at least in the medical treatment and abortion contexts, can best be understood as an aspect of one's interest in self-determination, and so at heart a facet of autonomy. As Jean Cohen has observed in connection with privacy reasoning, recognising the importance of bodily integrity to privacy reasoning does not entail a property analysis of the body, but rather a recognition that bodily integrity is central to individual identity. So for a pregnant woman "the experience of pregnancy constitutes a fundamental change in her embodiment on the physical, emotional, and symbolic levels, and thus in her identity and sense of self", illustrating the intimate connection between bodily integrity and "inviolate personality".[44]

In a similar vein Catriona MacKenzie has argued that it is insufficient to view bodily autonomy (the term she uses) in pregnancy and abortion "simply as a matter of preserving the integrity of one's bodily boundaries".[45] Rather, MacKenzie draws attention to a woman's "reflective perspective" in which she is aware not only that the fetus is somehow inside her own "subjectivity", based on the physical connection between the two, but also that, if the pregnancy continues, the being within her will become a separate being for whom she is morally responsible.[46] MacKenzie stresses that although biologically pregnancy is a passive process, this process is mediated by pregnancy's cultural meanings, a woman's personal and social context and by the manner in which she shapes herself in response to these by means of her decisions. In this way, MacKenzie suggests that bodily autonomy in the context of pregnancy is unhelpfully seen only as the right to bodily integrity, since what is important is that a woman should be able to shape what she dubs "an integrated bodily perspective" through which she can respond to the physical realities of pregnancy in a way with which she identifies and in a way compatible with her decisions concerning her future moral relationship with the fetus.[47]

To the extent that the term bodily integrity may tend to imply simply the importance of being free from invasions, whereas bodily autonomy captures the active and perhaps emotional aspects of one's involvement and decisions relating to one's

[43] C MacKenzie, "Abortion and Embodiment", (1992) 70(2) *Aust J of Phil* 136, 150.

[44] JL Cohen, "Rethinking Privacy: Autonomy, Identity, and the Abortion Controversy", in J Weintraub and K Kumar (eds.), *Public and Private in Thought and Practice: Perspectives on a Grand Dichotomy* (Chicago, IL: University of Chicago Press, 1997) 133–65, 160.

[45] C MacKenzie, "Abortion and Embodiment", 149.

[46] *Ibid.* MacKenzie and Cohen draw on similar literature, such as M Merleau-Ponty, *The Phenomenology of Perception* (1945), C Smith (trans.) (London: Routledge and Kegan Paul, 1962).

[47] C MacKenzie, "Abortion and Embodiment", 151. But note that MacKenzie is working towards a right to fetal death view of abortion.

body, then it may be that bodily autonomy is the richer term, at least in the pregnancy context. Since the term bodily autonomy is also employed in the literature of medical ethics and law, however, there are not the problems of terminology adverted to above with reference to terms other than "self-determination". Note, however, that the term familiar to the legal debate is "bodily integrity" and thus I shall continue predominantly to use that term.

Following this brief introduction to the idea and value of autonomy and its relation to the liberalism–communitarianism and feminist debates on the one hand and to the concepts of self-determination and bodily integrity on the other, to which I shall return at various points, I now briefly consider the meaning and basis of rights and duties and their place in moral thought. In moving from the idea of autonomy to that of rights, note that autonomy is not necessarily rights-based.[48]

B. The Meaning and Basis of Rights

What does it mean to say, for instance, that a fetus either has or lacks a right to life or that a woman has a right to self-determination or bodily integrity?[49] The proposition that "*X* has a right to *Y*" was most famously analysed in relation to legal rights by W. Hohfeld, who proposed four possible models with which to understand rights.[50] Using his analysis, it makes little sense to say that the fetus has a Hohfeldian *bare liberty*, (no duty not to live); or a *power* to alter a legal arrangement, or an *immunity* from legal change. It would appear that if the fetus has a right to life it means that someone, *Z*, has a duty to let the fetus live. This relation has been dubbed a *claim-right*. An immediate question is what is implied when we say that *Z*, perhaps the pregnant woman, has a duty to let the fetus live? It may mean that *Z* has a positive duty to help the fetus, or only that *Z* has the negative duty to refrain from harming the fetus and I shall return to this point later. It appears that such rights as those to self-determination or bodily integrity (whatever these may in fact entail) are, similarly, best characterised as *claim-rights*, as such rights are generally considered most closely to approximate the notion of individual rights employed in political morality. Thus, at a purely logical level, to say that a patient has the right to self-determination is to say that others, for instance doctors, have a duty not to interfere with that right.

Whilst Hohfeld's analysis gives us a starting point with which to understand the concept of a right, it does little to clarify the notion of a duty and this is particularly apparent when we wish to use his originally legal analysis in moral, rather than legal, theory. If a person's right to self-determination implies that some other has a duty of some kind not to obstruct the right-holder's exercise of his right, then how

---

[48] See discussion in ch. 2.
[49] The discussion in this section greatly benefits from the "Introduction" by J Waldron (ed.), to *Theories of Rights*, (Oxford, Oxford University Press, 1984).
[50] WN Hohfeld, *Fundamental Legal Conceptions as Applied in Judicial Reasoning* (New Haven, CT: Yale University Press, 1919).

is it that the right and the duty in this case come to be so related? Essentially, there have been two theories about this relation.

On Bentham's theory of legal rights, X has a right if Y has a duty to perform some act (or omission) which is in X's interest.[51] In a utilitarian system, all duties are intended to advance some individual benefit; it is only where a *particular* individual will benefit from the performance of some duty, however, that there will be a correlative right. Since it is the immediate, rather than some consequential benefit, which creates a right, this means that identification of the benefit determines the content of the duty. This theory has been refined to suggest that X:[52]

> "can be said to have a right (in a moral theory or a legal system) whenever the protection or advancement of some interest of his is recognized (by the theory or the system) as a reason for imposing duties or obligations on others (whether duties and obligations are actually imposed or not)."

The author of this passage suggests there are two particular strengths of this view. First, we can recognise a person's interest in a certain benefit, for example medical care, without having to determine in advance who owes him that duty. Second, individual rights can be better understood by concentrating on the *interest* which grounds various duties rather than by adopting a strictly Hohfeldian approach. For instance, the right to life is not exhausted by the description of a "claim-right" but may in fact invoke other aspects of Hohfeld's analysis, such as an "immunity" from legal change. So, the idea is that we should concentrate on the individual's interest in life which gives rise to the Hohfeldian elements rather than on the detail of the duties which this grounds. I shall return to the Interest approach subsequently.

The Choice Theory, as represented by the work of HLA Hart, asserts that having a right and benefiting from the performance of a duty are not—as the original Benthamite Benefit or Interest Theory would have it—the same.[53] This, Hart says, is demonstrated by the case of promise-making. Thus, if X promises Y to look after his aged mother then, Hart maintains, it is Y, not his mother, who gains a right against X that X will fulfil his promise, notwithstanding that both Y and his mother stand to benefit from this arrangement. Although Y's mother is a person "concerning whom"—to use his phrase—X has an obligation, the point is that the obligation to look after the aged mother is *owed to* Y, *to whom* wrong will have been done if the promise is breached. Moreover, given that Y has a moral claim against X, Y can choose to *release* X from his duty. Thus, to say that Y has a right against X is to say that, morally speaking, Y can determine how X shall act, thereby limiting X's freedom of choice: this, rather than the idea of benefit, is the core of the notion of "a right". The force of this particular promise-making example is in its

---

[51] This analysis is taken from Waldron, who draws on Hart's "Bentham on Legal Rights", in AWB Singer (ed.), *Oxford Essays in Jurisprudence*, Second Series, (Oxford: Oxford University Press, 1973) 171–9 and notes thereto.

[52] J Waldron (ed.), "Introduction", *Theories of Rights*, 10, footnote omitted.

[53] HLA Hart, "Are There Any Natural Rights?", in J Waldron (ed.), *Theories of Rights*, 77–90, 81.

separation of the right-holder from the party who will be the object of the beneficial action; but often, of course, the only person who will benefit is the person to whom the promise has been made.

Hart's thesis, then, is that rights are intrinsically connected with the justified limitation of the freedom of one individual by another. This justification is achieved, not by virtue of any moral quality inherent in the action that one individual is entitled to demand of another (such as that Y's aged mother will be cared for), but rather because "a certain distribution of human freedom will be maintained"[54] if one party has the power to determine how another shall act. He distinguishes between "special" and "general" rights: the former arise within special relationships or transactions such as the promise-making example and, he asserts, *indirectly* invoke the principle that all men have an equal right to be free; in the absence of such special conditions or relationships, general rights are asserted defensively in the light of some threatened action and amount to the *direct* claim of an equal right to be free.

Part of his concern is to accord to rights a "special force"[55] which he considers is lost in the benefit theory. If we consider *any* capacity to benefit as giving rise to rights and correlative duties, then Hart suggests we may mistakenly conclude that babies (presumably also fetuses) and animals have rights. In Hart's theory, given that rights can only be held by beings with the power of choice, neither animals, very small children, nor fetuses can be right-holders. The question of their ill-treatment, however, can be "simply and adequately described . . . by saying that it is wrong or that we ought not to ill-treat them or, in the philosopher's generalized sense of 'duty', that we have a duty not to ill-treat them."[56] In this way he highlights the importance of moral codes in which rights have no place, but which rely instead on such evaluations as *right* or *wrong*, *decency* or *indecency*, *good* or *bad*.[57] Whilst there is scope in his system for this "generalized sense of 'duty' ", however, its application in his argument is only explicitly directed towards beings incapable of choice. Yet it seems hard to believe that Hart would not in fact acknowledge a broader application of this sense of duty towards beings who *can* choose.

The most striking difference between Hart's Choice Theory and the Interest Theory is that the former relates the idea of rights to the active or autonomous aspect of persons: as we have seen, it is those with the ability to *choose* who bear rights—adults, for instance, rather than babies; further, rights are intrinsically related to freedom and, in particular, the justified proscription thereof. It is the right to freedom which underpins all other rights in Hart's theory. On some views correlated with *laissez-faire* conceptions of political morality, the association of rights with choice and autonomy will mean that correlative duties will tend to be negative in character: a duty not to interfere (in the absence of some justification) rather than a duty to provide positive assistance;[58] although, at least in so far as

---

[54] *Ibid.*, 80.
[55] *Ibid.*, 82.
[56] *Ibid.*, 82.
[57] *Ibid.*, 78.
[58] J Waldron (ed.), "Introduction", *Theories of Rights*, 11.

Hart's analysis is concerned, perhaps this negative quality really relates to the defensive character of his "general rights". By contrast, the Interest Theory, hinging as it does on the essential notions of interest and benefit—which are not intrinsically connected with the active rather than the passive sides of moral personality—inclines more to accommodate the latter, positive kind of duty.

As the debate on rights has progressed, however, this difference between the theories has become less marked, as few would now endorse a purely *laissez-faire* libertarian conception of rights imposing only negative duties. Further, as the Interest approach has become more refined, the distinction between the active and the passive has been replicated within the Interest Theory itself, so that, on some approaches, it is particularly those interests associated with autonomy or self-determination which are sufficiently important to ground the ascription of rights.

I do not have the scope here to enter into a sophisticated discussion of these theories. Instead, I now consider whether the Choice or the Interest theory of rights provides a better theoretical basis with which to analyse the maternal–fetal relationship.

C. The Basis of Rights in the Maternal–Fetal Relationship

I shall take the middle ground and thereby endorse both the ideas of interests and autonomy as these are brought together in formulations of the Interest Theory which consider our interests in autonomy to be of particular importance. Conscious of a vast theoretical dispute as to the strengths and weaknesses of the respective theories which would take me far beyond my present concerns,[59] I shall not support my choice in any generally defensible way. Instead, I make some brief points about why this approach seems well suited to the maternal–fetal relationship. The former relate to the fetus, the latter to the pregnant woman.

To begin, it is only on the Interest approach that the fetus—at least at some point in its development (the acquisition of sentience)—is able to enter the debate on its own terms, rather than purely as the object, say, of Hart's "generalized philosopher's 'duty' ".[60] As shall be apparent when I reflect, at various points, upon the importance of imperfect (or non–instrumental) duties, it may in fact prove not to be a handicap that on the Choice Theory the fetus does not enter the debate "in its own right", as it were. Yet, so far as the question of maternal–*fetal* conflict is concerned, to settle for an analysis which gives us no way of determining what stake the fetus *itself* may have in health and life, seems at best conceptually limiting

---

[59] For instance, the Interest Theory appears to be in difficulty in accounting for the relations pertaining to third party beneficiaries of correlative duties; moreover, on this theory, conflicts of rights appear inevitable. For discussion of these issues, see e.g. H Steiner, *An Essay on Rights* (Oxford: Blackwell, 1994) ch. 3.

[60] Unless, that is, one asserts that all human beings (including fetuses) have rights by virtue of being human. For an example of such an approach see e.g. the discussion of the human species argument in s. III(A) *infra*.

and at worst potentially to prejudge the issue. If the fetus acquires interests at some stage, does it also acquire rights? On the original Interest approach we might say, for instance, that its interests in life and health are sufficient to ground the ascription of rights. Yet to grant the fetus rights because it has a clear capacity to benefit will possibly be to lose sight of the fact that benefiting the fetus may well implicate its mother, possibly in adverse ways. This would suggest that some importance is still due to the idea of autonomy in the ascription of rights, since autonomy is an important hallmark of an independent being (small infants excepted, but they are physically detached from their mother, unlike the fetus). Thus, on a hybrid Interest–autonomy account of rights we might instead argue that, as a being which exists inside a person and is incapable of autonomous choice, at some point the fetus has *strong interests* rather than rights. I shall consider this further in due course. As we shall shortly see when considering the moral status of the fetus, these points should not obscure the important ways in which the fetus may in any event be the subject of moral concern, but not on its own terms, so to speak.

As for why a hybrid Interest–autonomy account of rights may be best suited to our analysis of the pregnant woman's situation in the treatment context, our understanding of the right to refuse medical treatment is enhanced not so much by the idea of the justified limitation of the freedom of one individual by another—the essence of the Choice Theory—as by the idea that any patient has a strong *interest* in being able to refuse or consent to medical treatment, in the sense that such a choice is one aspect of an individual's interest in making significant choices in his or her life. The Interest Theory, in effect, necessarily gives *content* to rights. In other words, if we were to try to explain the right to refuse medical treatment *solely* in terms of the distribution of human freedom as between doctor and patient, it would seem hard to explain why a patient should want to have a say in limiting what treatment a doctor administers. Of course, we could point to the idea of freedom—the right which underpins all others in Hart's system—but then so on refined interpretations of the Interest approach can we give particular weight to those interests connected with autonomy. Thus it is unclear what the Choice Theory could offer over the hybrid Interest–autonomy theory in this context. Indeed, given its assumption of a right to freedom, although Hart's theory could be said to offer a good explanation of how at least some rights operate—such as the rights arising from promises—his theory does not appear well-placed to explain the *value,* or *justification*, of a right such as the right to refuse medical treatment. As we have seen, this is because on his approach rights have no intrinsic connection with the moral qualities of the actions that individuals can ask of one another: the concept of freedom underpinning his theory encompasses equally the freedom to wear differently coloured clothes each day of the week as it does the freedom to refuse medical treatment. By contrast, in the close connection between the latter right and issues of importance in a person's life, the Interest theory seems better able to explain such a right. Such rights are necessarily *moral* in character in a way that Hart's rights (other than the right to freedom) are not. Indeed, Hart has acknowledged that the Choice Theory cannot adequately explain either all legal rights or, more particularly, those which are part of social and political morality.[61]

In its emphasis on control, however, the Choice Theory has advantages over the original formulation of the Interest Theory, as the latter would appear hard-pressed to explain the purpose of a right to refuse unquestionably beneficial medical treatment, given its emphasis on passive benefit rather than active, autonomous choice. In the light of the importance and value of the idea of autonomy explored above, the hybrid Interest–autonomy approach seems most constructive in this context, a point which will be brought out in different ways in discussion throughout.

D. The Place of Rights and Duties within Moral Theory

There is one other question which should be highlighted in introduction, particularly in the light of the way in which I shall thread my ethical and legal arguments together. Thus, we should note the divergence of views regarding, in particular, the importance to be attached to the idea of rights within moral theory.

Moral requirements are sometimes thought to be fully satisfied by the recognition of rights, beyond which lies the domain of the morally optional. Thus, on some views, given that rights are the principal constituents of morality, so long as rights are not violated, no moral wrongs are committed.[62] Alternatively, beyond or even prior to rights may lie a no less important arena of moral requirements or duties. Such contrasting visions draw attention to the differing importance attached to rights and duties in various moral theories. In this regard, for instance, Ronald Dworkin has suggested that political theories can be classified according to whether they are *right-*, *duty-* or *goal-based*: a *right-based* theory would regard a right, such as the right to equality, as fundamental; in a *duty-based* theory some duty, such as the duty not to harm others would be primary; and a *goal-based* approach would focus attention on some goal, such as enhancing general welfare.[63] Alternatively, some philosophers may hold a conception of morality in which neither rights nor duties (nor goals) predominate. For instance, in Joseph Raz's work rights and duties are to be understood as embedded within his wide theory of individual well-being,[64] an aspect upon which I touch in due course. For now, let me very briefly outline two contrasting conceptions of morality.

A writer well known for his rights-based approach is Robert Nozick, whose theory is developed particularly in opposition to utilitarianism, on the basis of the common criticism that the latter fails to recognise the separateness of persons.[65]

---

[61] HLA Hart, "Bentham on Legal Rights", 196–8, as noted by J Waldron (ed.), "Introduction", *Theories of Rights*, 9.

[62] See e.g. R Nozick, *Anarchy, State and Utopia* (Oxford: Blackwell, 1974).

[63] R Dworkin, *Taking Rights Seriously*, 2nd impression (corrected) with appendix (London: Duckworth, 1978) 171.

[64] J Raz, "Right-based Moralities", in J Waldron (ed.), *Theories of Rights*, 182–200.

[65] R Nozick, *Anarchy, State and Utopia*. It is beyond my scope to determine the merits of this criticism.

Nozick posits that morality is constituted by a closely restricted group of almost absolute individual rights, such as the right not to be killed or assaulted (provided one does not violate the rights of others), the right to be free from any kind of coercion or limitation upon one's freedom and the right not to have legitimately acquired property taken or its use restricted. In essence, a rights-based theory such as this assumes that we can reduce morality down to some sort of individualist core in which, broadly speaking, the violation of rights is the sole form of moral wrong. On this view, the exercise of our rights is always morally acceptable. Nozick's model for these basic moral rights appears to be a legal one: in the same vein that there can be no *legal* objection to the exercise of a legal right, so the exercise of a moral right is always inherently unproblematic.[66] Yet this leaves us with no moral vocabulary with which to condemn many kinds of conduct, including, I would emphasise, the moral acceptability of the exercise of legal rights, a point of concern here. Indeed, the implication is that there are no morally relevant considerations beyond the core that is constituted by rights, a position few philosophers would accept.

Turning to a very different conception of morality and rights, Onora O'Neill has argued that both utilitarian and liberal thought have emphasised justice at the expense of charity and other virtues and have thereby broken the link between the ideas of obligation and virtue.[67] Whilst obligations were fundamental in Locke's thought, they tend now to be understood merely as the "perfect" obligations which are the correlation of rights. Further, she argues that since there are no rights to charity, so charity—concern for the needs of others—has all but disappeared from our ethical map. In this light, charity is conceived either as personal preference, so that "callous and kindly actions to others in need are equally permissible, provided that justice is not breached" or as superogatory, so that "mundane help to others in need will be in the same category as saintly or heroic action".[68] (I touch on this theme in chapter two when I consider an important article by Judith Jarvis Thomson regarding the issue of abortion which effectively considers what is morally required of a woman who is pregnant.) But helping others in need *is* an obligation, O'Neill argues, in the light of the fact that we are both rational and needy agents. The notion of agency is central to this argument because, whereas "perfect" obligations consist in *relationships*, "imperfect" obligations are intrinsically related to *agents* in that they are principles which underlie and define the virtues of agents.[69] As rational and potentially vulnerable agents we could not universally adopt, in the Kantian sense, a principle of self-centred indifference to others because such a principle could well undermine our agency. In other words, if we all adopt the principle that we are under no obligation to help each other when in need, then, given that most of us need help at some point or points, we would be

---

[66] As HLA Hart notes in his "Between Utility and Rights", (1979) 79 *Colum L Rev* 828, 834.

[67] O O'Neill, "The Great Maxims of Justice and Charity", in her *Constructions of Reason: Exploring Kant's Practical Philosophy* (Cambridge: Cambridge University Press, 1989) 219–33.

[68] *Ibid.*, 225.

[69] On this argument they are also intrinsically related to agencies and traditions.

setting ourselves up for the undermining, perhaps destruction, of our own agency. As rational beings, as rational *agents*, we simply cannot endorse such a principle; rather, we are duty-bound to be charitable, to assist others in need. Significantly, while Kant's emphasis on autonomy has often been interpreted as being rights-based, in linking the concepts of autonomy, agency and duty, O'Neill seeks instead to suggest a duty-based tenor to his work.

Further to discuss these important issues on their own terms, however, would seriously delay beginning the substantive moral and legal questions which the book must address. I therefore rely upon discussion in various parts to highlight, in particular, the inadequacies of a rights-based conception of morality. Moreover, it will be seen that a moral justification of the law cannot be made by reference solely to the concept of rights, or not that concept at "face value", as it were, highlighting the need to deepen our understanding of the legal rights here in question. I touch on these issues at appropriate points. I now turn to explore the moral relationship between a pregnant woman and the unborn child she carries.

II. THE FETUS OR THE FUTURE CHILD?

Most of the literature on the maternal–fetal conflict construes the parties in issue as the woman and the "fetus", so that the harm that may be done if a woman refuses treatment needed by the fetus, say, is seen as harm inflicted on the "fetus". Similarly, as will be seen in Part II, the legal cases refer to the "fetus". One scholar, however, has persistently criticised this language. John Robertson, writing in 1994, reiterates his suggestion that at least in some cases of maternal–fetal conflict, "the real party in interest is not the fetus itself but the child that the fetus will become".[70] Robertson is addressing the issue not just of treatment refusal but also of maternal general conduct regarding which harm—for example through smoking or alcohol consumption—will likely be to the future child, given that these activities do not typically result in fetal death *in utero*. Nevertheless, sometimes the result also of a refusal of treatment may be harm—such as brain damage—to the child who will in due course be born. With these points in mind, Robertson holds that to discuss the conflict in terms of the *fetus* confuses and biases the issue in favour of the mother. Rather, on his view, if the real party in some cases is instead recognised as the subsequently born child then, he argues, we should speak in terms of maternal duties to "expected offspring".[71] In this light he suggests that the interests which are to be weighed against the woman's may appear rather stronger than those, particularly, of a relatively early fetus.

The exception to the idea that the real party in issue is the future child generally occurs with the *viable* fetus. At this point, Robertson argues, the interests in issue are indeed those of the fetus, not the subsequently born child. The difference to

[70] J Robertson, *Children of Choice: Freedom and the New Reproductive Technologies* (Princeton, NJ: Princeton University Press, 1994) 176.
[71] *Ibid.*, 177.

which he appears to be drawing attention is that where maternal and fetal interests are in conflict at fetal viability, the most likely cause is that a woman is refusing delivery by caesarean section, thereby most probably endangering fetal life (though brain damage is also a possibility). Thus, whereas in general during a pregnancy which a woman intends to carry to term the well-being of the fetus matters because it will in turn determine or affect the well-being of the born child, where fetal death is in issue, a child may in fact never be born whose interests will have been affected *in utero* (which is not to presume that abortion may not wrong a being). Of course, fetal death may also be in issue with the refusal of treatment *pre-viability*, for instance in the case of maternal refusal of a blood transfusion.

Thus, it seems that Robertson is arguing that there is sometimes a difference in the *identity* of the "other" that is in issue. (The term "identity" is used here for want of a better word: there is no suggestion that the fetus would not become the born child if it were subsequently born.) In effect, it appears that Robertson is arguing that, morally (and legally), the "other" party is on occasion the subsequently born child. By identifying the interests in issue in this way, he may consider that the need to determine the morality (and legality) of actions affecting that child when *in utero* (effectively, in the past and inside another person) becomes obsolete, in the sense that the subsequently born child is generally accepted as a moral (and legal) person with interests and rights. But the real difficulty is precisely to determine the moral (and legal) weight to be given to that other's interests *when still in utero*. Thus, even if we did recognise the "identity" of the other along Robertson's lines, we would still need to "remember" that it had been *in utero* in order to determine the legitimacy of actions affecting it in that time and place, which would be highly contorted.

Importantly, it should be noted that the term "future child" is thus capable of two different meanings: first, Robertson's notion of the *subsequently born child* and second, my notion of the child *who will be but is not yet born*. I adopt the latter meaning because, from the pregnant woman's perspective, since—looking forward—she carries the child who will be born and—looking backward—the born child was within her body, I do not think it possible to debate the morality of her choices and actions as these affect that child other than in a way which acknowledges its place, for a certain period, within her body. By contrast, the morality of the detached third party's actions could well be debated in such a way that the term "future child" only meant the subsequently born individual. Critically, this is because the *body* of the third party is not implicated in actions affecting that child. As between the "future child" and the pregnant woman, however, and the question of the way in which what she does affects it, it is impossible to leapfrog over gestation and birth to the time when the child is a physically separate being. So far as the maternal–fetal conflict goes, then, as opposed to the relationship between the future child and a detached third party, I consider that the term "future child" is best understood as the child *who will be but is not yet born* (thus, who is now *in utero* but will be born alive). By contrast, my use of the term "fetus" tends to imply that the unborn child will die *in utero* (as indeed it does for Robertson).

Indeed, it cannot be stressed too strongly that the relationship between a pregnant woman and the future child is importantly different from that between the same child and a third party (such as the father) in that only in the former case does the future child currently exist *within* the other party of the relationship. Hence, if the father harms the future child, he does not do so through his body (since the future child is not inside him) but rather, for instance, by means of his general conduct. For example he might carelessly drive a car in which the mother is a passenger, thereby causing an accident as a result of which the future child is born harmed. As we shall see, the fact that the future child exists inside the mother means that the moral status of a human being still *in utero*—the fetus—may be relevant in considering the moral obligations of a pregnant woman to the future child in a way that it would not be in considering, for instance, the relationship between the same child and its father, *at least when the obligation to the future child seriously involves the woman's body*. This latter condition is usually satisfied regarding the medical treatment context with which I am principally concerned. By contrast, I shall note that where a woman might harm the future child as a result of some instance of her "general conduct"—for instance by driving in a careless manner—her obligations might well be commensurate with those of the "detached" third party. The possibility of a woman causing prenatal harm in this way will principally be discussed in chapter six, when I address arguments from the law of tort. For present purposes, the important distinction to note is between the idea of obligations which are to be realised "by means of" the body, as in the case of the pregnant woman whose unborn child requires certain medical treatment, and obligations attaching to the domain of general conduct (acts or omissions). With regard to some (limited) sorts of harm that a pregnant woman may do to the future child, she may be akin to a "*detached* third party"; with regard to the context of medical treatment, by contrast, a woman and her fetus are very much *attached*. These differences affect the nature and quality of her obligations to the *future child* (as well as, of course, to the fetus) in the treatment context in a way that requires us to review the *moral status of the fetus*.

Accordingly, I shall briefly examine four key arguments which originate in the abortion debate regarding the fetus's moral status. The abortion debate clearly concerns the issue of fetal death and in this way is necessarily and exclusively about the fetus. Yet in saying this, we might reflect that to some degree the question of the fetus's moral status with regard to abortion attracts so much attention because a fetus is a developing human being who will, after a certain finite period of time (barring other events or actions) be born. In other words, in any case it may be misconceived to construe arguments which discuss the moral status of the fetus as ones which necessarily concern the fetus *qua* fetus. Moreover, the fetus changes, both physically and mentally and is, on some arguments, a being of changing moral status.

In considering the implications of these arguments for the issue of maternal refusal of treatment, I refer particularly to the issue of refusal of surgical delivery by caesarean section, partly because this is in fact the most common instance of maternal–fetal conflict within the medical arena and partly because such surgery implicates a woman's interests in self-determination and bodily integrity very seriously. Similarly, from the fetus's viewpoint, a great deal is at stake. So far as refusal of treatment at the stage of fetal viability is concerned, of course, Robertson himself identifies the "other" in issue as the fetus, but the question of the strength of the fetus's interests in this scenario remains to be determined. I am also concerned to address the idea of maternal refusal of treatment more generally. Thus, she might refuse medical treatment such as a blood transfusion, surgery other than a caesarean,[72] forceps delivery or a therapy[73] that is estimated to enhance fetal well-being or preserve fetal life. She might also refuse to be examined when this is apparently needed in the interests of the fetus. A possible instance of treatment refusal which goes to the question of the future child's interests being affected is the refusal of corrective fetal surgery. In such a case, it is clear that the interests in question are those of the future child, that is, the child who will be but is not yet born. Still, as suggested above, the weight of that future child's interests needs to be determined. In this regard, a highly relevant consideration will be its location inside its

[72] In the early days of fetal surgery the two most commonly performed operations were for hydrocephalus (whereby fluid accumulates in the brain) and fetal hydronephrosis (in which the urinary tract is obstructed). K Knopoff, "Can a Pregnant Woman Morally Refuse Fetal Surgery?", 79 (1991) *Calif L Rev* 499, 503–4. As noted by A Ouellette, fetal surgery has since been used to treat lung tumours, congenital diaphragmatic hernia (a hole in the diaphragm allowing the liver to be pushed into the chest cavity which may lead to respiratory failure), fetal chylotorax (where chyle, a milk-like substance usually found in the digestive tract forms in the pleural cavity or chest), sacrococcygeal teratoma (a tumour in the lower spinal cord), cleft lip and palate and simple types of congenital heart disease. Corrective procedures involve shunting blocked or fluid filled areas, patching holes, correcting deformities or removing tumours. A Ouellette, "New Medical Technology: A Chance to Reexamine Court-Ordered Medical Procedures during Pregnancy", (1994) 57 *Alb L Rev* 927, 932–3 drawing on M Longaker *et al*, "Update on the Status of Fetal Surgery" (1991) 23 *Surgery Annals* 53, 55. Clearly the pregnant woman must be treated as well as the fetus and for all types of surgery she must undergo a general anaesthetic. Following the surgery, premature labour is always a risk and hence the woman must take drugs to allay this (Ouellette at 933 citing Longaker *et al* at 64). Further, experts apparently agree that a woman who has fetal surgery must deliver by caesarean-section in order to avoid rupture of the prior surgical incisions (Ouellette at 933 citing M Harrison and N Adzick, "The Fetus as a Patient: Surgical Considerations", (1991) 213 *Annals Surgery* 279, 290). Risks associated with the surgery include haemorrhage, damage to surrounding tissue and organs, sepsis, death or other complications. K Knopoff, "Can a Pregnant Woman Morally Refuse Fetal Surgery?", 527, citing N Hacker and J Moore, *Essentials of Obstetrics and Gynaecology* (1986) 238–9. The technique of fetoscopy is much less invasive, however: it would not have to be followed by a caesarean but would still involve a general anaesthetic (Ouellette at 935 citing R Quintero *et al*, "Brief Report: Umbilical-Cord Ligation of an Acardiac Twin by Fetoscopy at 19 Weeks of Gestation", (1994) 330 *New Eng J Med* 469, 469–70.) Further details are given by Ouellette.

[73] On developments in this field, see e.g. E Reece and C Homko, "Embryoscopy, Fetal Therapy and Ethical Implications", (1994) 57 *Alb L Rev* 709. Embryoscopy is "a recently introduced technique which consists of either transcervical or transabdominal fiberoptic endoscopy of the first trimester embryo/fetus, has the potential for early and accurate prenatal diagnosis without the drawbacks of CVS [chorionic villus sampling]". (At 713.) The technique can be performed from five weeks menstrual age. and hence the practice will place more emphasis on the first trimester in fetal medicine. The authors note that whilst various diagnoses of embryonic malformations have been achieved through endoscopy, "the diagnostic and therapeutic potential is just beginning to unfold" (at 713) and suggest the time is ripe for ethical, legal and regulatory debate (at 724). The authors further note that embryonic organ-tissue biopsy and/or embryonic blood sampling appear possible and observe the progress being made in developing techniques for human cell and gene therapy. (At 718.) The ethical issues surrounding the latter techniques are beyond my current scope, except to note that the spectrum of fetal therapy which a mother might refuse is clearly ever broader. Overall, the authors note "that the perfection of embryoscopy will provide access to the entire conceptus, permitting both early diagnosis and, potentially, early treatment." (At 719, footnote omitted).

mother (which Robertson may perhaps acknowledge)[74] and, concomitantly, the extent to which the satisfaction of its medical needs impinges upon her body, though arguably its own state of current development may also affect the strength of its claims.

III. THE MORAL STATUS OF THE FETUS

Consider the following statements by obstetricians: "There are two patients with competing interests: the woman who refuses the cesarean and the fetus whose health depends upon it", and "the fetus is established as our second patient with many rights and privileges comparable to those previously achieved only after birth".[75] These statements are illustrative of the view that the scientific possibility of treating the fetus confers upon it the status of a patient with rights. Whether the fetus has the status of a "patient", however, and whether it has rights, is properly the subject not of scientific but of ethical and legal enquiry.

In this section I examine four key, even "classic", arguments concerning the fetus's moral status and outline a fifth view which captures something of the import of the other views and provides two bases upon which to consider fetal interests or claims. Each brief section is divided into three parts: the first outlines the argument; the second comments on it; the third considers the implications of the argument for the maternal–fetal conflict, notably what assistance each argument might or might not offer regarding the questions there arising. Rather than try to address all the possible implications or scenarios in each third section, which would be both repetitive and at times unenlightened, I shall try to develop a picture of the maternal–fetal conflict as the chapter progresses. By the end, when I shall be exploring those arguments which are most helpful, I shall attempt to give preliminary answers to the questions arising. Whilst the strength of the last arguments I consider lies in the joint attention they pay to maternal and fetal interests, conclusive answers cannot be given until the next chapter, in which I focus on the maternal–fetal conflict from the woman's point of view, that is, specifically in terms of those interests and rights of hers that are implicated and affected in pregnancy, as well as in terms of her duties.

---

[74] For instance, in comparing a parent's duty to provide an experimental medical technique for a born child with the idea of a pregnant woman's to do so for what he describes here as "the fetus" he notes that the fetus's "legal claim is traditionally less compelling than that of a child, *particularly* when the intervention must be done to the *body* of the mother who opposes it". The surrounding passages indicate that Robertson might here be concerned both with avoiding fetal death and with preventing harm to the future child. J Robertson, "The Right to Procreate and *in utero* Fetal Therapy", (1982) 3 *J Leg Med* 333, 346.

[75] Respectively from E Raines, "Editorial Comment", to R Jurow and RH Paul, "Caesarean Delivery for Fetal Distress Without Maternal Consent", (1984) 63 *Obstet & Gyn* 596, 599; and J Pritchard *et al* (eds.), *John Whitridge Williams, Williams Obstetrics*, 17th edn. (Nowalk, CO: Appleton Century Crofts, 1985) at xi, 867–71. These are very common views amongst obstetricians. For a powerful account of the development of fetal surgery and of the centrality of the fetus therein, see MJ Caspar, *The Making of the Unborn Patient* (New Brunswick, NJ: Rutgers University Press, 1998).

Finally, neither of the first two arguments (human species and personhood) can help us with the distinction between the interests of the fetus and the future child. Rather, they focus solely upon the fetus. The question of the interests of the future child will be picked up as we leave the third argument (the interest view) and enter the fourth (the argument from potential).

A. Conservative Position—Human Species Argument

"The most fundamental question involved in the long history of thought on abortion is: How do you determine the humanity of a being?"[76]

1. The Argument

The first argument is one of two based on Catholic thought. I have chosen the writer JT Noonan as an exponent of this argument, for whom the morally pertinent issue is to establish the "criterion of humanity".[77] In the following discussion, the principal points of the human species argument are his.

The argument first asserts that a human being exists from the moment of conception and defends this view in two ways. First, there is the "positive argument" that at conception the human genetic code attaches to the new being: "A being with a human genetic code is man."[78] On the face of it, it is unclear how this statement is different from the tautologous one: "A being with a human genetic code is human." But the purpose is to attribute to the zygote, embryo or fetus the full moral status and hence full rights of a born human being. In order to do this, the morally relevant quality must be humanity itself. Thus, although the argument seeks to establish the "criterion of humanity", the real point is to establish the criterion of moral status *as* humanity. On such a view, the fetus is seen as a being with full moral status: to be a member of the human species is all that counts, morally speaking.

The second argument in support of the significance of conception is a negative one. In effect, the strength of this position is tested by challenging the view that any morally relevant lines can be drawn after conception. The most commonly proposed distinction is that of viability, the point at which—usually after about 24 weeks—the fetus is able to live independently of the woman. Attributing significance to viability, it is argued, denies humanity to the fetus on the basis of its dependence. The criticism here is that dependence continues after viability, as a premature baby and very young children are utterly dependent on the care of another for their continuing existence.

[76] JT Noonan Jr., "An Almost Absolute Value in History", in JT Noonan Jr. (ed.), *The Morality of Abortion: Legal and Historical Perspectives* (Cambridge, MA: Harvard University Press, 1970) reprinted in J Arras and N Rhoden (eds.), *Ethical Issues in Modern Medicine,* 3rd edn. (Mountain View, CA: Mayfield Pub. Co., 1989) 261–5, 261.

[77] *Ibid.*

[78] *Ibid.*, 264

2. Commentary

My commentary in this section focuses on the "negative" argument, as the "positive" one will be considered in relation to the argument from potential, considered later. Turning to the negative argument, it might be argued that the significance of viability is not independence *per se*, but independence in the sense of the *ability to be separate from the mother's body*: in other words, at viability the fetus no longer exclusively depends on another's *body*. Thus, in criticising the viability benchmark, the conservative may fail to distinguish between care on the one hand and the life-supporting physical assistance provided by the body of the woman on the other: the last invokes the bodily integrity of a woman; the first does not. This failing is not uncommon. For instance, according to one scholar who specifically addresses the issue of maternal–fetal conflict, the argument that:[79]

> "there is a fundamental difference between the fetus in an incubator and a fetus *in utero*, no matter what its stage of development . . . hinges on two claims: 1) *where* an entity is determines *what* it is, and 2) the fact of biological dependence reduces an individual from person to non-person".

It is instructive to note the use of language such that the term "fetus" is used with regard both to the being *in utero* and the one in the incubator. By definition, however, a fetus is an *unborn* human in the sense of a being which is still within the body of the woman. That the writer in question uses the term "fetus" to apply also to a *born* human being accounts for his failure to notice certain important moral distinctions. For instance, with reference to his first point (that where an entity is determines what it is), he asserts that "no *place* other than a uterus is ascribed similar status-altering properties",[80] and in succeeding passages he repeatedly refers to the idea of a uterus as a place, his goal being to reject the notion that the uterus should in any way be "ethically special".[81] Yet this misses the point that, while an incubator is a place, it is also a *thing*. With the uterus, by contrast, we are talking not just of a location, but of a *part of a person's body*. Importantly, this means that in the latter case a *person's interests* are directly implicated.[82]

The writer elaborates his second point (that the fact of biological dependence reduces an individual from person to non-person) in terms of the fetus being "dependent on a biological support mechanism that involves *the mother—another biological support mechanism*."[83] Yet here again, as with Noonan, there is a failure to distinguish between technological assistance on the one hand and the assistance provided quite

---

[79] E-HW Kluge, "When Cesarean Section Operations Imposed by Court are Justified", (1988) 14 *JME* 206, 208.

[80] *Ibid.*, my emphasis.

[81] *Ibid.*

[82] See further ch. 2.

[83] *Ibid.*, my emphasis. The use of language here is tantamount to the idea, captured critically by G Annas, of women being perceived as "fetal containers". "Pregnant Women as Fetal Containers", (1986) 16 (Dec) *Hastings CR* 13. This idea, which is particularly pertinent to this article, is a general theme of Annas's essentially legal writings on the topic, to which reference is made in Pt. II.

literally *through* a person's body on the other. In other words, with regard to the fetus, it is neither the idea of place nor that of dependence, but the way in which these two points come together in the fetal dependence on the *body* of another person that is the morally significant feature affecting fetal moral status, meaning the fetus's need to be inside and draw upon the physical help of its mother's body. Concomitantly, the significance of fetal viability is that, although the fetus is still inside the pregnant woman, since at this time it becomes *capable* of independent existence it may therefore be accorded greater moral weight. Thus, so far as abortion is concerned, as opposed to writers such as Noonan and others who argue that the fetus has full moral status from conception onwards, viability (understood solely as the point at which fetal dependence on the woman may cease) is a significant distinction which from this time arguably lessens the strength of the woman's interests and increases those of the fetus, precisely because the fetus no longer needs the woman's body to the same extent. That is, the fetus need no longer depend on the woman's body for survival and hence need no longer implicate her interest in bodily integrity (although it will clearly benefit from going to term and implicates her interest in bodily integrity as long as it remains within her). Indeed, this position will later be seen to be reflected in the law. Yet what about the issue of maternal–fetal conflict?

3. Implications for the Maternal–Fetal Conflict

With regard to the refusal of caesarean delivery at viability the situation may be rather different, in the sense that the "treatment" which the fetus needs very seriously impinges upon the bodily integrity of the pregnant woman: it requires that she be cut open. Indeed, a caesarean section is viewed as major surgery. For this reason, there may not be quite the same lessening of a woman's interests and strengthening of those of the fetus that arguably occurs with regard to viability in the abortion context. Yet viability remains significant in the treatment refusal context in another (related) way, namely in the degree of fetal development. We can understand this by considering the following point.

Several writers have argued that technological developments which enable the fetus to survive outside the womb with artificial aid may mean that viability reaches earlier into pregnancy, which could be interpreted as destroying the moral significance of the distinction.[84] Yet such an approach fails to distinguish between

---

[84] See e.g. R Gillon, "Editor's Reply" to C Strong and G Anderson, "The Moral Status of the Near-Term Fetus", (1989) 15 *JME* 25, 27. Gillon describes the implications of the concept of viability as counter-intuitive in that "[i]n principle any fetus and indeed any embryo is viable given only technology to replace the natural support system provided by the mother's uterine-placental 'incubator'". Gillon's insistence upon viability's "indeterminacy" in the light of changing technology fails to acknowledge the intuitive aspect of viability as a *normative* concept. The idea that viability is an entirely medical or biological notion is quite common. See e.g. AE Doudera, "Fetal Rights? It Depends", (1982) 18 *Trial* 38: "Upon viability, a medical concept and essentially a matter of medical determination, the fetus is entitled to the full protection of the law. As such it should be proper for the courts to act to protect fetal life and rights while it is *in utero*". (At 44). As the book seeks to demonstrate, such questions as what protection the fetus merits and against whom are a complex of ethics and law (and legally, of principle and policy).

two senses of viability.[85] The first is the idea of independence from the mother's body made possible by technological development, such that as a matter of fact fetuses may be viable at increasingly early dates. The second sense captures the *moral* or *normative* import of viability. It is fair to say that on this latter approach the moral significance of viability is assumed to depend upon its natural attainment. At the same time, however, a fetus attains "natural viability" after it has been allowed to develop for some (approximately) six months. In this way, the significance of the moral or normative sense of viability is that since a fetus has developed to such a degree that it can survive outside the womb *without* artificial assistance, it may thereby have some claim to protection inside the womb. Hence, even though cae-sarean delivery seriously impinges upon a woman's body, at the same time arguably the claims of the "naturally" viable fetus at least require serious consideration. The fact that its claims will be tempered by our determination of the extent to which fetal needs at this time impinge upon a woman's interests highlights an important moral point, namely the *interlocking* nature of maternal and fetal interests: the way in which the strength of each must be viewed in relation to and partly determined by the strength of the other, a point inherent in the viability benchmark. This understanding represents the first element in our picture of the maternal–fetal relationship in the treatment context.

Returning briefly to Noonan's original argument, of the further distinctions which are criticised by the human species argument, one is particularly notewor-thy, namely that of "social visibility".[86] The target here is the view that since moral reasoning concerns the relationships between members of society, we cannot rea-son about a being who is not such a member: "Excluded from the society of men, the fetus is excluded from the humanity of men."[87] In fact, it is unclear that our moral reasoning only concerns the relationship between human beings as, for instance, we also reason about our treatment of animals and the environment. This is not a point which an exponent of the human species argument would readily acknowledge, since it is likely to threaten the view that genetic humanity is a nec-essary condition for moral status and in turn opens up the possibility that the pos-session of humanity itself might not guarantee the fetus a place as a member of the moral community. Rather, an exponent of the human species view would deny that being a member of a moral community in fact requires the possession of cer-tain characteristics, such as consciousness, reasoning and the ability to communi-cate. I now turn to an argument built upon this view.

B. The Personhood Argument

"The question which we must answer in order to produce a satisfactory solution to the problem of the moral status of abortion is this: How are we to define the moral commu-

---

[85] N Rhoden, "Trimesters and Technology: Revamping *Roe* v. *Wade*", (1986) 95 *Yale LJ* 639, 671.
[86] JT Noonan, Jr., "An Almost Absolute Value", 262.
[87] *Ibid.*, footnote omitted.

nity, the set of beings with full and equal moral rights, such that we can decide whether a human fetus is a member of this community or not?"[88]

1. *The Argument*

In this section I examine what is known as the "personhood argument", by considering the work of its original exponent, Mary Ann Warren, whose (early) views are expressed in the first section.[89]

This approach criticises the human species argument for failing to consider why the moral community should be identified with the set of all human beings. The suggestion is that the neglect of this question results from the failure to distinguish two senses of the term "human". In the *genetic* sense, "*any* member of the species is a human being"; by contrast, in the *moral* sense, a being is human, it is argued, so long as it is a "full-fledged member of the moral community".[90] Such a member is possessed of "full and equal rights", it is claimed, and thus the question of determining the (moral) humanity of the fetus involves asking whether the fetus has such rights. It is alleged that the human species argument both needs and fails to show that fetuses are human in precisely this sense, "the sense in which it is analytically true that all human beings have full moral rights".[91] Of course, to be fair to the human species view, it is not considered necessary to demonstrate this analytic truth because—on this view—to be human simply is to be a moral being: humanity *is* the criterion of moral status. The radical proposal inherent in the personhood argument was to challenge this view by redefining the moral community as follows.

Rather than consisting of all and only *human beings*, the moral community instead comprises all and only *persons*. To determine the content of such a community, a rough list is drawn up of the most obvious criteria of personhood: primarily consciousness, rationality and agency, but also the ability to communicate and self-consciousness. Whilst the possession of only some of these criteria may be sufficient for personhood and it may not be necessary to possess any *one* criterion from this list, it is asserted that all that is needed to demonstrate that the fetus is not a person is the proposition that a being with none of these characteristics is not a person. If the fetus lacks these characteristics then, for instance, abortion is not seriously morally wrong: even anti-abortionists "ought to agree", not only that the five criteria are

---

[88] MA Warren, "On the Moral and Legal Status of Abortion", (1973) 57(1) *The Monist* 43, reprinted in J Arras and N Rhoden (eds.), *Ethical Issues in Modern Medicine*, 276–86, 280.

[89] The argument as summarised here can be found in *ibid.* 280–3. Warren's more recent reflections are touched upon in due course.

[90] JT Noonan, Jr., "An Almost Absolute Value", 281.

[91] MA Warren, "On the Moral and Legal Status of Abortion", 281. To be fair to Noonan, it should be noted that terminological imprecision is a common failing in this area. See e.g. R Wertheimer, "Understanding the Abortion Argument", (1971) 1 *Phil & Pub Aff* 67, who begins his article: "First off I should note that the expressions "a human life", "a human being", "a person" are virtually interchangeable in this context." (At 69.) However, unlike Noonan, Wertheimer recognises that the concept of a human being both is and is not a moral concept, so that the term can be both descriptive and normative. (At 70.)

crucial to the idea of personhood, but "also that it is a part of this concept that all and only people have full moral rights".[92] Thus, the personhood argument hinges upon a normative understanding of the term "person", in a sense to be explored below.

2. Commentary

The first point is that in effect the argument has simply shifted the moral frame of reference from "humanity" to "personhood". Does it give us any reason to accept this? It may be right to assert that the concept of a person is "very nearly universal (to people)"[93] and is common to (at least in the sense of being understood by) those for and against abortion. Yet Warren also suggested, at the time of her writing, that neither group had properly grasped the relevance of this idea to the resolution of their dispute, implying that the reflection she recommends could well promote such an outcome.[94] Although the argument may have correctly drawn attention to the differences between "humanity" and "personhood", has it convinced us that only personhood counts, that we have only to consider *persons*—and their rights—in our moral deliberations? For to pronounce that a being is not a person and hence a bearer of rights may well have some of the question-begging faults of the genetic humanity theory.

The response is that it is "self-evident"[95] that the moral community is one of persons.[96] Yet an explanation of the moral significance of personhood is surely desirable. In fact, Warren does hint at—if not explain—the connection between descriptive and normative personhood when she asserts that to grant full moral rights to a being which is not a person is as ridiculous as to consider that such a being has "moral obligations and responsibilities".[97] The implied link between descriptive and normative personhood here may be the idea of moral agency. In this regard, in the first part of the chapter we saw that the Choice theory of rights is clearly based upon the power of the individual to be a conscious, rational chooser; moreover, it was stressed that the more flexible Interest approach could be interpreted so as to emphasise the active dimension of moral personality, which in turn would be associated with the ascription of rights. In this way the idea of moral agency—invoking the notion of a right-holder with the capacity to exercise or waive rights—gives a certain plausibility to the personhood argument.

Nevertheless, a personhood or "actual-possession criterion" approach to moral status carries some striking implications, in particular the moral permissibility of the infanticide of unwanted children. In this regard, it may not be surprising that

---

[92] MA Warren, "Moral and Legal Status of Abortion", 282.
[93] *Ibid.*, 281.
[94] *Ibid.*
[95] *Ibid.*
[96] Here she is criticised by B Steinbock in her *Life Before Birth: the Moral and Legal Status of Embryos and Fetuses* (New York, NY: Oxford University Press, 1992) 54, who alleges that Warren fails to explain the moral significance of the criteria of personhood.
[97] MA Warren, "Moral and Legal Status of Abortion", 283.

philosophers committed to variations of the argument find themselves compelled to oppose infanticide on the basis of utilitarian reasons which address the public interest. For instance, Warren responded to criticisms of her original argument by adding a postscript to her article accounting for the wrongness of infanticide on consequentialist grounds: in particular that even if a baby is not wanted by its natural parents there are potential adoptive parents who would lose much pleasure if the infant were destroyed.[98] She also suggests that infants are generally *valued*, so that most people would rather pay taxes toward orphanages than allow the destruction of unwanted infants.[99]

The point of most interest here is the way in which an exponent of the personhood argument must look beyond the rights language of that argument in order to explain a feature which appears morally embarrassing when viewed from a wider moral perspective. This is necessary given the rather narrow, "technical" nature of personhood arguments with their emphasis on the actual possession of certain characteristics as guaranteeing the possession of full and equal rights. Importantly, by their very nature, such arguments tend to exclude, except as tidying footnotes, any other terms of moral reference: it is in this way that Warren adds the notion of "valuing" infants only as a postscript. Yet, as touched upon in the first section of the chapter, moral analysis need neither begin nor end with the concept of rights. In this light, we might view with some scepticism the extent of the assistance to be gained from the concept of a person when we consider the moral status of the fetus and moral questions relating to its treatment. (Indeed, more recently, in work which postdates my original formulation of the ideas here, Warren has argued that we cannot determine the moral status of (embryos and) fetuses solely by considering their intrinsic properties. Rather, attention must be paid to their "unique relational properties", that is, their location within and total physiological dependence on a (usually) sentient moral agent. She also argues that the moral status of women is likewise relevant to the abortion debate, in addition to certain other issues.[100])

3. *Implications for the Maternal–Fetal Conflict*

With regard to the maternal–fetal conflict, as many questions will be raised as answered by the conclusion offered by the personhood argument to the effect that a fetus is not a person and therefore lacks rights. The implication of such an approach in the treatment context would seem to be that hence the fetus has no legitimate claim to consideration.

I have already noted the argument's failure to acknowledge or give importance to the widespread recognition of other moral concepts besides rights and the duties they ground. In addition, the personhood argument's exclusive focus is upon the

---

[98] *Ibid.*, 285.

[99] *Ibid.*

[100] MA Warren, *Moral Status: Obligations to Persons and Other Living Things* (Oxford: Oxford University Press, 1997) 201–2. She also refers to the human species' ability to maintain sustainable population levels in the light of resource constraints.

current possession of certain capacities, as witnessed most dramatically in the *prima facie* moral permissibility of the infanticide of unwanted infants. In this way, the argument cannot give any special significance to the *viable* fetus (that is, one capable of surviving outside the woman's body), one implication of which may be a concomitant lack of recognition of the arguable moral differences between a human being within, rather than without, the body of a pregnant woman. A further implication of the narrow focus on current capacities is that the argument has nothing to bring to our understanding of the way in which the maternal–fetal conflict may result in harm to the future child and the question of how to weigh the interests of that child against those of the pregnant woman.

My discussion of viability in connection with the human species argument has already drawn attention to developmental changes in the fetus, such that at viability the fetus may have a greater claim to protection than before. Conceptually, these changes may be morally accommodated and explained by a third argument, the "interest view".

C. The Interest View and the Relevance of Sentience

"Nothing matters to nonsentient, nonconscious beings."[101]

1. The Argument

I now turn to an argument originating in the work of Joel Feinberg based on the link between the possession of interests and rights, and consider its exposition by Bonnie Steinbock.

On this approach, to have an interest is to have a stake in something, to care about something, so that conscious awareness is a "prerequisite" for the possession of interests.[102] If consciousness is sufficient for the possession of interests and hence minimal moral status, then a sentient fetus is such a being. Importantly, the argument distinguishes two senses of "interest": first, those things which promote the good of a being may be said to be *in* its interests; second, there are those things one seeks, that is, those things in which one *takes* an interest.[103] Although a sentient fetus cannot *take* an interest in its welfare, arguably it *has* such an interest in the sense that it may feel both pleasure and pain.[104] If life is *in* its interest, then it might be argued that it has a right to life, notwithstanding its present inability to take an interest in that life. This approach thus rejects the argument, put forward by

---

[101] B Steinbock, *Life Before Birth*, 14.

[102] The idea of "having a stake" in something is Joel Feinberg's, as outlined for instance in his *Harm to Others* (New York, NY: Oxford University Press, 1984) at 34: "In general, a person has a stake in X . . . when he stands to gain or lose depending on the nature or condition of X."

[103] B Steinbock, *Life Before Birth*, 56.

[104] "[P]erhaps late fetuses, like babies, are capable of sensuous pleasure, from sucking their thumbs, from the warmth of the womb, from the sound of their mothers' heartbeats, from motion as the mother moves around." *Ibid.* 69. She further draws attention to studies indicating that the fetus both hears extrauterine sounds and finds some sounds more pleasurable than others. *Ibid.*, 69–70.

Michael Tooley, that a being can only possess a serious right to life if it has a self-concept, that is, if it perceives itself as a continuing subject of experiences and other mental states, and believes that it is such a continuing entity.[105] Rather, on this view, rights protect two kinds of interest, so that a being can have a right to life even if it is unable to take an interest in its continued existence.

Yet an important qualification in the case of the fetus is that it resides inside the body of a person, a woman. For reasons which will be developed more particularly in the next chapter, when I focus on a woman's moral interests, the fetus's location inside its mother may affect its status. On Steinbock's view, its existence inside the pregnant woman qualifies the rights which its possession of interests may ground, giving it "weak rights".

Recent scientific and moral work builds on this view. On the scientific front, Vivette Glover and Nicholas Fisk have explored the complex question of the fetus's capacity to feel pain, noting that "[t]he fetus is currently treated as though it feels nothing, and is given no analgesia or anaesthesia for potentially painful interventions".[106] Pain in the fetus cannot be measured directly but, on the basis of the available anatomical and physiological evidence, these authors suggest that it is "likely" that the fetus can feel pain from 26 weeks, that it is "possible" that it can feel pain from 20 weeks and is caused distress by interventions from 15 or 16 weeks, suggesting that analgesia for the fetus might be considered from this time, although the "[a]dministration of safe and effective analgesia to the fetus, without adverse effects in the mother, is a considerable challenge".[107] Overall, the authors highlight the need for much more research in this area.[108] As regards the moral debate, Mary Ann Warren has recently suggested that the fetus's possible sentience means that

---

[105] M Tooley, "Abortion and Infanticide", (1972) in P Singer (ed.), *Applied Ethics* (Oxford: Oxford University Press, 1986) 57–85, 64. The first step in this argument is the proposition that people's obligations to respect one's rights are conditional upon the right-holder possessing certain desires, which are related to states of consciousness. On this analysis, to say that a being has a right to X is to say that it is the subject of experiences and other mental states. Such a being is able to desire X and this grounds its right in X. It follows, so it is argued, that the "right to life" is not simply about the continuation of a biological organism but is instead the right of a subject of experiences and other mental states to continue to exist. Now, in order to possess the desire to continue to exist, a being must have a concept of such a continuing entity and must believe itself to be such an entity. Thus, a being which does not perceive itself as the continuing subject of mental states does not have a right to life. The argument as summarised here can be found at 64–7.

[106] V Glover and NM Fisk, "Fetal Pain: Implications for Research and Practice", (1999) 106 *British J of Obstet and Gyn* 881, 884.

[107] *Ibid.*, 885.

[108] *Ibid.* "The physical system for nociception is present and functioning by 26 weeks and it seems likely that the fetus is capable of feeling pain from this stage. The first neurones to link the cortex with the rest of the brain are monoamine pathways, and reach the cortex from about 16 weeks gestation. Their activation could be associated with unpleasant conscious experience, even if not pain. Thalamic fibres first penetrate the subplate zone at about 17 weeks of gestation, and the cortex at 20 weeks. These anatomical and physiological considerations are important, not only because of immediate suffering, but also because of possible long term adverse effects of this early experience." (*Ibid.*) One of the questions the authors consider is the experience of the baby during birth, either by natural or surgical means, noting the levels of various hormones present following either means of birth and speculating that in the future analgesia might be administered immediately before or after instrumental deliveries. *Ibid.*, 884.

what she dubs "the Anti-Cruelty principle" is invoked, "establishing a claim to protection from the needless infliction of pain or death."[109]

2. Commentary

A particular strength of the interest view is that, in ascribing moral status to the fetus following sentience, which broadly coincides with viability,[110] it gives us a way of considering the fetus "in its own terms", as it were, at a point when legally the balance of interests between a woman and her fetus notably shifts: as will be seen for instance in chapter four, in the United States a woman loses her right to abortion at viability.[111] Hence, there appears to be some coherence between the interest account of fetal status and aspects of the legal regulation of abortion. Further, the sentience criterion of moral status is considerably less restrictive than a personhood account, which we saw to require the actual possession of such characteristics as rationality; rather, on the interest view the link between sentience and interests grounds the ascription of (weak) rights.[112]

However, I prefer to stop short of granting the fetus rights, even weak ones, partly because of my earlier endorsement of a hybrid Interest–autonomy understanding of rights, but more particularly because to grant rights to a fetus, as opposed to a newborn infant, is to give others a reason to protect the fetus in ways which may conflict, particularly, with a woman's interest and right in bodily integrity (the importance of which is explored in the next chapter). The importance of the fetus's location is a point I have stressed since consideration of Noonan's human species argument. Thus, as Mary Ann Warren has noted, *not* to grant rights based solely upon the intrinsic properties of an individual is to be aware of the "variety of sound reasons" for the ascription of moral rights.[113] Indeed, as Warren argues, although both sentience and (Tooley's) self-awareness are properties generally relevant to the ascription of moral rights, neither can explain (in their own terms) the moral significance of birth as the moment when a biologically separate human being is born who can be protected without implications for a woman's interests and rights.

Importantly, however, as noted toward the end of my discussion of Warren's personhood argument, the denial of fetal personhood or weak rights based on the

---

[109] MA Warren, *Moral Status*, 214.

[110] As noted earlier, viability is generally thought to occur at approximately 24 weeks and, as Ronald Dworkin observes, even conservative scientists hold that the fetal brain is insufficiently developed to feel pain until roughly the 26th week. R Dworkin, "Unenumerated Rights: Whether and How *Roe* v. *Wade* Should be Overruled", (1992) 59 *U Chic L Rev* 381, 403, citing C Grobstein, *Science and the Unborn: Choosing Human Futures* (Basic, 1988). Compare Glover and Fisk on the "likely" and "possible" timings.

[111] Although English abortion law is not framed in terms of a woman's rights, viability is likewise an important benchmark which significantly further reduces the availability of abortion.

[112] Note that whilst the law recognises that the fetus has interests "in its own right", as it were, at viability, the law does not grant the fetus *legal rights* against its mother, as shall be explored in Parts II and III.

[113] MA Warren, "The Moral Significance of Birth", (1989) 4(3) *Hypatia*. Reprinted in HB Holmes and L Purdy (eds.), *Feminist Perspectives in Medical Ethics* (Indianapolis, IN: Indiana University Press, 1992) 198–223, 200.

interest view does not mean that a woman does not have imperfect (rather than instrumental) duties to the developing fetus. Rather, as we shall see especially in Part II, the true significance of not bestowing moral or legal personhood upon the fetus is that others are given no licence to override a woman's rights in order to protect those of the fetus (since it has no such rights).

3. Implications for the Maternal–Fetal Conflict

a) Treatment Refusal from Viability Onwards

Clearly, the interest view predominantly recognises the claims of the sentient/ viable fetus. In considering a woman's refusal of caesarean delivery, for instance, it would give us a way of understanding the fetus's interests in such delivery and the moral weight we may attach to these. Thus, whilst a viable fetus cannot *take* an interest in its need for delivery by caesarean section, arguably it has such an interest, given its ability to feel pleasure and pain. On Steinbock's view, such a fetus has a weak right to life, and hence (I presume) to caesarean delivery, which in turn is to be weighed against such interests and rights as the pregnant woman possesses. On my view, the fetus has a strong interest in the caesarean which must be assessed in relation to the woman's interests (and rights). Now, as we noted earlier, paradoxically the viable fetus can easily "need" or at least "invoke" its mother's body (such as by needing access to the outside world via the surgical route) to an extent which belies its attainment of a state of development enabling it to live free of her body. In these circumstances, its interests will be particularly tempered by the strength of the woman's interests in bodily integrity.

b) The Pre-viable Fetus and the Future Child

A strict application of the interest view to the maternal–fetal conflict implies that where treatment is refused *pre-viability*, this is of no moral consequence because, on this argument, a pre-sentient being has no interests. Moreover, as regards the previable fetus this would appear to be the case, with regard either to the questions of fetal death or harm to the future child. With regard to the death of the fetus, whilst the interest view denies moral *status* (in the form of interests) to the pre-sentient fetus, it admits that it may have a moral *value* (presumably prompting imperfect obligations in others) if there are moral reasons to support its preservation.[114] With regard to the child who is not yet but may later be born harmed (the future child), Steinbock suggests that since the interest view acknowledges that the interests of born children can be damaged *in utero*, it can also recognise the idea of duties to future offspring. Specifically, she writes: [115]

> "Although the obligation is to the born child, and it is the born child who has the right not to be injured, there is a sense in which the interest view can accommodate 'fetal rights' since the fulfillment of these obligations occurs while the child is still a fetus."

---

[114] B Steinbock, *Life Before Birth*, 166.
[115] *Ibid.*, 129.

Although the purpose of such accommodation is understandable, since at this point the argument no longer hinges upon the idea of sentience, the interest view seems somewhat stretched on its own terms (as Steinbock implicitly acknowledges). It may instead be better to regard the interest view as being compatible with or amenable to other moral explanations. For instance, the fact that a pre-sentient fetus is physically continuous with the born child—and therefore "carries", in some sense, the interests of that child—could be seen as a reason for moral obligations to be owed to it, notwithstanding its current lack of interests qua fetus. Such reasoning takes us close to aspects of the argument from potential, the fourth major argument regarding the fetus's moral status, to which I now turn.

D. The Argument from Potential

"Once conceived, the being was recognized as man because he had man's potential."[116]

1. The Argument

Here I discuss the work of two Catholic writers: JT Noonan and John Finnis.[117] Although each typifies the traditional Catholic view of the fetus by combining the argument from potential with the human species argument, yet the points are logically distinct.[118] So in this section I consider the argument from potential in itself, despite its deployment in connection with the human species argument.

On the argument from potential, conception is the crucial moment as it marks the beginning of a *new* human being. On this theme, Finnis writes that "it is to point to a perfectly clear-cut beginning to which each of us can look back and in looking back see how, in a vividly intelligible sense, 'in my beginning is my end' ".[119] This beginning is so profound for Finnis that he rejects the notion that asserting that this is when a person's life began is "to work backwards from maturity, sophistically asking at each point 'How can one draw the line *here*?' ".[120] Rather, the point of the argument lies in the *continuity* of development from the zygote to the embryo to the fetus. As a zygote is potentially a fully-fledged human being, so it has full human rights. Noonan emphasises that the fetus's rights are equal to those of a born individual,[121] and Finnis reiterates the point by empha-

---

[116] JT Noonan, Jr., "An Almost Absolute Value", 261, my emphasis.

[117] J Finnis, "The Rights and Wrongs of Abortion: A Reply to Judith Thomson", (1973) 2 *Phil & Pub Aff* 117–45. Reprinted in R Dworkin (ed.), *The Philosophy of Law* (Oxford: Oxford University Press, 1977) 129–52.

[118] One could for instance employ a potentiality argument to the effect that those beings from any planet who are or will potentially possess those characteristics associated with moral *personhood* should be counted as normative persons.

[119] *Ibid.*, 151.

[120] *Ibid.*

[121] JT Noonan, Jr., "An Almost Absolute Value", 261, 264.

sising that there is "no rhyme or reason" in delaying the attribution of these rights.[122]

2. Commentary

The argument from potential has been criticised on two main grounds. The first takes issue with the line that is drawn at the zygote and asks how it is that a zygote is a potential person but the sperm or the egg which are about to meet are not? In response, one can point to the unique genetic constitution of the zygote that results from the fusion of the sperm and egg, "not the father's, not the mother's, and not a mere juxtaposition of the parents", which will play a substantial role in determining the kind of individual who develops.[123] It can be argued that the main link between the sperm and egg on the one hand and the zygote on the other is that the zygote is the *product* of the two sex cells and will in turn produce sperm or eggs itself. The conception of a child, then, is "no *mere* germination of seed".[124] Finnis supports this argument by means of an analogy with the development of an oak tree: an acorn we pick from the ground can remain such for many years but, if we plant it, it will produce a new oak sapling. From that moment the sapling will, slowly, become an oak. Thus, there is a *qualitative* difference between the kinds of process in issue: the sperm and the egg only have the potential to *produce* a zygote (when combined), whereas the zygote itself *is* potentially a descriptive person and, all going well, will *become* one. These differences in the kinds of potentiality in issue in turn give us a reason to keep the demarcation line at the zygote.[125]

Is the first principal objection to the potentiality argument thus overcome? It has been argued that the idea of a "moment of conception when a new human being is miraculously created is over-dramatized, and results from ignorance of modern biology."[126] The point of this criticism is that in fact the alleged "moment" when the sperm and ovum fuse is a series of stages which may last 24 or more hours: "However you date man's beginning, it is, like his ending, a process."[127] This charge of "over-dramatization" has some force, but perhaps something of the

---

[122] J Finnis, "The Rights and Wrongs of Abortion", 152.

[123] *Ibid*.

[124] *Ibid*., emphasis in original.

[125] This would seem to foil John Harris's criticism, who writes: "If we remind ourselves that whatever value the embryo has . . . derives not from what it is but rather from the fact that it has the potential to become a person, then one problem . . . becomes clear—that if this is the source of its value, then we must value everything with that potential in that way—which means taking the same view of birth control as we take of abortion, and taking the same view of failure to procreate as we take of birth control!" J Harris, "A Woman's Right to Choose", in his *The Value of Life* (London: Routledge and Kegan Paul, 1985) 162. See also MA Warren, *Moral Status*, 207: "If an entity may *develop* into a human being, then surely it is a potential human being—even if the developmental processes would alter it so greatly that we might reasonably wonder whether it has remained the selfsame entity." (My emphasis.) Her point is apparently that identity is irrelevant to potentiality. But her notion of "develop" does not seem to account for the difference in kind emphasised by Finnis.

[126] G Williams, "The Fetus and the Right to Life", (1994) 53 *CLJ* 71, 76.

[127] *Ibid*.

symbolic significance of conception can still be retained in the argument from potential: scrupulous attention to the raw facts of biology may not suffice.[128]

The second principal objection to the argument from potential has more force, and concerns the argument that the zygote or fetus, although only potentially a descriptive person, already has full human rights. Dubbed the "logical error" in the potentiality argument, this objection charges that it is illogical to deduce *actual* rights from *potential* qualification for those rights. In other words, potential qualification entails *potential*, not *actual* rights. The criticism is clearly enunciated by Stanley Benn:[129]

> "For if *A* has rights only because he satisfies some condition *P*, it doesn't follow that *B* has the same rights now because he *could* have property *P* at some time in the future. It only follows that he *will* have rights *when* he has *P*. He is a potential bearer of rights, as he is a potential bearer of *P*. A potential president of the United States is not on that account Commander-in-Chief."

Although this objection has considerable logical force, the conservative has two avenues of response. First, he might well maintain that, rather than being based on a logical error, the argument from potential stands for the normative proposition that those who are potentially persons *ought* to have the same rights as actual persons. Such a proposition requires justification, but does not itself depend on a logical mistake.[130] Second, it has been suggested that the fact that the fetus is potentially a descriptive person is arguably a basis, not for the ascription of rights to it, but for (non-correlative, or imperfect) *duties* which we may owe it.[131]

This last point has obvious links with topics touched upon in the first section of the chapter, in particular the concept of duties that are independent of, that is, not instrumental to, rights. Thus, the fact that the fetus lacks the characteristics which would confer on it the *rights* associated with personhood does not of itself determine the moral permissibility of our treatment of it. Rather, amongst other things, we might argue that we owe duties to the fetus because it has the potential to be a person, descriptively understood. In this case, we may in fact be saying that a potential person is a being of *value* and deserves our consideration. The use of the "valuation principle" in connection with the potentiality principle has been sharply criticised by Michael Tooley, who asserts that the latter "should not be confused with [the] principle . . . the value of an object is related to the value of the things into which it can develop".[132] Indeed, he suggests that the principles must be kept firmly distinct, since the fact that a being's life is of value does not grant it a right to life. Yet this objection loses all force if we do not insist upon the language of

---

[128] As no doubt Williams would acknowledge. On the moral status of the fetus, he writes: "The answer cannot be given by studying . . . the proven facts of biology." *Ibid.* 73.

[129] S Benn, "Abortion, Infanticide and Respect for Persons", in J Feinberg (ed.), *The Problem of Abortion* (Belmont: Wadsworth, 1973) 135–44, 143, emphasis in original.

[130] B Steinbock, *Life Before Birth*, 59.

[131] J Feinberg, "Abortion", (1979) in his *Freedom and Fulfillment* (Princeton, NJ: Princeton University Press, 1992) 37–75, 49.

[132] M Tooley, "Abortion and Infanticide", 77.

rights (and instrumental duties). Instead, we may speak of intrinsic duties toward the fetus, or perhaps of *reasons* for taking the fetus into account in our moral deliberations. We shall shortly see that in this way we would be entering into what Joel Feinberg has dubbed a "modified potentiality" argument.

3. Implications for the Maternal–Fetal Conflict

a) Treatment Refusal Pre-Viability

Earlier, I argued that the interest view was of particular assistance in considering the claims of the fetus from viability onwards, but lacked solutions regarding the pre-viable fetus. A *modified* form of the argument from potential—one which does not give the fetus rights based on its potentiality but rather recognises that the fact that a fetus will become a person is a *reason* to take its needs into account, or to owe it certain duties—may be best placed to offer assistance in our moral assessment of the *pre-viable* fetus in two situations. The first is that in which a fetus may die as the result of the refusal of medical treatment; the second is that in which the fetus will survive, becoming later a born child who has been damaged by its mother's refusal of medical treatment whilst *in utero*.

Where the result of a treatment refusal will be the *death* of a pre-viable fetus, on a "modified" version of the potentiality argument, we might consider the extent of the fetus's development as partly determinative of its moral weight. In this sense, we would take note of the "gap" between its current development and, under normal circumstances, its birth as a fully-fledged moral person: *the greater the development, the greater the moral weight*.[133] In such a case, arguably the most important, if not the only, consideration is the extent of its development in relation to its "aim" of becoming, after birth, a full moral person.

Where instead the result of a maternal treatment refusal may be fetal *harm*, we are considering harm to a being which is not only a potential person but which will in fact become one. Whilst we may attach some weight to the extent of its progress in becoming that born child, given our assumption that it will in fact become that child, we must look beyond the extent of its development *per se* to its physical connection with its mother, inside her uterus. The point I am making is that a highly significant, albeit not the only, morally relevant difference between the child who will (in the future) be born harmed and its born brother or sister is that the former is still inside the pregnant woman's body.

Nevertheless, the closer the future child is to being free of her body—to being able to survive independently of it—then the stronger may be its moral claims. (Recall that we are here discussing a pre-viable future child, as a viable future child can, on the interest view, be seen as one with current interests.) As a matter of fact,

---

[133] This modification to the argument from potential is suggested by J Feinberg, in his "Abortion". I focus on his formulation of this argument in the next section, which specifically links the development of the fetus with the justification of harm to it, by considering the question of *reasons* on a woman's part; whereas here I concentrate solely on the idea of the fetus's moral claim growing during pregnancy, coupled with the question of the interests of the future child.

the closer the (pre-viable) future child is to this point, the more developed it will be. Thus, the dual questions of the stage of the future child's development and its location inside a pregnant woman are importantly connected.[134] Of course, this is also true of the fetus *qua* fetus, in the sense that the closer it is to viability, the stronger may be its claims. The point here is that the strength of the future child's interests may be understood in a similar, but not identical way. Thus, regarding the two issues of pre-viable fetal death and harm to the (pre-viable) future child, it is as though we might seek the answers by looking through opposite ends of the same moral lens. With regard to *fetal death*, we start from the viewpoint of fetal development *per se*; with regard to *harm* to the *future child*, we start from the future child's current location inside the pregnant woman's body. Yet at some point in each case the other "angle" enters into our deliberation of the strength of the fetus's or future child's claims.

Moreover, (as observed previously regarding the viable fetus's likely medical needs) in considering the issue of the future child's location within the woman's body, we must also take note of the extent of the demands upon her body posed by any treatment issue. Given the predominance of the issue of location *per se* in our consideration of the interests of the future child (when compared with those of a born child), it follows that the strength of its interests will ultimately be affected by an assessment of the severity of the demands its "treatment" would impose upon the woman's body. An example to consider here may be that of corrective *in utero* surgery which will benefit the future child. On the one hand, if this can be performed by means of the minimally invasive "keyhole" techniques, the future child's interests in such surgery *prima facie* appear quite strong, although such surgery would still involve a general anaesthetic for the woman and post-operative drugs. (Also relevant may be the question of religious objections on the woman's part, an issue discussed in chapter two). On the other hand, attention must be paid to the purpose of the surgery. For instance, surgery to correct a facial deformity, although desirable, does not seem as important as that to repair a malfunctioning organ which would otherwise result in poor health for the born child.[135]

Since both the modified potentiality and interest[136] views ask that we pay attention to the woman's moral interests, I now wish to turn, lastly, to two "gradualist" arguments. Both of these might be said to develop a modified potentiality account of the fetus's status and one also accommodates the idea of fetal interests at viability. The strength of these views lies in the *joint attention* they pay to maternal and fetal claims. In considering these arguments at the end of this chapter I shall try to develop further our understanding of the claims of the fetus/future child in the

---

[134] The fetus's location and its current stage of development are considered irrelevant on the *strict* potentiality argument.

[135] In fact, K Knopoff comments that fetal surgery is performed only to correct defects which will either kill the fetus or which will cause it progressive and irreversible damage unless treated. K Knopoff, "Can a Pregnant Woman Morally Refuse Fetal Surgery?", 503.

[136] As formulated by Steinbock and in the previous section.

treatment context, as well as to prepare the ground for an explicit consideration of maternal interests in pregnancy in the next chapter.

E. A Gradualist Approach

1. A "Claim"

"Potential possession of . . . [descriptive personhood] . . . confers not a right, but only a claim, to life, but that claim keeps growing stronger, requiring ever stronger reasons to override it, until the point when . . . [descriptive personhood] . . . is actually possessed, by which time it has become a full right to life."[137]

a) *The Argument*

This is Joel Feinberg's formulation of what he dubs the "modified or gradualist potentiality" argument. The following summary is based on his account.

This gradualist view starts from the proposition that unless one has a religious basis for doing so, it is hard to believe that immediately upon conception the zygote is the kind of being which possesses a right to life; in similar fashion, at the other end of the spectrum, the proposition that the nearly born fetus has no such right may seem equally implausible. Likewise, it may be hard to accept (notwithstanding, I might add, the coherence of the interest view and its emphasis upon sentience) that at one moment the fetus has no rights and at another suddenly gains them.[138] Instead, on the gradualist approach the fetus's potential personhood is a steadily strengthening reason against destroying it, which necessitates an ever stronger countervailing reason. This account fits with the widely held perception that the moral seriousness of abortion grows with the fetus. On this gradualist approach the fetus has "immature" or "weak" rights; it has "a *claim* with some moral force proportional to its degree of development but not yet as much force as a fully matured right".[139] The essence of this view is the idea of a claim which deserves serious consideration: if on balance there are reasons not to recognise the claim, then we might say it is an invalid claim or right.

Yet this account shares the (not necessarily significant) logical error of the argument from potential.[140] Although we can observe that a late-gestation fetus is very much closer to being a descriptive person—and hence a candidate for moral personhood—than the earlier zygote, we saw previously that it would be logically invalid to infer that a being which is almost qualified for full rights thereby possesses

---

[137] J Feinberg, "Abortion", 49.

[138] In this regard, note Steinbock's endorsement of a gradualist approach to abortion: "[A]s the fetus develops, it gets closer to becoming an individual that will have moral claims on us. It seems reasonable that the considerations offered to justify terminating a pregnancy should be stronger at the end of pregnancy that at the beginning. This . . . approach . . . is compatible with the interest view." *Life Before Birth*, 62.

[139] J Feinberg, "Abortion", 49–50, my emphasis.

[140] As Feinberg notes, *ibid.*, 51.

weak rights. But does this matter? In discussing the argument from potential earlier, it was noted that this objection could be met with two defences, one of which
is that the argument really stands for the normative proposition that those who are
potentially persons *ought* to have the same rights as actual persons. Whilst Feinberg
considers that if our sole concern is with the narrow question of the *criteria of moral
personhood*, then the logical objection has force, he suggests that the gradualist
account is a better answer to the broader question of the *morality of abortion* and,
presumably, other issues relating to treatment of the fetus. In so doing, ultimately
he stresses that the morality of abortion does not depend on the fetus's possession
of rights (full or weak). Rather, the fetus's potential personhood is a *reason* against
harming or killing it which requires an ever stronger reason on the woman's part
to justify such harm or death. Earlier we saw that this approach amounted to the
second defence of the argument from potential to the objection of logical error.

b) *Commentary*

The idea that we should be concerned with the fact that, as pregnancy progresses,
so the fetus becomes more like us has been sharply criticised in the early work of
Mary Ann Warren. Although she considers that we should take "seriously" the idea
that, just as a human being develops in a continuous fashion, so might his or her
rights, she insists we recall that whether or not an entity is sufficiently like a person
to be considered as possessing some moral rights will turn on whether it has those
attributes relevant to determining whether or not it is fully a person.[141] In short,
only the concept of personhood is morally determinative regarding an issue such as
abortion and so we must consider to what extent a being has Warren's five criteria
(as listed in section B above). On this view, a seven- or eight-month-old fetus is
"*somewhat*" but "not significantly more personlike" than a very early embryo:[142] it
may have the rudiments of consciousness, but lacks the characteristics of moral personhood (such as rationality, the ability to communicate and self-awareness). To be
sure, she insists that "in the *relevant* respects, a fetus, even a fully developed one, is
considerably less personlike than is the average mature mammal, indeed the average fish".[143]

This argument raises questions about our *methods* of determining the criteria of
moral status. In particular, we might reflect—as does Feinberg—upon the limits of
empirical or scientific reasoning in relation to such a controversial question as the
moral status of the fetus.[144] Certainly whether the actual capacities of Warren's fish
and fetus are equivalent is a matter of scientific evidence. Yet here Warren completely misses the force of a gradualist account, which fully admits that even a late
fetus does not yet possess the five criteria of moral personhood. The point—the
force—of the gradualist account lies precisely in that aspect which she excludes as
irrelevant: that, day by day, the fetus progresses along a course which makes it

[141] MA Warren, "Moral and Legal Status of Abortion", 283.
[142] *Ibid.*, emphasis in original.
[143] *Ibid.*, emphasis in original.
[144] J Feinberg, "Abortion", 45.

increasingly like us. This is, in a sense, an aspect of the *definition* of a fetus. With respect to the fetus, then, likeness is anything but a static concept; rather, likeness goes hand in hand with the force of potentiality.[145] In this light, Warren's comparison of the fetus with "the average mature mammal, indeed the average fish" is misleading: it ignores the idea that, unlike the average mature mammal, but especially the fish, the fetus is on a distinctly finite journey of development within the womb which comes ever closer to its end as it nears parturition. Paradoxically, we speak of the fetus's moral *status*, but by definition the fetus is anything but a *static* being. In this light, can we truly hold our hands on our hearts and swear that to compare a fetus with the average fish is perfectly fair?

If we can, then the notion of "fairness" deployed here is decidedly narrow, but so is the question of the criteria of moral personhood: it is for this reason that Feinberg considers that the gradualist account is a better answer to the broader issue of the morality of abortion than the "actual possession" criterion, which he regards as better suited to the narrower issue of personhood. On the limitations of a criterion such as that of "actual possession", he writes that "[t]o point out these embarrassments for a given position is not necessarily to refute it but rather to *measure the costs of holding it to the coherence of one's larger set of beliefs generally*."[146] (Regarding Feinberg's methodology at this juncture, see my remarks on intuition, reflective equilibrium and coherence in chapter two.[147]) For instance, in discussing the "embarrassment" that the actual possession criterion itself gives no grounds for proscribing infanticide, he proposes various utilitarian reasons against the practice, such as that it would tend to weaken the "socially valuable response" of warmth and tenderness that adults have toward infants.[148] He continues by alerting us to the possibility of "acts . . . [which] would strike at our *respect* for living human persons (without which organized society would be impossible) in the most keenly threatening way".[149] Feinberg's argument perhaps has a less obviously utilitarian ring when he expresses his final reason for endorsing a gradualist account as an answer to the morality of abortion: advanced fetuses are "beings whose similarity to real persons is close enough to render them *sacred symbols* of the real thing."[150] It may be rather curious to think of a fetus as a symbol, but Feinberg's meaning at this point is clarified by his reference to the original leading US abortion case, *Roe v. Wade*.[151] In this case the State asserted an interest in the potentiality of life as represented by the fetus, which Feinberg suggests derives from its "plain interest . . . in preserving respect for *actual* human life".[152] His point is that the way in which a

---

[145] Warren, by contrast, seeks to separate the points by dealing with what she dubs the "Fetal Development and the Right to Life" and "Potential Personhood and the Right to Life" respectively in ss. 3 and 4 of her article "Moral and Legal Status of Abortion".

[146] J Feinberg, "Abortion", 45, my emphasis.

[147] Concluding s. III(A)(3)(b) and notes thereto.

[148] J Feinberg, "Abortion", 55.

[149] *Ibid.*, 53, my emphasis.

[150] *Ibid.*, my emphasis. It should be noted that, in addition to "well-developed fetuses", Feinberg's emphasis at this point is upon "all near-persons, including higher animals, dead people, infants".

[151] 35 L Ed 2d 147 (1973). This case is discussed in Part II.

[152] J Feinberg, "Abortion", 55, emphasis in original.

fetus is treated carries implications for the value of human life more generally. It is in this light that he concludes that although the fetus is not a person with a right to life, its potential personhood, with all its symbolic significance, can be seen as a "*reason*"[153] against killing it such that the justification of abortion will require an increasingly strong counterbalancing reason on the woman's part.

c) Implications for the Maternal–Fetal Conflict

Let me first note that, for simplicity, I shall not address the distinction between fetal death and harm to the interests of the future child in my discussion of Feinberg. Rather, I choose to do this (building particularly on the discussion in sections C and D above) solely when I turn to the second "gradualist" account. This is because the second account is more developed and hence may be better able to be adapted to this complexity.

Moving from Feinberg's concern with the issue of abortion to my concern with that of maternal–fetal conflict, Feinberg's argument highlights the narrowness of such questions as whether the fetus is a person with a right to life and medical treatment. If we were to approach and dismiss the conflict entirely on the basis of such questions, then we would be ignoring a much wider field of relevant moral considerations. Indeed we saw this earlier with my rejection of the early Warren's personhood argument (see section B). While Feinberg initially considers the idea of a "claim", in the final analysis he appears simply to endorse the idea of the fetus's advancing development being a "reason" against harming it which can only be dislodged by a reason of proportionate merit on the mother's side. The difference between the idea of a claim and a reason here is that the former idea is connected with the fetus's interests "in its own right", as it were, while the idea of a reason is linked to that of imperfect obligations which, by definition, are not correlated with rights in another. In effect, Feinberg thus shifts the debate away from the intractable extremes represented by a *strict* potentiality account on the one hand and a personhood account on the other—both of which stress the notion of fetal rights (by their presence or absence)—to the question of non-instrumental (or imperfect) duties on the woman's part.

In essence, applying his argument to the maternal–fetal conflict, the implication is that the greater the development of the fetus, the greater must be the reason on the woman's part for refusing the medical treatment which it needs. For instance, with regard to the viable fetus requiring delivery by caesarean section, a woman must have a very strong reason to justify her refusal. As has been touched upon at earlier points and as is to be explored in the next chapter, a woman has an interest in her bodily integrity. Moreover, unlike the fetus, the woman is a moral (and legal) person with moral (and legal) rights and her interest in bodily integrity is protected by at least a *prima facie* moral (and legal) right thereto. Now, given that a caesarean section necessarily seriously invades her interest in bodily integrity, she might well be thought to have a very strong reason to refuse surgical delivery of her fetus. In

---

[153] J Feinberg, "Abortion", emphasis in original.

this way, I draw attention to the likely *coincidence* between the cases where she has a *very strong* reason and those where she has at least a *prima facie right*.

Importantly, this leads me to suggest that, apart from emphasising that the fetus's lack of rights is not determinative of the morality of its treatment (in the light, for instance, of the imperfect duties that may be owed to it), Feinberg's approach may ultimately be extended to the question of the *theoretical justification* of certain rights on the woman's part. That is, although his argument is not directed to the notion of a woman's rights, I am suggesting that we may apply his approach to the effect that, in theory, a pregnant woman may be justified in refusing medical treatment for the fetus where she has a serious reason for so doing. Since the caesarean section would necessarily impinge upon a woman's bodily integrity, potentially giving her a serious reason to decline the surgery, then in such a case it is possible that she may be justified in exercising her right to bodily integrity (and self-determination) and thus in refusing the caesarean section (a point to be explored fully in chapter two).

By contrast consider, for the sake of argument, the purely hypothetical example of a woman refusing to swallow a pill which would greatly enhance fetal welfare and that of the future child. (In fact, fetal arrhythmias and vitamin deficiencies can be treated in this way.[154]) Vastly unlike major surgery, a pill impinges upon the body in the most minimal sense imaginable, in that it is merely something to be swallowed in the way that food or liquid is normally ingested. Moreover, if we assume, for the sake of argument, that the pill has no possible adverse effects on the woman, then it will be very hard to think of a *reason*, let alone a serious one, why she should refuse to swallow the same, notwithstanding that she may have a right to bodily integrity which is at least minimally implicated in the ingestion of any external substance. In such a case, then, there does not appear to be the coincidence, referred to above, of a serious reason with the right, which might otherwise be thought to justify a woman having, and in turn exercising, a right to bodily integrity in such a way that the fetus will suffer. To the contrary, the refusal of the beneficial pill which can have no adverse effects on the pregnant woman seems an entirely *arbitrary* choice. The implication, in effect, is that she would clearly have a moral duty to take the pill.[155] To observe that the *link* between the right and the existence of a serious reason can be broken is therefore to recognise that a *right can be exercised without good reason*. In this way, we become aware of the scope for reflection upon the *moral quality* of a decision to exercise a right such as that to refuse medical treatment needed by the fetus. This is an

---

[154] A Ouellette, "New Medical Technology", 932, drawing on M Longaker *et al*, "Update on the Status of Fetal Surgery", 53. Once the substance the fetus is lacking is ingested by the woman, it then passes from her to the fetus through the placenta.

[155] My conclusion regarding the case of the beneficial pill is supported by other writers, although none have tried to analyse this in the manner adopted here. See e.g. S Elias and G Annas, *Reproductive Genetics and the Law* (Chicago, IL: Yearbook Medical Publishers, 1987), who compare the need for fetal surgery on the one hand and the need for a drug satisfying the criteria I have delineated, concluding that the woman would be "morally wrong" not to take the drug (at 262).

extremely important—indeed a central—point, which will be developed as the book progresses.

A further important point should be noted regarding the refusal of the beneficial pill. Thus, whilst such a pill technically belongs to the domain of "medical treatment", in effect its refusal is much closer to an instance of general *conduct* on the woman's part, as no bodily or other very personal interests are seriously implicated.[156] In turn this would explain why it could be relatively easy to judge a pregnant woman's failure to take the pill as *unreasonable*, as I shall explore in chapter two. Nevertheless, since the pill is in fact "medical treatment", technically a "right" to refuse it is invoked on the woman's part.[157]

Notice that I have sought to explicate my point about the potential separation of the right and the justifying reason by reference to the two cases which are at the very extremes of the range of "treatment" which a fetus may "need" and a woman may refuse. Moreover, it is also the case that whereas the caesarean section example in fact represents the most frequently occurring instance of maternal refusal of medical treatment during pregnancy, the case of the refusal of the pill which will greatly enhance the future child's welfare but has no adverse effects upon the woman remains hypothetical. Whilst the benefits from such pills might become more developed, it is in fact much less likely that a pregnant woman would refuse such "treatment".[158] This highlights the extent to which the maternal–fetal conflict, despite speculation and fears in various quarters of the literature, in fact concerns serious maternal reasons which are likely to be coincidental with (at least *prima facie*) rights.

Importantly, my adaptation of Feinberg's argument to the situation of maternal treatment refusal is limited to the domain of theory. That is, his (adapted) approach tells us that a woman may have a serious reason to refuse the treatment, but not

---

[156] As will be apparent in ch. 6 on the relevance of the law of tort (which partly touches on such questions as a pregnant woman smoking, drinking more than minimal alcohol or behaving in other ways likely to injure the future child), a woman's *conduct* will tend to affect the *future child's* interests, rather than those of the fetus *qua* fetus. That is, it is less likely that instances of maternal conduct will lead to the *death* of the fetus.

[157] At this juncture, mention might be made of another "gradualist account", developed by G Gillett and MC Reid in their "The Case of Medea—a View of Maternal–Fetal Conflict", (1997) 23 *JME* 19, with particular reference to the situation of abortion. Arguing, as this chapter has tried to show, that rights-based approaches fail to capture the "essential features of the moral problem", their focus is "threefold": upon "the agent's reasons or motives for relevant actions, the significance of the life of the moral patient, and the rights of each of the moral participants" (*ibid.*, 19). The approach is thus in line with my adoption of a gradualist account of the maternal–fetal relationship. Importantly, however, the authors do not make the additional crucial step, which I have begun to formulate in this section of exploring the *connections* between the reasons/motives underlying a choice and rights, both in terms of their theoretical justification and in their exercise on any given occasion. Since they do not make these connections, the implication of their analysis is that the "right" is an empty, free-standing concept, with regard to which, to be sure, mere assertions of rights would be entirely question-begging.

[158] The American Medical Association is of a similar view on this point: "[A] woman conceivably could refuse oral administration of a drug that would cause no ill effects in her own body but would almost certainly prevent a substantial and irreversible injury to her fetus. Given the current state of medical technology, it is unlikely that such a situation would occur. In addition, as a practical matter, it is *unlikely* that a woman would refuse treatment in that situation." AMA Board of Trustees, "Legal Interventions During Pregnancy: Court-Ordered Medical Treatments and Legal Penalties for Potentially Harmful Behavior by Pregnant Women", (1990) 263 *JAMA* 2663, 2666, my emphasis.

how to determine the seriousness of her reason. In order to assess whether in any given case a particular woman's rights are absolute (whether her reasons will *in the event* be sufficiently strong to outweigh the claims of the fetus) we would first need better to understand her interests and rights in pregnancy. This is the first important task of the next chapter. Thus, I defer the ultimate question of the extent of a pregnant woman's rights until then.[159]

I now turn to the second account which may be dubbed "gradualist" in the sense that fetal moral status is considered to grow with the fetus. Ronald Dworkin's account is also about the circumstances in which harm to the fetus is justified. Moreover, as with Feinberg's account but particularly in this case, Dworkin's approach is ultimately about the justification of the right to abortion, notwithstanding that his discussion tends to avoid overt reference to a woman's rights.

2. Respect for Human Life

"[Abortion] is a controversy about whether human life itself is sacred, and why, and about which acts show respect and which disrespect for human life. . ."[160]

---

[159] Ian Kennedy has defined the extent of a woman's moral duty toward the fetus in pregnancy, discussing the fetus's position in a manner somewhat reminiscent of Feinberg's idea of a growing moral claim, in "A Woman and her Unborn Child", in his *Treat Me Right* (Oxford: Oxford University Press, 1992) 364–84. He argues that the fetus has *weak* rights because it is not yet, and may never be, independent of the woman's body; but that it also has *growing* rights because, although still *in utero*, at some point it will be capable of independent existence. He writes of a woman's *prima facie* right to autonomy—including the "right to privacy and to be free from unwanted bodily interference" (*ibid.*, 374), which is subject to the fetus's interests and weak rights, in particular the right "to be free from avoidable harm, to be free from that which may destroy or damage its potential for being born whole" (*ibid.*, 375). On this basis he argues that a pregnant woman is under a correlative "primary duty" to limit her conduct so as not to harm the fetus, unless she has "good reasons" for not doing so. (*Ibid.*) It appears that the problem of *judging* serious personal reasons is not addressed in this analysis, although Kennedy may mean that we must take the notion of "serious reasons" at "face value", as it were, such that, for instance, a religiously-based refusal is a serious reason. Moreover, although Kennedy notes that a woman's *prima facie* right to autonomy includes, as mentioned above, a "right to privacy and to be free from unwanted bodily interference", rights which would pertain particularly to the medical treatment context, he does not explicitly distinguish between this context and the domain of general conduct, although the inherent differences between these contexts may implicitly be accounted for within his analysis. Thus, he concludes: "[I]f the case for the fetus is strong and the reasons for the mother's conduct are weak or less strong, she has a duty as a matter of moral theory to submit to the stipulated regime or treatment . . . whether it be a specific diet or drug prescription, abstinence from a particular substance or conduct, or some intervention such as a blood transfusion or even surgery." (At 377.) There have been several attempts to analyse legally the extent of a woman's duty which approach the issue of duty in a similar way. See e.g. PL Hallisey, "The Fetal Patient and the Unwilling Mother: A Standard for Judicial Intervention", (1983) 14 *Pac LJ* 1065 in which it is proposed, in the treatment context, that a mother's choice regarding medical treatment of her fetus should *not* prevail only if the fetal therapy is a proven procedure that clearly would benefit the fetus, the use of which would prevent significant and irreversible physical or mental impairment of the fetus, no less intrusive treatment is available, and the treatment would not result in serious harm to the mother.

[160] R Dworkin, *Life's Dominion: An Argument about Abortion and Euthanasia* (London: Harper Collins, 1993) 27–8.

a) *The Argument*

Ronald Dworkin has likewise questioned the helpfulness of approaches which focus upon whether the fetus is a person with a right to life.[161] Following careful examination of both conservative and liberal views on abortion, he argues that on both sides of the debate people are really concerned with whether and why human life is "sacred", coupled with the ways in which human life may be respected or disrespected. In what follows I considerably simplify a complex argument.

In exploring the notion of the sacred, he takes as his starting point the idea that human beings are special,[162] accounting for this by means of two expressions (or "traditions"[163]) of the sacred, namely those of nature and art. As a creation of nature, human life can be understood as sacred either in the traditional religious sense that humans were made by God "in His own image" or, secularly, as the idea that, of all the species on the planet, humans have evolved to represent nature's most advanced creation. In this "natural" sense, human life is valued in terms of the "natural invest-ment" that has gone into the development and preservation of our species.

As nature's or God's most advanced creation, human beings also express an "artistic" aspect of the sacred. Whereas the natural aspect is expressed in the time from conception to birth, this second aspect finds expression in the *living of a life*. Thus, Dworkin suggests that the "deliberate human creative force"[164] that we value in art can also be recognised and valued in the life of a developed human being, who is not only a "natural creation", but also the "product" of parental and social influences as well as that individual's own choices and actions. This latter "biographical" picture thus captures the human effort and influence which shape and define our lives. The distinction between these two forms of the sacred—the natural and the human or creative—is reflected in the Greek distinction between *zoe*, meaning physical or biological life, and *bios*, the very living of a life.[165]

The fetus, which has not yet begun its "biographical life", can be understood in terms of *zoe*, physical or biological life. In this sense, what is important is the degree of development of any given fetus, as this demonstrates the amount of "natural investment": the transition from zygote to embryo to fetus reflects an ever-increasing stake in life which reaches a height with the late-gestation fetus.[166] The

---

[161] Note also Feinberg's observation: "In addition to the argumentative support for the right-to-choose position, one can cite some evidence supporting the position that hardly any of the antiabortionists *really believe* that a fetus has the full moral status of a typical postnatal person." J Feinberg, "Abortion", 72, emphasis in original.

[162] The idea that human beings are intrinsically special is of course open to philosophical challenge; but note that Dworkin defends his view.

[163] R Dworkin, *Life's Dominion*, 82.

[164] *Ibid.*

[165] *Ibid.*, 82–3, n. 7.

[166] I do not think, as A Plomer maintains, that Dworkin's opponents would necessarily consider that this view "fails to give adequate moral (and legal) weight to the fact that a nonviable human foetus, unlike other things which lack interests . . . has the potential to become a person." A Plomer, "Review of *Life's Dominion*", [1996] 59 *MLR* 479, 481. Rather, as compared with, for instance, the personhood or the interest view, Dworkin's concept of investment appears implicitly to acknowledge the fetus's path through to personhood, albeit not in the strict sense that the argument from potential would.

longer we allow this development, the greater the degree of respect fetal life is due.

In Dworkin's view, this dual account of the sacred establishes a defence of abortion which sustains respect for life's sanctity by sidestepping the traditional Judaeo–Christian view that destroying a fetus denies the sanctity of life. Essentially it is argued that abortion, which "wastes human life"[167] in the sense of "frustrating" a biological life, might sometimes be justifiable where continued pregnancy would frustrate the mother's or the family's lives in a way which would itself represent a waste of *bios*, of the human and creative force and investment which make up lives. Thus, where a woman has a "serious" or "substantial" reason for aborting her fetus, arguably not aborting might itself frustrate a form of the sacred. For instance, it may be that bearing a child at a particular time would prevent her from accepting the offer of a position which would represent a significant advancement in her life's work or seriously compromise her ability to take care of certain others in her life. By contrast, to abort her fetus late in pregnancy in order to accommodate the demands of an overseas trip could be seen as a trivial and hence disrespectful reason.

Dworkin does not claim, however, that abortion can be justified in this way throughout pregnancy.[168] He notes that, approximately at viability, the fetus becomes sentient and can henceforward coherently be said to have interests in its own right. This accords with my earlier endorsement of the interest view. On Dworkin's argument, fetal acquisition of interests at viability will constitute an important reason for limiting abortion after this time. At this point, not only will the State have what he dubs its "detached" interest in encouraging serious and responsible decisions which respect the sanctity of life, but also a legitimate "derivative" interest in protecting the interests of the fetus. Hence from this time, as I shall further examine in chapter four, the State may be justified in imposing legal restrictions upon a woman's right to abort (subject to certain exceptions) for three reasons: the development of fetal interests; the fact that to abort late when there had been the opportunity much earlier may be a flagrant affront to the intrinsic value of human life; and the fact that, prior to the six-month viability mark, a woman can fairly be said to have had a considerable period of time during which to make the decision to abort.

b) *Commentary*

Dworkin's argument goes primarily to the justification of the present state of US abortion law and will be touched on in Parts II and III, where I have occasion to draw on abortion law to examine the law relating to the maternal–fetal conflict. His belief in the irrelevance and unhelpfulness of the question of whether the fetus is a person with rights ties in with my (and Feinberg's) rejection of such an approach following consideration of the personhood argument. By means of his

---

[167] R Dworkin, *Life's Dominion*, 94.
[168] *Ibid.*, 169–70.

dual account of the sacred, he seeks to explain why and when a woman might be justified in aborting, even though human life is at stake, by reference to those considerations which go to the very meaning and value of her own life. Whilst no reference need be made to her *right* to abort, in fact his argument seeks to explain and justify why she should and does have (within limits) the right to do so. Indeed, ultimately, the argument is a moral justification or explication of the legal right to abort. As will be further developed in sections of the book which address the law, apart from the core idea of respect, the other crucial idea in this account is that of *responsibility*. Where the woman's reasons (for aborting) relate to the very meaning and value of her own life, then arguably she is not "disrespectful" of "nature's" or "God's investment" in fetal life. In such a case, the linking idea seems to be that of responsibility, a sense of responsibility which is at the same time directed both toward herself (and possibly her family's interests) and the fetus: that is, if she has serious reasons for aborting going to considerations of great importance in her own life, then arguably she is responsible toward the value of human life, by virtue of the fact that we can recognise its two expressions in the creative (biographical) and natural (biological).

c) *Implications for the Maternal–Fetal Conflict*

Dworkin acknowledges the distinction between harm to the fetus resulting in death (in his case regarding abortion) and harm to the fetus resulting in a damaged child.[169] Yet it is not his purpose to address this problem and nor does he. The task of considering the application of his argument to the maternal–fetal conflict (as with all the arguments considered to date in this chapter) falls to the writer.

i) Fetal Death: Maternal Reasons

First, let us focus on the idea of treatment refusal leading to fetal death, which will represent the simplest application of the argument. *Pre-viability*, that is, prior to the fetus's acquisition of interests, the overriding consideration must be that a woman will be justified in refusing medical treatment where she has a serious reason proportionate to the fetus's stage of development, meaning one which relates to the meaning and value of her own life. We have seen that the medical treatment context primarily touches on two interests or rights on the woman's part—bodily integrity and self-determination. For a start, we can immediately see that Dworkin's argument will speak not so much to a woman's interests in bodily integrity as to specific aspects of her interest in self-determination. That is, in the maternal–fetal conflict cases, Dworkin's argument will tend to explain or justify those cases where a woman has religious or value-based objections to certain kinds of treatment. These will constitute reasons coming within Dworkin's approach, reasons which may be duly respectful of the fetus's "investment" in life.

Post-viability, where fetal death is in issue, we have seen that Dworkin recognises that the fetus has interests in its own right and that, regarding abortion, this is one reason why restrictions are imposed after this time. So far as the maternal–fetal

---

[169] R Dworkin, *Life's Dominion*, 19.

conflict is concerned, the fact that the fetus now has interests (on the basis of its sentience—occurring, approximately, at viability) means that the stage of its development in relation to its "goal" of becoming a person—that is, the gap between its current development and its full personhood—is no longer an important consideration. Indeed, although the fetus is inside its mother's body, it is now capable of existing in the outside world. Yet the problem for the fetus, so far as treatment issues occurring after viability are generally concerned, is precisely to "leave" her body, not, as with regard to abortion, preferably to remain in it until term in order to strengthen its health and prospects. The fetus in the treatment context which needs caesarean section delivery is thus having to make a demand upon the woman which is rather different from the fetus which simply "needs" to be allowed to go to term following viability: the latter fetus asks that the woman continue to accommodate it for its last three months of development (and then give birth); but the fetus which, at or near term, needs a caesarean delivery demands something new and unpredictable (if not completely unforeseeable) of the woman, namely surgical delivery, to which she may have religious or other serious objections. The point is that, whereas prior to viability she may have had plenty of opportunity to abort if she considered that the carrying to term of a child would "frustrate" her own interests in self-determination, she does not have the opportunity to refuse the caesarean section delivery until it is needed by the fetus. This means that the arguments which justifiably limit abortion after viability on Dworkin's account cannot "bite" in the treatment context. Of course, one could argue that a woman who has "objections" to surgical delivery should not conceive, but I shall try to show in chapter two that such an approach is untenable. Arguably then, I suggest provisionally that where she has acute religious or "philosophical" objections to the surgery, she may well be refusing treatment, thereby harming the fetus, for reasons which are not "disrespectful" of fetal life.

ii) Harm to the Future Child: Maternal Reasons

The other case to touch upon with regard to Dworkin's approach is that of the fetus which is harmed but not killed by a treatment refusal, such that a child is born who suffers from harm incurred *in utero*. Regarding the *pre-viable* future child, I refer to my discussion of a "modified potentiality" account above, in which I emphasised that, compared with a born child, a highly significant consideration affecting the strength of its claims is its location inside the pregnant woman, but that this is in turn intrinsically related to the degree of its development. What of the reasons for refusal on the woman's part?

Where a child will later be born harmed, the idea of fetal "investment in life" does not have quite the same "hold" as it does either in the abortion context or those cases of maternal–fetal conflict which may result in fetal death. I have suggested that the future child's interests have less weight than those of the born child because of the location of the future child inside the woman, but that the issue of location is connected at some point with that of the future child's development. Still, given that we are talking not of a life being cut short, but of a life being harmed, and given that I have suggested (in section D(3)) that in such a case the issue of location is ultimately more important than that of the stage of development, then in turn the *reasons* for a maternal refusal must be connected with the issue of location: that is, they must confront and meet the future child's demands upon the woman's *body*.

In fact, this need not introduce any new elements, in the sense that where a woman refuses medical treatment because she believes she will forego eternal life if she accepts the treatment in question, then the religious reason, whilst apparently invoking her interest in self-determination rather than bodily integrity, is ultimately "about the body": the reason forbids certain action regarding the woman's body. Alternatively, we might say that in this way it also implicates her interest in bodily integrity. Either way, we thus see the *prominence of the body* in the "reasons" at stake in *both* the interests of self-determination and bodily integrity as they arise in the treatment context.[170] Of course, this is not surprising in the sense that it is the fact that the fetus or the future child is *in* the woman's body that precipitates the entire problem of maternal–fetal conflict. (An additional implication of the above, in effect, is that in the case of fetal death as a result of the refusal, say, of caesarean delivery, likewise a woman's interests in self-determination and bodily integrity are very closely entwined.) In this way, whilst it transpires that no "new elements" are brought in by the suggestion that if a future child's interests are to be harmed then a woman's reasons must in some way "go" to the body, still it is conceptually significant to recognise this point. So, we might say that reasons for decisions which will affect the quality, rather than the existence of life, invoke questions, not so much of respect *per se*, but of *responsibility*. This latter idea has, for my purposes, an overarching aspect which allows it to embrace both the scenarios of fetal death and harm to the future child.

Apart from these comments, given the way in which Dworkin's argument is ultimately, albeit not explicitly, about the *theoretical justification* of a woman's rights, I refer again to the discussion regarding the *coincidence between rights and serious reasons* with regard to Feinberg's gradualist account. Rather than repeat those points here, which in any event required the consideration of a woman's interests "from her perspective" as it were, in order to determine whether in any *given case* a woman would be justifiably exercising her rights, I defer further discussion and development of these points until the next chapter.

3. A Virtue Ethics Approach

Finally, the analysis of the justification of harm to the fetus inherent in the gradualist approach may have a virtue-ethical component. I noted when I first introduced Feinberg's and Dworkin's arguments, that although they are writing about the circumstances in which harm to the fetus may be justified (that is, when there is reason on the woman's part of a moral weight proportionate to the fetus's development), their arguments may yet be used to explain when a woman is justified in

---

[170] This will be reinforced in ch. 2 when we compare the situation of a parent refusing medical treatment for a born child (for religious reasons) with the situation of a pregnant woman.

exercising a right. Indeed, this is the ultimate purpose of Dworkin's approach regarding abortion. Yet the key to their arguments lie in their attention to the *motives* or *reasons* on a woman's part. At this juncture, I shall briefly suggest several links with a virtue-ethical approach by considering the work of Rosalind Hursthouse, who has looked at the issue of abortion.[171]

Hursthouse's argument is not set within a rights framework. Rather, she puts to one side the idea of rights, in that she notes that in exercising a presumed moral right, one can do something "cruel, or callous, or selfish, or lightminded . . ."[172] and suggests that within virtue theory itself the question of whether one has a right is in fact irrelevant. (Hursthouse appears here to neglect the virtue of justice, although this is not to say that only considerations of rights are relevant to justice.[173]) Yet in effect her argument follows a similar pattern to that which I have developed so far, in the sense that she queries the assistance to be gained from arguments which focus entirely upon the "moral status of the fetus" and moves instead to an approach which focuses upon the intrinsic links between maternal and fetal interests.

Thus, she highlights the relevance of what she dubs the "familiar biological facts", such as that pregnancy involves only women and lasts for nine months, is "painful, dangerous and emotionally involving".[174] She then suggests that the first question the proponent of a virtue-ethical argument might pose is: "How do these facts figure in the practical reasoning, actions and passions, thoughts and reactions, of the virtuous and non-virtuous?".[175] In brief, she suggests that, *contra* Warren, whose personhood argument I rejected earlier, abortion is clearly not comparable to an appendectomy or a haircut. Rather, because abortion is the termination of a life, it is thereby connected with our beliefs and feelings about human life and death generally, which are necessarily serious matters. Here there may be some links with Dworkin's argument and his dual conception of the sacred. Further, Hursthouse alludes to the person who insists that a woman has a "right to her own life, her own happiness" and the way in which, unsatisfactorily, "discussion stops there".[176] Yet in Dworkin's *Life's Dominion* we can see precisely the kind of concern with "what constitutes a good human life" which Hursthouse shows would be paramount in virtue theory, namely through his concern with the way in which the flourishing of a woman's life (or indeed of others upon whom hers touches) may be at stake when she contemplates an abortion. Thus, Dworkin's argument might be said at

---

[171] R Hursthouse, "Virtue Theory and Abortion", in R Crisp and M Slote (eds.), *Virtue Ethics* (Oxford: Oxford University Press, 1997) 217–38. Reprinted from (1991) 20 *Phil & Pub Aff* 223–46.

[172] *Ibid.*, 227.

[173] See e.g. D Millar, *Social Justice* (Oxford: Clarendon Press, 1976) who argues that the criteria of justice are the distinct and irreducible ideas of rights, needs and desert.

[174] R Hursthouse, "Virtue Theory and Abortion", 229. Consideration of what I dub the "social context" of pregnancy forms an important part of my examination of a woman's duties to the fetus, in ch. 2.

[175] *Ibid.*

[176] *Ibid.*, 233.

least to touch on the question Hursthouse poses, namely "And is this life of hers a good one? Is she living well?".[177]

In fact there are two senses of "good" at stake here, on the one hand a life that is good morally speaking and on the other a life which promotes the individual's well-being. On one interpretation of Aristotle, these two senses will come together in the virtuous life, such that the life in which the individual flourishes is also the life which is morally good as regards others.[178] The point I am trying to make is that where the need for an abortion, or more particularly for the refusal of treatment, relates to factors of very great import within the woman's life, then it may be that we can say that she does not have the duty to carry the unborn child to term, or to submit to medical treatment on its behalf. In this way, what is good for the individual (the woman) is balanced with or weighed against the needs of others (the fetus), by means of a justification of a refusal to assist based upon needs and values within the life of the woman.

The final and perhaps key element in Hursthouse's approach which ties in with Dworkin's but also Feinberg's arguments lies in Hursthouse's point that "[a]bortion for shallow reasons in the later stages of pregnancy is much more shocking than for the same reasons in the early stages".[179] Applied to the context of the maternal–fetal conflict, the suggestion is that the woman with shallow or trivial reasons for refusing treatment which would result in considerable harm to the fetus/future child would not be displaying the characteristics of the virtuous or wise or emotionally attuned person: given the seriousness of the issues at stake, to refuse treatment lightly would be to have the "wrong *attitude* not only to foetuses, but more generally to human life and death, parenthood, family relationships".[180] Such a refusal could be the subject of moral condemnation.

The significance of noting this "conceptual analogy", if you like, between the gradualist view of the maternal–fetal relationship, particularly as formulated by Dworkin, and a virtue-ethical approach lies in giving further substance to the idea that whether a pregnant woman is morally justified in exercising her right to refuse medical treatment on any given occasion will depend upon the circumstances, including the stage of fetal development or the type of harm it would suffer on the one hand and the woman's reasons or motivations on the other. Although I shall very briefly revisit these ideas, it is beyond my scope to consider virtue ethics in detail, other than to observe Roger Crisp's and Michael Slote's observations about the possible development of virtue theory within law and politics:[181]

> "[I]f a virtue theory like Hursthouse's were *somehow extended into the sphere of law and politics*, it might find the resources to claim that, even if some sorts of abortions are morally wrong, *the State has no moral right to prohibit them*. This might be a sufficient concession to feminism and liberalism to make Hursthouse's view seem plausible, despite its denial of

---

[177] R Hursthouse, "Virtue Theory and Abortion", 233.
[178] I am grateful here to Roger Crisp.
[179] *Ibid.*, 231.
[180] As Hursthouse expresses this point regarding abortion. *Ibid.*, 230, my emphasis.
[181] In their "Introduction" to *Virtue Ethics*, 22, first emphasis added; second in original.

ground-floor rights. After all, even if there is a significant right of abortion, a woman who has an abortion solely in order, say, to spite her husband might plausibly be thought to be acting in a morally unacceptable way. Clearly, though, such possibilities need to be explored further."

IV. CONCLUSIONS

This chapter began with a brief theoretical introduction to the idea of autonomy and its place within liberalism–communitarianism and feminist debates, the nature of rights and duties (I endorsed a hybrid Interest–autonomy account of rights) and their place in moral thought. Here I observed the inconclusiveness of rights-based reasoning in moral theory. Thereafter I distinguished maternal treatment refusal which results in harm to the future child and that which results in fetal death, acknowledging that in the first case, given that a child will be born who suffers from damage incurred *in utero*, the real party in issue is not the fetus but the future child, understood as the child who will be but is not yet born. The difficulty, however, was to determine the *weight* to be given to the future child's interests when in conflict with those of the woman in whom it is currently situated, so that we must look to arguments about the moral status of the fetus. In this light, I considered four key arguments regarding fetal moral status, noting that in any event what happens to the fetus is generally of such moral importance to us because a fetus is an unborn human being on a finite journey toward becoming a born human being: in other words, a fetus is of moral interest because of what it is becoming. Consideration of fetal moral status was also essential in attending to those cases where treatment refusal in any event results in fetal death rather than harm to the future child.

The *human species* argument had little to contribute to the current discussion, except that my attempt to expose the weakness of its negative argument—particularly its rejection of the attainment of fetal viability as a relevant benchmark—was the first indication that arguments which take no account of the fetus's location inside the woman are inherently weak. Since such arguments tell us only about the fetus but not the woman in whom it necessarily resides, they only reveal part of the moral picture. In this regard, in discussing the viability benchmark, I drew out the different implications in the abortion and the treatment contexts, such that the viable fetus needing caesarean birth may well impinge on its mother's interests to a greater extent than the viable fetus whose need was "simply" to go to term and be delivered "naturally" (notwithstanding the considerable physical demands of the latter). Thus, in the treatment context there may be a much more intricate interplay of maternal and fetal interests after viability than with regard to abortion. This point was developed later in the chapter when it was noted that fetal medical needs can call upon a woman's bodily integrity or self-determination in novel and unforeseen ways at any time, including from viability onwards.

The human species argument was an important stepping stone to consideration of the *personhood* argument which immediately followed. This latter approach was in part flawed by its failure to give importance to the fetus's location. This arises because the argument amounts to claims about personhood of any species and is therefore not tailored specifically to considering the circumstances, in particular, of human gestation and birth. The "technical" finesse of the argument also accounted for its rigidity, as a result of which it is inclined to leave a trail of embarrassing conclusions needing to be "touched up" (for example, regarding infanticide in relation to unwanted infants). (Comments of Bernard Williams on the distinction between abortion and infanticide might be noted here.[182]) The reason for this lies in the exclusivity of an approach which focuses upon the crucial link between personhood and rights, such that notions of moral wrongness beyond the violation of rights appear only as tidying footnotes. Hence I rejected the personhood argument as an excessively narrow basis upon which to consider the maternal–fetal conflict: to conclude that the fetus is not a person with rights and therefore has no entitlement to consideration in the treatment context is a simple, and hence inadequate, answer to a very complex moral problem.[183]

The argument which attributes *interests* to the fetus at sentience/viability is legitimate and helpful, giving us a way to consider the fetus's claims from viability onwards, which we shall later see to be consistent with abortion law. The concept of interests can readily accommodate the idea that claims based on fetal interests may be weakened by the fetus's location inside the woman, an important reason to stop short of attributing the rights to the fetus which possession of interests would normally underpin. Yet the interest approach could tell us little in its own terms of the pre-viable fetus or the future child. Accordingly I turned to the argument from *potential*. Here I rejected the view that potential possession of personhood is a ground for the ascription of rights to the fetus in favour of the idea that potential personhood may instead be a reason for us to consider the fetus, perhaps a reason to owe it imperfect (or non-instrumental) duties.

In order to begin to develop this idea, I explored a *modified potentiality* account (as a prelude to the gradualist accounts developed in the last section) in which I focused only on the idea of the fetus's growing moral status (rather than also addressing the question of the strength of the interests required to justify harm on the mother's side which the gradualist accounts in the last section develop). At this point, with the benefit of having now considered four of the principal arguments regarding the fetus's moral status, I explored the difficult question of the distinction between harm to the future child and harm to the fetus *qua* fetus (in the latter sense, that is, harm

---

[182] "[A] distinction between abortion, which is permitted, and infanticide, which is not, is one which can probably be naturally sustained in a certain context of shared moral sentiment without further reason being needed. The fact that further reason is not needed does not mean that that distinction is *irrational*. It means only that the basic distinction is more directly convincing than any reason that might be advanced for it . . ." B Williams, "Conflicts of Values", in his *Moral Luck: Philosophical Papers 1973–1980* (Cambridge: Cambridge University Press, 1981) 81, emphasis in original.

[183] H Draper suggests that arguments against enforced caesareans generally rely on the idea that the fetus is not a person and that this argument may put us on the "slippery slope" to infanticide. H Draper, "Women, forced caesareans and antenatal responsibilities", (1996) 22 *JME* 327, 328. I hope to have shown why rejecting fetal personhood need not have this consequence.

that would result in fetal death). The combination of a modified potentiality account with, at fetal viability, the idea of fetal interests, may between them give us the conceptual tools to deal with the distinction between harm to the future child and the death of the fetus, with the latter (interest view) applying from viability onwards.

The complex conclusions are too detailed to repeat here, but I explicated the crucial moral distinction between a future child and a born child noted at the start of the chapter, namely a future child's location in and continuing impingement upon a woman's body. In the course of the discussion I drew attention to the links between not only the fetus's but also the future child's *location* and its *degree of development*. I argued that where the party in issue is the fetus, the degree of its development is the primary consideration, but that this is inevitably connected to the question of its location inside the woman; and that, so far as the interests of the future child are concerned, the primary consideration is its location (as this distinguishes it from the born child), but that at some point the degree of its development may be partially relevant to the strength of its claims. (A viable fetus, of course, also has interests "in its own right".) A "modified potentiality" account such as I have developed in relation to the maternal–fetal conflict therefore necessarily touches on the woman's interests. Since either the fetus or the future child is necessarily a being inside another person, this is a positive indication of the moral wisdom that we may find in such a view.

To further explore such an approach I examined two gradualist accounts, the strength of which lay in the *simultaneous* attention paid to maternal and fetal interests: the essence of each account was the idea that the greater the development of the fetus, the stronger the reason on the woman's side needed to justify harm to it. Dworkin's argument was seen to be more developed than Feinberg's, as it also acknowledged the difference in the character of fetal claims from sentience onwards. I explored the implications of this argument for the maternal–fetal conflict (a topic not addressed by Dworkin), drawing attention to the way in which the strength of the fetus's but also the future child's interests, at least so far as they are in conflict with its mother's, are always tempered to some degree by its location inside her body, given that through its medical needs it is likely to call upon her interests in bodily integrity or self-determination or both. With regard to either interest the body is always implicated where invasive treatment is in issue. This is the kind of treatment at stake in the caesarean cases.

Both Feinberg's and Dworkin's approaches, which address the justification of harm to the fetus, may ultimately be speaking about the *theoretical justification* of rights in the abortion context. This discussion was adapted to the maternal–fetal conflict. In Dworkin's more developed account, the idea of respect toward the value of life (an idea touched on in Feinberg's argument) seems ultimately to invoke the idea of responsibility in the justification and exercise of rights which concern this value. With regard to both accounts we saw the likely coincidence between the idea of a serious reason and the existence of an area of interest protected by a right: for instance, in the case of the refusal of a caesarean section on the basis of religious objections and/or its serious impingement upon the body and its imposition of physical risks. We also saw the potential break between the serious reason and the right: for instance, in the hypothetical case of the refusal of the harmless pill, highly beneficial to fetal welfare, which there appears to be no reason to refuse. (Of course, if the pill did have serious side-effects on a pregnant woman, she may thus have serious reason to refuse it.) These observations raise the highly important question of the scope for reflection upon the *moral quality* of the decision to exercise a right. In the next chapter we shall encounter the difficulty of determining, *in practice,* whether any given reason is in fact sufficiently serious to outweigh the fetus's claims. Here it should be noted that reasons do not present themselves with the labels "serious" or "trivial", a difficulty also addressed in a section of chapter four which seeks to give practical guidance in the situation of a pregnant woman's treatment refusal. Regarding my analogy with virtue ethics, although virtue theory does not start from rights, it may well be able to contribute to arguments about rights, precisely with regard to the question of the moral justification for their exercise.

To develop our understanding of these points, we need now to turn to consider a woman's interests in self-determination and bodily integrity and so to appreciate the maternal–fetal conflict as it occurs within the medical treatment context directly from her viewpoint. Given the complexities of the argument to follow, I shall generally leave to one side the question of the distinction between harm to the future child and death of the fetus which has been an important focus of this chapter. In so doing, note that regarding the typical case of refusal of caesarean delivery, in any event the moral strength of the claims of either the fetus or the future child are very similar, if not indistinguishable. This means that not knowing whether the refusal of a caesarean will result in fetal death or brain damage to the future child should not be an obstacle to the determination of the moral position on such treatment refusals. The distinction between the fetus and the future child will resurface at later points, especially in chapter six, on the relevance of arguments from tort law where I consider both the treatment context and the issue of a woman's general conduct.

2

The Relation of the Pregnant Woman to the Fetus: The Interface Between Her Moral Rights and Duties

I. INTRODUCTION

THIS CHAPTER looks at a woman's relationship to the fetus she carries in two principal ways: first, in terms of the idea of *rights*—by considering, in particular, her moral interest in self-determination and touching on her moral interest in bodily integrity which are the grounds of her rights in pregnancy; second, in terms of the idea of *duties*—by considering, in particular, the idea of the extent of a duty that might be owed through or via the body. Thus, her interest in and right to bodily integrity is particularly explored with reference to the concept of duty. On questions of definition, recall that in the previous chapter I suggested that an interest in self-determination be understood as concerning a person's interest in reflectively making significant personal choices, whilst an interest in bodily integrity concerns being able to decide what happens to one's body which is important because one's body is a central part of oneself and so of one's sense of self.

To contemplate the maternal–fetal conflict from the woman's perspective, first in terms of her rights and second in terms of her possible duties is, in a sense, to approach her relationship to the fetus from opposite ends of the same moral lens. In the first case, in considering the strength or otherwise of her rights, at some point the possibility of a right "giving way" to a duty is in issue; in the second case, consideration of an argument directed towards the concept of duty must at some point address the question of how any duty that might be owed relates to those rights which she has. This structure is justified in two ways. First, to look at the problem in this way is not only to break down some very difficult conceptual issues into manageable parts, but ultimately to make clear that the problem of the maternal–fetal conflict is a problem of the relationship between a woman's rights and duties. Second, this structure is subsequently mirrored in Parts II and III of the book in which I explore, at various points, the ideas of a pregnant woman's *legal* rights and duties, sometimes separating and sometimes bringing together these points. The structure thus underscores the *conceptual* links between the ethics and the law relating to the maternal–fetal conflict.[1]

---

[1] Aristotle appears to emphasise the connections between moral and legal judgment, describing the law as "a rule proceeding from a sort of practical wisdom and reason". He also notes that "intelligence

II. THE ARGUMENT FROM RIGHTS

A. Self-Determination

The ideas of self-determination and autonomy were first introduced at the start of chapter one in the context of the preliminary discussion of rights, duties and the kinds of interests that may be implicated in the maternal–fetal conflict. There I observed the long-standing philosophical recognition of the value of autonomy and cited, amongst other work, that of Joseph Raz, in whose ethical framework autonomy plays a crucial role.

In this section I want to distinguish between three senses of autonomy. The first is autonomy in the sense of a *value*, as explicated, for instance, by Joseph Raz. Well-being, according to Raz, largely ". . . consists in the (1) whole-hearted and (2) successful pursuit of (3) valuable (4) activities."[2] Although each of these points is explained and defended, it is only with the last idea that I am concerned at present, that is, the understanding of the intrinsic relation between the good and the active life. The activity that is conducive to well-being can take many forms, for instance pursuing a lifetime interest, or forming close and loving friendships. What these have in common is that they each require a certain amount of doing: they require *activity*. For instance, friendship requires, amongst other things, the activity of understanding: we do not serve our friends well if we rarely bother to consider them or reflect on their perspectives or problems, or, more light-heartedly, share in mutual activities together. Raz suggests that "[t]he ideal of personal autonomy is the vision of people controlling, to some degree, their own destiny, fashioning it through successive decisions throughout their lives".[3]

On the basis of his view that the individual has an interest in being autonomous it might be asked whether it is also his *right*? Does the individual have a right to what Raz dubs the "collective goods" which enable autonomy? Raz argues that to say that an individual has a right means, "other things being equal, an aspect of *x's* well-being (his interest) is a sufficient reason for holding some other person(s) to be under a duty."[4] Moreover, (simplifying a complex argument) he suggests that given that society at large is involved in facilitating the existence of the conditions which enables the pursuit of an autonomous life, it is unlikely that the interest of

---

. . . and right judgment . . . [are] . . . the greatest thing" in the selection of the best laws. Aristotle, *The Nicomachean Ethics*, D Ross, (trans.) (Oxford: Oxford University Press, 1980), Bk X, ch. 9 at 1180a and 1180b respectively. It is beyond my scope further to consider his ideas in this regard. Note, however, that in the Introduction to this work I observed that, as regards the links between the ethics and the law of the maternal–fetal conflict, I was concerned with the question of the moral criticism of the law or, put another way, its moral justifiability.

[2] J Raz, "Duties of Well-Being", in his *Ethics in the Public Domain: Essays in the Morality of Law and Politics* (Oxford: Oxford University Press, 1994) 3–28, 3.

[3] J Raz, *The Morality of Freedom* (Oxford: Oxford University Press, 1986) 369.

[4] J Raz, "Right-based Moralities", (1982) in J Waldron (ed.), *Theories of Rights* (Oxford, Oxford University Press, 1984) 182–200, 183.

any *one* individual can justify imposing such an onerous duty on so many. It follows that there can be no right to personal autonomy as such, which means personal autonomy is one example of an *ideal* or *value* at the heart of our morality.[5]

The second sense of autonomy I have in mind is the most specific and pertains to the individual's interest in autonomy—or what we may dub "self-determination"—in *particular contexts*, such as regarding the issue of medical treatment. There are two important points to note about this sense of autonomy. First, autonomy here becomes very *personal*—invoking issues about the body or the religious beliefs of the individual. Second, the interest in self-determination invoked here is so strong and so particular to the individual—in the sense of going very much to the person—that it in turn merits the protection of at least a *prima facie right*. Indeed, this would be consistent with Raz's argument that autonomy is a value from which specific rights may be derived: on his view, there are "derivative rights"[6] which protect and advance aspects of the individual's autonomy and contribute to making autonomy possible.[7] Hence we might see the right to self-determination in the medical context as derived from the broader value of autonomy.

It is this very personal dimension of autonomy which is at stake regarding the issue of maternal treatment refusal: as we have already begun to appreciate, the fetus's medical needs impinge upon a woman's self-determination in ways which go to quite specific religious or secular beliefs about the value and meaning of life. Thus, a pregnant Born-Again Christian believes that it is a serious sin to submit to surgery, whilst the religious beliefs of a Jehovah's Witness will preclude the acceptance of a blood transfusion. An alternative scenario, which does not go to the idea of a woman's religious beliefs but which implicates her life in a very personal way, may be represented by the scenario of a pregnant woman dying of a terminal condition. She may have a few days to live and prefer to die as comfortably and peacefully as possible rather than submit to caesarean surgery.[8] The point here is that, perhaps even more than the abortion context (where somewhat broader issues to do with family size or a woman's work may be at stake), the medical treatment context implicates the interest in and right to self-determination in its most personal and particular guise.

The third sense of autonomy covers the idea of day-to-day general conduct introduced early in chapter one, an aspect closely related to the idea of liberty. Notably, on the views of legal philosophers such as Joseph Raz (following on from

---

[5] *Ibid.*, esp. 186–95. In addition to the sense of autonomy as a value, Raz distinguishes between two further senses of autonomy. The first sense refers to the life in which autonomy is achieved or realised—and is only found where an individual has been able to choose between various significant options in such a way as to shape his or her life. In the second sense, autonomy is seen as the capacity to achieve an autonomous life: whether the conditions of autonomy exist will depend both on the capacities of the individual as a rational agent and on the conditions of his life and the choices available to him. In this last sense, autonomy is only possible if various collective goods, such as that a society is a tolerant one, exist. J Raz, "Right-based Moralities", 191.

[6] J Raz, *The Morality of Freedom*, 247.

[7] J Raz, "Right-based Moralities", 195.

[8] This is the case of *Re AC*, 533 A 2d 611 (DC App 1987); 573 A 2d 1235 (DC App 1990), discussed in Parts II and III.

the above) and Ronald Dworkin, this very general sense of autonomy or liberty does not merit the protection of any particular right.[9] Colloquially of course, one might speak of a "right to do as one pleases, so long one does not harm others", but this is really to cite the general idea of freedom or liberty, rather than any particular right. So, although we may have an interest, in a very loose sense, in doing as we please so long as we do not "harm" others, it need not be thought that we necessarily have a serious right so to do. For instance, to take a very simple example, although I may wish to be able to travel from London to Bath by whatever means are available to me (by car or train, say), although we might say that I have some kind of a right to travel to Bath, I do not think this is true in any very meaningful or significant sense. The point comes particularly to the fore when we consider the possible harm to others that might attend the *manner* in which I might achieve this goal. Suppose I need to arrive in Bath by 10 o'clock on a Saturday morning for a friend's wedding and that I cannot leave London on Friday night because of another commitment and must therefore travel early on the Saturday. Suppose further that there is a train strike, so that the quickest means of transport (barring air-travel) is unavailable to me, and so I will have to travel by car. I do need to get to Bath, indeed to the church, on time, but even if I had a (not particularly meaningful) right to travel to Bath, I certainly do not have a right to speed down the motorway at breakneck speed, endangering other road-users in the process. Moreover, I think most people would agree that it would be *unreasonable* on my part to subject others to serious risks in order to reach the wedding on time.

We might note three additional points of considerable importance here. The first is that in fact I have a moral *duty* to other road-users to drive safely (which is recognised in law). Second, "other road-users" would here include fetuses present within any female travellers who happen to be pregnant. Third, if *I* were pregnant, my moral duty to take care in the *conduct* of my car would, at least in some jurisdictions, also find recognition as a legal duty owed to the fetus/future child within me.[10] Importantly, in these cases—which I am arguing fall within the realm of "general conduct"—there is a broad coincidence of the idea of *reasonableness* with the idea of *duty*, such that if I breached a duty to take care I might also be said to be acting unreasonably, including towards "my" fetus.[11] In other words, the oblig-

---

[9] As observed in the previous chapter, it is the right to equality which is fundamental in Dworkin's work. I take it that therefore the general day-to-day conduct which is the subject of this section would not be the subject of a right in the way that certain kinds of quite specific choices within a life might be. Dworkin explicitly attacked the idea that liberty is of value in "What Rights Do We Have?" in *Taking Rights Seriously* (2nd impression (corrected) with appendix London: Duckworth, 1978) 266. I think it also follows from Raz's argument as noted above that one's general conduct would not merit the protection of a specific right. This is because, by definition, specific rights protect quite particular interests and choices.

[10] See ch. 6.

[11] Note that most instances of physical harm to others represent a breach of a *negative* duty—as in the example of driving in an unsafe manner to Bath. The idea of physically harming others by failing to assist them is discussed in connection with my argument from duty in section III *infra*. There, the idea of failing to assist, for instance, an injured other, is considered in connection with the idea of the woman assisting (or not assisting) the fetus through her body.

ation—moral or legal—of a pregnant woman to drive carefully, is one pertaining to the domain of general conduct, about which a judgment of reasonableness is relatively easily made. In such a case, a woman's and a third party's moral (and potentially legal) duties to her unborn child are commensurate.

The purpose of drawing attention to the distinction between self-determination in the personal sense which tends to merit the protection of a right on the one hand, and the individual's day-to-day conduct on the other, is to open up the problem of *judging* when, if ever, the individual's *prima facie* rights in self-determination should give way to the interests of others. Specifically of course, the question is when a pregnant woman's *prima facie* rights should give way to the interests of the fetus/future child. My point is that, regarding general day-to-day conduct, *at least so far as possibly physically harmful interactions with others* are concerned, there is usually something of a "yardstick" by which we can determine, to some degree, the "reasonableness" of a person's conduct. My example about travelling from London to Bath is a very simple one and in subtler cases there may well be dispute about what is and is not reasonable. Importantly, though, "reasonableness" will necessarily be *easiest* to determine where it is *furthest* from "personal" questions. This is the important point for my purposes. In other words, it may be uncontroversial to say that to insist upon speeding down the motorway in the circumstances described is unreasonable because no great *personal meaning* attaches to such a choice (notwithstanding that the purpose of my journey is to be at a close friend's wedding) and because of the risks to others.

I have suggested in this section that no particular *rights* are likely to be invoked with regard to the issue of a "detached" third party harming the fetus, or the woman harming the fetus in a manner akin to that of such a party (for instance, through her careless driving). Concomitantly, in these latter cases judgments about reasonableness are more accessible. Turning to the other end of the spectrum, to those areas which do raise questions of very personal meaning, we find (in the context under discussion) the interests in and rights to self-determination and bodily integrity. When we address the question of when, if ever, these *prima facie* rights should give way to the interests of the fetus, we are beginning to touch upon the interface between a woman's rights and duties. Here I think that ideas of "reasonableness" are much harder to formulate, as I shall now explore. In the section that immediately follows, the way in which the obstetric medical treatment context invokes a woman's right, in particular to self-determination, and the problems this presents, will be explored. Throughout the rest of this chapter, the important distinction I have identified between a pregnant woman's and a third party's relationship to the unborn child on the one hand and the distinction between a pregnant woman's duties to her unborn child in the medical treatment context and her duties in the course of her general conduct on the other should be recalled: these hinge upon a distinction between obligations realised via the body and obligations in the course of general conduct. This latter distinction is particularly pertinent to the argument from duty, in section III below.

B. The Interplay of Maternal and Fetal Interests

Let us return to the discussion of the "gradualist" accounts of the maternal–fetal relationship at the end of chapter one. There I suggested that these arguments either could be (in Joel Feinberg's case) or were essentially (in Ronald Dworkin's) explanations of the *justification* of certain rights regarding abortion and I sought to apply and adapt these approaches to the question of the maternal–fetal conflict. In the course of the discussion, I drew attention to the likely coincidence between a serious reason and a right, but also noted the possible break in this link. Thus I contrasted the refusal of a caesarean section for religious or other serious reasons with the hypothetical refusal of the pill (beneficial for fetal welfare by curing, for instance, a vitamin deficiency) apparently without reason. Alternatively, there is the (unlikely) possibility of the refusal of a caesarean section motivated solely by the desire to avoid an abdominal scar. In the latter case, it can be fairly confidently asserted that the wish to avoid a scar is not a *serious* or *appropriate* reason given what is at stake, that is, possible fetal death or brain damage. This example of the refusal motivated by the wish to avoid a scar is given by Bonnie Steinbock, who suggests that we can agree that this would be "appallingly selfish".[12] In a similar vein, regarding risks to the fetus's life or health, Nancy Rhoden suggests that "trivial reasons for running this risk may justify our casting moral aspersions" on the woman's choices.[13]

   Thus, using the "gradualist" and, to some extent arguably "virtue-ethical" approach formulated at the end of chapter one, we had reached the provisional conclusion that a woman may justifiably exercise her right to refuse treatment where she has a "serious" reason to do so (for instance, the religious reason) and that, correspondingly, she does so unjustifiably in the event that her reasons are trivial (the abdominal scar). The ease with which the abdominal scar example is so frequently cited lies in its relatively obvious moral inappropriateness: we, third parties, can easily condemn such a motivation.[14] It has to be said that it is also *immensely* unlikely that a woman would proffer such a reason to avoid the caesarean. Yet what of the serious religious reason? Although a religious reason must necessarily be "serious" *for the woman* (given the evident place of religion in her life) is it serious or strong enough to withstand the *claims of the fetus*?

---

[12] B Steinbock, *Life Before Birth: the Moral and Legal Status of Embryos and Fetuses* (New York, NY: Oxford University Press, 1992) 153–54. Of course, someone to whom physical appearance is crucial to employment, such as a model, may arguably be an exception here. I am grateful to Roger Crisp for this thought.

[13] N Rhoden, "Cesareans and Samaritans", (1987) 15 *Law Med & Health Care* 118, 121.

[14] In this connection, recall the following comment in R Crisp and M Slote's "Introduction" to Rosalind Hursthouse's piece (first cited in the last chapter) in their *Virtue Ethics* (Oxford: Oxford University Press, 1997) 22: "[E]ven if there is a significant right of abortion, a woman who has an abortion solely in order, say, to spite her husband might plausibly be thought to be acting in a morally unacceptable way." My point here is to notice that the editors cite a reason which we can readily agree, I think, makes the abortion morally wrong: the reason is "trivial", rather than "serious", and hence the question of *judging* the seriousness of a non-trivial reason is not encountered.

Now, the difficulty we are about to encounter is as follows. I have suggested that the gradualist accounts of the maternal–fetal relationship imply that where a woman has a serious reason to refuse treatment so she has the right to do so—in *theory*, so to speak. The same conclusion may be reached by incorporating a virtue-ethical gradualist approach within a rights framework. Yet in *practice*, if we wish to determine whether any given woman is justifiably asserting a right to refuse treatment, we will need to determine the "seriousness" or "strength" of her reason. It is as though the gradualist understanding of the relationship gives us only a major premise of an argument, the minor premise of which remains to be worked out. So the problem discussed in the next section is the problem of how to say, in any given *non-trivial* case, whether the reason in question is serious for *us*, meaning serious when we view the woman's interests and rights in relation to those of the fetus.

I will explore the problem with regard to a woman's interest in and right to self-determination, focusing upon the question of religious reasons for refusal of treatment.

1. *The Seriousness of a Woman's Religious Reasons for Refusing Treatment*

Consider the case where a woman wishes to decline the caesarean surgery for religious reasons, a very common reason for which obstetric interventions are refused, as evidenced by the legal cases considered in Part II. For instance, a pregnant woman may be a Born-Again Christian who believes that it would be a serious sin to submit to surgery, such that she would forego eternal life were she to do so. By its nature, then, such a religious reason is clearly not trivial. In this light, it is not surprising that we give people rights to religious freedom and that the desire to refuse medical treatment for religious reasons has played a not insubstantial part in the creation of a competent adult's (legal) right to refuse treatment as we know it. Yet how far can we allow a right to religious freedom when *physical harm to others*, here the fetus, is threatened? No doubt this is a question which would have greatly preoccupied John Stuart Mill.[15] Surely, we might say, the belief cannot be so important that it would justify or excuse the fetus's death *in utero*, or brain damage to the child who will be born (the "future child"). Others might ask why the pregnant woman should have the "right to sacrifice" the fetus in the interests of her religious faith. Ultimately, these questions require that we consider how serious a religious reason is when harm to another person or being is a likely consequence. To those who do not share the religious belief in question, it seems inevitable that it will seem less serious than to those whose belief it is. This is because the belief in question is not ours, meaning that we stand, in some sense, "outside" it. From

---

[15] "[T]he sole end for which mankind are warranted, individually or collectively, in interfering with the liberty of action of any of their number, is self-protection . . . the only purpose for which power can be rightfully exercised over any member of a civilized community, against his will, is to prevent harm to others." "On Liberty", (1859) in Mill, *Utilitarianism*, M Warnock (ed.), (Fontana: London, 1962) 135.

this perspective, how are we to determine what weight to give to the religious reason?

The problem adverted to here is that of how to take account, in our moral reasoning, of the reasons of others. One obvious way we do this is by according rights: hence, the rights to self-determination and bodily integrity that are implicated in refusing medical treatment. By granting the right to refuse medical treatment, for instance, we are partly saying that we recognise the individual's interest in making deeply personal choices in this area, including in decisions that affect his or her body: thus, we are acknowledging the significant interests of self-determination and bodily integrity. Ultimately this might be said to be a way, in turn, of *valuing individuals*. Yet where we are contemplating whether a *prima facie* right should not give way to a duty—whether the woman's interests ought not give way to those of the fetus—we no longer have the solid crutch of the idea of the "right" to hold on to and must take the matter back a stage further to the question of her *reasons* for refusing treatment. The problem here seems to lie in the interface between the subjective domain, which certain rights protect, and the objective—in the sense of interpersonal—quality that is inherent in the notion of duty.

More specifically, as far as religious reasons are concerned, it is a question of the interface between the domain of *religion* on the one hand and *ethics* or *moral reasoning* on the other. That is, the question is how to understand the religious interests of the pregnant woman from the moral perspective in which we are trying to compare her interests with those of the fetus. So we must determine what weight we give to her religious views by balancing these against the interests of the fetus and deciding, in effect, whether her religious interests outweigh the interests of the fetus. Let us first try to explicate the interface between religion and moral reasoning.

Broadly speaking, both philosophical ethics and religion are concerned with the project of giving meaning and shape to our lives, incorporating consideration of our relationships to others. Moreover, sometimes the processes that seem to be in issue in either religious or philosophical ethics may well share certain qualities. For instance, religious thought may involve stories from which religious/moral guidance is to be drawn (such as the story of the Good Samaritan); it may also involve piecing together the structure of religious belief from differing texts and differing accounts of the same events therein (such as the accounts of the life of Christ in the New Testament). Likewise, philosophers employ examples—even "stories"— from which they argue toward certain moral conclusions. On other occasions, philosophers try to establish the views of a given philosopher, such as Kant, reconciling his writings in various texts; moreover, since this process is a matter of interpretation, it is subject to disagreement. Likewise, there may be considerable disagreement within (Christian) religious thinking about what, for instance, Paul said.

But in other ways there may be important differences. For instance, rational argument may or may not be part of a religious faith, depending in part upon the religion and in part upon the character of the individual believer and his relationship to his faith. Rationality *per se*, however, is not generally taken to be a constitutive feature of religion: it is not, we might say, what is important about religion. The point is that we do not *expect* religion to be rationally coherent in the way that we expect philosophically-developed moral positions to be, at least to a significant degree. Indeed, rational argument is a necessary part of philosophical ethics, although this is by no means to prejudge the considerations which will be relevant to this task. (Consider for instance the suggestion in the brief discussion in chapter one relating the gradualist accounts of the moral status of the fetus to a virtue ethics approach that there is an important element of emotional attunement in the idea of an appropriate or proportionate response to the developing fetus.[16])

Perhaps most significantly, however, where religion and philosophical ethics truly diverge is in the question of outcomes: the development of religious thought is part of the process of forming a set of beliefs which amounts to a religious *faith*. Where seriously held, this faith will form a crucial part of a person's life and her beliefs about the world. Indeed, it might be said that in some sense ultimately faith drives and binds religion.[17] By contrast, with regard to philosophical ethics, although philosophers want to be able to draw moral conclusions about particular issues or problems, those conclusions do not typically amount to a faith as such. That is, although a philosopher might strongly hold certain views, or feel that the views of a particular past philosopher, such as Aristotle, are particularly astute, she is unlikely to *believe* in Aristotle in the strong sense which would make the arguments of Kant, say, in some sense irrelevant to her task of trying to determine "the good", although no doubt examples of highly dogmatic philosophers of whom this would not be true could be found. Rather, generally speaking, part of the philosophical process of upholding Aristotle's conception of the good is just as likely to lie in a discussion and criticism of Kant's ideas in this regard, and vice versa. The point I am trying to make is that a religious faith amounts, in some sense, to an *internal system* (regardless of its rationality or otherwise) which makes it hard to criticise from "outside".

---

[16] Thus, other considerations beyond reason may well be relevant to or part of our moral reasoning. For instance, in ch. 1 I touched on Michael Tooley's argument regarding abortion and infanticide: his argument has been the subject of particularly interesting criticism by Genevieve Lloyd, who has suggested that "the emotional contexts of pregnancy and infancy form part of the proper subject matter of adequate moral theorizing on these issues." As Lloyd notes, this is not to suggest that emotions may themselves be the judge of the moral issues—a possibility which Tooley considers and rejects—but rather to acknowledge their relevance to the issues in question. G Lloyd, "Review of M Tooley's *Abortion and Infanticide*" (1986) 64 *Aust J of Phil*, Supplement "Women and Philosophy", 144.

[17] This may account for a remark such as that of Mr Harding in Anthony Trollope's *Barchester Towers* (1857), to the effect that "where there is no mystery, there is no faith". And see the entry of Nicholas Dent in T Honderich (ed.), *The Oxford Companion to Philosophy* (Oxford: Oxford University Press, 1995) on "irrationalism", where he writes that "St Thomas Acquinas, for all his demonstrated powers of reasoning, conceded some truths to the sole competence of faith. Even Kant . . . confessedly found it necessary to 'deny *knowledge* in order to make room for *faith*' ". (At 418.) See also Isaiah Berlin's discussion of the counter-Enlightenment thinker, JG Hamann, in his *The Magus of the North: JG Hamann and the Origins of Modern Irrationalism* (London: Fontana, 1994). On Hamann's relationship to religion, Berlin writes: "There cannot be any peace between faith and reason. So far from religion being reason *in excelsis* as Thomism teaches, one must make up one's mind either for faith or for criticism; either to complete commitment or to open scepticism." (At 68.)

In the light of the above points and given that my discussion falls within the domain of philosophical ethics rather than within a religious faith, it appears that we cannot both step inside the religious belief *and* retain the external perspective from which we wish to weigh the belief against the interests of the fetus. Therefore, we are left pondering the significance of the belief for the pregnant woman, that is, the place of religion in her life and what it would mean for her, in the light of her religious faith, to be subjected to surgery against her will.[18] This approach would be consistent with Julian Savulescu's suggestion that the way to understand religion in this context is as a "construct which gives meaning to people's lives".[19] His discussion of religiously based refusals occurs within the broader context of an argument to the effect that we respect a person's autonomy when we respect desires which are or which satisfy her *rational* desires, rather than merely her expressed desires.[20] On his argument, the desire to refuse life-saving medical treatment can be seen as rational when the person's religious faith has a valid purpose in her life: in these circumstances, she has what we might dub a psychological reason to hold the belief. Moreover, on this understanding, since the religious belief is autonomously held, it will be crucially connected to the person. Applying this point to the context in question (not one discussed by Savulescu), where a pregnant woman for whom religious faith has a valid purpose wishes to refuse caesarean delivery with the likely consequence that the fetus will die (and the possible consequence that she will), her religious faith is clearly a fundamental, indeed central, aspect of her life and its meaning. So, by recognising the important *role* religion plays in her deliberations about how to live, we can accord significant weight to the question of religion in moral argument without ourselves being religious (or sharing the same religious faith). To put the point another way, although we cannot place ourselves in the position of feeling and holding the particular religious beliefs ourselves, we can recognise the importance of the belief for the other person.[21]

In a similar vein, Michael Wreen has argued that religious beliefs and values have a "pervasive, supremely important integrating and reconciling function . . . in a person's life", such that not respecting a religious refusal would amount to "a personal insult of a very deep and cutting nature".[22] In other words, Wreen likewise stresses the connection between religious belief and the person, a connection which is unlikely to be fundamentally present between the person and the irrational belief (say) that medical treatment involving red objects (for example, blood trans-

---

[18] Note that others, namely conscientious objectors, have been excluded from the duty to assist in the fighting of wars on the basis of the place of their beliefs within their lives. But this example has only limited parallels with our concerns.

[19] J Savulescu, "Rational Desires and the Limitation of Life-Sustaining Treatment", (1994) 8 *Bioethics* 191, 220.

[20] *Ibid.*, 191. His discussion of these conditions in the body of the article is touched on in Part II.

[21] In this sense, as Isaiah Berlin recognised, understanding does not necessarily involve agreement. This means that we can criticise and refuse certain values in addition to understanding and sympathising with them. CJ McKnight, "Pluralism, Realism and Truth", in D Archard (ed.), *Philosophy and Pluralism* (Cambridge: Cambridge University Press, 1996) 87–99, 91.

[22] MJ Wreen, "Autonomy, Religious Values and Refusal of Lifesaving Medical Treatment", (1991) 17 *JME* 124, 128.

fusions) should be rejected.[23] Importantly, this is not to deny that we would be likely to harm such a patient if, following discussion and clarification that he understood the consequences of a refusal, we disregarded his wishes and administered treatment against his will. The point is rather that the value of the religious belief within the woman's life is one possible moral reason, for our purposes, to respect her refusal. Ultimately, given the centrality of religion in our pregnant woman's life, such that it is intrinsically connected to *herself,* if we do not attach weight to her beliefs sufficient to allow her to refuse the surgery, then it might be said that we are not valuing, or respecting, her humanity. (Note that I am not giving weight to religious values over other values which give meaning to and shape a person's life, as Wreen may be doing. If this is Wreen's position, I would probably reject his adjective "supremely" if that is meant specifically in comparison with non-religious values. Thus, broadly speaking, I would probably favour Julian Savulescu's position that "[f]or ethics, religious values are just another set of values, to be treated in the same way as other relevantly similar values".[24])

In this way, my argument may have some connection with a point of Christine Korsgaard's regarding the work of Kant and Thomas Nagel (albeit regarding the somewhat different context of a person's ambitions).[25] She argues that we should promote the ends of others, not because we recognise the value of those ends (although we may come to do so), but out of respect for the humanity of those who have them.[26] Obviously, such an argument would have limits: we would not want to promote Hitler's ends, for instance. But religious ends came to be particularly protected in the twentieth century, as liberal societies granted individuals the right to religious freedom, because of the specially important place of religion in a person's life. In the case of the pregnant woman, promotion of her ends would amount to allowing her to refuse medical treatment on religious grounds.[27] In respecting her in this way, it may be that we would be recognising what Mary Midgley has

---

[23] The "red-object" example is Wreen's. He does not address the problem of maternal–fetal conflict. See discussion of the notions of legal competence in ch. 3.

[24] J Savulescu, "Two Worlds Apart: Religion and Ethics", (1998) 24 *JME* 382, 383. Savulescu suggests that "[n]on-religious values can perform the same 'integrating and reconciling' function in atheist lives as religious values can perform for theists". *Ibid.*

[25] C Korsgaard, "The Reasons We Can Share: an Attack on the Distinction between Agent-Relative and Agent-Neutral Values", in her *Creating the Kingdom of Ends* (Cambridge: Cambridge University Press, 1996).

[26] This point is located in the context of a discussion in which Korsgaard criticises the distinction between agent–neutral and agent–relative values and reasons. (Like Nagel, she equates reasons and values). She argues that, rather than being either objective or subjective, reasons and values are instead *intersubjective*, supervening on the structure of personal (i.e. all human) relations. In other words, she rejects the "objective realist" view that one only has reason to help another realise their ends if one first sees those ends as ones that one can share. Rather, the "intersubjectivist" first sees the other as human and then shares or tries to share their ends. (See 289–90.) It is beyond my scope to enter into her argument in any detail, but I touch on deontological reasons at the end of Part III, where I consider rescue law and the moral appropriateness or inappropriateness of compelling the donation of a bodily organ or part (independently, that is, of the question of what, if any, moral duties may lie).

[27] This view is supported by FC Chervenak and LB McCullough, who conclude that a pregnant woman's desire to refuse treatment should prevail where her reasons relate to fundamental values and beliefs, such as in the case of a religious refusal. "Perinatal Ethics: A Practical Method of Analysis of Obligations to Mother and Fetus", (1985) 66 *Obstet & Gyn* 442, 443.

called the "otherness of others". Writing on Kant, Midgley notes that for Kant respect is a feeling distinguished by its function—by what it *shows*—namely a "worth which we did not make and cannot alter".[28]

An important point to note in passing is the question of to what extent the woman's religious faith was chosen "autonomously". Whilst I have argued that a narrow notion of rational autonomy is out of place here and that the important point is the place of religion in her life, it might be queried whether or not she truly chose that faith. People are either born into faiths and then keep or reject (or feel ambivalent about) them or adopt a certain faith, or change faiths, later in life. The processes involved in this are obviously enormously complex and raise questions, alluded to at the start of chapter one in the brief discussion of autonomy, of the relationship between the self, her ends and society. Some people may well be able both to question and maintain their faiths, others may go through life doing so rarely, if at all. I do not see that it would be possible to make these evaluations of a particular pregnant woman without risking harming her by threatening the place of religion within her life, thereby potentially disjointing her from her family and social fabric and breaking up what had been, for her, a comprehensive life perspective. Unless, in other words, we see clear evidence of undue influence, for instance by members of her family or her religious organisation,[29] then we must accept her faith as an important constituent of her life.

Yet what of the fetus? Although I have argued that it is not a moral person, I have also noted the moral inconclusiveness of this point: the fetus is also "another" of some considerable moral worth. Notwithstanding the light I have tried to shed on the question of religious belief in this context, we must still consider whether we should not intervene (override a woman's refusal) given that without the caesarean section this other—the fetus—will probably die. However much *weight* we give to the pregnant woman's interests, however much we thereby *value* her, we still need to reconcile her claims with those of the fetus.

Now, in the above discussion we have been "going behind", so to speak, the right to self-determination to explore the issue of serious (here religious) reasons for the exercise of this right. We now need to resurface in order to acknowledge the significance of the other right that is seriously implicated with reference to the caesarean section—the right to bodily integrity. At this juncture, then, let us recall that in our scenario, it is not just religious belief *per se* that is implicated, but a special conjunction of religious belief and the body, in the sense that, as noted toward the end of chapter one, where treatment is refused for religious reasons, those reasons touch on the body; moreover, that the "other" in question—the fetus—is

[28] M Midgley, *Heart and Mind: The Varieties of Moral Experience* (London: Methuen, 1981) 96.
[29] *Re T (Adult: Refusal of Treatment)* [1992] 4 All ER 649, mentioned early in ch. 3. For a recent debate on the autonomy of Jehovah's Witnesses and the relationship between the individual and his/her religious organisation, see the three articles by O Muramoto entitled "Bioethics of the Refusal of Blood by Jehovah's Witnesses" in vols 24 and 25 of *JME*. The first is at (1998) 24 *JME* 223. By contrast, for a ringing defence of Jehovah's Witness practices and their relationship to individual conscience see D Ridley, "Jehovah's Witnesses' Refusal of Blood: Obedience to Scripture and Religious Conscience", (1999) 25 *JME* 469.

inside that body. In this regard, it may be instructive to consider the way in which we might approach the analogous, but by no means identical, situation of a *parent and a born child*. In fact, it is unlikely that we would grant a parent the (legal) right to refuse life-sustaining medical treatment for a minor child on the basis of the same kind of religious belief.[30] As one court put the matter as long ago as 1962, "this right [of a parent to practise her religion] ends where somebody else's right begins".[31] In such a case "somebody else's right"—that of the minor child—begins upon birth when it is deemed a moral (and legal) person.

Yet there are obvious and important differences between such a case and that of a pregnant woman. In the former case, whilst a right of parental autonomy is at stake, no personal right of self-determination is, because the medical treatment in question would be on a physically separate other, the born child. Moreover, since the religious belief pertains to the born child and his/her body, no interest in and right to bodily integrity is implicated for the parent. By contrast, in the latter case of the pregnant woman, both the interests in, and rights to, self-determination (rather than the determination of a born child through the exercise of parental autonomy) and bodily integrity are clearly implicated. Ultimately, the point is that in overriding a parent's religious objections to her born child's medical treatment, although we may be insulting the parent *qua* parent and even as an individual, we do not touch the parent's (the objecting party's) *body*. This is not so with the pregnant woman: in her case, because the fetus is inside her, we act both against her as an individual *and* upon her body. In the final analysis, then, it is the fact that the fetus is inside the pregnant woman that morally distinguishes the two cases: this means that the woman's self-determination and bodily integrity are both in issue, making her interests and rights very much stronger than those of the parent with religious objections to the medical treatment of a born child.[32] Conversely, the physical separation of the born child and the parent in turn enables us to separate their interests, both conceptually and morally, in turn weakening those of the parent in comparison with those of the born child. Indeed, the harm to the born child would truly be harm to "another", in Mill's sense, whilst the sense in which harm to the fetus (or future child) is harm to "another" is qualified by the fetus's/future child's location within the body of the pregnant woman. (That the born child is deemed a legal person, but the fetus is not, is a related aspect of these differences, as indicated at the end of the last paragraph.) The implication, then, is that our duty

---

[30] See the brief discussion of this point in ch. 3. In adverting to the law at this juncture, naturally I do not mean to imply that the state of the law necessarily provides an indication of the moral situation in this scenario. Still, the basic point is that I take it as "given" that morally speaking a parent should not be able (for religious reasons) to refuse life-sustaining treatment for an otherwise healthy incompetent child. For enunciation of the relevant English principles see e.g. the judgment of Waite LJ in *Re T (a minor) (wardship: medical treatment)* [1996] 35 BMLR 63.

[31] *In re Clark* (1962) 185 NE 2d 128, 132.

[32] For an example of a philosopher arguing that the strength of rights depends upon the importance of the interests at stake, see JJ Thomson, *The Realm of Rights* (Cambridge: Cambridge University Press, 1990), for whom the distinctiveness of rights does not lie in any notion of their absoluteness, but rather in their responsiveness to the value concerns of the individual.

not to intervene in the case of the pregnant woman with religious objections to certain medical treatment ultimately hinges upon the strength of her interest in and right to bodily integrity. This is so notwithstanding that in this case the *reasons* for her treatment refusal (and so her *justification* (toward the fetus) for exercising her right) apparently relate to her interest in and right to self-determination, albeit in a way which implicates her body, in the sense that her religious reasons concern the body.

In effect, the significance of the woman's body and her interest in bodily integrity is that it brings into view *our relationship to the pregnant woman* through the question of our duty not to invade her body against her will. (The moral problems of nonconsensual bodily invasions are addressed specifically in chapter seven.) In terms of *her relationship to the fetus*, however, and the *justification* of harm to it through the refusal of the caesarean-section, in the scenario discussed here it is the woman's interest in self-determination—expressed through a sincerely held religious faith which partly consists in beliefs about the body—which means, as we have said, that she cannot be said to have the moral duty to submit to the treatment in question, or, put another way, that she justifiably asserts the right to refuse the surgery. (This is the case both with respect to the fetus and to the future child, in the light of the degree to which also the latter must impinge upon the mother's body to be delivered by caesarean section, as discussed in chapter one.)

While the exercise of the woman's right might thus be justified this is not to deny that, from her perspective, there may also be what John Gray, writing on Isaiah Berlin, has called an "irreparable loss of value".[33] As Gray notes, Berlin is critical of arguments for rational autonomy, partly on the basis that for any one person "valued goods and projects may not be reconcilable in a harmonious individuality".[34] Hence, although one woman's refusal may be clearly governed by the belief that medical intervention is not required (for instance a Born-Again Christian), for another her religious faith may, in effect, compel her to renounce or risk renouncing fetal life (a Jehovah's Witness refusing a transfusion). No principle of practical reason can solve this dilemma for her since, as noted above, to a strong degree a religious faith constitutes a system unto itself. Indeed, it is quite possible that a woman will later come to regret her decision, although this will more likely occur where the refusal has been for non-religious reasons and is accordingly touched on in the second half of the chapter.

It is time to leave the argument from rights and turn to that from duty. I suggested earlier that the problem I am discussing lies in the interface between the subjective domain, which certain rights protect, and the objective quality that is inherent in the notion of duty. Moreover, as we recalled above, where medical treatment is refused for religious reasons, those reasons themselves touch upon the body. Thus, in turning to the argument from duty, I shall focus on the idea of a duty being owed via the body, in the course of which the important distinction

---

[33] John Gray, *Berlin* (London: Fontana, 1995) 33.
[34] *Ibid.* This is part of Berlin's argument for value-pluralism, which I cannot explore here.

between duties of general conduct and duties which seriously invoke the body will be particularly in point. Hence, if the above discussion has concentrated on the issue of a woman's interest in self-determination, through the example of the religious reason for refusing medical treatment, the next section concentrates on her interest in bodily integrity. At the end of the next section, I shall draw together the conclusions from the forthcoming argument with those from the argument from rights examined in this first section of the chapter.

III. THE ARGUMENT FROM DUTY

In exploring the maternal–fetal relationship in terms of the idea of a woman's duties, I pay particular attention to a seminal article which amounts to the exploration of the idea of a duty being owed via the body. I approach the argument from duty in this way because ultimately, as I have noted at various points, perhaps the most significant fact distinguishing the maternal–fetal relationship from any nearest analogy, such as between a parent and a born child, is that a "fetus" or "future child" is a being inside the body of another, specifically its mother. This is a fact utterly unique in human relationships, notwithstanding that this specific relationship is fundamental to human life. It means that the duties of pregnancy (at least in the medical treatment context) are ultimately duties attaching to the *body* of the pregnant woman, moreover, that these duties invoke a woman's interest and right to bodily integrity.

I shall not try to justify the idea that a woman has such an interest and right, partly in the light of the introduction to the ideas of interest, choice and rights in the first part of chapter one, partly because such a right is widely accepted in moral theory (and also in law),[35] but really because in any event the truly important and difficult questions arise when we wish to determine the *extent* of this right or, put another way, the degree of duty which may attach to the body. Thus, as Feinberg expresses this point: "There is . . . a 'clear intuition' in support of a basic right 'to decide what happens in and to one's body', . . . though the limits of that right are lost in the fog of controversy."[36] Recall here that in chapter one I did not find a property analysis of bodily integrity helpful or necessary but suggested instead that we have a moral interest in bodily integrity based on the centrality of the body to our sense of self.

The argument I am about to consider explores the question of whether a woman has a duty not to abort by analogy with an example from the realm of conduct (acts and omissions). As we shall see, given the argument's analogical structure, little attention is paid to the reality of pregnancy. Nevertheless, consideration of the argument throws some important light upon the idea of a bodily duty toward the fetus.

---

[35] For an argument seeking to establish an individual's personal body rights, see ch. 3 of SR Munzer, *A Theory of Property* (Cambridge: Cambridge Univesity Press, 1990).

[36] J Feinberg, "Abortion", (1979) in his *Freedom and Fulfillment* (Princeton, NJ: Princeton University Press, 1992) 37–75, 66.

A. The Argument from Bodily Integrity

"[H]aving a right to life does not guarantee having either a right to be given the use of or a right to be allowed continued use of another person's body—even if one needs it for life itself."[37]

1. The Argument

Scholars and judges inclined to favour the fetus over the mother in the maternal–fetal conflict within the medical treatment context often refer to the fetus as though it were an abstract entity, without a physical location inside the body of a woman, whose important interests in self-determination and bodily integrity it thereby affects and may be affected by.[38] Similarly, prior to the 1970s there was a tendency on both sides of the abortion debate to consider that the essential question was whether it was wrong to destroy a fetus, without consideration of the necessarily implicated interests of the pregnant woman.

In 1971 Judith Jarvis Thomson shifted the debate's focus from the moral status of the fetus to the moral rights of a pregnant woman. She challenged the view that although a woman may have a right to bodily autonomy, the fetus is a person with a right to life which is more fundamental and hence overrides the woman's right. She criticises this argument, not by questioning whether the fetus is a person with a right to life, which she accepts for the purposes of her argument, but by focusing on the *nature of the right to life*. Thus, she asks us to consider the following intriguing scenario:[39]

"You wake up in the morning and find yourself back to back in bed with an unconscious violinist. A famous unconscious violinist. He has been found to have a fatal kidney ailment, and the Society of Music Lovers has canvassed all the available medical records and found that you alone have the right blood type to help. They have therefore kidnapped you, and last night the violinist's circulatory system was plugged into yours, so that your kidneys can be used to extract poison from his blood as well as your own."

The hospital director apologetically acknowledges that it was wrong of the society to kidnap you, but points out that he cannot now unplug you as this would kill the violinist, but, not to worry, it's only for nine months. Yet it could be for nine years. Regardless of whether it would be nice or kind of you to stay plugged in, Thomson

---

[37] JJ Thomson, "A Defence of Abortion", (1971) 1 *Phil & Pub Aff* 1, reprinted in P Singer (ed.), *Applied Ethics* (Oxford: Oxford University Press 1986) 37–56, at 46.

[38] This tendency has been observed by J Gallagher, who notes that such opinions tend to depict it as an "*independent entity, abstracted from the reality of the woman's body*, much as though commentators had encountered it upon the street." J Gallagher, "Fetus as Patient", in N Taub and S Cohen (eds.), *Reproductive Laws for the 1990s* (Clifton, NJ: Humana Press, 1989) 185–235, 187, my emphasis. For a personal account of this phenomenon, in which the author recounts the observation that she, the pregnant woman, was not "in the picture" which was the sonogram of her developing fetus, see A Cherry, "Maternal–Fetal Conflicts, The Social Construction of Maternal Deviance, and Some Thoughts about Love and Justice", (1999) 8 *Tex J Women & L* 245, 247–8.

[39] JJ Thomson, "A Defence of Abortion", 38–9.

asks, *are you morally required to do so?* She suggests we would regard this situation as "outrageous".[40] And yet, the director might argue, the violinist, as a person, has a right to life and this is stronger than your right to bodily autonomy. (Notice that the violinist is "plugged into" the person; whereas the fetus is of course *inside* the pregnant woman. This may account for Thomson's term "bodily autonomy" rather than "bodily integrity", in that it would seem that a highly significant impact of having the violinist plugged into one would be the restriction of one's movement. Thus, in recounting Thomson's argument I use the term "bodily autonomy"; but as the discussion of her argument develops I adopt the term "bodily integrity". This seems appropriate since both Thomson and I are really concerned with a being—the fetus—which is inside the body of the pregnant woman. This is not to deny that the more advanced the pregnancy, the greater the restriction of movement.)

Thomson's response is to argue that the right to life does not entitle the violinist to whatever he needs to remain alive, particularly to the use of your body, unless you have granted him that right; nor does it give him a right against third parties that they should give him the use of your kidneys.[41] The "right to life does not guarantee having either a right to be given the use of or a right to be allowed continued use of another person's body—even if one needs it for life itself".[42] So, even though you will kill the violinist, you do not violate his right to life when you reach round and unplug yourself: to do this you would have to kill him "unjustly", but since he had no right to your body, his right to life is not violated when you unplug yourself. Although the violinist has thus invaded your bodily boundaries, Thomson's scenario also implicitly requires that we imagine what it is like to be "taken over" in this way and how we would then perceive ourselves, in a way not inconsistent with Jean Cohen's, Catriona MacKenzie's and my thoughts on the importance of bodily integrity/autonomy expressed in chapter one.

a) *Moral Requirements*

Thomson's analysis of moral requirements focuses upon rights, which she sees as the principal component within justice, a conception which is itself open to challenge.[43] Central to her argument is the idea that to possess the right to use another's body one must have been granted it by that other. (Indeed, on her view, to possess any right one must have been granted it by another, a view which surely cannot apply to the right to bodily integrity and autonomy.) The surprise, perhaps, is to discover that even the fetus's right to life must depend on such grant. In the abortion context, this raises the question how a pregnant woman might be said to have given such a right to the fetus. The answer will lie in whether the mother

---

[40] *Ibid.*, 39.
[41] *Ibid.*, 45.
[42] *Ibid.*, 46.
[43] For a different view of justice see D Millar, *Social Justice* (Oxford: Clarendon Press, 1976) who argues that the criteria of justice are the distinct and irreducible ideas of rights, needs and desert.

voluntarily became pregnant.[44] Now, as Thomson recognises, whether a pregnancy is voluntary is by no means a clear-cut thing: the spectrum from the involuntary (with rape at one end) to the voluntary (deliberate planned pregnancy) is obviously complex.[45] Nevertheless, she admits that where pregnancy *is* the result of a voluntary act undertaken in full knowledge of the possible consequences then, having been partly responsible for bringing this dependent fetus into existence, a woman has "a special kind of responsibility for it, a responsibility that gives it rights against her which are not possessed by any independent person—such as an ailing violinist who is a stranger to her."[46] In such a case (assuming for the sake of argument that the fetus is a person) abortion would be unjust killing, that is, would violate the fetus's right to life. Here the woman's "special responsibility" (arising from her voluntary conduct) implies or is tantamount to a duty owed by her to the fetus through which the fetus gains rights to her body. In other words, where there is a special responsibility for the fetus there is a duty and, following from this, a correlative right.

b) *Moral Decency*

Yet this is not necessarily to suggest that where there is no special responsibility/duty and correlative right, people should not assist others. Indeed, Thomson argues there may well be circumstances in which you "ought" to assist someone: for instance if the violinist only needed your kidneys for an hour; or if a fetus—even one that is the product of rape—only needed the use of your body for a similar period. But the difference lies in the sense of "ought" here employed. The idea here is that you *ought* to let your body be used; not in the sense that you are *required* to do so, but rather in the sense that it would be morally *decent* of you. The difference between the cases of "special responsibility" and those of moral decency is that in the latter neither the violinist nor the fetus gains rights from the fact that you "ought" to help them. It might be "self-centred, callous, indecent in fact, *but not unjust*",[47] if you decline to assist: Thomson insists that although moral indecency might be just as serious as injustice, the two charges are different, as one invokes the issue of rights and the other does not. On Thomson's view, then, morality is primarily about respecting rights, a position which is controversial and which I shall later question.

   In explicating these ideas, Thomson goes so far as to allow her imaginary critic to derive a right from the "morally decent" ought, but insists it is crucial we acknowledge there are occasions when you are not morally required to assist the violinist, just as there are occasions when the woman is not morally required to

---

[44] JJ Thomson, "A Defence of Abortion", 48.

[45] Between these extremes, Joel Feinberg discusses the varying degrees of responsibility (or lack of it) that may attach in different scenarios ranging from contraceptive failure which is entirely the fault of the manufacturer to pregnancy resulting from indifference at the time of intercourse. J Feinberg, "Abortion", 68–9.

[46] JJ Thomson, "A Defence of Abortion", 48.

[47] *Ibid.*, 51, my emphasis.

carry the fetus to term. On these occasions neither the violinist nor the fetus acquires rights against you or the woman. She writes:[48]

> "Except in such cases as the unborn person has a right to demand it—and we were leaving open the possibility that there may be such cases—nobody is morally *required* to make large sacrifices, of health, of all other interests and concerns, of all other duties and commitments, for nine years, or even for nine months, in order to keep another person alive."

In fact, all this amounts to is a restatement of her position that we can derive a right from an ought when the ought implied a morally required duty, as is the case in the special responsibility scenario discussed earlier: that is, where a woman is voluntarily pregnant and so has a duty to a dependent fetus which thereby acquires rights to her body. In the ensuing discussion, however, the contrast between the two moral domains is sharpened and it becomes clearer that the domain of the morally *decent*, while important, is in Thomson's view the domain of the morally optional. Further, we do now have more information about the requirements of the "special responsibility" case in which rights are implicated, as it appears that a woman who has taken on this "special responsibility" has an obligation to make large sacrifices (assuming that the fetus is a person).

As her article develops,[49] her analysis of the abortion issue hinges upon the distinctions between the "Good" or "Splendid" and the "Minimally Decent" Samaritan. In essence, Thomson holds that you are not required to be (as good as) a Good Samaritan unless you have assumed special responsibility for someone (become voluntarily pregnant, say). Yet this does not mean that where you have *not* assumed that responsibility (where, say, you did all you could to avoid becoming pregnant) it is necessarily morally appropriate to seek an abortion: "[t]here may well be cases in which carrying the child to term requires only Minimally Decent Samaritanism of the mother, and this is a standard we must not fall below."[50] In other words, in the imaginary case in which continued pregnancy only calls for a relatively small level of sacrifice, then you "ought" not to abort in the sense that it would be morally indecent of you to do so. In such a case the fetus has no rights against you and hence, on Thomson's argument, you could do as you wish with it: after all, you are not required to be morally decent. All the same, notwithstanding your "technical freedom" to do so, it would be decent of you not to abort.

2. Commentary

a) *Thomson's View of Morality*

In explicitly excluding the idea of moral decency from the realm of justice, Thomson may well be invoking the concept of other virtues, such as charity. Importantly, however, although she claims that a charge of a lack of moral decency

---

[48] *Ibid.*, emphasis in original.

[49] S. 6, 51*ff.* My discussion concentrates upon those sections of her article most relevant to my concerns, but note that she also considers, for instance, self-defence arguments about abortion at length.

[50] *Ibid.*, 55.

may be no less grave than one of "injustice", her entire argument—which is intended to show that no *rights* are violated when a woman (who is involuntarily pregnant) aborts—in fact marginalises the notion of imperfect duties which are, by definition, not instrumental to the protection of rights. She thus assumes such duties to be optional, in a manner which incorrectly suggests that imperfect obligations are supererogatory.

If Thomson argues (and her article is not clear on this point) that the general right to life, rather the than fetus's (assumed) right, entails only negative duties, this does seem excessively libertarian. Indeed, few would now endorse the *laissez-faire* libertarian idea that the duties correlating to rights are only negative in character.[51] In this light, she could well have allowed a correlating positive duty to the right to life but limited this to one to provide "manageable" levels of assistance, rather than "large" sacrifices. Yet at heart this is a methodological point about Thomson's way of limiting what we can fairly ask of pregnant women. That is, if she had instead emphasised the point that pregnancy *always* or generally entails large burdens and risks, then she could alternatively have argued that the fetus's right to life does not entail the right to be carried for nine months inside the body of a woman, which, in effect, would be to say that the fetus does not have a right to life. It was, of course, because Thomson wished to *accept* the claim that the fetus has a right to life but challenge what this *entails,* that her argument evolved as it did.

Thus, although one might criticise Thomson for so sharply dividing the moral territory into the zone of rights/moral requirements on the one hand and general intrinsic duties/moral decency on the other, and then apparently marginalising the latter to the point of optionality, she does this because she is addressing a rights argument: namely, that the fetus has a right to life. As a result, the significance of moral decency, which she claims to be just as important as the domain of justice (as she has defined the latter), is reduced: as moral requirements are translated in terms of correlative rights and duties, and as Thomson's object is to limit moral requirements, so moral decency can only be optional, notwithstanding her evident desire that we should take moral indecency as seriously as injustice. As others have noted, rights arguments have a tendency to diminish the significance of other virtues.[52] In this sense Thomson's explanation of a pregnant woman's duties in terms of the distinction between the Good and the Minimally Decent Samaritan can be seen as a pertinent illustration of the way in which rights-based arguments, as Onora O'Neill observes, make "callous and kindly actions to others in need . . . equally permiss-

---

[51] An obvious exception would be R Nozick. See e.g. his *Anarchy, State and Utopia* (Oxford: Blackwell, 1974).

[52] See e.g. O O'Neill, "The Great Maxims of Justice and Charity", in her *Constructions of Reason: Exploring Kant's Practical Philosophy* (Cambridge: Cambridge University Press, 1989) 219–33. As noted in ch. 1, she argues that both utilitarian and liberal thought have emphasised justice at the expense of charity and other virtues and have thus severed the link between the ideas of obligation and virtue. Whilst obligations were fundamental in Locke's thought, they tend now to be seen merely as the "perfect" obligations which are the correlation of rights. Further, since there are no rights to charity, so charity has all but vanished off our ethical map. (At 225.)

ible, provided that justice is not breached".[53] (As we saw in chapter one, in a similar vein consideration of the personhood argument as to fetal moral status indicates that rights arguments tend to obscure other important moral duties and concepts.) Thus, Thomson leaves us with a narrow, rights-based morality in which the contrast between self and other is at its sharpest, softened only by her acknowledgment of the realm of the "morally decent". Such a morality is of course disputed in different ways by legal philosophers such as John Finnis[54] and Joseph Raz.[55]

3. *Limiting the Obligations Pregnancy Imposes*

Reminded of the importance of imperfect duties, let us leave to one side the rights argument which prompted Thomson's approach and focus instead on this other domain of moral thinking. Although the fetus may well not be a person (in that it lacks those characteristics of moral persons, namely consciousness, rationality and agency, the ability to communicate and self-consciousness), in any event pregnancy imposes duties which are unrelated to personhood and hence rights. As noted, I favour a gradualist account of fetal status which makes its lack of personhood/rights irrelevant to its appropriate moral treatment. But are the (imperfect) duties of pregnancy "absolute" or can they be limited? Showing that we can lay down certain limits is, after all, the ultimate point of Thomson's article. Thomson does this by means of the notion of "voluntariness", which she ties into the rights argument. Yet if the imperfect obligation is not a matter of choice, these obligations—those that are not correlated to rights—are potentially boundless. In this light, can we limit the obligations entailed in a voluntary pregnancy, recognising that these are typically large, without relying on ultimately question-begging arguments about what the fetus's personhood/rights (or rather lack thereof) would entail?

To see what Thomson's argument offers to an understanding of the maternal–fetal conflict within the treatment context, I shall draw out some of the crucial distinctions which are by no means explicit in her text, thereby appreciating the strengths and weaknesses of her argument. Thomson's argument is built upon two rather thorny philosophical distinctions, namely that between positive and negative duties and between special and ordinary ones.

a) *Duties of the Body and Duties of Conduct*

My overarching distinction between duties which seriously invoke the body and duties of day-to-day conduct will now emerge. As noted, this is a distinction which Thomson does not herself make, perhaps to her cost. Indeed, unlike the issue of the moral duties of the Good Samaritan, the question of whether there is a duty to

---

[53] *Ibid.*, as noted originally in ch. 1. For a reminder that considerations of justice only constitute part of morality, see also B Barry, "And Who is my Neighbour?", Review of C Fried, *Right and Wrong* (Cambridge, MA: Harvard University Press, 1977) (1979) 88 *Yale LJ* 629, 642.

[54] See subsequent discussion *infra*.

[55] See e.g. his "Right-based Moralities", (1982) in J Waldron (ed.), *Theories of Rights* (Oxford: Oxford University Press, 1984) 182–200, and discussion in the first part of this chapter.

carry a fetus to term or, for my purposes, to submit to a caesarean section on its behalf, is complicated—though not necessarily answered—by the fact that such a duty rubs up against the moral interest in and right to bodily integrity (and self-determination). This is not true of the Good Samaritan, who acted in the course of general conduct: on my view (which, as explored earlier in the chapter, appears consistent with aspects of Joseph Raz's thought) the latter domain does not invoke these moral interests but only a very general sense of autonomy which thus does not merit the protection of any particular right.[56]

As we have seen, however, it is just possible to conceive of treatment beneficial to the fetus which does not implicate these interests. For this reason, in due course it will be revealing to compare the idea of a maternal duty to submit to a caesarean section (which clearly does implicate these interests) with that of a duty to take the pill that is highly beneficial for the unborn child's welfare but does not have adverse effects for the pregnant woman.[57] It is also instructive to reflect in passing upon the idea of a pregnant woman's duties not to harm the unborn child she carries *outside* the treatment context.

i) Positive and Negative Duties: Bringing out Ideas about *Reasonableness*
We have seen that Thomson regards the right to life *only* as a right not to be killed directly (or at least "unjustly"). Although it seems excessively libertarian to consider that the right to life invokes only negative obligations, her use of the distinction between positive and negative duties may be designed to bring out the following highly important point. At some level, she is drawing attention to the important differences in the way the right to life tends to operate in the differing cases of a fetus and a born person. Regardless of whether or not the right to life entails a right to positive assistance from others, not killing (or not physically harming) one's fellow citizens is *most usually* about not killing them in the sense of the negative duty not to harm. That is, only rarely does the right to life (for those of us who are not doctors, firemen, etc., who may thereby have a special duty to assist to an extensive degree)[58] entail the *saving* of a life. Whilst every day we fulfil the obligation not to kill in the first sense, most of us will never be called upon to save another human being's life in any truly immediate sense, as the Good Samaritan apparently was. That is, whilst we might frequently be called upon to make a financial donation to a charity supporting a famine-stricken people and indeed can save lives in this way, or to give to homeless people begging on the street, generally speaking we may rarely, if ever, come across dying people in the street to whom we can render immediate one-to-one life-sustaining aid.

With regard to the fetus, the situation is different. It is one thing to say, as we shall see that John Finnis would, that abortion is killing, but one must also accept that not aborting is not merely not killing in the same way that I refrain from killing

[56] Note my rejection of Hart's Choice theory of rights, at least in this context, in ch. 1, s. I(C).

[57] On some occasions of course, if it had adverse effects upon the woman, it may also do so upon the fetus.

[58] Here of course I ignore contingencies of the current English *legal* position in *Capital & Counties plc* v. *Hampshire* [1997] 2 All ER 865.

the passers-by on the street. Rather, not aborting (and hence not killing) means continuing to absorb and respond to the demands of the growing fetus and its impact upon one's health, both psychological and physical. In other words, at some level killing a fetus is *also* a matter of not continuing to do something.[59] More particularly, as the discussion in the next section will highlight, it is a matter of not continuing to render bodily aid, as well as emotional assistance. Thus, in some sense that may not be sufficiently clear in her text, Thomson has very appropriately drawn attention to the way in which carrying a fetus to term can, to some extent, be seen as an instance of a positive duty to assist.

I say "to some extent" because I think there are limits to this argument regarding abortion. Thus, once a woman has decided to take an unplanned pregnancy to term (or has deliberately conceived) and has let the fetus keep on growing, thereby taking on a commitment towards her fetus, we might say that aborting thereafter (except to protect her life or health) is morally different such that, even if such an abortion can still at some level be described as "not assisting" the fetus, it might more appropriately be construed as harming it and thus breaching a negative duty in relation to it.[60] (Importantly, however, it might be noted that for some women abortion is never an option due to religious, financial, emotional or some other constraints, such as lack of awareness of their legal rights.[61]) However, this intuition would require further defence which is beyond my current scope. In any event, regarding the issue of a caesarean section, this is much more easily describable (in comparison with not having a late abortion where there is no sudden risk to life or health from continued pregnancy) as being asked further to assist the fetus.

But why is it so important to emphasise this distinction between positive and negative duties and the way in which the breach thereof may harm others? I argue in this section that we can judge the reasonableness of the negative duty more easily than we can that of the positive duty. In other words, we can say more easily where there is a negative duty than where there is a positive duty. As touched on

---

[59] JC Callahan and JW Knight also recognise this point, observing "[t]he duty to avoid harming others is generally discharged by simply refraining from running them over with cars, avoiding dropping things on them, and so on." By contrast, if pregnant women are not to harm their fetuses, then they must "nurture" them. "Women, Fetuses, Medicine and the Law", in HB Holmes and L Purdy (eds.), *Feminist Perspectives in Medical Ethics* (Indianapolis, IN: Indiana University Press, 1992) 224–39, 232. However, the authors do not further draw out the differences between these negative and positive duties, although they do note that both parents and pregnant women have special positive duties toward children/fetuses. On women's special responsibilities for the fetus, see the last section of this chapter.

[60] The sense in which abortion may arguably breach a negative duty is one which might profitably be discussed in the context of an examination of the relevance of the law of abortion to questions of maternal treatment refusal, on which see esp. ch. 5.

[61] As noted by A Ouellette, "New Medical Technology: A Chance to Reexamine Court-Ordered Medical Procedures during Pregnancy" (1994) 57 *Alb L Rev* 927, 950–1, who cites religious and financial constraints. K Knopoff, "Can a Pregnant Woman Morally Refuse Fetal Surgery?", (1991) 79 *Calif L Rev* 499, also cites "fear of invasive medical procedures . . . inadequate knowledge of their options and legal rights, or . . . shame, familial or societal pressure . . . or lack of access to abortion clinics". (At 509). For further discussion of this point and other relevant examples, see F Baylis, "Case Comment And Note: Dissenting With The Dissent: *Winnipeg Child And Family Services (Northwest Area) v. G (DF)*", (1998) 36 *Alberta L Rev* 785, 787–9.

earlier in this chapter, this may be because not breaching a negative duty not to physically harm others, for instance driving a car in a careful rather than a careless way, is unlikely to have any very personal significance for the driver. By contrast, with regard to the issue of a positive duty, questions about the person who may be called upon to fulfil this duty may well be relevant to the existence and extent of the duty.[62] Consider the following example.

A man cycling along a path by a river knocks into a small child, thereby pushing the latter into the water. This man has clearly broken a negative duty which he owed to this child not to cause physical harm to it. Now let us contemplate the rescue of this child by another man.

This second man is passing by and sees the child knocked into the river. Since he can swim, surely he should jump in and save the child. Indeed, in such a case there would not appear to be any physical risks to him involved in the rescue. So let us factor these in by adding that the river is flowing fast, and over rocks. Should he still jump in? His swimming skills, which will affect the degree of risk to which he thereby subjects himself, may be relevant. Let us assume he can swim well and is fit and strong. Surely he should jump in and attempt the rescue. Suppose instead that he has only had a few swimming lessons or cannot swim at all; moreover, he is just recovering from a bad flu which has left him distinctly weak. Now the physical risks to himself are clearly greater than in the first example in which the river was not flowing fast, or in the second, in which he could swim well and was very strong, and so on.

The degree of risk to the rescuer thus varies depending not just upon the circumstances of the rescue (the slow/fast river, etc.), but also upon his ability. Through these examples, we can see that the risks to the rescuer are slowly increasing, to the point where, regarding the last case, there may be disagreement about whether the man should jump in at all. In effect, here there may be disagreement about whether he has a (positive) duty to rescue the child, perhaps reflecting the understanding that "ought implies can". (This is not to deny that there may be various intermediate cases regarding which, even if the person probably could rescue the child, there will be disagreement about whether the duty lies.) To some extent, if we say that in this final case the man should not jump in, we may have in mind that in any event his rescue attempt is unlikely to be successful, apart from the point that he may catch pneumonia, or whatever, in the process. But this is to make an observation about the outcome, not the duty which may or may nor lie.

[62] Most importantly, my argument does not hinge on a distinction between negative and positive duties *per se*, for an example of which in this context see K Knopoff, "Can a Pregnant Woman Morally Refuse Fetal Surgery?" 518, footnotes omitted: "If we consider a pregnant woman's refusal of treatment to be harming another person—namely, the fetus—her right to autonomously refuse could justifiably be curtailed. If, on the other hand, the woman's refusal is not considered harm but simply failing to aid, curtailing her autonomy becomes of questionable legitimacy." Note further that Knopoff assumes the fetus would have to be a person to justify restrictions on maternal autonomy. She also argues that since "natural causes" are responsible for fetal medical needs then a woman is not responsible for the harm, whatever the cost to her, including taking vitamin supplements, just as a potential swimmer rescuer is never responsible for the harm when someone drowns (at 522). As the following discussion makes clear, I disagree with this position.

This example shows that factors about the *person* and his or her *abilities/capacities* may be relevant to the determination of the positive, but not the negative, duty. With regard to the reckless cyclist, for instance, if we later learn that he was speeding to the hospital to give blood to his own child, this may be relevant to his degree of culpability for the harm to the child he knocked into the river,[63] but does not of itself mean that he had no negative duty not to harm the child by the river, nor that he did not breach such a duty. It may be objected that where the rescue could only be effected at great cost, in some sense the rescuer's personal circumstances "excuse" him if he declines, rather than that he has no positive duty; but the point is stronger than this because these facts about him actually affect the existence or degree of his positive duty.[64] In turn these observations may be bound up with the view, propounded for instance by Philippa Foot, that positive duties are less stringent than negative ones.[65] The suggestion is that the negative duties under discussion are ultimately more fundamental than the positive ones. Note further that the duties discussed here pertain to the domain of general conduct and so do not invoke the individual's moral interests in self-determination and bodily integrity.

In fact Thomson herself illustrates her Samaritan argument with an example which, when compared with the bodily "plugged-in" violinist scenario, is very much from the domain of general conduct (although she does not explicitly make this distinction herself). She is considering whether the right to life entails the right to be given the bare minimum:[66]

> "But suppose that what in fact *is* the bare minimum a man needs for continued life is something he has no right at all to be given? If I am sick unto death, and the only thing that will save my life is the touch of Henry Fonda's cool hand on my fevered brow, then all the same, I have no [such] right".

---

[63] For instance, legally we may take facts about a person into account in determining whether they should be guilty of murder or manslaughter holding, for example, that in effect their responsibility was diminished.

[64] My approach might be described as "appealing to costs" by a consequentialist. See e.g. M Menlowe's discussion "The Philosophical Foundations of a Duty to Rescue", in M Menlowe and A McCall Smith (eds.), *The Duty to Rescue: the Jurisprudence of Aid* (Aldershot: Dartmouth, 1993) 5–54. Menlowe is primarily concerned with the appraisal of various consequentialist arguments. Within his argument my position would appear aligned with that of the "moderate", who is concerned that "an appeal to costs must be allowed because a moral system that does not allow such an appeal (a system without options) fails to reflect important facts about the nature of persons"; and particularly with the "positive argument [that] attempts to demonstrate that an adequate morality must recognise subjective reasons as a source of value". (At 43.) Menlowe endorses the consequentialist approach of S Kagan, *The Limits of Morality* (Oxford: Clarendon Press, 1989) who argues that any moderate position is inherently unstable because it will collapse into extremist accounts. Whilst I cannot address this further here, I note Menlowe's observation that "[c]onsequentialism requires at least that the option of favouring one's own interests is very limited" (at 40) and direct the reader forward to my next section, where the kind of duty with which I am truly concerned—the duty to aid another by submitting to surgery for that other's benefit—comes to the fore: this is a very specific kind of aid entailing very personal interests on the part of the rescuer.

[65] P Foot, "The Problem of Abortion and the Doctrine of Double Effect", in B Steinbock (ed.), *Killing and Letting Die*, (Englewood Cliffs, NJ: Prentice-Hall, 1980) 156. Reprinted from the (1967) 5 *Oxford Review*, 156.

[66] JJ Thomson, "A Defence of Abortion", 45, emphasis in original.

She compares the situation in which Fonda would have to fly in from the West coast on the one hand with that in which he would merely have to cross the room to touch my brow on the other, and says:[67]

> "Is it to be said . . . that I have a right to it when it is easy for him to provide it, though no right when it's hard? It's rather a shocking idea that anyone's rights should fade away and disappear as it gets harder and harder to accord them."

Since my concern is not with the rather narrow issue of rights but with moral requirements beyond their call, I shall ignore the rights focus of this passage and instead focus upon what Henry Fonda would have to do to save my life here. After all, as Brian Barry has suggested, rather than being forced into conclusions about rights, "why can't we simply say that the further Fonda would have to come the less badly we would think of him if he doesn't?".[68] Barry suggests we could condemn him for not crossing the room just because it would be so easy for him; in other words, that our praise or blame of Fonda—or any rescuer—will vary according to how easy it was to help, which supports my argument with regard to the swimming rescuer above. Thus, the ease of the assistance will depend upon the situation (as in Fonda's case) or the ability (as in my swimming rescue case) of the person. If Henry Fonda is sitting in an armchair across the room, then he most surely breaches a positive duty to come to my aid if he does not cross the room and cool my brow. By contrast, if he has to fly from the United States to London to do so, then I suggest no such positive duty is breached in his case.

Unaware of these problems as regards a pregnant woman's duty to submit to medical treatment, one leading scholar has simply suggested that the question is whether she is being "reasonable". John Robertson weighs the risks of surgery to a woman against the benefits to the fetus, writing "a clear medical need that *reasonable* persons would not refuse would have to be established."[69] Importantly, in Robertson's work the concept of reasonableness is strongly linked to the idea of conduct. Indeed, his emphasis on reasonableness is highly reminiscent of the legal tort of negligence—concerned with the idea of a duty of care—which largely goes to issues of conduct, by act or omission.[70] He argues that a pregnant woman has duties to prevent harm to the future child when she may "reasonably" do so, con-

---

[67] JJ Thomson, "A Defence of Abortion", 51.

[68] B Barry, "And Who is my Neighbour?", 653.

[69] J Robertson and JD Schulman, "Pregnancy and Prenatal Harm to Offspring: The Case of Mothers with PKU", (1987) 17 (Aug) *Hastings CR* 23, 28. See also K Kinlaw, "Commentary: Maternal Rights, Fetal Harms", (1991) 21 (May/June) *Hastings CR*, 22. On the risks of a caesarean section, she writes: "These . . . are apparently medically 'reasonable' . . . as cesarean sections are regularly recommended by the medical team and accepted by expectant parents in order to promote the health and safety of the woman and fetus." (At 23.)

[70] See also J Parness, "Duty to Prevent Handicaps: Laws Promoting the Prevention of Handicaps to Newborns", (1983) 5 *West Eng L Rev* 431, in which one of the opening questions is "what constitutes *unreasonable conduct* or perhaps reasonable but unwarranted *conduct* toward the unborn?" (At 432, my emphasis.) See further ch. 6.

comitant with those of a parent to a born child, suggesting that "the timing of the *conduct*" does not affect the nature of the duty.[71]

Robertson's reasoning misses two important points. First, the difficulty of determining reasonableness with regard to a positive duty to assist is not appreciated. As the next section shows, these difficulties are accentuated when that positive duty literally means helping another through one's body, a supremely personal domain (protected by at least *prima facie* rights). Second, Robertson's argument obscures the fact that it is not *time*, so much as *place*, that is in issue (at least regarding the medical treatment context), in the sense, unlike the born child, that the fetus or the future child is within the woman's body.

Importantly, however, Robertson's ideas about reasonableness may well have validity in two ways. First, they may be relevant *outside* the medical treatment context, where we are considering a woman's general conduct and the way this may harm, particularly, the future child. For instance, given the certainty that extensive maternal smoking or alcohol abuse will harm the future child, it seems highly arguable that a pregnant woman has moral duties not to smoke or consume more than minimal alcohol (subject to arguments about addiction noted in chapter six). Similar arguments might be made about participation in certain sports such as bungee-jumping, or about mundanely ordinary conduct, such as failing to take care in crossing a street or driving a car. By harming the fetus or future child in these ways a woman would arguably be breaching negative duties not to harm it, regarding which the most important issue may well be the appropriateness or otherwise of legal compulsion.[72] (She may also have a positive duty to follow a certain diet.)

Second, Robertson's ideas may have validity in the case of the pill beneficial to fetal welfare. The spectrum elaborated in the swimming rescue case indicates that not all positive duties meaningfully invoke questions about the person and, in particular, their moral interests in self-determination and bodily integrity. Thus, vastly unlike major surgery, taking a pill impinges upon the body in the most minimal sense imaginable. In this sense, referring back to my criticisms of Robertson, "place" is not in issue. Indeed, swallowing a pill is very much akin to an instance of conduct. Moreover, given our assumption that the pill has no possible adverse effects on the woman, it will be very hard (though not necessarily impossible) to think of a reason, let alone a serious one, why a pregnant woman should refuse to take it. Importantly, this means that she indeed has the moral duty to take the pill for the benefit of the fetus or future child.[73] Put another way, since swallowing the

---

[71] J Robertson and JD Schulman, "Pregnancy and Prenatal Harm", 24, my emphasis. For a physician's view, see J Phelan, "The Maternal Abdominal Wall: A Fortresss Against Fetal Health Care?" (1991) 65 *S Cal L Rev* 461, who suggests that at a legal hearing "factors can be introduced to determine the reasonableness of a proposed bodily intrusion before medical treatment is mandated over the objections of the pregnant woman". (At 487, footnote omitted.)

[72] See further chs. 6 and 7.

[73] For this reason, it begs the question somewhat to comment, as one scholar has, that "[e]ven if the fetus can be treated with vitamins, the woman has to swallow them before they can help". K Knopoff, "Can a Pregnant Woman Morally Refuse Fetal Surgery?", 525. Elsewhere Knopoff notes that a woman might have a severe allergic reaction to a vitamin (at 526) but this is a separate point in

pill does not appear seriously to invoke her interests either in self-determination or bodily integrity, then arguably she would unjustifiably assert a right to refuse it.

ii) Special and Ordinary Duties: Bringing out the Further Idea of a Duty *Through the Body*

I now move from a positive duty of conduct with attendant physical risks to the idea of a duty that can only be realised through the body. The generally extensive nature of the burdens in pregnancy are here taken as given, such that there will be few/no pregnancies in which carrying the fetus only calls for a woman to be "minimally decent" toward the fetus. Indeed, Thomson's imaginary pregnancy in which carrying the fetus to term only requires minimal burdens belies the reality that, as Donald Regan writes, "[i]t is very large burdens or nothing".[74] Moreover, he notes, "[t]he fact that many women willingly undertake the burdens of pregnancy, for reasons of their own, is no reason to discount the burdens as they affect women to whom they are unwelcome".[75] In any event, the caesarean section with which I am here principally concerned makes serious invasive demands. That natural birth is itself physically burdensome is not in point when a woman has no serious objections, religious or otherwise, to natural delivery.

For Thomson, we have seen that where a woman is morally required not to abort—where she has accepted responsibility for a pregnancy—she has a special duty to carry the fetus to term (make a large sacrifice) and thereby act in a manner which we would normally associate (it is considered) with the conduct of a Good or Splendid Samaritan. John Finnis is strongly critical of this view, alleging that the duty not to abort is not "special", but is instead "a straightforward incident of an ordinary duty everyone owes to his neighbour".[76] He argues that she has failed to understand the relationship between special and ordinary duties for the following reasons: she thinks the entire problem is to do with rights and that these depend on grant or assumption; she considers that special responsibilities also depend on assumption or grant and hence that the entire problem has to do with special responsibilities.[77] Let us take these criticisms in turn.

First, as observed before, although Thomson insists that moral indecency may be as serious as injustice, the entire purpose of her use of this distinction is to focus on what she sees as the narrow core of moral requirements which involve rights. Finnis is therefore correct to consider that she thinks the whole problem is to do with

her argument. Overall, however, Knopoff concludes that "any special relationship that the pregnant woman may have with the fetus requires only that she act with reasonable care under the circumstances, or at most undertake minimally burdensome measures of aid." Thus it would seem she may admit a duty to take the vitamin pill or such like.

[74] D Regan, "Rewriting *Roe* v. *Wade*", (1979) 77 *Mich L Rev* 1569, 1591. He cites these burdens over some two and a half pages of text, concluding (at 1582), that he "suspect[s] it is an unusually lucky woman who does not put up with enough pain, discomfort and disruption of appearance and emotional state to add up to a major burden".

[75] *Ibid.*, 1635.

[76] J Finnis, "The Rights and Wrongs of Abortion: A Reply to Judith Thomson", (1973) 2 *Phil & Pub Aff* 117–45. Reprinted in R Dworkin (ed.), *The Philosophy of Law* (Oxford: Oxford University Press, 1977) 129–52, 134.

[77] *Ibid.*

rights. Further, on her argument, it appears that special responsibilities—such as that of continuing a pregnancy—also depend on grant or assumption, as the duty not to abort arises where one has assumed responsibility for the fetus, that is, become voluntarily pregnant. Finnis is thus right that Thomson is ultimately concerned with what is morally required, such that rights are effectively no more than a "technical device" used by her to delineate the domain and extent of moral requirements. Thomson thus "needs" a distinction which is of less concern to Finnis because, on his view, what is morally required of us is rather more considerable.

Indeed, there is considerable disagreement between Thomson and Finnis as to whether the Good Samaritan was doing more than the "minimally decent thing" (Thomson); or whether he was only doing his "ordinary neighbourly duty" (Finnis). Fortunately, I need not settle this difference. Rather, it is more to my point to question the extent to which a woman carrying a fetus to term can in fact be likened (to employ Thomson's terms) to the actions of the Good Samaritan; or, (to use Finnis's terms) to question whether it is a matter of a woman's "ordinary neighbourly" duty that she carry the fetus to term or, by implication, submit to whatever medical treatment is needed by the fetus (or future child).[78]

It should already be apparent that I think we have an "ordinary duty" to assist others which may involve physical risks, notwithstanding my discussion of the difficulties of determining the existence or extent of this duty in complex cases. Similarly, I presume that Finnis would consider that his "ordinary duty" will on occasion entail some degree of physical risk, such as rescuing a drowning child. Yet in such cases, while there may be physical *risks* to the rescuer, the rescue in itself will be effected by (possibly strenuous) swimming—an activity: thus, the rescuer is called upon to engage in an activity which he has likely partaken of before, albeit under pressure when performed as part of a rescue. This is a duty of *conduct*, if you like, which may carry some degree of physical risk.

There is something different, I suggest, about a duty which necessarily *inheres in* the body. It is very rare that one may have the opportunity to assist another in a way which makes serious and invasive demands of one's body—in effect, to *use* one's body to help or save another—such that it is quite hard to think of a suitable example, other than the cases of pregnancy and organ or tissue donation. Indeed, this accounts for the utterly unreal nature of Thomson's original example of the ailing violinist who is "plugged in" to another person in order to survive. In the case of the donation of an organ, such as a kidney, the donor will run certain physical risks. But more than this, I emphasise here the sense in which the *aid* to the other truly occurs through the body—it is my kidney that someone needs. The incursion into the body, a very personal domain, which *necessarily* brings a certain degree of

---

[78] In general, as I now move away from the abortion issue to that of "maternal–fetal conflict", unless fetal death *in utero* is specifically in issue, the following discussion concerns either the fetus or the future child; but for simplicity I shall henceforth generally refer to the "fetus". Occasionally, I use the term "unborn child" to cover both.

pain and discomfort, is important in itself, independently of the fact that, as a secondary issue, physical risks may attend this process.

There are several important aspects to this bodily rescue which distinguish it from the swimming case. Assuming at least that one has swum before, one can relatively easily imagine jumping into the river to save the child, even if one has never rescued whilst swimming; moreover, unless things "go wrong", one will not encounter physical problems (rather than the demands of the swimming *per se*). By contrast, since the opportunity for a truly "bodily rescue" is so rare, to the extent that few (except pregnant women) will ever be called upon to assist another in this way, it is very likely that a potential "bodily rescuer" will find it quite hard to imagine what this type of rescue will be like. Here the necessary pain and physical incursion into the body come to the fore. While some people may have few concerns about the donation of a kidney, I do not think we immediately assume that anyone who *is* concerned about this prospect is necessarily callous and thereby shirking his or her moral duty. A potential "bodily rescuer" may or may not have experienced severe pain, with or without surgery: if he has, he knows that pain can be a completely overwhelming experience in which all else loses significance, so that in some sense the body dominates the mind; if he has not, then its prospect is simply an unknown quantity. In essence, the point in this section is that there is something more complex in the determination of the duty in the case of the "bodily rescuer" than in the case of the "swimmer rescuer". There may be a specially psychological or emotional dimension because the means of rescue is so intimately part of the self. This difference means that there is some quality of empathy or understanding called for in our contemplation of someone being faced with a request, say, to donate a kidney, which would make us slow to condemn a person who was very apprehensive about such a procedure. I do not mean so much that we "forgive" them given their difficulties, but rather that we have no *basis* on which to condemn or criticise them.[79] (Since thinking about the matter in this way, I have found a number of resonances within the literature on ethics. For instance, some feminist work emphasises the complexities of listening and hearing, particularly across diversity, as an activity in which people might fail for numerous reasons.[80] Further, Marilyn Friedman has suggested that emotional sensitivity to others' feelings and attitudes is essential if we are to have "deep concern for their moral situations".[81] Friedman also

---

[79] Regarding these ideas of empathy or understanding, one physician has observed of the "maternal–fetal conflict" cases that "these cases are testimony to a concern for the well-being of the fetus". W Meeker, MD, Letter to the Editor, (1987) 317 *New Eng J Med,* 1224. Meeker criticises G Annas's view that the cases "betray a profound suspicion of pregnant women and a failure to identify with them" in his "Protecting the Liberty of Pregnant Patients", (1987) 316 *New Eng J Med* 1213 at 1213. Annas's response (at 1224–5) is to note that Meeker's view depends on compassion for the fetus, but that he fails to extend this to the woman involved.

[80] See A Jaggar, "Feminism in Ethics: Moral Justification" in M Fricker and J Hornsby (eds.), *The Cambridge Companion to Feminism in Philosophy* (Cambridge: Cambridge University Press, 2000) 225–44, 238 for a discussion of relevant work. These points may also relate to Christine Korsgaard's argument regarding our conception of the ends of others, noted *supra* these notes.

[81] M Friedman, "Feminism in Ethics: Conceptions of Autonomy", in M Fricker and J Hornsby (eds.), *The Cambridge Companion to Feminism in Philosophy,* 205–24, 213.

suggests that one understands oneself and one's situation partly by appreciating the significance of one's emotional reactions, a point of relevance here to the pregnant woman.) Importantly, with regard to the donor herself, the point is not that the prospect, say, of donating an organ will necessarily make someone lose all capacity for rational reflection, but rather, given the intensely personal and physical nature of such rescues, that it will be very understandable (in one sense, one might even say rational) that someone may have intense doubts and fears about such a prospect.[82]

Perhaps something of this complexity is captured in a story reported early in 1997 in which the sister of a woman dying of leukaemia initially refused to donate bone marrow. The sister whose bone marrow was needed had a "terror of hospitals". When it emerged that she was reconsidering her decision not to donate (in which she was influenced by the realisation that the procedure would not have to be performed in a hospital), the dying sister said she bore her sister no ill-will. She continued: "I hope she loves me enough to do it, but everyone has a phobia and *no one can tell how that person is feeling.*"(A true phobia could raise competence issues.[83]) Importantly, the dying sister did not condemn the other's reluctance to

---

[82] I do not mean here to endorse, as for instance *per* Descartes, sharp distinctions between "mind" and "body", aligned in turn with "reason" and "non-reason" and, ultimately, ideas relating to "male" and "female", (for a critique of which see G Lloyd, *The Man of Reason: Male and Female in Western Philosophy* (London: Methuen, 1984). Rather, in suggesting that there are complex psychological elements pertaining to the determination of a very bodily duty, it might instead be argued that "good" or "true" reasoning must in this case attend to these considerations, which in turn here become "part of" reason. However, it is beyond my scope to develop this point. For further thought on this theme, see e.g. S Callahan, *In Good Conscience: Reason and Emotion in Moral Decision Making* (New York, NY: Harper Collins, 1991), who argues that a significant problem of the moral life is not, as is often thought, that our reason is tainted by our emotions, but rather that we are deficient in emotional responses. See also M Nussbaum, "An Aristotelian Conception of Rationality", in her *Love's Knowledge: Essays on Philosophy and Literature* (New York, NY: 1990) 54–105, discussing the place and validity of the emotions in Aristotle's conception of practical reason. It is important to note, however, that it is very hard to say anything about these ideas without immediately begging questions about our definition of the terms "reason" and "emotion". Indeed, as M Nussbaum has expressed the point in connection with the thought that emotion may have a valid role to play in moral reasoning, the traditional distinction between reason and emotion should not be taken "on trust". M Nussbaum, "Feminists and Philosophy", A Review of LM Anthony and C Witt, *A Mind of One's Own: Feminist Essays on Reason and Objectivity* (Boulder, CO: Westview Press, 1993), *NYRB*, 20 Oct. 1994, 59, 63.

[83] *The Guardian*, 19 Apr. 1997, 7, my emphasis. Importantly, the word "phobia" is not used here in the precise sense which usually means a paralysing fear. Rather, I think the phrase connotes a recognition of deep fears and uncertainty. Thus, I do not mean to imply that where someone has a phobia, this is the end of the matter. In this regard, note should be taken of the decisions in *Re MB* [1997] 8 Med LR 217 and *Re L* [1997] 1 FCR 609 (discussed in ch. 3) in which the women in question wished to have caesarean surgery, but had needle phobias which prevented them consenting to the anaesthesia. These cases of truly paralysing phobias are different, I think, from those in which there are deep fears and doubts. I argue in ch. 3 that the judgment that it would be lawful to operate on these (incompetent) women notwithstanding their lack of consent was, exceptionally, justifiable in their best interests in the light of the fact that neither objected to the surgery itself. See also JS Mill, "On Liberty", (1859) in M Warnock (ed.), *Utilitarianism*, (Fontana: London, 1962), 206–7, reasoning that the individual "is the person most interested in his own well-being: the interest which any other person . . . can have in it, is trifling compared with that which he himself has . . . with respect to his *own feelings and circumstances*, the most ordinary man or woman has means of *knowledge immeasurably surpassing* those that can be possessed by any one else." (My emphasis.) The point is of interest notwithstanding that Mill's concern here is not with determining duties toward others. W Kymlicka has questioned the truth both of Mill's position and of the Marxist perfectionist position that the good of each person consists in a

donate, as she had some awareness that she could not really appreciate what the other felt in her contemplation of the procedure. Morally speaking, this "gap" or "haze" complicates our determination of the duty in these very personal situations.

These reflections are brought home by the US case of *Re AC*.[84] Ms C was dying of cancer and, on medical estimates, had at most two days to live. Her fetus was near viability. In these circumstances, the hospital sought an order for a caesarean delivery to which—in a state of great distress and slipping in and out of consciousness—she first consented and then refused. Apart from the legal questions which arose in the case (discussed in Parts II and III), could we even say that a woman in this position clearly has the moral duty to submit to the caesarean? Whilst one woman may be content to submit to the surgery in these circumstances, if another thinks differently and reluctantly chooses to die in as comfortable and peaceful a manner as possible, I do not think we can fairly say she is breaching a duty to give the unborn child the best chance of survival. Notice that in this example we have begun to flesh out the particulars of a given case, so that details about the circumstances of the person potentially owing the duty have come to light.

Regarding a woman's possible feelings in preferring not to submit to a caesarean birth, note might be taken of the increasing recognition of Post Traumatic Stress Disorder following a bad birth experience, including natural delivery. Interestingly, the research into this phenomenon has highlighted that the degree of distress suffered by women is:[85]

> "less related to any specific procedure (such as forceps delivery) than to factors such as lack of consent for interventions, inadequate information, feeling ignored or powerless, hostility on the part of staff, and the degree of physical pain suffered."

This indicates the range of issues surrounding birth and attendant medical procedures which may affect a pregnant woman. Thus, it is apparent that not just a caesarean but also a "natural" birth can be a traumatic experience. The reasons for this may in part be related to the way a given mode of delivery is "handled" by medical staff since issues such as information and consent are clearly crucial to a woman's birth experience, a point which has been confirmed by other research.[86] (Related to this is the question of what women (and their partners) have been

---

capacity she shares with everyone else, suggesting that "[o]ur good is neither universal nor unique". W Kymlicka,*Contemporary Political Philosophy: An Introduction* (Oxford: Oxford University Press, 1990) 203. Nevertheless, as regards the very personal domain of the body I suggest that Mill's position captures something important. In any event, Kymlicka himself suggests that "[e]ven if I am not always right, I may be more likely to be right than anyone else". *Ibid*.

[84] 533 A 2d 611 (DC App 1987); 573 A 2d 1235 (DC App 1990).

[85] This research, published in the *British Journal of Psychiatry*, was conducted by Dr Janet Menage, a GP and counsellor. It is estimated that up to 1.5% of women who felt they had had a bad birth experience suffered symptoms consistent with PTSD. According to Dr Fiona Blake, a consultant psychiatrist at the John Radcliffe Infirmary in Oxford, the syndrome is under-recognised. She stresses that many women who do not suffer the full-blown syndrome would still benefit from a "debriefing" following a traumatic labour. *The Guardian*, 15 Oct. 1996, 11.

[86] H Churchill, *Caesarean Birth: Experience, Practice and History* (Hale: Books for Midwives Press, 1997) 56–61.

"schooled" to expect during their antenatal classes and in this regard several commentators have suggested that the possibility of the need for caesarean delivery is not made clear enough to pregnant women, with the result that they have particularly negative perceptions of caesarean birth.[87] This is not to deny that physically a caesarean birth has consequences which a natural birth does not, but the evidence on the psychological effects of a caesarean are inconclusive. I return to these points in chapter four.) Note that the refusal of a caesarean is most unlikely to be related to physical risk alone, notwithstanding the greater risks of death from a caesarean section, coupled with the possibility of damage to other organs.[88] So it is both unnecessary and misleading to defend a woman's right to refuse such surgery with particular reference to the increased risks it imposes, as scholars supporting this right have typically done.[89] Indeed, there is only one known case in which a woman has refused a caesarean *because of* its physical risks, which in her case were accentuated by her morbid obesity.[90] By contrast, the swimmer who declines to jump into the river to save the drowning child is much more likely to be doing so purely on the basis of a risk calculation, albeit a hasty or even subconscious one.

Ultimately, then, an important component in determining the duty of the pregnant woman is the process of seeking to understand her difficulties (where these exist). At some level, this means that somewhere in the complex determination of her duty lies the question of our relationship—and duty—to her. These observations are relevant to a recent English decision, in which a Bangladeshi woman who, like her fetus, was also at risk of death without a caesarean and who had previously

[87] *Ibid.*, 90, 103, citing literature on point.

[88] The *Baby Boy Doe* decision cited above described the risk of death from caesarean birth as 1 in 10,000, compared with 1 in 20,000 to 50,000 in normal birth. 632 NE 2d at 328. The court noted the "other complicating factors such as damage to other organs". *Ibid.*, 329. A woman is twelve times as likely to become ill when she delivers by caesarean rather than natural birth: National Institute of Health, US Dep't of Health and Human Services, Pub. No. 82–2067, *Cesarean Childbirth: Report of a Consensus Development Conference* (1981) 268. Note further that because of the risk of uterine rupture at the site of a caesarean scar, women who have had caesareans are generally committed to future caesareans. *Colautti* v. *Franklin* 58 L Ed 2d 596 (1979) 399 (a US Supreme Court abortion decision discussed in ch. 5) in which this was accepted in relation to the future pregnancies of women who have had a hysterotomy (a type of caesarean)). For a recent English assessment of the risks see e.g. H Churchill, *Caesarean Birth: Experience, Practice and History*, 93–7 regarding the risks of a caesarean itself (rather than the anaesthesia). In 9 to 15% of caesareans, according to some studies, women suffer serious morbidity, the principal causes being endometriosis, urinary tract infections and wound infections. It is also more likely that a woman who has had a caesarean will have problems in future pregnancies, labours and deliveries. Further, despite the decreasing risk of death from caesarean surgery, it is still between 2 and 11 times greater than for vaginal delivery. Churchill also notes that caesareans may also have adverse psychological effects on women, including depression and guilt and "could possibly have long term effects on the mother–child relationship" (at 89, citing literature on point). (But see further below.) Of course, in different ways I suggest these psychological consequences might also be the result of not having a caesarean where this results in fetal harm or death. Further, as noted above, Post Traumatic Stress Disorder can accompany *any* bad birth experience, including natural delivery. Churchill also notes, however, that evidence about the negative effects of caesareans is inconclusive, noting that some studies have suggested that levels of depression amongst women who had surgery were not significantly different from those who delivered vaginally. (At 91.)

[89] See e.g. N Rhoden, "The Judge in the Delivery Room".

[90] An unreported decision. J Robertson, "Procreative Liberty and the Control of Conception, Pregnancy, and Childbirth", (1983) 69 *Va L Rev* 405, n. 165. The woman weighed more than 157.7kg.

experienced a caesarean birth said she "would rather die" than have another. This very strong feeling was surely more significant than the particular issues of "back pain" and "pain around the scar" which she raised.[91] By contrast, we are not called upon to seek to *understand* the person, such as the cyclist who knocks the child into the river, who breaches a negative duty not to harm.[92] (It is, of course, possible to think of instances of rescue by conduct which might risk harm to the rescuer in ways which would require us carefully to reflect on his concerns—for instance, the case of rescuing a bleeding AIDS victim. The case in which a rescuer fears catching a serious disease may be something of a hybrid between rescues by conduct and rescues by means of the body, albeit perhaps still closer to the former.[93])

In the light of the above, I now return to consider whether Finnis is right to categorise pregnancy—in which the fetus "invades" (in a sense) and burdens the woman's body in an increasingly apparent way—within the domain of "ordinary duty". Rather obviously perhaps, one could argue that the essence of any ordinary duty is that it should only require *non-extraordinary* sacrifices and risks. Finnis's view that the demands of pregnancy are only those of the "ordinary neighbourly duty" may stem from the fact that pregnancy is very much an "ordinary" state of affairs which carries "ordinary", in the sense of "inherent" or "usual", sacrifices and risks for pregnant women. Crucially, however, this is not to say that those sacrifices and risks might not be *extraordinary* by comparison with what must, by definition, be the more regular demands that incidences of Finnis's ordinary neighbourly duty impose. The assistance to the fetus involves increasingly extensive physical invasion, burdens, risks, pain and emotional involvement over a remarkably long period of time, culminating in what is generally considered an immensely painful experience—childbirth—which also carries a 1 in 20,000 to 50,000 risk of death.[94] As noted, the pain and risks of a caesarean section are deemed even greater.[95] Thus, it is misleading to characterise the duties of pregnancy as "ordinary", notwithstanding the ordinary place of pregnancy in biological life.

By asserting that the duty not to abort or, (presumably and more importantly for my purposes) the duty to submit to a caesarean section where required by the unborn child, is an ordinary neighbourly duty, Finnis has effectively "moved the goalposts". He implies that very physical sacrifices and burdens can be part of that ordinary duty, a position I have questioned.[96] In effect, Finnis gives no guidance

---

[91] *Rochdale (NHS) Trust* v. *C* [1997] 1 FCR 274, discussed further in chs. 3 and 4.

[92] Note two other points. First, the question of the legitimacy of the State *imposing* increased risks or burdens by compelling treatment is a separate (moral and legal) point, distinct from the question of the woman's moral *justification* toward the fetus for the exercise of her right (absence of duty). Second, in one of the classic scenarios in which caesarean delivery is needed, both the woman and the fetus may be at risk without this (as in *Rochdale*).

[93] I am grateful to Jonathan Glover for pointing out this case.

[94] As observed in the notes *supra*, this was a finding of fact in the *Baby Boy Doe* decision, 632 NE 2d at 328.

[95] *Ibid*.

[96] Feinberg argues that although we all have general duties to assist strangers in danger, these do not require that we make "enormous sacrifices" or "run *unreasonably* high risks". J Feinberg, "Abortion", 66, my emphasis.

on the topic which most concerns Thomson, namely how much can *fairly* be required of someone, and of a pregnant woman in particular. At the same time, however, he cannot legitimately make use of the idea of an "ordinary neighbourly duty" without giving some moral content to the idea of a "special duty". Yet, so far as the current discussion is concerned, he leaves us in the dark as to what a special duty would entail or how it might arise. It may be that Finnis ducks these issues because, while he questions and puzzles over the nature of *both* the rights to life and bodily autonomy, ultimately he accepts that the fetus has a right to life, but doubts a woman's interest in and possible right to bodily autonomy.

I have argued that Finnis fails to distinguish duties of ordinary conduct from duties seriously involving the body. More significantly, by analogising the abortion issue to the range of Samaritan problems, the above discussion has revealed that Thomson herself may fail to give due significance to the body in general and the physical demands of pregnancy in particular. The story of the Good Samaritan is a story about the *conduct*, not the *body*, of the Good Samaritan.[97] (Of course, the story of the plugged-in violinist is very much about the body, but it is the story of the Good Samaritan that does Thomson's moral work.) In this way she may have provided an opening for Finnis's argument that the duty not to abort is an ordinary neighbourly duty.

Yet the situation of the pregnant woman is markedly different from that of the Good Samaritan, who was simply in the course of a journey when he stopped to help the injured man. Although his assistance was considerable and in this sense he "went out of his way", it was a one-off involvement in which no important personal beliefs about himself were implicated (rather than beliefs about the good of helping others); nor were demands made upon his *body* in any serious way: the story is about the domain of general conduct. For this reason we do not face the problem of a reconciliation of his actions with the very personal domain that tends to be protected by rights (to self-determination and, in particular, bodily integrity). In this way, although he was fulfilling a positive duty to assist, it was a positive duty at the other end of the spectrum from that which would impinge upon these rights. Of course, none of this is meant to deny the goodness of the Samaritan; rather it is to point out that his story is much simpler than that of the pregnant woman, a point undermined by Thomson's otherwise powerful analogy.[98] I further develop these points in the next and final section, arguing that in determining the extent of a

---

[97] Likewise Heather Draper, writing on the caesarean issue, does not see any obstacle to the application of Good Samaritan reasoning in this context. H Draper, "Women, Forced Caesareans and Antenatal Responsibilities", (1996) 22 *JME* 327, 328.

[98] Like Thomson, Donald Regan is concerned with the issue of abortion. He writes: "If we bear in mind that no other potential samaritan is required to bear burdens as physically invasive as the burdens of pregnancy and childbirth, and if we bear in mind also that no other potential samaritan . . . is subjected to burdens remotely comparable in magnitude to the burdens imposed on the pregnant woman, we conclude that laws forbidding abortion are at odds with the general spirit of samaritan law". D Regan, "Rewriting *Roe* v. *Wade*", 1610, footnote omitted. Although these points are directed to the law, I suggest they apply equally at the level of moral theory, that is, concerning our determination of the moral duties of the pregnant woman to the fetus.

pregnant woman's duties, attention must also be paid to the context of pregnancy and hence of the duties in question.

To introduce this last argument, notwithstanding the above discussion, it may well be objected that the (voluntarily) pregnant woman's duties to the fetus are more stringent, for instance, than those the man walking by the river owes to the drowning child, because she is *specially related* to the fetus (having either deliberately conceived or declined to abort). Indeed, this ties in with Thomson's intuition that to be obliged to make large sacrifices a woman must be voluntarily pregnant. So, despite my arguments distinguishing the stringency of these duties (such as that ideas relating to reasonableness and the body may account for variations in stringency), it may well be harder to defend the idea that positive duties are less strict in the case of a special relationship, such as would appear to exist in the case of a woman's planned pregnancy. Thus, building upon and confirming some important aspects of the above discussion, I turn to the last significant point to be brought out about the duties of pregnancy.

b) *The Social Context of Pregnancy*

In effect, the context of that special relationship may make a difference to the degree of obligation thereby imposed. I turn first to Feinberg's argument that social organisation may in some circumstances mean that positive duties are less strict than negative ones. Feinberg argues that the right to life does entail a right to positive assistance; but where, as in the case of pregnancy, the right's fulfilment requires large sacrifices then, presumably in the interests of reason and fairness, responsibility must have been assumed by the woman.[99] This conclusion relates generally to his views of the distinction between positive and negative duties. While, like Finnis,[100] he criticises the view that negative duties are more stringent than positive ones, he argues that positive duties are less stringent where social organisation would make the imposition of strict positive duties on everyone chaotic.[101] For instance, where certain individuals, such as firemen, have accepted special duties to assist others and thereby run exceptionally high (what passers by would regard as unreasonably high) risks for others, then the (positive) duties of passers-by are reduced.[102] He argues that voluntarily pregnant women are in a situation analogous to that of firemen. Although a little bizarre, this comparison is worth developing.

---

[99] J Feinberg, "Abortion", 68.

[100] J Finnis, "The Rights and Wrongs of Abortion", 150–1, 142–3.

[101] Similarly, HLA Hart has written about what he dubs "role-responsibility": "A sea captain is responsible for the safety of his ship . . . a sentry for alerting the guard at the enemy's approach . . . These examples of a person's responsibilities suggest the generalization that, whenever a person occupies a distinctive place or office in a social organization, to which specific duties are attached to provide for the welfare of others . . . he is properly said to be responsible for the performance of these duties, or for doing what is necessary to fulfil them." HLA Hart, *Punishment and Responsibility* (Oxford: Oxford University Press, 1976) 242. The implication is that people with such "role-responsibilities" have a strict positive obligation to fulfil them.

[102] J Feinberg, "The Moral and Legal Responsibility of the Bad Samaritan", (1984) in his *Freedom and Fulfillment* (Princeton, NJ: Princeton University Press, 1992) 175–96, 195–6.

Let us first note society's interests in each case. Put simply, if people are to be rescued from fires effectively (or to the best of society's ability), then society must appoint firemen. Further, if society wants to continue to exist, then some people— women in fact—have to bear children. Whilst it is true that society does not have an interest in *all* women reproducing, nevertheless the importance of deciding what the burdens upon any one woman can fairly be said to be lies partly in the implications for women more generally, including those contemplating pregnancy and those who are not planning or are unable to bear children. Thus, the issue ultimately has a political component, raising questions of justice.[103] With this aspect in mind, what can we say about the respective burdens upon the fireman and the pregnant woman?

From the fireman's point of view (rather than that of society) he can choose other ways of helping people that involve as much, lesser or different kinds of risk, although his job will then need to be filled by someone else. If the original fireman chooses to fight fires, however, he clearly knows he is obliged to take large risks to perform his job—thereby fulfilling his strict positive duty—while passers-by have a less strict obligation to help. The choice to have a child is different in that it is not so much the choice to help another being (though it will entail this) as to create one. Although a woman can choose whether or not to have a child, she cannot choose another way of having a child other than by going through a nine-month period of gestation ending in childbirth. (There is of course the possibility of surrogate motherhood, but this is largely irrelevant for our purposes since in such a case another woman simply takes on the risks and sacrifices.) Still, notwithstanding these differences, if a woman chooses to bear a child, is she under as strict an obligation to help (such as to accept whatever medical treatment is required by the fetus) as the fireman, as Feinberg's argument would seem to imply?

In fact the argument about social organisation and strict positive duties, as exemplified by the case of the fireman, works differently if we apply it to the case of the pregnant woman. Society can choose whether to have a fire-service or to leave the job to those on hand to help, say, to a reasonable degree. There is at least a chance of success if the job is left to passers-by which is simply non-existent in the case of reproduction. Thus, although some women can choose to have children and others not, just as some people can choose to be fireman and others not, there remains the point that, in the case of fires, unqualified third parties can at least *try* to assist in a way that is impossible when it comes to reproduction: carrying a child for nine months only directly involves one woman for each child (usually) in the course of a process which is both dramatically essential to the continuation of society and an almost mundanely ordinary part of our social and biological lives. What then are the implications for the stringency of (voluntarily) pregnant women's positive duties toward the fetus? Does their peculiarly essential role heighten the degree of

---

[103] Donald Regan's argument regarding abortion appears in line with mine at this point: "[T]he fact that some women must bear children if the nation is to continue is no reason to impose the burdens of pregnancy on women who are unwilling, so long as there is an adequate supply of volunteers." "Rewriting *Roe* v. *Wade*", 1635.

duty to which they are subject? After all, since they are the only people able to help fetuses directly, there is no question of chaos or confusion arising about who should be doing the rescuing which might arise (as Feinberg's argument implies) were we not to appoint firemen.

Here I note again the paradox that despite the ordinary and essential place of pregnancy in society, it may well invoke physical burdens and risks for the pregnant woman which are extraordinary by comparison with the bounds of what people are normally expected to do for one another, including those closely or specially related. For instance, we may think it desirable if a parent (the only compatible donor, say) agrees to donate a kidney to his ailing child, but I do not think we assume it necessary or unquestionably reasonable in the way that some may think it necessary or reasonable that the pregnant woman submits to the caesarean section as "a matter of course", if you like.[104] This seems connected with the fact that the possibility of a parent being called upon to donate a kidney is very much the exception, rather than the norm. The underlying point here, as we have already seen, is that serious bodily assistance is rather extraordinary outside the context of pregnancy.[105] Importantly, this is not to deny that we might well wish to argue that a parent has such a duty to his or her born child. But in reality such an argument would encounter at least some of the difficulties that we have met in seeking to determine the extent of a pregnant woman's rights and duties. Moreover, there is an underlying imbalance here: whereas we would probably have to mount an argument to establish parental bodily duties, conversely we must mount an argument to question assumptions regarding certain maternal prenatal duties.

In short, it is neither fair nor just that a person (a woman) be considered to assume obligations which override her rights to self-determination and, especially, bodily integrity. If it is harder to see this in the case of pregnancy, this is simply because fetal needs impinge upon a woman's body as a matter of course. Hence, rather than insisting that voluntarily pregnant women owe a duty to the fetus entailing large sacrifices (and that women should not become pregnant unless they are prepared to make such sacrifices), biological facts at the heart of our social life may here lessen, rather than intensify, the positive duties to promote fetal welfare imposed upon pregnant women in this regard, so that these are indeed (as previous sections argued) less stringent than the negative ones. The implications are that a

---

[104] One author has suggested "that the exception to the common law rule of non-subordination operates in the context of a woman's relationship to her fetus reflects a lack of regard for her bodily integrity and a *pervasive belief in the propriety of woman's maternal, self-sacrificing behaviour*". Note, "Rethinking (M)otherhood: Feminist Theory and State Regulation of Pregnancy" (1990) 103 *Harv L Rev* 1325, 1336, my emphasis. On the law relating to a duty to rescue see ch. 7. For a discussion of the idea of "maternal deviance" in this context, see A Cherry, "Maternal–Fetal Conflicts", 255 *ff*.

[105] That it is unlikely that a parent's refusal to donate a kidney to a born child would be called unreasonable seems implicitly supported by a passage in the latest English caesarean decision, *St George's Healthcare NHS Trust v. S, R v. Collins and others, ex parte S* [1998] 3 All ER 673. There is speculation in the judgment as to the possibility that one day medical advances could mean that a parent could save the life of his/her child by undergoing a very *minor* procedure, the refusal of which could (morally) be described as *unreasonable*. However, the court carefully distinguished moral duty from legal compulsion. (At 692.)

woman who either declines to abort or embarks upon a planned pregnancy does not thereby undertake to submit to *any* medical intervention deemed necessary for the fetus.[106] Indeed, in reality it is impossible to predict what special needs any given fetus will have during the course of its gestation. Thus, a woman has no opportunity to choose in advance—in order to avoid the question of certain fetal needs arising—without aborting: this is the only safe way to rule out the possibility of the fetus needing certain sorts of treatment, or a certain kind of delivery. Yet this, in effect, is to say that unless a woman is prepared to do anything for the fetus, notwithstanding, for instance, her religious faith, then she must either abort or decline to conceive. This would ignore the place of pregnancy within our (indeed any) society. Given the acute personal importance to the woman (and partner) of reproduction, we cannot say that either a pregnant woman must accept any treatment required by the fetus, in particular the highly invasive and potentially religiously problematic caesarean section, or not reproduce. The possible objection that such a woman should adopt, rather than reproduce, is highly unsympathetic to the reality of a woman's (or couple's) emotional involvement in reproduction. (Similar difficulties might attach to the suggestion that a woman should instead use a surrogate.)

This recognition of the social context of pregnancy (echoes of which can be found in relevant law)[107] is noticeably absent from Thomson's approach and there are two principal reasons for this. First, her argument is at heart a response to a rights argument. Second, her argument works, and powerfully so, by analogy. Her use of the Good Samaritan argument skilfully brings into play a series of distinctions (albeit ones which have required considerable teasing out) on the one hand between positive and negative duties, and on the other between special and ordinary ones. Yet, just as the story of the Good Samaritan is a story about conduct, rather than the body, which means perhaps that Thomson does not give due

---

[106] I thus disagree with E-H Kluge, "When Cesarean Section Operations Imposed by Court are Justified", (1988) 14 *JME* 206, who suggests that the fact that a woman has the opportunity to abort earlier in her pregnancy justifies the compelled caesarean section (at 209–10). As my discussion should show, this is too simple an answer to the problem.

[107] This "social context" of pregnancy finds recognition in US cases on abortion and maternal liability for prenatal injury. Regarding abortion, see e.g. *Planned Parenthood of Southeastern Pennsylvania* v. *Casey*, 120 L Ed 2d 674 (1992) *per* the joint opinion: "The mother who carries a child to full term is subject to constraints, to pain that only she must bear. That these sacrifices have from the beginning of the human race been endured by the woman with a pride that ennobles her in the eyes of others and gives to the infant a bond of love cannot alone be grounds for the State to insist that she makes that sacrifice. Her suffering is too intimate . . . for the State to insist . . . upon its own vision of the woman's role, however dominant that vision has been in the course of our history and . . . culture. [Her] . . . destiny . . . must be shaped to a large extent on her own conception of her spiritual imperatives and her place in society." (At 698–9.) This reasoning is further developed in Blackmun J's opinion. On the question of maternal liability for prenatal injury, see *Stallman* v. *Younquist*, 531 NE 2d 355 (Ill 1988), in which Cunningham J observed: "As opposed to the third-party defendant, it is the mother's every waking and sleeping moment which, for better or worse, shapes the prenatal environment which forms the world for the developing fetus. That this is so is not a pregnant woman's fault: it is a fact of life. In practice, the reproduction of our species is necessarily carried out by individual women who become pregnant. No one lives but that he or she was at one time a fetus in the womb of its mother." (At 360.) See further chs. 4 and 6.

significance to the body, so too it is a story which cannot tell us anything particular about the context of the relationship between the pregnant woman and her fetus. In this way her argument fails to acknowledge the extensive, indeed extraordinary, nature of the bodily burdens in pregnancy.

In the light of my conclusion that the "social context" of pregnancy is relevant to this discussion, some comment is in order regarding what a context-attentive form of reasoning may or may not entail. The validity of moral, social and political reasoning which emphasises context has been endorsed, in particular, by some feminist philosophers. The idea of attending to the features of a particular context is sometimes contrasted with abstract, universal forms of reasoning such as those exemplified in different ways by Kantian and Utilitarian approaches. As Virginia Held has argued,[108] although a Kantian approach may develop ways of dealing with specific cases and contexts, still it tends to assume that abstract reasoning is, by definition, truer. Similarly, in the Utilitarian approach, one abstract idea (the Principle of Utility) is theoretically applicable to any moral problem, regardless of the context. Of course, these observations are generalised, but they highlight an underlying belief in an abstract reason typically shared by Kantians and Utilitarians alike. Importantly, in attending to the "social context" of pregnancy and to the particular context of treatment refusal within this, my reasoning has not sought to reject the application of abstract principles *per se*. My point has rather been that in reasoning about the extent of maternal duties we must acknowledge the context of the maternal–fetal relationship; it is not that the context can provide "the answer", as it were, in itself.[109]

Given these observations it is somewhat paradoxical that the "context" to which I have drawn attention is in fact so "widespread". Pregnancy *is* the means by which the human race reproduces and the women who either potentially or actually bear children make up approximately half the population. To attend to the "social context" of pregnancy is thus to attend to an enormously significant feature of human life, such that to recognise the facts and demands of pregnancy is at the same time to "get things right", morally speaking. Thus, the hugeness of this "context" brings

[108] V Held, "Feminist Transformation of Moral Theory", (1990) 50 *Philosophy and Phenomenological Research* (Autumn Supplement 321–44). Extracts reprinted in P Singer (ed.), *Ethics* (Oxford: Oxford University Press, 1994) 166–70, 168. Held first expressed these views in her *Rights and Goods: Justifying Social Action* (New York, NY: The Free Press, 1984). Virginia Held's work is particularly prominent here; but other philosophers who might be mentioned in connection with context-attentive reasoning (and related themes) are: S Sherwin, "Feminist and Medical Ethics: Two Different Approaches to Contextual Ethics", in HB Holmes and L Purdy (eds.), *Feminist Perspectives in Medical Ethics* (Indianapolis, IN: Indiana University Press, 1992) 17–31; C Gilligan, *In a Different Voice* (Cambridge, MA: Harvard University Press, 1982) and C Gilligan, J Ward and J Taylor (eds.), *Mapping the Moral Domain* (Cambridge, MA: Harvard University Press, 1988).

[109] My position would be consistent with Held's view that "[s]atisfactory principles for areas such as . . . family relations . . . cannot be derived from simple universal principles, but must be arrived at *in conjunction with* experience in the domains in question." V Held, "Feminism and Moral Theory", in E Kittay and D Meyers (eds.), *Women and Moral Theory* (Savage, MD Rowman and Littlefield, 1987) 111–28, my emphasis. Held is thus critical of Nel Noddings's overly simplistic and hence somewhat unhelpful rejection of principles in her *Caring—A Feminine Approach to Ethics and Moral Education* (Berkeley, CA: University of California Press, 1984).

out the point that there need be no intrinsic conflict or tension between context-sensitivity (however specific and unique the context may be) and "moral truth". It is beyond my scope to embark upon a detailed study of this theme.[110] Importantly however, these brief points support the pattern of the argument with regard to the strength of positive duties and social organisation developed at the start of this section.

Discussion of the importance of a context-sensitive approach is an appropriate point at which briefly to comment upon my reasoning generally. My approach may be an example of what Robert Audi has dubbed "ethical reflectionism", which holds principally that reflection is and should be our "basic method for justifying ethical judgments, especially general moral principles or general judgments of what has intrinsic value, and among our basic methods for discovering such judgments".[111] I cannot discuss this in detail here but, in essence, intuitions may provide what Audi dubs the "prima facie justified inputs"[112] within the process of ethical reasoning, which are then extended and systematised by means of "reflective equilibrium".

Finally, I advert again to the possibility of regret touched on in the first half of the chapter. Indeed, Celia Wells has noted the story of a woman with cerebral palsy

[110] For another discussion which stresses the importance of context, see H Smith, "Fetal–Maternal Conflict", in A Buchanan and JL Coleman (eds.), *In Harm's Way: Essays in Honour of Joel Feinberg* (Cambridge: Cambridge University Press, 1994) 324–43. Smith distinguishes between a causal and a contextual analysis of harm to the fetus/future child, rejecting a utilitarian analysis in favour of an approach which distinguishes between harming and rendering a lower level of aid. But in the light of the discussion here, her interesting analysis seems limited in several respects: for instance, in its emphasis upon rights to the exclusion of imperfect moral duties; and in its failure to distinguish between the moral duties of parents to born children on the one hand and pregnant women to the fetus/future child on the other. Moreover, her analysis ceases at what is perhaps the most difficult point, with which I have tried to grapple, namely the *determination of the level of care required* of pregnant women, or rather, as she puts it, of "parents" generally.

[111] R Audi, "Intuitionism, Pluralism, and the Foundations of Ethics", in W Sinnot-Armstrong and M Timmons (eds.), *Moral Knowledge: New Readings in Moral Epistemology* (New York, NY: Oxford University Press, 1996) 101–36, 121. Reflective equilibrium is of course the approach advocated by John Rawls in ss. 3–4 of his *A Theory of Justice* (Cambridge, MA: Belknap Press of Harvard University Press, 1971). Note Ian Kennedy's observation, from "The Moral Status of the Embryo", in his *Treat Me Right*, (Oxford: Oxford University Press, 1992) 119–39, at 126, my emphasis: "There is a perfectly proper place for intuitive response in the sum total of moral views and values. Equally, there is a perfectly respectable argument for taking account of a strongly held and widely held sense of moral outrage or repulsion when considering any scheme for ordering affairs. Furthermore, the fact that such moral outrage can draw on some *reasoned argument as well as intuition* makes it doubly valid as a ground of objection." Kennedy may assume that reason and intuition are independent of each other, whereas Audi's point would be that Kennedy's intuition has a valid place *within* his reasoning when coupled with a process of reflective equilibrium.

[112] R Audi, "Intuitionism, Pluralism, and the Foundations of Ethics", 129. See also G Sayre-McCord, "Coherent Epistemology and Moral Theory", in W Sinnot-Armstrong and M Timmons (eds.), *Moral Knowledge*, 137–89, who defends the coherence theory of justification by defending the epistemic value of the method of reflective equilibrium. As Sayre-McCord defines it, the coherence theory of justification can be described as holding that "a belief is justified if, and then to the extent that, it coheres well with the other things a person believes . . . [who] is justified in holding some belief if and only if the belief itself is justified and she holds it because it is justified". In dealing with various criticisms, Sayre-McCord notes that the link between justification and truth is not provided by coherence itself, but by the "evidential relations that bind beliefs into coherent sets" (at 178).

who wrote (to a national newspaper) of her mother's regret that her fear of a caesarean section led her to refuse this. The caesarean would have avoided her daughter's cerebral palsy.[113] Wells suggests that evidence of a woman's regret or of a
woman who has later thanked medical staff for obtaining a declaration as to the
lawfulness of operating in the face of a needle-phobia refusal (as in *Re L*, discussed
in chapter three)[114] should "at least . . . raise a doubt about the wisdom of this
respect of 'autonomy' ".[115] I think this is right, but the appropriate way to deal with
this is not to say that in some cases it might be better to override refusals, a view to
which Wells is by no means committed (how can we know who will regret or
thank and who will not?), but rather to put the subject of refusing surgery such as
a caesarean on the prenatal agenda as early as possible, with the follow-up of discussion and counselling both nearer and at the time of the prospective birth (when
fears will loom larger). This issue is particularly discussed in chapter four.

IV. CONCLUSIONS

The maternal–fetal conflict is in some sense a problem located at the interface
between a woman's rights and duties. Accordingly, the first part of this chapter has
looked at the maternal–fetal relationship in terms of a woman's rights, whilst the
second has examined the relationship in terms of her duties.

In concluding chapter two, I return first to the idea of her *rights*. In section II.B,
I developed further the "gradualist approach formulated at the end of chapter one,
the essence of which was the idea that, as the fetus develops, so an increasingly serious reason is needed to justify harm to it. So far as a pregnant woman's *rights* are
concerned, the argument put forward in chapter one was that she justifiably exercises her right to refuse treatment when she has serious reasons for doing so. If the
moral acceptability of exercising this right thus depends on the reasons for so doing,
I noted that this could be, in effect, to incorporate a virtue–ethical approach into
the rights framework. The residual problem we encountered in chapter two was
that of determining the "seriousness" or "strength" of a woman's reasons in non-
trivial cases, given that we do not share her religious beliefs and that it is her body,
not ours, which will be the subject, for instance, of surgery. In essence, I concluded
that we must accept the seriousness of her religious beliefs, taking note of the place
of religion in her life. Ultimately, we must also consider the place of the fetus within
her body and the implications for our helping the fetus (against her will) that this
latter point seems to entail. In the final analysis, then, we must place faith or trust[116]

---

[113] C Wells, "On the Outside Looking in: Perspectives on Enforced Caesareans", in S Sheldon and
M Thomson, *Feminist Perspectives on Health Care Law* (London: Cavendish Publishing, 1998) 237, 247,
n. 58. The letter was apparently to the *Independent* between 21 and 27 Feb. 1997.

[114] [1997] 1 FCR 609.

[115] C Wells, "On the Outside Looking in: Perspectives on Enforced Caesareans", 251.

[116] For interesting work on the notion of *trust* in moral theory see e.g. A Baier, *Moral Prejudices*,
(Cambridge, MA: Harvard University Press, 1994) ch. 1, in which she discusses the idea of "appropriate trust" as mediating between love and obligation, reason and feeling.

in the moral responsibility of the pregnant woman. In turn I suggested that there may be scope here for further adapting a virtue–ethical approach into a rights framework, in the sense that to coerce a pregnant woman into accepting medical treatment which she refuses and thereby override her right, may be to deny her the opportunity of responsible autonomy which is so crucial to her well-being, her flourishing, a point briefly touched on further in chapter four.

With regard to the argument from duty, as examined through Thomson's argument, I sought to limit the obligations pregnancy imposes, other than by reasoning about what the fetus's hypothetical rights would entail (the latter being Thomson's approach). This was particularly important given the potentially enormous scope of those obligations which Thomson had somewhat marginalised under the description of "moral decency". Concerning a pregnant woman's *duties*, the important points to emerge during or as a result of examination of her argument were that rescuing another involves a positive duty with regard to which questions about the potential rescuer appear to become relevant in a way that they do not with regard to the breach of a negative duty not to harm others, in turn creating areas of potential disagreement about the existence or extent of a duty in particular cases. Next, in discussing the idea of the ordinary neighbourly duty, I drew attention to the fact that whilst such duties may subject us to physical risk, they do not seriously invade the body in the special sense of a duty that is, quite literally, to be realised through the body. In this regard, in the light of the intensely personal nature of a prospective (positive) duty to rescue another through one's body (such as in the case of an organ donation, or the caesarean) I tried to highlight the increased *complexity* in our determination of the existence and extent of such duties. This arises in the light of the emotional or psychological elements that are likely to be present in these intensely physical and intimate cases.[117] It is important to note that my argument does not hinge on a distinction between duties of the body and duties of conduct *per se*, just as it does not hinge on that between positive and negative duties *per se*. Rather, the point is that *generally* judging reasonableness is harder in relation to positive duties to aid than negative duties not to harm, and this is acutely accentuated where a positive duty seriously implicates bodily integrity. Finally, having drawn out these points, I argued that whilst certain extraordinary burdens or risks may be an inherent part of pregnancy, they cannot therefore be assumed to be part of a woman's duty (notwithstanding her special relationship to the fetus) in the light of my points about the "social context" of pregnancy: namely, its ordinary but truly essential place within society.

Let me conclude chapter two by "bringing together" the argument from duty, the end result of which was to recognise the social context of pregnancy, with the argument from rights. First, an emphasis upon the idea of "context" is entirely consistent with, in fact may be said to go hand in hand with the "gradualist virtue-ethical" approach developed earlier. Indeed, we saw previously that Hursthouse

---

[117] For further thought particularly relevant here and to n. 82 *supra* see M Nussbaum, *Upheavals of Thought: the Intelligence of Emotions* (Cambridge: Cambridge University Press, 2001).

laments the fact that the "familiar biological facts", or what I have in effect included within the idea of "context", are more often than not ignored in philosophical arguments about abortion. This is not true of Dworkin's work on abortion (which postdates Hursthouse's); nor, I suggest, is it true of my approach to the different but related problem of maternal–fetal conflict.

One might also notice that recognising the "context" within which a woman will be asked to accept medical treatment for the fetus also involves the recognition that her interests and rights in self-determination and bodily integrity will thereby be called into play. This is where the argument from rights "marries" that from duty. My discussion contrasted the considerable but relatively brief nature of the Good Samaritan's non-bodily assistance (in the course of a journey) to the injured man, with the lengthy and intensely physically demanding nature of the pregnant woman's bodily assistance to the fetus. Although the Bible tells us that those who passed by before the Samaritan failed to stop and assist the injured man, implying that the conduct of the Samaritan was *exceptional*, we can also say that it was *unreasonable* of the priest and the Levite not to assist.[118] Additionally, it was a dereliction of a moral duty on their part. This is something which the discussion about a woman with serious reasons (and rights) suggested we could not say of the pregnant woman who does not "rescue" the fetus through her body.

With regard to the fact that rights are implicated in the situation of pregnancy, we should also notice that these may come into play for the first time at any point in pregnancy and will do so, very often, quite late: for instance, a caesarean birth will make demands on a pregnant woman in an unpredictable, if not totally unforeseeable, way at the very end of gestation. This is the "context", in a sense, of the rights that are implicated in the maternal–fetal conflict. To allow the woman her rights in self-determination and bodily integrity, then, is another way of saying that she cannot fairly be said to have the duty, in becoming pregnant, to make extraordinary sacrifices on the fetus's behalf.

This is not to say that she does not have a duty to "do all she can". This much is only "reasonable". Yet, by definition, doing all she can will be doing all those things which she does not have serious reason to refuse to do (including serious doubts grounding such reasons). In other words, to say that she must "do all she can" is at the same time to allow for the constraints of her religious faith or her concerns and fears in relation, for instance, to invasive surgery, though clearly the latter must be the subject of discussion with relevant parties, a question touched upon in chapter four. Crucially, "doing all she can" will entail seriously considering the interests of the fetus or future child and trying to bring herself to accept the relevant treatment. In this sense, we might say that her trying or striving here fulfills her duty to her unborn child. Ultimately, it seems unfair to say that, despite such attempts, she is failing in her moral duty. This may be related to my social context argument.

[118] I cannot discuss here the point that the priest and the Levite may have thought the traveller "dead and defiling to the touch of those whose business was with holy things", thereby displaying a "preoccupation with petty-fogging rules" implicitly criticised by Jesus. See GB Caird, *The Pelican New Testament Commentaries: The Gospel of St Luke* (Harmondsworth: Penguin, 1963) 148.

Thus, in the hypothetical case of the woman refusing to swallow the highly beneficial pill (which has no adverse effects on her) for no apparent reason, she indeed has the duty to take the pill for the benefit of the future child. Moreover, since swallowing the pill does not appear seriously to invoke her interests either in self-determination or bodily integrity, then arguably she would unjustifiably assert a right to refuse it. That she has a "right" to refuse the pill is thus really only true in the weak sense that it is her choice, rather than a matter also invoking an important interest on her part. In this regard, it may be recalled that in the first section of chapter one the Choice theory of rights was rejected in favour of a hybrid approach which combined the ideas of interest and autonomy, on the basis that the former approach could do nothing to explain the significance of rights in a context such as that of maternal–fetal conflict. The current discussion vindicates that stance. In essence, as regards these hypothetical refusals, the presence of a moral duty demonstrates the potential gap between the theoretical justification of a pregnant woman's rights and their exercise in practice.

Staying with the hypothetical but troublesome case of the woman refusing to swallow the beneficial pill, in this instance it may be more morally significant to emphasise, not that she has the moral right to refuse the pill in question, which indeed we may prefer to deny (consistent with my earlier point that the example of the pill more readily falls within the domain of general conduct), but rather that we have some kind of an obligation to grant her the choice, perhaps based on the importance of allowing people a domain of responsibility, as adverted to above. Importantly, in the light of her apparent irresponsibility (in the initial rejection of the pill) this idea would not preclude attempts on our part to encourage or even persuade her to take the pill, a point which is developed in chapter four. Legally, broad policy considerations discussed in chapters six and seven are also in point here.

Finally, in observing that the actions of the Samaritan seem quite "other-directed", it cannot be assumed that in refusing treatment for religious or other serious reasons, a woman is thinking only of herself. Where a woman believes that it would be a serious sin to accept surgery as a result of which she will forego eternal life, she may well be concerned for the shame that might thereby fall upon her family. Indeed, in one reported case concerning a Nigerian couple, a husband committed suicide following his wife's forced caesarean birth.[119] In this way, the maternal–fetal conflict may well resist description or analysis in terms of a self/other dichotomy. This observation will be developed in chapter four.

---

[119] This case is cited in VEB Kolder, J Gallagher and MT Parsons, "Court-Ordered Obstetrical Interventions", (1987) 316 *New Eng J Med* 1192, 1193.

Conclusions to Part I

IN THE LIGHT of the detailed conclusions to each of the two chapters in Part I, it would be both inappropriate and cumbersome to conclude Part I at any length. So I confine myself to a few key points.

The discussion and argument in Part I has shown that the maternal–fetal conflict can only be understood by exploring the way in which the fetus or future child's interests *relate to* those of the pregnant woman and vice versa. This has been the essence of the "gradualist" picture endorsed at the end of chapter one, in which ("in theory") harm to the fetus or future child was seen to be morally justifiable only where there was a serious reason on the woman's part proportionate to the degree of development on the part of the fetus/future child. Regarding the question of recognising that on occasion the real party in issue is not the fetus but the future child (who is not yet but will be born), it was observed at the start of chapter one that the difficult question was that of the moral weight to attach to that future child's interests. In the course of the first chapter, I highlighted the important difference between a born child and a future child, namely the latter's current location inside its mother. I argued that this fact necessarily affects the weight to be accorded to its interests, at least when those interests are in conflict with those personal and particularly bodily interests of its mother, rather than a "detached" third party, or, concomitantly, the mother's *outside* the treatment context, a point developed particularly in chapter six. With regard either to the fetus or the future child, I stressed the links between the questions of its location inside the mother's body and the degree of its development, noting that the issue of location was in itself of more significance for the "future child"—so that maternal reasons for refusing medical treatment must address this point—and vice versa.[119]

---

[119] The important distinctions summarised in this paragraph have not been made by J Savulescu in his "Liberalism, Harm to Others and Involuntary Medical Treatment in Pregnancy", (unpublished, 1997, on file with author). This is an interesting study of the ethics of the conflict which also touches upon the law, which takes as its starting point that Mill's harm principle should be extended to include "future others". He argues that if "(1) a parent's action or (inaction) will likely result in serious harm of a child who will likely exist in the future; (2) the harm to the parent of foregoing the present action (or acting in another way) will likely be acceptably small; then the State is justified in requiring that the parent now refrain from acting (or act differently) so as to prevent serious harm to the child", suggesting that this could justify compulsory treatment of pregnant women in some circumstances. At face value, this sounds plausible enough, but the weaknesses in this argument—the difficulties it would ultimately encounter—are highlighted by his statement that "[t]here is no reason to treat the interests of future individuals any differently to those of present individuals". The point here is that it all depends upon whose interests those of future individuals are being compared with, coupled with the nature of those interests: thus, I have distinguished between maternal *general conduct*, which may harm the future child in a manner akin to a detached third party on the one hand and the particular and very personal interests in self-determination and bodily integrity which will usually be invoked in the treatment context on the other. In the latter case, the importance of the kinds of maternal reasons which will arise for refusing treatment will be a legitimate consideration affecting the strength of the future child's (or fetus's) interests.

The "gradualist" picture was further developed in the first half of chapter two, in which I examined the relationship in terms of the idea of a woman's *rights*, drawing attention to the difficulties in judging the strength of a "serious" reason on the woman's part. Importantly, the gradualist argument, with the arguably virtue-ethical components to which I drew attention, ultimately "opens the door" on the moral quality of the decision to exercise a right by attending to a woman's motives or reasons for so doing. This "door" will remain open in Part II, where the recognition of the serious reasons for which a woman may refuse treatment will in turn enable me to defend the idea of a woman's *legal* right to refuse treatment; further, the somewhat unlikely possibility of a woman seeking to exercise the right for trivial reasons may in turn lead us to note the opportunity, in the maternal–fetal conflict, for appropriate discussion, counselling and, rarely, persuasion. Whether a woman who continues to assert a trivial reason for refusing certain treatment with the possible consequence of death of the fetus or harm to the future child should nevertheless retain the right to do so is answered by a complex of issues of principle and policy addressed in different ways in chapters four, six and seven.

In turning to explore the relationship in terms of the idea of *duty* in the second half of chapter two, I suggested that it was harder to determine the reasonableness—hence in particular the extent—of positive duties to assist others; moreover, that we could not readily determine the reasonableness of duties to aid another through one's very body. I concluded that attentiveness to the context of the maternal–fetal conflict is crucial in reaching appropriate and fair moral conclusions regarding the maternal–fetal relationship. It was in this way that I sought to limit the positive duty to assist the fetus that treatment questions invoke. Despite a woman's "special" relationship to the fetus, following consideration of the ordinary but essential place of pregnancy in society at large and the extraordinary (by comparison even with other special relationships) nature of the peculiarly bodily burdens in pregnancy, I concluded that such intense burdens, while customary or inherent within pregnancy itself, cannot be assumed to be part of a woman's duty to her fetus. These arguments in turn provide the foundations for discussion of the idea of a woman's *legal* duty to the fetus, discussed particularly in Part III.

Lastly, to clarify my terminology in the remainder of the book, note that for simplicity from now on I generally use the term "fetus" (as do the legal cases in Parts II and III), unless the interests of the "future child" need specifically to be delineated. Sometimes I also use the term "unborn child" to cover both.

PART II

The Legal Arguments from Rights

Introduction

THE FIRST chapter of Part II introduces the legal cases of compelled obstetric intervention. From the outset, it is important to note that the cases discussed span a considerable period of time, in which different legal results have obtained. Rather than commencing chronologically with the earliest cases in point, I begin with one American and one English case from the "middle period" (the late 1980s and early 1990s). For various reasons which are discussed in this section, in the early 1990s the only English and the leading American authority were at odds on the question of a competent pregnant woman's legal right to refuse medical treatment; moreover, the circumstances in which she was clearly thought to have such a right were also unclear. Thereafter I explore the "early" cases (1960s to early 1980s). I adopt this approach because it is a more pointed way of exposing the slim legal foundations for compelled obstetric intervention. Thus, when we turn to the earliest maternal–fetal cases, it is apparent that this thin line of authorities largely developed along a parallel but somewhat distinct path from the principal cases of the law of treatment refusal, with the result that the maternal–fetal cases have tended to fail to take into consideration a patient's important interests and rights in self-determination and bodily integrity.

The latter half of the chapter introduces the most prominent recent American and English maternal–fetal cases: the American case of *Baby Boy Doe* (1994)[1] clearly endorses a pregnant woman's legal right to refuse treatment as invasive as a caesarean section, but leaves open the question of less invasive treatment. This question was picked up in *Re Fetus Brown* (1997), which holds that a pregnant woman can also refuse treatment as invasive as a blood transfusion. The English Court of Appeal decision of *Re MB* (1997)[2] holds that a pregnant woman has the absolute right to refuse any medical intervention, assuming her presumed competence, as an adult, is not rebutted (a position affirmed by the Court of Appeal in *St George's Healthcare NHS Trust* v. *S, R* v. *Collins and others, ex parte S*).[3] The issue of competence has assumed a particular importance in English law, as consideration of other English decisions reveals. In discussing these most recent English and American authorities, I review the legal status of the fetus.

Despite clarification of the law in England and in at least some US states, several questions remain: first, *Re MB* establishes that "a competent woman who has the capacity to decide may, for religious reasons, other reasons, or for no reasons at all, choose not to have medical intervention".[4] However, the case expressly

---

[1] 632 NE 2d 326 (Ill App 1 Dist 1994).
[2] [1997] 8 Med LR 217.
[3] [1998] 3 All ER 673.
[4] [1997] 8 Med LR at 227, *per* Butler-Sloss LJ.

acknowledges that ethical dilemmas remain. This is consistent with the fact that, apart from reiterating that the fetus is not a legal person, the case did not address the question of why a *pregnant* woman—who is clearly not identical to one who is not pregnant—should have the same right as any other competent woman to refuse medical treatment. This was not seen as a task appropriate for a court of law. Yet, as the Court of Appeal virtually admits in this case, a reconciliation of the law and ethics by means of a moral justification of the law is highly desirable. This is particularly so in the light of the widespread public awareness of this issue as well as the increasing scope for interventions to benefit the fetus, both of which may in the future put pressure on a pregnant woman's legal right to refuse medical treatment. I embrace the task of a moral justification of this legal right particularly in chapter four, building on ethical foundations laid in Part I.

Second, in the light of a flush of English cases which preceded *Re MB* it is conceivable that, at some level and in ways which I shall outline, judgments about the irrationality/immorality of beliefs which form the basis of a woman's decision to refuse medical treatment may illegitimately come to bear on the determination of a pregnant woman's competence to decide treatment issues for herself, particularly in the light of the test of competence in English law and the way this operates in the situation of maternal–fetal conflict. Once again, this points to the need for a justification of a pregnant woman's right to refuse treatment, in which, particularly, the difficulty of judging her serious reasons (first discussed in Part I) is highlighted also within the legal (rather than the purely moral) debate.

Third, since only some US states have decided this issue and then, at least in Illinois, only to the extent that "invasive" treatment is in issue, the question of whether a pregnant woman should have the legal right to refuse medical treatment in the United States remains very open. Each of these questions points towards the need for a justification of a pregnant woman's legal right to refuse medical treatment, a task begun legally in chapter four, where I start to build upon arguments from Part I, and continued, in different ways, through to the end of the book.

Thus in chapter four I incorporate Part I's insights into a woman's interests in pregnancy into our understanding of the idea of her legal right to refuse medical treatment. The discussion confirms the likely coincidence between her legal right to refuse treatment and her serious reasons for exercising this right based on her interests in self-determination or bodily integrity or both. I focus particularly on her interest in self-determination (in the sense of reasons for refusal going to questions of meaning or value in her life) rather than the issue of the risks of medical treatment, which I touch upon in Part III. I build upon the idea, first formulated in chapter one, that increasingly serious reasons are necessary to justify harm to the fetus as it develops. The chapter seeks to analyse two State interests and the intersections between these: first, the State's interest in the *preservation of life*—the interest the State asserted against a competent adult's *prima facie* right to refuse treatment before an almost absolute right became established; second, the State's interest in the *potential life of the fetus*, the primary State interest in the early US maternal–fetal cases which derives from abortion law and on the basis of which a woman's *prima facie* right to refuse medical treatment was often overridden in the earliest cases. In this process, I highlight certain threads common to both these State interests— notably a concern that choices regarding human life are appropriately respectful and responsible—and argue that they come together in the maternal–fetal conflict in the form of an interest in the *moral quality* of a pregnant woman's decision to refuse medical treatment. There is no suggestion that this interest is asserted *explicitly* in the latest cases themselves. But this analysis provides a way of exploring a pregnant woman's right to refuse medical treatment in terms of the ideas of respect and, especially, responsibility toward fetal life emphasised in a leading US Supreme Court abortion decision in a way which enables us to defend the *principle* of her right to refuse medical treatment, even though this will likely be detrimental to the fetus. Whether in *practice* her exercise of this right in fact attends to these values will depend upon the nature of her reasons for refusal.

Whilst the analysis in chapter four is to a large extent in terms of US law, given the way in which the discussion focuses both upon the very personal nature of the rights in question and upon the idea of responsibility in their exercise, the ideas are highly relevant to a defence and understanding of a pregnant woman's right to refuse medical treatment in any jurisdiction. Moreover, in the light of the arguably unlikely possibility that a pregnant woman might seek to exercise her right to refuse medical treatment for clearly trivial reasons, the place of counselling and/or persuasion is also touched upon. Importantly, in this regard, the possibility of persuasion was explicitly sanctioned, but not fleshed out, in the leading English case of *Re MB*.

The last important point to note here is that the maternal–fetal cases are introduced and discussed within the framework of the medical law of treatment refusal, where they most clearly belong. Although a judge in one of the maternal–fetal conflict cases dubbed the law of treatment refusal one of the "closest legal analogues",[5] I would support the argument of a leading scholar that in fact the law relating to treatment refusal provides the "more appropriate" framework in which to analyse these cases and hence is more than an analogy.[6] However, unlike the customary cases of treatment refusal (which concern the life of only one individual), the maternal–fetal cases obviously involve two lives (of differing legal status). It is for this reason that the cases and literature have drawn upon and sought to apply arguments from the law of abortion, tort and rescue, areas of law which are more appropriately classed as analogues. I draw upon arguments relating to abortion in a novel way in chapter four. Following this, Part III looks at arguments from the three legal analogues I have identified. In this process I will frequently return to some of the maternal–fetal cases first introduced in chapter three in order to explicate the points from other areas of law upon which they draw.

---

[5] *Re AC*, 533 A 2d 611 (DC App 1987), *per* Nebeker AJ at 615.
[6] N Rhoden, "The Judge in the Delivery Room: The Emergence of Court-Ordered Cesareans", (1986) 74 *Cal L Rev* 1951, 1968–9.

3

Introduction to the Maternal–Fetal Cases and the Law of Treatment Refusal

A. Two Forced Caesareans

THE PHENOMENON of court-authorised obstetric intervention reached England in 1992. This came as something of a surprise, as in 1990 a US court had apparently turned the tide on a wave of such cases occurring principally in the 1980s.[1] Indeed, the two cases introduced here reach somewhat different conclusions about a woman's legal right to refuse medical treatment, despite the fact that the English case purported to rely on the earlier American authority. Whilst it was initially considered that this may have stemmed in part from the different factual situations at stake, it is now apparent that the judge in the English case probably relied upon an "incomplete reference"[2] to the American decision. This section has two purposes: to introduce the facts of these two very different cases, one English and one American, and to introduce, through the American authority in particular, some of the difficulties, hence limitations, of the reasoning in these cases.

In the space of two and a half months in 1992, English law both recognised and realised the possibility of a controversial exception to the principle that a competent adult can refuse life-sustaining medical treatment. Reviewing this area of the law for the first time at appellate level in *Re T*,[3] Lord Donaldson MR suggested a

---

[1] One 1987 study reports 21 instances of doctors seeking court orders for caesareans since 1981, of which the doctors were successful in all but three. VEB Kolder, J Gallagher and MT Parsons, "Court-Ordered Obstetrical Interventions", (1987) 316 *New Eng J Med* 1192. The study also found that in 88% of the cases the order to operate was received within six hours, and in nearly one-fifth it was received in less than an hour. An additional finding was that 81% of the women were black, Asian or Hispanic, 44% were unmarried and 24% did not speak English as their primary language. This relevance of this last aspect is touched on later in the chapter. The study also found that most cases in which a physician sought a court order for treatment on behalf of the fetus had not been reported because of time constraints on the courts and the methods by which the orders were obtained (at 1192).

[2] *Re MB* [1997] 8 Med LR at 227, *per* Butler-Sloss LJ.

[3] *Re T (Adult: Refusal of Treatment)* [1992] 4 All ER 649, in which a 34-week pregnant Jehovah's Witness who had been in a car accident contracted either pleurisy or pneumonia. In the first stages of labour, she refused a blood transfusion (as subsequent to the forthcoming caesarean section) following discussions with her mother. Although she had been raised by her Jehovah's Witness mother, she was not herself of that faith. After she became unconscious her father and boyfriend applied to the court

"possible qualification" to the autonomy of a competent adult where respecting a treatment refusal may lead to the death of a viable fetus.[4] It was perhaps only a matter of time before a party would test the water and, shortly after, the issue received disturbingly swift attention in an *ex parte* hearing in *Re S*.[5] There, Sir Stephen Brown P was called upon to decide whether it would be lawful for doctors at a London hospital to override the refusal, on religious grounds (the woman and her husband were Born-Again Christians),[6] of a fully competent 30-year-old woman to undergo an emergency caesarean section. Without such a declaration it would have been a criminal and tortious assault to touch Mrs S without her consent, regardless of whether this was deemed to be in her best interests.[7] The surgeons were convinced that the operation was the only way to save the lives of both the woman and the fetus.[8] In granting the declaration, Sir Stephen Brown P was clearly

---

for assistance. The Court of Appeal held that doctors were justified in administering a transfusion of necessity on the basis that, at the time of the refusal and thereafter, she lacked the capacity to consent and had been subject to undue influence by her mother, which vitiated her refusal.

[4] *Re T (Adult: Refusal of Treatment)* [1992] 4 All ER, 653.

[5] *Re S (Adult: Refusal of Treatment)* [1992] 4 All ER 671. The application came to the notice of the court at 1.30 pm, came on for hearing shortly before 2 pm and the order was issued at 2.18 pm. *Ibid.* 672. The procedural problems affecting these cases have long been recognised (see e.g. J Gallagher, "Prenatal Invasions and Interventions: What's Wrong with Fetal Rights?", (1987) 10 *Harvard Women's LJ* 9, 49). For an astonishing physician view of procedural requirements in these cases see J Phelan, "The Maternal Abdominal Wall: A Fortresss Against Fetal Health Care?", (1991) 65 *S Cal L Rev* 461, who notes: "When the situation is so urgent that there is no time to appoint a guardian *ad litem* or counsel, due process may not require a similar level of protection [as in the non-emergency setting]". (At 488, footnote omitted.) What this author surely means is that the same scale of hearing may not be *possible* without maternal and/or fetal death, not that such is not *required*. By highlighting the impact of procedural problems on the substantive law, such an approach only emphasises the need for legal clarity in this area, rather than case-by-case decision-making. Remarkably, this physician seriously suggests that it might be sufficient on occasion for two physicians or a physician and a nurse in the absence of a second physician to ascertain that there is "clear and convincing evidence of fetal distress" (at 488, footnote omitted). C Wells has noted that these cases "cannot be de-emergencied by the magic means of suspension of reality (or suspension of labour)". She suggests that "[t]he length of the proceedings has to be judged against that context", one in which one or two deaths may be in issue. C Wells, "On the Outside Looking In: Perspectives on Enforced Caesareans", in S Sheldon and M Thomson (eds.), *Feminist Perspectives on Health Care Law* (London: Cavendish Publishing, 1998) 237–57, 246. But once again this highlights the need for clear law, not case-by-case law.

[6] Heather Draper suggests an additional reason, namely that this was Mrs S's second delivery, that she had likewise refused a caesarean in relation to her first and that the outcome then had been a successful vaginal delivery. The implication is that Mrs S doubted the need for a caesarean in the second case. Draper does not cite a source for this information. H Draper, "Women, Forced Caesareans and Antenatal Responsibilities", (1996) 22 *JME* 327, 332. It is also unclear that the religious reason would still not have been the governing reason. In this sense, the successful outcome in the first case might have been seen by Mrs S as "vindicating" her faith.

[7] See discussion of these principles in the section on *Re MB* in s. III(B) *infra*. For a disturbing account of compelled obstetric examination and interventions apparently occurring in England before *Re S*, see L Miller, "Two Patients or One? Problems of Consent in Obstetrics", (1993) 1 *Med Law Int* 97, 97–8. The case she discusses did not involve a caesarean (or the courts), but did involve imposing a refused vaginal examination. The woman was apparently held down by six people while she kicked and screamed.

[8] The fetus was in a position of "transverse lie" with the elbow projecting toward the cervix and the head on the right side: [1992] 4 All ER at 642. This meant that, without intervention, there was a risk of the uterus rupturing, leading to shock, internal bleeding and possible death; the fetus would then have died of oxygen starvation as the walls of the uterus closed in: *The Times*, 15 Oct. 1992.

responding to the exception outlined in *Re T*, though his judgment, of less than a page, masks the situation's "considerable legal and ethical complexity".[9]

Less clearly, Sir Stephen Brown P drew upon recent American authority on point in *Re AC*,[10] a case involving very different facts. There the District of Columbia Court of Appeals initially upheld the authorisation of a hospital to perform a caesarean on a terminally ill woman—with at best two days to live—in an attempt to save her fetus. One year later, however, the same court had vacated its order;[11] and three years later the court held a full hearing on the merits.[12] The distressing chronology of Ms C's case, coinciding as it does with the last days of her life, reveals subtle and complex changes in her desires for herself and her fetus as her condition worsened, changes with which the trial court never got to grips. Given that the District of Columbia Court of Appeals' subsequent vacation of the order arose out of the uncertainty surrounding her wishes, the following account focuses on this aspect.

Ms C was in approximately her 25th week of pregnancy when she learned, following a routine check-up, that her teenage cancer was no longer in remission and that she had an apparently inoperable tumour in her right lung. Following admission to hospital two days later her condition temporarily improved and she confirmed that she really wanted to have her baby. Over the space of a weekend, however, her condition rapidly deteriorated and she was informed that her illness was terminal, at which time she agreed to palliative treatment intended to extend her life to at least the 28th week of her pregnancy, on the basis that the potential outcome at 28 weeks would be much better for the fetus if it were necessary to "intervene".[13] While Ms C knew that there were some risks for the fetus in this treatment, she chose this course both to prolong her life and to ensure her comfort during this time. No doubt associated with her extreme distress, her relationship with the fetus now begins to change: when asked if she still wanted to have the baby, she said "something to the effect of 'I don't know, I think so.' "[14] Shortly thereafter her condition further deteriorated so that she required sedation in order to breathe and the next day the hospital sought a declaratory order as to what course of action should be followed.

The trial court, sitting at the hospital but not in the presence of Ms C, made the following findings of fact: that she would die within 24 to 48 hours, that the fetus had a 50 to 60 per cent chance of survival if a caesarean were performed as soon as possible and, most significantly, that the court was unclear as to whether or not Ms

[9] [1992] 4 All ER at 653, *per* Lord Donaldson MR.

[10] 533 A 2d 611 (DC App 1987).

[11] According to B Steinbock, this was in response to a request from 40 organisations, including the American Civil Liberties Union, the American Medical Association and the American College of Obstetricians and Gynecologists. B Steinbock, *Life Before Birth: the Moral and Legal Status of Embryos and Fetuses* (New York, NY: Oxford University Press, 1992) 159.

[12] 573 A 2d 1235 (DC App 1990).

[13] *Ibid.*, 1238, *per* Terry AJ.

[14] *Ibid.*, 1239.

C would wish the caesarean to be performed at that time.[15] Although she had not indicated opposition to the idea of intervention at 28 weeks, the possibility of intervention before that time had not been discussed. One physician testified that in the light of her medical problems he did not consider that "she would have chosen to deliver a child with a substantial degree of impairment" associated with premature delivery.[16] When the court's decision to authorise the operation was relayed to a conscious Ms C by a physician[17] she agreed to the surgery. Shortly afterwards, however, when the same physician sought to confirm her consent to the procedure, Ms C, who was unable to speak on account of the breathing tube, "very clearly mouthed words several times *I don't want it done. I don't want it done*".[18]

Back at the court hearing one of the physicians questioned whether the right conditions existed to obtain a valid consent, but he also expressed the view that Ms C was "in contact with reality" and able to make the kind of decision in issue;[19] the other physician stated that her sedation had worn off and that she was "quite reactive" and "much more alert than she had been earlier in the day".[20] Despite her apparent change of heart in the form of a refusal, the court still found her intention to be unclear and, notwithstanding this perceived lack of clarity, authorised the operation, citing as legal authority *Roe* v. *Wade*'s[21] interest in protecting the potential life of the fetus and another decision relating to a caesarean section, *Re Madyun*.[22] The motion for a stay of the order having been denied,[23] the operation was performed. Mother and child both died, the mother after two days, the child after a few hours. It should be noted that the physician who had treated Ms C's cancer for several years was not informed of the hearing; if he had been, he "would have come to the hospital immediately and would have testified that a caesarean section was medically inadvisable *both for AC and for the fetus*."[24]

When in 1990 the District Court of Appeals issued its new decision, it found that the trial court had failed properly to determine the factual issue of Ms C's competence or, if she were deemed incompetent, the correct application of the doctrine

---

[15] S Martin and M Coleman scathingly note that although the trial judge "did not clearly know what Angela's present views were, . . . he did not go down the hall and ask her." S Martin and M Coleman, "Judicial Intervention in Pregnancy", (1995) 40 *McGill LJ* 947, 966.

[16] Dr Hamner, 573 A 2d at 1239; 533 A 2d at 613.

[17] Dr Hamner.

[18] Dr Weingold, having observed the conversation between Dr Hamner and AC, 573 A 2d at 1241, emphasis in original.

[19] Dr Weingold, *ibid*.

[20] Dr Hamner, *ibid*.

[21] 35 L Ed 2d 147 (1973) 183. This leading case is discussed especially in ch 4.

[22] 114 Daily Wash L Rptr 2233 (DC Super Ct July 26 1986). (Published as appendix to *Re AC*, 573 A 2d 1259.) (Refusal of a caesarean section by a Muslim woman, supported by her husband, on the basis of her faith. "When questioned . . . Mrs Madyun reiterated her preference for a natural delivery and expressed her belief that a Caesarean section was not necessary. She understood the risks of infection to the fetus resulting from continuation of labor without delivery, but sought to explain her decision to decline a Caesarean section by reference to her religious beliefs. Mrs. Madyun testified that a Muslim woman has the right to decide whether or not to risk her own health to eliminate a possible risk to the life of her undelivered fetus." (At 1269, *per* Levie AJ) Aspects of the case are discussed *infra*.

[23] 533 A 2d 611 (DC App 1987).

[24] 573 A 2d at 1252, n. 17, emphasis in original.

of substituted judgment. Much of the majority and dissenting judgments are taken up with these issues, so that comparatively little judicial energy is left for the merits or otherwise of forced intervention. Towards the middle of the majority judgment, the court highlighted the significance of the concept of bodily integrity, which meant, the court suggested, that there must be "truly extraordinary or compelling reasons to override"[25] the patient's wishes. But what *counts* as such a reason in these circumstances is precisely what is in issue and this is unanswered. (For a case which pick ups on this aspect of *Re AC*, see *Pemberton* v. *Tallahassee Memorial Regional Medical Center*,[26] discussed in the next chapter.) Having reviewed the legal arguments from cases and literature, but without adding arguments of its own, the court declared that in "virtually all cases", the patient's wishes, however determined, "will control":[27]

> "We do not quite foreclose the possibility that a conflicting state interest may be so compelling that the patient's wishes must yield, but we anticipate that such cases will be extremely rare and truly exceptional. This is not such a case."

This passage is a reflection of language used earlier in the judgment, including that noted above, as Associate Judge Terry himself stressed in the paragraph which succeeded the above passage:

> "Throughout this opinion we have stressed that the patient's wishes, once they are ascertained, must be followed in 'virtually all cases,'. . . unless there are 'truly extraordinary or compelling reasons to override them,' . . ."

This repetition or reiteration naturally adds force to the judgment. Importantly, however, it should catch our attention for another reason: although the majority judgment outlines and rejects the legal arguments for intervention in such a case, it never fully analyses the *application* of these arguments in the maternal–fetal context. The court is clearly impressed by the anti-interventionist literature; clearly too the extreme nature of the case had tremendous impact. At the end of the day, however, at the end of the *judgment*, we find the court repeating itself rather than explaining *why* the State's interest in the fetus should not have been deemed sufficiently compelling to override Ms C's apparent refusal. Although *Re AC* is a distressing and tragic case, saying so is not enough: it would have been preferable if the majority in *Re AC* had gone beyond rejecting the arguments for intervention to explain in detail why, at least in Ms C's case, her apparent refusal should have been upheld despite the adverse consequences for the fetus.[28] As we shall see, the later American case of *Baby Boy Doe* spelt out the reasons more fully. The *Re AC*

---

[25] *Ibid.*, 1247.

[26] 66 F Supp 2d 1247 (1999).

[27] *Ibid.*, 1252, *per* Terry AJ, footnote omitted. The court's conclusion is consistent with the American College of Obstetricians and Gynecologists Committee Opinion No. 55 of October 1987, entitled "Patient Choice: Maternal–Foetal Conflict", which concluded that "[t]he use of the courts to resolve these conflicts is *almost never* warranted". My emphasis.

[28] M Diamond notes the seemingly disproportionate space the court gave to the issue of substituted judgment, "Echoes from Darkness: The Case of Angela C.", (1990) 51 *U Pitt L Rev* 1061, 1072.

court did note two important but somewhat secondary reasons against compelled interventions: first, court-ordered treatment erodes trust within the physician–patient relationship and drives women with high-risk pregnancies out of the health care system to avoid coerced treatment; second, and more significantly, the court noted that any judicial hearing in such cases would normally take place under circumstances in which it would be "difficult or impossible" for the pregnant woman to receive proper legal representation, which is highly undesirable given the importance of her implicated interests. These points were supplemented with a review of the procedural inadequacies in this case.[29]

B. Who Is At Risk? Different Factual Scenarios

At this point, it may assist to outline and clarify the possible factual scenarios of cae-sarean cases. There appear to be at least three: *first*, the *Re S* situation where the life of both the mother and fetus are deemed at risk if a caesarean section is not per-formed, though the probabilities of death without surgery are usually cast differently, and the risks to the mother from the caesarean section are those which are "normal" to this surgery; *second*, the scenario in which only the fetus is deemed at risk without a caesarean section and again the risks to the mother are those inherent in the surgery itself. *Third*, there is the rare but clearly possible situation demonstrated by *Re AC*, in which only the fetus is at risk without the caesarean section, it is thought that the mother will shortly die in any event, and in these circumstances the surgery will likely hasten her death.

Having outlined these differences it is apparent that, notwithstanding the recent judicial suggestion (in *Re MB*) that the judge in *Re S* was appraised of an incom-plete reference to *Re AC*, *Re S* could well have been the result of a specific aspect of *Re AC's* reasoning, to which attention has been drawn elsewhere.[30] The 1990 *Re AC* court referred to the case of *Re Madyun* in a footnote. In *Madyun*, the cae-sarean carried no risk of harm to the woman over and above that inherent in the procedure itself, unlike in *Re AC* where the operation actually hastened Ms C's death due to her poor physical condition: the facts of *Re AC* are exceptional while

---

[29] 573 A 2d at 1248. Regarding the first point, the court drew on the American Public Health Association's *amicus curiae* brief. (This argument is touched on in ch. 7.) On the difficulties of obtaining balanced medical evidence as would normally be required under the adversarial model, see S Martin and M Coleman, "Judicial Intervention in Pregnancy", 966. These authors suggest that there may also be a tendency to defer to the professional judgment of doctors, which may be inaccurate or outdated such that the medical procedure in question is not in fact necessary (*ibid.*). (On the last point see further discussion in s. III(D)(2).) For further comment on the issue of procedural inadequacies, see JK Levy, "Jehovah's Witnesses, Pregnancy, and Blood Transfusions: A Paradigm for the Autonomy Rights of All Pregnant Women", (1999) 27 *J of Law, Med. and Ethics* 171, 184, who notes the difficulties for the patient of presenting a well-rounded case when her health is already compromised. Further (depending on the jurisdiction) poverty (or, conversely, insufficient poverty to qualify for legal aid coupled with lack of sufficient resources of her own) may prevent access to her own legal counsel.

[30] See I Kennedy and A Grubb, *Medical Law* 3rd edn. (London: Butterworths, 2000) 933.

those of *Re Madyun* are the norm. In purporting to leave aside exceptional cases, *Re AC* thus implies that a different result may obtain in what are actually normal cases, which seems inconsistent with the tenor of the judgment. It is on precisely this "misstatement"[31] of the exception and the norm that Sir Stephen Brown P may have relied in *Re S*:[32]

"There is, however, some American authority which suggests that if this case were being heard in the American courts the answer would likely be in favour of granting a declaration *in these circumstances*: see *Re AC*".

That the *Re AC* court misstated the exception and the norm is one matter; but the question remains whether it intended its result also to hold for the properly identified norm, namely the *Re S/Madyun* scenario?

To answer this question let me now introduce a third caesarean case which could, in theory, have contributed to the decision in *Re S*. The "normal" circumstances of *Re S* and *Madyun* were also those of the 1981 appellate case of *Jefferson v. Griffin Spalding County Hospital Authority*.[33] Here, a pregnant woman in her 39th week who had regularly presented herself to the hospital for prenatal care, was found to have a complete *placenta praevia* (with the placenta between the baby and the birth canal). Medical opinion considered it was "virtually impossible"[34] that the condition would correct itself, that the chances of the fetus and the woman failing to survive vaginal delivery were 99 and 50 per cent respectively, and that delivery by caesarean section prior to the onset of labour would have an almost 100 per cent chance of success for both. On the basis of her religious beliefs, Jessie Mae Jefferson advised the hospital that she would not need a caesarean and for this reason declined to consent (either to surgery or blood transfusions). Having denied the application for a stay of the trial court's order, the Supreme Court of Georgia ordered her to submit to the caesarean section and such related procedures as her physician considered necessary to save the fetus. A few days later Mrs Jefferson successfully gave birth to her child vaginally.

Both the 1987 and 1990 appeal courts in *Re AC* distinguished *Jefferson*. The 1987 court observed:[35]

"*Jefferson* is of limited help for our purposes. Here, the mother was not near term for delivery; in *Jefferson*, the mother was at term. Furthermore, the performance of a Caesarean section would not clearly prevent the death of the mother or the child in this case; in *Jefferson*, both the mother and child would almost certainly have survived the performance of the Caesarean section."

The 1990 court adopted a similar view, holding that "*Jefferson* is of limited relevance, if any at all, to the present case"[36] and emphasised that in *Jefferson* "the caesarean was

---

[31] Kennedy and Grubb capture the error in this way, arguing that given *Re S*'s reliance on this, the decision cannot be upheld. *Ibid.*

[32] [1992] 4 All ER at 672, my emphasis.

[33] Ga 274 SE 2d 457 (1981).

[34] *Ibid.*, 458.

[35] 533 A 2d at 614, *per* Nebeker AJ.

[36] 573 A 2d at 1243, *per* Terry AJ.

in the medical interests of both the mother and fetus".[37] Further, regarding *Madyun* the 1987 court in *Re AC* simply observed that the trial court had expressly relied on that case.[38] The 1990 *Re AC* court, having declared that it considered it "sufficient for now to chart the course for future cases resembling this one", observed in its footnote on *Madyun*:[39]

> "In particular, we stress that nothing in this opinion should be read as either approving or disapproving the holding in *In re Madyun, supra*. There are substantial factual differences between *Madyun* and the present case. In this case, for instance, the medical interests of the mother and the fetus were in sharp conflict; what was good for one would have been harmful to the other. In *Madyun*, however, there was no real conflict between the interests of mother and fetus; on the contrary, there was strong evidence that the proposed caesarean would be beneficial to both."

This view of *Madyun* reads remarkably like the assessment both courts made of *Jefferson*. This need not surprise us, as it was only a third court, the trial court in *Re AC*, which expressly relied on *Madyun*; nor need it trouble us that both hearings of the District of Columbia Court of Appeals distinguished *Jefferson* and yet came to different conclusions about Ms C's case: both courts accepted that Ms C's case entailed exceptional risks; it is just that the 1990 court decided that, if Ms C had made a competent refusal, her wishes should have been respected, while the 1987 court apparently did not.

What *is* striking is that the 1990 court should have placed its views about *Madyun* in a footnote. *Madyun*, of course, was also a District of Columbia decision, whereas *Jefferson* came from Georgia, which may account for the direct manner with which the court put the latter to one side. Having done this, however, there was still the decision in *Madyun* to address. Its presence in a footnote might be explained on two grounds. First, Terry AJ, who was one of three judges to affirm the appeal in *Madyun* and who delivered the majority judgment in *Re AC*, might well have wished to avoid embarrassment at what was really a change of heart by him in the latter case. Second, in the light of the considerable public and academic pressure to vacate the 1987 order in *Re AC*, the majority may have been reluctant, at the end of the judgment, to emphasise the extent to which its decision effectively only applied to "a situation in which a pregnant but dying patient is either incapable of consenting to treatment or affirmatively refusing treatment",[40] as the opening section of the judgment, which stresses the "reasonable expectation that the challenged action in this case . . . may occur again",[41] makes clear. Technically then, the judgment only covers *Re AC*-type cases: whatever the court *wanted* to say about forced treatment of pregnant women in general, its judicial hands were in some ways tied by the particular facts of the case. Although the court bizarrely implies,

---

[37] 573 A 2d at 1243, *per* Terry AJ.
[38] 533 A 2d at 613.
[39] 573 A 2d at 1252, n. 23, *per* Terry AJ.
[40] *Ibid.*, 1242, *per* Terry AJ.
[41] *Ibid.* In this regard, reference was made to the fact that the hospital in this case operated a "high-risk" pregnancy clinic, which would increase the likelihood of it again facing a *Re AC*-type case.

in the sentence which carries the footnote to *Madyun*, that consideration of the ordinary *Madyun* scenario (which is in effect also that of *Jefferson*) could demand that "it sail off the chart into the unknown",[42] in a sense the subliminal judicial desire to turn the tide on forced treatment of pregnant women can be seen to explain the characterisation of the norm as the exception: in some sense the court wants to say that it has the norm well in mind, and that it is only something other than the norm, something "extremely rare and truly exceptional"[43] which could prompt the overriding of a woman's refusal. What is all too apparent, however, is that, in distinguishing *Jefferson* and neither approving nor disapproving *Madyun*, strictly speaking the court left open the legal answer regarding whether or not a pregnant woman can refuse a caesarean section (or, presumably, other surgery or treatment) which carries "only" inherent risks. The rather startling implication is that *Re S*, contrary to some views,[44] could well have been in line with the letter, if not the spirit, of *Re AC*.[45]

However, from the tone of the judgment it is apparent that the decision in *Re AC* was intended to call a halt to compelled obstetric intervention in general rather than solely in the particular circumstances of the case, and it is now apparent that subsequent cases have interpreted it as doing just this, although in the United States

[42] *Ibid.*, 1252, *per* Terry AJ.

[43] *Ibid.*

[44] E.g. M Thompson notes the same passage of Sir Stephen Brown P's reasoning which I cited earlier to the effect that *Re AC* implied that if Mrs S's case were an American case, her refusal would likely be overridden "in these circumstances". On this, Thompson writes: "This assertion is erroneous. *Re AC* . . . does not validate, or support, compelled medical treatment against the wishes of a competent patient in order to save or benefit the life of a fetus." M Thompson, "After *Re S*", (1994) 2 *Med L Rev* 127, 128, footnote omitted. My argument implies that, so far as the spirit of the decision is concerned, Thompson is surely right; regarding the letter, however, Sir Stephen Brown P may, after all, have been so. If so, his decision cannot quite be said to rely on a "misreading of the tragic, now discredited case of Angela Cardner" as, for instance K de Gama has suggested in "A Brave New World? Rights Discourse and the Politics of Reproductive Autonomy", in A Bottomley and J Conaghan (eds.), *Feminist Theory and Legal Strategy* (Oxford: Blackwell, 1993) 114–30, 122. She continues: "Ironically, lost to Stephen Brown J, giving judgment, was the fact that after her death the decision was overruled, a victory which marked a turning-point in the United States . . . for reproductive autonomy." *Ibid.* Indeed, at one time some commentators held the view that Sir Stephen Brown P had relied on the 1987 case: if we refer to the reports of *Re S* on this point, *The Times* report of 16 Oct. 1992 only refers to *Re T*; the All ER report refers to the 1990 case of *Re AC*, but see the comments on this in the English caesarean decision of *Re MB*, as discussed in s. III(B).

[45] Note that Belson AJ dissented in part and concurred in part. For instance, he agreed that "with respect to surgical procedures, the pregnant woman's wishes, either as stated expressly or as discerned through substituted judgment, should ordinarily be respected and carried out unless there are compelling reasons to override them." 573 A 2d at 1253. He does not define, however, what would be the "ordinary" case in which he considers the woman's wishes should prevail. Later, however, he stated his "disagreement with the very limited view the majority opinion takes of the circumstances in which the interests of a viable unborn child can afford such compelling reasons. I would hold that in those instances, fortunately rare, in which the viable unborn child's interest in living and the state's parallel interest in protecting human life come into conflict with the mother's decision to forgo a procedure such as a caesarean section, a balancing should be struck in which the unborn child's and the state's interests are entitled to substantial weight." *Ibid.*, 1254. It seems, then, that Belson AJ would broaden the potential application of the notion of compelling reasons. Aspects of his judgment are discussed further in chs. 4 and 6.

it is understood, as we shall see, that *Re AC* only precludes treatment as invasive as a caesarean.[46] In this light, *Re S* can clearly be seen to be wrong. This in turn vindicates the assessment of the *Re S* decision by the Royal College of Obstetricians and Gynaecologists, which issued guidelines shortly after the case, stating in part:[47]

> "Obstetricians must respect the women's legal liberty to ignore or reject professional advice, even to her own detriment or that of her fetus . . . We conclude that it is inappropriate, and unlikely to be helpful or necessary, to invoke judicial intervention to overrule an informed and competent woman's refusal of . . . treatment, even though her refusal might place her life and that of her fetus at risk."

Moreover, we shall see that subsequent US authority has suggested that those maternal–fetal cases pertaining to the norm, such as *Jefferson* and *Madyun*, are wrong.

Before discussing the most recent caesarean section cases, in the next section I briefly examine the history of precedents of forced treatment of pregnant women and the way in which these bore little relation to the primary body of the law of treatment refusal. Two related strands of cases, upon which the maternal–fetal cases have sometimes relied, are also touched on at this juncture. In the subsequent discussion (section II) I shall outline the basis for the right of competent patients to refuse medical treatment, in the United States and England, following which I shall then be in a position to explore the latest caesarean decisions. Unlike the early maternal–fetal cases, the recent cases will be seen clearly to draw upon the principal body of the medical law of treatment refusal (in section III).

C. Analysis of Original Precedents for Forced Obstetric Intervention

The forthcoming discussion shows the unprincipled basis for the original precedents which spawned the subsequent spate of compelled obstetric cases in two principal ways: first, by highlighting the scant attention that was paid to the developing principles of the medical law of treatment refusal; second, by showing that the first

---

[46] *Baby Boy Doe*, 632 N E 2d 326 (Ill App 1 Dist 1994). *Re MB* [1997] 8 Med LR 217 also interprets the decision in this way.

[47] RCOG Guidelines, "A Consideration of the Law and Ethics in Relation to Court-Authorised Obstetric Intervention", No. 1, April (1994) at 15. In 1996 the College issued guidelines confirming that doctors have a duty to respect a patient's refusal of any procedure by advance directive: Supplement to "A Consideration of the Law and Ethics in Relation to Court-Authorised Obstetric Intervention" (December, 1996), para. 2.1. See also the similar views of the American College of Obstetricians and Gynecologists, "Patient Choice: Maternal–Fetal Conflict", ACOG Committee Opinion, No. 55 (October, 1987). Although discouraging court involvement, the ACOG guidelines nevertheless leave the door open by stating that "[t]he use of courts to resolve conflict is *almost never* warranted". (My emphasis.) The question of whether court involvement is warranted in some cases will thus depend on the physician's assessment. Note that the AMA guidelines "Legal Interventions During Pregnancy", (1998) (Policy No. H–420.969) likewise are uncertain on the permissibility of legal interventions in the "exceptional circumstance" and do not rule out interventions "in which a medical treatment poses an insignificant or no risk for the woman, entails a minimal invasion of her bodily integrity, and would clearly prevent substantial and irreversible harm to her fetus". For further discussion of the role of professional guidelines see ch. 4, s. IV(D).

case in particular failed to consider the important factual and legal differences between a fetus and a born child, thereby obscuring the significance of the legal status of the fetus and the bodily integrity of the pregnant woman, issues which, as discussed in Part I, were repeatedly highlighted as being importantly connected so far as the moral status of the fetus was concerned.

In opening the judgment of the Supreme Court of Georgia in *Jefferson*, Presiding Justice Hill declared that "[t]he power of a court to order a competent adult to submit to surgery is exceedingly limited. Indeed, until this unique case arose, I would have thought such power to be nonexistent."[48] Hill PJ correctly identifies the exceptional nature of the power in issue. The question is whether such power does or should exist in what he characterised as the "unique" case then before him. This section examines the legal basis of the 1981 decision in *Jefferson* in terms of the law of treatment refusal and relates the decision to the earliest precedent in point, which predated *Jefferson* by some 16 years: the decision of the New Jersey Supreme Court in *Raleigh Fitkin-Paul Morgan Memorial Hospital* v. *Anderson* (1964).[49]

In *Jefferson*, it was only Justice Hill who made any reference to the law of treatment refusal[50] and his discussion amounts to barely two paragraphs: in the first he refers to a commentary in the Annotated Law Reports;[51] in the second he observes that one court has held that a woman in the last stages of pregnancy lacks the right to refuse what he terms "necessary life saving surgery and medical treatment"[52] where the fetus's life is at stake, citing *Raleigh Fitkin-Paul Morgan Memorial Hospital* v. *Anderson*. It is a little disconcerting at this point to turn to *Anderson* and find that, contrary to Justice Hill's assertion, surgery was not there in issue although, following the judgment, the right to refuse it arguably was. The case concerned an action by a hospital seeking to administer blood transfusions to a pregnant woman in her 32nd week, despite her refusal on religious grounds not to consent to the same. The judgment of the Superior Court was reversed and the matter remanded to the trial court for directions which included appointing a special guardian for the infant, who was ordered "to consent to such blood transfusions as may be required and seek such other relief as may be necessary to preserve the lives of the mother and the child".[53] Thus, although the court clearly held that the woman lacked the right to refuse the transfusions, it is not clear that her right to refuse other treatment—such as surgery—was simultaneously overridden. Indeed, the quoted passage might well be taken to imply that the guardian would have to reapply to the court in respect of her refusal of any other treatment. Hence, whilst it purports

---

[48] Ga 274 SE 2d at 460.

[49] 201 A 2d 537, cert denied, 12 LE 2d 1032 (1964). *Jefferson* also refers at this point to *Re Melideo*, 390 NYS 2d 523 (1976) and *Re Yetter*, 62 Pa D & C 2d 619 (1973) which do little to back *Anderson:* the former simply refers to *Anderson* and distinguishes itself by saying that a non-pregnant woman may refuse treatment; the latter concerned the competence of a female patient at a state mental hospital to refuse recommended surgery for breast cancer.

[50] Marshall J concurred in his opinion.

[51] 93 ALR 3d 67 (1979).

[52] Ga 274 SE 2d at 460.

[53] 201 A 2d at 538.

simply to rely on *Anderson*, *Jefferson* actually extends the ruling in that case: apart from surgery being considerably more intrusive than a blood transfusion, the court in *Jefferson* also authorised the State to take custody of the child.[54] It matters that *Jefferson* goes considerably further than *Anderson*, not only because of its own poor coverage of legal points, but also because *Anderson* itself appears to lack any principled basis.[55]

Indeed, one has the sense that the *Anderson* court felt inclined to put the problem in the "too hard" basket. As noted above, the court first addressed the question of whether the State's concern for the welfare of an infant justified blood transfusions despite the objections of its parents.[56] Having answered this in the affirmative, it turned to the harder question of whether an adult may be compelled to submit to medical procedures necessary to save her own life:[57]

> "Here we think it is unnecessary to decide that question in broad terms because the welfare of the child and the mother are so intertwined and inseparable that it would be impracticable to attempt to distinguish between them with respect to the sundry factual patterns which may develop."

Up to a point, the court is attuned to the difficulties: we saw in Part I that the physical bond of mother and fetus produces considerable complexity for conceptual analysis of the relationship. Two legal solutions appear to present themselves if we have to choose in a case such as *Anderson*: the first is that the woman's interests should prevail; the second favours the fetus. Although *Anderson* opts for the latter, it disguises this by proceeding to authorise the administration of transfusions to save the life of the woman "or the life of her child",[58] implying not only that to administer to one is in any event to administer to the other, but also, in a sense, that it is not favouring one over the other. The court's fudging of the issue here arises because it has failed to answer the preliminary question whether a competent woman can refuse life-saving treatment for *herself*,[59] (momentarily leaving to one side, that is, the question of fetal interests): the *Anderson* court has let the physical connection between the woman and the fetus cut short its legal analysis.

---

[54] These differences were observed shortly after by G Annas, "Forced Cesareans: the Most Unkindest Cut of All", (1982) 12 (June) *Hastings CR* 16, 17. See also EP Finamore, "*Jefferson* v. *Griffin Spalding County Hospital Authority*: Court-Ordered Surgery to Protect the Life of an Unborn Child", (1983) 9 *Am J L & Med* 83, 90.

[55] Drawing our attention to the length of the judgment in *Anderson* (one page), G Annas has perhaps charitably observed that there was "little policy discussion": "Forced Cesareans", 17. In fact it is unclear that the court recognised that it faced *any* policy issues.

[56] *State* v. *Perricone*, 181 A 2d 7851 (1962). Other cases of maternal–fetal conflict touch on this issue and are discussed *infra*. The *Anderson* court also considered a child's right to sue for negligently inflicted injuries before birth, regarding which see ch. 6 on arguments from tort law.

[57] 201 A 2d at 538.

[58] *Ibid*. The same approach can be seen in the judgment of the Superior Court in *Jefferson*, Ga 274 SE 2d at 458. By contrast the Supreme Court emphasises the potential separateness of the viable fetus (*ibid*., 459).

[59] By contrast, a later case involving a blood transfusion for a fetus admitted that, were only the woman's life at stake, she could refuse treatment (on the basis of her religious beliefs): *Re Jamaica Hospital*, 491 NY S 2d 898, 899 (1985).

Physically, if a pregnant woman refuses a caesarean "on" herself she necessarily refuses it for her fetus. By contrast, *conceptually*, two questions arise. First, can she refuse treatment for herself (whether or not she may die without it)? Second, can she refuse treatment for her fetus? The *Jefferson* court appears to have acknowledged this distinction. Its reasoning, which at least addresses the law on treatment refusal, is more sophisticated than that in *Anderson*, as the court acknowledges explicitly the existence of the mother's (separately identifiable) interests. Yet, in the final analysis, the *Jefferson* court orders compulsory treatment "[b]ecause the life of defendant and of the unborn child are, at the moment, inseparable":[60] here biological inseparability has not so much cut short the analysis as determined the outcome.

Another line of reasoning deserves mention here for its reinforcement of the sense in which the physical relationship between woman and fetus complicated and at times befuddled these early legal analyses: both *Jefferson* and *Anderson* considered the issue of the woman's religious freedom. In *Jefferson*, Justice Smith observed the distinction in the First Amendment to the US Constitution between absolute freedom of belief and freedom of action: the latter may be restricted insofar as practices may be detrimental to public health or welfare.[61] Smith J appears to have been struck by the following passage from *Reynolds* v. *United States*: [62]

> "Suppose one believed that human sacrifices were a necessary part of religious worship, would it be seriously contended that the civil government under which he lived could not interfere to prevent a sacrifice?"

Smith J adopts the customary approach on the basis of which a practice may be restricted where there is no less burdensome alternative, citing *Roe* v. *Wade*[63] as giving the State a compelling interest in the viable fetus and *Anderson* as justifying that interest in these circumstances. If we turn again to *Anderson*, however, we find that there the court only considered the exercise of religious freedom in the domain of parental refusal of treatment for children. The dynamics of the relationship between belief and action as between mother and fetus—rather than mother and child—are left unconsidered. Yet in both *Anderson* and *Jefferson* the "religious practice" does not involve harm to a *separate individual*; nor, for that matter, is it a threat to the public at large. Rather, belief, action and possible harm are all, as it were, *within* the woman, a point that appears to pass unnoticed by the *Jefferson* and *Anderson* courts. The question of the woman's bodily integrity demands attention at this point.

It is in connection with this failure to appreciate the significance of bodily integrity that it is conceptually apposite briefly to note that the State, acting as *parens patriae*, can in appropriate situations restrict a parent's decision-making power in relation to a child where the parent's claim is founded upon religious belief or on a more generalised right of parenthood. The leading American authority on point

---

[60]   Ga 274 SE 2d at 458, *per curiam*.
[61]   *Ibid.*, 461.
[62]   98 US 145 (1878) 166.
[63]   35 L Ed 2d at 183.

is the US Supreme Court case of *Prince* v. *Massachusetts*,[64] in which Rutledge J notably observed:[65]

"Parents may be free to become martyrs themselves. But it does not follow that they are free, in identical circumstances, to make martyrs of their children before they have reached the age of full and legal discretion when they can make that choice for themselves."

The case has been drawn upon in subsequent jurisprudence to support the proposition that whilst a parent or guardian can consent to medical treatment for a child, he or she cannot deprive it of life-sustaining treatment, however well-intentioned.[66] Several of the maternal–fetal conflict cases draw upon this line of cases to support the proposition that a pregnant woman cannot refuse medical treatment for the fetus she carries. Indeed, the *Jefferson* court based its decision in part on the idea that "this child is a viable human being and entitled to the protection of the Juvenile Court Code of Georgia", but did not present arguments as to why that Code should be deemed to apply to the fetus.[67] In the case of *Crouse Irving Memorial Hospital* v. *Paddock*[68] the Supreme Court of Onondaga County was particularly influenced by cases concerning the treatment of born children to conclude that the hospital and attending physician had authority to perform a (religiously refused) blood transfusion on a pregnant woman during or following a caesarean section. But the court did not even consider the crucial difference between born and unborn children, namely that in the latter case overriding a parental refusal means treating a pregnant woman herself against her will for the sake of a being which is not yet a legal person. The maternal–fetal conflict case of *Re Madyun* also places strong support on the precedents for the treatment of born children, attempting to bridge the gap between the cases concerning the born child and the maternal refusal of caesarean section delivery with which it was presented with the conclusion that the relevant law applied also to a fetus on the basis that the State has an "important and legitimate interest in protecting the potentiality of human life", citing the abortion case of *Roe* v. *Wade* and noting that, according to *Roe*, this

---

[64] 331 US 158.

[65] *Ibid.*, at 170.

[66] See e.g. *Re Kevin Sampson*, 323 NYS 2d 253 (1971); *Custody of a Minor*, 379 NE 2d 1053 (1978). For the relevant English principles see esp. the judgment of Waite LJ in *Re T (a minor) (wardship: medical treatment)* [1996] 35 BMLR 63.

[67] Ga 274 SE 2d 457 (1981), 459, *per curiam*. But note that Justice Smith, concurring in the judgment, observed: "I believe the legislature intended that the juvenile courts exercise jurisdiction only where a child has seen the light of day. I am aware of no 'child deprivation' proceeding wherein the 'child' was unborn." (At 461–2, footnote omitted.) He noted that the Code simply defined a "child" as "any individual under the age of 17 years".

[68] 485 NYS 2d 443 (1985). The court also seemed to invoke the now largely defunct State interest in the ethical integrity of the medical profession, citing a law review article which observed that "[a] hospital is not the patient's servant, subject to his orders . . . to let a patient die runs counter to the reason for the hospital's existence". "Lifesaving Treatment for Unwilling Patients", (1968) 36 *Fordham L Rev* 695, 701. At 445. The court thus seems to have held that this State interest overrode the woman's acknowledged right, based on cases such as *Schloendorff*, to refuse unwanted medical treatment.

interest becomes compelling at the point of viability.[69] I shall consider the question of what the State's interest in the potential life of the fetus from the law of abortion might entail in the different context of the maternal–fetal cases in chapter four.

To return to *Anderson*, given that the case arose in the early 1960s, it is perhaps not surprising that the court's scant legal analysis did not address the law in relation to treatment refusal, as courts had not yet begun to develop patients' rights in this regard.[70] Yet one should perhaps feel a twinge of alarm at the court's failure to think worthy of mention long-standing and dearly cherished principles of US law: the interests in and rights to self-determination and bodily integrity. Moreover, it can fairly be said that the 1980s decisions of *Jefferson* and *Madyun* failed to recognise either the magnitude or the constitutional dimensions of a woman's right to refuse treatment, as the recent caesarean section case of *Baby Boy Doe* concludes. I therefore turn to outline the basis of the current law of treatment refusal.

II. THE LAW OF TREATMENT REFUSAL

A. The United States

Despite the frequency of their citation, two profound statements of law readily withstand repetition. The first is from *Union Pacific Railway Co.* v. *Botsford* (1891):[71]

> "No right is held more sacred, or is more carefully guarded by the common law, than the right of every individual to the possession and control of his own person, free from all restraint or interference of others, unless by clear and unquestionable authority of law . . ."

The second is from Justice Cardozo in *Schloendorff* v. *Society of New York Hospital Schloendorff*, namely that "[e]very human being of adult years and sound mind has a right to determine what shall be done with his own body".[72] It is the concepts of self-determination and bodily integrity which are simultaneously so absent from the analysis in *Anderson* (particularly) and yet so much at stake in that case and the others which are the subject of discussion here.[73] This is not to imply, as some

---

[69] 114 Daily Wash L Rptr 2233 (DC Super Ct 1986). Published as appendix to *Re AC*, 573 A 2d 1259, at 1262, *per* Levie AJ.

[70] In the United States perhaps the case which could best be said to mark the true beginning of medical law was *Canterbury* v. *Spence* 464 F 2d 772, dated 8 years after *Anderson* in 1972. G Annas has these chronological points well in mind, noting that *Anderson* predates *Roe* by 8 and *Re Quinlan*, 355 A 2d 647 (1976) (see ch. 4) by more than 10 years: "Forced Cesareans", 17.

[71] 141 US 250, 251, (1891).

[72] 211 NY 125, 129–30 (1914).

[73] The significance of the principles of bodily integrity and associated autonomy in the maternal–fetal conflict cases is widely noted by scholars. Notable examples are G Annas, "Forced Cesareans", 16; N Rhoden, "The Judge in the Delivery Room", 1969*ff*; L Nelson, B Buggy and C Weil, "Forced Medical Treatment of Pregnant Women: 'Compelling Each to Live as Seems Good to the Rest'", (1986) 37 *Hastings LJ* 703, 745*ff*; D Johnsen, "The Creation of Fetal Rights: Conflicts with Women's Constitutional Rights to Liberty, Privacy, and Equal Protection", (1986) 95 *Yale LJ* 599, 614*ff*.

have,[74] that recognising these interests and rights necessarily answers the questions here in issue; rather, it is to acknowledge that analysis can only begin once their significance has been realised.

In the United States, the right to refuse medical treatment is supported by common law and constitutional reasoning, both of which seek to protect the individual's rights to self-determination and bodily integrity as expressed respectively in the *Union Pacific Railway* and *Schloendorff* cases. At common law, the right to refuse medical treatment appears to exist as a corollary of the *Canterbury* v. *Spence* (1972)[75] right of informed consent: for instance *Re Conroy* (1985)[76] observed that the "right of a person to control his own body" had long been recognised at common law,[77] finding protection more recently through the doctrine of informed consent, which is "a primary means developed in the law to protect this personal interest in the *integrity of one's body*."[78] Having discussed the prerequisites of informed consent, the court observed that the significance of the doctrine becomes fully apparent in the appreciation that it encompasses a right to "informed refusal".[79] Later the *Conroy* court referred more broadly to the principle of *self-determination* in its assessment that life-sustaining treatment could be withheld or withdrawn from an incompetent patient when it was established that this would have been consistent with the patient's wishes. As the court put it, "[t]he standard we are enunciating is a subjective one, consistent with the notion that the right that we are seeking to effectuate is a *very personal right to control one's own life*."[80] (These interests in self-determination and bodily integrity were discussed in chapter two and, so far as the maternal–fetal conflict is concerned, in turn underlay the argument from rights

[74] As much as anything it is the *tone* in which some write that implies an absoluteness to the very concepts in issue. While this absoluteness may ultimately be legally justified, I find too certain assertions of rights question-begging and unhelpful, including to those intended to benefit from such an approach, namely women. For an explicit example of such an approach, see K de Gama, "A Brave New World?", who writes: "Interventions ordered by the courts, which disdain women's decisions about care of the *self*, reveal women can still be excluded from the ideology of universal rights whenever expedient." (At 127, my emphasis.) Her use of the word "self" seems to assume that there is only one set of interests at stake and hence no conflict to reconcile. For a different and rather troubled view, see C Wells, "On the Outside Looking In: Perspectives on Enforced Caesareans".

[75] 464 F 2d 772 (1972). "True consent to what happens to oneself is the informed exercise of a choice, and that entails an opportunity to evaluate knowledgeably the options available and the risks attendant upon each." At 780, *per* Robinson J, footnote omitted. (In this case, a 1% chance of paralysis resulting from a laminectomy was considered a risk of sufficient magnitude to prompt a duty of disclosure.)

[76] 486 A 2d 1209 (N J 1985). In this case, the guardian of an 84-year-old incompetent nursing home patient sought permission for the removal of the woman's nasogastric feeding tube. The bedridden patient had serious and irreversible physical and mental disabilities and a short life expectancy. The Supreme Court of New Jersey held that a competent adult has the right to decline medical treatment, including artificial nutrition, and did not lose that right upon becoming incompetent (*ibid.*, 1236).

[77] *Ibid.*, 1221 *per* Schreiber J. Reference was made here to the principles in *Union Pacific Railway* and *Schloendorff*.

[78] *Ibid.*, 1222, *per* Schreiber J, my emphasis. The US Supreme Court has backed this understanding. See *Cruzan* v. *Director, Missouri Department of Health* (1990) 111 L Ed 2d 224, 236.

[79] "Thus, a competent adult person generally has the right to decline to have any medical treatment initiated or continued." 486 A 2d at 1222, *per* Schreiber J.

[80] *Ibid.*, 1229, *per* Schreiber J, my emphasis.

(where I focused on the religious reason for refusal) and the argument from duty (where I explored the intersection of the right to bodily integrity with the idea of a bodily duty).)

Constitutionally, the federal right of privacy (explored further in chapter four) has for some time protected both bodily integrity and self-determination by upholding the individual's right to make certain decisions which concern his/her own body and a realm of personal decision-making.[81] The 1976 case of *Re Quinlan*[82] gave the right to refuse medical treatment a privacy grounding, based on *Roe* v. *Wade*. Privacy reasoning was relied upon in the two treatment refusal cases immediately following: *Superintendent of Belchertown State School* v. *Saikewicz*[83] and *Re Quackenbush*.[84] However, doubts were expressed in *Re Storar*,[85] where the court noted that the Supreme Court had "repeatedly declined" to consider the issue. In *Cruzan, by Cruzan* v. *Harmon*, Robertson J in the Supreme Court of Missouri suggested that *Roe* v. *Wade* "itself counsels against such a broad reasoning".[86] When the United States Supreme Court was finally faced with the issue in *Cruzan* v. *Director, Missouri Department of Health*,[87] it seems in fact to have assumed the right to refuse treatment, but to have shifted the analysis, holding that the question whether a person's right to refuse medical treatment is protected by the Federal Constitution is properly analysed in terms of the person's liberty interest under the Due Process Clause of the Fourteenth Amendment, rather than in terms of a generalised constitutional right of privacy.[88] On this analysis, the court considered that a competent person has a constitutionally protected liberty interest in refusing medical treatment.[89] Subsequent cases have gone both ways, adopting either the more traditional privacy analysis or the *Cruzan* approach, although some have suggested that there is no such liberty interest at all, holding that it was assumed in *Cruzan*.[90]

---

[81] Notable examples are *Griswold* v. *Connecticut*, 14 L Ed 2d 510 (1965) (married couples have a constitutional right to use contraceptives); *Roe* v. *Wade*, 35 L Ed 2d 147 (1973) (women have constitutional right to abortion until viability when the State's interest in the potential life of the fetus becomes compelling).

[82] 355 A 2d 647 (1976) 663.

[83] Mass, 370 NE 2d 417 (1977). In this case, an incompetent resident of a state School (a facility of the Dept of Mental Health) suffered from acute myeloblastic monocytic leukaemia. Following appointment of a guardian with authority to make decisions regarding requisite care and treatment, the Supreme Judicial Court of Massachusetts held that, in appropriate circumstances, both competent and incompetent patients have a general right to refuse treatment for a terminal illness and proceeded to apply the substituted judgment doctrine, by which it claimed to have established that Joseph Saikewicz himself would have refused the chemotherapy which was in issue. The case has been widely criticised for its use of the substituted judgment doctrine in relation to a patient who had never been competent. On other aspects of this case, see ch. 4.

[84] 383 A 2d 785 (1978), on which see ch. 4, s. II(B).

[85] 420 NE 2d 64 (1981), 70.

[86] 760 SW 2d 408 (Mo banc 1988), 418.

[87] 111 L Ed 2d 224 (1990).

[88] *Ibid.*, 242.

[89] *Ibid.*, 241–2.

[90] See e.g. *Compassion in Dying* v. *State of Washington* (1995) 49 F 3d 486. In the US Supreme Court hearing in *Washington et al* v. *Glucksberg et al*, 138 L Ed 2d 772 (1997) Rehnquist CJ, in his majority opinion, held that the notion of a liberty interest in, for instance, refusing medical treatment or assisted suicide was not consistent with the nation's history. Thus: "In light of that history, this

Conroy's discussion of the "right to control [one's] own body" and the "right to control one's life", relating in turn to bodily integrity and self-determination, captures the law's recognition of the individual's principal interests in medical treatment decisions. The notion of "control[ling] one's own life" is necessarily broader than the concept of bodily integrity and it would be appropriate at this juncture to remind ourselves why self-determination is generally perceived as a good for the individual. In the first section of chapter one I drew attention to the significance of autonomy in ethics, for instance in the work of the legal philosopher Joseph Raz. We saw that the concept of "autonomy" is central to his account of well-being, which is defined by an active life. Here I briefly draw attention to a discussion of autonomy particularly in the medical context.

The philosopher Roger Crisp (reflecting on the importance of informed consent) similarly links autonomy with well-being, though perhaps less forcefully than Raz, arguing that "[o]ne's well-being is constituted partly by the very living of one's life, as opposed to having it led for one by others."[91] Indeed, in the light of autonomy's "intrinsic" and "high" value, he suggests that anyone who surrenders control of his life to others on the basis of their promise to make better choices for him than he has so far made for himself, makes a very serious mistake.[92] Crisp is keen to emphasise the value that lies in the individual choosing and acting for himself, in order to explain or account for the harm that is done to someone when he is prevented from doing so. He discusses the fictional case of a patient whose surgeon failed to inform him of a serious (12 per cent) risk of paralysis from an operation and argues that, even though the patient would have consented if he had known of this risk and even though the patient considers that, despite the risk's materialisation, the operation benefitted him overall, the law should recognise that the patient was harmed either on the basis of battery or negligence. (In English law such an action would only sound in negligence.[93]) For my purposes, the important point is that, although the patient considers that, on balance, he is better off, without full information he was effectively deprived of the opportunity to make a vital choice himself. As Crisp puts it, he has "suffered a violation of his autonomy [which is] a harm to his well-being".[94] In *Conroy's* terms, his "very personal right to control [his] life" has been overridden.

Re Conroy went a long way towards both affirming and developing important principles of medical law and is frequently cited in later cases. For instance, the case was the first to outline the countervailing State interests to which the right to refuse treatment was originally subject. Thus, judicial reasoning in the earliest cases on

Court's decisions lead to the conclusion that respondents' asserted 'right' to assistance in committing suicide is not a fundamental liberty interest protected by the Due Process Clause." For a discussion of the case and arguments as to its true significance, see e.g. R Dworkin, "Assisted Suicide: What the Court Really Said", *NYRB* 25 Sep. 1997, 40.

[91] R Crisp, "Medical Negligence, Assault, Informed Consent, and Autonomy", (1990) 17 *J Law & Soc* 77, 82.

[92] *Ibid.*, 81–2.

[93] *Chatterton* v. *Gerson* [1981] 1 All ER 257.

[94] R Crisp, "Medical Negligence, Assault, Informed Consent, and Autonomy", 87.

point employed a "balancing approach" in which the patient's right to refuse treatment was weighed against such of the State interests as were considered applicable in the circumstances.[95] So, for instance, the 1977 case of *Superintendent of Belchertown State School* v. *Saikewicz* asserts:[96]

> "As distilled from the cases, the State has claimed an interest in: (1) the preservation of life; (2) the protection of the interests of innocent third parties; (3) the prevention of suicide; and (4) maintaining the ethical integrity of the medical profession."

In the next chapter, where I have reason to explore the *values* underlying the right to refuse medical treatment, I shall examine a few of the cases prominent in the *development* of this right in terms of the most important State interest, namely in the preservation of life. At this point, however, I shall outline the present state of Anglo-American law.

As it currently stands, medical law has developed such that a competent adult patient can refuse even life-sustaining medical treatment for whatever reason he chooses or for no reason at all: in other words, such a patient has the almost absolute *legal right* so to do. Self-determination came of age in this context in the 1993 case of *Thor* v. *Superior Court*.[97] Here, an irreversibly quadraplegic prisoner had no sensation

---

[95] English law appears at times to have adopted both the US approach and an "absolute right with exceptions" approach, as I Kennedy and A Grubb have noted regarding the judgment of Lord Donaldson MR in *Re T*. First Lord Donaldson states: "An adult patient who . . . suffers from no mental incapacity has an *absolute right* to choose whether to consent to medical treatment" ([1992] 4 All ER at 652–3, my emphasis). (The only possible "qualification" at that time was, of course, the issue which precipitated *Re S*.) Second, in his conclusion he refers to the patient's "*prima facie*" right, which is to be balanced against possibly countervailing interests of society (*ibid.*, 664). Kennedy and Grubb further note that the latter view is reflected in the judgment of Butler-Sloss LJ. See their *Medical Law*, at 916.

[96] 370 NE 2d at 425 *per* Liacos J. The second State interest mentioned—in the protection of innocent third parties—was noted in the maternal–fetal conflict cases of *Re AC* (1987 and 1990) and *Re Fetus Brown* (1997). The leading authority is *Re President and Directors of Georgetown College*, (1964) 331 F 2d 1000, in which the District of Columbia Court of Appeals ordered a mother to submit to a religiously-refused blood transfusion for the sake of her 7-month-old child, purporting to rely upon such authorities as *Jacobson* v. *Massachusetts* (1904) 197 US 11 (adults can be required to submit to compulsory treatment or prophylaxis, at least for contagious diseases). In effect, given the medical emergency and the mental state of the patient in *Georgetown*, the court invoked the State's *parens patriae* power and applied it to the mother, thus viewing her as incompetent. The case spawned a line of subsequent authorities in which differing results obtained. Given the undeveloped nature of patients' rights in 1964 and doubts as to the patient's competence in this case, *Georgetown* is a highly dubious authority and indeed recent cases have come to recognise the strength of a parent's interest and right in refusing treatment. See e.g. *Fosmire* v. *Nicoleau*, 551 NE 2d 77 (1990), in which Wachtler CJ acknowledged the State's interest in "maintaining family unity and parental ties", but concluded that "[t]he citizens of this State have long had the right to make their own medical care choices without regard to their physical condition or *status as parents*". (At 84, my emphasis.) In any event, *Georgetown* represents a dubious policy initiative subject to numerous questions, notably whether the State has authority to compel treatment of one individual for the sake of another, rather than the public at large. Finally, application of this line of reasoning to the maternal–fetal cases immediately raises the question of whether the fetus can be considered a third party when it exists inside the pregnant woman, a point recognised, for instance, by the author of the Note, "Developments in the Law: Medical Technology and the Law", (1990) 103 *Harvard L Rev* 1519, at 1569–70. For further discussion of *Georgetown* itself, see e.g. Case Comment, "Constitutional Law—Transfusions Ordered for Dying Woman over Religious Objections", (1964) 113 *U Penn L Rev* 290. For recent discussion of this line of cases, see R Scott, "Autonomy and Connectedness: A Re-evaluation of *Georgetown* and its Progeny", (2000) 28(1) *J of Law, Med and Ethics* 55.

[97] 855 P 2d 375 (1993).

in or control of his body below his shoulders, needing assistance with the performance of all his bodily functions. He began to refuse feeding and medical treatment necessary to his health, which created a substantial risk of death. On psychiatric examination he was found to be depressed but mentally competent. The Supreme Court of California denied the attending physician's petition to be allowed, in the light of the prisoner's refusals, to use a surgical tube to feed and medicate him. Arabian J held that health-care decisions essentially concern one's own subjective sense of well-being and hence that the patient's right to refuse treatment stands regardless of the opinion of others, including doctors.[98] He asserted that it was for the patient to determine what he or she can bear: "For self-determination to have any meaning, it cannot be subject to the scrutiny of anyone else's conscience or sensibilities."[99] In short, a competent adult patient can now refuse whatever treatment she wants and for whatever reason she chooses.

B. England

Thor's approach is broadly consistent with the English Court of Appeal's stance in *Re T*[100] the preceding year, to the effect that a competent adult has the right to refuse treatment, even where this will permanently damage health or lead to premature death. Lord Donaldson MR further observed:[101]

> "The right of choice is not limited to decisions which others might regard as sensible. It exists notwithstanding that the reasons for making the choice are *rational, irrational, unknown or even non-existent.*"

This was in line with the view of Lord Templeman in *Sidaway* v. *Board of Governors of the Bethlem Royal Hospital*, that "a patient is entitled to reject . . . [medical] advice for reasons which are rational, or irrational, or for no reason."[102]

The right of a competent adult to refuse treatment was approved in *Airedale NHS Trust* v. *Bland*,[103] in which the House of Lords held that it would be lawful for doctors to withdraw artificial nutrition and hydration from the persistent vegetative state patient Anthony Bland, for whom it was considered such treatment could be of no benefit. The Law Lords considered that it was not in his "best interests" to continue to be treated (*per* Lord Goff, Lord Lowry and Lord Browne-Wilkinson), alternatively that, as a PVS patient, he no longer had any interests (*per* Lord Mustill and perhaps Lord Keith). *Re T*'s statement of the law was

---

[98] This was in answer to the argument that the patient in *Bouvia* v. *Superior Court*, 225 Cal Rptr 297 (Cal CA 1986) (discussed in the next chapter) had suffered "unending agony".

[99] *Per* Arabian J, as cited in I Kennedy, "Commentary: Refusal of Treatment: Adult Prisoner: *Thor* v. *Superior Court*", (1994) 2 *Med L Rev* 220, 224.

[100] [1992] 4 All ER 649.

[101] *Ibid.*, 653, my emphasis.

[102] [1985] 1 AC 871, 904. The case concerned a claim in negligence for non-disclosure of the risks of a surgical operation.

[103] [1993] 1 All ER 821.

implicitly endorsed by three of the Law Lords[104] and explicitly by Lord Goff, who alone referred to that decision.[105] Moreover, Lord Goff, in drawing attention to the Canadian case of *Nancy B* v. *Hotel-Dieu de Quebec*,[106] in which the patient suffered from an incurable but not life-threatening condition, emphasised that the recognition of the right in *Bland* is not limited to terminally ill patients. (In fact, it should be noted that none of the Law Lords appeared to envisage the *Re S* exception to the right to refuse treatment. This was evidence of the dubious nature of the exception in English law,[107] a position confirmed by the 1997 decision in *Re MB* discussed later in this chapter.)

Following *Re T* and *Bland*, several subsequent decisions can be seen to have reinforced the position now reached in English law. In *Re C*[108] a 68-year-old Broadmoor patient suffered from paranoid schizophrenia but refused to consent to the amputation of his foot, the need for which was suggested because of life-threatening gangrene. He received alternative treatment to avert the threat to his life, after which the hospital refused to give him an undertaking that it would in future honour his refusals. C's application to the court for an injunction preventing the hospital from amputating without his consent was successful and *Re C* thus became the first English case actually to give effect to the right to refuse treatment.[109]

Most importantly, Thorpe J developed a three-stage test on competence for use in future cases: (1) could the patient comprehend and retain the necessary information; (2) did he believe it, and (3) had he weighed the information, balancing risks and needs, to arrive at a choice? In this regard, Thorpe J noted the similar approach then recently recommended by the Law Commission.[110] On the basis of this test, the judge decided that C was competent even though he suffered from schizophrenic delusions: his mental condition did not mar his understanding of the proposed treatment. However, as Andrew Grubb notes, American authority (and, presumably, *Re T*) would suggest that even if C had irrationally believed that surgery would for instance kill him, he would still be competent and in possession

---

[104] Lords Keith, Mustill and Browne-Wilkinson.

[105] [1993] 1 All ER 821, 866.

[106] 86 DLR (4th) 385 (Qu Sup Ct 1992).

[107] I Kennedy and A Grubb, "Commentary: Withdrawal of Artificial Hydration and Nutrition: Incompetent Adult: *Airedale NHS Trust* v. *Bland*", (1993) 1 *Med L Rev* 359, 361.

[108] [1994] 1 FLR 31.

[109] For a discussion of this case, see A Grubb, "Commentary: Treatment without Consent: Adult: *Re C (Refusal of Medical Treatment)*", (1994) 2 *Med L Rev* 92.

[110] Law Commission, Consultation Paper 129, "Mentally Handicapped Adults and Decision-Making", para. 2.20. After *Re C*, in 1995 the Law Commission published its report No. 231 on "Mental Incapacity", in paras. 3.2–3.32 of which, it recommended that a person lacks capacity at the material time if he is unable by reason of mental disability to make a decision for himself on the matter in question either because: "(a) he is unable to understand or retain the information relevant to the decision, including information about the reasonably foreseeable consequences of deciding one way or another or failing to make the decision; or (b) he is unable to make a decision based on that information." The Commission defined "mental disability" as a disability or disorder of the mind or brain, whether permanent or temporary, which results in an impairment or disturbance of mental functioning. Crucial to this understanding of capacity is the notion that a patient's inability to decide must flow from a mental disability.

of the right to decide for himself.[111] More recent decisions applying the *Re C* test include *Re JT (Adult: Refusal of Medical Treatment)* (1998) in which a 25-year-old patient with a mental disability was deemed competent to refuse life-saving renal dialysis,[112] and *R v. Ashworth Hospital Authority, ex parte Brady* [2000],[113] in which a prisoner's decision to refuse food by means of a hunger strike was not regarded as a competent refusal because of the patient's personality disorder. By contrast, competence was not in issue in the 1995 case of *Secretary of State for the Home Department v. Robb*,[114] which concerned a 27-year-old prisoner on a hunger strike and the lawfulness of currently refraining from force-feeding (and possibly abstaining from administering potentially life-sustaining medical treatment). The case reiterated the precedence of the principles of bodily integrity and self-determination over any possible countervailing State interests.[115] (Note that in the *Brady* decision Judge Maurice Kay left undecided whether force-feeding a competent prisoner on hunger strike might be lawful in the public interest, for instance, of safeguarding institutional discipline. Andrew Grubb has suggested that the decision in *Robb* might be distinguished on the basis that it only held that the prison authorities had no duty to intervene.[116])

Having outlined the current state of the law of treatment refusal as it relates to competent adults, I can now discuss the most recent caesarean decisions. As noted above, the *development* of the legal right to refuse medical treatment, in particular its relation to the State's interest in the preservation of life, will be briefly explored in the next chapter as part of the process of determining why a pregnant woman should have the right to refuse medical treatment granted in the recent maternal –fetal cases, to which I now turn.

III. THE MOST RECENT CAESAREAN CASES

On both sides of the Atlantic, the most recent maternal–fetal conflict decisions interpret the 1990 decision in *Re AC* as recognising and supporting any pregnant woman's right to refuse medical treatment (that is, not just a woman in the situation of Ms C in that case), for whatever reason, regardless of the effects on the

---

[111] A Grubb, "Commentary: *Re C*", 95. See e.g *Re Quackenbush*, (discussed in ch. 4, s. II(B)) and *Re Yetter*, 62 Pa D & C 2d 619 (1973) which, as noted earlier in these notes, concerned the competence of a female patient at a state mental hospital to refuse recommended surgery for breast cancer and particularly her irrational beliefs in relation thereto.

[112] [1998] 1 FLR 48.

[113] [2000] Lloyd's Rep Med 355.

[114] [1995] 1 All ER 677.

[115] Thorpe J appears to have drawn on the decision in *Thor, supra* n. 97, to give a medical law analysis to this case; but as I Kennedy has noted, the quadraplegic prisoner in *Thor* was necessarily a patient refusing medical treatment, whereas in *Robb* the prisoner was simply refusing food, although the need to administer life-sustaining medical treatment may have arisen in the future. See I Kennedy, "Commentary: Consent: Force-feeding of Prisoners: *Secretary of State for the Home Department v. Robb*", (1995) 3 Med L Rev 189, 190.

[116] I Kennedy and A Grubb (eds.), *Principles of Medical Law* (3rd cumulative supplement) (Oxford: Oxford University Press, 2000) 27–8.

fetus/future child. (But note the unsatisfactory exception in the 1999 *Pemberton* v. *Tallahassee Memorial Regional Medical Center* based on the notion of "extraordinary circumstances" left open by *Re AC*, discussed in the next chapter.[117]) Whilst the latest US decisions apply only to the refusal of caesarean sections and blood transfusions, the English decision covers any medical treatment. I shall explore these cases in turn.

A. Baby Boy Doe

In the Illinois decision *Baby Boy Doe*, a competent woman expecting her first child refused a medically advised caesarean section on the basis of her religious beliefs. As with Mrs Jefferson, given her "abiding faith in God's healing powers, she chose to await natural childbirth".[118] In this she was supported by her husband. In the obstetrician's opinion, there was a reduction in the flow of oxygen to the fetus and the Circuit Court found, amongst other facts, that the chances of the 36.5 week old male fetus being born alive were "close to zero" and that if he survived natural delivery he would be retarded. Regarding "Doe" herself, whom the court deemed competent, it found that the chances of a mother dying in a caesarean delivery are approximately 1 in 10,000, compared with 1 in 20,000 to 1 in 50,000 in normal delivery; that she would have "much more pain" due to a caesarean delivery than natural birth; that there could be "other complicating factors such as damage to organs" and that she would have to recuperate for about six weeks after the operation, which it described as "major surgery".[119] The Circuit Court denied the application to compel "Doe" to undergo the surgery and appeal was taken. For the Appellate Court of Illinois, Presiding Justice DiVito, who gave the opinion of the court,[120] held that "a competent woman's choice to refuse medical treatment as invasive as a cesarean section during pregnancy must be honored, even in circumstances where the choice may be harmful to the fetus".[121] (As an aside here, it might be observed that the court noted that in due course the woman gave birth naturally.[122]) I now discuss the key elements in this decision.

1. Rights—not Duties

Foremost in DiVito PJ's judgment was the rejection of the State and Public Guardians' argument to the effect that the Circuit Court should have *balanced* the rights of the unborn but viable child against its competent mother's choice,

---

[117] 66 F Supp 2d 1247 (1999).

[118] 632 NE 2d 326 (Ill App 1 Dist 1994), 327.

[119] *Ibid.*, 329. For a different view, see B Sachs *et al*, "Cesarean Section Related to Maternal Mortality in Massachusetts", (1988) 71 *Obst Gyn* 385, 388 on a study indicating that vaginal birth is riskier for the pregnant woman.

[120] In which Hartman and McCormick JJ concurred.

[121] 632 NE 2d at 326.

[122] *Ibid.*, 329.

principally for religious reasons, to refuse the caesarean. In this respect, the court drew upon the District of Columbia case of *Re AC*, introduced at the start of this chapter.[123] In particular, attention was drawn to the Court of Appeals' criticism of the lower court's actions in that case, whereby, rather than determining Ms C's wishes by means of the doctrine of substituted judgment, it balanced the "fetus's rights" against those of Ms C. The decision in *Re AC* was interpreted by DiVito PJ to mean that "[t]he woman's decision, not the fetus's interest, is the only dispositive factor".[124] He then observed that the Court of Appeals in *Re AC* held that a competent woman's decision would hold in "virtually all cases"; moreover that the court, "[w]hile not deciding the question, . . . expressed doubt as to whether there could ever be a situation extraordinary or compelling enough to justify a massive intrusion into a person's body, such as a cesarean section".[125] In this regard, he rejected the Public Guardian's argument that the situation in *Baby Boy Doe* was one such case. He thus ruled out the possibility, albeit only *technically* left open in *Re AC*, that in more usual circumstances of maternal refusals of caesareans[126] the right upheld in *Re AC*—which concerned the specific situation of a dying woman—may not be upheld. He noted, however, that the court in *Re AC* did not express an opinion about a woman's right to refuse a less invasive procedure, such as a blood transfusion, and likewise left this question open for another case.[127]

The court upheld a competent pregnant woman's right to refuse a caesarean (thereby rejecting any balancing approach) in two main ways. First, it emphasised the right of any competent adult to refuse medical treatment. Second, it held that a woman is not under a duty to guarantee either the mental or physical health of her child at birth and hence cannot be compelled to do or not do anything purely for the fetus's benefit. I shall discuss each of these lines of thought in turn. Before this, however, it might be noted that the court has adopted an approach similar to that which I spelt out in Part I: in chapter two I explored a woman's relationship to the fetus in two ways, first in terms of her rights, and second in terms of her duties, bringing these together at the end of that chapter.

On the question of the right of any competent adult to refuse medical treatment, DiVito PJ begins by citing the two prominent decisions to which I made reference in section II above, namely the *Union Pacific Railway* and *Schloendorff* cases, with their statements of the rights to self-determination and bodily integrity respectively. He then notes various Illinois authorities which protect a competent person's right to refuse even life-sustaining treatment, and observes that this right holds independently of whether the treatment is seen as risky or beneficial to the individual.[128] Next, he refers to the US Supreme Court's decision in *Cruzan* v. *Director, Missouri Department of Health*, in which (we saw earlier) the Court held that the Due Process

[123] 632 NE 2d at 332.
[124] *Ibid.*
[125] *Ibid.*
[126] This is not the "norm" identified in *Madyun*, but a third situation as described in section I(B) *supra*.
[127] *Ibid.*, 332, 333.
[128] *Ibid.*, 330.

Clause of the Fourteenth Amendment confers a significant liberty interest in avoiding unwanted medical procedures. DeVito PJ chooses to emphasise an aspect of the judgment of Justice O'Connor to the effect that the liberty guaranteed by the Due Process Clause protects, "if anything", a person's "deeply personal" decision to refuse unwanted medical treatment. He then cites the following passage from O'Connor J's judgment:[129]

> "Because our notions of liberty are inextricably entwined with our idea of physical freedom and self-determination, the Court has often deemed state *incursions into the body* repugnant to the interests protected by the Due Process Clause."

Having drawn attention to the individual's underlying interests in self-determination and especially bodily integrity, DiVito PJ turned to the individual's interest in religious liberty, noting that this was protected by both the federal and the Illinois constitutions, and cited an Illinois case on point in which it was stressed that religious liberty and the right to shape one's own destiny are among the rights "most valued by civilized man"; moreover, that the right existed regardless of whether the individual's beliefs were considered "unwise, foolish or ridiculous, in the absence of any overriding danger to society".[130]

The *Baby Boy Doe* court did not elaborate upon these interests and rights as they might apply to the pregnant woman in particular. Rather, it drew attention to the state right of privacy and the way this had been conceptually linked with the right of bodily integrity in the case of *Stallman* v. *Youngquist*,[131] in which the Illinois Supreme Court held that a pregnant woman did not owe a duty of care to her fetus in respect of unintentional prenatal injuries. This was the case which the court relied upon for its argument from *duty*. The ratio of the decision in *Stallman* v. *Youngquist* addresses both the rights and the duty points.

The *Stallman* court rejected a maternal duty of care toward the fetus in two ways. First, it said that such a cause of action would establish a legal duty on the woman's part "to effectuate the best prenatal environment possible".[132] On this point, the *Baby Boy Doe* court highlighted *Stallman*'s emphasis upon the *uniqueness* of the relationship between a pregnant woman and her fetus, particularly its observation that:[133]

> "No other plaintiff depends exclusively on any other defendant for everything necessary for life itself. No other defendant must go through biological changes of the most profound type, possibly at the risk of her own life, in order to bring forth an adversary into the world."

Second, *Stallman* made an important distinction between the idea of fetal rights assertable against third parties on the one hand, which it said advanced the interests of the mother and fetus but did not intrude upon a third-party defendant's right to

---

[129] 111 L Ed 2d 224, 249, my emphasis.
[130] *In re Estate of Brooks*, 32 N E 2d 435 (1965).
[131] 531 NE 2d 355 (Ill 1988).
[132] *Ibid.*, 359, *per* Cunningham J.
[133] *Ibid.*, 360.

control his/her life and, on the other, the idea of fetal rights assertable against its mother. In the latter case, the *Stallman* court held that a woman did not owe a tortious duty of care toward the fetus because this would "subject to State scrutiny all the decisions [she] must make in attempting to carry a pregnancy to term, and infringes on her *right to privacy and bodily autonomy*".[134] This is the "conceptual linking" of the rights of privacy and bodily integrity to which the *Doe* court refers. For these reasons, *Stallman* held that a woman cannot be under a legal duty to guarantee the mental and physical health of her fetus. Applying this position to the situation of compelled obstetric intervention, the *Doe* court considered that *Stallman*:[135]

> "directs that a woman's right to refuse invasive medical treatment, derived from her rights to privacy, bodily integrity and religious liberty, is not diminished during pregnancy. The woman retains the same right to refuse invasive treatment, even of lifesaving or other beneficial nature, that she can exercise when she is not pregnant. The potential impact upon the fetus is not legally relevant."

The thrust of the "no duty" argument therefore lies in the question of the extensive impact of legal duties upon, especially, the *rights* of the pregnant woman.

Importantly, in one sense, to argue that a woman does not owe a legal duty to the fetus because of her rights is to beg the question, why does she still have the right and not owe the duty? It is for this reason that, in Part I, I sought to draw apart these closely connected threads, trying to establish independently first, why she has the moral right and second, why she does not have the moral duty (in the first and second sections of chapter two respectively and in both cases where she has serious reasons for her refusal) before reuniting the arguments at the end of that chapter. The *Doe* court gives the barest hint, in fact, of why she has the legal right, namely because these interests in self-determination and bodily integrity are "deeply personal" (as *per* O'Connor J in *Cruzan*), and why she does not have the legal duty, namely because to subject her to such would be to intrude so greatly upon her life ("no other defendant" as *per* the *Stallman* court) through her interests in bodily autonomy and privacy. Ultimately, giving either of these reasons is tantamount to saying that she has the right but not the duty, and yet the whole process of justifying that right (or absence of duty) lies in the *expansion* of our understanding of the personal interests which support her right, coupled with a recognition of the context of pregnancy and any duties it may or may not create. This is the task I attempted and these are the kernels of the points upon which I elaborated at the level of moral theory in chapter two. The rest of the book builds upon these points in legal terms, through discussion of the maternal–fetal and other relevant legal cases themselves.

Returning briefly to my exposition of the decision in *Doe*, regarding the maternal–fetal cases of *Jefferson* and *Madyun* (which we saw earlier both denied pregnant women the right to refuse a caesarean section), the *Doe* court held that these were contrary to the rationale of both *Stallman* and *Re AC*, both of which reject any

---

[134] 531 NE 2d at 360, my emphasis.
[135] 632 NE 2d at 332.

balancing of maternal and fetal rights; further, that the courts in *Jefferson* and *Madyun* failed to recognise not only the "constitutional significance" but also the "magnitude" of a pregnant woman's rights.[136] These observations are in tune with my discussion particularly of *Jefferson* (in the early part of this chapter), notably in the scant attention such early cases paid to important principles of medical law. Moreover, as for the earliest case of *Raleigh Fitkin-Paul Morgan Memorial Hospital* v. *Anderson*, which concerned a blood transfusion, DeVito PJ stressed that "the court's decision regarding a forced transfusion cannot be persuasive in a case involving a forced caesarean section".[137] In this regard, it may be recalled that earlier in the chapter I traced the way back through *Re AC* and *Jefferson* to *Anderson* (a blood transfusion case), highlighting not only the way in which the invasion in *Anderson* could hardly have licensed that in *Jefferson* (surgery), but also the unprincipled basis of *Anderson* itself.

As for what the law should be regarding maternal blood transfusions, a matter left undecided in *Baby Boy Doe*, this is a question which was subsequently decided by the Appellate Court of Illinois in *Re Fetus Brown* (1997).[138] In this case, in an analysis which closely followed that of *Baby Boy Doe* and *Stallman*, the court held that *Baby Boy Doe* was wrong to characterise a blood transfusion as "relatively non-invasive and risk-free"[139] and thus ruled that a pregnant woman can refuse treatment as invasive as a blood transfusion. Presumably, however, a question-mark still surrounds treatment which cannot be characterised as invasive and invokes no religious beliefs or (if this were possible) privacy questions upon the part of the pregnant woman, in the light of the way *Doe* rests a woman's right to refuse treatment upon the rights to bodily integrity, religious liberty and privacy. I shall discuss this further in chapter four.

2. The Legal Status of the Fetus

Although the question of the legal status of the fetus received little overt attention in the *Baby Boy Doe* decision, the case made an important distinction between the maternal–fetal relationship on the one hand and the relationship between the fetus and third parties on the other. In this way, the decision implicitly recognised that the legal status of the fetus is affected by its location within a pregnant woman's body, particularly when its interests are being compared with hers, a point perhaps more clearly expressed in English law, as discussed below.

Thus, as we saw above, the court emphasised the uniqueness of the maternal–fetal relationship, citing in this regard the passage from *Stallman* (quoted above), to the effect that "[n]o other plaintiff depends exclusively on any other defendant for everything necessary for life itself". Importantly, however, the court stressed that the law

---

[136] *Ibid.*, 333.
[137] *Ibid.*, 334.
[138] 294 Ill App 3d 159 (Ill App 1 Dist 1997). The judgment was given by Theis J. Greiman and Zwick JJ concurred.
[139] 632 NE 2d at 333.

in Illinois did not regard the fetus only as part of its mother, noting that the fetus has:[140]

> "the legal right to begin life with a sound mind and body, assertable against *third parties* after it has been born alive. This right is *not* assertable *against its mother*, however, for the unintentional infliction of prenatal injuries."

In other words, the physical relation between the woman and the fetus is highly relevant to the determination of any liability on her part in respect of unintentional injury. This reasoning closely mirrors my arguments at the level of moral theory in Part I, where I distinguished the relationship between a pregnant woman and the fetus she carries on the one hand and a "detached" third party and that same fetus on the other. The *Stallman* court insisted that, whilst the "error" of considering the fetus as *only* a part of its mother had been corrected with regard to third-party liability for prenatal harm, it would not now make the error of "treat[ing] the fetus as an entity which is entirely separate from its mother".[141]

I shall discuss the other, secondary, arguments upon which *Baby Boy Doe* bases the right of a pregnant woman to refuse a caesarean section in Part III, notably certain arguments from the law of abortion and rescue, in addition to further points regarding the law of tort and the *Stallman* decision.[142] Regrettably the US Supreme Court declined to hear *Baby Boy Doe*, which means that the chance for a federal ruling on point was lost.[143] This lack, coupled with inconsistent state case law, means that US attorneys from states which have yet to decide this issue have difficulty providing legal advice on point.[144]

I now turn to the most important English decision on point.

B. *Re MB*

In *Re MB*, the English Court of Appeal held that a competent pregnant woman has the right to refuse *any* medical treatment needed by the fetus, rather than solely treatment as invasive as a caesarean section. The judgment of the court was given by Lady Justice Butler-Sloss, who stated:[145]

---

[140] 632 NE 2d at 332, my emphasis.

[141] 531 NE 2d at 359.

[142] Questions about the use of force were also raised, an issue I address at the end of ch. 4 and in ch. 7.

[143] The Public Guardian petitioned the US Supreme Court for an order remanding the matter to the circuit court. The petition was denied and two months later the US Supreme Court denied *certiorari*.

[144] As noted by JK Levy, "Jehovah's Witnesses, Pregnancy, and Blood Transfusions: A Paradigm for the Autonomy Rights of All Pregnant Women", 173.

[145] [1997] 8 Med LR 217 at 227, albeit technically in *obiter*. The court was considering an appeal upon the judgment of Hollis J. The court also comprised Saville and Ward LJJ. Butler-Sloss LJ gave the judgment of the court. It is worth noting that in principle a woman could also make an advance refusal to cover, say, the situation of her becoming unconscious after an accident. As with all advance refusals, however, it would have to be very clear that she intended the refusal to apply in the circumstances, following the principles laid down in *Re T* [1992] 4 All ER 649. Note that the Law Commission, in its Report No. 231 on "Mental Incapacity" recommended that "in the absence of any indication to the contrary it shall be presumed that an advance refusal of treatment does not apply in circumstances where those having care of the person who made it consider that the refusal: (a) endangers that person's life or (b) if that person is

"The law is, in our judgment, clear that a competent woman who has the capacity to decide may, for religious reasons, other reasons, or for no reasons at all, choose not to have medical intervention, even though . . . the consequence may be the death or serious handicap of the child she bears or her own death . . . The fetus up to the moment of birth does not have any separate interests capable of being taken into account when a court has to consider an application for a declaration in respect of a cesarian section operation. The court does not have the jurisdiction to declare that such medical intervention is lawful to protect the interests of the unborn child even at the point of birth."

The court reiterated and approved the view of Balcombe LJ in *Re F (in utero)*[146] (discussed below) that it was for Parliament, not the judiciary, to change the law if it saw fit.

The facts of the case are rather different from any maternal–fetal conflict case discussed so far. In essence, Miss MB, who was 40 weeks pregnant, "clearly"[147] understood and consented to the need for a caesarean delivery of her unborn child, but had a needle phobia which prevented her from consenting to the necessary anaesthesia. A great deal of the case, therefore, is taken up with the question of her capacity to decide and whether her needle phobia effectively rendered her incompetent. On these facts Miss MB was deemed incompetent, an aspect discussed below.

1. Rights and Article 8 of the ECHR under the Human Rights Act

The Court of Appeal first noted that it is both a criminal and tortious assault to perform physically invasive treatment, whatever the degree of invasion involved, unless a patient consents.[148] Second, it reiterated the position in *Sidaway* v. *Bethlem Royal Hospital*, outlined earlier, that a competent patient has an absolute right to refuse medical treatment "for any reason, rational or irrational, or for no reasons at all".[149] Next, the judgment observed that in an emergency medical treatment can be administered even where, because of a lack of capacity to decide, no consent had been competently provided, so long as the treatment is necessary and does no more than is reasonably required in the best interests of the patient (*Re F*).[150] The judgment then turns to consider the issue of capacity to decide, which I shall discuss in due course.

The court referred to American authorities, notably *Re AC* and *Baby Boy Doe*, concluding that they "do not point to a clear conclusion from which this Court might derive assistance . . . although we detect in the most recent trend in appellate decisions a move towards the approach of the English courts."[151] This is a somewhat ironic assessment of the American cases, when in reality it is only in *Re*

a woman who is pregnant, the life of the fetus". (Para. 5.26.) For recent related thoughts see N Peart *et al*, "Maintaining a Pregnancy Following a Loss of Capacity", (2000) 8 *Med L Rev* 275.

[146] [1988] 2 All ER 193.
[147] [1997] 8 Med LR at 220, *per* Dr F.
[148] *Collins* v. *Wilcox* [1984] 1 WLR 1172, *per* Goff LJ at 1177, cited with approval in *Re F (Mental Patient: Sterilisation)* [1990] 2 AC 1.
[149] [1985] 1 AC at 904.
[150] [1990] 2 AC 1.
[151] [1997] 8 Med LR at 227.

MB that English law can be said to come into line with one of the latest American cases on point: *Re S* essentially followed the approach in *Jefferson* and *Madyun*. Indeed, it is at this point of the judgment that Lady Justice Butler-Sloss takes the opportunity clearly to reject the approach of Sir Stephen Brown P in *Re S*, suggesting that he "was invited to rely upon an incomplete reference to *Re AC* (1990)".[152]

Lady Justice Butler-Sloss might also have referred to the jurisprudence pertaining to the European Convention on Human Rights in relation to a competent adult's right to refuse medical treatment, although neither the (then existing) European Commission of Human Rights nor the European Court of Human Rights had yet faced the question of a pregnant woman refusing medical treatment.[153] Indeed, she probably would have done had *Re MB* occurred a couple of years later in the light of the Human Rights Act 1998. The first part of Article 8 of the Convention provides: "Everyone has the right to respect for his private and family life, his home and his correspondence". If an applicant can show an interference with this right,[154] then, so far as Strasbourg jurisprudence is concerned, it falls to the state in question to try to justify this under Article 8(2):

> "There shall be no interference by a public authority with this right except such as is in accordance with the law and is necessary in a democratic society in the interests of national security, public safety or the economic well-being of the country, for the prevention of crime and disorder, for the protection of morals, or for the protection of the rights and freedoms of others."

Until recently (see below) it was understood that there is no right to privacy in English law,[155] but with the incorporation of the European Convention into English law by means of the Human Rights Act 1998 privacy reasoning will become an important feature of the law, since by virtue of the Act all courts will have to decide cases compatibly with the Convention (unless primary legislation prevents them from doing so or provisions under such legislation cannot be read compatibly with the Convention).[156] Further, courts considering a "question which has arisen in connection with a Convention right must take into account" Strasbourg jurisprudence insofar as the Court considers it "relevant to the proceedings" in question.[157] It should be noted, however, that the courts' obligation

---

[152]   [1997] 8 Med LR at 227.

[153]   To date the Court still has not; the Commission has, of course, been abolished.

[154]   Otherwise an applicant has no case, as *Dudgeon* v. *United Kingdom* 4 EHRR shows, in which the applicant alleged Northern Ireland's criminalisation of all homosexual behaviour was a breach of Article 8. Despite the fact that no proceedings had been brought in recent years, the Court noted: "In the personal circumstances of the applicant, the very existence of this legislation continuously and directly affects his private life: either he respects the law and refrains from engaging (even in private with consenting male partners) in prohibited sexual acts to which he is disposed by reason of his homosexual tendencies, or he commits such acts and thereby becomes liable to criminal prosecution". (Para. 41, footnote omitted.)

[155]   *Kaye* v. *Robertson* [1991] FSR 62.

[156]   S. 6(1)–(3).

[157]   *Ibid.*, s. 2(1). This does not mean that courts are bound to follow ECHR jurisprudence.

to interpret English law in ways which are compatible with the Convention does not create free-standing new rights.[158]

As regards the development of the right to privacy in English law, in 1997 the Lord Chancellor claimed that a right to privacy was about to emerge, since the judges were "pen-poised, regardless of incorporation of the convention to develop a right to privacy to be protected by the common law".[159] In the 2001 decision of *Douglas and others* v. *Hello! Ltd*[160] a right to privacy was recognised in two alternative ways. First, Lord Justice Sedley held that the claimants had a right to privacy protected by English law: "To say this is in my belief to say little, save by way of a label, that our courts have not said already over the years".[161] Thus, he held that the right is grounded in the equitable doctrine of breach of confidence. But a right to privacy:[162]

> "accord[s] recognition to the fact that the law has to protect not only those people whose trust has been abused but those who simply find themselves subjected to an unwanted intrusion into their personal lives. The law no longer needs to construct an artificial relationship of confidentiality between intruder and victim: it can recognise privacy itself as a legal principle drawn from the fundamental value of personal autonomy."

Alternatively he held that if he was wrong on the first point, then he would accept counsel's submission "that this is precisely the kind of incremental change for which the Human Rights Act is designed: one which without undermining the measure of certainty which is necessary to all law gives substance and effect to s. 6 of that Act".[163] Thus, it can now be asserted with some confidence that English law will recognise and give effect to a right to privacy. The remaining question concerns the meaning and scope of such a right.

With regard to this last point, the Strasbourg Court has generally avoided the need to define a core meaning of "private life", which has been interpreted in various ways, for instance[164] as including the right to "establish and develop relationships with other human beings especially in the emotional field, for the development and fulfilment of one's own personality",[165] as including sexual orientation and activity,

---

[158] J Wadham and H Mountfield, *Blackstone's Guide to the Human Rights Act 1998* (London: Blackstone, 1999) 32.

[159] HL Deb vol 583, col 784, 24 Nov 1997, as cited in KD Ewing, "The Human Rights Act and Parliamentary Democracy", (1999) 62 *MLR* 79, 94.

[160] [2001] 2 All ER 289.

[161] *Ibid.*, para. 125.

[162] *Ibid.*, para. 126.

[163] *Ibid.*, para. 129.

[164] D Feldman, "Privacy-related Rights and their Social Value", in P Birks (ed.), *Privacy and Loyalty* (Oxford: Oxford University Press, 1997) 15–50, 41. In turn this is consistent with the notion that the Convention is a "living instrument", the interpretation of which requires that the notion of "private life" will create new rights as social conditions require it: *Tyrer* v. *United Kingdom* (1978) 2 EHRR 1, para. 31. Indeed, the process of trying to produce an "exhaustive list" does not, as E Barendt observes, look "very sensible". E Barendt, "Privacy as a Constitutional Right and Value", in *Privacy and Loyalty*, 1–14, 13.

[165] Appl. no. 6825/74, 5 DR 86. The applicant wished to keep a dog, which certain regulations prohibited. See also *Niemietz* v. *Germany* (1992) 16 EHRR 97, para. 29, regarding the first part of this definition. The applicant's law offices were searched by German police looking for information about

which concern "an intimate aspect of private life",[166] and as protecting a person's "physical and moral integrity".[167] Overall, it has been held that the essential purpose of the article is to protect the individual from arbitrary action by the public authorities.[168]

As regards physical integrity several cases relevant to the issue of medical treatment have been brought under Article 8. In 1979 in *X* v. *Austria*,[169] for instance, which concerned a compulsory blood test, the Commission held that "[a] compulsory medical intervention, even if it is of minor importance, must be considered as an interference with the right." In *Herczegfalvy* v. *Austria*,[170] the Court decided that Article 8 was applicable in the context of the forced administration of food. More recently, the European Court of Justice has held that "the right to respect for private life requires that a person's refusal be respected in its entirety".[171] Thus, it can safely be stated that Article 8 encompasses the issue of physical interference with the person and decisions relating to bodily integrity.[172] It has been suggested that the article also covers self-determination more generally.[173] As regards the treatment context a recent Court of Appeal decision has recognised that "Article 8 protects the right to personal autonomy, otherwise described as the right to phys-

a third party who was the subject of a criminal investigation. The Court held it "would be too restrictive to limit the notion to 'an inner circle' in which the individual may live his own personal life as he chooses and to exclude therefrom entirely the outside world". At para. 29. For a defence of Art. 8 based on the notion of personality, see LG Loucaides, "Personality and Privacy under the European Convention on Human Rights", (1990) 61 *BYBIL* 175, who argues that freedom can only be effective if the individual can be self-defining and self-determining, hence that the relationship between the individual and the State or society must not be conceived in abstract terms but in a way which takes account of the personal qualities of the individual. This conception, it is argued, has been influential in the interpretation of the Convention. (At 177.)

[166] *Laskey, Jaggard and Brown* v. *United Kingdom*, (1997) 24 EHRR 39, para. 36. The applicants appealed against their conviction in the UK for various offences including assault and wounding relating to sado-masochistic activities over a 10-year period which were filmed on videotape on the basis that this was a violation of Art. 8. The Court found the convictions did not unjustifiably interfere with their private life. See further ch. 4, s. IV(C)(5) for a discussion of the notion of interference and its justification.

[167] *Costello-Roberts* v. *United Kingdom* (1995) 19 EHRR 112 (which concerned an unsuccessful application in respect of corporal punishment at a private school) para. 35, citing *X and Y* v. *Netherlands* (1986) 8 EHRR 235 (which concerned an application on behalf of a mentally handicapped young woman of 16 who had been raped at a special-needs home and the fact that the Netherlands' criminal law only recognised a complaint if made by the victim herself, of which she was incapable).

[168] *Kroon* v. *Netherlands* (1994) 19 EHRR 263.

[169] Appl. no. 8278/78, 18 DR 154, 156. See also Appl. no. 8239/78, *X* v. *Netherlands*, 16 DR 184, against the Netherlands, in which the Commission found that the compulsory taking of blood samples after a positive breathalyser test was an interference with private life. The Commission held that "[p]hysical interference, even minimum physical interference with a person against his will may raise problems in connection with this Article." (At 189.)

[170] (1993) 15 EHRR 437.

[171] *X* v. *Commission of the European Communities* (Judgment of 5 October 1994) Case C-404/92 P [1994] ECR I–4737, para. 23. The case concerned the refusal of a pre-employment AIDS screening test by an applicant wishing to work for the European Commission.

[172] See also L Doswald-Beck, "The Meaning of the 'Right to Respect for Private Life' under the European Convention on Human Rights", (1983) 4 *HRLJ* 283, 293; and H Nys, "Physician Involvement in a Patient's Death: A Continental European Perspective", (1999) 7 *Med L Rev* 209, 214.

[173] H Nys, "Physician Involvement in a Patient's Death", 214.

ical and bodily integrity . . . [and] a *patient's* right to self-determination".[174] But how would the European Court of Human Rights view the issue of treatment refusal during pregnancy?

One might first look to relevant jurisprudence on abortion. In the relatively early decision of *Brüggemann and Scheuten* v. *Germany* (1978),[175] the Commission considered that whilst the abortion decision invokes a woman's private life, some regulation of pregnancy was nevertheless consistent with respect for private life, since pregnancy "cannot be said to pertain uniquely to the sphere of private life".[176] The implication is that abortion regulation does not need to be justified under Article 8(2).[177] This approach has been widely criticised. In particular, the Commission reasoned that all Member States of the Convention regulate abortion in some way.[178] Louise Doswald-Beck, who notes in general "the extent to which the Commission is in practice affected by deep-seated attitudes", observes that not only is the notion that practice can determine the boundaries of rights troubling, but that the Commission also failed to consider that regulation of abortion might also be consistent with justified interference under Article 8(2).[179] The reasoning of the dissenting Mr Fawcett is generally preferred.[180] He rejected the majority's holding that "pregnancy does not pertain uniquely to the private sphere", holding that "'private life' . . . must in my view cover pregnancy, its commencement and termination: indeed it would be hard to envisage more essentially private elements".[181] He nevertheless held a certain degree of regulation of abortion to be justified under Article 8(2).[182] (In later decisions, the Court has avoided the problems of relying on a notion of a "private sphere" by adopting a value-based approach to the issue of respect for private life.[183])

Although the abortion jurisprudence is clearly relevant, I suggest that the issue of maternal refusal of medical treatment during pregnancy would be recognised as

---

[174] *NHS Trust A* v. *M; NHS Trust B* v. *H* [2001] 2 WLR 942, 954, *per* Dame Elizabeth Butler-Sloss P, my emphasis.

[175] (1981) 3 EHRR 244.

[176] *Ibid.*, para. 59.

[177] But see the strong dissent of Mr Fawcett, considered in ch. 4, s. IV(C)(5).

[178] *Ibid.*, para. 61.

[179] Of the decision, she writes: "It is clear that this case involved a highly controversial issue and therefore likely that the majority of the Commission came to their conclusion in order to avoid some acute problems." "The Meaning of the 'Right to Respect for Private Life'", 291. On the sensitivity of the abortion issue see also the decision of the Commission in *RH* v. *Norway*, Appl. no. 17004/90 (1992) in which the Commission observed, in relation to Art. 2, that it did "not have to decide whether the foetus may enjoy a certain protection under Article 2 . . . but it will not exclude that in certain circumstances this may be the case notwithstanding that there is in the Contracting States a considerable divergence of views on whether or to what extent Article 2 . . . protects human life." Observing the diversity of national views and assuming the relevance of the Convention, the Commission noted that "in such a delicate area the Contracting States must have a certain discretion." (Para. 1.) Art. 2 is discussed further below.

[180] E.g. by L Doswald-Beck, "The Meaning of the 'Right to Respect for Private Life'", 291; D Feldman, "Privacy-related Rights and their Social Value".

[181] (1981) 3 EHRR 244, para. 1.

[182] See further ch. 4, s. IV(C)(5).

[183] D Feldman, "Privacy-related Rights and their Social Value", 31.

being closer to the situation of treatment refusal and hence that Article 8 would be deemed, *prima facie* at least, to include a pregnant woman's right to refuse medical treatment. It is true that the Court has indicated (in the context of assisting suicide), that "the acts of aiding, abetting . . . are excluded from the concept of privacy by virtue of their trespass on the public interest in protecting life as reflected in the criminal provisions of the [Suicide Act 1961]".[184] Yet it has been suggested that the Court does not consider the right to life under Article 2 as more "fundamental" than any other right under the Convention.[185] (The jurisprudence in relation to Article 2 is considered in the next section, whilst Article 8 and the Human Rights Act are discussed further in the next chapter.)

This is the kind of analysis, then, in which the *Re MB* court might have engaged if it had considered the ECHR jurisprudence (beyond that which it considered in relation to abortion, as discussed below) when considering a pregnant woman's rights.

2. The Legal Status of the Fetus and Article 2 of the ECHR under the Human Rights Act

Returning directly to *Re MB*, the grounds for not distinguishing between the medical law rights of pregnant and non-pregnant women appear to lie in the legal status of the fetus, a topic addressed toward the end of the judgment. In other words, the essence of the decision in the passage cited earlier, is that a pregnant woman has the same right as any ordinary (non-pregnant) patient because the fetus has no separate interests until it is born and becomes a legal person. This is so "even at the point of birth". In this way the Court of Appeal appears implicitly to highlight the bodily integrity of the pregnant woman: since the fetus is inside her it cannot be protected by others against her. This becomes more apparent if we review the court's discussion of the legal status of the fetus.

In *Re MB* Lady Justice Butler-Sloss reviewed the English authorities on point, beginning with *Paton v. BPAS Trustees* (1979),[186] in which a husband failed to obtain an injunction restraining an abortion being carried out on his wife. In that case Sir George Baker P declared:[187]

---

[184] *R* v. *United Kingdom,* Appl. no. 10083/82, para. 13. The applicant, an employee of the Voluntary Euthanasia Society, had been convicted of two offences of conspiring with another to aid and abet suicide and two offences of aiding and abetting suicide, in contravention of s. 2 of the Suicide Act 1961. One of his allegations was that this breached his right to private life under Art. 8. Although it rejected this argument, the Commission did suggest that the private life of someone seeking to commit suicide (rather than someone aiding and abetting) might be invoked by this scenario. (Para. 13.)

[185] M Blake, "Physician-assisted Suicide: A Criminal Offence or a Patient's Right?" (1997) 5 *Med Law Rev* 294, 306, relying on *Open Door Counselling and Dublin Well Woman* v. *Ireland* (1992) 15 EHRR 244 (an abortion decision in relation to Art. 10). Note further that the reference to the protection of the rights and freedoms of others does not necessarily mean only the rights and freedoms under the Convention. L Doswald-Beck, "The Meaning of the 'Right to Respect for Private Life'", 308.

[186] [1979] QB 276.

[187] *Ibid.*, 279. The position in Canada, the United States and Australia is still in line with English law. The relevant authorities are: in Canada—*Tremblay* v. *Daigle* (1989) 62 DLR (4th) 634 (Can Sup Ct) and *R* v. *Sullivan* [1991] 1 SCR 489 (Can Sup Ct); in Australia—*Attorney General (Qld), ex rel Kerr* v. *T,* (1983) 46 ALR 275 (Aus H Ct); and the US—*Roe* v. *Wade,* 35 L Ed 2d 147 (1973) and *Planned Parenthood of Southeastern Pennsylvania* v. *Casey,* 120 L Ed 674 (1992). The last two cases are discussed in

"The foetus cannot, in English law, in my view, have a right of its own at least until it is born and has a separate existence from its mother. That permeates the whole of the civil law of this country . . . and is, indeed, the basis of the decisions in those countries where law is founded on the common law, that is to say, in America, Canada, Australia."

This position was reiterated in the 1987 case of *C* v. *S*,[188] in which a father, named as first plaintiff, sought to prevent his girlfriend from having an abortion of their unborn child, named as the second plaintiff. Heilbron J reiterated the views of Sir George Baker P and cited Canadian authority, to the effect that the unborn child is not a person and that any rights accorded to the fetus are held contingent upon its subsequent live birth.[189] Heilbron J emphasised that in various contexts, such as that of inheritance or prenatal injury, the claim of an unborn child "crystallises" at birth: only then, and not prior to this, could it be a party to a legal action exercising legal rights.[190]

The next prominent case on point is the decision in *Re F (in utero)*, in which the Court of Appeal had to decide whether it had the power to make an unborn child a ward of court in the light of a local authority's concerns about the lifestyle and mental condition of its mother. Lord Justice Balcombe[191] referred to the passages from the judgments in *Paton* and *C* v. *S* cited above, and to the position under the European Convention on Human Rights as established in the important case of *Paton* v. *UK*,[192] discussed below. Balcombe LJ observed that the only purpose of extending the wardship jurisdiction to include a fetus was to enable the mother's actions to be controlled.[193] In this regard, he took note of academic suggestions that a court would be able to prevent a mother from engaging in various activities, such as smoking or drinking or any other activity that might harm the unborn child. He also noted the possibility that a court might be asked to order that a fetus be delivered by caesarean section.[194] He observed that a judge could not make such a determination without legal guidance, stressing that it was for Parliament to amend the law if it saw fit.[195] The purpose of extending the wardship jurisdiction to cover a fetus was also addressed by May LJ, who noted that the orders that a court might make in such a case could only be against the mother, whose liberty would therefore be restricted. Thus, until birth, "there must necessarily be an *inherent incompatibility* between any projected exercise of wardship jurisdiction and the rights and welfare of the mother".[196] Finally, the sensitivities and complexities of

ch. 4. In ch. 6 note is made of a recent New Zealand decision—*In the Matter of Baby P (An Unborn Child)* [1995] NZFLR 577—in which a different legal view of the fetus was taken.

[188] [1987] 1 All ER 1230.

[189] In particular, *Medhurst* v. *Medhurst* (1984) 46 OR (2d) 263.

[190] *C* v. *S* [1987] 1 All ER at 1234.

[191] [1988] 2 All ER at 197–8. May LJ likewise referred to these decisions, at 195.

[192] (1980) 3 EHRR 408.

[193] [1988] 2 All ER at 200.

[194] This was noted by J Fortin, "Legal Protection for the Unborn Child", (1988) 51 *MLR* 54, 81, who refers to the US case of *Jefferson* in n. 16.

[195] [1988] 2 All ER at 200. May LJ made the same point at 196–7.

[196] *Ibid.*, 184, my emphasis.

the situation were well captured by Staughton LJ's statement that "[t]he court cannot care for a child, or order that others do so, until the child is born; *only the mother can*".[197]

Turning to *Paton* v. *UK* itself, here the unsuccessful plaintiff had sought to rely on Article 2(1) of the Convention, which states that "[e]veryone's right to life shall be protected by law". In considering whether Article 2 applied to the fetus, the Commission first considered whether the term "everyone", which it noted is not defined in the Convention, included the fetus and decided that, given the nature of limitations to the right to life, such as "[i]n defence of any person from unlawful violence", it did not.[198] Next, the Commission considered whether the term "life" (also not defined) in the first sentence of Article 2(1) only covers the life of those already born or includes also the fetus. In this regard, the Commission stated that attention must be paid to the "context of the Article as a whole" and noted that the term "life" may be interpreted differently in different legal instruments, depending on the context in which it is used in the relevant instrument.[199] Given that the *express* limitations upon the right to life clearly do not apply to the fetus, the Commission then considered whether Article 2 does not apply to the fetus at all, whether it recognises a fetal right to life with certain *implied* limitations, or whether the fetus has an absolute right to life.[200] Taking the last point first, the Commission rejected the notion of an absolute right to life on the basis that:[201]

> "The 'life' of the foetus is intimately connected with, and cannot be regarded in isolation from, the life of the pregnant woman. If Article 2 were held to cover the foetus and its protection under this Article were, in the absence of any express limitation, seen as absolute, an abortion would have to be considered as prohibited even where the continuance of the pregnancy would involve a serious risk to the life of the pregnant woman. This would mean that the 'unborn life' of the foetus would be regarded as being of a higher value than the life of the pregnant woman. The 'right to life' of a person already born would thus be considered as subject not only to the express limitations [in Articles 2(1) and (2)] but also to a further, implied limitation."

This would, however, "be contrary to the object and purpose of the Convention". Here the Commission noted that at the time the Convention was signed almost all the contracting states allowed abortion when necessary to save the life of the mother; moreover, that since then "the national law" on abortion had moved toward further liberalisation.[202]

The Commission then considered which of the two remaining interpretations of Article 2 was correct. In this regard, given that the abortion in question was carried

[197] [1988] 2 All ER at 201, my emphasis.
[198] (1981) 3 EHRR 408. Paras. 8 and 9.
[199] *Ibid.*, para. 16.
[200] *Ibid.*, para. 17.
[201] *Ibid.*, para. 19. This was stressed by Staughton LJ in *Re F (in utero)* [1988] 2 All ER at 201. The point is reminiscent of the *Stallman* court's emphasis on the intimate physical connection between a fetus and a pregnant woman. For a recent case of a father seeking to prevent an abortion, this time in Scotland, see *Kelly* v. *Kelly*, 1997 SLT 896.
[202] (1981) 3 EHRR 408, para. 20.

out when the applicant's wife was ten weeks pregnant and upon the medical ground of protecting her life or health, the Commission considered (and again it is worth citing the reasoning in full) that it was:[203]

> "not concerned with the *broad* question whether Article 2 recognises a 'right to life' of the foetus during the whole period of the pregnancy but only with the *narrower* issue whether such a right is to be assumed for the initial stage of the pregnancy. Moreover, as regards implied limitations of a 'right to life' of the foetus at the initial stage, only the limitation protecting the life and health of the pregnant woman, the so-called 'medical indication', is relevant for the determination of the present case and the question of other possible limitations (ethic indication, eugenic indication, social indication, time limitation) does not arise . . . The Commission considers that it is not in these circumstances called upon to decide whether Article 2 does not cover the foetus at all or whether it recognises a 'right to life' of the foetus with implied limitations. It finds that the authorisation, by the United Kingdom authorities, of the abortion complained of is compatible with Article 2(1), first sentence because, if one assumes that this provision applies at the initial stage of the pregnancy, the abortion is covered by an implied limitation, protecting the life and health of the woman at that stage, of the 'right to life' of the foetus."

Thus, assuming that the fetus might at least have a right to life during the initial stages of pregnancy, this is by implication limited in order to protect the life and health of the pregnant woman. Importantly, the decision in *Paton* v. *UK* thus leaves the question of to what extent Article 2 applies to the fetus very open.[204] Indeed, so far there is only authority for saying that the early fetus has at best a limited right to life in the light of threats to the woman's physical or mental health. Following the decision in *Paton,* P van Dijk and G van Hoof have observed with regard to the reasonable weighing of the rights and interests involved, "[a]s long as the question of whether Article 2 is applicable to the unborn life has not been answered in the negative, this reasonableness will have to be reviewed in each individual case".[205]

The Court of Appeal in *Re MB* also noted the decisions in *RH* v. *Norway* (1992) (extending *Paton* to abortions for social rather than health reasons)[206] and *Open Door and Dublin Well Woman* v. *Ireland* (concerning the suppression of communication of information in Ireland about the availability of abortions in the United Kingdom and thus invoking Article 10, the right to freedom of expression).[207]

As always, it will be harder to defend a woman's right to refuse treatment than to abort (assuming the generally voluntary nature of pregnancy in the former case). In the light of the judicial sensitivity to the interests of pregnant women which is certainly evident in cases such as *Re F (in utero)* it is difficult to evaluate how much

---

[203] *Ibid.*, para. 22, my emphasis.

[204] Of the decision FG Jacobs and RCA White observe: "It is difficult to conclude other than that the Commission was anxious to sidestep a controversial case." *The European Convention on Human Rights* 2nd edn (Oxford: Clarendon Press, 1996) 43. They also note, however, the lack of consensus amongst Member States of the Council of Europe on the moral and legal issues surrounding abortion.

[205] P van Dijk and G van Hoof, *Theory and Practice of the European Convention on Human Rights*, 3rd edn. (The Hague: Kluwer, 1998), 301.

[206] Appl. no. 17004/90 (1992), *supra* n. 179.

[207] (1992) 15 EHRR 244.

we should be concerned that the incorporation of the Convention into English law could bring with it the grant of a right to life to the fetus under Article 2. Some clearly think this a real possibility. Thus, Aileen McColgan has suggested that:[208]

> "whatever the approach taken . . . in *Re MB*, there are strong grounds to suspect that incorporation of the Convention may change the approach of the higher English courts in this area, while reinforcing the instincts of those confronted with medical declarations of impending doom."

At the same time, McColgan acknowledges that a caesarean section or a forceps delivery is far more invasive than the blood tests the Commission has previously authorised to protect the rights of others under Article 8(2).[209] More problematic, I suggest, might be a refusal of a less or non-invasive procedure, although such a refusal would presumably be motivated by reasons of "thought, conscience or religion" which might thus also merit the protection of Article 9.[210] Further, as regards a blood transfusion, the *Re Fetus Brown* court's recognition of the invasiveness of this procedure could be used in argument. Regarding the caesarean, a further line of reasoning which we could draw out from UK abortion law (briefly outlined below) could be that the risks (to the mother) of a caesarean being greater than those of natural birth, as discussed earlier, any right to life that also the late-term fetus might have would be subject to the need to avert risks to the mother's physical health. Indeed, noting the undeveloped nature of the relevant case law, Ian Kennedy and Andrew Grubb have suggested, with regard to the *abortion* context, that however Article 2 is understood, it is "most unlikely" that it would be interpreted in a way which fails to allow for a pregnant woman's rights to life and privacy, at least where remaining pregnant affected her *health*.[211] (On the question of the illegality of tradeoffs between maternal and fetal health in US abortion law in particular see chapter five.) As regards the *treatment* context, however, where physical health is not threatened by the proposed treatment, the question might then arise as to what "mental health" in the treatment, as opposed to the abortion, context might mean. Finally, since in any event Strasbourg jurisprudence in the form of the Commission's decision in *Paton* clearly rejected the suggestion that a fetus

---

[208] A McColgan, *Women Under the Law: The False Promise of Human Rights* (Harlow: Longman, 2000) 276–7.

[209] *Ibid.*, 279. *X* v. *Austria* (1980) and *X* v. *The Netherlands* (1979) mentioned *supra* n. 169.

[210] This might be implied from the European Court of Human Right's decision in *Hoffman* v. *Austria* (1994) 17 EHRR 293. The case concerned the issue of custody of children, rather than the refusal of medical treatment, but it was accepted in the Court's judgment that the applicant's position against blood transfusions was a direct result of her religious beliefs. The first part of Art. 9 reads: "Everyone has the right to freedom of thought, conscience and religion; this right includes freedom to change his religion or belief and freedom, either alone or in community with others and in public or private, to manifest his religion or belief, in worship, teaching, practice and observance." Limitations in the second part are "such . . . as are prescribed by law and are necessary in a democratic society in the interests of public safety, for the protection of public order, health or morals, or for the protection of the rights and freedoms of others."

[211] I Kennedy and A Grubb, *Principles of Medical Law* (Oxford, Oxford University Press, 1998) para. 11.92. Note that Art. 2 clearly imposes positive as well as negative obligations, as recognised most recently in *NHS Trust A* v. *M; NHS Trust B* v. *H* [2001] 1 All ER 801.

could have an absolute right to life, stating, as we saw above, that "the 'life' of the foetus is intimately connected with, and cannot be regarded in isolation from, the life of the pregnant woman", it would be possible to maintain the current legal position under *Re MB* and yet decide a case compatibly with the Convention. Of course, a new case on abortion (or a case on treatment refusal during pregnancy) could yet go to Strasbourg.

Returning to the reasoning in *Re MB* itself, the court also referred to the decision in *Burton* v. *Islington*,[212] a prenatal injury case, which gave no indication that the court should take into account the interests of the unborn child. This case is discussed in chapter six with regard to the relevance of arguments from the law of tort.

Lastly, certain statutory authorities were mentioned, notably the Offences Against the Person Act 1861, which makes it an offence to procure an abortion; the Infant Life (Preservation) Act 1929, section 1 of which establishes a criminal offence for the intentional destruction of a child, capable of being born alive, before it has an existence independent of its mother; and the Abortion Act 1967, section 1 of which (as amended by the Human Fertilisation and Embryology Act 1990) allows the termination of pregnancies up to 24 weeks in certain defined circumstances, and after 24 weeks where necessary to prevent "grave permanent injury to the physical or mental health" of the pregnant woman, or where continued pregnancy would "involve risk to the life of the pregnant woman greater than if the pregnancy were terminated" (as well on grounds of serious fetal abnormality up until the point of birth).[213] Here the court noted that although it might be "illogical" that abortions after 24 weeks are illegal (except in certain circumstances) but that a competent pregnant woman can (irrationally) refuse medical treatment even at the point of birth, this "appears to be the present state of the law".[214] I shall refer to this aspect again toward the end of the chapter. Lastly, the court referred to the Congenital Disabilities (Civil Liability) Act 1976, section 1 of which provides that if a child is born disabled due to certain specified occurrences, it may have a cause of action in respect of the wrongful act, but not against its mother, except in relation to her driving. (This legislation is considered in chapter six.)

In effect, then, both English and American law deny any legal personality to the fetus until birth, at which point any claims it may have had before birth crystallise, giving it legal rights assertable against third parties in certain contexts. Thus, with slightly different emphases, English and American law both recognise the impact fetal legal rights would have upon a mother's interests in self-determination and bodily integrity. As will be evident at various points in the book, the denial of fetal legal personhood is ultimately a choice against coercion of pregnant women. Although the extent to which her interests and rights in self-determination and bodily integrity would be affected would depend upon the nature of the restriction

---

[212] [1993] 3 All ER 833.
[213] Relevant aspects are discussed in ch. 5.
[214] [1997] 8 Med LR at 226.

or invasion in question,[215] the denial of fetal legal personhood is effectively recognition that, as Mary Ann Warren has written, "[t]here is room for only one person with full and equal rights inside a single human skin".[216]

3. Capacity

While my overall concern is with the right of a *competent* pregnant woman, it is pertinent to consider *Re MB*'s discussion of the question of capacity for two reasons. First, despite the legal presumption of an adult's competence, of the seven (reported) caesarean cases in England, competence has been in issue in six, including in the 1998 decision of *St George's*.[217] Second, with regard to two of these—*Re L*[218] and *Rochdale (NHS) Trust* v. *C*[219]—it has been suggested that the judges misapplied the *Re C* test by evaluating competence by reference to the irrationality of the woman's decision.[220] Indeed, as Andrew Grubb has observed and as the ensuing discussion is intended to show, "*Re S* may have gone, but all now turns on a woman's competence".[221] As an introduction to the following discussion, I outline the basis of the decisions in *Re L* and *Rochdale*, aspects of which will be considered below.

In *Re L*, another "needle phobia" case which pertained to the need for a drip prior to a caesarean section, Kirkwood J was of the view that the woman in question

---

[215] A similar point was recently made by the Court of Appeal for Manitoba in the 1996 Canadian case of *Winnipeg Child and Family Services (Northwest Area)* v. *DFG*, [1996] 10 WWR 111, affirmed on appeal by the Supreme Court of Canada, [1997] 152 DLR (4th) 193, which I discuss in ch. 6, as this case was concerned with the issue of maternal *conduct*, rather than with the medical treatment context.

[216] MA Warren, "The Moral Significance of Birth", (1989) 4 *Hypatia* 3. Reprinted in HB Holmes and L Purdy (eds.), *Feminist Perspectives in Medical Ethics* (Indianapolis, IN: Indiana University Press, 1992) 198–223, 213, emphasis in original. See also MA Warren, *Moral Status: Obligations to Persons and Other Living Things* (Oxford: Oxford University Press, 1997) 218, arguing that "birth is still the most appropriate point at which to begin fully to enforce the moral rights that the Human Rights principle accords to sentient human beings".

[217] The remaining cases not previously identified are: *Tameside and Glossop Acute Services Trust* v. *CH* [1996] 1 FLR 762, in which the patient suffered from paranoid schizophrenia and was admitted under s. 3 of the Mental Health Act 1983. Applying the three-part *Re C* test to the extensive evidence before him, Wall J held that the woman in question lacked the capacity to consent to or refuse the recommended caesarean. This is discussed *infra*. In a second case, *Norfolk and Norwich Healthcare (NHS) Trust* v. *W* [1996] 2 FLR 613, a woman with a history of psychiatric treatment arrived at hospital denying she was pregnant, but in a state of arrested labour. Johnson J held that although she was not suffering from a mental disorder within the meaning of the 1983 Act, she was unable to weigh the issues involved. In determining her best interests, S Michalowski has suggested that he effectively took account of the interests of the fetus, since, at the end of his judgment, he notes that his references to the "foetus" were meant to emphasise that it was only the patient's interests which were relevant, but continued: "However, the reality was that the foetus was a fully formed child, capable of normal life if only it could be delivered from the mother." (At 616.) S Michalowski, "Court-Authorised Caesarean Sections—The End of a Trend?", (1999) 62 *MLR* 115, 124. She suggests that in the light of the scarcity of decisions questioning the competence of adult patients "one might detect some judicial bias toward the incompetence of women in labour". *Ibid.*, 126. Of course only women can become pregnant.

[218] [1997] 1 FCR 609.

[219] [1997] 1 FCR 274.

[220] Mr Francis QC for Miss MB, in *Re MB* [1997] 8 Med LR at 223.

[221] A Grubb, "Commentary: Medical Treatment (Competent Adult): Pregnant Woman and Unborn Child: *Winnipeg Child and Family Services (Northwest Area)* v. *DFG*", (1997) 5 *Med L Rev* 125, 130.

suffered from "an affliction of a psychological nature that compelled [her] against medical advice with such force that her own life would be in serious peril".[222] On this basis he deemed her incapable of weighing the relevant information (the third element in the *Re C* test) and therefore lacking in the mental competence to make the decision to consent to or refuse the requisite caesarean.

In the *Rochdale* case, Mrs C refused a caesarean for reasons related to her previous experience of surgical delivery, particularly backache and pain around the scar. In particular, she said that she would "rather die" than have another caesarean. Despite the consultant obstetrician's view that Mrs C was competent to refuse the surgery, Johnson J concluded that she was not capable of weighing the information she had been given, thus failing the third strand of the *Re C* test. He said:[223]

> "The patient was in the throes of labour with all that is involved in terms of pain and emotional stress. I concluded that a patient who could, in those circumstances, speak in terms which seemed to accept the inevitability of her own death, was not a patient who was able properly to weigh up the considerations that arose so as to make any valid decision, about anything of even the most trivial kind, surely still less one which involved her own life."

As Andrew Grubb has noted, Johnson J's implicit suggestion that a woman in labour is *ipso facto* incompetent was received with considerable alarm, following which the Court of Appeal's judgment in *Re MB* represents a "calming voice".[224] It is therefore important to explicate the judgment in *Re MB* on this point. In this process, I shall submit that the decisions in the "needle phobia" cases of *Re L* and *Re MB* to override the women's refusals of the anaesthesia are defensible, but that the decision in *Rochdale* to override the refusal of a caesarean was probably not.

In formulating her conclusions on the issue of capacity, Lady Justice Butler-Sloss holds that a competent pregnant woman can refuse medical treatment "for religious reasons, other reasons, for rational or irrational reasons or for no reasons at all".[225] With regard to the issue of irrationality, she states:[226]

> "Irrationality is here used to connote a decision which is so outrageous in its defiance of logic or of accepted moral standards that no sensible person who had applied his mind to the question to be decided could have arrived at it."

---

[222] [1997] 1 FCR 609, 612.

[223] [1997] 1 FCR at 274. Discussed further in ch. 4.

[224] A Grubb, "Commentary, *Winnipeg Child and Family Services*", 130. An example of the alarm that followed the 1996 caesarean decisions, notably that of *Rochdale*, can be found in the writings of Barbara Hewson (now QC) a barrister subsequently involved in this case. Of Johnson J's decision in this case, she wrote that "he had effectively redefined when a woman was competent to take decisions over her treatment, and had ruled that a woman in labour was not". *The Times*, 16 Sep. 1996, 1. Additionally, writing early in 1997 after the ruling in *Re MB* (overriding the refusal of the anaesthesia) but before the Court of Appeal issued its judgment in that case, she wrote: "In future, pregnant women who reject their doctor's advice could be tried by judges, as witches were centuries ago . . . Pregnant women are seemingly a new class of 'incompetents', like coma victims, small children and the severely mentally disabled, over whom the state can claim total dominion." *The Independent,* 5 Mar. 1997.

[225] [1997] 8 Med LR at 224.

[226] *Ibid*.

At this juncture she drew upon the work of Andrew Grubb and Ian Kennedy to observe that a misperception of reality (for example, the blood is poisoned because it is red) will possibly be accepted as a disorder of the mind.[227] Importantly, it was stressed that irrationality, panic and indecisiveness do not in themselves constitute incompetence, but may be *evidence* of such. In this regard, she noted, the level of competence must increase commensurate with the gravity of the decision.[228]

a) *Impairment or Disturbance of Mental Functioning*

Turning to the test on capacity Butler-Sloss LJ held that: [229]

> "A person lacks capacity if some impairment or disturbance of mental functioning renders the person unable to make a decision whether to consent to or to refuse treatment: That inability to make a decision will occur when:
>
> (a) the patient is unable to comprehend and retain information which is material to the decision, especially as to the likely consequences of having or not having the treatment in question.
>
> (b) the patient is unable to use the information and weigh it in the balance as part of the process of arriving at the decision. If, as Thorpe J observed in *Re C* . . . a compulsive disorder or phobia from which the patient suffers stifles belief in the information presented to her, then the decision may not be a true one. As Lord Cockburn CJ put it in *Banks* v. *Goodfellow* . . . 'One object may be so forced upon the attention of the invalid as to shut out all others that might require consideration.'"

Reference was then made to the "temporary factors" discussed in *Re T*, notably confusion, shock, fatigue, pain or drugs. While these may "completely erode" capacity, she held that others must be satisfied that these factors are so powerful that the ability to decide is not present. On the question of "panic induced by fear", Butler-Sloss LJ stated that it would be necessary carefully to review the evidence, holding that "*fear* of an operation *may be a rational reason* for refusal to undergo it . . . [but] *may* also . . . paralyse the will* and thus destroy the capacity to make a decision".[230]

---

[227] [1997] 8 Med LR at 224. I Kennedy and A Grubb, *Medical Law: Text with Materials*, 2nd edn. (London: Butterworths, 1994).

[228] *Re T* [1992] 4 All ER at 661; *Sidaway* [1985] 1 AC at 904; and *Gillick* v. *West Norfolk and Wisbech Area Health Authority* [1986] 1 AC 112, 169, 186.

[229] *Ibid.* [1997] 8 Med LR at 224. The reference to *Banks* is (1870) LR 5 QB 549 at 569.

[230] *Ibid.* On this point, S Michalowski comments: "[I]t is surprising that the Court . . . distinguished between fear of an operation that may be a rational reason for refusing to consent to medical treatment, thus not excluding capacity, and fear that paralyses the will and therefore voids the patient's competence. It is submitted that the rationality of the patient's fear can be of no more significance than the rationality of other reasons of the patient. While it is perfectly true that fear can exclude capacity if it overrides the patient's ability to understand and weigh treatment information, the Court should not betray its own principles, *as irrational fear does not necessarily negate the patient's ability to consent to medical treatment.*" S Michalowski, "Court-Authorised Caesarean Sections", 118, my emphasis. In fact, I do not think the court is here suggesting that fear should be, as it were, checked for rationality. Rather, at this point the court seems to be acknowledging the rational foundations of an emotional reaction such as fear. Nevertheless, Michalowski is right that it does not matter, for the court's purposes, whether the fear is irrational or not. It only matters whether the fear is overriding capacity, for instance in the sense of paralysing the will. Michalowski also questions whether in fact the court simply found her "attitude to desire a Caesarean section but not at the price of having to endure a needle prick so irrational as to justify the conclusion that the patient was temporarily incompetent?" (At 119.) Given that a phobia

In seeking to explain the application of these ideas to Miss MB herself, Lady Justice Butler-Sloss reviewed the evidence and drew certain conclusions from this:[231]

> "She could not bring herself to undergo the cesarian section she desired because, as the evidence established, 'a fear of needles . . . has got in the way of proceeding with the operation.' 'At the moment of panic . . . her fear dominated all.' ' . . . at the actual point she was not capable of making a decision at all . . . at that moment the needle or mask dominated her thinking and made her quite unable to consider anything else.' On that evidence she was incapable of making a decision at all. She was at that moment suffering an impairment of her mental functioning which disabled her. She was temporarily incompetent."

It might have been desirable if the court had fleshed out somewhat more the link between the stated principles and the evidence. But perhaps it felt this was in some way obvious, given its reliance on the evidence of the consultant psychiatrist, Dr F. Miss MB had agreed to have the caesarean no less than five times in total. The operation did not proceed on either of the first two occasions because she did not want to give requisite blood samples. At the time of the third consent the anaesthetist visited her to insert a venuflon which she refused and the operation was cancelled. Later, a consultant anaesthetist visited her to discuss the possibility of anaesthesia by mask only, explaining the dangers of this (namely the increase in the risk that the patient may regurgitate and inhale stomach contents during the induction of the anaesthesia). She consented on this basis. Two days later she was again visited by the consultant anaesthetist who explained the risk of aspiration with the mask and she then refused consent. At this time "she was refusing to discuss her problems with anyone".[232] Labour then began and she was visited by her GP, who advised that "she was happy to go for the operation provided she did not feel or see the needle; did not have an IV line and did not have a catheter 'post-op' " (the fourth consent).[233] She was then visited by Dr F, the consultant psychiatrist, with whom she again agreed to consent to the operation. When she saw the mask in the operating theatre, however, she again refused consent. Before the court Dr F gave evidence that she was suffering from needle phobia which he described as an abnormal fear inducing a panic reaction in the face of a needle. His affidavit evidence makes repeated reference to the notion of panic, observing, for instance, that "[a]t the moment of panic, her fear dominated all". This is precisely the language Butler-Sloss LJ then employs in her judgment.

Applying *Re F* to the case at hand, Butler-Sloss LJ noted that best interests are not confined simply to medical interests. She observed that both parents wanted the child born alive and that Miss MB wanted the operation, apart from her

---

is an "abnormal" or "irrational" fear, *per* Dr F, even if the court did find her fear "irrational" this would not be significant in itself nor inconsistent with the stated principles of the judgment. Rather, the significance of her fear would consist in its paralysing effect on her decision-making capacity.

[231] [1997] 8 Med LR at 224.
[232] *Ibid.*, 220.
[233] *Ibid.*

needle phobia (discussed further below). She referred to psychiatric evidence which "strongly supports" medical intervention since she was "likely to suffer significant long term damage if there is no operation and the child was born handicapped or died".[234] She also noted: [235]

> "She would not suffer lasting harm from the anaesthesia being administered to her to achieve a desired result of the safe delivery of her child. She faced with fortitude, but equanimity, the pain and the risk inherent in the invasive surgery."

S Michalowski has suggested in relation to this aspect that the risks of anaesthesia were not sufficiently explored. I think, however, that this was not really necessary as part of the best interests assessment in this case given that Miss MB had no objection to anaesthesia *per se*, as opposed to the method of its delivery, as well as, of course, no objection to the burdens or risk of the surgery. Most interestingly, however, Michalowski suggests that the likely effects of enforced anaesthesia should have been explored (in conjunction, she suggests, with the risks of anaesthesia). Noting that Miss MB had avoided seeking prenatal care, she observes that this behaviour is confirmed by case studies on patients with needle phobia. She also notes that the phobia is apparently increased by exposure to needles in traumatic settings[236] and that treatment for the phobia must be based on trust.[237] Michalowski observes that consideration should also be given to alternatives to treatment involving needles (of course this was done in *Re MB* when the alternative of a mask was suggested) or to the possibility of assisting the patient in overcoming his or her phobia, citing a discussion of a case of a woman with extreme needle phobia which was sufficiently reduced in an hour that she was able to consent to treatment which involved needles. Her anxiety about future treatment was also decreased.[238]

Ian Kennedy has also written on the court's findings on capacity and their application to Miss MB,[239] and addresses with considerable concern the way in which the Court of Appeal may have succeeded in confusing, rather than clarifying, this issue. Yet he notes that—with further analysis—it may be thought that a patient's decision made on the basis of "needle phobia" is one which it is legitimate to disregard. To use the language of *Re MB* in which, as noted, Miss MB had no objection to the caesarean surgery in itself ("[i]t was never a case of her wanting natural childbirth. She wanted the surgical procedure to be over and done with")[240] her needle phobia may have "paralyse[d] her will"[241] in a way that made it impossible

[234] [1997] 8 Med LR at 225.

[235] *Ibid*.

[236] S Michalowski, "Court-Authorised Caesarean Sections", 121, citing J Ferguson *et al*, "A Rapid Behavioural Treatment for Needle Phobics", (1978) 166 *Journal of Nervous and Mental Disease* 294.

[237] *Ibid*., citing B Dennis, "Care Study: Severe Needle Phobia", (1994) *Midwives Chronicle & Nursing Notes* 58.

[238] *Ibid*., citing J Ferguson *et al*, 'A Rapid Behavioural Treatment for Needle Phobics'.

[239] I Kennedy, "Commentary: Refusal of Consent, Capacity: *Re MB (Medical Treatment)*", (1997) 5 *Med L Rev* 317. See further MJ Gunn *et al*, "Decision-Making Capacity", (1999) 7 *Med L Rev* 269.

[240] [1997] 8 Med LR at 221.

[241] *Ibid*., 224.

for her to consent to the requisite procedures. The way her actions relate to her autonomy are touched on below.

b) *Competence and Autonomy*

Moving back from the particular circumstances of Miss MB to the principles on capacity enunciated in the decision itself, in effect the judgment holds that those involved in a situation of treatment refusal must recognise that:

(a) Where a pregnant woman is refusing, say, a caesarean section for rational, irrational or non-existent reasons, she has the right to do so.
(b) However, they must also consider whether "some impairment or disturbance of mental functioning renders [the woman] unable to make" a treatment decision, either by interfering with her ability to comprehend and retain information or with her ability to use and weigh it.
(c) As part of this process, they must consider:
    (i)   whether any irrationality, panic and indecisiveness are, in fact, *evidence* of incompetence; and/or
    (ii) whether any fear and possible consequent panic are in effect paralysing the pregnant woman's will to decide in accordance with her own true desires; or whether any temporary factors such as confusion, shock, pain or drugs are completely eroding the capacity to decide.

Given that where obstetric intervention is not refused for religious reasons, the reasons for refusal may well relate to questions such as fear of the surgery in itself or of death as a result of it, this aspect of *Re MB* is extremely important and highlights the sense in which competence may in some circumstances be called into question by such issues. In practice, this will be an extremely delicate point.

i) Fear and Paryalsis of the Will

Re MB's discussion of competence can be related to my discussion of autonomy and reasons in chapter two and, in particular, my reference to the work of Julian Savulescu. He argues that we respect an individual's autonomy only when we respect her rational desires and, elaborating upon this further now, that an individual "rationally desires a course of action if that person desires it while being in possession of all the available facts, without committing relevant error of logic, and 'vividly imagining' what its consequences would be like for her".[242] This ethical analysis may capture something of the elements in the *Re C/Re MB* tests. The point I wish to make is that, consistent with Julian Savulescu's idea that, in effect, we may only pay lip-service to a person's autonomy when we grant a right based on their *expressed* desires, the needle phobia cases of *Re L* and *Re MB* can be seen as ones in which a person was not in fact choosing *autonomously*. In these cases, the women's phobias can be seen to have "paralysed their wills", so that their expressed desires— "I do not want the drip or the anaesthesia that will facilitate the caesarean", or

---

[242] J Savulescu, "Rational Desires and the Limitation of Life-Sustaining Treatment", (1994) 8 *Bioethics* 191, 191.

"I do not want the anaesthetic"—do not reflect truly autonomous choices. For this reason it was acceptable for the courts to override their rejections of the anaesthesia as refusals which were not in accordance with what the women themselves *ultimately*, rather than *immediately*, wanted.[243] Most importantly, neither of these women rejected the caesarean surgery in itself. This means that the involuntary invasion was only of the needle, not the surgeon's scalpel. In *Re L* itself Kirkwood J notes that, following the safe surgical delivery of her child, the woman in question "was delighted with the outcome, and . . . had expressed apology that she had caused many people so much trouble".[244] This reaction, which must always be closely considered, was consistent with her earlier statements that "she wished to be safely delivered of her child".[245] Similarly, in *Re MB*, "[i]t was never a case of her wanting natural childbirth. She wanted the surgical procedure to be over and done with".[246] In these cases, then, arguably others are actually *helping* the women achieve their own goals. Paternalism here, to use language of Ronald Dworkin's is "volitionally" rather than "critically" paternal.[247] Interestingly, it may be that approaching the cases in this way is an instance of the "care perspective", [248] touched on in the next chapter, in the sense that care should "facilitate" rather than "undermine" autonomy.[249]

ii) Irrationality—Evidence of Incompetence?
The case of *Rochdale*, however, is importantly different and, whilst it preceded *Re MB*, may highlight complexities in the application of *Re MB's* findings on the issue of capacity.

    In *Rochdale* the consultant obstetrician was clearly of the view that Mrs C was "fully competent" and that she could comprehend and retain the medical information as well as believe it. As Johnson J observed, she therefore satisfied the first two elements in the *Re C* test. However, in the judge's opinion, she failed the third

---

[243] This acceptance of a degree of paternalism would probably also be supported by a philosopher such as Joel Feinberg, who has been particularly preoccupied with autonomy—which he sees as being closely associated with making important life decisions—and paternalism, endorsing the latter where a person's choice is not fully voluntary. See e.g. *Harm to Self* (New York, NY: Oxford University Press, 1986).

[244] [1997] 1 FCR at 612.

[245] *Ibid.*, 610.

[246] [1997] 8 Med LR at 221.

[247] See S Guest, *Ronald Dworkin*, 2nd edn. (Edinburgh: Edinburgh University Press, 1997) 72. By contrast, if we prevented someone having homosexual relations we would be being "critically" paternal. For further thought suggesting that in these cases the women are not being coerced, see I Berlin, "Two Concepts of Liberty", in *Four Essays on Liberty* (Oxford: Oxford University Press, 1969) 122: "If I am prevented by others from doing what I could otherwise do, I am to that degree unfree . . . Coercion implies the deliberate interference of other human beings within the area in which I could otherwise act."

[248] M Verkerk, "A Care Perspective on Coercion and Autonomy", (1999) 13 *Bioethics* 358, 366: "In the care perspective, respecting autonomy involves coming to understand individuals in the light of their own self-conceptions and trying to see the world form [*sic*] their point of view. But respect for persons also involves taking account of both our connectedness and interdependence. Again respect requires not so much refraining from interference as recognising our power to make and unmake each other as persons and exercising this power wisely and carefully."

[249] *Ibid.*, 367.

element, in that he considered she was unable to "weigh up" the information. In other words, on his view, she could not appropriately balance her desire to avoid the pain and her feeling that she would rather die than have another caesarean, against both her own death and the death of her unborn child.

At this juncture, we come to a highly significant point about the application of the *Re C* test (essentially endorsed in *Re MB*) in cases of maternal–fetal conflict. In the case of the refusal of treatment by a *non-pregnant* woman, her *weighing* of the information only involves balancing the risks and needs as these concern herself. With regard to a doctor's or judge's concern that the patient is/is not able to weigh the information, the concern is only with the patient. By contrast, as we have already seen in different ways, the situation of a pregnant woman is considerably more complex, in that a pregnant woman must consider the effects of a refusal, not only on herself, but also upon her unborn child: two lives may be at stake, in respect of one of which the woman decides *qua* parent. This means that the question which others must consider, of whether she is able to weigh the information, is in turn much more complex. Indeed, when third parties consider her decision to refuse treatment in the light of the third element in the *Re C* test, it is likely that at some level they will weigh the connected, but also to some degree separable, interests of the woman and her fetus. Thus, whereas the "weighing up" by a non-pregnant patient is akin to a *rational* assessment of the medical options and consequences, in the case of a pregnant woman the weighing process becomes highly morally charged: reason here becomes deeply *moral*.

Moreover, in the light of the two lives that may be at stake in the case of a treatment refusal by a pregnant woman, *Re MB's* endorsement of the point in *Re T* to the effect that the level of competence must increase commensurate with the gravity of the decision, takes on an added dimension: a pregnant woman may, in effect, be required to be "more competent" than the "ordinary competent" patient because she is "speaking for" two lives, notwithstanding the lack of legal status of the fetus. Hence, although legally the effect of her refusal upon the fetus is irrelevant, the question of the impact of her decision upon the fetus may come in "through the back door", in the determination of her competence.[250]

---

[250] In the United States the issue of competence in this context has apparently been connected with the issue of ethnic diversity: the high proportion of women of colour whose refusals have been over-ridden, including the 25% for whom English was a second language, may be in point here. On this point, note an unsigned "Letter to the Editor" in response to the article by Kolder *et al* ("Court-Ordered Obstetrical Interventions"), asserting that these authors "skate over the issue of maternal competence . . . by declaring that "[c]ompetency is assumed by the law, and even a medically 'irrational' decision does not necessarily allow an inference of incompetency". As a matter of US (and English) law, Kolder *et al* are quite correct. The letter continues: "Maternal competency was established by a psychiatrist in only 3 of the 20 cases reported . . . No evidence is given that the other 17 mothers were fully competent in deciding against medical intervention . . . Yet, in 5 of the 21 cases in which the mother's first language was not English, maternal competency may well have been impaired by the women's difficulty in understanding the proposed obstetrical intervention." (1987) 317 *New Eng J Med* 1223. Whilst the letter obscures the point that competence is, of course, a rebuttable presumption, it does perhaps raise questions about the issue of competence in these cases. I touch briefly upon the ideas of race and sex discrimination toward the end of ch. 4.

To return to the *Rochdale* case, in deeming Mrs C incapable of "weighing up the information" (which included the likely death both of herself and her unborn child) Johnson J may well have effectively *balanced* the fetus's interests against hers. We saw that such a judicial weighing or balancing by a judge was rejected in *Baby Boy Doe* (based, particularly, on *Re AC*) which was approved in *Re MB*. I suggest, then, that *Rochdale* (which, we have seen, preceded *Re MB*) was wrongly decided, in that the issue of capacity here appears essentially to have been determined by reference to moral judgments inherent in the weighing or balancing in such a situation. On the facts of *Rochdale*, given that Mrs C said that she "would rather die" than submit to another caesarean, this aspect of *Rochdale* is actually obscured, in the sense that she would have preferred to die rather than have the caesarean which would most likely have prevented her, and her fetus, from dying.

In support of my supposition that Johnson J made the wrong decision in *Rochdale*, there is good and relevant evidence to suggest that Mrs C was able to "weigh up" the consequences herself. In the light of her prior experience of a caeasarean, she was clearly very able indeed to imagine the pain and general caesarean experience for herself. In this regard, we should note Thorpe J's conclusion in *Re C*, with regard to an anticipatory rather than a present refusal, that the patient in that case could make an anticipatory refusal "because in weighing the consequences of facing a future acute phase [of gangrene] without amputation he has the experience of a recent acute attack to guide him".[251] In the light of her previous experience of a caesarean, Mrs C's refusal of a second one is somewhat akin to the question of the anticipatory refusal discussed in *Re C*. Applying Thorpe J's view to her case, she could be said to be able to weigh up the consequences *at least regarding herself* (although it would of course be impossible to remember dying). As for the possibility of the death of her unborn child, by contrast, this was certainly an outcome that she had to *imagine*, rather than recall. Nevertheless, thinking of Julian Savulescu's idea of a patient being able "vividly to imagine" the consequences of a refusal (though not meaning to suggest that he would necessarily endorse this reading of *Rochdale*), it would seem that she should have been deemed competent in this respect: asked what would happen to her *first-born* child if she were to die, she said that her mother would look after her.[252] In other words, there was good evidence that she had realistically contemplated the outcome of her death.

Nevertheless, it may well trouble us that a woman could refuse a caesarean in the light of the backache and pain around the scar. What is significant about Mrs C's case, however, is not that she was offering *these* as reasons which she deemed sufficient to justify her own and the fetus's death, but rather that she actually felt she would "rather die" than have another caesarean. In other words, it is important to focus upon her feelings and what they reveal about her prior experience and the way in which this in turn affects her perception of a future caesarean: it is in this way that we appreciate the way her reasons relate to and are part of her. Indeed,

---

[251] [1994] 1 FLR at 36.
[252] [1997] 1 FCR at 275.

it may well be that the reasons of "back pain" and "pain around the scar" were simply the "tip of an iceberg", the core of which consisted in ideas and feelings she felt unable to articulate, at least to others. These were issues I touched on toward the end of chapter two. Given the intensity of these feelings, one may seriously question how a *forced* caesarean would affect her. In this connection, although Johnson J reports that during the hearing of the case (back at the hospital following attempts at persuasion) she in fact consented to the surgery, Mrs C is understood to have felt very pressured to do so.[253] This would in turn raise the question of undue influence, as discussed, for instance, in the case of *Re T*,[254] an aspect I consider in the next chapter when I turn to look at the issues of counselling and persuasion, when I shall touch upon the *Rochdale* decision again. In leaving *Rochdale* for the present, I note that, perhaps even more important than the issue of a woman's rights that such a case raises, may be the question of our intrinsic moral responsibilities to her. I refer to this aspect again elsewhere.

C. The Last of the English Caesarean Cases?

In *St George's Healthcare NHS Trust* v. *S, R* v. *Collins and others, ex parte S*[255] the Court of Appeal thoroughly condemned a series of events in which a pregnant woman who was refusing a caesarean was detained under the Mental Health Act 1983 and a judicial declaration was obtained to operate on her against her will. I hope that this will prove to have been the last of the English caesarean cases. The case is deeply shocking and deserves discussion in its own right. Importantly, it also illustrates the use of the Mental Health Act 1983 in this context.

Upon registering as a new patient at an NHS hospital in 1996, Ms S was diagnosed, at 36 weeks of pregnancy, with pre-eclampsia, and advised that she needed urgent medical attention, bedrest and admission to hospital for an induced delivery, without which both her life and that of the fetus were in real danger. Ms S (a veterinary nurse) fully understood the risks but rejected the advice. She was seen by a social worker, Ms C, approved under the Mental Health Act 1983 and two doctors, also rejecting their advice. After this, Ms C applied for her to be admitted to a mental hospital for assessment under section 2 of the Act. In due course, once again contrary to her wishes, Ms S was transferred to another hospital, which made an *ex parte* application to the court for a declaration dispensing with the need for her consent to medical treatment. This application was granted by Hogg J., and thereafter the recommended medical treatment, including a caesarean section to deliver Ms S's baby, was carried out. Ms S was returned to the mental hospital and two days later her detention under section 2 was terminated, at which point she discharged herself.

At the hearing in 1998, Ms S sought relief both by way of appeal against the grant of the declaration dispensing with the need for her consent to treatment, and by

---

[253] Personal communication: conversation with Ms Barbara Hewson (now QC), 24 Jan. 1997.
[254] [1992] 4 All ER at 662.
[255] [1998] 3 All ER 673.

way of judicial review of the decision that she should be admitted and detained in the mental hospital under section 2 of the Mental Health Act 1983, her transfer, detention and treatment at the second hospital, and her return to the mental hospital.

I shall first summarise the court's findings. Judge LJ[256] held that given the individual's right to autonomy and self-determination, a competent adult was entitled to refuse even life-sustaining medical treatment. Where the adult is a pregnant woman, her right is not diminished simply because her decision to exercise it may seem morally repugnant. In this case, the declaration entailed the removal of Ms S's baby from her body under physical compulsion, a procedure amounting to trespass. Further, the declaratory order was made on the basis of an *ex parte* application which had not then been instituted by the issue of a summons, had been made without Ms S's knowledge or any attempt to inform her or her solicitor of the application, without any evidence (oral or by way of affidavit) and without any provision for Ms S to apply to vary or discharge it.[257] Hence, she was entitled to have the order set aside, and thereafter to sue for damages two of the trusts involved in the case.

Judge LJ held further that the 1983 Act could not be deployed to detain a person against his or her will merely because her thought processes seemed bizarre and irrational and against the views of most members of society. Thus, detention on the basis of mental disorder could only be justified if the case fell within the prescribed conditions of the Act. Further, a person detained under the Act for mental disorder could not be forced to receive medical treatment unrelated to his or her mental condition unless he or she lacked capacity to consent to such treatment. Accordingly, Ms S's detention, treatment and transfer were all unlawful. Hence, the application for judicial review would be granted and appropriate declaratory relief ordered.

1. The Right of a Pregnant Woman to Refuse Medical Treatment

Although the facts of this case can fairly be described as a shocking example, however well-intentioned, of the deprivation of vitally important liberties, so far as the legal rights of pregnant women are concerned, one may ponder the significance of the decision given that, in one sense, the Court of Appeal in *St George's* is simply affirming its earlier finding in *Re MB* that a "competent woman who has the capacity to decide may, for religious reasons, other reasons, or for no reasons at all, choose not to have medical intervention, even though . . . the consequence may be the death or serious handicap of the child she bears or her own death".

So far as *St George's* contribution to the jurisprudence relating to this legal right is concerned, as we have seen, Miss MB was of course deemed incompetent on the basis of a needle phobia that led her to "refuse" the anaesthetic needed prior to the caesarean that was deemed necessary in her case. The Court of Appeal's decision

---

[256] The court also comprised Butler-Sloss and Walker LJJ.

[257] A declaration defines the legal rights of various parties and hence can only be effective if all parties are present.

in *St George's*, by contrast, related to criticisms of decisions which had already occurred. In this regard, chronologically speaking these decisions were made during the "legal limbo" obtaining between *Re S*, decided in 1992, and *Re MB*, decided in 1997, although, as noted before, the Law Lords in *Bland* had made no reference to an exception to the right to refuse treatment in the case of a pregnant woman. At the initial hearing in *St George's*, Hogg J was told of Ms S's admission for assessment of her mental and psychiatric condition under section 2 of the Act (see below); was incorrectly told that at the time of the hearing Ms S had been in labour for 24 hours; and was *not* told certain "highly material"[258] facts, such as that Ms S was thought to be competent, had been in touch with a solicitor and had not been told of the application, lapses which Judge LJ deemed "highly regrettable".[259] In these circumstances, he notes, Hogg J "decided that she should follow *Re S*".[260] One must assume that the arguable relevance of *Bland* on the question of a pregnant woman's right to refuse medical treatment was not drawn to her attention.

Having outlined the way in which the decision in *St George's* "relates to" that in *Re MB*, we can move on to reflect upon the discussion in *St George's* of a pregnant woman's right to refuse medical treatment, and then turn to consider the use of the Mental Health Act 1983 in this case.

In giving judgment on the appeal on this question, Judge LJ emphasised the importance of autonomy, noting, in particular, what one might call the "underlining" of this principle by various of the Law Lords in the case of *Bland*. Importantly, however, he held that "[i]t does not follow without any further analysis"[261] that the principle of autonomy entitles a woman to put the fetus she is carrying at risk. In due course he was to review and approve Butler-Sloss LJ's consideration of the legal status of the fetus in *Re MB*, (in such cases as *Paton, Re F (in utero)* and *C v. S*, none of which were cited in *Re T* or *Re S*), on the basis of which she held that, as in the different contexts at stake in these first three cases, the fetus's lack of legal personality until birth precluded its protection by the law against its mother.

Prior to this, however, Judge LJ noted the idea of the sanctity of life which was of concern in *Re T*, in which Donaldson LJ had (somewhat infamously) articulated the possibility of an exception to the right to refuse medical treatment in the case of a pregnant woman, an exception which, as we have seen, was realised—within a matter of weeks—in the case of *Re S*.

Thus, exploring—in a sense—the "limitations" of the idea that the fetus is not a legal person and hence is of no legal relevance, Judge LJ drew on another authority of interest which was not available to the court in *Re MB*. Turning to the House of Lords decision in *Attorney-General's Reference (No. 3 of 1994)* (which concerned the criminal liability of a man who stabbed his pregnant girlfriend),[262] Judge LJ

---

[258] *Ibid.*, 700.
[259] *Ibid.*, 701.
[260] *Ibid.*, 682.
[261] *Ibid.*, 686.
[262] [1997] 3 All ER 936. In particular, the Lords' rejection of the argument that the fetus was a part of its mother entailed a reconsideration of the application of the doctrine of transferred malice in this context. On this point, Lord Mustill held that "the defendant's malice is directed at one objective,

noted that "[w]hatever else it may be, a 36-week foetus is not nothing; if viable it is not lifeless and it is certainly human".[263] In this case, the House of Lords had criticised the Court of Appeal's conclusion that the fetus should be regarded as an integral part of its mother in the same way as if it were part of her body. Judge LJ cited Lord Mustill's rejection of:[264]

> "the reasoning which assumes that since (in the eyes of English law) the foetus does not have the attributes which make it a 'person' it must be an adjunct of the mother. Eschewing all religious and political debate I would say that the foetus is neither. It is a unique organism. To apply to such an organism the principles of a law evolved in relation to autonomous beings is bound to mislead."

This, coupled with a relevant observation of Lord Hope, prompted Judge LJ to make the important point, so often ignored in discussions of the maternal–fetal conflict, that "the interests of the foetus cannot be disregarded on the basis that in refusing treatment which would benefit the foetus, a mother is simply refusing treatment for herself".[265] Indeed, to make such a claim is ultimately both unhelpful and antagonistic, paradoxically doing nothing to further understanding of the needs, interests and rights of pregnant women in the medical treatment context, a point further considered toward the end of the chapter.

On what basis, then, does Judge LJ uphold a pregnant woman's right to refuse medical treatment when the pressure is on to protect fetal life? The answer is twofold. First there is the fetus's lack of legal personality. Thus, notwithstanding Judge LJ's wish to acknowledge that there is another being who clearly is not "nothing" inside a pregnant woman's body, legally speaking—as indeed Lords Mustill and Hope reiterate in *Attorney-General's Reference (No. 3 of 1994)*—there is no "other" whom the law can here protect against its mother whilst *in utero*. At various points I have suggested that the fact that the fetus is not a legal person is a point which is conceptually connected with its location inside her body: to protect the fetus in such a situation could only be achieved by means of a (non-consensual) incursion into her body. The law (when applied rightly) shrinks from this. Why? This takes us to the second reason upon which Judge LJ upholds a pregnant woman's right.

This, as might be expected, inheres in the principle of self-determination. At this juncture we should recall that Ms S refused medical treatment on the basis that she had "always held very strong views with regard to medical and surgical treatments for [herself]", wished to let "nature . . . 'take its course'", saw "death as a natural and inevitable end point to certain conditions", and was of the view "that natural

---

and when after the event the court treats it as directed at another object it is not recognising a 'transfer' but creating a new malice which never existed". It is beyond my scope to explore the complexities of this issue. See the discussion of the decision in A Grubb, "Commentary: Killing the Unborn Child: Abortion and Homicide: *Attorney General's Reference (No. 3 of 1994)*", (1998) 6 *Med L Rev* 256.

[263] [1998] 3 All ER at 687.

[264] *Ibid.*, (citing from *Attorney-General's Reference (No. 3 of 1994)* [1997] 3 All ER 936 at 943).

[265] *Ibid.*, 688. Andrew Grubb suggests that this "is a judicial statement of the 'Not-One-But-Not-Two' approach—of *de jure* unity but *de facto* separateness", citing I Karpin, "Legislating the Female Body: Reproduction Technology and the Reconstructed Woman", (1992) 3 *Columbia J of Gender and Law* 325 at 329. A Grubb, "Commentary: Killing the Unborn Child: Abortion and Homicide", 259.

events should not be interfered with".[266] In terms of my analysis overall (for instance in chapters two and four), it may be that these views could be seen as serious personal (rather than religious) reasons or values, but more would have to be known about the views of Ms S, who was of course suffering from "moderate depression".[267] Attention is drawn here to the particular gloss which Judge LJ puts on the principle of self-determination, which is worthy of note. Thus, he suggests that where the reasons for interfering with individual liberty are "readily understandable, and indeed to many would appear commendable",[268] it is all the more important to recall the "salutary warning"[269] of Lord Reid in the case of *S v. McC, W v. W*,[270] in which he explained English law's concern to protect the liberty of the individual, noting "[w]e have too often seen freedom disappear in other countries not only by coups d'etat but by gradual erosion: and often it is the first step that counts. So it would be unwise to make *even minor concessions*". Of course, as no doubt Judge LJ would acknowledge, in Ms S's case the concessions were anything but minor, but he was partly adverting, at this juncture, to the possibility that medicine may in the future develop to the point where a very minor procedure undergone by one person could save the life of another. In further support of the importance of not interfering with the individual's freedom to make his or her own treatment choices, including those which might benefit "another", he drew on relevant American authority from rescue law, namely *McFall v Shimp* (1978),[271] a decision discussed in chapter seven.

Additionally, Judge LJ's defence of a pregnant woman's medical treatment rights hinges upon the multiplicity and magnitude of the rights at stake in her case: he cites particularly the recent decision of the Supreme Court of Canada in *Winnipeg Child and Family Services (Northwest Area) v. G*,[272] in which the Court allowed an appeal against the detention under the relevant mental health legislation for treatment of a pregnant woman who was addicted to glue sniffing. In this case, McLachlin J, for the majority, took note of a Canadian Royal Commission report which stressed that judicial intervention to protect an unborn child against its mother "ignores the basic components of women's fundamental rights—the right to bodily integrity, and the right to equality, privacy, and dignity", noting, as had Balcombe LJ in *Re F (in utero)*, that it would be inappropriate for the courts to make such a radical change in the law. *Winnipeg* is discussed further in chapter six.

2. The Use of the Mental Health Act 1983

Consistent with the liberal underpinnings of the judgment and in line with a proper construction of the Act, Judge LJ deplored the use of the Mental Health Act 1983 to achieve the detention of a person such as Ms S simply because her thought

[266] [1998] 3 All ER at 681.
[267] *Ibid.*, 682.
[268] *Ibid.*, 688.
[269] *Ibid.*, 686.
[270] [1972] 2 AC 24, 43, my emphasis.
[271] 10 Pa D & C 3d 90.
[272] [1997] 152 DLR (4th) 193, 210.

process is "unusual, even apparently bizarre and irrational" and against the views of "the overwhelming majority of the community at large".[273] In this connection, he cited the case of *Re S-C (mental patient: habeas corpus)*,[274] in which Sir Bingham MR had drawn attention to the importance of the circumstances in which mentally ill people can be detained being very carefully defined by statute. In line with this point and, in a sense, with his emphasis (in discussion of the common law) upon the need to avoid "even minor concessions" being even stronger when the motives for doing so may be "readily understood", Judge LJ outlines what he dubs the "prohibited reasoning" which is "readily identified and easily understood": namely that "no normal mother-to-be could possibly think like that", that her "bizarre thinking" represented a danger to her life and that of her fetus, and hence that Ms S "*must* be mentally disordered".[275] It was this chain of reasoning which led, in Ms S's case, to her detention under the Act for her sake and that of her unborn child.

So far as Ms S's admission for assessment was concerned, Judge LJ carefully reviewed the provisions of section 2(2):

> "An application for admission for assessment may be made in respect of a patient on the grounds that—(a) he is suffering from mental disorder of a nature or degree which warrants the detention of the patient in a hospital for assessment (or for assessment followed by medical treatment) for at least a limited period; and (b) he ought to be so detained in the interests of his own health or safety or with a view to the protection of other persons."

As Judge LJ stressed, these two grounds are cumulative. In this regard, and crucially, he found that those involved in the decision to make an application for admission failed to keep separate the question of Ms S's urgent need for treatment arising from her pregnancy and the very different question of whether her mental condition— the depression which each doctor diagnosed—warranted her detention in hospital.

---

[273] [1998] 3 All ER at 692. For a US case with a broadly similar flavour, see *Re Steven S*, 126 Cal App 3d 23 (1981). In this case, a pregnant woman was originally certified to receive intensive psychiatric treatment for a maximum of 14 days, against which she requested judicial review. Her petition for writ of *habeas corpus* was later discharged when a district attorney advised the juvenile court that there was insufficient evidence regarding her mental illness. On this point, the California Court of Appeal (2nd Dist) observed that "[t]he District Attorney could have proceeded . . . but, by not proceeding, was in effect conceding that appellant was in fact sufficiently able to care for herself and not a danger to others". (At 528.) At the same time, a dependent child petition was filed on the basis that "she was unable to care for herself and for the unborn child" (at 528) which alleged that the fetus was a minor within s. 300 of the state's Welfare and Institutions Code and that the pregnant woman had an undiagnosed psychiatric illness. Whilst the latter application was awaiting a full hearing on the merits the juvenile court ordered the fetus and hence the woman to be detained under s. 320, but not after the birth of the child (which it had wrongly been told was imminent). At the hearing on the merits, the detention order was continued. The California Court of Appeal held that the fetus is not a "person" within the meaning of the statute conferring jurisdiction on the juvenile court to adjudge any "person under the age of 18 years" a dependent child of the court on certain specified grounds. The court also observed: "DPSS [Department of Public and Social Services] should not have been permitted to use a dependent child petition in the juvenile court as a basis for confining appellant to protect the fetus. We disapprove of the use of the juvenile court proceedings in the instant case which effectively detained the mother for approximately two months in circumvention of the state's mental health laws." (At 528–9.)

[274] [1996] 1 All ER 532.

[275] [1998] 3 All ER at 692, emphasis in original.

Thus, reviewing the evidence, he found that if Ms S had not been suffering from pre–eclampsia, an application for her detention would not have been considered, "let alone justified".[276] Hence, although he found that the requirements of section 2(2)(b) might have been fulfilled, the cumulative grounds prescribed in section 2(2)(a) were not established. Accordingly, Ms S's detention was unlawful.

Further, Judge LJ noted that even if Ms S had rightly been detained under the Act, she would not thereby have lost all her autonomy. As he makes clear, Part IV of the Act carefully sets out the circumstances of non–consensual treatment: under section 63 treatment may only be given *without* a patient's consent where it is treatment for the mental disorder from which he/she suffers and is given under the direction of the responsible medical officer, as, for instance, in *B* v. *Croydon Health Authority*.[277] In that case, the patient suffered from a borderline personality disorder, the symptoms of which included a compulsion to self-harm, which entailed a refusal to eat. The Court of Appeal found that treatment in the form of tube feeding was just as much a part of treatment for the disorder as that directed to remedying its underlying cause and hence fell within the ambit of the power conferred by section 63. In the *St George's* case, however, as Judge LJ notes, Ms S was "neither offered nor did she refuse treatment for mental disorder";[278] and, as a patient detained under the Act, she could only have been compelled to accept treatment *unconnected* with a mental disorder (by implication following the principle of necessity under *Re F*) if her capacity had been diminished, but it had not.

3. How Could this Case Have Arisen?

It is what Judge LJ dubs the "prohibited reasoning" which provides the key to understanding both how this case could ever have arisen and why it was wrong in law. As Judge LJ notes, the prohibited reasoning must be avoided both in relation to *consent* and in relation to *admission and detention under the Act*.[279]

As we have seen, in effect those originally faced with Ms S's refusal of a caesarean and her reasons therefor, concluded that she must be mentally disordered, deciding to detain her under the Act further to investigate their suspicions. Yet a person detained under the Act is not *ipso facto* incapable of consenting to medical treatment.[280] Nor, for that matter, was it assumed that Ms S *was* incompetent. Rather, as Judge LJ notes, beyond it being drawn to Hogg J's attention that Ms S had been admitted under section 2 for assessment, which was ongoing, with only "moderate depression"[281] being diagnosed to date, the question of her competence or incompetence *was never properly addressed*; indeed, as noted earlier, Hogg J was not informed that Ms S was thought to have the capacity to refuse medical treatment. To be sure, at some level those involved in the treatment of Ms S in *St George's*

---

[276] *Ibid.*, 697.
[277] *Ibid.*, 683. (*Croydon* is at [1995] 1 All ER 683.)
[278] *Ibid.*, 693.
[279] *Ibid.*
[280] See e.g. *Re C* [1994] 1 All ER 819.
[281] [1998] 3 All ER at 682.

were well aware that she was competent since, moments before the operation, she was still being asked if she consented to it. As Judge LJ notes, "if she was not thought competent at that stage, the exercise was a complete waste of time".[282] Whilst she had decided that to "struggle physically and be overcome would be undignified" in the face of the court order, as Judge LJ makes plain, "[t]his was not consent but submission".[283] In any event, whatever Hogg J may have thought on the issue of competence, it has been seen that she decided to follow *Re S*, which of course concerned a *competent* pregnant woman's refusal.

Thus, the "prohibited reasoning"—which in a sense amounts to an approach whereby capacity is judged by reference to the *outcome* of a patient's decision—on the one hand wrongly led to Ms S being detained under section 2 of the Act and, on the other, may have succeeded in obfuscating the legal issues at stake under the common law, perhaps subliminally increasing the pressure on Hogg J (in what she was falsely told to be an emergency situation) to follow *Re S* and thereby achieve the outcome in which both Ms S and her baby would live. That is to say, with more time or in the case of a pregnant woman regarding whom no "mental disorder" issues were (illegitimately) clouding the need seriously to consider and decide the competence issue, the implicit criticisms of *Re S* in *Bland* may well have come to light. By contrast, in the *St George's* case *it is as though*, given that the ongoing assessment of her mental condition under the Act might in due course have resulted in the conclusion that she had a mental disorder, those involved felt that *in any event* this was a case in which it would be "justifiable" to order a caesarean. *Legally speaking*, however, *this would be a nonsense*. First, any subsequent finding of a mental disorder would *not* preclude the need to determine her competence to consent to or refuse medical treatment. Second, as noted earlier, she could only be compelled to receive treatment unconnected with her mental disorder if she were incompetent. Moreover, in such circumstances, treatment could only be justified under the principle of necessity in *Re F*, a decision not considered at the hearing before Hogg J.

At this juncture, note might be taken of the much–criticised decision in *Tameside and Glossop Acute Services* v. *CH*,[284] which was not a decision mentioned by Judge LJ. In this case, which concerned a schizophrenic pregnant woman detained under the Act (and who was clearly incompetent), Wall J held that a caesarean section was treatment for the woman's mental disorder within section 63 of the Act. Yet, despite some evidence that the successful outcome of her pregnancy would benefit her mental health, as Penney Lewis has noted:[285]

"this interpretation gives an excessively broad scope to s. 63, potentially allowing non-consensual treatment for a wide range of conditions which are neither consequences nor symptoms of the mental disorder (as in *B* v *Croydon HA*) and yet could be said to affect the patient's mental disorder if not treated. This broad interpretation should be avoided."

[282] [1998] 3 All ER at 684.
[283] *Ibid.*
[284] [1996] 1 FLR 762.
[285] P Lewis, Law Notes, "*Tameside and Glossop Acute Services* v. *CH*", (1996) 7(1) *Dispatches* 4, 4.

Thus in *Tameside*, rather than finding that the caesarean was treatment for her mental disorder, it would have been preferable, if there were sufficient evidence to support the caesarean as being in the woman's best interests, to permit the surgery under the principle of necessity derived from *Re F*.

In its earlier stages, then, *St George's* might be seen as a case in which Ms S's choice was rejected in favour of an outcome driven by the desire to save her life and that of her unborn child. The events and decisions were fuelled and befuddled by confused and incorrect legal reasoning. In this process, although there was no explicit link between the common law position and the 1983 Act (nor could there properly be), at some level the misguided use of the latter may both have affected the quality of the consideration of the substantive position at common law and encouraged a rash of gross procedural errors.

There is much else that cannot be touched upon here, including the question of Ms S's transfer between hospitals, but note should be taken of the guidelines relating to the determination of capacity and the importance of *inter partes* hearings which the court included at the end of its judgment.[286]

Finally, insofar as the case adds to the jurisprudence relating to refusal of medical treatment during pregnancy, whilst the Court of Appeal can be seen in *St George's* to have made an important liberal statement about the limits of legal authority, stressing that a pregnant woman's right to refuse medical treatment is not diminished if others find her decision morally objectionable, it leaves unanswered, as indeed it must, the question of the moral justifiability of a pregnant woman's choice to exercise her legal right to refuse medical treatment. In this regard, Judge LJ simply suggests that "while pregnancy increases the personal responsibilities of a woman it does not diminish her entitlement to decide whether or not to undergo medical treatment".[287] In so doing, he could be said to be drawing attention to a woman's moral responsibilities toward the fetus, whilst stressing that her legal rights remain intact. In this way, the potential—though arguably by no means necessary—divergence between the moral acceptability of a woman's treatment decision (where this results in fetal harm or death) and her legal right in this regard is thrown into relief in a way which calls out, as far as possible, for an alignment of the two. Likewise the US decision of *Re Fetus Brown*, which we saw held that a pregnant

---

[286] With regard to these guidelines, however, John Grace QC has suggested that unfortunately "the issue of competence used to be, and still may be, in an emergency, decided on the basis of whether or not the obstetrician thought the woman was competent". J Grace QC, "Should the Foetus Have Rights in Law?", (1999) 67 *Medico-Legal J* 57, 62. A member of the audience, Dr Susan Bewley, an obstetrician, observed during debate following his talk: "[W]e have to see that our patient is competent every single time we operate, in our judgment. I think that we may not be there on the finer points of competence, and in most hospitals where you perform a Caesarean you can also get urgent psychiatric opinion to help you". (*Ibid.*, 64.) John Grace was counsel for the health authority in *Re MB*.

[287] [1998] 3 All ER at 692. Judge LJ also notes, at 687, that "[i]n the present case there was no conflict between the interests of the mother and the foetus; no one was faced with the awful dilemma of deciding on one form of treatment which risked one of their lives to save the other. Medically, the procedures to be adopted to preserve the mother and her unborn child did not involve a preference for one rather than the other." However, I do not think that anything turns on this, particularly since he proceeds to endorse the principle of self-determination.

woman has the right to refuse treatment as invasive as a blood transfusion, noted what it dubbed a woman's "apparent disparate ethical and legal responsibilities".[288] Similar concerns were voiced in *Re MB*.

D. The Remaining Ethical Dilemmas and Legal Perplexities

We have seen that in English law a pregnant woman has the legal right to refuse any medical treatment, for whatever reason or for no reason at all, whatever the consequences. Although she may do no *legal* wrong in exercising this right, how-ever, it does not follow that she necessarily does no moral wrong. Rather, as Brian Barry reminds us, "the exercise of either a moral or legal right is always open to moral appraisal and, potentially, to moral condemnation".[289] Indeed, to say that a pregnant woman is "within her rights" to refuse medical treatment may beg as many questions as it answers.[290] In this sense, although the observation of one prac-titioner (in 1988), that "[i]n Britain, fortunately, medical decision-making where the patient is competent is still a matter for the individual concerned and nobody else",[291] remained correct in 1997, as another writer observes in relation to patients who are pregnant women, "this simple rationale does not seem adequate".[292] Thus, despite the recent clarification of the law pertaining to the maternal–fetal conflict, Lord Donaldson MR's reflection in *Re T* to the effect that an instance of this conflict would present courts with a "problem of considerable legal and ethi-cal complexity" remains true.

1. The Importance of Justifying the Law

In *Re MB* itself, having both cited this observation and called into question the cor-rectness of the decision in *Re S* which immediately followed *Re T*, Lady Justice Butler-Sloss drew attention to the remaining ethical dilemmas.[293] Since consistency between ethics and law in such an area is highly desirable, making for broadly

---

[288] 294 Ill App 3d at 171. Here the court referred to an aspect of the US Supreme Court's decision in *Planned Parenthood of Southeastern Pennsylvania* v. *Casey*, 120 L Ed 2d 674 (1992), to which I shall refer toward the end of ch. 5.

[289] B Barry, "And Who is my Neighbour?", Review of Charles Fried, *Right and Wrong* (Cambridge, MA: Harvard University Press, 1977) (1979) 88 *Yale LJ* 629, 641, footnote omitted.

[290] The phrase "within [his] rights" is Barry's. *Ibid*.

[291] D Brahams, "A Baby's Life or a Mother's Liberty: a United States Case", (1988) *The Lancet* 1006, 1006, as cited in D Meyers, *The Human Body and the Law* (Edinburgh: Edinburgh University Press, 1990) 16.

[292] D Meyers, *The Human Body and the Law*, 17. Or, as the Royal College of Obstetricians and Gynaecologists has expressed the point, if somewhat unclearly: "A woman's 'right to decide' must surely be balanced by her obligation to her dependent fetus and renders her *morally accountable* if knowingly the child is harmed by her decision or indecision." RCOG Guidelines, "A Consideration of the Law and Ethics in Relation to Court-Authorised Obstetric Intervention", No. 1, April (1994) at 13, my empha-sis. I take this statement, which is a little unclear, to mean that whatever her *legal* rights, a woman is morally responsible for her decision to exercise these rights.

[293] [1997] 8 Med LR at 225.

socially acceptable law, it is most important that we can *defend*, and not just *assert* or plead for, a pregnant woman's legal right to refuse medical treatment, as for instance Sara Fovargue and Jose Miola have recently done, stating that "a competent woman *must* legally have the right to refuse a caesarean section".[294] The defence of a woman's right was a task which Butler-Sloss LJ suggested was beyond the role of the court,[295] but which I have suggested might be seen as the overall purpose of this book. As observed in the Introduction to Part II and elsewhere, that there is a need for such a justification is particularly apparent in the light of the increasing scope for medical intervention on behalf of the fetus. Thus, JK Mason and RA McCall Smith observe that the issue "is becoming more controversial as the opportunities become ever more feasible"[296] and M Oberman observes the "frenzied effort to analyze and resolve a burgeoning series of new 'conflicts'" during the 1990s.[297] Further, as a result of the publicity which has attached to these cases, there is now considerable public awareness of this issue. It is also conceivable that the issue could increase the pressures surrounding the issue of abortion, since, as Mason and McCall Smith also observe, an issue such as maternal refusal of medical treatment encourages people to rethink their views on the status of the fetus.[298] These points combine to suggest that a pregnant woman's right to refuse medical treatment is one which needs strengthening, by virtue of a clear justification, if it is to resist possible erosion in the future. This need within medical law is not unusual: in *Bland* Lord Browne-Wilkinson observed that, to be acceptable, the law relating to the termination of life support must "reflect a moral attitude which society accepts".[299]

More to the point for current purposes, as we have observed in the preceding discussion, within English law the *present* erosion of the right is clearly possible by means of a finding of incompetence. Margaret Brazier is similarly alert to this possibility and I find support for my observations and concerns in her work. She points out that of the factors which the Court of Appeal in *Re MB* suggested might induce temporary incompetence (such as confusion, shock, fatigue and pain) all are in many cases an "inevitable part" of giving birth, so that few women in labour could truthfully declare themselves to be fully competent in these terms.[300] Noting, as I have done, the higher degree of competence that may effectively be required of a pregnant woman in labour, she writes:[301]

---

[294] S Fovargue and J Miola, "Policing Pregnancy: Implications of the *Attorney-General's Reference (No. 3 of 1994)*", (1998) 6 *Med L Rev* 265, 295. (Emphasis in original.)

[295] [1997] 8 Med LR at 225.

[296] JK Mason and RA McCall Smith, *Law and Medical Ethics*, 4th edn. (London: Butterworths, 1994) 137.

[297] M Oberman, "Mother's and Doctors' Orders: Unmasking the Doctor's Fiduciary Role in Maternal–Fetal Conflicts", (2000) 94 *Nw UL Rev* 451, 453, citing home-births, mandatory HIV testing and the question of a pregnant woman's use of a living will.

[298] JK Mason and RA McCall Smith, *Law and Medical Ethics*, 110.

[299] *Airedale NHS Trust* v. *Bland* [1993] 1 All ER 821 at 877.

[300] M Brazier, Guest Editorial, "Hard Cases Make Bad Law?", (1997) 23 *JME* 341, 343.

[301] *Ibid.* Elsewhere Brazier has expressed her concerns as follows: "Foetus never equals child in theory. Yet at the very threshold of transformation from dependent foetus to independent living infant, the law and medicine may covertly combine to prevent a healthy foetus from suffering harm where any aspect of maternal behaviour can be seized on as evidence of her inability make [*sic*] an independent judgment." M Brazier, "Parental Responsibilities, Foetal Welfare and Children's Health", in C Bridge

"The way is left open to establish in a great many cases where women and doctors disagree about childbirth that the woman was incompetent so that what others consider in
her best interests and her child's interests can lawfully be done."

Strikingly, she continues: "Hard cases can be dealt with at doctors' and judges' discretion, ultimately undermining women's autonomy perhaps more significantly
than if formal recognition had been afforded to fetal status."

Further, extra-judicially Lord Justice Thorpe has suggested that, regardless of
commitment to patient autonomy to be found in legal principle, "at some level"
judges will be influenced by expert evidence about which treatment will result in a
live mother and child and that "[u]nless the recognition of this consideration is legit-
imated there is an obvious risk of strained reasoning".[302] Later he makes clear that
society must resolve this issue "through its democratic and legislative processes."[303]

These thoughts bolster the case for the need of a justification of the current law,
coupled with further consideration of the way in which maternal refusals should be
handled in practice. Indeed, given that the decision in *Re MB* was in effect clarifying the existing law, rather than deciding what it should be once and for all—in the
light of the endorsement of the view (first expressed in *Re F (in utero)*) that it was
for Parliament to change the law if it deemed this appropriate—then we might also
see the residual task as one of reasoning why Parliament should, or rather should
not, in my view, amend the current law. The arguments relevant to such a task are
necessarily broader than those pertinent to a strictly judicial enquiry.[304]

Additionally, with regard to the law in itself, as it were, I observed earlier that in
discussing the relevant statutory provisions, Lady Justice Butler-Sloss took note of
the apparently "illogical" state of the law, to the effect that whilst the fetus is protected from an abortion after 24 weeks (with exceptions) it is not protected from
the (irrational) refusal by its mother of medical treatment which would prevent its
death. In other words, it is desirable that the law's approach in these different areas
is explained, a task upon which I embark particularly in chapter five. A proper
explanation of the law also requires that the approach in different areas is defended.

2. The Tension between the Legal Right and the Manner of its Exercise

With regard, in particular, to the possibility of the *present* erosion of a pregnant
woman's right to refuse treatment, we have seen that *Re MB* holds that a competent pregnant woman may refuse any medical intervention needed by the fetus for
any reason, including an "irrational" one, or no reason at all. I described how the

---

(ed.), *Family Law Towards the New Millenium: Essays for PM Bromley* (London: Butterworths, 1997)
263–93, 280.

[302] Thorpe LJ, "The Caesarean Section Debate", [1997] *Fam Law* 663, 664.
[303] *Ibid.*
[304] As noted, for instance, by the court in *Tremblay* v. *Daigle* (1989) 62 DLR (4th) 634 (Can Sup Ct)
at 650, where it stated: "Decisions based upon broad social, political, [and] moral . . . choices are more
appropriately left to the legislature." A similar point was made by Lord Browne-Wilkinson in *Bland*,
who referred to the "moral, social and legal issues" which were appropriate for Parliament, not the
courts, to consider. [1993] 1 All ER at 879.

court stressed that the term "irrationality" might cover a decision which is outrageous not only in its "defiance of logic", but also of "accepted moral standards".[305] In other words, a pregnant woman has the right to make what might be
seen as an utterly immoral decision—the right to make a quite capricious choice.
We have also seen that "all now turns on the finding of the woman's competence".
In this connection, I noted earlier that the court in *Re MB* was of the view that irrationality may be evidence of incompetence and the way in which this aspect could
find expression, as for instance in the case of *Rochdale*. As has been noted, the decision in *Rochdale* is arguably evidence that it is not inconceivable that others might
evaluate competence by reference to the perceived irrationality-immorality of the
decision.[306] Thus, whilst it would now be clearly wrong under English law to
adopt such an approach, it is surely possible that at some level judgments about the
rationality or, particularly, *moral appropriateness* of a woman's reasons for refusing
medical intervention (given what is at stake for the fetus) might infuse the determination of her competence to decide, in turn prompting otherwise unnecessary
applications to the court for a declaration as to competence.[307] In such cases there
would, in effect, be a *tension between the idea of the woman's legal right and the manner
of its exercise.*

One way to account for the tensions or areas of residual concern to which I
allude here is in terms of the distinction between our *de jure* and *de facto* conceptualisations of the fetus and its relationship to its mother, an issue discussed by
Andrew Grubb.[308] To observe this distinction is to recognise that although the
fetus is not a legal person and thus has no legal rights assertable against its mother,
de facto we can distinguish in certain ways between its interests and those of its
mother. It is an approach which echoes, for example, Catharine MacKinnon's
description of the maternal–fetal relationship:[309]

> "More than a body part but less than a person, where it is, is largely what it is. From the
> standpoint of the pregnant woman, it is both me and not me. It 'is' the pregnant woman
> in the sense that it is in her and of her and it is hers more than anyone's. It 'is not' her in
> the sense that she is not all that is there."

Whilst in chapters one and two I rejected the idea of a fetus "abstracted", as it were,
from its very physical location *in utero*, with concomitant rights assertable against its
mother, I also dismissed as unhelpful the argument that since the fetus is not a person, it has no moral claims until birth. I stressed that maternal and fetal interests are
best understood in relation to each other and for this reason endorsed a gradualist

---

[305] [1997] 8 Med LR at 224.

[306] As noted earlier, this was argued by Mr Francis QC, for Miss MB in *Re MB*.

[307] The fact that attempts to secure court orders in the United States have disproportionately affected
women who are black, Asian or Hispanic (*supra* n. 1), for whom English may sometimes be a second
language, may well be relevant to this point. Indeed, the woman in the *Rochdale* case was Bangladeshi.

[308] A Grubb, "Commentary, Unborn Child (Pre-Natal Injury): Homicide and Abortion: *Attorney-
General's Reference (No. 3 of 1994)*", (1995) 3 *Med L Rev* 302, 307. (On the decision of the Court of
Appeal, not the House of Lords.)

[309] CA MacKinnon, "Reflections on Sex Equality Under Law", (1991) 100 *Yale LJ* 1281, 1316.

approach which, in addition to crucially linking maternal and fetal interests, acknowledged the question of maternal responsibility for fetal harm and hence the need for the justification thereof.

In a sense, then, just as the fetus's arguable lack of *moral* personhood was not the end of the matter *morally* speaking, so with regard to the law the fetus's lack of *legal* personhood need not be conclusive.[310] Indeed, that the law *does* already take account of the fetus's interests in various contexts is a point stressed by Andrew Grubb. Discussing the relevance and application of the distinction between *de jure* unity but *de facto* separateness to English law, he makes three points: first, the extent to which such an approach is more flexible than either the "unity of persons"[311] or the "separate persons" approach, in that it allows for a "sensitive accommodation" of maternal and fetal interests; second, that it reflects our popular conception of the maternal–fetal relationship; and third, that it is in fact already reflected in the law. For instance:[312]

> "when an abortion may be carried out; that the contingent interests of a fetus may justify a pre-natal injury action in tort or inheritance by as-yet-unborn children and *why the courts have genuine concerns when a pregnant woman's refusal of medical treatment may harm her fetus.*"

With regard to the last example, this passage was written prior to the decision in *Re MB*. In this connection, we might note that in *Re MB* the court (rightly) reiterated the *de jure* understanding of the fetus as a being with no legal interests before birth. Indeed, not to do so would have been to license invasions into those rights of the pregnant woman which the court wished to uphold, an approach which the court might be said to adopt on grounds both of principle and policy. Yet something of the concern with the *de facto* distinctness of the woman and the fetus may well be thought to linger in Lady Justice Butler-Sloss's reference to the remaining ethical dilemmas.

Further, we saw that in *St George's* Judge LJ noted that "[w]hatever else it may be, a 36-week foetus is not nothing; if viable it is not lifeless and it is certainly human" and that "the interests of the foetus cannot be disregarded on the basis that

---

[310] For a recent example of a writer assuming that all turns on personhood, see F DeCoste, "Case Comment and Note: *Winnipeg Child and Family Services (Northwest Area)* v. *DFG*: The Impossibility of Fetal Rights and the Obligations of Judicial Governance", (1998) 36 *Alberta L Rev* 725, 730: "Whether the fetus is, or is not, a person has of course everything to do with the moral consideration it is owed."

[311] This was the approach adopted by the Court of Appeal in *Attorney-General's Reference (No. 3 of 1994)* [1996] 1 Cr App R 351, in which the court had to consider whether the defendant could be charged with the murder or manslaughter of an unborn child, following his stabbing of its mother. It held that the requisite intent in the case of murder was an intention to kill or cause really serious bodily injury to the mother because, as Lord Taylor LCJ put it, "[i]n the eyes of the law the foetus is taken to be a part of its mother until it has an existence independent of the mother". (At 362.) The position in respect of manslaughter was appropriately modified. However, as noted in the text *supra*, the House of Lords subsequently rejected this position. Lord Mustill (with whom the other Lords agreed) held that "the relationship was one of bond, not identity. The mother and the foetus were two distinct organisms living symbiotically, not a single organism with two aspects. The mother's leg was part of the mother; the foetus was not."

[312] A Grubb, "Commentary, *Attorney-General's Reference (No. 3 of 1994)*", 307, my emphasis. See also the discussion in J Seymour, *Childbirth and the Law* (Oxford: Oxford University Press, 2000) 199*ff.*

in refusing treatment which would benefit the foetus, a mother is simply refusing treatment for herself". Sara Fovargue and José Miola have suggested that this latter observation shows a "lack of substance" in the judgment,[313] which, I think, is a misinterpretation of this point. As we saw, Judge LJ drew on the judgments in *Attorney-General's Reference (No. 3 of 1994)*, notably Lord Mustill's statement that the fetus "is a unique organism". Fovargue and Miola argue that these views are an attempt to "personalise" the fetus which "could lead to it being viewed as a separate 'patient' from the pregnant woman",[314] with attendant rights and interests[315] and consequently the erosion of pregnant women's autonomy. In particular, Fovargue and Miola are concerned that in *Attorney-General's Reference (No.3)* the House of Lords restricted the effect of the judgment to the facts of that case and thus left open the possibility of maternal liability for fetal welfare as a result of the criminal or grossly negligent conduct of the mother.[316] Indeed, these authors state that "[t]he intellectual gap left by the House of Lords . . . serves only to further personalise the foetus and *thus grant it the interests and rights of a legal person*".[317] Importantly, however, Lord Mustill observes of the fetus that "[t]o apply to such an organism the principles of a law evolved in relation to autonomous beings is bound to mislead",[318] a point which might well be interpreted as indicating some sensitivity as to the necessity of *not* granting the fetus a legal status, despite recognising its *sui generis* status. Fovargue and Miola also juxtapose two passages from Judge LJ's judgment in *St George's*, in the "first" of which he affirms his commitment to the principle of autonomy and in the "second" of which he observes that "each woman is entitled to refuse treatment for herself", but "[i]t does not follow without any further analysis that this entitles her to put at risk the healthy viable foetus which she is carrying."[319] But this juxtaposition is misleading, since in reality the latter passage comes before the former.[320] This means that in the second passage quoted, Judge LJ is effectively announcing an analysis of the issue which he is then "concluding" in the passage cited first.

As for Fovargue and Miola's concerns about the possible effects of the fetus being recognised as "not nothing", to deny that the fetus is "something" is much more likely to lead to this result, either through abuse of the concept of competence, or through a threat to the legal position on a woman's rights enunciated in *Re MB*. By contrast, a concern that the fetus is "something" might be said to capture what

---

[313] S Fovargue and J Miola, "Policing Pregnancy: Implications of the *Attorney-General's Reference (No. 3 of 1994)*", 287.

[314] *Ibid.*, 288.

[315] *Ibid.*, 287.

[316] *Ibid.*, 279, 289. For an excellent discussion of the uncertainties surrounding maternal liability following this case see M Brazier, "Parental Responsibilities, Foetal Welfare and Children's Health".

[317] S Fovargue and J Miola, "Policing Pregnancy: Implications of the *Attorney-General's Reference (No. 3 of 1994)*", 290, my emphasis. Thus, I do not share their concerns about the development and application of the law relating to unlawful manslaughter by pregnant women against their fetuses either in the "treatment" or "lifestyle contexts".

[318] [1997] 3 All ER 936 at 943.

[319] [1998] 3 All ER at 686.

[320] The latter is at 686, the former at 692.

JK Mason and RA McCall Smith describe as "an expression of an intrinsic public concern for the status of the fetus".[321] They highlight the need to find what they dub a "middle view"[322] in which, on the one hand, a woman is not reduced to a "maternal environment", as may well be the tendency if the fetus is treated as a patient with its own rights, and, on the other, the fetus is recognised as having an intrinsic value, such that it cannot simply be viewed as a part of the woman's body. Indeed, I rejected both these polarised views in chapters one and two in my formulation of a gradualist account of the maternal–fetal relationship. Strikingly, the language of rights, both maternal and fetal, has the tendency to heighten the sense of conflict, as the tone of my argument overall should make clear.[323] In the immediate and longer term, then, paying attention to and acknowledging the real concerns about the potentially damaging effects of a maternal refusal on the fetus/future child is much more honest and hence helpful to the debate than suppressing these. In this light, it is somewhat disingenuous of Dawn Johnsen to state of forced surgery that "[t]he *purported* justification for this extraordinary interference with women's liberty and bodily integrity has been the well being [*sic*] of the fetus",[324] as though the fetus might not very possibly be harmed by a refusal of treatment. Thus, to deny the possibility of a very real conflict is to sweep over the real concerns and tensions and thus to submit the current legal position to doubt and criticism.[325]

This is not to deny that the law should stand by a pregnant woman's legal rights, nor, a point which might be noted in passing, that there may be medical uncertainty

---

[321] JK Mason and RA McCall Smith, *Law and Medical Ethics*, 109.

[322] *Ibid.*, 110. The authors refer here to two quotations from a Swedish Government Official Report, "The Pregnant Woman and the Fetus—Two Individuals", SOU 1989.51.

[323] "Note: Rethinking (M)otherhood: Feminist Theory and State Regulation of Pregnancy", (1990) 103 *Harv L Rev* 1325, 1333: "The emergence of this language of rights . . . has fostered the characterization of pregnancy as an *inescapable conflict* between the fetus and the mother, a characterization that has come to define the parameters of the debate over women's reproductive freedom." My emphasis. Indeed, the conflict is surely not inescapable, but may on occasion be very real. The author continues: "Positing the woman and fetus as adversaries, this discourse has both obscured the degree to which state regulation reinforces gender hierarchy and undermined the development of effective policies for protecting maternal and fetal health". On this last point, see esp. ch. 6, which touches upon the notion of inadequate availability of prenatal care and the lack of treatment programs for pregnant addicts.

[324] D Johnsen, "Shared Interests: Promoting Healthy Births Without Sacrificing Women's Liberty", (1992) 43 *Hastings LJ* 569, 596, my emphasis. This article promotes a "facilitative" rather than an "adversarial" approach to the maternal–fetal relationship which makes sound policy sense but tends to obscure the very real moral conflict that may be presented in the medical treatment context as opposed, for example, to broader social concerns about drug-addiction or the different issue of *access* to medical care. See also K Knopoff, "Can a Pregnant Woman Morally Refuse Fetal Surgery?", (1991) 79 *Calif L Rev* 499, 502, who refers to "the doctor's perception of the fetus's needs".

[325] Compare M Oberman, "Mother's and Doctors' Orders", who argues that the term "maternal–fetal conflict" is inappropriate and should be replaced with "maternal-doctor conflict", since "these conflicts originate in the context of the relationship between the doctor and the pregnant woman . . . they result from doctors' seemingly well-motivated efforts to promote maternal or fetal well-being by imposing their perception of appropriate medical care on their pregnant patients." (At 454.) Whilst there is some merit in this view, I do not think that redescription in these terms can completely hide the fact that there may be a very real conflict between the pregnant woman and the fetus when she refuses treatment which, on the best medical judgments available, it apparently needs. This is not to deny the interest and value of a fiduciary duty analysis of this scenario in the US context.

about obstetric outcomes.[326] As Rhoden rightly notes, however, in discussing the *principle* of a pregnant woman's legal right to refuse a caesarean section or other treatment we must assume, for the sake of argument, that we are dealing with a clear medical need on the fetus's part and hence discount the issue of medical uncertainty.[327] John Seymour has written very clearly on the issue of risks:[328]

"[T]here exist well-recognised obstetric risks, which may or may not eventuate and may or may not be reduced or avoided by medical intervention. It is only in rare obstetric situations that it can be asserted with certainty that harm will occur if intervention is not undertaken. It can never be asserted that medical treatment will inevitably prevent it. What can be demonstrated in a particular situation is the existence of a *statistically verifiable risk* to the woman or her fetus. The fact that it does not occur in this situation does not mean that it will never do so. The fact that medical advice is not always correct does not mean that it is never correct. Overlooking these obvious propositions can lead to the misuse of anecdotal evidence. . . When harm does not eventuate, it is fallacious to assert that no risks existed."

It is thus unclear whether we can truly say that doctors are over-inclined to recommend caesareans,[329] although it does seem that the fear of litigation (in obstetric cases

[326] In this regard, it was earlier noted that in the case of *Jefferson*—in which doctors estimated that the chances of the fetus and the woman failing to survive vaginal delivery were 99 and 50% respectively—the woman subsequently gave birth vaginally to a healthy child.

[327] N Rhoden, "The Judge in the Delivery Room", 1960. Later in her article, however, she discusses "some of the limitations of the technology upon which doctors rely in predicting fetal harm" (at 2010). She notes that many of the instruments used to detect fetal abnormality have a significant error rate (at 1957, 2012-2013). Doctors thus tend to err on the side of safety. It is beyond my scope to review this technology.

[328] J Seymour, *Childbirth and the Law* (Oxford: Oxford University Press, 2000) 208, emphasis in original. On the question of "anecdotal evidence", note that Kolder *et al* allude to six cases in which doctors sought orders for caesareans which turned out to be unnecessary, including *Jefferson*. VEB Kolder *et al*, "Court-Ordered Obstetrical Interventions", 1195. Seymour thoughtfully comments on the possible conflict between a woman refusing recommended intervention and the health professionals as a "collision between two different perspectives". He continues: "Doctors are trained to anticipate and minimize risk. They will frequently take the view that it is good medicine to seek to avoid a known risk, even a statistically remote one; their instinct will therefore be to err on the side of intervention." (At 220.) For a different view, see B Steinbock, "Maternal–Fetal Conflict and *in utero* Fetal Therapy", (1994) 57 *Alb L Rev* 781. Steinbock notes the increase in caesarean rates from approximately 5% in the mid-1960s to more than 25% in 1988 (citing medical literature on point) and notes that "experts estimate that more than half of the one million cesareans performed in the United States each year are unnecessary". (At 792, footnote citing a *New York Times* report omitted.) She continues: "In light of these facts, a woman's skepticism about whether her cesarean is necessary may be entirely reasonable." See also L Miller, "Two Patients or One? Problems of Consent in Obstetrics", (1993) 1 *Med Law Int* 97: "The rates of and indications for Caesarean sections vary from country to country, hospital to hospital and clinician to clinician." (At 102, footnotes citing medical literature and reports omitted.) M Oberman, "Mothers and Doctors' Orders", lists the caesarean rates for countries ranging from the United States (at 24.7%) to the Czech Republic (at 7.8%) with the United Kingdom standing at 10%. (At 478, citing M Gabay and S Wolfe, *Unnecessary Cesarean Sections: Curing a National Epidemic* (1994)). Given the prevalence of medical negligence litigation in the United States it seems hard to discount the thought that the fear of litigation plays some role in the US rates. In the United Kingdom, rates have risen from 4.9% in 1970 to 11.8% in 1989. C Wells, "On the Outside Looking in: Perspectives on Enforced Caesareans", 247. Wells reports the US rate as having risen from 5.5% to 24.7% in the same period.

[329] Thus, although H Draper suggests that since a woman's decision is completely dependent on the skill of her medical advisers, they are obliged "to be sure" about their advice, it does not seem that certainty is possible. H Draper, "Women, Forced Caesareans and Antenatal Responsibilities", 332.

generally) is often relevant here. In this context, note that the ACOG has recommended that physicians obtain a second opinion on the risks.[330] Clearly a caesarean, partly in view of the increased risk of death it creates, should never be recommended out of fear of litigation, for financial reasons or for reasons of convenience but only in cases of best-judged medical need.[331]

The residual tensions which I have been discussing and which will—in theory and in practice—surround the application of *Re MB* (or, for that matter, *Baby Boy Doe*), have always been present in the maternal–fetal cases and literature.[332] Indeed, it is these which effectively account, in the early cases, for the court orders of prenatal interventions. I believe that at some level it is ultimately a tension between the assertion of a woman's legal right to refuse treatment and the way her exercise of that right may be viewed by others: is the right being exercised in a morally appropriate way, given the probable consequence of harm to the fetus or future child? The underlying tension can be seen in the work of two authors which predates the most recent cases, both of whom sought to resolve it by advocating compelled treatment in certain cases. For instance, as observed in Part I, John Robertson's work is strongly concerned with the "reasonableness" of maternal choices and the language of reason peppers his argument.[333] Importantly, and somewhat paradoxically, it might be noted at this juncture that there is an element of Robertson's "reasonableness" in the gradualist account of the maternal–fetal relationship which I have endorsed, in the sense that the notion of reasonableness seems to hinge upon some sense of *proportionality* between the interests and reasons of the pregnant woman on the one hand and the fetus's medical needs on the other.

---

[330] "Patient Choice: Maternal–Fetal Conflict", ACOG Committee Opinion, No. 55 (October, 1987).

[331] H Churchill, *Caesarean Birth: Experience, Practice and History* (Hale: Books for Midwives Press, 1997) 97.

[332] As we shall see in the next chapter, they also inhere in the abortion debate. Consider the following statement: "[W]e must not let anyone speak for women, for that is what speaking for the foetus is about: *speaking of/within a woman is to speak for the woman* . . . It is not the case that foetuses do not have a voice; it is simply that their voices—mother's voices—are ones that patriarchy does not want to hear." D Greschner, "Abortion and Democracy for Women: A Critique of *Tremblay* v. *Daigle*", (1990) 35 *McGill LJ* 633, 654, emphasis in original. Whilst my argument defends the view that women should be able to "speak for" their fetuses, it also tries to recognise, as others have acknowledged, that sometimes the woman may not always speak for the fetus in the positive sense which this scholar implies (and needs), namely when her choices or actions (unjustifiably) harm it.

[333] J Robertson, *Children of Choice: Freedom and the New Reproductive Technologies* (Princeton, NJ: Princeton University Press, 1994) 173–94. For example, with my emphases: "[I]f a medical procedure is moderately or minimally risky and intrusive, but will prevent great harm to offspring, it may *reasonably* be demanded of her, because of her obligation to act for the good of the person that she is choosing to bring into the world." (*Ibid.*, 179, regarding moral duties.) "Neither her procreative liberty nor right of bodily integrity give her the right to cause or avoid preventing *reasonably* avoidable harms to offspring that she chooses to bring into the world." (*Ibid.*, 180.) See also J Robertson and JD Schulman, "Pregnancy and Prenatal Harm to Offspring: The Case of Mothers with PKU", (1987) 17 (Aug.) *Hastings CR* 23. Despite recognising that caesarean sections impose an increased risk of death upon the mother, they observe: "However, one could argue that willful refusal of cesarean section is so irresponsible as to justify prenatal child abuse charges when the child is born with extensive brain damage that the cesarean section would have prevented." They add, as though the point were entirely secondary: "But a clear medical need that *reasonable* persons would not refuse would have to be established." (At 28, my emphasis.) The use of the word "willful" is questionable.

Yet the difficulty with Robertson's analysis may lie in its links with a utilitarian framework in which, broadly speaking, there may be no grounds for giving special weight to certain kinds of interests and reasons. Indeed, since his approach assumes that any reasons can be assessed by the standard of reasonableness, his analysis does not appreciate the difficulty of attempting to judge the serious personal reason. As will be confirmed in the next chapter, it is this difficulty which partly accounts for the grant of legal rights in such contexts.

Another scholar, Robert Blank, tries to resolve the underlying tensions by setting the maternal–fetal cases *within* the tort framework, considering the law of treatment refusal *along the way*, as it were.[334] He sees his purpose, then, as *defining the standard of care* in pregnancy.[335] Such an approach is akin to that which is foundational in the law of negligence. Yet, so far as physical harm to others is concerned, the law of negligence, as we shall observe in chapter six, is geared toward setting limits to what I dubbed "general conduct" in Part I. In this process, it hinges upon the judgment of the conduct of the hypothetical "reasonable person". As discussed in Part I, this is precisely the kind of judgment that is often inappropriate, if not impossible, in the face of the very personal interests and rights with which we are concerned in the medical law context.

As the discussion in the next chapter is intended to show, however, there are other ways of resolving these tensions than by overriding a pregnant woman's rights, or—which amounts to the same—by (incorrectly) deeming a woman to be incompetent. Thus, the critical issue is to give some consideration to the fetus's medical needs in ways which do not override a pregnant woman's rights.

3. Starting to Link the Ethics and the Law

In the following chapter I begin to attempt the critical legal synthesis of the ethics and the law relating to the maternal refusal of medical treatment. So far as the forthcoming chapter is concerned, this has two central components.

a) *Recognising the Likely Connection between the Serious Reason and the Right*

First, the connections between the serious reason for refusing treatment and the right to do so—and hence the justification of harm to the fetus—must be developed and understood within the law itself. Otherwise ethical dilemmas about the "*de facto* fetus" are likely to remain, if not multiply, particularly in the light of the increasing scope for *in utero* interventions. This will not be good for the law, for pregnant women, or, indeed, for society at large. In other words, without recognition of this point of connection, discomfort is likely to surround the result in *Re MB, St George's* or *Baby Boy Doe*, prompting criticism of the law and perhaps a lack of ease in its application, either in hospitals or at court in the event of a declaration as to competence being sought. Reflecting on the legal cases of maternal–fetal

---

[334] R Blank, "Emerging Notions of Women's Rights and Responsibilities During Gestation", (1986) 7 *J Leg Med* 441.
[335] *Ibid.*, 443.

conflict introduced in this chapter, we might note that in these cases, the pregnant woman's reasons for refusing medical treatment were apparently serious, in the sense that the reasons were either religious (the cases of *Jefferson, Madyun, Re S, Baby Boy Doe, Re Fetus Brown*) or concerned an important aspect of her self-determination, such as the question of the manner of her death (*Re AC*). As I argued in Part I, where a woman's reasons for refusal are seriously connected with her bodily integrity or self-determination, rights can be seen to protect important *interests* on her part. Thus, her right to refuse treatment is not simply about protecting her *choice*, though the exercise of the right is of course a matter of choice on her part. These ideas are developed in explicitly legal terms in the next chapter.

b) *Exercising the Right—the Scope for Third-Party Involvement*

Second, I also took note in Part I of the hypothetical case of a pregnant woman's trivial or non-existent reason for refusing treatment and suggested that in such a case—given our concerns for the *de facto* interests of the fetus—then counselling and even persuasion (in circumstances to be strictly defined in the following chapter and which exclude the caesarean section where a woman's own life is *not* at risk without it) may be appropriate because no important maternal interests seem to be invoked. Importantly, with regard to the issue of counselling and persuasion, the court in *Re MB* considered that where a competent woman refuses medical intervention doctors could "attempt to persuade her", but that anything more than this would be unlawful. Thus, *Re MB* effectively legitimises persuasion, but without specifying in which cases this is more or less appropriate or what form this can take. Since it does not detail these points, the decision thus leaves open the critical question of what degree of persuasion is *consistent with* a competent pregnant woman's possession of the legal right to refuse medical treatment. In this respect, a health professional interviewed in connection with the publicity surrounding the most recent English caesarean decision described how in most cases there was a consensus of views about treatment between pregnant women, obstetricians and midwives, but in those few cases where this was not so "heavy duty persuasion usually works" although, at the end of the day, the "woman's wishes" must be accepted.[336] As we shall see in the next chapter, the important question of the circumstances in which persuasion is appropriate, its strength and its relation to and effect upon a woman's rights has been the focus of considerable attention in American (abortion) law.

IV. CONCLUSIONS

This chapter has introduced the leading maternal–fetal cases, exploring the weak basis for the early precedents for forced obstetric intervention and the extent to which these were at odds with the developments in the medical law rights of the

---

[336] Interviewed on BBC 1 *News* at 9pm, 7 May 1998. (No name given.)

ordinary competent patient. Consideration of the most recent maternal–fetal cases in the latter half of the chapter has shown that the legal rights of pregnant women in England and in some US states are now, in theory at least, as sure as those of her non-pregnant counterparts (save that the question of refusals of non-invasive treatment appears to remain open in the United States and numerous states have yet to consider the issue). Yet, in the light of the undeniable difference between a pregnant and a non-pregnant patient—that one carries a fetus or future child and the other does not—an ethical justification (beyond the denial of the legal personality of the fetus) of why a pregnant woman should have the legal right to refuse medical treatment is surely desirable. For, as Robin West has written with regard to rights generally and reproductive rights in particular, although the possession of such "insular rights" is ultimately a mark of freedom, "those same rights distance their holder from the society against which they are exercised".[337] In the next chapter, I will explore the reduction of this distance within the law itself, building upon the ethical arguments of Part I.

Justifying a woman's *right* in this way is to attend to her relationship toward and responsibility for the fetus, a topic which forms the heart of chapter four. The remainder of the book consolidates our understanding and acceptance of the current legal position by approaching the issue in terms of the idea of *duty*. Thus, for instance in Part III, determining that there can be no legal duty to accept treatment for the fetus is established through reflection on the difficulties of determining whether a duty (moral or legal) lies—the problem of the interface between rights and duties which I have suggested lies at the heart of the maternal–fetal conflict in the medical treatment context. Finally, upholding a pregnant woman's right (*whatever* the reasons for refusal) in the light, say, of her interest in bodily integrity, is to attend to the strength of this interest and, in particular, to the moral problems, explored in chapter seven, of invading a woman's body against her will. The conclusion that pregnant women should have medical law rights throughout pregnancy can also be defended in policy terms, by attending to the wider effects on expectant mothers of compelling medical treatment for the sake of the fetus, an issue touched upon in chapters six and seven.

---

[337] R West, "Taking Freedom Seriously", (1990) 104 *Harvard L Rev* 43, 106. I return to this important article in ch. 4.

4

Understanding the Values Underlying and Justifying a Pregnant Woman's Legal Right to Refuse Treatment

A. The State Interests at Play

T HIS CHAPTER seeks to explore and justify a pregnant woman's legal right to refuse medical treatment, surgery or therapy needed by the fetus by examining aspects of the values inherent in the right of any competent adult patient to refuse medical treatment on the one hand, and in a woman's right to abort on the other, as these are explicated within the relevant US law. This does not mean that the discussion is of no relevance to the English position. Rather, as this introduction outlines, it is simply that it is primarily in the US law that we find discussion of these values. I suggest that the process of understanding why a pregnant woman should have the legal right to refuse medical treatment properly begins with a consideration of the development of the ordinary competent patient's right to refuse life-sustaining medical treatment. In briefly reviewing the latter, I explore the State's interest in the *preservation of life*. This was the primary interest which the State formerly arrayed against the *prima facie* right of a competent adult to refuse, in particular, life-sustaining medical treatment. Hence I shall, in part, be exploring the values underlying the justification of the now established right of the ordinary patient to refuse such treatment. In this process, I am not exploring constitutional reasoning in any general sense, but reasoning regarding the values and interests asserted in the relevant medical law contexts.

Moving to the specific case of the pregnant woman, the principal State interest originally asserted in the US maternal–fetal cases against the *prima facie* right of a pregnant woman to refuse medical treatment was the interest in the *potential life of the fetus*: for instance in *Jefferson*, *Re Madyun* and *Re AC* (1987). Thus, in *Re Madyun* the Superior Court of the District of Columbia observed that the State has an "important and legitimate interest in protecting the potentiality of human life", citing *Roe* v. *Wade* (which held, amongst other things, that the fetus is not a person),[1]

---

[1] 35 L Ed 2d 147 (1973).

and noted that this interest becomes "compelling" at the point of viability.[2] Reference was also made to *Jefferson* and *Re Jamaica Hospital*[3] on this point.

Having observed this, however, it is important to recognise the differences—as some judges have not—between the contexts of abortion and maternal treatment refusal. Possibly seeking to address this point, in *Re AC* (1987) the District of Columbia Court of Appeals noted:[4]

> "It is appropriate here to state that this case is not about abortion. The Supreme Court has made clear that state legislation may not altogether prohibit a woman from making the decision to terminate her pregnancy. *Roe* . . . However, when a fetus becomes viable, that is, when the fetus is 'potentially able to live outside the mother's womb albeit with artificial aid', . . . the state has a compelling interest in protecting the 'potentiality of human life' . . . Thus, as a matter of law, the right of a woman to an abortion is different and distinct from her obligations to the fetus once she has decided not to timely terminate her pregnancy."

This passage is distinctly unclear, but the court seems to be alluding to the idea of moral and, given the result that obtained in *Re AC* (1987), *legal* obligations which arise once a woman has decided to carry the fetus to term (and not abort pre-viability). In any event, the court seems to have seen itself as "presented with a woman whose significant interest in her bodily integrity must be balanced against the state's interest in potential human life".[5] Another passage of relevance can be found in the (partly) dissenting judgment of Belson AJ in *Re AC* (1990), where, having noted, as does the majority, that the case is not about abortion, he states:[6]

> "Rather, we are dealing with the situation that exists when a woman has carried an unborn child to viability. When the unborn child reaches the state of viability, the child becomes a party whose interests must be considered."

Aspects of this will be discussed in chapter five with regard to the distinction between negative and positive legal obligations as these might be derived from abortion law, but the important point for present purposes is that these judges are acknowledging, but not getting to the heart of, important differences between the contexts of abortion and maternal treatment refusal. By the late 1990s this issue remained unresolved.

In the 1997 case of *Re Fetus Brown*, in which the woman's right to refuse a blood transfusion was weighed against the State's interest in the fetus, the Illinois Court of Appeals disposed of the point by noting that this was not an abortion case and by saying that "without a determination by the Illinois legislature that a fetus is a

---

[2] 114 Daily Wash L Rptr 2233 (DC Super Ct 1986). Published as appendix to *Re AC*, 573 A 2d 1259, at 1232, *per* Levie AJ.

[3] 491 NYS 2d 898 (1985), in which the Superior Court of Queens County ordered the transfusion of blood to a Jehovah's Witness 18-weeks pregnant, who objected on religious grounds, finding that the State's interest in the not-yet-viable fetus outweighed the patient's interests.

[4] 533 A 2d 611 (DC App 1987), 614, *per* Nebeker AJ.

[5] *Ibid.*

[6] 573 A 2d 1235 (DC App 1990), 1255.

minor . . . we cannot separate the mother's valid treatment refusal from the potential adverse consequences to the viable fetus".[7] In effect this was to decide the matter, at least in part, by relying upon the fetus's lack of legal personhood.

More recently still, the jurisprudence in this area has shown signs of regression, since in 1999 in *Pemberton* v. *Tallahassee Memorial Regional Medical Center*[8] the US District Court for the Northern District of Florida (Tallahassee Division) failed even to recognise that maternal refusal of medical treatment cannot simply be equated with the context of abortion. The case concerned an appeal against a state court's order of a caesarean upon a non-consenting pregnant woman who disputed its necessity.[9] Judge Hinkle rejected various of Ms Pemberton's arguments, including that her constitutional rights had been invaded, citing *Roe* v. *Wade* as authority for the proposition that at viability the State's interest in the fetus outweighs the woman's constitutional interest in determining whether to have the child, stating that here the woman wanted "*only* to avoid a particular procedure for giving birth, not to avoid giving birth altogether".[10] Overall, the judgment in this as yet most recent of cases is deeply disappointing, revealing as it does a lack of sensitivity to the different issues at stake in the treatment refusal and abortion contexts respectively. In finding against the pregnant woman in this case, somewhat bizarrely Judge Hinkle purports to "pick up" on the way in which the District of Columbia Court of Appeals in *Re AC* left open "the possibility that a conflicting state interest may be so compelling that the patient's wishes must yield" but suggested "that such cases will be extremely rare and truly exceptional", noting that *Re AC* itself was "not such a case".[11] In Judge Hinkle's view, *Pemberton* was "such a case":[12]

"In anything other than an extraordinary and overwhelming case, the right to decide would surely rest with the mother, not with the state. But based on the evidence disclosed by this record, this was an extraordinary and overwhelming case; no reasonable or even unreasonable argument could be made in favour of vaginal delivery at home with the attendant risk of death to the baby (and concomitant grave risk to the mother). On the clear and uncontradicted evidence, the interests of the baby required a caesarean section."

[7] 294 Ill App 3d 159 (Ill App 1 Dist 1997) at 171. The point here was that a refusal to consent to a blood transfusion for a minor would constitute neglect.

[8] 66 F Supp 2d 1247 (1999).

[9] Ms Pemberton had previously had a caesarean section with a vertical incision. For her current pregnancy she wished to give birth vaginally but had not been able to find a physician who would assist her in this, as it was thought that there was a risk of uterine rupture and fetal death. She tried to give birth at home with the assistance of a mid-wife but after some time needed an intra-uterine drip which she sought at her local hospital with a view to then returning home. The physicians by whom she was seen would not take part in this plan and began proceedings legally to compel a caesarean. Ms Pemberton was retrieved against her will from her home (to which she had returned) and a court hearing was held at the hospital. On appeal, one expert for the hospital, Dr O'Bryan, estimated the risk of uterine rupture at 4–6%. Ms Pemberton's expert witness, Dr Wagner, estimated the risk of uterine rupture lower, at between 2–2.2%, stating that if the uterus were to rupture the risk of death would be 50% (at 1253). The question the case raises but which Judge Hinkle does not appreciate, is *who* should decide the acceptability of the risk to the fetus. This is intrinsically related to the question of whether the pregnant woman should have the right to decline the caesarean.

[10] *Ibid.*, 1251, my emphasis.

[11] 573 A 2d at 1252, *per* Terry AJ, footnote omitted.

[12] 66 F Supp 2d at 1254, footnote referring to *Re AC* omitted.

He concluded that, in the light of the very substantial risks to the fetus, requiring her to undergo a caesarean did not violate her constitutional rights.[13] In other words, in his view her rights were outweighed by those of the State in the fetus.

Although English law does not explicitly have an interest in the potential life of the fetus, the judicial and public concern with the *de facto* fetus was noted toward the end of the previous chapter, for instance in Lord Justice Judge's idea in *St George's* that the fetus is "not nothing". Further, there is undoubtedly a State concern with the potential life of the fetus given the restrictions on abortion in English law. What is striking about English abortion law as compared with the US position is that English law is not framed in terms of a woman's *right* to abort; rather, the question is always whether certain conditions—what we might also construe as reasons or justifications—exist on her part.[14] Thus, as noted in chapter three, the Abortion Act 1967 (as amended by the Human Fertilisation and Embryology Act 1990) allows the termination of pregnancies up to 24 weeks in certain defined circumstances, and after 24 weeks where necessary to prevent "grave permanent injury to the physical or mental health" of the pregnant woman, or where continued pregnancy would "involve risk to the life of the pregnant woman greater than if the pregnancy were terminated" (as well as on the grounds of serious fetal abnormality).[15] This is one factor which helps to make English abortion law less conflict-ridden than its US counterpart, although the medicalisation of the English position, which is built on the idea that abortion is essentially a medical matter, is legitimately the subject of criticism. For instance, Sally Sheldon observes:[16]

> "The Woman of the Abortion Act is clearly treated as someone who cannot take decisions for herself, rather responsibility is handed over to the reassuringly mature and responsible (male) figure of the doctor. The legislation assumes that the doctor is far better equipped to judge what is best for the woman, even though he may never have met her before, and have no real knowledge of, nor interest in, her concrete situation."

---

[13] 66 F Supp 2d at 1254.

[14] The connections between US abortion law and English laws on reproduction, including on abortion, are also to some extent supported by reference to their partly shared legal history. Thus, John Seymour notes that "[g]iven the nature and origins of" the English statutory position on abortion "it would be unconvincing to assert that these laws do not rest on a recognition of the special status of the fetus and an acceptance of the view that the state has an important interest in protecting it." J Seymour, *Childbirth and the Law* (Oxford: Oxford University Press, 2000) 172–3. (He is also concerned with Australian law at this juncture.) The English position on abortion is touched on further in ch. 5.

[15] The relevant portion of s. 1(1) reads: "Subject to the provisions of this section, a person shall not be guilty of an offence under the law relating to abortion when a pregnancy is terminated by a registered medical practitioner if two registered medical practitioners are of the opinion, formed in good faith—(a) that the pregnancy has not exceeded twenty-four weeks and that the continuance of the pregnancy would involve risk, greater than if the pregnancy were terminated, of injury to the physical or mental health of the pregnant woman or any existing children of her family; or (b) that the termination is necessary to prevent grave permanent injury to the physical or mental health of the pregnant woman; or (c) that the continuance of the pregnancy would involve risk to the life of the pregnant woman, greater than if the pregnancy were terminated; or (d) that there is a substantial risk that if the child were born it would suffer from such physical or mental abnormalities as to be seriously handicapped".

[16] S Sheldon, "Who is the Mother to Make the Judgment?: The Construction of Woman in English Abortion Law", (1993) 1 *Fem Leg Stud* 17.

Sheldon does acknowledge, however, the role of medicalisation in depoliticising abortion in the United Kingdom.[17] In this light, it may be seen that the decision in the US Supreme Court case of *Planned Parenthood of Southeastern Pennsylvania* v. *Casey*,[18] which is examined extensively in this chapter, might represent the best approach, since it combines the idea of a right, which English law does not, with the idea of responsibility, which is implicitly contained in aspects of the English law. In other words, the notion of justification is important with regard to an abortion and perhaps this entails that reasons are discussed at some point. This does not, however, require that doctors should necessarily be the gatekeepers.

Returning directly to the issue of the State's interest in the fetus, although—be it in the abortion context or that of treatment refusal by pregnant women—this is in both cases the State's interest in the "potential life of the fetus", the critical question is what this interest should *mean* and *how it should relate to* a woman's interests and rights in either context.[19] Whilst in the US abortion law context the State's interest in the fetus becomes compelling at viability, I argued in chapter two that, given that a woman has no opportunity to refuse medical treatment such as a caesarean prior to viability—and could not certainly avoid the need arising other than by aborting/not conceiving—her interest in refusing treatment is not diminished at this stage, although morally she must have a very strong reason to justify doing so. We can see that there is thus no ready justification for the State's interest to become "compelling" at viability, as it does with abortion, which in turn lends support to the conclusion that a pregnant woman should have the legal right to refuse medical treatment up to and including the point of birth, in line with the decision in *Baby Boy Doe* (and *Re MB*) introduced in the last chapter. Indeed, *Baby Boy Doe* does not pit the State's interest in the potential life of the fetus against a pregnant woman's rights, granting her the absolute right to refuse treatment as invasive as a caesarean. But since the decision is limited in this way, and the subsequent decision in *Re Fetus Brown* decided that a blood transfusion is invasive and hence that a pregnant woman can refuse such treatment, we have seen that in Illinois the spectrum of less invasive treatment remains unclear. Further, many states have yet to consider the issue in any form.

In the first place, therefore, reflection upon the values inherent in the State's twin interests in the *preservation of life* (from the context of treatment refusal) and in the *potential life of the fetus* (from the abortion context) may offer guidance as to what the US law should be in relation to treatment which is less invasive than caesareans or blood transfusions (for instance in Illinois, which has considered this

[17] S Sheldon, "The Law of Abortion and the Politics of Medicalisation", in J Bridgman and S Millns (eds.), *Law and Body Politics: Regulating the Female Body* (Aldershot: Dartmouth, 1995) 105, 119.

[18] 120 L Ed 2d 674 (1992).

[19] As S Martin and M Coleman note, "the same governmental interests in fetal life and public morality asserted in relation to the criminalization of abortion are often invoked to support state-imposed restrictions on pregnant women." S Martin and M Coleman, "Judicial Intervention in Pregnancy", (1995) 40 *McGill LJ* 947, 986. Apart from suggesting that the "conflict paradigm" pertaining to abortion should not determine and may not be relevant to the situation of "maternal–fetal conflict", these authors are not concerned with the *articulation* of the State interests in these different contexts.

issue) and in relation to maternal refusals more generally in those states which have yet judicially to address this question or may be called upon to revisit it (for instance if Georgia were to encounter "another" *Jefferson*). Second, and much more significantly in the light of the tensions surrounding a woman's legal right to refuse treatment adverted to at the end of the last chapter, reflection upon the values inherent in these State interests as they apply to the situation of maternal–fetal conflict may enable us to understand what the State's interest in the treatment cases might be in a way which *supports* the principle of a pregnant woman's legal right to refuse medical treatment. These are the central tasks of this chapter. If the last chapter tended to focus upon the *patient's* interests in its discussion of the right to refuse treatment, this chapter might in some sense be said to concern the *public* interest in a patient's treatment refusal decision, relating a patient's interests to the latter.

In essence, I argue that there are important links between these two State interests from the treatment refusal and abortion law contexts, namely—in each case—a concern that decisions about life and death are in some sense appropriately respectful and responsible toward the value of human life. Further, given that a pregnant woman's decision to refuse treatment has ramifications for the potential life of the fetus—that is, a life other than that of the right-holder—I suggest that at some level her right, and the way she chooses to exercise it, invokes both the State's interests in the preservation of life and in potential life, or some "hybrid" of the two. I argue that, rather than being in conflict with or otherwise undermining her right to refuse medical treatment, the combined force of these interests can instead be seen to support it (subject, in practice, to her reasons for refusal), thus strengthening the legal right to refuse medical treatment that she has been held to have in England and in some US states.[20] In effect, I suggest that the State's concern is ultimately that a pregnant woman's treatment refusal be responsible, and that in this regard the public interest is satisfied where her reasons for refusal are serious and considered, but arguably not in the (most) unlikely event that these are trivial or non-existent. In the latter case, third parties may therefore have a legitimate interest in counselling and, in some very limited circumstances, persuasion.

Importantly, in shifting the debate beyond the conflict of legal rights and duties in which it is typically structured, I hope to pay attention to aspects of the problem which are lost on a strictly rights-based approach. Capturing the importance of this task in general, Scott Veitch has suggested that "the notion that there are 'rights without remainder' as perceived by the legal system works to preclude in law

---

[20] In turn this is consistent with the fact that, as Janet Gallagher has put the point, "*Roe* has emerged as one of the key legal precedents in the development of legal protection for an individual's right to make personal decisions about medical care", which is the "real irony" of using *Roe* (in the early cases) to override women's rights in the treatment context. J Gallagher, "Fetus as Patient", in N Taub and S Cohen (eds.), *Reproductive Laws for the 1990s* (Clifton, NJ: Humana Press, 1989) 185–235, 196, my emphasis.

possible sources of different *types* of reasoning that do not match up to those recognised by law".[21]

Although my approach is novel so far as the maternal–fetal conflict is concerned, it is likely that at least some scholars working on this topic would see its merits. Consider, for instance, Janet Gallagher's statement:[22]

> "Fetal rights theorists assume that *Roe's* analysis of the scope of the abortion right also determines a woman's rights in the coerced medical treatment context. But the pregnant woman's right to shape her own medical care and that of her unborn child draws upon a wider range of precedents, demands a distinct analysis and balancing test, and requires a *fresh examination of* Roe *itself.*"

Moreover, at the level of theory, it should be noted that the approach I adopt is by no means novel, as Ronald Dworkin has argued that where rights are called into question or are in conflict with other rights, we should look to the underlying values and deep ideas that support them.[23] This is, in effect, the approach he adopts in his *Life's Dominion.*[24]

Beyond the moral and conceptual links to which I shall draw attention as outlined above, a further important parallel between the abortion right and the right of a pregnant woman to refuse medical treatment should be noted. At the end of the previous chapter, I suggested that although a pregnant woman's legal right to refuse medical treatment is now relatively clear in England and in some US states (barring issues clouding competence especially in England but also perhaps in the United States),[25] given the lack of an ethical justification for this within the law itself, there remains a tension which is ultimately a concern, I think, about the *reasons* for which she may choose to exercise this right. In a similar fashion, we shall see that *Roe* v. *Wade's* establishment, in 1973, of a woman's legal right to abort (whilst more clearly articulated than the right at issue in the most recent maternal–fetal cases) left a residual tension about the abortion right, as evidenced in the cases of the ensuing 20 years, which frequently sought to chip away at this right. (Some of these are discussed in chapter five. Note here that it is beyond my scope

---

[21] S Veitch, *Moral Conflict and Legal Reasoning* (Oxford: Hart Publishing, 1999) 183, emphasis in original. The phrase "rights without remainder" comes from the work of Jean-François Lyotard, as cited by Veitch. Veitch's book defends Isaiah Berlin's agnostic liberalism, at the centre of which lies conflict regarding values, and examines whether liberal legal structures can deal sufficiently with moral conflict or whether they are the victims of professional interests and techniques which obscure the possibilities for meaningful dissensus especially regarding conflicts of values. It is beyond my scope to assess this line of thought.

[22] J Gallagher, "Prenatal Invasions and Interventions: What's Wrong with Fetal Rights?", (1987) 10 *Harvard Women's LJ* 9, 14–15 (footnote omitted, my emphasis). Gallagher does not herself embark upon this analysis.

[23] R Dworkin, *Taking Rights Seriously*, 2nd impression (corrected) with appendix (London: Duckworth, 1978) 191*ff.*

[24] *Life's Dominion: An Argument about Abortion and Euthanasia* (London: Harper Collins, 1993).

[25] Importantly, discussion with an American bioethicist and a psychiatrist working in the clinical setting suggests that the issue of competence will also be critical to these cases in the United States, although this has not been reflected in the relevant legal decisions so far. (Discussion with Dr Rosamond Rhodes (a bioethicist) and Dr James Strain (a psychiatrist), Mount Sinai School of Medicine, New York, April 2000.

to address the important issue of lack of funding for abortions.[26]) In this sense, it is not so surprising, contrary to Katherine de Gama, that "it is from the very case which . . . enshrines the principle that a foetus cannot be a legal person that the discourse of foetal rights has emerged".[27] Thus, as with the abortion debate, the denial of a tension regarding a pregnant woman's right to refuse medical treatment is inclined to provoke dogmatic and ultimately question-begging assertions about a woman's rights, with possible consequent backlash against these. Such backlash may consist in overly rigid assertions of fetal rights which do not attend sufficiently to a woman's interests and difficulties in pregnancy or to the context of the conflict in question. Indeed, these patterns reflect the character of a considerable portion of the relevant literature.

As we shall see in this chapter, 20 years after *Roe*, in *Planned Parenthood of Southeastern Pennsylvania* v. *Casey,* the US Supreme Court has, in part, tried to resolve the unease which *Roe* created but *without* denying women the right to abort (within limits). *Casey* tries to do this in two ways which are, I believe, pertinent to the justification and acceptance of the current law regarding the maternal–fetal conflict. First, it explains *why* a pregnant woman should have the right to abort (other than by saying that the fetus is not a legal person). Second, it acknowledges and accommodates the interests of others that the abortion right will be exercised in an appropriately considered way. This chapter tries to show that both these aspects can assist our understanding of the maternal–fetal conflict, reconciling ourselves to the fact that, as Stephen Macedo has expressed the point, "fully public justifications on controversial issues (ones that all reasonable people really do accept) will often be impossible to come by", yet at the same time recognising that "public reflection can help us identify and rule out unreasonable options. It can, as well, help us narrow the gaps and negotiate the *tensions* among public and personal values."[28]

B. The Liberal Backdrop to the Cases

These last thoughts raise the issue of the liberal foundations of the treatment refusal and abortion cases under discussion here. There has been little discussion, or sometimes even acknowledgement, of the links between medical law and the liberalism in which it is grounded, perhaps due to the complexity and enormity of the debate on liberalism, which is daunting. Not only do contemporary theorists back different overriding values, such as justice (Rawls), equality (Dworkin) and freedom

---

[26] Regarding *federal* funding, in *Harris* v. *McRae* 476 US 747 (1986) the US Supreme Court held that the Hyde amendment, which forbids federal medical welfare funds from being used even for medically needed abortions, was constitutional; regarding *state* funding, in *Maher* v. *Roe* 432 US 464 (1977) the Court held that a state can deny financial assistance for non-therapeutic abortions, notwithstanding that it may help pay for childbirth.

[27] K de Gama, "Case Note on *Re S*", [1993] *J Soc Welf & Fam Law* 147.

[28] S Macedo, *Liberal Virtues: Citizenship, Virtue and Community in Liberal Constitutionalism* (Oxford: Clarendon Press, 1990) 75, my emphasis. See also B Williams, *Moral Luck: Philosophical Papers 1973–1980* (Cambridge: Cambridge University Press, 1981) 82.

(Raz),[29] but the theoretical complexity of their different positions requires considerable intellectual investment. In chapter one we barely glimpsed the sheer complexity of the arguments about liberalism itself, let alone the liberalism–communitarianism debate noting, for instance, Joseph Raz's development of a perfectionist liberal position.[30] Ronald Dworkin's *Life's Dominion* is a notable exception to the lack of work connecting medical law and liberalism,[31] but of course this is itself built upon and fits within a theoretical framework which is the fruit of many years' work on law and political theory. As noted in chapter one, Dworkin's liberalism is "a theory of equality that requires official neutrality amongst theories of what is valuable in life". Thus, as regards the individual's conception of the good, the State should be neutral.[32] Importantly, this does not mean that liberalism is based on scepticism. For instance, Dworkin writes of liberalism:[33]

> "Its constitutive morality provides that human beings must be treated as equals by their government, not because there is no right or wrong in political morality, but because that is what is right."

Although neutral about the good, however, liberalism is not required to be neutral as regards questions of justice or "the right".

There is not scope here satisfactorily to endorse one theory of liberalism over another, nor to determine the success of liberal neutrality (although, given the diversity of societies such as ours, it may be that the principle of liberal neutrality is best placed to achieve public assent)[34], but nor is this necessary. Rather, it is important to attend to the context of concern—the medical treatment context—and to note the appropriateness of State neutrality in that context, centrally invoking as it does very personal interests, including in the body. (Below I discuss the connections

---

[29] Indeed, as Joseph Raz observes: "It is probably true to say that no political cause, no one vision of society nor any political principle has commanded the respect of all liberals in any given generation, let alone through the centuries." J Raz, *The Morality of Freedom* (Oxford: Clarendon, 1986) 1.

[30] Note Raz's rejection of the distinction between first- and third-person ethics, believing it a "mistake . . . to think that one can identify . . . the rights of others, while being completely ignorant of what values make a life meaningful and satisfying and what personal goals one has in life". J Raz, *The Morality of Freedom*, 214. His objection to "morality in the narrow sense" underlies his rejection of the notion that morality is rights-based.

[31] On the purely philosophical front see also M Charlesworth, *Bioethics in a Liberal Society* (Cambridge: Cambridge University Press, 1993) in which these links are briefly discussed.

[32] Note, however, that one can support liberalism and yet consider that some ways of life are objectively better than others, as noted in A Swift and S Mulhall, *Liberals and Communitarians*, 2nd edn. (Oxford: Blackwell, 1996) 25.

[33] R Dworkin, *Law's Empire* (Cambridge, MA: Harvard University Press, 1986) 441. One reason for the liberal rejection of scepticism, suggests Kymlicka, is that scepticism does not support self-determination. If all choices are equally good, such that no-one can be mistaken in their choices, then there would be no reason to object to government choosing for us. W Kymlicka, *Contemporary Political Philosophy: An Introduction* (Oxford: Oxford University Press, 1990) 201–2.

[34] W Kymlicka, *Contemporary Political Philosophy*, 229. But note that, according to John Gray, the key problem with the standard approach "is in the assumption that principles of liberty or justice can be insulated from the force of value-incommensurability. If Berlin is on the right track, this is an illusion, since there are conflicting liberties, rival equalities, and incompatible demands of justice". J Gray, *Isaiah Berlin* (London: Harper Collins, 1995) 147. Thus Berlin does not make the distinction between the right and the good.

between self-determination, bodily integrity and privacy.) My point here is that it is difficult to make the body (rather than the body as an instrument in the course of conduct) the subject of moral discourse in the sense of being subject to moral duties, an idea explored in chapter two. There I examined the limited scope for judging reasonableness as regards the body. Importantly, refusal of treatment by a pregnant woman, of course, very much affects the fetus. Thus, notions about her good in the treatment context potentially involve treating another unjustly, at which juncture liberalism would cease to be neutral.[35] To the extent that notions of justice hinge partly on notions of rights, this raises the question of the legal status of the fetus. This conjunction of issues—on the one hand concerning the woman's body and on the other concerning the fetus's legal status—is also raised with regard to abortion. If the fetus were a person, State neutrality would not be possible in either case in the sense that a woman's decision about the *good* for herself (or her and her family) would trespass on the *rights* of the fetus. Yet given that the fetus is not deemed a legal person in the United States (a position the origins of which are constitutional)[36] nor in England and elsewhere, in effect priority is given to the woman's need (and right) to decide matters centrally affecting her body and life herself. My point is that whilst the lack of fetal personhood is essential to State neutrality on these questions, this lack does not preclude a woman's interests in these contexts in fact being the predominant issue, thus making the fetus's lack of personhood of secondary importance.

We should briefly note here the position of the future child, that is, the child who will be but is not yet born. Whilst the child when born will acquire legal rights, I argued in chapter one that the morality of its prior treatment *in utero* cannot be resolved by consideration of those rights alone, since, at the time the injury may occur, it is within the body of the pregnant woman, thereby invoking her rights to self-determination (which may here be "about the body") and bodily integrity. The significance of these is not so much that she has these rights *per se*, as that it is hard to determine the duty which is owed through the body (as opposed to the detached third party's duty to avoid causing harm to the future child. In this sense, the morality of the actions affecting the future child is influenced by what is possible for the pregnant woman. Likewise at law.

Overall, the point for present purposes has been briefly to acknowledge the liberal backdrop to the cases discussed here. At the same time, and by no means inconsistently with this, the chapter is committed to Macedo's idea of reflection aimed at "narrowing the gaps and negotiating the tensions" surrounding the issue of maternal treatment refusal.

---

[35] As noted in a general sense in A Swift and S Mulhall, *Liberals and Communitarians*, 301.

[36] See R Dworkin, *Life's Dominion*, 109–17 for a discussion of why a fetus is not a person within the US constitution and why individual states cannot declare it to be a person or protect fetal interests where this would interfere with an individual's constitutional rights.

C. Privacy, Liberty or Autonomy?

We shall shortly see that in *Casey* the abortion right was understood by the joint opinion as deriving from the Due Process Clause. In connection with this point, a key issue surrounding the debate on abortion has concerned Justice Blackmun's derivation of the abortion right in *Roe* from the right to privacy (by citing the Court's decisions on contraception), an aspect of the decision which has been both criticised and supported.[37] Yet although in both *Cruzan* and *Casey*, the Court has shifted its analysis from privacy to liberty, a development consistent with a move away from privacy by some (but not all) academic defenders of abortion and the right to die,[38] it is too early to predict that the Court has permanently moved from a privacy to a liberty interest approach.[39] Whether the law on treatment refusal or abortion is properly related to privacy or to liberty is an important question related to the interpretation of these rights, a point in turn related to the role and scope of the activity of interpretation. It would be beyond my scope to resolve this here, since the literature on this subject is vast, but the parameters of the debate should be noted.

The idea of a right to privacy or a right to respect for private life need not imply a distinction between public and private spheres, despite the European Commission's suggestion to this effect in the now more than 20-year-old abortion case of *Brüggemann*, introduced in the last chapter. Indeed, after the *Brüggemann* decision the ECHR has generally avoided the problems of delineating public and private spheres by considering a variety of underlying values.[40]

[37] For a variety of critical arguments, see e.g. C MacKinnon, "Reflections on Sex Equality under Law", (1991) 100 *Yale LJ* 1281; T Halper, "Privacy and Autonomy: from Warren and Brandeis to *Roe* and *Cruzan*", (1996) 21 *J of Med and Phil* 124; M Nussbaum, "Is Privacy Bad for Women? What the Indian Constitutional Tradition can Teach us about Sex Equality", (2000) 25 (April/May) *Boston Review*, 42. For a supportive argument see JL Cohen, "Rethinking Privacy: Autonomy, Identity, and the Abortion Controversy", in J Weintraub and K Kumar (eds.), *Public and Private in Thought and Practice: Perspectives on a Grand Dichotomy* (Chicago, IL: University of Chicago Press, 1997) 133–65.

[38] See e.g. J Ely, "The Wages of Crying Wolf: Comment on *Roe* v. *Wade*", (1973) 82 *Yale LJ* 920; CL Neff, "Woman, Womb and Bodily Integrity", (1991) 3 *Yale J of Law and Fem* 327. Interestingly, in connection with the European Convention, Aart Hendriks observes that the European Court of Justice has recently (in effect) identified two aspects of an employment applicant's right to privacy: the right to physical integrity and the right to protection from disclosure of personal information. *X* v. *Commission of the European Communities* (Judgment of 5 October 1994), Case C–404/92 P, [1994] ECR I–4737. Para. 23 of the judgment reads in part: "Since the appellant expressly refused to undergo an Aids screening test, that right precluded the administration from carrying out any test liable to point to, or establish, the existence of that illness, in respect of which he had refused disclosure." A Hendriks, "Commentary", on this case in (1995) 2 *Euro J Health Law* 180. The case demonstrates the way in which privacy can protect both bodily or physical integrity and information in the same context. At the same time, however, it might be objected that it is unclear why notions of autonomy and consent cannot do this work. (In English law, for instance, arguably one must be aware that one's blood is to be tested for HIV for the necessary touching (via the needle) to be lawful. I Kennedy and A Grubb, *Medical Law: Text with Materials*, 3rd edn. (London: Butterworths, 2000) 662.) On the other hand, it could also be argued that this case confirms the close connection between autonomy and privacy in this context.

[39] T Halper, "Privacy and Autonomy", 128. Case-law touched on in ch. 3 bears this out.

[40] D Feldman, "Privacy-related Rights and their Social Value", in P Birks (ed.), *Privacy and Loyalty* (Oxford: Oxford University Press, 1997) 15–50, 31. Feldman observes that the judges have looked to

At the level of political theory, of course, the "public–private" distinction has been the subject of sustained feminist criticism. In essence, the thought has been that the distinction fosters social hierarchies and social inequities between the sexes across all spheres of life.[41] The critique relates to the supposed liberal conception of the domain of justice or right on the one hand and a private realm of value or the good on the other. Thus Seyla Benhabib questions the supposedly unproblematic nature of this distinction, noting that it has effectively excluded various questions of particular concern to women from moral scrutiny, such as pornography, domestic violence and abortion.[42] More recently, however, feminist scholarship has questioned some feminists' critique of the public–private distinction.[43] Indeed, as Jean Cohen has argued, the abstract concepts of public and private do not need to be mapped onto a dichotomous model of our social structure and the concepts do not need to be employed in stereotypically gendered ways since, as with all hotly debated concepts, they are open to reintrepretation.[44] Cohen's detailed argument rejects Catharine MacKinnon's criticisms of privacy reasoning in the US Supreme Court's reproduction decisions, arguing that these, far from reinforcing institutions which keep women from having "identity, autonomy, control, and self-definition",[45] have begun to grant these goods to women by protecting the choices of women as *individuals* rather than protecting the family privacy associated with traditional power relations and gender norms.[46] She also rejects the communitarian criticism of the Court's privacy reasoning, exemplified for instance by Michael Sandel and Mary Ann Glendon,[47] which she suggests hinges upon the mistaken assumption that the ascription of legal rights of privacy to the individual presupposes an atomistic or voluntarist conception of the self. (Recall here Sandel's misplaced criticism of Rawls touched on in chapter one.) Rather, in protecting the

their own social and legal cultures and to comparative constitutional law, drawing on the values of personal autonomy, human dignity, physical and moral integrity, personal identity and the social importance of the family.

[41] See JL Cohen, "Rethinking Privacy: Autonomy, Identity, and the Abortion Controversy", 135, citing C Pateman, "Feminist Critiques of the Public/Private Dichotomy", in SI Benn and GF Gaus (eds.), *Public and Private in Social Life* (London: Croom Helm, 1983).

[42] S Benhabib, *Situating the Self: Gender, Community and Postmodernism in Contemporary Ethics* (New York, NY: Routledge, 1992), as discussed in A Jaggar, "Feminism in Ethics: Moral Justification", in M Fricker and J Hornsby (eds.), *The Cambridge Companion to Feminism in Philosophy* (Cambridge: Cambridge University Press, 2000) 225–44, 232.

[43] For a review see A Phillips, *Endangering Democracy* (University Park, PA: Pennsylvania State University Press, 1991) 92–119.

[44] JL Cohen, "Rethinking Privacy: Autonomy, Identity, and the Abortion Controversy", 135.

[45] *Ibid*., 141 citing MacKinnon, "Privacy and Equality", 101.

[46] Note M Nussbaum's suggestion that the problem with Rawls's and others' traditional pictures of the family, "is not that they are too individualist, but that they are not individualist enough". This is in the context of a defence of liberalism against various feminist charges. Here Nussbaum acknowledges some early blindness on liberalism's part to structures within the family which did not sufficiently attend to and value women's autonomy. M Nussbaum, "The Sleep of Reason", *Times Higher Ed Supp*, Feb. 1996, 17, 17.

[47] See e.g. M Sandel, "Moral Argument and Liberal Toleration: Abortion and Homosexuality", (1989) 77 *Calif L Rev* 521 and MA Glendon, *Abortion and Divorce in Western Law* (Cambridge, MA: Harvard University Press, 1987) and *Rights Talk: The Impoverishment of Political Discourse* (New York, NY: Free Press, 1991).

individual's decisional autonomy regarding certain vitally personal decisions, privacy rights are perfectly consistent with the appreciation that personal identity is formed by intersubjective processes as well as a perception of the way in which our values are historical and contextual in source.[48] This is in line with points made in chapter one about the view of the self held by liberals such as Dworkin and Rawls and is consistent with Iris Marion Young's suggestion that "[i]nstead of defining the private as what the public excludes . . . the private should be defined, as in one strain of liberal theory, as that aspect of his or her life and activity that any person has a right to exclude others from".[49] In redeveloping our conception of privacy, Cohen argues that:[50]

> "we can take up the concern for the situated dimensions of identity and argue that the new privacy rights protect both agency *and* identity, self-determination *and* self-realization, autonomy *and* authenticity, without prescribing a particular concept of the self on either level."

(On the close connection between privacy and autonomy supposed by this analysis, see below.) Enough has been said at this juncture to suggest that the recognition of privacy rights does not presuppose the public–private distinction, nor any particular conception of the self. Indeed, drawing on Young's work, Nicola Lacey has suggested that since the value of privacy is contextual it is possible to support the idea of privacy without thereby endorsing a private realm as that term is typically understood.[51]

One context in which privacy is clearly highly valuable, as Cohen explores, is that of reproduction.[52] Cohen argues that "[r]eproductive freedom is fundamental . . . because it involves the core of a woman's identity—her embodiment, her self-formative processes, her life projects, and her self-understanding are all at

---

[48] JL Cohen, "Rethinking Privacy: Autonomy, Identity, and the Abortion Controversy", 148–9.

[49] I Young, *Justice and the Politics of Difference* (Princeton, NJ: Princeton University Press, 1990) esp. ch. 4. (At 119.)

[50] JL Cohen, "Rethinking Privacy: Autonomy, Identity, and the Abortion Controversy", 153, emphasis in original.

[51] N Lacey, "Theory into Practice? Pornography and the Public/Private Dichotomy", in A Bottomley and J Conaghan (eds.), *Feminist Theory and Legal Strategy* (Oxford: Blackwell, 1993) 112. See also N Lacey, *Unspeakable Subjects*, (Oxford: Hart Publishing, 1998) 81–2; and D Feldman, "Privacy-related Rights and their Social Value", 16–17. See also W Kymlicka, *Contemporary Political Philosophy*, 261: "Once it is detached from patriarchal ideas of family autonomy, I believe that most feminists share the basic liberal motivations of respecting privacy—i.e. the value of having some freedom from distraction and from the incessant demands of others, and the value of having room to experiment with unpopular ideas to nourish intimate relationships", citing A Allen, *Uneasy Access: Privacy for Women in a Free Society* (Totowa, NJ: Rowman and Littlefield, 1988).

[52] On the questions of reasons for one's choices, Cohen argues that one is not obliged to give them, in effect that a privacy right to decisional autonomy "means that one cannot be obliged either to reveal one's personal motives for these ethical choices or to accept, as one's own, the group's reasons or evaluations . . . [t]hus the decisional autonomy of the legal subject in the domain protected by personal privacy rights involves informational privacy as well". JL Cohen, "Rethinking Privacy: Autonomy, Identity, and the Abortion Controversy", 155. My argument does not require this and, as this chapter progresses, it will become apparent that I think there are dangers in insisting too strongly on this point. See in particular comments on the work of Robin West towards the end of this chapter on the possible dangers of liberals seeming to insulate decisions relating to controversial ethical issues from others.

stake."[53] She also acknowledges Ronald Dworkin's argument that the issues at stake in issues such as abortion are quasi-religious. The link between abortion and privacy has also been defended in detail by Dworkin himself. Dworkin argues that Justice Blackmun, in respecting the precedent of *Griswold* v. *Connecticut*,[54] in which the Court explicitly recognised a right to privacy for the first time and applied it to a married couple's right to use contraceptives, was bound to hold that a right to privacy protects abortion as well as contraception "on the presumption that decisions affecting marriage and childbirth are so intimate and personal that people must in principle be allowed to make these decisions for themselves".[55] In this sense, privacy means "sovereignty over personal decisions".[56] The appropriateness of privacy reasoning to the abortion issue is even stronger than with regard to contraception, suggests Dworkin, because it concerns a woman's interest in controlling not only her sexual relations, but also changes in her body, noting that the Supreme Court has in different ways recognised the significance of bodily integrity.[57] As Cohen notes, the importance of bodily integrity to privacy reasoning does not entail a property analysis of the body, but rather a recognition that bodily integrity is central to individual identity.[58]

Dworkin's answer to the conservative argument that there is no right to privacy in the constitution is the jurisprudential one that constitutions are made up of abstract rather than specifically identified rights, embodying ideals which are to be interpreted in the light of changing social conditions.[59] Courts' decisions applying privacy to reproduction, contraception and abortion, he argues, in turn "have been collected" into the principle of *procreative autonomy*.[60] Here he cites Justice Brennan's oft-cited pronouncement from *Eisenstadt* v. *Baird*:[61]

---

[53] JL Cohen, "Rethinking Privacy: Autonomy, Identity, and the Abortion Controversy", 161.

[54] 14 L Ed 2d 510 (1965).

[55] R Dworkin, *Life's Dominion*, 106. For criticisms of this development in privacy reasoning and its application to abortion, see T Halper, "Privacy and Autonomy", 125–6.

[56] R Dworkin, *Life's Dominion*, 53. But note Dworkin's suggestion that privacy reasoning can be sensitive to the uniqueness of the relationship between a pregnant woman and her fetus and to the complexities of a pregnant woman's views and feelings regarding pregnancy and abortion in a way which writers such as Catharine MacKinnon may not have supposed, 54–7. (Here he cites C MacKinnon's "Reflections on Sex Equality Under Law".) Dworkin writes: "In fact, the best argument for applying the constitutional right of privacy to abortions . . . emphasizes the special psychic as well as physical costs of unwanted pregnancies." (At 56.)

[57] *Ibid.*, 106–7. See also JL Cohen, "Rethinking Privacy: Autonomy, Identity, and the Abortion Controversy", 161, also cited above in my text: "Reproductive freedom is fundamental . . . because it involves the core of a woman's identity—her embodiment, her self-formative processes, her life projects, and her self-understanding are all at stake."

[58] *Ibid.*, 160. (I noted this also in ch. 1.)

[59] R Dworkin, *Life's Dominion*, 129; R Dworkin, "Unenumerated Rights: Whether and How *Roe* v. *Wade* Should be Overruled", (1992) 59 *U Chic L Rev* 381.

[60] R Dworkin, *Life's Dominion*, 157. For a different view, see M Tushnet, "Legal Conventionalism in the US Constitutional Law of Privacy", in E Paul, F Miller Jr., and J Paul (eds.), *The Right to Privacy* (Cambridge, Cambridge University Press, 2000) 141–64. Tushnet argues that the US Supreme Court's decisions on privacy are best appreciated as being grounded in legal conventionalism, whilst at the same time identifying a number of puzzles in legal conventionalism.

[61] 405 US 438, 453 (1972), emphasis in original. The relevant literature is vast, but see also e.g. S Such, "Lifesaving Medical Treatment for the Nonviable Fetus: Limitations on State Authority under

"If the right of privacy means anything, it is the right of the *individual*, married or single, to be free from governmental intrusion into matters so fundamentally affecting the person as the decision whether to bear or beget a child."

At this point Dworkin is linking privacy with autonomy in the reproduction context.[62] This is not to say that autonomy and privacy are the same and the relationship between them has been the subject of considerable debate. On one view, for instance, although not a proxy for autonomy, privacy might be a subset of it.[63] On another view, however, a major flaw in work on privacy has been the notion that privacy and autonomy are synonymous concepts; rather, privacy should not be confused with, and indeed is unrelated to, autonomy.[64] The diversity of interpretations has been noted by David Feldman, who concludes that the debate centres around the question whether control over information on the one hand or notions of personal autonomy, dignity or moral integrity central to liberalism on the other lie at its heart.[65] In connection with the European Convention on Human Rights, Feldman has observed:[66]

"the idea of private life must not stretch to the point at which it subsumes other autonomy-related rights and loses its rationale. The interest in private life . . . is *related to*, but is not the *same as*, autonomy, moral integrity, dignity, or intimacy".

Noting the difficulties inherent in the question of whether privacy can be distinguished from "a broad liberty or personal autonomy",[67] Eric Barendt, who discusses privacy as a constitutional right and value, observes that those sceptical of privacy generally take one of two positions, "either that the development of the constitutional right has been misconceived, or more radically that privacy as a general concept is fundamentally incoherent".[68] Mindful of the huge literature on this

Roe v. Wade", (1986) 56 *Fordham L Rev* 961, n. 104: "The right to control matters concerning reproduction, including the right to decide to terminate a pregnancy, has been firmly established as one of the autonomy interests subsumed under the fourteenth amendment right of privacy", citing *Roe* v. *Wade* and *Griswold* v. *Connecticut*.

[62] For discussion of other work on the US context which analyses the importance of autonomy in the relevant privacy decisions, see LG Loucaides, "Personality and Privacy under the European Convention on Human Rights", (1990) 61 *BYBIL* 175. In particular, Loucaides cites Henkin "'Selective Incorporation' in the Fourteenth Amendment", (1963–4) 73 *Yale LJ* 74, who writes "[t]he court has been vindicating not a right to freedom from official intrusion, but to freedom from official regulation, i.e. a right to autonomy . . . . We will know which rights are and which are not within the zone only case by case, with lines drawn and redrawn in response to individual and societal initiatives and the imaginativeness of lawyers".

[63] T Halper, "Privacy and Autonomy: from Warren and Brandeis to *Roe* and *Cruzan*", 133.

[64] WA Parent, "Recent Work on the Concept of Privacy", (1983) 20 *Am Phil Q* 341, 345.

[65] D Feldman, "The Developing Scope of Article 8 of the European Convention on Human Rights", [1997] 3 *EHRLR* 265, 265–6. See also WA Parent, "Recent Work on the Concept of Privacy", who identifies no less than five interpretations of privacy, each with a band of supporters slightly varying the themes within these interpretations.

[66] D Feldman, "The Developing Scope of Article 8", 273, my emphasis,

[67] E Barendt, "Privacy as a Constitutional Right and Value", in P Birks (ed.), *Privacy and Loyalty* (Oxford: Oxford University Press, 1997) 1–14.

[68] *Ibid.*, 2. (In omitted footnotes within this passage, Barendt refers to H Gross, "The Concept of Privacy", (1967) 42 *NYUL Rev* 34 (a much cited piece), R Gavison, "Privacy and the Limits of Law", (1980) 89 *Yale LJ* 421 as being of the first view, and R Wacks, *Personal Information: Privacy and the Law* (Oxford: Clarendon Press, 1989) 18–19, as being of the second.)

topic, Barendt suggests that these "familiar objections"[69] are misplaced or exaggerated, on the basis that such uncertainties are the stuff of constitutions and Bills of Rights and that constitutional (rather than statutory) recognition of privacy will enable society better to realise its "*social* value and ethical force".[70] In turn this means that it does not much matter whether privacy is included in documents such as the US Bill of Rights (since this is explicable as a matter of social history)[71] or whether the right protects one or many ends, since uncertainty attaches to the justifications of numerous other rights.[72] Indeed, constitutional freedoms are not meant to be precisely defined in the way that statutory rights are.[73] If privacy has seemed more problematic, Barendt argues, this is because of the difficulties, on occasion, of separating it from liberty, fuelled by unclear judicial and other reasoning on point; it is possible, however, to conceive of examples which reveal a point of separation.[74]

The discussion so far suggests that the attempt to find a single interest underlying privacy is, as Feldman suggests, doomed.[75] Reflecting that rights are or should be granted based on reasons as to why they would be valuable,[76] Feldman argues that the weight and significance of privacy derives from its ability to facilitate the conditions for diverse forms of human flourishing.[77] For Feldman privacy is primarily a value, rather than a right, which spawns "privacy-related" rights which protect the conditions necessary for "valuable personal and social activity".[78] This conception of privacy is reminiscent of Joseph Raz's approach to rights, touched on in Part I, a point acknowledged by Feldman. Feldman suggests that purely autonomy-based justifications of privacy rightly create suspicion and that privacy-related rights become more attractive if the social role of humans receives more emphasis. In this conception, privacy is not conceived primarily as a way of elevating individual choices but rather for its potential to enable socially recognised goods.[79] Nevertheless, in fostering human flourishing, presumably a socially recognised good, privacy-related rights might also foster "desirable ends" such as

---

[69] E Barendt, "Privacy as a Constitutional Right and Value", 2.

[70] *Ibid.*, emphasis in original.

[71] *Ibid.*, 12.

[72] *Ibid.*, 8, e.g. freedom of expression. See also D Feldman, "Secrecy, Dignity, or Autonomy? Views of Privacy as a Civil Liberty", (1994) 47 *Current Legal Problems* 41, 58, who notes that whilst privacy is both autonomy- and dignity- related, so are many other civil liberties. However, Feldman also suggests that "the breadth of the idea, and its tendency to merge with the idea of liberty itself, produces a lack of definition which weakens its force in moral and political discourse." (At 49.)

[73] E Barendt, "Privacy as a Constitutional Right and Value", 12.

[74] *Ibid.*, 8–9, 10.

[75] D Feldman, "Privacy-related Rights and their Social Value", 21.

[76] *Ibid.*, 28.

[77] *Ibid.*, 21.

[78] *Ibid.*, 16.

[79] *Ibid.*, 21. (See further the discussion of Raz at the end of this chapter.) On autonomy Feldman notes: "Many of the features of individuals which make convincing the classical liberal notion of individual autonomy are themselves heavily influenced, if not determined by, the social circles in which we move." (At 22.)

autonomy.[80] As regards the move from privacy as a *value* to privacy-related *rights*, the protection of privacy by constitutional means is based, suggests Feldman, on the need to "permit choice, difference, and moral integrity (the ability to live according to one's conscientious moral judgements)", which is important to liberals and communitarians alike.[81] This means the State can only limit or interfere with privacy-related rights to advance legitimate public interests and other rights.[82] Although his defence of privacy-related rights emphasises the social nature of humans and hence may seem harder to apply to medical law issues primarily invoking, say, bodily integrity, in fact he envisages this conception of human flourishing as encompassing medical law issues, such as the refusal of medical treatment,[83] abortion and euthanasia,[84] and thus his argument is clearly of relevance here.

Feldman's analysis is attractive in the way that Raz's work is for its conception that particular rights should be granted on the basis of an understanding as to why they would be valuable,[85] a point which I think can be made about Dworkin's work as well. Such rights are more likely to be perceived as beneficial across a broad spectrum of political views, since thinking and arguing about why they are valuable is an attempt not only to justify arrangements supporting them, but also "pragmatically . . . to reduce what Rawls has called the 'strains of commitment' which may be felt in respect of the fundamental, constitutive principles governing political life".[86] Yet this understanding is not inconsistent with Cohen's analysis, nor with Dworkin's, particularly in his suggestion, noted above, that US court decisions on privacy in the reproduction context form the principle of procreative autonomy. On this understanding, privacy is valued for its protection of autonomy in a certain context.

One point which is emerging from this discussion, I think, is that (at least in the legal context)[87] it is not the right which is important *per se* so much as what it protects, such as a certain kind of decision. In turn this means that the debate about the *name* of the right, be it "privacy", "liberty" or "autonomy", may be of less significance. It is thus not surprising, perhaps, that, having affirmed the Supreme Court's

---

[80] In connection with privacy and its links with autonomy and dignity, elsewhere Feldman has written: "The combination of the idea of a right to be respected as a moral agent with the idea of social spheres of decision-making within which people or groups are entitled to regard themselves as free from outside coercion are, I suggest, of the essence of the notion of privacy as a civil liberty." "Secrecy, Dignity, or Autonomy?", 55.

[81] D Feldman "Privacy-related Rights and their Social Value", 27 (citing G Dworkin, *The Theory and Practice of Autonomy* (New York, NY: Cambridge University Press, 1988) 41).

[82] *Ibid.*, 27.

[83] D Feldman, "Secrecy, Dignity, or Autonomy?", 55

[84] D Feldman "Privacy-related Rights and their Social Value", 42. He does not elaborate here upon these suggestions.

[85] *Ibid.*, 28.

[86] *Ibid.*, 19. The reference is to J Rawls, *A Theory of Justice* (Oxford: Clarendon Press, 1972) 176.

[87] Issues of definition are likely more crucial to the philosophical debate and are hotly contested there. For an excellent review of the main philosophical issues relating to privacy and an introduction to several notable philosophical contributions, see F Schoeman, "Privacy: Philosophical Dimensions of the Literature", in F Schoeman (ed.), *Philosophical Dimensions of Privacy: An Anthology* (Cambridge: Cambridge University Press, 1984) 1 (adapted from his "Privacy: Philosophical Dimensions", (1984) 21 *Am Phil Quart*).

application of privacy reasoning to the reproductive context, Dworkin both suggests and acknowledges three other bases for the abortion right: first, as deriving from the First Amendment's protection of religious freedom, his principal argument;[88] second, as deriving from the Due Process Clause of the Fourteenth Amendment, the view adopted in *Casey*; and third, as deriving from the Equal Protection Clause,[89] a view supported particularly by Justice Blackmun in *Casey*. In Dworkin's view, the right to abortion can be linked with each of these bases, as well as with the principle of procreative autonomy deriving from the application of privacy in the reproduction context. For Dworkin, the question is not which is correct: he suggests that we should not be concerned about the diversity of possible homes for the right to abort. It should be noted, however, that none of the Court's abortion decisions, including *Casey*, connect the right with the First Amendment.

Similarly, the right to refuse medical treatment might, depending on the circumstances, be protected by relying on autonomy or decisional autonomy aspects of privacy. Given the number of Strasbourg decisions interpreting the right to respect for private life as including protection of physical integrity (noted in the previous chapter), then it does not seem inappropriate that English medical law should link the right to refuse medical treatment with Article 8 under the Human Rights Act. Indeed, apart from the possible reliance, on occasion, on Article 9, protecting freedom of thought, conscience and religion (as noted in chapter three), it is not clear what other constitutional home the right could find, since the right to liberty and security under Article 5 is clearly concerned with issues of lawful arrest and detention. The right to be free from inhuman or degrading treatment under

---

[88] Dworkin argues that a "textual home" can be found for the right to "procreative autonomy" in the First Amendment, since it does not require belief in God, as evidenced by *United States* v. *Seeger* 380 US 163 (1965). In this case a man had no belief in God but opposed war on general ethical principles. He was granted exemption from military service under a statute which only allowed religious grounds for claiming exemption. Thus Dworkin argues that, according to the First Amendment, the State cannot impose its own view on people about the ultimate point and value of life. Dworkin suggests that a "content" test of "religious beliefs" is preferable to a "subjective importance" test, and that the former is necessary and sufficient. The Court in *Seeger* was unclear on this point. R Dworkin, *Life's Dominion*, 162–3. For criticism of this approach see e.g. S Douglas-Scott's review of *Life's Dominion* in (1994) 2 *Med L Rev* 255: "It may be true that many feel that state laws prohibiting abortion violate religious freedom but so far attempts to pursue such an argument have failed, both in the Supreme Court and among constitutional theorists. However, in this context, we need not be well versed in the US Constitution to see a problem with Dworkin's argument. For how are we to identify the 'essentially religious'? Dworkin stresses that the convictions which endorse the objective importance of human life 'speak to the same issues—about the place of an individual human life in an impersonal and infinite universe—as orthodox religious beliefs do for those who hold them'. But might not the same be said about other moral ideas such as justice or liberty—are these not also 'essentially religious' on Dworkin's definition? The definition simply seems too indeterminate to prove of any value in the courtrooms or legislatures where abortion battles are fought." (At 258.) But overall Douglas-Scott considers that the book "does go a long way to persuade us of his central contention, that in the great moral issues of abortion and euthanasia, 'opinions divide not because some people have contempt for values that others cherish, but, on the contrary, because the values in question are at the centre of everyone's lives.' " (At 260.)

[89] R Dworkin, *Life's* Dominion, 166. This is discussed in my chs. 5 and 7. For a sex-equality perspective on abortion see RB Ginsburg, "Some Thoughts on Autonomy and Equality in relation to *Roe* v. *Wade*", (1985) 63 *N Carolina L Rev* 375.

Article 3 might on occasion be a possibility, as was suggested in *Herczegfalvy* v. *Austria*.[90] In the latter case, which concerned the forced administration of food and neuroleptics, isolation and handcuffing of a mentally ill incompetent patient convicted of various offences, the European Court of Human Rights emphasised that, although mental patients merit the protection of Article 3, "[t]he established principles of medicine are . . . in principle decisive in such cases; as a general rule, a measure which is a therapeutic necessity cannot be regarded as inhuman or degrading".[91] But the Court would have to be sure of the medical necessity. Since the patient in *Herczegfalvy* was incompetent, however, the case has no direct application to cases of competent patients.

In any event, in terms of the debate between liberty, privacy and autonomy as bases for the right to refuse medical treatment or to abort which was the focus of discussion here, assuming that a possible right is capable of receiving some constitutional protection, it has been suggested that ultimately the important question is whether that right can receive some constitutional protection, not whether one constitutional right provides its exclusive protection rather than another. It should be remembered, at this point, that rights can be subject to other interests and rights. The uncertainty surrounding the extent to which Article 2 of the European Convention (the right to life) might come to protect the fetus was noted in the previous chapter.

D. The US and English Aspects of the Discussion

The final background issue to touch on before the substantive argument of this chapter begins concerns the mixture of American and English law that follows. As should already be apparent from the above points, it is the American law which addresses the *justification* of the kinds of right here in issue, coupled with the relationship between the right-holder and others regarding the issue of persuasion, topics not addressed, for instance, in *Re MB*. With regard to these points, American law tends much more than English law to "go behind" the rights in question to the interests and values underlying and justifying them. No doubt this relates in part to certain differences in the legal systems. With regard to the somewhat more philosophical approach of the judges of the US Supreme Court, it is not suggested that English judges should necessarily embark on a process similar to that upon which I

---

[90] (1993) 15 EHRR 437 (first noted in ch. 3, in which the Court decided that Art. 8 was applicable in the context of the forced administration of food). Art. 3 reads: "No one shall be subjected to torture or to inhuman or degrading treatment or punishment."

[91] *Ibid.*, para. 82. A McColgan suggests generally that the absence of punitive motivation might count against a finding that Art. 3 has been breached. A McColgan, *Women Under the Law: The False Promise of Human Rights* (Harlow: Longman, 2000) 278. It was also relevant to the finding of no violation of Art. 8 that the applicant's psychiatric condition made him "entirely incapable of taking decisions for himself". (1993) 15 EHRR 437, para. 86.

embark in this chapter.[92] My purpose is rather to justify a pregnant woman's right to refuse medical treatment to the extent to which this currently exists and to promote that right where it does not, by showing the way in which, in various ways, it both has and might be done in the United States at the federal constitutional level.

It might be noted that JK Mason and RA McCall Smith have observed that there are "practical reasons" why, very unusually in medical law, American views regarding abortion have little influence on British thinking and that in the United States abortion is fundamentally a constitutional issue.[93] Nevertheless, my suggestion is that reflection upon the *arguments* within American abortion law (in addition to the values underlying the right to refuse treatment) can help us explain, evaluate and justify both the American and English law regarding the maternal–fetal conflict. Further, with the advent of the Human Rights Act 1998, the reasoning of English judges will indeed develop a more constitutional flavour, such that the American experience of delineating, weighing and protecting certain rights will come to seem that much more relevant to our own. (Later I make further reference to relevant ECHR jurisprudence.) Thus, the United States and now the United Kingdom both have a common law system alongside a system of essentially liberal entrenched rights.[94] With reference to the processes involved in relation to entrenched rights, we might note that when judges weigh rights against the interests of the State they are engaged in a process which is "essentially . . . political rather than judicial", as Justice McLachlin of the Canadian Supreme Court noted prior to her appointment.[95]

My concern, however, is not just with the theoretical justification of a pregnant woman's legal rights, but also with the operation of the law in practice. *Re MB* has given important guidance on this question, particularly with regard to the issue of competence, an aspect which will come to the fore in later stages of the chapter when I try to draw together the threads of the discussion, formulating a framework relating to the issues of discussion and counselling on the one hand and persuasion on the other. With regard to the issue of persuasion, however, I have noted that *Re MB* licensed but gave no guidance regarding persuasion whatsoever, notwithstanding that it may severely distort the way in which the pregnant woman reaches

---

[92] On the question of the less philosophical tenor of English medical law judgments, it might be noted that where reference is made to the question of the values and interests underlying the right, for instance, to refuse medical treatment, the reference is often to American or Canadian authority. See e.g. the judgment of Butler-Sloss LJ in *Re T*, 4 All ER at 665, where she states that she "agree[s] with the reasoning" of the Court of Appeal in Ontario in *Malette* v. *Schulman*, (1990) 72 OR (2d) 417 (which concerned a blood transfusion given to an unconscious card-carrying Jehovah's Witness) and she cites that part of Robins JA's judgment (at 432) in which self-determination is the relevant issue and discusses its value.

[93] JK Mason and RA McCall Smith, *Law and Medical Ethics*, 4th edn. (London: Butterworths, 1994) 104.

[94] As noted by A McColgan, *Women Under the Law*, 32. As McColgan notes, the same can be said of Canada, aspects of the law of which are considered in ch. 6. McColgan suggests that the fact that in theory US judges can trump politicians on a *de jure* basis but Canadian and English judges can do so only on a *de facto* basis is not as significant as it might be in practice. *Ibid.*, 28, 32.

[95] B McLachlin, "The Charter of Rights and Freedoms: a Judicial Perspective", [1988–89] *Univ of British Columbia L Rev* 579, 583–4, as cited by A McColgan, *Women Under the Law*, 27, n. 79.

her treatment decision.[96] Most importantly, in this way it is conceivable that the decision could paradoxically have the effect of licensing an interference with a woman's right to refuse medical treatment, potentially thereby contravening Article 8 under the Human Rights Act 1998. This critical issue is considered later in this chapter. Thus, broadly speaking, building upon the ethical discussion of the theoretical and practical issues first discussed in Part I, the rest of this legal chapter is a composite of the American/ECHR/theoretical and English/practical. Finally, it might be noted that the focus of the ensuing discussion is particularly upon a pregnant woman's interest in self-determination, as her interest in bodily integrity, though touched upon, is developed more in arguments in Part III.

I now begin the substantive work of this chapter by trying to uncover the rationale of the State's interest in the preservation of life of the ordinary competent patient.

II. THE DEVELOPMENT OF THE "ORDINARY" COMPETENT PATIENT'S RIGHT TO REFUSE TREATMENT

A. The State "Lets Go" of the Patient

In the development of the "ordinary" competent patient's right to refuse treatment, the State's interest in preserving the patient's life was the basis of the primary tussle between the individual and the State and is commonly accepted to be the most significant of the interests which courts typically balanced in these cases.[97] The preservation of life interest has two dimensions, as for instance the US case of *Re Conroy*[98] notes: an interest in the prolongation of the life of the particular individual and an abstract interest in preserving the "sanctity" of all life. In this regard, the traditional understanding was that "sanctity" was upheld where life was preserved.

Whilst English medical law does not speak explicitly of a "preservation of life interest", the State clearly has such an interest. Thus, what Lord Donaldson MR described as a "conflict of principle" lay at the heart of the rationale for the exception opened up in *Re T* and taken up in *Re S*. Lord Donaldson MR observed that "[s]ociety's interest is in upholding the concept that all human life is sacred and that it should be preserved if at all possible."[99] This passage reveals that, broadly consistent with the United States, English law generally considers that the value of life— expressed in the idea of "sanctity"—is upheld where life is preserved. Clearly opposing the individual's and society's interests, Lord Donaldson MR continued:[100]

---

[96] On what he calls "manipulation" (as distinct from coercion) J Raz writes that "it perverts the way that a person reaches decisions, forms preferences or adopts goals". J Raz, *The Morality of Freedom*, 377–8.

[97] See e.g. *Superintendent of Belchertown State School* v. *Saikewicz*, 370 NE 2d at 425; *Re Conroy*, 496 A 2d at 1223. These interests were listed in ch. 3.

[98] 486 A 2d at 1223.

[99] [1992] 4 All ER at 661.

[100] *Ibid.*

"It is well established that in the ultimate the right of the individual is paramount. But this merely shifts the problem where the conflict occurs and calls for a very careful examination of whether, and if so the way in which, the individual is exercising the right. In case of doubt, that doubt falls to be resolved in favour of the preservation of life, for if the individual is to override the public interest he must do so in very clear terms."

The perception, in English law, of an opposition between the individual and the public interest was reiterated in perhaps the most significant case of English medical law, *Airedale NHS Trust* v. *Bland*, in which Lord Goff suggested that the sanctity of life had to *give way to* the principle of self-determination.[101]

Indeed, as we saw in the previous chapter, English and American law regarding competent patients now grant competent adults the (almost absolute) right to refuse medical treatment, thereby apparently endorsing a fully "subjective" patient decision-making process. Thus, in *Re T* Lord Donaldson MR ultimately affirms the right of a competent adult to refuse medical treatment, observing that "[t]he right of choice is not limited to decisions which others might regard as sensible. It exists notwithstanding that the reasons for making the choice are rational, irrational, unknown or even non-existent". Further, I observed that in this way English law is in line with American authority, as expressed, for instance in the case of *Thor* v. *Superior Court*, with its statement that "[f]or self-determination to have any meaning, it cannot be subject to the scrutiny of anyone else's conscience or sensibilities." In this sense, patients' rights appear to have trumped the State's interest in the preservation of life.

Nevertheless, although competent patients now have the right to make treatment refusal decisions themselves, this does not mean that the values inherent in the preservation of life interest, which I shall now explore, have ceased to have a place in treatment refusal decisions. Rather, with the establishment of a near-absolute[102] legal right, the locus of power has shifted from the State to the patient, enabling the latter to have the final say. In this process, however, we shall see that the State's interest need not be seen as defunct, but can instead be understood as *supporting* patients' rights.

B. Understanding the State's Preservation of Life Interest as *Supporting* the Right to Refuse Treatment

As the right to refuse even life-sustaining treatment developed, a competent adult's right had to overcome two primary hurdles in order to outweigh the State's interest in preserving life. In the 1976 case of *Re Quinlan*, in which the Supreme Court of New Jersey had to consider the withdrawal of treatment from a patient in persistent vegetative state (and which was relied upon in subsequent cases concerning competent patients), Chief Justice Hughes put the matter thus:[103]

---

[101] [1993] 1 All ER 821, 866.
[102] Subject to exceptions which are not directly relevant to my purposes.
[103] 355 A 2d 647 (1976) 663, 664.

"We think that the State's interest *contra* and the individual's right to privacy grows as the degree of bodily invasion increases and the prognosis dims. Ultimately there comes a point at which the individual's rights overcome the State interest."

Invasiveness and a poor prognosis, then, were the joint tests by which the State sought to ensure that individuals did not refuse treatment—so opt out of life— without a "good reason", particularly when they might otherwise live relatively long lives. The need for a "good reason" was perhaps associated with the perception that the possession of life was a "good thing" and that, where a person chose to depart it, this carried implications for the value, the "sanctity", of life. This interpretation can be supported by the 1977 case of *Superintendent of Belchertown State School* v. *Saikewicz*,[104] which provides a passing yet significant gloss on the preservation of life interest which it appears to derive from the leading abortion case of *Roe* v. *Wade*,[105] and which we shall shortly see suggests the idea of an at least partly shared rationale for the State's interest in life as expressed in the abortion and treatment refusal contexts. Thus, referring to *Roe*, Liacos J suggests that an aspect of the preservation of life interest may express itself in the "additional interest in seeing that *individual decisions* on the prolongation of life do not in any way tend to *'cheapen' the value which is placed in* [sic] *the concept of living"*.[106]

Three cases—*Re Quinlan, Re Quackenbush*[107] and *Bouvia* v. *Superior Court*[108]— illustrate the way in which courts allowed patients to refuse treatment in ways which could also be thought not to take life lightly.

In *Re Quinlan* itself, a 21-year-old woman was in a persistent vegetative state and her father applied to be appointed her guardian with the express power of authorising the discontinuance of all "extraordinary treatment". The Supreme Court of New Jersey distinguished the case of *John F Kennedy Memorial Hospital* v. *Heston*,[109] which concerned not only much less invasive treatment (a blood transfusion), "but most importantly a patient apparently salvable to long life and vibrant health;—a situation not at all like the present case."[110] Suggesting that a putative decision by Ms Quinlan to allow a "noncognitive, vegetative existence to terminate by natural forces is regarded as a valuable incident of her right of privacy",[111] the court went on to declare that "[t]he only practical way to prevent destruction of the right" was to allow her guardian and family to decide what she would have chosen in the circumstances. The point is that a failure to allow them to "render their best judgment . . . as to whether she would exercise [the right] in these circumstances"[112] would effectively destroy her right to make crucial personal decisions.

---

[104] 370 NE 2d 417 (S Ct Mass 1977).
[105] Aspects of *Roe* are explored when I examine the State's interest in potential life.
[106] 370 NE 2d at 426, *per* Liacos J, my emphasis. No specific part of *Roe* is referred to.
[107] 383 A 2d 785 (1978).
[108] 225 Cal Rptr 297 (Cal CA 1986).
[109] 279 A 2d 670 (1971).
[110] 355 A 2d at 663, *per* Hughes CJ.
[111] *Ibid.*, 664.
[112] *Ibid.*

After *Quinlan*, from *Re Quackenbush* onwards, concern with one of the hurdles—prognosis—gradually gave way to an emphasis on invasiveness. Moreover, as the prognosis test slipped away, so the idea of invasiveness shifted from a notoriously problematic concern with extraordinary versus ordinary treatment to the concept of burden: was the treatment burdensome for the patient? "Quality of life" considerations, as we might call them, now began to play a more explicit role.

In the case of *Quackenbush*, the court observed that the extent of the bodily invasion required to overcome the State's interest was not defined in *Quinlan*. Regarding the joint test of a poor prognosis and significant bodily invasion, the court decided that the "extensive bodily invasion"[113] faced by Mr Quackenbush (either the amputation of both legs above the knee or both entirely) was "sufficient to make the State's interest in the preservation of life give way to the patient's right of privacy to *decide his own future* regardless of the absence of a dim prognosis".[114] The implication is that it was for the *patient*, Mr Quackenbush, to determine whether a future without his legs was consistent with his dignity and what he valued in life. But it is also apparent that the court itself readily understood that being forced to continue life in a far less mobile and "complete" form could well be seen as undignified and not in accordance with at least some valuable aspects of life. Thus, it seems to have been important in a case such as *Quackenbush* that *others* could perceive that continuing life without one's legs may, understandably, be undesirable. Hence, at this stage in the evolution of the right to refuse medical treatment, a sense of *shared values* seems to unite the position of patients and the State in such cases.

Likewise in *Bouvia* v. *Superior Court*, the patient's condition is the subject of ready sympathy: Elizabeth Bouvia was 28 and suffered from severe cerebral palsy and quadraplegia. Despite once being well enouh to obtain a college degree, she became completely bedridden and at the time of the case could only move a few fingers of one hand and make some small head and facial movements. Not only was she totally dependent on others for all her needs, but she also suffered from crippling and degenerative arthritis such that she was in continual pain. She was attached to a nasogastric feeding tube and another tube which administered only partially pain-relieving morphine. Apart from her great physical difficulties and discomfort, her broader interests in life had clearly diminished as her husband had left her and both her parents and various friends, with whom she had lived intermittently, were now unable to care for her, leaving her in the hands of a public institution. In these circumstances, she had repeatedly expressed the desire to die. However, it was estimated that, attached to her nasogastric tube, she would live for another 15 to 20 years. The Californian Court of Appeals expressed its understanding of her position as follows:[115]

---

[113] 355 A 2d at 789, *per* Muir J.

[114] *Ibid.*, my emphasis.

[115] 225 Cal Rptr at 305, *per* Beach AJ, my emphasis. The decision reinforced the irrelevance of prognosis by pointing to the Californian Natural Death Act which, although addressed to terminally ill patients, could be seen as an expression of State policy to the effect "that adult persons have the fundamental right to control the decisions relating to the rendering of their own medical care". Natural Death Act, Health and Safety Code s. 7186.

"It is incongruous, if not monstrous, for medical practitioners to assert their right to preserve a life that someone else must live, or, more accurately, *endure*, for '15 to 20 years'. We cannot conceive it to be the policy of this State to inflict such an *ordeal* upon anyone. It is therefore immaterial that removal of the nasogastric tube will hasten or cause Bouvia's eventual death. Being competent, she has the right to live out the remainder of her natural life in *dignity and peace*."

This passage, with its language of endurance and ordeals, highlights the sense in which the State's recognition that a patient led an appalling life could allow it to let such a patient die.

The above discussion shows that, in these relatively early cases, the State effectively granted patients the *right* to refuse treatment by endorsing their *reasons* for wishing to exercise this right. Indeed, reflecting on the *Quinlan* decision, the *Conroy* court noted that "the underlying concept was an individual's right to behave and act as he deems fit, *provided that such behavior and activity do not conflict with the precepts of society*."[116] Yet we have also seen that the privacy right relied upon in *Quinlan* arguably protects intimate, personal decisions. (The point can also be said to apply to the "liberty interest" in terms of which, as we saw in chapter three, many subsequent cases have analysed the right to refuse treatment. Indeed, given the conflicting interpretations of the scope of privacy discussed earlier, it may be that decisional autonomy is better or equally well understood as falling within a liberty interest rather than within a right to privacy. Whether this arena is better protected by a liberty interest rather than a privacy right does not affect what follows.) The idea of intimate personal choices was likewise stressed in *Conroy*, in which the court observed that "[t]he question is not what a *reasonable or average* person would have chosen to do under the circumstances but what the *particular patient* would have done if able to choose for himself."[117] At first sight, these aspects of *Quinlan* to which the *Conroy* court refers—which refer on the one hand to the patient's interest and on the other to the public's interest in the patient's decision—appear inconsistent, indeed contradictory; but they can be reconciled if we observe two important points about the right to refuse treatment.

First, the establishment of such a right means that the treatment decision is for the individual to make, which of course implies that the individual can decide as she sees fit. But notice that second, whilst a decision is the individual's to make, she may well *exercise* that right in a way in which many of us can understand or share in. So it is that in *Quinlan*, in referring to the decision of Ms Quinlan's guardians, Chief Justice Hughes states:[118]

"If their conclusion is in the affirmative this decision should be accepted by a society the overwhelming quantity of whose members would, we think, in similar circumstances, *exercise such a choice in the same way for themselves* or for those closest to them. It is *for this reason* that we determine that Karen's right of privacy may be asserted in [*sic*] her behalf ".

[116] 486 A 2d at 1228, *per* Schreiber J, my emphasis.
[117] *Ibid*., *per* Schreiber J, my emphasis.
[118] 355 A 2d at 664, my emphasis.

Whilst in the *Quinlan* case the grant of the right seems at some level to depend on, or at least be supported by, the choice being in accordance with what *others* would have chosen, we have seen that by the time of *Thor* in 1993 the strength of the legal right to refuse treatment no longer depends on choosing in a way which others can understand or support. This is not to say, however, that there might not be—and very often—a congruence of the two: that is, patients may exercise their right in ways many of us would endorse or understand. Of course, this is not surprising, for we have seen that the legal right arose out of interests and concerns which touch us all, in particular our interests in self-determination and bodily integrity, the sense in which we all—or most of us—want to decide, so far as possible, "how our lives go" and "what happens to" our bodies. In turn this relates to the point (made early in chapter one) that such rights, whilst an expression of individual *choice*, protect important and common *interests*.[119]

In the light of these reflections, we can make an important distinction between the idea of a positive and a negative choice to exercise the right to refuse medical treatment, as follows.

1. A Positive Choice—A Serious Reason

So far, I have suggested that an individual may very well make a treatment decision which many (though not necessary all) of us would support, for instance that it is better to die than to live as Elizabeth Bouvia was having to "live" before her death. Let us call this a "positive" choice. To the extent that such a choice may acknowledge or express what we consider "valuable in the concept of living", then arguably the exercise of the right of self-determination could well endorse or be in tune with notions of the "sacred", for instance as explored with regard to Ronald Dworkin's work in chapter one. There I noted his distinction between the biological, religious or natural sense of the sacred on the one hand and the human, creative, biographical sense on the other. In line with this distinction, where a patient refuses treatment for reasons connected with the lack of "flourishing" of her own life, then arguably she is doing so in a way which does not insult our sense of life being something valuable which is not to be discarded lightly. The case of Elizabeth Bouvia is here in point. Someone in her situation can readily be seen to be making a choice consistent with broadly shared ideas about what is good or worthwhile in life: apart from her bedridden state in great physical pain, we saw that her husband had left her and that her family and friends could no longer care for her. Thus, her reasons for wanting to decline further medical treatment were effectively expressions of her interests both in self-determination and bodily integrity. In essence, her condition was such that it would have been tantamount to a *perversion*

---

[119] To have a right *is* to be able to choose, of course. But it might be noted that when in *Re T* Lord Donaldson MR endorses the right of a competent adult to refuse medical treatment, he refers to this right as a "right of *choice*", concomitant with the fact that he is, of course, endorsing the right to refuse treatment for reasons which are "rational, irrational, unknown or even non-existent." Indeed, he refers to these as "reasons for making the *choice*". *Re T* [1992] 4 All ER at 653, my emphases.

of the values inherent in the State's preservation of life interest *not* to grant her the right to die. While such a right was not yet clearly established at the time of her case, the point is that by recalling a case such as that of *Bouvia* in our reflections upon the subsequent establishment of a near-absolute right to refuse life-sustaining treatment, we can see that this right can well be understood as upholding or being consistent with ideas about the value or "sanctity" of life which in turn may be associated with the public interest.

Now, a competent woman in Miss Bouvia's situation would thus have a clear legal right to reject further treatment. In one sense, as an argument of the communitarian Mary Ann Glendon implies, her *right* tells us that her choice is none of our business: Glendon is concerned about the language of rights weakening people's concern for one another.[120] The point of my argument so far, however, has been to try to show that the fact that an individual has a certain right can *also* be seen as telling us that it is very important that certain personal areas be in her control and that reflection upon her circumstances—and hence the reasons for her exercise of a given right—will likely make us appreciate her predicament, sometimes to the extent that some or many, but not necessarily all, would endorse or share in the choice being made. Where others would not make the same choice, they may at least appreciate that such a patient has serious reasons for choosing as she does, related to her underlying moral interests.

2. A Negative Choice—A Trivial Reason

Yet it is also important to recognise that the connection between the reasons for the exercise of a right and the underlying moral interests is a contingent one. For I have noted that the legal right to refuse treatment for oneself is now so firmly established that an individual can very well refuse life-sustaining treatment for an apparently spurious or trivial reason, such as a dislike for the name of the hospital in which he is located. Regardless of the patient's *right* to make that choice, such a decision may well not only puzzle us, but also seem a pretty poor *reason* to (effectively) die. We can call this a "negative" choice. In this latter example, the exercise of the right to refuse treatment and hence die seems to have little connection with anything that seems important in life. In particular, to refuse life-sustaining medical treatment because one does not like the name of the hospital, say, apparently has no association with the individual's very personal interests in bodily integrity and self-determination. It is apparently a choice with no great *meaning*. It is, moreover, a most unlikely choice.

As I explored in Part I, we can recognise the same distinction between positive and negative choices in the case of a pregnant woman. This was an important component of chapters one and two, in which I explored the *reasons* for a woman's treatment refusal, noting that in theory these can be either serious or trivial. Understanding whether her refusal can be conceived in a positive light is much

---

[120] MA Glendon, *Rights Talk*.

more complex than in the case of the "ordinary competent patient" because of the presence of the fetus. Indeed, no doubt on some views a pregnant woman's refusal could only be viewed as negative. I now turn to explore these complexities in order to try to show that we can understand the idea of a pregnant woman's legal right to refuse medical treatment in a positive or morally defensible light. Whether a woman chooses to exercise the right in a way consistent with its theoretical justification is another matter which may in turn open the way for third-party involvement in her decision. In exploring these issues, I shall first set the decision in *Casey* in context. Then I shall explicate the State's interest in the potential life of the fetus.

III. SETTING *CASEY* IN CONTEXT

A. The Structure of the Interests at Stake

The US law of abortion is a much-debated area of constitutional law concerned with a complex balance of interests: it addresses the rights of a pregnant woman, the State's interests both in her life and health and in the fetus she carries and, finally, the interests of the state in which that woman resides in regulating abortions. Considerably simplifying the 1973 abortion case of *Roe* v. *Wade*,[121] in that case the State asserted two important interests: an interest in the potential life of the fetus and an interest in the health or life of the pregnant woman and structured these such that, notwithstanding the State's interest in the potential life of the fetus, prior to viability, a woman had the right to abort, which we have seen was considered to be an aspect of her right to privacy. At viability, however, the State's interest in the fetus became compelling, such that thereafter abortion would only be legal if needed to protect the mother's life or health. Thus, the case delineated, weighed and balanced these interests, in the process establishing a woman's legal right to an abortion (within limits). Subsequent decisions of the Supreme Court have generally arisen when individual states have created abortion legislation which has been the subject of legal challenge. In such cases, the Court has considered the legality of various regulations and restrictions in the light of *Roe* and intervening decisions.

The relation between constitutional rights and other interests raises the question of whether and to what extent a given right can be legitimately subject to other interests. The standard to be applied by the Supreme Court in considering this question has been the subject of heated and at times bitter dispute. Whilst a detailed discussion of the legitimacy of these differing standards is beyond my current scope, something of the importance of the process at stake in the weighing and balancing of the different interests in question can be gleaned from the comments of Justice Blackmun in one of the important abortion cases.

---

[121] 35 L Ed 2d 147. The opinion was given by Blackmun J, who expressed the views of seven members of the court. Separate concurring judgments were given by Burger CJ and Douglas and Stewart JJ. White J, joined by Rehnquist J, gave a dissenting judgment, as did Rehnquist J (in a separate judgment).

Thus, in the 1989 case of *Webster* v. *Reproductive Health Services*,[122] Justice Blackmun railed against the novel "permissibly furthers" test created by the plurality in that case, stating that "[w]hether a challenged abortion regulation 'permissibly furthers' a legitimate state interest is the *question* that courts must answer in abortion cases, not the standard for courts to apply."[123] He described the plurality's standard as a "dressed up version of rational-basis review",[124] observing that the rational-basis standard, which tests whether a regulation is *rationally* related to the State interest it is designed to further, is the Supreme Court's most lenient level of review.[125] This standard should be compared, at the other end of the scale, with "strict scrutiny": this is the standard to which Justice Blackmun has repeatedly argued that restrictions on the right of privacy, from which he originally derived the abortion right in *Roe*, should be subject. By this standard a state must show that the restriction in question is "both necessary and narrowly tailored to serve a compelling state interest".[126]

Although Justice Blackmun expressed this view most recently in 1992 in *Planned Parenthood of Southeastern Pennsylvania* v. *Casey*,[127] the joint opinion in that case adopted the "undue burden" standard, emphasising that the abortion right protects the woman from unduly burdensome interference with her decision.[128] This is the standard employed in relation to the Due Process Clause of the Fourteenth Amendment, which declares that no state shall "deprive any person of life, liberty, or property, without due process of law",[129] and is thereby consistent with the joint opinion's view that the abortion right derives from this clause: the opinion stresses that "the controlling word in the case before us is 'liberty'".[130] A state regulation imposes an "undue burden" if it "has the purpose or effect of placing a substantial obstacle in the path of a woman seeking abortion of a nonviable fetus".[131]

As regards *Casey's* impact on abortion law, in essence the Supreme Court upheld *Roe's* "most central principle",[132] namely that a woman has a right to abort her fetus at any time before viability. Its judgment, based both on an explication of individual liberty and the force of precedent, drew upon its recognition of the individual's rights to make deeply personal decisions and to bodily integrity. It was the individual's

---

[122]   106 L Ed 2d 410.

[123]   *Ibid*., 460, concurring in part, dissenting in part, emphasis in original.

[124]   *Ibid*.

[125]   In *Casey* Rehnquist CJ, White, Scalia and Thomas JJ (concurring in the judgment in part and dissenting in part) endorsed a "rational basis" test.

[126]   *Griswold* v. *Connecticut*, 14 L Ed 2d 510 (1965), as cited by Blackmun J in *Casey*, 120 L Ed at 749.

[127]   *Ibid*.

[128]   *Ibid*., 713–15.

[129]   As cited by the joint opinion at 120 L Ed 2d at 695. The standard originates from the judgment of O'Connor J in *Webster*, 106 L Ed 2d 410.

[130]   120 L Ed 2d at 695

[131]   *Ibid*., 714.

[132]   *Ibid*., 710, *per* the joint opinion of O'Connor, Kennedy and Souter, JJ. Separate judgments were given by Stevens and Blackmun JJ (concurring in the judgment in part and dissenting in part); by Rehnquist CJ, joined by White, Scalia and Thomas JJ (concurring in the judgment in part and dissenting in part); and by Scalia J (concurring in the judgment in part and dissenting in part) joined by Rehnquist CJ and White and Thomas JJ.

"deeply personal" interests in bodily integrity and self-determination that were high-lighted by Justice O'Connor in the US Supreme Court case of *Cruzan*, as noted in the previous chapter. The Court also affirmed *Roe*'s holding that on the basis of the State's interest in the potential life of the fetus, after viability the State may regulate and proscribe abortion except where it is necessary, according to medical judgment, for the preservation of the life or health of the mother.[133] The Court did uphold certain restrictions on abortion: it also found "reasonable" certain regulations during the second trimester of pregnancy, namely the mandatory provision of literature on the risks of and alternatives to abortion, a 24-hour waiting period before the operation and limits on its availability to minors. (The issue of lack of federal or state funding of abortion is of course also relevant to the availability of abortion, but it is beyond my scope to address this here.) In contrast, the Court struck out an obligation that married women seek the formal consent of their husbands. In fact, it is disputable whether the restrictions which the Court upheld do not in fact create an undue burden on a woman's abortion right. Although I shall consider an aspect of these regulations subsequently, however, these aspects are not directly relevant to my concerns. Thus, notwithstanding these restrictions, broadly speaking the triangle of interests as originally delineated in *Roe* continues, such that a woman has a non-absolute right to abortion, while the State has interests in the potential life of the fetus and in the woman's health and life.

IV. THE RELATIONSHIP BETWEEN A WOMAN'S RIGHT TO REFUSE
TREATMENT (OR ABORT) AND HER RESPONSIBILITY TOWARD THE FETUS

I now explore the ideas of respect and responsibility toward the unborn as they are developed in *Casey* itself in a discussion which is directed both to the justification and the exercise of a pregnant woman's rights in the treatment context. I start by exploring what is at stake in the State's interest in potential life.

A. The State's Interest in the Potential Life of the Fetus

Although *Roe* held that the fetus is not a person for the purposes of the Fourteenth Amendment and therefore lacks a right to life, a position affirmed in *Casey*,[134] it might be recalled from Part I that the conclusion that the fetus is not a person is by no means definitive of the moral position in relation to it. Likewise, in this chapter we shall see that the fetus's lack of legal personhood is not necessarily an obstacle to giving it at least some legal consideration. Indeed, Justice Blackmun noted in *Roe* that the Court's conclusion that the fetus is not a person "does not of itself fully

---

[133] *Roe*, 35 L Ed 2d at 183–4. *Casey*, 120 L Ed 2d at 716, *per* the joint opinion.
[134] 35 L Ed 2d at 180. This position appears to have been implicitly affirmed in *Casey*, 120 L Ed 2d at 738 *per* Stevens J.

answer the contentions raised".[135] Further, he expressly disagreed with the view that a woman's right to an abortion is absolute, stating that a woman is not "entitled to terminate her pregnancy at whatever time, in whatever way, and for *whatever reason she alone chooses*".[136] Although part of his concern at this point is with the State's interests in protecting maternal health and safeguarding medical standards, he also cites the State's interest in potential life. He described this latter interest as an "important and legitimate"[137] one which is, it would seem, derived from the State's interest in life *per se*. As with the State's interest in the preservation of human life explored in section II(A), the State's interest in potential life appears in part to embody a concern to ensure respect for human life. In this way, that there should be a limit to a woman's right to abort seems partly connected with the sense in which, at some level, society has an interest in her reasons and a stake in decisions about life, although this is an aspect of *Roe* only developed, as we shall see, in *Casey*.

In a sense, the State's interest in the potential life of the fetus might be seen to "pay attention to" the important domain of intrinsic duties—those which are not instrumental to the protection of rights—which we saw to remain, if not come to the fore, when the fetus's arguable lack of rights was highlighted in Part I. Indeed, we might here recall Judith Jarvis Thomson's distinction between "moral requirements" and "moral decency" which I criticised in chapter two. In effect, the law's expression in terms of *rights* might be said to correspond to the rather narrow domain of "moral requirements": thus, a fetus does not have legal rights and hence there are no legal duties upon a pregnant woman (notwithstanding restrictions on abortion after a certain time); rather, she has rights which generally trump the fetus's interests. To be sure, the law has to define certain boundaries and set certain limits and underlying this in the case of pregnancy is the important goal of not coercing pregnant women within a very personal and bodily arena. Yet there is scope for the operation of "moral decency" in the law in the way that it may attend, in ways to be explored in this chapter, to the manner of the *exercise* of a woman's rights. We can also relate these points to the distinction noted toward the end of the last chapter between the *de jure* and *de facto* conceptualisations of the fetus: although the *de jure* position is that the fetus is not a legal person, the State's interest in the potential life of the fetus in some sense embodies its concern with respecting or valuing the life of the *de facto* fetus.

This theme of respecting or valuing fetal life was one I touched upon with regard to the "gradualist accounts" for the justification of harm to the fetus, which I developed in terms of the justification of a woman's rights, an aspect which I explored toward the end of chapter one. For instance, I observed that, reflecting on *Roe*, Joel Feinberg notes that "[w]hatever interest the state has in 'the *potentiality of human life*' must be derivative from the plain interest it has in preserving and promoting

---

[135] 35 L Ed 2d at 180.
[136] *Ibid.*, 183, my emphasis.
[137] *Ibid.*, 175.

respect for actual human life."[138] So far as the potential life of the fetus is concerned, we saw that Feinberg suggests that while *Roe* held that the fetus is not a legal person, the decision also implies that we can and should respect the fetus, as a "being whose similarity to real persons is close enough to render [it a] sacred symbol . . . of the real thing".[139] More recently, we have seen that Ronald Dworkin, writing with particular reference to the decision in *Casey*, has suggested that the abortion debate is not so much about the question whether the fetus is a person with a right to life, a view to which Feinberg also subscribes,[140] as about the importance of properly respecting life, writing that "it is a controversy about whether human life itself is sacred, and why, and about which acts show respect and which disrespect for human life".[141] I developed these points to apply to the maternal–fetal conflict and suggested that the idea of respect toward the value of human life seems ultimately to invoke the concept of *responsibility* (rather than solely respect) in the justification and exercise of rights which concern this value (particularly given that I am concerned, not just with the prospect of fetal death, but also on occasion with harm to the future child (who will be but is not yet born)).

Now developing this theme with reference to the State's interests in the preservation of life and in potential life as these come together and relate to the idea of a woman's legal right to refuse medical treatment needed by the fetus, we could say, in the language of the *Saikewicz* decision discussed in connection with the development of the right to refuse treatment—which itself referred to *Roe*—that a maternal refusal of treatment needed by the fetus for serious reasons (which by definition go to considerations of great importance in her own life) does not "cheapen the value that is placed in the concept of living".

I now turn to explore in detail the two senses in which *Casey* is important to the maternal–fetal conflict, namely, first: the support which it can give to the principle of a pregnant woman's right to refuse treatment; second, the way *Casey* provides for a framework in which such a right can be exercised.

B. The Theory—The *Justification* of the Right

Although the maternal–fetal conflict case of *Baby Boy Doe*, for instance, draws upon *Cruzan* in order to support the principle of a pregnant woman's right to refuse medical treatment (citing O'Connor J's emphasis upon "deeply personal" interests), in the latter case and others like it, the life of the patient making the decision

---

[138] J Feinberg, "Abortion", (1979) in his *Freedom and Fulfillment* (Princeton, NJ: Princeton University Press, 1992) 37–75, 55, emphasis in original.

[139] *Ibid*. See ch. 1 for a discussion of Feinberg's arguments on the moral criteria of personhood.

[140] "In addition to the argumentative support for the right-to-choose position, one can cite some evidence supporting the position that hardly any of the antiabortionists *really believe* that a fetus has the full moral status of a typical postnatal person." J Feinberg, "Abortion", 72, emphasis in original.

[141] R Dworkin, *Life's Dominion*, 27–8. For a contrary view, see D Callahan, *Abortion: Law, Choice and Morality* (New York, NY: Macmillan, 1970) 474: "It is all but impossible to extrapolate from attitudes towards fetal life attitudes toward [other] existing human life."

is the only life at stake. By contrast, *Casey*'s defence of the abortion right—which is addressed to the situation in which it is not the life of the woman making the decision which will be destroyed, but rather that of the fetus—is highly pertinent to a defence of a pregnant woman's right to refuse medical treatment, notwithstanding the different issues of abortion and treatment refusal at stake. Indeed, reflecting upon *Casey* in this way will enable us to take account of *Re Conroy*'s suggestion that the State's interest in the preservation of life is stronger where it concerns "some other actual or potential life that cannot adequately protect itself",[142] an aspect recalled in the American maternal–fetal conflict decision of *Re Fetus Brown*. Although in the latter case the court deemed that the State's only interest could be in the life of the pregnant woman, it might be recalled that it resolved the case by relying on the fetus's lack of legal personhood. In this way, of course, whilst *Re Fetus Brown* adheres to the *de jure* position of the fetus in law, it leaves untouched the *de facto* questions inherent in the State's interest in potential life, an interest in the moral quality of decisions affecting fetal life. My suggestion, as I have said, is that this interest combines with the State's interest in the preservation of life to give the State an interest in the moral quality of a pregnant woman's right to refuse medical treatment.

1. The Right to Define One's Own Concept of Existence

As touched upon with reference to the Supreme Court case of *Cruzan*, one of the most important areas of US law is the substantive sphere of liberty protected by the Due Process Clause of the Fourteenth Amendment. Associating the abortion right with the Due Process Clause, the Court in *Casey* adopted the view that the liberty protected by the clause "is not a series of isolated points" but is instead "a rational continuum",[143] determining the flow of which is a matter of "reasoned judgment".[144] Given that the joint opinion considered the issue of abortion to be the object of "profound moral and spiritual disagreement",[145] the Court saw its obligation as being "to define the liberty of all, not to mandate our own moral code".[146] The fundamental constitutional problem was "whether the State can resolve these philosophic questions in such a definitive way that a woman loses all choice in the matter".[147]

To start, the Court emphasised that at the time of both *Roe* and *Casey* it was settled law that the constitution limits the right of the State to interfere with a person's

---

[142] 486 A 2d 1209, 1223 (1985). This aspect of *Conroy* was noted in *Norwood Hospital* v. *Munoz*, 564 NE 2d 1017, 1023 (1991), which related to the State's interest in protecting innocent third parties and the question of a parent of a minor child or children refusing life-sustaining treatment. On this interest see the notes to ch. 3, s. II(A).

[143] *Per* the joint opinion, 120 L Ed 2d at 696. The court was citing Harlan J, dissenting, in *Poe* v. *Ullman*, 6 L Ed 2d 989. This position was adopted by the court in *Griswold* v. *Connecticut*, 14 L Ed 2d 510 (1965).

[144] 120 L Ed 2d at 697.

[145] *Ibid.*

[146] *Ibid.*

[147] *Ibid.*, 697–8.

bodily integrity,[148] and in a "person's most basic decisions about family and parent-hood".[149] The significance of the latter precedents to which the Court here referred is that they protect the most "intimate and personal decisions a person may make in a lifetime, choices central to personal dignity and autonomy".[150] In other words, such choices underlie the liberty of the Fourteenth Amendment. Notably, the joint opinion observed that "[a]t the heart of liberty is the right to define one's *own concept of existence, of meaning, of the universe, and of the mystery of human life.*"[151] (As noted, Dworkin has suggested that this reasoning would also be consistent with his First Amendment freedom of religion argument for the abortion right, observing the "striking overlap" here between the Due Process Clause and the First Amendment.[152]) This was the dimension of liberty which *Roe* sought to protect.[153] The joint opinion stressed that intimate decisions such as that of abortion, which concern the "meaning of procreation" are the subject of *reasonable disagreement*, stating that "reasonable people will have differences of opinion about these matters".[154] In contrasting different views about abortion, it emphasised that "[t]hese are *intimate* views with infinite variations" and stressed "their *deep, personal* character".[155] In another passage, the joint opinion concluded that "[t]he destiny of the woman must be shaped to a large extent on her own conception of her spiritual imperatives and her place in society".[156] The decision in *Re Fetus Brown* makes reference to this aspect of *Casey* and to the joint opinion's description of the way a woman's liberty is at stake in an "utterly unique" way in pregnancy.[157] (These thoughts can in turn be related to my argument in chapter two about the "social context" of pregnancy, which we shall see to find expression within the law itself in chapters five and six.)

a) *Application to the Maternal–Fetal Conflict*

i) Serious Reasons and Self-Determination

Consideration of the application of these ideas to the maternal–fetal conflict brings forward into this legal discussion ideas discussed in Part I with regard to a woman's reasons for refusing treatment, in particular the idea of religious or philosophical objections on her part relating to her interest and right in self-determination. These points were discussed with particular reference to Dworkin's "gradualist" approach, an approach which was ultimately directed to the justification of the

---

[148] 120 L Ed 2d at 697. E.g. *Winston* v. *Lee*, 84 L Ed 2d 662 (1985), briefly discussed in ch. 7. (Supreme Court held that to remove surgically a bullet from a suspect's body against his will for use as evidence against him would violate his constitutional rights.)

[149] 120 L Ed 2d at 696–7. E.g. *Carey* v. *Population Services International*, 431 US 678 (1977).

[150] 120 L Ed 2d at 698.

[151] *Ibid.*, my emphasis. Somewhat disparagingly, this has been called the "mystery passage". See e.g. FJ Beckwith and JF Peppin, "Physician Value Neutrality: A Critique", (2000) 28(1) *J of Law, Med and Ethics* 67, 72.

[152] R Dworkin, *Life's Dominion*, 171.

[153] 120 L Ed 2d at 699.

[154] *Ibid.*

[155] *Ibid.*, my emphases.

[156] *Ibid.*, 699.

[157] 294 Ill App 3d at 171.

abortion right. With regard to the maternal–fetal conflict, I explored in chapter one the idea that the prospect of serious harm to the fetus or future child necessitated a serious justifying reason on the woman's part, a reason which we saw would relate to her interests in self-determination and/or bodily integrity (the latter being especially important in the case of harm to the future child, given the way the issue of location particularly bears upon the morality of choices affecting it). In chapter two, it may be recalled, I observed our difficulties in judging whether a non-trivial reason for refusing treatment was sufficiently serious—the problem of reconciling the "subjective" and "objective" viewpoints which may partly explain why we grant rights in these areas in the first place.

Following that discussion, so far in Part II, particularly in the *Baby Boy Doe* decision discussed in chapter three, I have examined the legal recognition of a pregnant woman's interests in self-determination and religious liberty (in addition to that in bodily integrity) which underpin her right to refuse medical treatment. And in this chapter I have examined the serious reasons—consistent with aspects of the values underlying the State's interest in the preservation of life—for which patients generally refuse life-sustaining treatment.

In fact, the discussion at the level of *moral* theory about the difficulties of judging the serious reason foreshadowed the difficulties that we would have if we were to attempt to decide (in non-trivial cases) whether a woman has a legal right to refuse treatment or whether her interests should be overridden for the sake of the fetus. Thus, I now draw attention to the links between my argument to this effect and *Casey*'s emphasis, outlined above, upon the scope for *reasonable disagreement* which surrounds these intimate areas of personal decision-making and which in turn justifies the granting of legal rights in these contexts.[158] Indeed, this aspect of *Casey* is tantamount to a legal recognition, or rather expression, of my argument in chapter two to the effect that we simply cannot judge whether a serious reason is "sufficiently serious" to outweigh the fetus's claims, but must instead accept such reasons at face value, observing their important connection with the pregnant woman. This was particularly stressed in relation to religious reasons, with regard to which my discussion concentrated on the relation between the pregnant woman and her religious faith, hence the place of religion in her life. I argued that where a woman refuses treatment, such as a caesarean section, for religious reasons, we must accept these as sufficiently serious, in effect recognising the way in which such reasons relate to and are an important part of her. In the language of *Casey*, we might describe maternal refusal of medical treatment for religious reasons as one of

---

[158] Noting the preponderance of religious and "cultural" reasons for maternal refusals, one scholar aptly notes: "In a nation that thrives on cultural diversity in so many respects, it is naïve to expect that these differences magically disappear in medical settings." JC Fletcher, "Drawing Moral Lines in Fetal Therapy", (1986) 19 *Clin Obstet & Gyn* 595, 600. The same point is surely true of countries such as England, Canada and Australia. In another passage, Fletcher writes: "In a society that cherishes so highly the values that underlie . . . self-determination and respect for persons . . . any proposal for coercion of a competent adult for medical reasons needs justification on clear moral grounds shared in a consensus by many with a high degree of certainty. These . . . are not likely to be present . . . [as regards] fetal interests". (At 600.)

the "most intimate and personal decisions a person may make in a lifetime, . . . central to personal dignity and autonomy". As is apparent in this passage and in passages cited above, *Casey*'s explication of the individual's interests in self-determination, including in decisions about family and parenthood, stresses their deeply personal nature: the decision speaks of the right to define one's "own concept of existence, of meaning, of the universe, and of the mystery of human life". In this way, the case confirms in *legal terms* the way in which reasons which express an individual's deeply personal interest in self-determination form an important part of the person.

This conception of a woman's interests from abortion law, coupled with my earlier exploration of the individual's deeply personal interests in the medical law contexts, come together to support the legal right of a pregnant woman to refuse medical treatment (for which I argued morally in Part I) in a manner attuned to the "public interest" in such cases. Thus, where a woman has serious reasons for refusing treatment which reflect these strongly personal interests, I do not think our interest extends beyond the "passive" recognition of these serious reasons. It is in this way that our concern with the idea of responsibility toward the fetus (or future child) must be satisfied in such cases. This was an idea with which I was concerned in purely moral terms in Part I, which we have seen to be implicated in the State's interest in potential life in *Roe* in connection with the idea of respect toward fetal life and which will be seen to be an aspect of the abortion right particularly developed in *Casey*.

At this point, in the context of this current discussion which is concerned, particularly, with the individual's interest in self-determination, I would like to touch upon the question left open in the 1994 decision of *Baby Boy Doe*—namely whether a woman can refuse treatment which is less invasive than a caesarean section. We noted in chapter three that in 1997 in *Re Fetus Brown* the Appellate Court of Illinois decided that a blood transfusion should be characterised as invasive treatment and hence that a pregnant woman has the right to refuse a transfusion. An alternative justification of the right to refuse treatment such as a transfusion or less or non-invasive treatment could be made in terms of the reasoning outlined above. This would suggest that where a transfusion or non-invasive treatment is being refused for religious reasons (or reasons reflecting important personal values), then the pregnant woman should have the right to refuse it: in the light of the intrinsic connections between such reasons and the person, to deny her this right would be unacceptably to coerce her. Indeed, given that *Baby Boy Doe* partly bases a woman's right to refuse medical treatment upon her right to religious liberty, this line of thought would be a natural development flowing from *Doe* itself.

Yet what of the possible case of a pregnant woman who refuses minimally or non-invasive treatment for a spurious reason, one which is trivial or "outrageously" irrational or inappropriate? Indeed, as recognised at various points in my argument, clearly it is possible (though I have suggested *most unlikely*) that a pregnant woman might refuse treatment for what seems an obviously trivial or clearly inappropriate reason (such as the hypothetical case of the refusal to swallow the beneficial pill).

In cases which seem blatantly irresponsible, then our interest might take a more "active" form than in those cases in which, for instance, serious religious or other reasons are invoked. In order to develop this point, I turn to that dimension of *Casey* which developed the *practical* implications of the theoretical understanding of the abortion right. On the basis of its view that these rights concern the "meaning of procreation", and hence invoke questions about "human responsibility and respect for it",[159] the Court laid the foundation for its argument, to which I now turn, that although a woman has the right to abort pre-viability, the State can take steps to ensure her decision is "informed".[160]

C. The Practice—The *Exercise* of the Right

The true significance of *Casey* is that it manages to uphold *Roe* whilst taking account, to some degree, of concerns raised in the abortion cases of the 20 intervening years. In effect, *Casey* reviews the way in which *Roe*, which *expressed* certain State interests in the woman and the fetus, in fact provides for the *realisation* of these. Whilst the *Casey* court was concerned with the State's interests in the life and health of the mother, it focused particularly upon the State's interest in the potential life of the fetus. In this regard, writing on abortion and the decision in *Casey*, Ronald Dworkin has distinguished between the State's "derivative" interest in the fetus, which applies in the abortion context from viability onwards as the fetus acquires interests in its own right, and the State's "detached" interest, developed in *Casey*, in encouraging responsible decisions which are duly respectful of the value of fetal life.[161] With regard to this interest, Justices O'Connor, Kennedy and Souter held that states are free to take steps to ensure that a woman's choice is thoughtful and informed and may therefore enact laws providing for a reasonable framework within which a woman can make a decision of such import.[162] The joint opinion was supported in this respect by Justices Stevens and Blackmun.[163] Let us first clarify the relevance of this aspect of *Casey* to the maternal–fetal conflict and then specifically examine *Casey*'s provisions in this regard.

1. Relevance to the Maternal–Fetal Conflict

My discussion of this aspect of *Casey* relates to our concerns about the way in which a pregnant woman may choose to *exercise* her legal right to refuse medical treatment and hence in the scope for education, counselling and persuasion in the maternal–fetal conflict cases. In the light of the connections between treatment refusal and abortion law, and given that the early maternal–fetal cases drew upon

---

[159] 120 L Ed 2d at 699.
[160] *Ibid.*, 716.
[161] R Dworkin, *Life's Dominion*, e.g. at 11, 24, 169–70.
[162] 120 L Ed 2d at 711–12.
[163] *Ibid.*, 740 and 751 respectively.

abortion law to assert some kind of interest in the fetus, just as in the abortion context the State has an interest in ensuring respectful choices, so too it may have such an interest in the cases of maternal–fetal conflict. In other words, because another life is at stake—not just that of the woman—the State seems once more to have an interest in the *moral quality* of the treatment refusal decision. As we have seen, the State no longer has such an interest in the case of the refusal of treatment by the "ordinary competent adult": that is, in the latter case the only concern of third parties is that a patient is competent and has been appropriately informed about the consequences of a treatment refusal. Regarding the maternal–fetal conflict, by contrast, the State has an interest in the moral quality of a woman's treatment decision which is satisfied where a maternal refusal hinges upon serious reasons grounded in her underlying moral interests, thus supporting the principle of her right, but not in (unlikely) cases of trivial or non-existent reasons for refusal.

It may be pertinent to recall at this point that in the English case of *Re F (in utero)*, discussed in the last chapter, Staughton LJ observed that "[t]he court cannot care for a child . . . until the child is born; *only the mother can*".[164] Thus, whilst the law will not intervene to protect the child against the mother, the upshot is that responsibility for fetal welfare lies with her. (This means, of course, that where she refuses treatment or surgery and this results in fetal harm, legally she cannot seek to place liability on health professionals treating her.) In all likelihood she will do all she can. (In fact, health care providers have expressed concern that pregnant women are actually too willing to jeopardise their own health to submit to procedures that may be of benefit to their fetuses.[165]) But, in the unlikely event that she does not, we have seen that the Court of Appeal in *Re MB* has effectively legitimised persuasion in relation to a pregnant woman's refusal of treatment. Since that case is not concerned with the issue of the relationship between a woman's right and her responsibility toward the fetus, however, it does not tell us anything about the scope for third-party involvement in her decision, a question of central concern in *Casey*. This is why it is important and helpful to explore this aspect of *Casey*. Thus, exploring the issue of third-party involvement in the abortion choice, as this has been conceived in the United States, and trying to apply these ideas to the situation of maternal–fetal conflict to see the extent and limits of third-party involvement under *Casey*, in turn helps us to formulate guidelines for consideration also beyond the United States. In particular, we will want to know when involvement must rest with education, discussion and counselling and when it may go beyond this to persuasion—a *question* not addressed and, perhaps more significantly, a *distinction* not made in *Re MB* itself. Indeed, whilst various scholars advocate persuasion at most, there have been no serious attempts to formulate guidelines in this regard.[166]

---

[164] [1988] 2 All ER 193, 201, my emphasis.

[165] AMA Board of Trustees, "Legal Interventions During Pregnancy", (1990) 263 *JAMA* 2663, 2663.

[166] E.g. John Fletcher writes that as a matter of social policy coercion, which may do great harm to pregnant women, should be rejected in favour of persuasion and education. Elaborating upon the latter options, he suggests that this "will entail clear warning about the moral consequences . . . of proven fetal therapy". "Drawing Moral Lines in Fetal Therapy", (1986) 19 *Clin Obstet & Gyn* 595, 601. Another discussion mentioning the idea of persuasion occurs in FC Chervenak and LB McCullough,

2. *The Right to Make the Ultimate Decision, Not to Do So in Isolation*

In this section I consider the joint opinion's view that a woman's right to abort is not a right to do so in ignorance of society's views on the matter and the alternatives open to her. *Casey*'s argument that states can facilitate a reasonable framework within which the abortion decision occurs is bound up with several questions: the validity of the trimester framework established in *Roe*, the operation of the State's interests in the fetus and in the life and health of the woman, the ways in which various state abortion regulations in *Casey* and other cases sought to influence a woman's decision and the question of whether or not such regulations actually interfered with her choice. The joint opinion considers the trimester framework to be excessively rigid, such that it fails to allow due weight to be given to the State's own interest in the potential life of the fetus which we saw was originally asserted in *Roe* and was there described as "important and legitimate".[167] I do not wish to pursue the intricacies of the arguments in favour of (*per* Blackmun and Stevens JJ) or against (*per* the joint opinion) the trimester framework. However, there appears to be some elision in the joint opinion which refers, on the one hand, to *Roe*'s assertion of an "important" State interest in the fetus which in turn becomes "compelling" at viability and, on the other, to the idea that *Roe* in fact stands for "a substantial State interest in potential life *throughout* pregnancy":[168] that is, it glides over the change in the *strength* of the State interest at viability.

Notwithstanding these differences and problems, Justices Stevens and Blackmun agreed with the principle at stake in the joint opinion's finding that "[s]tates are free to enact laws to provide a reasonable framework for a woman to make a decision that has such profound and lasting meaning".[169] The joint opinion considered this to be consistent with *Roe*'s central holding and, indeed, an "inevitable consequence" of the State's assertion of an interest in the potential life of the fetus.[170] Justices O'Connor, Kennedy and Souter also suggested that states could enact regulations which would inform the woman of the "philosophic and social arguments of great weight that can be brought to bear in favour of continuing the pregnancy".[171] Most significantly, we should note the joint opinion's view that "what is at stake is the woman's *right to make the ultimate decision, not a right to be insulated from all others in so doing*".[172] In this light, it was considered that states might enact laws designed to create a "structural mechanism" by which third parties, such as the

---

"Clinical Guides to Preventing Ethical Conflicts Between Pregnant Women and their Fetuses", (1990) 162 *Am J Obstet & Gyn* 303. These authors advocate a paradigm of "respectful persuasion", beginning with informed consent, moving on to negotiation and concluding with respectful persuasion (at 305–6), but posit that this may not be effective. They suggest that doctors must convey that when a pregnancy has reached full term, a fetus is also a patient. (At 305.)

[167] 35 L Ed 2d at 182.
[168] 120 L Ed 2d at 714, my emphasis.
[169] *Ibid.*, 712.
[170] *Ibid.*
[171] *Ibid.*
[172] *Ibid.*, 715, my emphasis.

State, or family members in the case of minors, may themselves "express profound respect for the life of the unborn".[173]

There was disagreement, however, as to how far the State could go in effecting such a mechanism. Thus, while Justice Stevens agreed that the State could express a preference for childbirth over abortion, he considered that "serious questions" arose if it were to attempt to "persuade" her to choose the former.[174] He was supported in part in this criticism by Justice Blackmun,[175] who did not voice any agreement with the idea that the State may express a preference for normal childbirth, but concentrated instead on Justice Stevens's concerns about persuasion.[176] Justice Blackmun noted that states may not try to assert their preference for childbirth over abortion "under the guise of securing informed consent".[177] Thus, he seems to have been alert to the possibility that the concept of "informed consent" might be used illegitimately to import unnecessary burdens upon the exercise of a woman's abortion right. Moreover, Justice Stevens considered it questionable whether the regulations concerning counselling provisions which were in issue in *Casey* in fact had anything to do with the "philosophic or social" arguments which the court legitimised in principle.[178] In other words, both justices were aware of the need to distinguish *neutral medical information* legitimately related to *health* on the one hand and information concerned with *moral consequences*, coupled with the question of *persuasion* in relation thereto, on the other. This would equally be an area of legitimate concern in relation to the treatment context: indeed, toward the end of chapter three I drew attention to the *moral questions* that are ultimately at stake in addition to what we might dub the "neutral medical consequences" in *Re MB's* application of the *Re C* test to the maternal–fetal cases, as discussed, for instance, with reference to the *Rochdale* case. I now turn again to the maternal–fetal conflict itself.

a) *Application to the Maternal–Fetal Conflict*

Regarding the maternal–fetal conflict, we might consider which of the positions in *Casey* would be justifiable: on the one hand there is the joint opinion's finding of the legitimacy of a "reasonable framework" within which the State can seek to ensure that a woman's choice is thoughtful and informed, the principle of which

---

[173] 120 L Ed 2d at 715.

[174] Rather than "inject into a woman's most personal deliberations its own views of what is best", he considered that, at most, the State could promote its preferences by funding childbirth and creating and maintaining alternatives to abortion. *Ibid.*, 740–1. The question of the State expressing a preference for childbirth had been debated in *Webster*, 106 L Ed 2d 410. In that case, the Court observed that "the Constitution does not forbid a State or city, pursuant to democratic processes, from expressing a preference for normal childbirth" (opinion of the Court, 106 L Ed 2d at 431, citing *Poelker* v. *Doe*, 432 US 519, 521 (1977)).

[175] 120 L Ed 2d at 752.

[176] *Ibid.*

[177] *Ibid.* (He referred here to *Thornburgh* v. *American College of Obstetricians and Gynecologists*, 90 L Ed 2d 779 (1986) and *Akron*, 76 L Ed 2d 687 (1983).)

[178] *Ibid.*, 744. He thereby concluded that the information requirements in point served no useful purpose and therefore constituted an unnecessary and hence undue burden on a woman's liberty.

was supported by Justices Stevens and Blackmun. Applying this to the context of the maternal–fetal conflict, it would seem that not only must third parties—doctors and health professionals generally—inform women of the risks and benefits of certain sorts of treatment to herself and the fetus, but also that a third party such as a doctor or, preferably, a counsellor, should be able, subject to time constraints, to discuss the likely implications of a woman's refusal with her. But could such a person legitimately seek to *persuade* the woman to accept the treatment under *Casey*?

Regarding the legitimacy of persuasion *per se*, judging by other aspects of the decision in *Casey*,[179] the joint opinion would seem to support the idea. Yet we should recall the important concerns of Justices Stevens and Blackmun that while the *Casey* framework should "enhance the deliberative quality" of a woman's decision, the State must not "inject into a woman's most personal deliberations its own view of what is best . . . but . . . must respect the individual's freedom to make such judgments".[180] Nevertheless, in the light of the moral argument in Part I to the effect that the fetus's (and to some extent the future child's) claim grows throughout pregnancy, and of Justice Blackmun's position in *Roe* (affirmed in *Casey*), that the State's interest in the fetus becomes compelling at viability,[181] might it not be arguable that a post-viability refusal of treatment could be the subject not only of discussion but also attempted *persuasion* (presumably with some view to the moral consequences) even on Justice Blackmun's terms? After all, persuading a woman to accept treatment (which she has no serious reason to refuse) is very different from persuading a woman not to abort (where the consequence will be that she will give birth to a child that she would not otherwise have had).

i) Treatment Refusal *after* Viability

At this juncture, we should recall the important contextual differences between the situations of abortion and maternal–fetal conflict noted in Part I: regarding the former, a woman has many months prior to viability during which she can abort and, concomitant with the fetus's development of interests at viability, this partly justifies the restriction of the abortion right from viability onwards. In the case of maternal–fetal conflict, however, we saw that treatment issues often make demands upon a woman's interests and rights for the first time quite (even very) late in pregnancy. This would suggest, following the approach of Justices Blackmun and Stevens, that persuasion would only be justifiable in the maternal–fetal conflict (after viability)

---

[179] Notably the fact that the joint opinion upheld the mandatory provision of literature on the risks and alternatives to abortion and a 24-hour waiting period before an abortion.

[180] *Per* Stevens J, 120 L Ed 2d at 741.

[181] This is to be distinguished from the joint opinion's views in this regard: as touched upon earlier, the joint opinion does not appear to address clearly the issue of the changing strength of the State's interest in the fetus. Note that prior to *Casey* one author considered whether the State's interest in the nonviable fetus could be compelling in the treatment context but merely "protectible" in the context of abortion. As this author notes, however, this would imply that the significance of a woman's interest in bodily integrity is less than her interest in abortion. Rather, although not perfectly symmetrical, these interests should be considered as broadly equivalent, particularly given the primacy of the right to bodily integrity as a form of autonomy. S Such, "Lifesaving Medical Treatment for the Nonviable Fetus", 976.

where the woman is refusing treatment for an obviously *trivial, outrageously inappropriate* reason. This is because the justification for third-party involvement would lie not so much in the State's compelling interest in the fetus—because a prior opportunity for refusal had not arisen—but rather in the triviality/inappropriateness of the reason. Importantly, this was in fact precisely the area where I suggested that there was an opening for involvement in her treatment choice, as I shall discuss further below.

ii) Treatment Refusal *before* Viability

One might at first argue that prior to viability, although persuasion might be authorised on the joint opinion's views in *Casey*, it is unlikely that it would be sanctioned by Justice Blackmun and probably not by Justice Stevens.[182] Yet pre-viability there is also the possibility of a treatment refusal resulting in harm to the future child, not just in fetal death. This would suggest that even on the views of the more liberal judges, where a woman is refusing treatment for the trivial or non-existent reason, the State would legitimately have an interest in persuasion prior to viability. In the light of my reasoning in Part I, which emphasised the significance of location in the determination of the strength of the future child's interests, the future child's interests can be seen as particularly strong where the relevant treatment is non-invasive and hence does not make severe demands of the woman's body (and the woman's reasons for refusal are trivial or non-existent).

Where fetal death is in issue as the probable result of a treatment refusal (for trivial/non-existent reasons), the State's interest in the fetus and hence the grounds for persuasion would tend to strengthen with the development of the fetus.

3. Persuasion and the Clearly Trivial or Non-Existent Reason

Most importantly, recall that I am not suggesting that women *do* refuse medical treatment for trivial reasons, but only that we should have some moral/conceptual tools to deal with this possibility. This is important because of the tensions underlying these cases to which I first drew attention at the end of chapter three: people worry about *why* a pregnant woman might refuse treatment and hence whether she should have the legal right to do so. Overall, the important point about the scope for persuasion with regard to trivial or non-existent reasons is that, as I observed in Part I, if a woman were to seek to exercise her right to refuse treatment in such a way the reasons do not appear to be intrinsically related to the *interests* which underpin the rights in self-determination or bodily integrity. To return to the example used in my explication of this point in Part I, if a pregnant woman were to refuse to swallow a pill highly beneficial to the unborn child's welfare (with no religious or other such reason at stake), neither her interests in self-determination nor in

---

[182] However, in this regard it should be recalled that where harm to the future child, rather than fetal death, is at stake, viability ceases to have such significance. In this regard, I refer to my discussion in Part I to the effect that where harm to the future child is in issue, a woman must have strong reasons relating to her body. See that discussion for further clarification of this point.

bodily integrity are invoked in any but the most superficial sense. As I put it earlier, there is not the "coincidence" between the serious reason and the right which would normally justify a woman having and exercising the right to refuse the treatment. I pointed out that, since the case does not invoke an important *interest* on her part, to say that she has the "right" to refuse the pill is really only correct in the weak or one-dimensional sense that it is her *choice*. On this basis, I suggest that attempts at persuasion may well be appropriate in cases of *clearly trivial and irresponsible* reasons; in particular, this may include discussion as to the *moral appropriateness* of the reason in relation to the prospective harm to the unborn child.

Thus, with regard to an aspect of the question left open following *Baby Boy Doe* and *Re Fetus Brown* (namely whether a woman has the right to refuse non-invasive treatment), if a woman were to refuse such treatment for trivial and hence inappropriate reasons or for non-existent reasons with potentially harmful consequences for the fetus/future child, both counselling and persuasion would be permissible under *Casey*. But if she were still to refuse, she should have the legal right to do so.

Yet why should she retain the ultimate right to decide in such a case? After all, to insist in such a case on the idea of her *right* seems in some way to debase our carefully understood concept of the right in question. In this connection, Dworkin has suggested that one possible ground for limiting the definition of a particular right might be that "the values protected by the original right are not really at stake in the marginal case, or are at stake only in some attenuated form".[183] In the light of the unjustifiable way in which the right is to be exercised in the case of the refusal to swallow the pill, I suggested in Part I that one reason for granting her the right lies not in the "meaning" for her (given that her *interests* are not seriously invoked), but rather in the importance of not forcing her. In other words, whilst legally she is being granted the right to refuse the pill (subject to our attempts to persuade her to take it), it is important to allow her the chance to make the choice herself and thereby to realise—or fail to realise—an opportunity for responsible agency. On this note, as hinted in chapter two, one way in which virtue theory may be developed within law and politics may be in providing important grounds for proscribing coercion in such cases, but it remains beyond my scope to develop this theme. Instead, let us recall what Justice Stevens said in the US Supreme Court abortion decision of *Thornburgh* v. *American College of Obstetricians and Gynecologists*:[184]

> "In the final analysis, the holding in *Roe* v. *Wade* presumes that it is far better to permit some individuals to make incorrect decisions than to deny all individuals the right to make decisions that have a profound effect upon their destiny."

It may be that if we were not to grant the right in such a case there would also be a symbolic significance that might attach to the denial of any one pregnant woman's right, as discussed in the final section of this chapter. The question of

---

[183] R Dworkin, *Taking Rights Seriously*, 200.
[184] 90 L Ed 2d 779 (1986), 807. Aspects of this decision are discussed in ch. 5

whether we should endorse forced treatment in the (unlikely) event of "trivial refusals" is further discussed in chapter seven, which deals with the law of rescue and is mainly concerned with the arguments for and against coercion and the use of force (imposition of a legal duty) in cases where a moral duty seems clear. Additionally, there are important policy considerations at stake (discussed both in chapter six and chapter seven) which appear to weigh against forced prenatal treatment. Part of what emerges from chapter seven is that maternal rights to refuse treatment are always necessary to protect the "vague but powerful idea of human dignity" and/or political equality, one or both of which Dworkin has suggested are central to the valuing of rights.[185]

By contrast, in the (equally hypothetical) case of the refusal of a caesarean section (rather than the beneficial pill) for reasons relating to the abdominal scar, third-party involvement should stop at information and discussion for the important reason that, unlike in the case of the beneficial pill, there is a risk that a caesarean section will have fatal implications for a woman. In this case, regardless of the fact that these fears are apparently not part of her reasons, I suggest that others would not be justified in advocating a course which could result in physical harm—death—of the woman. Further, as *Baby Boy Doe* has recently confirmed, caesarean surgery always results in pain and generally delayed recovery (compared with "natural birth") in the post-operative stages.[186]

The exception to this will be in the case where the chances are that the woman herself will die without the surgery. Persuasion will be acceptable in such cases assuming the reasons for her refusal are trivial (rather than religious, as discussed above, or very deeply held, as in the case of *Rochdale,* discussed below).

Importantly, the occasion for treatment refusals which allow for persuasion will therefore be very few; but so too, I believe, will be the occasions on which women do refuse treatment for clearly trivial and hence morally inappropriate reasons. The discussion therefore tends to confirm that where a pregnant woman refuses medical treatment it will most likely be for an appropriately serious reason. This in turn supports the moral justification of her possession of the legal right to do so.

4. Reasons and Competence—Moral Infusions

As highlighted at the end of chapter three, there are difficulties in the practical application of aspects of *Re MB* which inhere in the relationship between the issue of reasons and that of competence. Although a woman does have the legal right to refuse medical treatment even for irrational or non-existent reasons, the determination of her competence to do so is related at one level to her reasons.

In this regard, I return briefly to the case of *Rochdale,* in which I suggested that Johnson J effectively weighed the interests of mother and fetus, to observe the way in which *moral* questions might come into play in the crucial "weighing-up"

---

[185] R Dworkin, *Taking Rights Seriously,* 198, 199.
[186] 632 NE 2d at 328. Indeed, the court found that "[t]he mother will have much more pain due to a C-section delivery than birth from the laboring process".

process, rather than purely *medical* ones. I suggested at the end of the last chapter that in this case it would have been important to attend to Mrs C's feelings about the question of the caesarean, which probably underlay the explicit reasons she gave, in particular her feeling—which was before the court—that she would "rather die" than have another caesarean. I suggested above, in the abdominal scar example, that persuasion in the case of a caesarean is not defensible in the light of the increased risk of death to the woman over natural childbirth and noted that the exception to this will be in the case where the chances are that the woman herself will die without the surgery. The acceptability of persuasion in the latter cases will depend, I think, on the reasons for the woman's refusal. In fact, as we saw earlier, Mrs C was indeed at risk of death without a caesarean. Nevertheless, in her case, bearing in mind the strength of her reasons, there appears to have been no scope for persuasion, as opposed to discussion intended to clarify the issues and objections, as evidenced by the fact that Mrs C is understood (having consented to the caesarean) to have felt extremely pressured to do so, resulting in much post-birth stress and trauma.[187]

In section D I distil this discussion into a framework for use in the maternal–fetal conflict. Whilst the English cases discussed in this section would not of course be binding on US courts, the problems encountered in these cases offer important reflections to those dealing with situations of maternal refusals in the United States just as much as in England. Indeed, discussion with US health professionals indicates that similar factual scenarios to those experienced in England have been and are likely to be encountered in the United States;[188] moreover, that some of the ideas from the English cases are in practice considered important in determinations of capacity in the United States. Indeed, recent American work on the notion of capacity suggests that certain "legal standards" for competence have developed which focus, as English law does, on particular *functional abilities*. These include:[189]

> "(1) *understanding* of information that is disclosed in the informed consent process, (2) *appreciation* of the information for one's own circumstances, (3) *reasoning* with the information, and (4) *expressing a choice*."

Courts may test for one or more of these abilities in determining competence.[190] With regard to the reasoning requirement, there is general agreement that the patient is not required to make a wise choice and in this sense the focus is on how the choice is made—the process—rather than normative considerations of what choice is made.[191] Nevertheless, the quality of the patient's choice is not irrelevant

---

[187] Personal communication: conversation with Ms Barbara Hewson (now QC), counsel for Mrs C, 24 Jan. 1997.

[188] As noted previously, in particular with Dr Rosamond Rhodes (a bioethicist) and Dr James Strain (a psychiatrist), Mount Sinai School of Medicine, New York.

[189] T Grisso and PS Applebaum, *Assessing Competence to Consent to Treatment: A Guide for Physicians and Other Health Professionals* (New York, NY: Oxford University Press, 1998) 20, emphasis in original.

[190] *Ibid.*, 59.

[191] *Ibid.*, 33, 53.

to a determination of competence, since it is very often the possibly dangerous outcome of an apparently inadvisable choice that points to the need to determine competence. Since in part the patient will be evaluated for her ability to weigh risks and
benefits,[192] and since the risks of a refusal will typically fall on the fetus whereas the
benefits will often accrue to the pregnant woman, as indicated earlier, moral
considerations are at stake in her reasoning process. This means that others must be
specially careful that it is her reasoning (amongst other functional abilities, where
appropriate) that is evaluated, not her choice. It is possible, however, that either
health professionals or a judge or both will incorrectly perceive that her reasoning
process is at fault, as in the English case of *Rochdale*, thereby illegitimately deeming
her incompetent and so removing her right "through the back door".[193]

5. Guaranteeing Rights in Practice as well as in Theory—Article 8 of the ECHR under the Human Rights Act 1998 and the Issue of Persuasion

As we have seen through discussion of *Casey* in particular, US case-law has shown
an acute awareness on the part of some judges of the crucial difference between the
theoretical existence of a right and its exercise in practice, free from undue interference. Following the Human Rights Act 1998, it would appear that English
judges will, somewhat belatedly, have to wake up to this difference (with the
exception, perhaps, of Lord Donaldson in *Re T*, as explained in the next section).

As we saw in the last chapter, under *Re MB* (although there had to date been no
right to privacy in English law) since a pregnant woman has the right to refuse
treatment for any reason—which I suggested could also be protected by Article 8
of the ECHR—then theoretically at least the legal principles in *Re MB* are consistent with Article 8 of the Convention under the Human Rights Act 1998. I have
also stressed, however, that *Re MB* freely licensed others to persuade a pregnant
woman to accept medical treatment or surgery for the fetus but gave no guidance
on this whatsoever. In the light of the Strasbourg and US jurisprudence (apart, in
the latter case, from the restrictions upheld in *Casey* and the question of lack of
funding noted elsewhere which could well discourage abortion)[194] this is somewhat remarkable. What are we to make, then, of the situation in which others seek
to persuade a pregnant woman to accept treatment? Could she then allege an interference with her right under Article 8, assuming the English law on treatment

---

[192] T Grisso and PS Applebaum, *Assessing Competence to Consent to Treatment: A Guide for Physicians and Other Health Professionals* (New York, NY: Oxford University Press, 1998), 54. For further extremely interesting work on competence see B Cox White, *Competence to Consent* (Washington, DC: Georgetown University Press, 1994). It is beyond my scope to discuss competence in depth in itself. The early leading and well-known cases on the issue of competence are *Department of Human Services v. Northern* 563 SW 2d 197 (Tenn Ct App 1978) and *Lane v. Candura* 376 NE 2d 1232 (Mass App 1978).

[193] A McColgan likewise notes the fragility of autonomy in childbirth, observing that "[t]he problem lies not so much in the letter of the law as in its application (or otherwise) at the front-line".
A McColgan, *Women Under the Law*, 110.

[194] I.e. during the second trimester of pregnancy, the mandatory provision of literature on the risks
of and alternatives to abortion, a 24-hour waiting period before the operation and limits on its availability to minors.

refusal is interpreted to be consistent with the right to respect for private life? (After all, the second part of the article makes clear that "there shall be no interference by a public authority with the *exercise* of this right" except under certain conditions.[195]) This is hugely important, for "[t]he Convention is intended to guarantee not rights that are theoretical or illusory but rights that are practical and effective".[196]

Of course, attempts at persuasion may or may not be found to be an interference with the right. For instance, in *Costello-Roberts* v. *United Kingdom* "slippering" at a private school was not deemed to be disrespectful of private life on the basis that it did not reach a sufficient level of seriousness.[197] But this has been criticised as "conceptually unsatisfactory" given the lack of method in determining "levels of seriousness or degrees of due respect".[198] The level of seriousness in our case will depend on the degree of persuasion since the existence of interference under Article 8(1) (and, as I shall consider shortly, the justifiability of interference under Article 8(2)) is always a question of degree. In this light, it is conceivable that the "heavy duty persuasion" advocated by one health professional in the previous chapter could be deemed an interference.

Assuming there is a *prima facie* interference, a court would then have to consider the traditional threefold test: first, whether the interference is "prescribed by law" or "in accordance with the law"; second, whether it serves a legitimate objective (set out in the second part of the article); and third, whether it is necessary in a democratic society.

For the interference to be "in accordance with law" there must be an "ascertainable" legal regime regulating the relevant interference.[199] In *Sunday Times* v. *United Kingdom*, which concerned the right to freedom of expression under Article 10, the Strasbourg court stated:[200]

> "Firstly, the law must be adequately accessible: the citizens must be able to have an indication that is adequate in the circumstances of the legal rules applicable to a given case. Secondly, a norm cannot be regarded as 'law' unless it is formulated with sufficient precision to enable the citizen to regulate his conduct."

In essence, this case shows that the law must not only be accessible and clear but also predictable in its application.[201] The judicial authorisation of persuasion in

---

[195] My emphasis.

[196] *Airey* v. *Ireland* (1979–80) 2 EHRR 305, para. 24. Mrs Airey sought a decree of judicial separation from her husband based on his alleged cruelty to herself and their children. There was no available legal aid and she lacked the resources to finance legal assistance. The Court decided there was a breach of Art. 6(1) on the basis of the effective denial of access to a court.

[197] E.g. in *Costello-Roberts* v. *United Kingdom* (1995) 19 EHRR 112 (introduced in the notes to ch. 3, s. III(B)(1)) corporal punishment was not considered an interference. But note that the question of a possible violation of Art. 3 was the more prominent in the case.

[198] D Feldman, "Privacy-related Rights and their Social Value", 41.

[199] J Wadham and H Mountfield, *Blackstone's Guide to the Human Rights Act 1998* (London: Blackstone, 1999) 12.

[200] (1970) 2 EHRR 245, para. 49.

[201] FR Jacobs and RCA White, *The European Convention on Human Rights* 2nd edn. (Oxford: Clarendon Press, 1996) 33.

Re MB may appear at least *prima facie* to count as legal regulation as compared with the situation in the telephone-tapping case of *Malone* v. *United Kingdom*, in which the Court found there was no proper statutory code governing interceptions of communication.[202] But the lack of definition or guidance in Butler-Sloss LJ's suggestion that others may "attempt to persuade" the pregnant woman and hence the potential breadth of this statement casts doubt on the clarity and predictability of the law's application. Moreover, if there are to be limitations on a given freedom then there must be procedural safeguards.[203] There are none on persuasion in *Re MB*. Note, however, that the Court's review of the question of whether the interference is "prescribed by law" is quite deferential, particularly where national judicial interpretation is involved;[204] further, of particular relevance to the domestic context, this argument is usually only successful where there is no statutory scheme *and* no basis for judicial review.

The second question would be whether a legitimate aim is being served by the attempt to persuade a pregnant woman to accept medical treatment. Here we may be on firmer ground. Possible aims might be the protection of health or morals or the protection of the rights and freedom of others as allowed in Article 8(2), but as regards the latter it should be recalled that it has been suggested that the Strasbourg court has not indicated that the right to life is stronger than any other right,[205] nor, of course, that the fetus has a right to life (at least in the abortion context). In connection with the protection of health or morals, the strong dissent of Mr Fawcett in the *Brüggemann* case is worthy of attention once more. As we saw in the previous chapter, he rejected the majority's holding that "pregnancy does not pertain uniquely to the private sphere", holding that "'private life' . . . must in my view cover pregnancy, its commencement and termination: indeed it would be hard to envisage more essentially private elements".[206] Nevertheless he held that "pregnancy has also

---

[202] (1984) 7 EHRR 14, para. 79. "[I]t cannot be said with any reasonable certainty what elements of the powers to intercept are incorporated in legal rules and what elements remain with the discretion of the executive. In view of the attendant obscurity and uncertainty as to the state of the law in this essential respect, . . . the law . . . does not indicate with reasonable clarity the scope and manner of exercise of the relevant discretion conferred on the public authorities."

[203] In *Klass* v. *Germany* (1978) 2 EHRR 214, which concerned a degree of secret surveillance "in the interest of public safety", the Court held that states do not "enjoy an unlimited discretion to subject persons within their jurisdiction to secret surveillance. The court, being aware of the danger such a law poses of undermining or even destroying democracy on the ground of defending it, affirms that the Contracting States may not, in the name of the struggle against espionage and terrorism, adopt whatever measures they deem appropriate. The Court must be satisfied that, whatever system of surveillance is adopted, there exist adequate and effective guarantees against abuse." (Paras. 49–50.)

[204] See e.g. *Open Door Counselling and Dublin Well Woman* v. *Ireland* (1992) 15 EHRR 244, in which the Court found that the Government's interference with the freedom of the counselling centres to provide abortion information was prescribed by law: "Taking into consideration the high threshold of protection of the unborn provided under Irish law generally and the manner in which the courts have interpreted their role as the guarantors of constitutional rights, the possibility that action might be taken against the corporate applicants must have been, with appropriate legal advice, reasonably foreseeable." (Para. 60.)

[205] As noted in ch. 3, in M Blake, "Physician-assisted Suicide: A Criminal Offence or a Patient''s Right?" (1997) 5 *Med Law Rev* 294, 306, relying on *Open Door*.

[206] (1981) 3 EHRR 244, para. 1. Such reasoning would appear to bolster the connection between bodily integrity and Art. 8 observed in ch. 3.

responsibilities for the mother towards the unborn child, at least when it is capable of independent life".[207] For this reason he considered legislative intervention "in sexual morality may have the purpose of preventing abortion being often reduced simply to a form of contraception or, alternatively, of inducing a sense of *moral responsibility* in the commencement of pregnancy".[208] In the light of my arguments in this chapter relating to the theoretical justification of the right and its responsible exercise in practice, this reasoning is striking. Thus, it is conceivable that an English judge could hold that attempts at persuasion were justifiable under Article 8(2) in the interests of encouraging moral responsibility.

Yet, given the State's aim, there would have to be limits to the persuasion in order for an interference to satisfy the principle of proportionality—namely whether, according to the Court in *Handyside* v. *United Kingdom*, the interference is "necessary in a democratic society".[209] In *Handyside*,[210] the Court observed that whilst "necessary" is not the same as "indispensible", nor is it as flexible as words such as "ordinary", "useful", "reasonable" or "desirable". Rather, "necessity" must imply a "pressing social need". Here the Court referred to the doctrine of "margin of appreciation", by which the Court allows states some leeway in the protection of Convention rights having regard to national traditions and conditions.[211] As an international doctrine this will not, however, have any place under the Human Rights Act[212] (although there is also a domestic sense to the doctrine, whereby national judges defer to the national executive or legislature or other public authority, particularly one with expertise). Thus, our courts will likely find themselves looking more closely at issues which the Strasbourg court could in effect avoid by

---

[207] *Ibid.*, my emphasis.

[208] *Ibid.*, para. 6, my emphasis, although he considered the legislative interventions were not in fact justified in this case.

[209] (1976) 1 EHRR 737. This case concerned the English publication, for children, of the *Little Red School Book*, which contained a part on sex. The police seized the book and obtained a forfeiture order on the basis that the book was contrary to the Obscene Publications Act 1950. The applicant pleaded a violation of Art. 10 (freedom of expression) whilst the government argued that the restriction was necessary for the "protection of morals". Accepting that the limitation was "prescribed by law" the Court had to consider whether it was proportionate and "necessary in a democratic society". In answer with reference to the doctrine of the margin of appreciation (see text following), the Court noted that "the domestic margin of appreciation . . . goes hand in hand with a European supervision". (At para. 49.) See also *Dudgeon* v. *United Kingdom* (1981) 4 EHRR 149, in which the applicant alleged that Northern Ireland's criminalisation of all homosexual behaviour was a breach of Art. 8. The Court agreed on the basis that the legislation, "by reason of its breadth and absolute character, is, quite apart from the severity of the possible penalties provided for, disproportionate to the [government's] aims". (At para. 61.) At para. 53 the Court said that "a restriction on a Convention right cannot be regarded as 'necessary in a democratic society' (two hallmarks of which are tolerance and broadmindedness) unless, amongst other things, it is proportionate to the legitimate aim pursued". (Footnote omitted.)

[210] (1976) 1 EHRR 737, para. 48.

[211] In practice, this doctrine meant that the Court or the Commission would allow governments "the benefit of the doubt", L Doswald-Beck, "The Meaning of the 'Right to Respect for Private Life' under the European Convention on Human Rights", (1983) 4 *HRLJ* 283, 307.

[212] J Wadham and H Mountfield, *Blackstone's Guide to the Human Rights Act 1998*, who are of the view of "the majority of commentators, that the margin of appreciation should be regarded as an international doctrine". (At 18.) But note that there is also a domestic sense to the term, whereby national judges defer to the national executive or legislature or another public authority, particularly one with expertise.

reference to local conditions. In so doing, they will have to balance the interests of the individual with those of the community at large, consistent with the Court's approach to these issues in recent cases.[213] The Court in *Handyside* reflected on the principles characterising a democratic society, identifying these as "pluralism, tolerance and broadmindedness",[214] which meant, for instance, that "every 'formality', 'condition', 'restriction' or 'penalty' imposed in this sphere must be proportionate to the legitimate aim pursued".[215]

Encouraging moral responsibility toward fetal life is an important and legitimate aim which is arguably consistent with these democratic values in a way which coercion would not be. But if persuasion is so heavy that the will of the patient is obliterated (such as the "heavy duty persuasion" advocated by one health professional) then we will have succeeded not in encouraging moral responsibility but in negating the patient's right to refuse medical treatment: "persuasion" has here become coercion. "Persuasion" of this degree could not be deemed proportionate for, if it were, the reality would then be that a pregnant woman does *not* have the right to refuse the treatment in question. This would be a very different legal result from our starting point. That is, given that *Re MB* grants a pregnant woman the absolute right to refuse medical treatment needed by the fetus and assuming this is upheld under Article 8, then interference cannot legitimately negate the right, that is, effectively force treatment on her. Here, then, we see the way in which what Butler-Sloss LJ presumably thought of as "the situation on the ground" might in reality nullify the supposedly absolute right laid down in *Re MB*. In this sense, this aspect of *Re MB* could be open to challenge. It is with these points in mind that I have sought to identify certain limits to persuasion in the framework which follows shortly.

A final point to consider here, however, is who might the "others" be and to what extent the State has responsibility for their actions in relation to the right of the pregnant woman patient. As regards health professionals employed by an NHS Trust hospital, as representatives of a public authority they would have a duty, by virtue of section 6(1) of the 1998 Act, to act in ways compatible with Convention rights.[216] What about the actions of private healthcare providers, or the actions of a woman's family? Could these be actionable under the Convention? An application before the Strasbourg court is an application against the State alleging either an infringement of a right or rights or the failure positively to protect against

---

[213] E.g. *Keegan* v. *Ireland* (1994) 18 EHRR 342 and *Stjerna* v. *Finland* (1994) 24 EHRR 194, as noted in D Feldman, "Privacy-related Rights and their Social Value", 41.

[214] (1976) 1 EHRR 737, para. 49. For application of these principles, see *Dudgeon*, the case concerned with the illegality of homosexuality in Northern Ireland, in which we have seen that the Court noted that two "hallmarks" of a democratic society are tolerance and broadmindedness. (Para. 53.) The issue of homosexuality obviously raises questions about majority and minority public opinion and central to democracy is the notion of protecting minorities against oppression by the majority, as noted by FG Jacobs and RCA White, *The European Convention on Human Rights*, 33.

[215] (1976) 1 EHRR 737, para. 49.

[216] Note that s. 6(3) says that "'public authority' includes . . . (b) any person certain of whose functions are functions of a public nature".

infringement by a third party, including by a private person.[217] Whether the 1998 Act is purely "vertically effective" (between individuals on the one hand and the State or public authorities on the other) or whether it is "horizontally effective" (that is, between private individuals) by virtue of the courts' obligation, as public authorities under section 6(3), to act compatibly with Convention rights, is a question which has been the subject of considerable academic debate.[218] I cannot examine this question in detail here. Essentially, however, where in litigation between private parties there is a relevant statutory right, the courts have a clear obligation under section 3(1) of the Human Rights Act to interpret the right, "so far as it is possible", in a way that is compatible with the Convention. There is no clear obligation as regards common law rights or other judicial discretion, apart from the courts' general obligation under section 6(3) of the Act to act compatibly with the Convention. Ultimately then, it is for the courts to decide to what degree the Act affects the common law or other judicial discretion as regards private parties. But the possibility of a subsequent Strasbourg decision to the effect that the State has breached a positive obligation to protect one private party from the acts of another will give the courts a strong incentive to develop common law rights in a way that avoids such breaches, as recently occurred in *Venables and Thompson* v. *New Group Newspapers Ltd* in relation to the law of confidence.[219]

To return directly to the maternal–fetal context in the light of these observations, as we saw in chapter three, English law has recently recognised that Article 8 of the Convention protects a patient's right to self-determination and bodily integrity (*NHS Trust A* v. *M*; *NHS Trust B* v. *H*). Thus, the State could conceivably have an obligation to prevent private individuals such as members of the pregnant woman's family, or actions of the staff (or independent contractors) of a private hospital from infringing her rights in the manner discussed in this section. But although the European Court of Human Rights finds positive obligations in the Convention, it does so cautiously, or may find an obligation but no breach thereof.[220] It is more likely to find a positive obligation where the duty is to "respect" the patient's right, as for instance under Article 8, than in the case of a free-standing negative right.[221] Further, in positive obligation to act rather than

---

[217] J Wadham and H Mountfield, *Blackstone's Guide to the Human Rights Act 1998*, 25.

[218] *Ibid.*, 25–6. See further M Hunt, "The 'Horizontal Effect' of the Human Rights Act", [1998] PL 423.

[219] [2001] 1 All ER 908. The law of confidence thus defeated freedom of expression under Art. 10, in order to protect Venables' and Thompson's (notorious child-murderers) right to life under Art. 2.

[220] See e.g. *Osman* v. *United Kingdom* (1998) 5 BHRC 293, in which it was held that the police had a duty of care to protect members of a family from harm in the light of certain reports about a campaign of harassment by a school teacher who had become infatuated with the son. Controversially, the case decided that, by upholding a strike-out claim, the United Kingdom had not complied with the right to a fair trial under Art. 6. In *Z* v. *United Kingdom* ([2001] FCR 246, the appeal from *X* v. *Bedfordshire County Council* [1995] 2 AC 633), however, the ECHR found no breach of Art. 6 in relation to strike-out proceedings concerning social workers. See also *TP & KM* v. *United Kingdom* [2001] 2 FCR 289. The decision in *Osman* is thus in doubt.

[221] I Kennedy and A Grubb, *Medical Law*, 31.

negative obligation to refrain from interfering cases, the analysis under Article 8(1) and (2) is merged, as in *Rees* v. *United Kingdom*, in which the Court observed:[222]

> "In determining whether or not a positive obligation exists, regard must be had to the *fair balance* that has to be struck between the general interest of the community and the interests of the individual, the search for which balance is inherent in the whole of the Convention. In striking this balance the aims mentioned in the second paragraph of Article 8 may be of a certain relevance, although this provision refers in terms only to 'interferences' with the right protected by the first paragraph—in other words is concerned with the negative obligations flowing therefrom."

Thus, the Court performs a balancing test in which it weighs the individual's and the community's interests, either finding or not finding a positive obligation in principle and then turning, in the former case, to consider the issue of breach on the facts of the case. Hence, although the European Court of Human Rights could well hold that there is an obligation to protect a pregnant woman against excessive persuasion to accept medical treatment, it could still find that there had been no breach on the facts, either because the State had done all it could or because the persuasion in question was not excessive on the facts.

I now distil the discussion so far into a framework relating to the issues of discussion, counselling and persuasion.

D. A Framework relating to Discussion/Counselling and Persuasion— Some Pointers

On the basis of the discussion so far in Parts I and II, the following considerations would be relevant to doctors or health professionals generally in reviewing a woman's treatment refusal decision with her. In the light of the time constraints inherent in medical emergencies, these issues should—where possible—be dealt with before a birth becomes a matter of medical emergency, but not so long before the birth that a woman has not gained a real sense of her wishes.[223] Overall, as

---

[222] (1987) 9 EHRR 56, para. 37, my emphasis.

[223] For a thoughtful discussion regarding the issues of a pregnant woman's competence in labour, see R Ladd, "Women in Labour: Some Issues about Informed Consent", (1990) 4(3) *Hypatia* 37–45. Reprinted in HB Holmes and L Purdy (eds.), *Feminist Perspectives in Medical Ethics* (Indianapolis, IN: Indiana University Press, 1992) 216–223. Ladd argues that the use of very general pre-admission consent forms, which become effective when a woman enters hospital, implies that pregnant women will subsequently lack competence to give informed consent; further, that a pregnant woman may in fact be better able to make treatment decisions once labour has begun, when she "learns how [various] factors play out in her case and how she feels, both physically and emotionally" (at 221); hence that the use of general consent forms is not appropriate. These points might be related in turn to the issue of what has been dubbed "decisional authenticity", meaning the degree to which a decision is in tune with a person's long-term values and preferences. On this see e.g. JJ Finer, "Toward Guidelines for Compelling Cesarean Surgery: of Rights, Responsibilities and Decisional Authenticity", (1991) 77 *Miss L Rev* 239. The implication of Finer's views is that it is the long-stated preference (e.g. to have or not have a certain kind of treatment) that is a person's truly held view (at 286). As Ladd's article points out, however, it is arguable that a pregnant woman knows her own mind more clearly closer to the moment when

argued in chapter two, it is crucial that third parties seek to understand the woman's difficulties where these exist.[224] Although the primary aim of this framework is to protect pregnant women and, where compatible with this, the fetus, another aim is to encourage doctors and other health professionals not to feel powerless in the face of a maternal refusal,[225] but at the same time—and this is critical—closely to define the limits of their involvement, since doctors can have great influence over their patients.[226] Indeed, it is possible that the power imbalance between doctor and patient may result in coercion, particularly where there is the suggestion of a

treatment must be accepted or refused. This is a difficult issue and in reality patients may vary. Additionally, as Finer notes, such factors as shock, pain and confusion, to which I refer in the text following, further complicate matters. But the implication of Finer's views is that a woman's decision could be overridden because such factors are deemed to diminish her competence. It is to avoid this outcome (except in the cases of genuine phobia of the precondition to the surgery) that I am here formulating a detailed framework. In any event, perhaps these difficulties highlight the need for pregnant women to be aware, so far as possible, of the difficulties of others in interpreting and responding to their treatment decisions.

[224] S Martin and M Coleman have suggested that "[r]arely is there even an attempt to understand the decision from the perspective of the woman involved. Sometimes, the woman's own reasons for refusing the surgery are not even sought . . . and if provided, they are often trivialized." "Judicial Intervention in Pregnancy", 965, citing VEB Kolder, J Gallagher and MT Parsons, "Court-Ordered Obstetrical Interventions", (1987) 316 *New Eng J Med* 1192 as authority for the view that women are often labelled as irrational.

[225] For a powerful account of the frustrations of this viewpoint see J Phelan, "The Maternal Abdominal Wall: A Fortresss Against Fetal Health Care?", (1991) 65 *S Cal L Rev* 461. On the acuteness of these frustrations the author writes (at 472): "Depending on the clinical situation, the physician can often remedy the fetal health problem easily, with a cesarean, a fetal blood transfusion, or another available medical procedure. The 'hands off' alternative implies that physicians and nurses should 'discard all that experience, knowledge and skill' because a competent pregnant woman's right to bodily integrity permits her to decide whether her potentially viable fetus will live or die . . . That physician is in the most unenviable of positions, as she is *wrong if she does perform a cesarean and wrong if she does not* . . . Under these circumstances, the physician's individual integrity, as well as that of the entire medical profession, is questioned whether or not the cesarean is performed, and *liability could flow from either decision.*" (Footnote omitted, my emphases.) Regarding the last point, at a legal level, this cannot be right: if a caesarean is refused with consequent fetal harm, then the woman takes responsibility for this. For detailed discussion of this and related matters see e.g. J Seymour, *Childbirth and the Law* (Oxford: Oxford University Press, 2000). At a moral level, whilst the "hands off" position might conflict with the physician's own ethical stance, my work here seeks to provide a moral justification for such a position. Apart from these points, however, this physician's observations suggest that, in an ideal world, it is not just pregnant women, but also health professionals, who might benefit from a counsellor's attention in this context. See also S Goldbeck-Wood, Editorial, "Women's Autonomy in Childbirth", 314 *BMJ* (1997) 1143.

[226] Note K Knopoff, "Can a Pregnant Woman Morally Refuse Fetal Surgery?", (1991) 79 *Calif L Rev* 499: "Courts probably will not decide many of the forced fetal surgery cases. That is to say, even without a court order, doctors may have a great deal of power to pressure women into consenting to the recommended surgery. Psychological factors intensify that pressure so that, in many cases where women finally give consent, they do not give it freely and voluntarily". (At 535, footnote citing the 1983 President's Commission Report, *Making Health Care Decisions: The Ethical and Legal Implications of Informed Consent in the Patient–Practitioner Relationship* omitted). Note further that in the survey by Kolder *et al* nearly half the obstetricians surveyed (who all directed fellowship programs in maternal–fetal medicine) considered that when persuasion is unsuccessful, judicial authorisation should be sought. Further, 47% thought the then existing precedents for court-ordered caesareans should be extended to other procedures with the potential to save fetal life once those became the standard of care. VEB Kolder, J Gallagher and MT Parsons, "Court-Ordered Obstetrical Interventions", 1193. It is unclear whether the (unfounded) threat of legal liability for fetal harm influenced these figures.

possible court order, such that a woman may "change her mind" through fear of legal action.[227] A woman might also submit through fear of the physical consequences of refusing and the procedure being forced on her.[228] Further, it might be noted that doctors may, for instance in the United States, breach a fiduciary duty owed to their pregnant women patients if they seek to induce or coerce them into accepting the recommended treatment.[229] This framework should also assist in those US states in which the issue of maternal–fetal conflict in the treatment context is as yet undecided, since cases may well not reach the courts. It is also hoped that this framework, which "takes account", to some extent, of the fetus/future child might be helpful in dealing with the possible lack of physician commitment to professional guidelines such as those promulgated by the ACOG and AMA.[230]

a) *The Serious Reason—Discussion and Counselling:* with regard to the refusal of treatment for serious reasons, counselling and discussion, at most, are permissible, in order to ensure that the treatment options and consequences—"neutral medical information" as it were—are clearly understood.[231] (On the

[227] For recognition of this point see e.g. S Martin and M Coleman, "Judicial Intervention in Pregnancy", 968, n. 90. On the improper use that doctors might make of the idea of legal action, see M Oberman, "Mother's and Doctors' Orders: Unmasking the Doctor's Fiduciary Role in Maternal–Fetal Conflicts", (2000) 94 *Nw UL Rev* 451,481, who notes that in interviews following the *Baby Boy Doe* decision doctors at Chicago's Rush-Presbyterian Medical Center admitted that they had recently had 5 or 6 similar cases but that in all of these the women had backed down at the threat of legal action.

[228] JK Levy, "Jehovah's Witnesses, Pregnancy, and Blood Transfusions: A Paradigm for the Autonomy Rights of All Pregnant Women", (1999) 27 *J of Law, Med and Ethics* 171, 183.

[229] M Oberman, "Mother's and Doctors' Orders", 478. She suggests doctors "almost invariably will subject her to a series of informal and formal sanctions designed to induce, if not to coerce her into consenting to the operation". As she observes, however, it may be difficult to establish the requisite harm (489–90). She also notes the breach of confidentiality which may occur when doctors enlist "unrelated third parties" to put pressure on a woman to consent (at 481).

[230] *Ibid.*, 491*ff* in which the author notes various problems on this front including that the AMA guidelines "Legal Interventions During Pregnancy", (1998) (Policy No. H–420.969) have not been incorporated into the AMA's Code of Ethics and thus do not carry an enforcement mechanism. Oberman notes the view of Dr S Latham (former director of the Ethics Division of the AMA interviewed in Chicago, Ill, (12 Jan. 1999) that currently the political climate regarding abortion is so charged that it would be difficult to pass a policy specifically dealing with obstetric interventions (at 493). Nevertheless, Oberman suggests that even with explicit professional guidelines rejecting compelled interventions, these would only be effective if they became part of standard medical practice, drawing on discussion of the relationship between professional guidelines and behaviour in D Orentlicher, "The Influence of Professional Organization on Physician Behavior", (1994) 57 *Alb L Rev* 583. Orentlicher notes: "The medical profession's experience with standard-setting suggests [that] . . . professional regulation can have a substantial impact on physician behaviour, but professional guidelines alone are generally insufficient to change physician behaviour. The guidelines must be combined with other measures to ensure compliance." (At 591.) Somewhat depressingly Orentlicher further notes that physicians may be more inclined to follow practice guidelines when they contain clear rules with a "credible threat of enforcement from outside of the profession", and when "violations [can] . . . be detected with relative ease" (at 596, 598). In response to the limits to the role of professional guidance, Oberman recommends (at 496 *ff*) that physicians disclose their views on maternal autonomy at the outset of the maternal–physician relationship, an idea she discusses in some depth, although she notes the potential difficulties for women in finding other prenatal care, for reasons related to insurance on the one hand (potentially only a short list of accepted providers) or the restrictions associated with poverty on the other (at 498).

[231] On this point, note the view of one author that "from a purely information standpoint, the pregnant woman's physical and psychological position with respect to the fetus makes her a uniquely appropriate decisionmaker. She alone has full information about the risks and benefits of a particular course

important question of identifying serious reasons see (g) below; and on the issue of information and consent see my comments on this in section (i) at the end of the framework.)

i) Note that *persuasion* is not appropriate in these cases because where the reason is "serious", in ways elaborated in earlier argument, the reasons have an intrinsic connection to the woman and her underlying moral interests in self-determination and/or bodily integrity;[232] further, that in such cases a pregnant woman will likely have in mind the effect of her choices upon the fetus (see further the factors noted in section (e) (i) to (iii) below) so that her reasons will be able appropriately to "answer" to these considerations.

ii) Are the woman's reasons religious or ("quasi-religious")? If so, and this is a highly complex matter, are these beliefs autonomously held, in the sense that they appear to enhance the woman's ability in the process of the determination of the shape and meaning of her life? If not, there may be the prospect of discussion beyond "neutral medical issues" in relation to religious reasons, as non-autonomously held religious beliefs may not be "part" of the person in the way that such beliefs generally are. It should be noted, however, that in practice this may be impossible to determine except in obvious cases of undue influence, as in the English case of *Re T*.[233]

iii) Do the reasons relate to her fears, and if so, of what? Thus, is it considered that these are negating her competence, effectively paralysing her will, such as in the English "needle phobia" cases of *Re MB* and *Re L*? In these exceptional cases, when a woman consents to the caesarean, for instance, but cannot consent to the necessary anaesthesia, then it may be in her best interests to legitimise surgery (subject to good evidence on this point). But where the fears concern the treatment in itself (the caesarean section), rather than a precondition to it (the anaesthesia), as in the "needle phobia" cases, I think that such fear should be understood as a *serious reason*: in this light, counselling and discussion, but not persuasion, are permissible.

of conduct." In the note to this, the author observes "[f]ocusing primarily on the medical implications the doctor is unlikely to give sufficient weight to a woman's religious objections to surgery, for example." "Note: Rethinking (M)otherhood: Feminist Theory and State Regulation of Pregnancy", (1990) 103 *Harv L Rev* 1325. Whilst the last part of this is surely right, I do not think it can be that the woman certainly knows best about the risks or problems not only in relation to herself but *also* in relation to the fetus. See further s. (i) below.

[232] Compare the approach of L Nelson and N Milliken, "Compelled Medical Treatment of Pregnant Women: Life, Liberty and Law in Conflict", (1988) 259 *JAMA* 1060, who suggest that it would be "ethically acceptable to try to persuade a pregnant woman refusing medical treatment to change her mind." (At 1061.) I think this is acceptable in *limited* cases, as outlined in this framework.

[233] In particular, the idea of attempting to demonstrate to, for instance, a Jehovah's Witness, the *irrationality* of their religious beliefs, as Julian Savulescu has recently suggested, is a matter requiring extensive ethical consideration. He discusses such an approach in J Savulescu and RW Momeyer, "Should Informed Consent be Based on Rational Beliefs?", (1997) 23 *JME* 282. I suggest that to expose the inconsistencies in biblical texts on the point, for instance, of consuming blood, may either do a patient a great service or disservice, depending on the person in question. For instance, if religion is a great comfort within a person's life, exposing such inconsistencies could do great harm. See further my discussion of religious reasons in ch. 2. See also R Gillon, Editorial, (2000) 26 *JME* 299.

Indeed, whilst this framework distinguishes between serious and trivial reasons and the scope, respectively, for discussion and counselling as opposed to persuasion, clearly on occasion there may be a temptation to consider that *fear* cannot be a serious in the sense of an "appropriate" reason (for example, in the light of third parties' reflections upon the degree of risk to the woman in the caesarean surgery) but is instead a "trivial" or "insufficiently serious" one. It is to avoid this possibility that I am suggesting that fear (that is, of surgery in itself, not the anaesthesia) should always be understood as a serious reason.[234] In this connection, we should recall that in *Re MB* the Court of Appeal noted that fear may constitute a "rational reason" for refusing treatment.

b) *Irrationality and Competence:*

i) Is the decision to refuse treatment considered irrational, for instance "outrageous" either in its "defiance of logic", or of "accepted moral standards", to use the terminology of the decision in *Re MB*? With regard to the issue of *irrationality*, it is hard to know how health professionals will distinguish between irrationality *per se* and that which is evidence of incompetence. It seems likely (and in some sense understandable) that the more irrational (outrageous, illogical etc.) the decision, then the greater the risk that it will be deemed evidence of incompetence. Moreover, as noted in chapter three, that two lives may be at stake in a pregnant woman's decision to refuse treatment, and especially one for which the woman "speaks" (the fetus) may at some level increase the degree of competence that others expect a pregnant woman to demonstrate. Importantly, however, they must resist the temptation to conclude that the woman cannot "weigh" the information before her—that is, is *incompetent* to do so—on the basis that at some level her reasons seem an "inappropriate" basis upon which to refuse medical treatment such as a caesarean. Such weighing is not permissible—for instance, in Illinois under *Baby Boy Doe* and in England under *Re MB*. Cases will vary, and problems about the different degrees of articulateness of some patients will compound this issue: it may be relevant for instance that Mrs C in *Rochdale* was Bangladeshi.

ii) Nevertheless, whilst the woman has the *right* to refuse treatment, including for apparently *irrational or morally inappropriate reasons* in England, in those (hypothetical) cases where the decision is "outrageous" either in its "defiance of logic", or of "accepted moral standards", others are permitted under *Re MB* to try to persuade the pregnant woman to accept the treatment in ways on which I give guidance in sections (d), (e) and (f) below. But note that persuasion was not appropriate in the *Rochdale* case itself, where the result was that Mrs C felt very pressured to accept the caesarean which she had "serious reasons" to reject. Indeed, let us remind ourselves that in this

---

[234] JJ Finer, who advocates overriding refusals in some circumstances, himself makes an exception for the case of the pregnant woman with "pathologically high levels of fear regarding . . . surgery". JJ Finer, "Toward Guidelines for Compelling Cesarean Surgery", 294.

framework I am *excluding* as candidates for persuasion the cases where, in the best judgment of third parties, a woman has serious reasons for her refusal of treatment. Clearly, however, in some cases third parties will mistakenly deem a serious reason which should properly be seen as the subject of "reasonable disagreement" to be exceedingly irrational. Where possible this should be avoided. In order to help third parties reflect upon whether reasons with which they strongly disagree are nevertheless "intrinsically connected to" the pregnant woman, we might reflect upon a passage from the work of Michael Wreen (who is not specifically concerned with the maternal–fetal conflict) in which he writes that "when autonomy is isolated from other values, an autonomous patient might refuse treatment for utterly trivial, laughably whimsical, or *grossly irrelevant* reasons".[235] Note that it is in this way that I have at times characterised the "trivial reason" (specifically identified below). In other words, establishing whether the perceived irrationality–immorality has a connection with other values and beliefs within a person's life will help to establish whether these are "serious reasons" which should only be the subject of discussion, for clarificatory purposes, rather than persuasion. Reasons pertaining to a clearly defined religious faith will likely receive the swiftest recognition.

iii) Where a decision to refuse treatment *is* considered irrational in the sense that it is "outrageous" either in its "defiance of logic", or of "accepted moral standards", *and* has no apparent place or purpose within the woman's life more generally, third parties should be permitted to draw to a woman's attention the impact of her choice upon the fetus (see section (e) below). What they are *not* permitted to do is to *deem her incompetent—hence take away her right—on the basis of the perceived irrationality–immorality of her decision*, unless her reasons are deemed to be evidence of incompetence. Of course, deciding whether the character of her reasons reflects incompetence will often be precisely where the difficulty lies.[236] In this light, given the temptation that may exist to deem the woman incompetent (as in *Rochdale*), emphasising and closely defining the scope for *persuasion* in such cases should in theory *strengthen* a pregnant woman's right to refuse treatment. (But note the limitations upon persuasion and questions to do with its strength below, limitations not observed in *Rochdale* itself.) In other words, if others have a legitimate involvement in a woman's choice through the

[235] MJ Wreen, "Autonomy, Religious Values and Refusal of Lifesaving Medical Treatment", (1991) 17 *JME* 124, 128, my emphasis.

[236] In *St George's Healthcare NHS Trust* v. *S, R* v. *Collins and others, ex parte S* the Court formulated guidelines relating to cases of treatment refusal which include provision for the consultation of a psychiatrist on the issue of competence. In *Re MB* in the section on "Procedure" which concludes its judgment, the Court of Appeal holds, at para. 8, that "[t]here should in general be *some evidence* preferably but not necessarily from a psychiatrist, as to the competence of the patient, if competence is in issue." [1997] 8 Med LR at 228, my emphasis. It appears that the Court of Appeal in *St George's* is contemplating a more *active* role for psychiatrists in the determination of competence than that contemplated by the court in *Re MB*, at least in "serious or complex cases involving difficult issues about the future health and well-being or even the life of the patient". [1998] 3 All ER 673 at 703.

avenue of persuasion, then it is probably less likely that a woman will *wrongly be deemed incompetent*. Thus, up to a point (see here the *extremely important* comments in sections (d) and (f) below) the possibility of persuasion may protect a woman's right by helping to prevent an inappropriate finding of incompetence.

    iv) Where a judgment that she is incompetent *is* appropriate, there should be some, possibly psychiatric, evidence to support this, other than that of the "irrationality" of the decision to refuse treatment. (See for instance the guidelines in *Re MB* and *St George's*.)

c) *Clearly Trivial or Non-existent Reasons:* in the unlikely event that the woman's reasons for refusal are clearly trivial, or non-existent, then *persuasion*, as detailed and limited in sections (d), (e) and (f) below, may be appropriate. However, prior to this, naturally the reasons (where these exist) should be carefully discussed, in the course of which it may become apparent to others that the reasons cannot in fact be put in the rather narrow category of "the trivial".

d) *Persuasion Generally:* As a preliminary point in all cases: does the treatment impose greater risks to the pregnant woman, or usually greater pain, upon the woman than non-treatment? If so, I suggest that third-party involvement should be restricted to counselling and discussion, rather than persuasion.

e) *Attending to the Fetus/Future Child:* Key elements to consider in connection with "outrageously irrational or morally inappropriate *and* insufficiently serious reasons, or clearly trivial or non-existent reasons" may be:

    i) The stage of development of the fetus: the more advanced, then, on the basis of my argument in Part I and of the position of the US (and English) law in Part II, the greater may be the interests of third parties in seeking to persuade, particularly where refusal of treatment may result in fetal death (rather than harm to the future child). In this connection, the gradualist underpinnings of the State's interest in potential life are well captured by Justice Stevens in an abortion decision following *Roe* but prior to *Casey*:[237]

> "I should think it obvious that the State's interest in the protection of an embryo—even if that interest is defined as 'protecting those who will be citizens' . . .—increases progressively and dramatically as the organism's capacity to feel pain, to experience pleasure, to survive, and to react to its surroundings increases day by day. The development of a fetus—and pregnancy itself—are not static conditions . . . Recognition of this . . . is supported not only by logic, but also by history and by our shared experiences."

    ii) Where harm to the future child is in issue, arguably the stage of development, whilst important, is not as important as the question of the extent to which the relevant treatment may impinge upon the woman's body, consistent with my reasoning on this point in Part I. The greater the degree of invasion for the woman, the weaker the interests of the future child, in the

[237] *Thornburgh*, 90 L Ed 2d 779 (1986), concurring in the majority opinion, at 805, footnote omitted. The phrase "those who will be citizens" is a reference to the judgment of Rehnquist J, dissenting.

light of the significance of the issue of location *per se* in relation to the strength of the future child's interests as compared with its mother's (rather than those of a "detached" third party).

iii) If the treatment is life-enhancing, rather than life-saving, how desirable is it? For instance, as noted in Part I, surgery to correct a facial deformity does not seem as important as that to correct a malfunctioning organ.

f) *The Strength of Persuasion:* However, with regard to the issue of persuasion and its effects on the pregnant woman, note should be taken of the guidance of Lord Donaldson MR in *Re T*, upon the relationship between the questions of persuasion and undue influence, particularly the possibly vitiating effects of the latter (such that a battery might then be committed), in which he said:[238]

> "It matters not how strong the persuasion was, so long as it did not overbear the independence of the patient's decision. The real question in each case is: does the patient really mean what [she] says or is [she] merely saying it for a quiet life, to satisfy someone else or because the advice and persuasion to which [she] has been subjected is such that [she] can no longer think and decide for [herself]? In other words, is it a decision expressed in form only, not in reality?"

Of the issues highlighted as very important, most relevant is that of the "strength of will" of the patient. Here he noted that a patient who is "very tired, [or] in pain . . . will be much less able to resist having [her] will overborne . . .".[239] These points are obviously highly relevant to the case of a pregnant woman, particularly the common scenario concerning the need for an emergency caesarean section. Indeed, in chapter three I noted that Margaret Brazier has drawn attention to the way in which such factors as confusion, shock, fatigue and pain are in many cases an "inevitable part" of labour.[240] Here the importance of rights under the European Convention being "guaranteed" in practice, not just in theory, comes to the fore.

Thus, although the English law is that if a woman is still refusing treatment after persuasion she must be allowed to do so, in reality it is very possible that third parties will have succeeded, not in *changing her mind* but rather in *overbearing her will*. Her *right*, in other words, will have been negated. It is for this reason that I am suggesting that what we saw one health professional (in chapter three) to describe as "heavy duty persuasion" should be limited to situations in which the treatment refused does not impose greater pain or risks upon the pregnant woman *and* to situations where the reasons for refusal seem "insufficiently serious" or "trivial", "irrational/inappropriate *and* purposeless" or are "non-existent". As we saw before, these kinds of reasons arguably lack the fundamental connection to the person (which, say, the religious reason has or deeply held life values have) which in turn means that such reasons are not linked with a person's moral interests in self-determination and/or bodily integrity which are the principal foundation of the right to refuse treatment.

---

[238] [1992] 4 All ER at 662.
[239] *Ibid.*
[240] M Brazier, Guest Editorial, "Hard Cases Make Bad Law?", (1997) 23 *JME* 341, 343.

Essentially this may rule out many caesarean deliveries as the targets of persuasion, rather than discussion and counselling, in the light, say, of *Baby Boy Doe*'s factual finding about the greater pain and risks of such surgery over natural birth. Whilst on different facts these points may not apply—for instance, where a woman will likely die as the result of a refusal—in such cases it is of course extremely unlikely that she has only trivial, highly inappropriate and purposeless or nonexistent reasons for the refusal in question.

g) *Distinguishing the Serious from the Trivial:* It is implicitly accepted above that reasons do not come with labels bearing the words "serious" or "trivial". Sometimes a reason may not seem trivial, but third parties may nevertheless be concerned about the "seriousness" of the reason, in the sense of whether it has been sufficiently thought out. The case of *Pemberton*, introduced earlier in the chapter, may be an illustration. Ms Pemberton had previously had a caesarean section with a vertical rather than a horizontal incision. For her current pregnancy she wished to give birth vaginally but had not been able to find a physician who would assist her in this, as it was deemed that there was a risk of uterine rupture and fetal death. She attempted to give birth at home with the assistance of a midwife but after some time needed an intra-uterine drip which she sought at her local hospital with the aim of then returning home. The physicians by whom she was seen would not be party to this plan and instigated proceedings legally to compel a caesarean. Ms Pemberton was retrieved against her will from her home (to which she had returned) and a court hearing was held at the hospital which resulted in a compelled caesarean. On appeal, one of five experts for the hospital, Dr O'Bryan, estimated the risk of uterine rupture at four to six per cent. Additionally, Dr Clark, "a national expert", stated that current medical opinion places the risk at between 6 to 10 per cent at the low end, and as high as 60 per cent. Ms Pemberton's expert witness, Dr Wagner, put the risk of uterine rupture lower, at between 2 and 2.2 per cent, stating that if the uterus were to rupture the risk of fetal death would then be 50 per cent (effectively a one per cent risk).[241] Judge Hinkle declared the risk to be "substantial", regardless of whether it be one or 60 per cent. The question the case raises, however, but which he does not acknowledge, is *who* should decide the acceptability of the risk to the fetus (or indeed to the pregnant woman herself, regarding whom the risks of complications following uterine rupture were not quantified). The question of who should decide the acceptability or otherwise of risk to the fetus is intrinsically connected to the question of whether the pregnant woman should have the right to decline the caesarean. Arguably *Pemberton* is a prime example of a case in which discussion and counselling were appropriate to find out more about Ms Pemberton's objections, who apparently considered that vaginal delivery would not pose an "appreciable"[242] risk to her unborn child. For instance, perhaps there were unresolved traumas to do with

---

[241] 66 F Supp 2d at 1253.
[242] *Ibid.,* 1252.

her previous caesarean. (Rights to religious freedom were also asserted on appeal but no specific religion was identified.)

h) As might be expected in the light of the attention to the issue of persuasion regarding US abortion law, the question of persuasion has long been recognised as an important and difficult one regarding patients generally as they contemplate treatment options. The following comment from the 1983 President's Commission Report, *Making Health Care Decisions*, aptly captures the complexities which have here been under discussion regarding the maternal–fetal conflict:[243]

> "The difficult distinction, both *in theory and in practice*, is between acceptable forms of informing, discussion and rational persuasion on the one hand, and objectionable forms of influence or manipulation on the other."

i) *General Issues relating to Information and Consent in Practice:* In chapter two I noted that issues such as lack of information about and consent to medical procedures during birth are capable of contributing to "bad birth experiences". Clearly it is crucial that women are kept as informed as possible of how their labour is progressing and what options are open to them and so forth. Indeed, the principal recommendations of the English Department of Health's report *Changing Childbirth* were that women should be given enough information for them to make decisions regarding care and that continuity of care is crucial in facilitating communication between health professionals and their patients.[244] Strikingly, one consultant obstetrician has written of the need, so far as possible, for *joint* decision-making between health professionals and pregnant women, acknowledging the fallibility of medical judgment:[245]

> "Doctors would not need to practise defensively if they were willing to say: 'This is the situation as I see it: we could do this or that, but I am not really sure what is best. Under these circumstances, what would you prefer me to do?' In my experience, by sharing responsibility like this I am more likely to make the best decision and furthermore (although this is a secondary consideration), I am less likely to be blamed when the outcome is tragedy. Being truthful and sharing responsibility is not opting out. It does not absolve us from responsibility. It is the more difficult course to follow, since it requires more time, more emotional involvement and more consideration of the wishes of others rather than of our own."

As regards the process of "joint" decision-making, one health writer has suggested that although women do not have a medical education (unless health professionals of some kind themselves), they "do have varying degrees of intuitive knowledge about their bodies and many have experiential knowledge about pregnancy and labour".[246] The question of "intuitive knowledge" is a difficult one. Women may

---

[243] In its discussion of "Manipulation", as cited in I Kennedy and A Grubb, *Medical Law,* 3rd edn. (London: Butterworths, 2000) 755, my emphasis.

[244] H Churchill, *Caesarean Birth: Experience, Practice and History* (Hale: Books for Midwives Press, 1997) 58.

[245] Peter Huntingford in 1985, as cited in *ibid.*, 165.

[246] *Ibid.*, 56.

have some "intuitive" knowledge of how their pregnancy is progressing, though it is hard to evaluate this point. Sometimes women realise they are pregnant before a test establishes this and other times they do not. And sometimes women are aware that something is wrong with their pregnancy and other times are not. The question of how to "blend" such knowledge with medical knowledge is also difficult and raises a number of complex questions. But once again these points highlight the importance of information, consent and, as far as possible, joint decision-making. As regards information, one issue which sometimes causes problems is the question of who has responsibility for informing a pregnant woman of what.[247] A further issue relating to the question of information, touched on in chapter two, concerns the importance of clearer information earlier in pregnancy about the real risk of a need for a caesarean in some births.[248] In this regard it would seem that some of the negative psychological effects of having a caesarean are induced by a sense of "missing out" on a natural delivery.[249] It should be noted, however, that the conclusions on the negative psychological effects of caesarean sections *per se* (as opposed to forced ones) in comparison with natural delivery are inconclusive.[250] Overall, Helen Churchill concludes:[251]

> "[I]t appears that the negative effects of caesarean birth on women are related to: use of general anaesthesia, absence of a partner or friend during delivery, lack of detailed information about the events surrounding caesarean birth, missing out on vaginal delivery, having a longer recovery time, experiencing greater pain, routine separation of the infant from the mother at birth as is common practice, emergency rather than elective operations and most importantly, the increased risk of fatality from childbirth."

Although greater pain and longer recovery time are inherent in the procedure, some of the practices associated with caesareans could be modified, as discussed in detail by Churchill. This is not the place for such a discussion, but if the experience of caesareans could be made any less negative, then women refusing them on the basis of reasons related to fear or strong negative perceptions, may have less reason to do so.

Concluding this section, I note that one set of scholars has written of the difficulty of judging maternal reasons *tout court*, albeit with particular reference to the case of the religious reason, rather than the problems in judging the serious, personal

---

[247] H Churchill, *Caesarean Birth: Experience, Practice and History*, 59, 165.

[248] *Ibid.*, 90, 103.

[249] *Ibid.*, 90: "Unless women have a previous history of difficult labour, previous caesareans or are alerted during antenatal check-ups that a caesarean may be necessary, they will not usually seriously consider that they could need a section. They are therefore more disappointed when the outcome does not meet their expectations and are likely to suffer more in terms of depression because of this."

[250] "Evidence on the negative effects of caesarean section is not conclusive and some studies have suggested that mothers having caesarean birth are not significantly different on levels of depression than those delivering vaginally . . . and that many women perceive the operation to be a positive experience . . . Further, it has been suggested that the most important dimension of birth to the women involved is a healthy baby and not the delivery process." *Ibid.*, 91, citing literature on point.

[251] *Ibid.*, 102.

reason.[252] The authors do not appear to acknowledge the possibility of a trivial reason for a refusal (as writers such as Nancy Rhoden and Bonnie Steinbock have done, as noted in chapter one), referring to the idea of a woman's *"perceived* 'callousness' ",[253] as though we could *never* make the judgment that a refusal was in fact callous or capricious, no matter what the reason for the refusal. Moreover, since the authors are not concerned with exploring the connections between the *reasons* and the *right* which is an important aspect of the current discussion, they conclude rightly but in a somewhat question-begging fashion that the woman's right trumps the fetus's interests and/or others' concerns for the fetus. This is correct, but, as this chapter has tried to show, the justification of that right will be enhanced and concomitantly the right will be strengthened by the recognition of the way in which serious reasons theoretically ground the right. Similarly, where a refusal is trivial, or thought to be trivial, allowing others a legitimate way to express concerns through discussion and, very rarely persuasion (where the best judgment of others is that the reason is utterly irrational and "purposeless", truly trivial or effectively non-existent), will do most to enhance women's interests and rights in medical decision-making in pregnancy. In general, however, given that pregnant women do refuse treatment for serious reasons, these authors are right, in one sense, to characterise the task of attempting to evaluate their decisions as "hopeless and unprincipled".[254] Indeed, I think they capture part of the difficulty regarding the religious reason, saying, "[t]here is no meaningful way to evaluate the reasonableness or merit of a belief in the authority of the Scriptures or of a judgment that receiving a blood transfusion is the equivalent of an activity prohibited by the Scriptures".[255] Yet, once again one could make the further and crucial step, as I have tried to do, of saying that, although we cannot judge the *reasonableness* of this kind of serious reason, its *meaning* and *value* lies in its connection with the woman's interest in self-determination, which partly grounds her right in the medical treatment context.

To complete the discussion regarding the relationship between a pregnant woman's medical law rights and her responsibility toward the fetus, I would like to reflect upon what this discussion of *Casey* generally reveals about the kinds of rights in issue in the maternal–fetal conflict.

E. The Significance of a Responsibility-based Right: a Synthesis of Justice and Care

We have seen that, in drawing out and deepening our understanding of the right to an abortion established in *Roe*, the joint opinion did not merely say that those who possess rights must exercise them responsibly, but also that the justification for

---

[252] L Nelson, B Buggy and C Weil, "Forced Medical Treatment of Pregnant Women: 'Compelling Each to Live as seems Good to the Rest' " (1986) 37 *Hastings LJ*, 720–1.

[253] *Ibid.*, 721, my emphasis.

[254] *Ibid.*

[255] *Ibid.*, n. 57.

a right such as the abortion right lies in its association with the meaning of procreation and the question of human responsibility and respect for it. Thus, to have the right to abort, as *Casey* makes clear, or to refuse medical treatment needed by the fetus, is to have the responsibility—we might even say the duty—to make a thoughtful and respectful choice. This is because the justification of either right lies partly in a woman's responsibility toward herself, the fetus and the society which, up to a point, lets her abort or otherwise harm it.

To appreciate the contribution of *Casey* it is important to note, however briefly,[256] that until this time two ways of understanding the relationship between the individual and the community had predominated in such cases, reflecting approaches in debates beyond the law and ethics of reproduction. The first, a rights-based approach, essentially hinges upon the understanding that the individual can have her way, so long as no compelling countervailing harm can be demonstrated.[257] Even if this approach is not absolutist, in the sense that it takes account—to some degree—of society's interests, if a claim of a right is understood as vindicating the interests of the individual *against* society, such an approach may be hard-pressed to explain or acknowledge the way in which decisions relating to reproduction necessarily concern the interests of more than one (or even two) individuals. This is the approach that has dominated the relevant case-law to date. But, as noted at various points, the liberal jurisprudence of such cases has been the subject of a communitarian critique, which suggests that giving precedence to reproductive rights comes at the expense of the well-being of the community, emphasising the way in which such rights are thought merely to concern and satisfy the interests and desires of the individual. In the area of medical ethics, such ideas have been echoed particularly in the approach known as an "ethics of care", which values connection, relationships and the idea of interdependent community.[258]

Now in one sense, of course, given the nature of human reproduction (by definition and in various senses involving more than one individual) an "ethics of

---

[256] See further ch. 1, s. I for a brief introduction to some of these themes.

[257] A good example of such an approach in the field of reproductive law can be found in J Robertson's *Children of Choice: Freedom and the New Reproductive Technologies* (Princeton, NJ: Princeton University Press, 1994).

[258] The work of Carol Gilligan has been of particular importance here. See e.g. C Gilligan, *In a Different Voice: Psychological Theory and Women's Development* (Cambridge, MA: Harvard University Press, 1982) and C Gilligan, J Ward and J Taylor (eds.), *Mapping the Moral Domain* (Cambridge, MA: Harvard University Press, 1988). In the latter work Gilligan withdrew the suggestion, prominent in the former, that there is some intrinsic connection between being female and taking up the care perspective. For a critique of Gilligan's earlier work, see C MacKinnon, *Feminism Unmodified: Discourses on Life and Law* (Camb., MA: Harvard University Press, 1989) 39, who argues that "[w]omen value care because men have valued us according to the care we give them . . . Women think in relational terms because our existence is defined in relation to men." Note that the relationship between care and justice has not yet been generally agreed on. According to M Friedman, "[a] wise working strategy for the present time is to regard care ethics as at the very least an account of a distinctive style or approach to ethical problems and concerns." "Feminism in Ethics: Conceptions of Autonomy", in M Fricker and J Hornsby (eds.), *The Cambridge Companion to Feminism in Philosophy*, 205–24, 208.

care" perspective may seem a more appropriate model. Yet, given our need ultimately to determine the degree of freedom we allow individuals (or couples) at law,
the justice perspective, which concentrates on autonomy and non-interference, is
not just relevant but crucial.[259] The law (and ethics) relating to reproductive autonomy would thus seem to cry out for some kind of *synthesis* of these two
approaches.[260] Indeed, concerning the *justification* of reproductive autonomy generally and rights specifically, reflection upon the values at stake in reproduction
reveals what might be labelled a "dual" feature: first, that reproductive choices are
intensely personal; second, that at the same time such choices raise questions—for
all of us—about the value of human life. Thus, whilst choices relating to reproduction reflect the individual's (or couple's) interests and values, at the same time
they express judgments about particular values to the community beyond.
Crucially, the Court in *Casey* appears implicitly to have understood this point of
connection and has effectively developed an account of the abortion right based
upon the idea of responsibility. In this process, the Court has recognised that a
woman's important freedom to decide about abortion is at the same time an opportunity to express and acknowledge responsibility, not only to herself, but also to
others—even, we might say—toward the value of human life itself.

---

[259] Hence it is particularly unhelpful to deride liberalism on the one hand and yet to chastise the legal
system for overriding pregnant women's rights (in the early maternal–fetal cases) on the other, as
L Purdy does in her article "Are Women Foetal Containers?", (1990) 4(4) *Bioethics* 273, 287, 289. See
also "Note: Rethinking (M)otherhood: Feminist Theory and State Regulation of Pregnancy", in which
the author writes (at 1337): "Whatever political value the notion of rights may have, the paradigm of
conflicting rights seems singularly inappropriate to describe pregnancy, a condition of continuous connection and dependence. Despite, or *arguably because of*, the prevailing discourse of rights and autonomy,
women continue to be coerced into a culturally defined maternal role of nurturance and self-sacrifice."
(My emphasis.) It is hard to see how the notion of *maternal* rights forces women into this role. Further,
the author does not appear to reconcile or explain the connection between these points and the
acknowledgement of the "political value" of rights. One might also note that, although a condition of
"continuous connection", pregnancy is one-sided in its dependency. An important aspect of this
author's contribution to the debate, however, lies in the suggestion that a change of emphasis from rights
to connection and responsibility shifts attention to the mother's and fetus's "conflicting as well as shared
needs" (at 1342). The author is confident that this will enlarge, rather than reduce women's autonomy
which will in turn promote both maternal and fetal health, suggesting that "[t]he answer to the dilemma
can no longer be simply to privilege either maternal or fetal rights. Rather, the solution must involve
some means of meeting these needs." (At 1343.) Sometimes, however, surely we will have "simply to
privilege" maternal needs or insist on maternal rights. Indeed, on the "disastrous limitations" of ethical
viewpoints which are hostile to rights and which "offer no serious discussion of justice or its borders,
. . . dismiss justice as an ethically inadequate, 'male' concern, or . . . ignore the import and importance
of the institutions of the public domain . . . in favour of celebrating the caring virtues of domesticity
and intimacy", see O O'Neill, *Towards Justice and Virtue: A Constructive Account of Practical Reasoning*
(Cambridge: Cambridge University Press, 1996) 141. (But note that O'Neill is not concerned with a
synthesis of justice and care in certain contexts, since she thinks each of value in different contexts, on
which see e.g. her "Justice, Gender and International Boundaries", in M Nussbaum and A Sen (eds.),
The Quality of Life (Oxford: Clarendon, 1993) 303–23, 311.

[260] Some philosophical work has touched on the idea of such a synthesis in *other* areas of ethics: see
e.g. M Stocker, "Duty and Friendship: Toward a Synthesis of Gilligan's Contrastive Moral Concepts",
in E Kittay and D Meyers (eds.), *Women and Moral Theory* (Totowa, NJ: Rowman and Littlefield, 1987)
56–68. However, the approach is largely unexplored in ethical and legal debate regarding reproduction;
for a legal exception see the next note.

In this way, the Supreme Court appears, in effect, to have taken the path advocated, for instance, by Robin West in 1990.[261] In an article which reviewed the state of liberal individualism following the US Supreme Court's 1989 term, she suggested that new arguments which highlight the connections between the individual and others were needed to defend the liberal's commitment to individual freedom, arguments which would focus upon the moral quality of reproductive decisions rather than "insulating" them from the understanding of others; and that a failure to build reproductive freedom on a theory of responsibility could lead to an erosion of reproductive rights. West suggested that "[l]iberals and feminists must develop alternative, *public-regarding* arguments supporting [these] rights and the liberty they protect that transcend the circular and increasingly false insistence that they simply exist."[262] This echoes my concern, made at the end of the last chapter and at the beginning of this one, that merely asserting a maternal right to refuse medical treatment during pregnancy is ultimately question-begging, including when premised upon the fetus's lack of legal personhood: hence the project of this chapter—to explain and justify the right in a way which attends at some level to the public interest. West thus appears to be wary of the possible limitations of a privacy rationale for reproductive rights, highlighting the capacity for an intrinsically insulating approach to increase the sense of conflict surrounding deeply controversial areas.

Ronald Dworkin might be said to have taken up West's call for new arguments in an article in 1992 which preceded the Supreme Court's decision in *Casey* (although this is not to suggest that there is any necessary connection between his article and West's). Indeed, Dworkin discussed the possibility of the Court relying on the arguments it subsequently developed in *Casey*, focusing upon the important distinction between the governmental goals of coercion and encouraging responsibility which can be said to underpin the subsequent decision.[263] Thus, it could be said that in *Casey* the Court has effectively developed a "responsibility-based argument for reproductive freedom that . . . justi[fies] rather than supplant[s] the rights-based claim

---

[261] R West, "Taking Freedom Seriously", (1990) 104 *Harvard L Rev* 43.

[262] *Ibid.*, 84, my emphasis. And see generally the discussion at 81–5.

[263] Thus: "These goals of responsibility and conformity are not only different; they are antagonistic. If we aim at responsibility, we must leave citizens free, in the end, to decide as they think right, because that is what moral responsibility entails. If, on the other hand, we aim at conformity, we deny citizens that decision. We demand that they act in a way that might be contrary to their own moral convictions, and we discourage rather than encourage them to develop their own sense of when and why life is sacred." R Dworkin, "Unenumerated Rights: Whether and How *Roe* v. *Wade* Should be Overruled", (1992) 59 *U Chic L Rev* 381, 408. As noted earlier, Dworkin argued that whilst the cases relating to procreative autonomy are generally understood as pertaining to the Due Process Clause of the 14th Amendment, they might also be understood as resting upon the Religion Clauses of the 1st Amendment. He also suggested, however, that it would be "remarkable" if the right of procreative autonomy were not also protected by the Due Process Clause or the Equal Protection Clause (at 425). In *Casey* itself, as we have seen, the Court situates the abortion right within the Due Process Clause. While there are some implications relating to the Equal Protection Clause in the joint opinion, this is an aspect specifically taken up by Blackmun J, on which see ch. 5 s. II(E). Note that Stevens J made reference to Dworkin's article on the question of whether the fetus should be deemed a person. 120 L Ed 2d at 739, n. 2.

of *Roe* v. *Wade*",[264] thereby halting what many had perceived would be the eventual demise of *Roe*.

Strikingly, this development rather gives the lie to Sheila Noonan's reflections upon (an earlier piece of) West's work, who wrote that "[i]n an era in which the last vestiges of *Roe* v. *Wade* are subject to constant judicial erosion, West's articulation of the connection thesis may result in its hastening demise."[265] Noonan's reference to the "connection thesis" is to West's reformulation of the work of Carol Gilligan in an earlier article.[266] In effect, Noonan, who describes herself as a radical feminist, criticises West for the way she "colludes"[267] with liberalism and defends ideas of freedom, autonomy, choice and equality.[268] Noonan is concerned that liberalism does not pay sufficient attention to what she dubs "concrete dynamics of power".[269] This reflection is worthy of mention because of the way in which, as Kolder and others originally highlighted (noted in chapter three), the instances of forced caesareans have disproportionately affected women of colour and/or women for whom English was not the first language. (It might be noted here that one author has suggested that the statistics in this survey might be skewed since the survey was only sent to teaching hospitals, which tend to run clinics treating the poor and uninsured, but nevertheless acknowledges that the survey raises the important issue that physicians might listen less to people from some sections of society because they are seen as "uneducated, ignorant, shortsighted, or simply because they come from backgrounds with which a physician cannot identify".[270]) The idea that the maternal–fetal conflict may be particularly subject to problems of race (and sex) discrimination is troubling and should be taken seriously. I do not think, however, that it is possible to analyse these issues other than by rigorous scrutiny and argument. Indeed, as Martha Nussbaum has persuasively argued, to believe instead in the "play of social and political forces" is to opt for a vision in which the stronger force will dominate, noting that in such a conception liberalism is simply another ideology.[271] Importantly, however, this does not mean that

---

[264] R West, "Taking Freedom Seriously", 84.

[265] S Noonan, "Theorizing Connection", (1992) 30 *Alberta L Rev* 719, 722.

[266] R West, "Jurisprudence and Gender", (1988) 55 *U Chic L Rev* 1.

[267] S Noonan, "Theorizing Connection", 722.

[268] *Ibid.*, 735.

[269] *Ibid.*, See also "Note: Rethinking (M)otherhood: Feminist Theory and State Regulation of Pregnancy", where the author notes (at 1335) that "some feminists have suggested that the language of rights is problematic in that it inadequately describes women's experience" (citing C Gilligan, *In a Different Voice,* and other works), "while masking issues of power" (citing C MacKinnon, *Toward a Feminist Theory of the State* (Cambridge, MA: Harvard University Press, 1989) 215–34). For a different view, this author cites M Minow, "Interpreting Rights: An Essay for Robert Cover", (1987) 96 *Yale LJ* 1860, who defends rights-based claims and suggests that "[b]y invoking rights, an individual or group claims the attention of the larger community and its authorities" (at 1874). I cannot examine these thoughts in detail here, although I think my approach tends to confirm that no one moral or legal language is sufficient in this context. On gender hierarchy note the discussion of coercion particularly in ch. 7.

[270] JK Levy, "Jehovah's Witnesses, Pregnancy, and Blood Transfusions", 183 (footnote omitted).

[271] M Nussbaum, "Feminists and Philosophy", A Review of LM Anthony and C Witt (eds.), *A Mind of One's Own: Feminist Essays on Reason and Objectivity* (Boulder, CO: Westview Press, 1993) NYRB, 20 Oct. 1994, 59, 60.

liberalism cannot recognise power asymmetries as part of the relevant facts in certain contexts.[272] Taking on board these reflections, in West's article on liberal individualism, in the US Supreme Court's decision in *Casey* and Ronald Dworkin's *Life's Dominion*, I think we see liberalism at its very defensible best.

Finally, with its insistence on the intrinsic link between a woman's right and her responsibilities, *Casey* seems to point towards an understanding in which the dichotomy between self and other, which seems such an unsympathetic basis upon which to review either abortion or, more particularly, the maternal–fetal conflict, is broken down: for the rights in these contexts are "about", in some sense, responsibility towards others, toward life itself. This is not to deny that where a person possesses a right, he or she can in fact choose to exercise it regardless of the interests of others; indeed, to have a right is to be able to do just this. Rather, the point is that the *justification* of such rights may at least partly lie in the individual's responsibility toward others. Yet the point also applies to the *exercise* of such rights in the sense that, in the unlikely event that a woman is unaware of any relevant moral or spiritual arguments, it is hard to see that she will be able to make a meaningful choice in these contexts. In fact, however, it is far more likely that she will be aware of various considerations, drawn from her religious, family or other experience:[273] these will influence her choice, making us see that the justification for and exercise of rights of these degrees of magnitude and meaning do not, at heart, involve only the individual. This again emphasises the social nature of autonomy discussed first in chapter one without denying that the woman's right is very much her own. In these ways the rights which we are inclined to recognise in the maternal–fetal context would seem to acknowledge and support, rather than deny, the interconnectedness of the woman and fetus and, ultimately, the woman and us.

Such an understanding may be reminiscent of Joseph Raz's understanding of the nature of morality, in which both rights and duties are to be understood as embedded within his wide theory of individual well-being.[274] We saw in chapter two that on his understanding there is no right to personal autonomy as such (in an ideal sense), although there may be rights to aspects of it (such as, for our purposes, the right to abort, or to refuse medical treatment including when pregnant). Although on some views it may seem an unattractive feature that a theory does not allow a

---

[272] As noted by M Nussbaum, "The Sleep of Reason", *Times Higher Ed Supp*, Feb. 1996, 17, 18. Here she discusses a 1994 case (which she does not name) in which the first woman to work in the tinsmith shop in the General Motors plant in Indiana brought a sexual harassment case. The lower court judge, ignoring the asymmetry of power between the male co-workers and the woman, held that the men's use of obscenities amounted only to the "ribald banter of the tinsmith's shop". On appeal, Judge Posner rejected the lower court's findings of fact and held that the asymmetry of power, with its historical social meanings, was a vital part of the facts of the case.

[273] This is a point which Stevens and Blackmun JJ are at pains to point out. See for instance the opinion of Stevens J with regard to the 24-hour delay regulation which the Court upheld but which he denounced: "The mandatory delay . . . appears to rest on outmoded and unacceptable assumptions about the decisionmaking capacity of women. . . Just as we have left behind the belief that a woman must consult her husband before undertaking serious matters, . . . so we must reject the notion that a woman is less capable of deciding matters of gravity." 120 L Ed 2d at 742.

[274] J Raz, *The Morality of Freedom*, 256.

right to personal autonomy, there is an important and arguably attractive implication of this argument of relevance to the discussion in this chapter. Thus, if the autonomous life is not "a life within unviolated rights"[275], then the activities and choices which make up a valuable life may equally be those associated with duties as they are with interests which support rights. Significantly, this means that our understanding of autonomy need not be confined to the interests of the individual, but may also encompass the *connections* between the individual's and other's lives. Indeed, Raz questions whether it is possible to define those principles of activities and goals which are concerned only with oneself independently from those which relate to others. In this way, his approach is intended to reunite the series of dichotomies underlying a rights-based understanding of morality: he rejects the dichotomy between egoism and altruism, self-interest and the moral claims of others and thereby rejects the dichotomy between the right-holder and others.[276] In many ways this chapter's examination of the justification and exercise of a pregnant woman's legal right to refuse medical treatment adopts a similar approach.

In the end, this picture of the moral problems presented in the maternal–fetal conflict raises the question of our responsibilities to the pregnant woman, a point to which I now turn.

V. POSTSCRIPT: FIRST THOUGHTS ON DENYING A PREGNANT WOMAN THE LEGAL RIGHT TO REFUSE TREATMENT

Many people will not be satisfied with the suggestion that a pregnant woman should have the legal right to refuse medical treatment needed by the fetus, for whatever reason. Indeed the law itself, as pointed out in chapter three, is by no means easy with this conclusion as evidenced, for instance, in Lady Justice Butler-Sloss's observations in *Re MB* about the residual ethical dilemmas. I have tried, so far, to show why a pregnant woman should indeed have this right, in the process of which I have paid attention both to her interests in having this right and to our interest in such rights being responsibly exercised. I wish finally to strengthen my case by exploring some of the implications, related to the arguments in this chapter, of *denying* a pregnant woman this right, with particular reference to the case of *Re AC*.

In essence, I suggest that the State's interest in protecting potential life to some extent at least precludes it acting in a way that *itself* diminishes our sense of life's worth. Given that the fetus is by definition within the woman, intervening *for* the fetus necessarily implies doing something *to* the woman against her will: in this way, I suggest that the State cannot help but be faced with questions about the value it

---

[275] J Raz, "Right-based Moralities", (1982) in J Waldron (ed.), *Theories of Rights* (Oxford: Oxford University Press., 1984) 182–200, 191.

[276] J Raz, "Rights and Individual Well-Being", first published in (1992) 5 (July) *Ratio Juris* 2, reprinted in his *Ethics in the Public Domain: Essays in the Morality of Law and Politics* (Oxford: Oxford University Press, 1994) 44–59, 58–9.

thereby seems to accord to the woman's life, indeed with what harm it may do her. In one sense, the argument in this section may be said to highlight the sense in which the maternal–fetal conflict is of "great symbolic importance because it determines what value and how much respect we accord to the autonomy of pregnant women".[277] But the point applies beyond that half of society made up by women.

A. The Paradox of the Maternal–Fetal Cases

Earlier in this chapter I drew a distinction between the "positive" and "negative" choices that a patient might make in refusing medical treatment. In the event that a pregnant woman insists on making an obviously "negative" or "trivial" choice, despite third-party efforts in this regard, and in the light of the State's interest in promoting respect for fetal life, her decision might well be thought to "cheapen the value that is placed in the concept of living" in the way first expressed (as we saw earlier) in the case of *Saikewicz*. So far from the woman's refusal of treatment diminishing life's worth, I would like finally to consider the way in which the State itself might do so by overriding her refusal and the way in which the State may thereby in some way undermine its own aims. In a striking and much-cited passage, the *Saikewicz* court shifts its focus away from the actions of the individual:[278]

> "The constitutional right of privacy, . . . is an expression of the sanctity of individual free choice and self-determination as fundamental constituents of life. *The value of life* as so perceived *is lessened not by a decision to refuse treatment, but by the failure to allow a competent human being the right of choice.*"

If the State were to intervene to override a woman's treatment refusal, on the basis of *Roe* v. *Wade*'s interest in potential life and, in some sense, its resurrected interest in the preservation of life (which have both been seen to encompass an interest in upholding choices which do not diminish the value of life) arguably the State may itself display a disrespectful attitude toward life, thereby partially frustrating its own purpose (particularly where fetal death, rather than harm to the future child, is in issue). This has two stages. The first—the harm that is done to the pregnant woman herself—is already well recognised in the literature: one scholar captures it well, if somewhat dramatically, in the perception that overriding a pregnant woman's refusal of treatment reduces her to the status of a "foetal container"[279] and a "non-person without rights to bodily integrity";[280] others have suggested that the value of a pregnant woman's life is "certainly diminished" if a court overrides her rejection of treatment.[281] These points naturally carry implications for the status of

---

[277] S Elias and G Annas, *Reproductive Genetics and the Law* (Chicago, IL: Yearbook Medical Publishers, 1987) 254.

[278] For citations see e.g. *Re Conroy*, 486 A 2d at 1224; *Re Farrell*, 529 A 2d 404, 411 (NJ 1987). The *Saikewicz* passage is at 370 NE 2d at 426, *per* Liacos J, footnote omitted, emphasis added.

[279] G Annas, "Pregnant Women as Fetal Containers", (1986) 16 (Dec.) *Hastings CR* 13, 13 .

[280] G Annas, "Protecting the Liberty of Pregnant Patients", (1987) 316 *New Eng J Med* 1213, 1214.

[281] L Nelson *et al*, "Forced Medical Treatment", 751.

all women. In this regard, a striking analogy from fiction has found a home in the maternal–fetal literature, as many writers have made reference to Margaret Atwood's *The Handmaid's Tale*, in which doctors and the State remove human rights from fertile women, so that these women come to see themselves as "two legged wombs, that's all".[282] Further, immediately following the English decision of *Re S*, Ian Kennedy observed that the case had "massive implications for the status of women, in regarding them as chattels and ambulatory wombs".[283] Elias and Annas have suggested that "[t]reating women as incubators while they are pregnant represses them and deprives them of their human dignity and autonomy, and so *dehumanizes us all*."[284] This is strong language but arguably this last aspect represents the "second stage" of the State's frustration of aspects of its own interest in life.[285]

B. Abandoning One Life to Save Another: *Re AC*

The case of *Re AC*, introduced in chapter three, is a particularly poignant illustration of the difficulties inherent in the State's assertion of an interest in life in the maternal–fetal cases. Ms C's life was ending and her interest in a peaceful death was entirely subsumed in the State's interests in the fetus: whatever one's sense of the sacred may be—whether seen as entirely independent of the way our lives are lived

---

[282] M Atwood, *The Handmaid's Tale* (Boston, MA: Houghton Mifflin, 1986). See also J Gallagher, "Fetus as Patient", 215: "The fetal rights demands *are* a symbolic affront to all women: a dismissal of our moral agency and full citizenship, reducing us to the status of potential 'motherships', or carriers of 'precious cargo'." Emphasis in original.

[283] *The Times*, 15 Oct. 1992.

[284] S Elias and G Annas, *Reproductive Genetics and the Law*, 261, my emphasis. Whilst their views may be said to be in line with mine, I am trying to give "flesh" to the dehumanisation argument by the development of the argument in this section. Without "flesh" the notions of women becoming incubators and such like have a slightly *in terrorem* quality, as F DeCoste has also noted. "Case Comment and Note: *Winnipeg Child and Family Services (Northwest Area)* v. *DFG*: The Impossibility of Fetal Rights and the Obligations of Judicial Governance", (1998) 36 *Alberta L Rev* 725, 746.

[285] For another argument on the State's preservation of life interest but only as applied to the fetus, see A Ouellette, who suggests that, in the case of fetal surgery, the State's interest in preserving the life of the fetus is minimal since risks to the woman would "balance out" the "potential benefits to the fetus and the surgery would not benefit the health of the pregnant woman". "New Medical Technology: A Chance to Reexamine Court-Ordered Medical Procedures during Pregnancy", (1994) 57 *Alberta L Rev* 927, 959. Ouellette writes: "Maternal health would *surely* be compromised and a woman's life threatened if she was forced to undergo fetal surgery on behalf of her fetus." (*Ibid.*, my emphasis.) We do not know this for sure. However the abortion cases (discussed in the next chapter) reject the idea of increased maternal risk for the sake of the fetus. Note also S Michalowski, "Court-Authorised Caesarean Sections—The End of a Trend?", (1999) 62 *MLR* 115, who writes with reference to the English jurisprudence: "If women could be forced to have Caesarean sections in the name of the protection of the foetus, it would also follow that the interests of the foetus would be of higher value than those of the pregnant woman, a concept difficult to justify." (At 126.) It is unclear that this is really true. Legally, to mandate treatment for the fetus is to assume a non-existent jurisdiction (in English law) to take its interests into account but it is not necessarily to assume that the fetus's life is of higher value, for instance if the risks to the fetus of not having the caesarean are very high whereas the risks to the woman are "only" the inherent ones. Needless to say, this does not mean I advocate forced interventions, particularly in the light of the literal and symbolic harms that may result.

(for instance associated with a religious interpretation) and/or, as Dworkin has suggested, as instantiated in crucial aspects of our lives—death is commonly recognised as a critically important time.

As noted at the start of this chapter, the District of Columbia Court of Appeals of 1987, in approving the trial court's overriding of Ms C's apparent refusal, clearly saw itself as "presented with a woman whose significant interest in her bodily integrity must be balanced against the state's interest in potential human life".[286] The court argued that the State could not intervene to protect the life or health of the fetus unless to do so would not "significantly" affect the mother's health and the fetus had a "significant" chance of being born alive.[287] Note was taken of medical literature relating to the effects of a caesarean on women: that it would usually bring some discomfort and complications which would be temporary in "otherwise normal" patients, but that sometimes the caesarean could result in the woman's death.[288] However, these considerations were not considered decisive:[289]

> "The Caesarean section would not significantly affect AC's condition because she had, at best, two days left of sedated life; the complications arising from the surgery would not significantly alter that prognosis."

As has been observed elsewhere,[290] clearly a lot depends on the term "significantly". Indeed, the entire justification for the decision rests on the fact of Ms C's poor prognosis: since she was going to die in any event, the State could wash its hands of any causal responsibility (potentially through the caesarean) for the fact of her death. In this assessment, the timing and manner of her death were seen as negligible considerations. At this juncture, we might consider whether Ms C's case could be seen in some way as a forewarning of the suggestion of the Supreme Court of Missouri in Cruzan (the following year) that the State might seek to end the lives of disabled people if it allowed quality of life arguments to play a role in treatment

---

[286] 533 A 2d at 614, per Nebeker AJ.

[287] Although the court does not give a legal source for this approach, it presumably derives from Roe v. Wade. For a discussion of the State's balancing of the interests of the mother and the fetus based on Roe, see ch. 5. On the complexities of the State's position in these cases, one scholar has suggested that the State has a shared interest in the mother's autonomy "which places it on both sides of the argument concerning the mother's right to refuse" medical treatment. JK Levy, "Jehovah's Witnesses, Pregnancy, and Blood Transfusions", 176.

[288] 533 A 2d at 617. It was noted that the death rate of women upon whom a caesarean section had been performed is between 0.1 and 1%, "significantly higher" than women who have given birth vaginally. The court cited C Gray, Attorney's Textbook of Medicine, 3rd edn. (1987) 308.50. Commentators have generally described a caesarean as increasing the risk of death by four. See e.g. N Rhoden, "The Judge in the Delivery Room: The Emergence of Court-Ordered Cesareans", (1986) 74 Cal L Rev 1951, 1959. See further Baby Boy Doe 632 NE 2d at 329, as noted in ch. 3.

[289] 533 A 2d at 617, per Nebeker AJ. George Annas has suggested that this reasoning reveals the court's perception that its actions could only be justified "as though she were already dead": indeed Annas notes that the lawyer for the fetus argued that AC had no important interests to consider since she was dying. "She's Going to Die: the Case of Angela C", (1988) 18 (Feb./March) Hastings CR 23, at 25 and 24 respectively.

[290] I Kennedy, "A Woman and her Unborn Child", in his Treat Me Right (Oxford: Oxford University Press, 1992) 364–84, 368.

refusal cases.[291] The Supreme Court of Missouri referred to an "arbitrary discounting" of the interests of either the patient or the State if quality of life arguments were allowed a role in treatment refusal cases. Yet, as we have seen, quality of life arguments have only ever *strengthened* the rights of competent patients following *Quinlan*, to the point where, whilst the burdens of treatment might be a very good *reason* for the patient to refuse treatment—Ms C supposedly refused the caesarean consistent with her desire, expressed in the course of earlier discussions, to be "kept as comfortable as possible through her pregnancy and to maintain the quality of her life"[292]—the patient's *right* to refuse treatment (conversely the strength of the State's interest) *no longer depends on quality of life considerations*. (That is, the patient does not now have to have a poor quality of life in order to be allowed to refuse life-sustaining treatment.) In this way George Annas's comment that *Re AC* was not a hard case seems very much to the point.[293] Indeed the law, both as it developed and as it stands, is succinctly caught by Associate Judge Terry (for the majority) in the 1990 hearing of *Re AC*: having observed that the right of bodily integrity was one possessed equally by competent and incompetent patients, he said "it matters not what the quality of a patient's life may be; the right of bodily integrity is not extinguished simply because someone is ill, or even at death's door."[294] Hence we might ask what accounts for what, in relation either to competent or incompetent patients, might legitimately be termed "the abuse of power" in *Re AC* (1987)? Why was the judgment so "lawless",[295] so much at odds with all stages of the development of the right to refuse treatment as we have observed this to relate to the State's interest in the preservation of life?

The explanation relates in part to my point that the biological inseparability of mother and fetus clouds the sense in which saving the fetus can be clearly aligned with upholding something important about life. The State's interest in the fetus necessarily incorporates an interest in Ms C's life *insofar as it supports the fetus*. It is apparently for this reason that Ms C was not accorded the respect that from an early stage attached to a patient with a poor prognosis. That is, the fact that she was dying would normally and for quite some time have protected her against the State overriding her choice; and in 1987 it should not even have been a consideration for the State. That the court acted in a way so counter to the history and meaning of the preservation of life interest shows what little concern it had for—what small value it attached to—Ms C's life in its own right. Indeed, despite the fact that she was rapidly dying of cancer, she was not recognised as a patient *herself*. This point seems obvious if we reflect that the physician who had for many years treated her cancer was not informed of the court hearing; he subsequently stated that if he had been

[291] 760 SW 2d at 420. Prognosis was seen by the Supreme Court of Missouri in *Cruzan* as an aspect of quality of life considerations instigated by *Quinlan*.

[292] 533 A 2d at 613.

[293] G Annas, "She's Going to Die", 25.

[294] 573 A 2d at 1247.

[295] Annas adopts this description in "She's Going to Die", 25. Similarly B Steinbock characterises the decision as "egregious judicial error" in *Life Before Birth: the Moral and Legal Status of Embryos and Fetuses* (New York: Oxford University Press, 1992) 159.

notified of the hearing he would have testified that the caesarean surgery interfered with Ms C's ability to receive potentially beneficial chemotherapy that could have let her live longer.[296] At the same time, although she was *dying* and the fetus was being taken from her, she was still *needed* to save it: the operation is *about the fetus*, but it is, after all, *on Ms C*. Rather than "letting her (and the fetus) go", in a sense consistent with respect for her choice, or try further to treat her cancer,[297] the State literally cuts her open, thereby at least symbolically using her to save the other being inside her.[298] In this way, the State seems to abandon her. If my argument so far is right, not only did the State harm Ms C's interests (physically, morally, legally), it thereby offended us all: to attempt to bring a child into the world by such treatment of its mother seems some kind of terrible shame.[299] Afterwards, Ms C's mother stated:[300]

> "[T]he hospital staff told us we were needed at a short meeting. They did not tell us it was a court hearing. It took all day. Poor Angie, first she's told she's dying and the next thing everybody abandons her and leaves her alone in her room . . . Then even before the hearing was over they started prepping her for surgery. She was already in so much pain. We told the judge she didn't want the surgery, that we didn't want her to suffer anymore, that we didn't think the baby would live. But they didn't listen. After the surgery and after they told her the baby was dead, I think Angie just gave up."

It is at this point that I would like to note that at some level, at some time, there may be a legitimate place for emotional considerations in legal reasoning. The suggestion here is that the legal decision to operate on Angela Carder without her consent was so poor partly because it did not attend to the physical and emotional reality of her predicament or of what was involved in ordering a caesarean upon her. I cannot develop this point here, but the contribution that the emotions can make to wise legal judgment has been discussed by others.[301] It may be recalled that I made related points with regard to moral reasoning in chapter two, where I suggested that some quality of empathy or understanding was required from us when reflecting upon whether a moral duty can be said to lie to donate a kidney or to submit to a caesarean, at which point I referred in particular to the case of

---

[296] Affidavit of J Moscow, MD, *Re AC*.

[297] That Ms C's doctors advocated chemotherapy raises the question of whether her life really should have been deemed in its final stages. Indeed, in one newspaper report, her father is quoted as asking "[f]or 14 years our daughter was considered terminally ill and what right did the court have to decide that her life was over?". "Drama in the Womb: A Matter of Life and Death Winds Up in Court", *Los Angeles Times*, 25 Dec. 1987, 5 A-5.

[298] On the question of the sense of "use" and for instance whether it could be said that the State uses her in the Kantian means/end sense, see related discussion in ch. 7.

[299] A thoughtful and striking argument against coercive treatment of pregnant women from the perspective of doctors' professional duties is made by S Mattingly, who concludes that "from the position of professional ethics the obstacle to fetal benefit is not maternal autonomy but maternal non-malificence." S Mattingly, "The Maternal–Fetal Dyad: Exploring the Two-Patient Obstetric Model", (1992) 22 (Jan./Feb.) *Hastings CR* 13, 16. See also JC Fletcher, "Healing Before Birth: an Ethical Dilemma", (1984) 87 *Tech Rev* 27, 35, reflecting that coercion to protect the fetus is morally self-defeating because it necessarily involves committing a moral wrong against women.

[300] "Drama in the Womb", 5 A-5.

[301] See e.g. P Gewirtz, "Aeschylus' Law", (1988) 101 *Harvard L Rev* 1043.

Re AC.[302] These points can in turn be related to my overall project of seeking to explain and justify the idea of the right to refuse medical treatment in pregnancy, since the process of reinforcing the connection between a woman's moral interests in pregnancy and the kinds of reasons that these will likely spawn has required us to understand the women who seek to exercise these rights. Without such understanding, as Robin West has eloquently written, "[w]e neglect our capacity to walk a mile in another's shoes".[303]

As we have seen, *Re AC* was unusual in that the surgery actually hastened Ms C's death: it hardly needs saying that it ill befits the State to try to preserve one (potential) life in a way which effectively speeds the death of another. *Re AC* was an exceptional case, but it should not be thought that this point has no application in the usual case: if we reflect that the death rate from caesarean sections is four times that of vaginal delivery then, through the imposition of this increased risk, the State's desire to preserve fetal life by overriding a woman's choice appears problematic, perhaps to different degrees, in the context of any caesarean. More particularly, as noted earlier, the surgery is always a physical harm in itself—painful and invasive— regardless of the lack of "adverse" consequences in most cases.[304] (As noted in chapter two, that natural delivery is itself physically burdensome is not in point where a woman has no serious objections, religious or otherwise, to natural birth.) Lastly, it is interesting to note that caesarean sections were originally developed to assist women who, for health reasons, could not survive "natural" delivery.[305]

C. The Use of Force

Finally, it should be noted that the issue of force was considered to be "of not insignificant concern" in the *Baby Boy Doe* decision.[306] De Vito PJ observed that even the Public Guardian, who had sought the order for a compelled caesarean in this case, opposed the use of force or other means to compel the woman in question to undergo the surgery. This meant, De Vito PJ noted, that "we have been asked to issue an order that no one expects to be carried out".[307] He went on to suggest that "as a simple matter of policy", the court would not issue an order that

---

[302] See s. III(A)(3)(a)(ii). As observed in the notes to ch. 2, however, it is very hard to say anything about these ideas without immediately begging questions—which need to be addressed— about our definition of the terms "reason" and "emotion".

[303] R West, "Taking Freedom Seriously", 72.

[304] N Rhoden, "Cesareans and Samaritans", (1987) 15 (Fall) *Law, Med & Health Care* 118, 122.

[305] W Mitchinson, "Agency, Diversity, and Constraints: Women and their Physicians, Canada, 1850–1950", in S Sherwin (coord.), *The Politics of Women's Health: Exploring Agency and Autonomy* (Philadelphia, PA: Temple University Press, 1998) 122–149. In the 19th century, women with heart disease and rickets leading to deformed pelvises (caused by malnourishment) were helped by caesareans. In time, despite better nutrition, caesarean section rates increased rather than decreased. Mitchinson suggests that three factors may account for this: an increase in the size of babies, a concern to save the fetus's life (when the mother's may not have been in danger) and the increased safety of the procedure. (At 138.)

[306] 632 NE 2d at 335, *per* De Vito PJ.

[307] *Ibid*.

was not intended to be enforced. (One scholar has suggested that it appears that Dr Meserow, the maternal–fetal medicine specialist seeking the order in fact hoped that the court would decide that he had no legal duty to perform the caesarean and thus had no legal liability for damage to the health or life of mother or fetus.[308])

If there could be no intention of enforcing an order for a compelled caesarean against a pregnant woman, the reasons must lie in the question of what such enforcement would entail. Indeed, De Vito PJ proceeded to consider this point, and cited the following passage from the decision of the Court of Appeals in the 1990 hearing of Re AC:[309]

"Enforcement could be accomplished only through physical force or its equivalent. A.C. would have to be fastened with restraints to the operating table, or perhaps rendered unconscious by forcibly injecting her with an anesthetic, and then subjected to unwanted major surgery. Such actions would surely give one pause in a civilized society, especially when A.C. had done no wrong."

Having further noted an academic description of what actually happened when a forced caesarean was carried out, De Vito PJ stated "[w]e simply cannot envision issuing an order that, if enforced at all, could be enforced only in this fashion".[310]

The issue of force was considered in Re MB in connection with a finding of incompetence. Although the Court of Appeal determined that the judge in Re MB was justified in granting the declaration that it would be lawful for reasonable force to be used in that case, it was noted that this would vary depending on the facts and, in particular, that in Miss MB's case, the "force" was only of the anaesthetic needle. Moreover, it was stressed that this was a "difficult issue which may have to be considered in greater depth on another occasion".[311] I discuss this issue further in chapter seven.

VI. CONCLUSIONS

This chapter has sought to defend a woman's legal right to refuse medical treatment needed by the fetus. It explored, first, the development of the "ordinary" (that is, non-pregnant) patient's right to refuse medical treatment by examining the State's interest in the preservation of life, arguing that the State's original concern that patients not opt of life without *good reason* was far from undermined when it allowed patients the *right* to do so, rather than test their *reasons* in each case. This is because patients generally do refuse medical treatment for what I dubbed "positive" reasons,

[308] JK Levy, "Jehovah's Witnesses, Pregnancy, and Blood Transfusions", 183.
[309] 573 A 2d at 1244, n.8.
[310] 632 NE 2d at 335. Here he cited a discussion in J Gallagher, "Prenatal Invasions and Interventions: What's Wrong with Fetal Rights?", 9–10. The point is aptly put by S Elias and G Annas, in their *Reproductive Genetics and the Law*, who ask: "Do we really want to restrain, forcibly medicate, and operate on a competent, refusing adult? Such a procedure . . . is certainly brutish and not what one generally associates with medical care." (At 259.)
[311] [1997] 8 Med LR at 225.

consistent with a recognition of the value and meaning of life, which may include considerations regarding the bodily burdens of certain kinds of treatment.

Turning to the more complex case of pregnant women, I explored the State's interest in the potential life of the fetus as derived from abortion law, an interest which the State originally balanced against the rights of the pregnant woman in those cases in which it denied her the right to refuse treatment. In essence, both the interests in potential life (from abortion law) and in the preservation of life (from the law of treatment refusal) were seen to find expression in the quasi-hybrid situation of maternal–fetal conflict. I explored the way in which both these interests at some level reflect a concern that decisions in these areas of life and death— which are very personal and yet which may "speak to" society at large—are duly respectful and responsible toward the value of human life.

With regard, first, to the personal nature of these decisions and the very personal interests in self-determination and bodily integrity which they implicate, I noted again the scope for reasonable disagreement first touched upon in Part I, such that where treatment is being refused for serious reasons, third parties could not make the judgment that a reason was not in fact sufficiently serious. Yet I also noted that in an important sense a serious reason "answers", on the woman's part, to the claims of the fetus. This aspect supports the principle of a pregnant woman's right to refuse medical treatment, thus fostering acceptance of that right where it currently exists and promoting it where it does not.

Second, with regard to the idea of encouraging responsibility toward the value of human life, I suggested that in the case of seemingly insufficiently serious, trivial or irresponsible reasons for the refusal of treatment, third parties may have a limited role in discussion, counselling and sometimes persuasion in the treatment context, to the extent that this is consistent with a pregnant woman's rights. (In this regard it was noted that rights, whatever their basis, must be guaranteed in reality, not just in the law reports, a point familiar to the US and ECHR contexts.) Lastly, I considered the moral difficulties for the State itself, in terms of its own interest in the acknowledgement of the value of human life, of overriding a woman's treatment refusal.

Overall, and importantly, the argument acknowledged, rather than denied, the reality of possible harm to the unborn child flowing from a treatment choice.[312] Notwithstanding this, however, it is suggested that ultimately respecting fetal life entails respecting the lives of pregnant women.[313]

---

[312] For thoughts of potential interest here, see M Nussbaum, *The Fragility of Goodness: Luck and Ethics in Greek Tragedy and Philosophy*, updated edn. (Cambridge: Cambridge University Press, 2001). Thus, the attempt has been to justify the right to refuse medical treatment in pregnancy in a way that does not "underdescribe or misdescribe" (*ibid.*, 49) the problem.

[313] Christine Overall, amongst others, has eloquently elaborated upon this point: "Whenever we reach a stage where interventions in a pregnant woman's body, against her will, allegedly for the sake of the foetus, appear to be necessary, then we should step back and look at the larger picture: in what ways have we failed to support, educate, care for, and appreciate the pregnant woman?" C Overall, *Human Reproduction: Principles, Practices, Policies* (Toronto: Oxford University Press, 1993) 42.

Conclusions to Part II

In England and in some US states a pregnant woman does and should have the legal right to refuse medical treatment needed by the fetus/future child. The discussion in chapter three has shown the extent to which she does now have this right, but that a number of tensions surround its existence. Accordingly, chapter four has sought to justify her right in ethical terms, building upon the analysis in Part I. Apart from justifying the right where this exists, an important purpose of this chapter has been to show why she should have that right in those US states which have yet to decide the issue.

Overall, the arguments have highlighted the extent to which the maternal–fetal conflict is likely to concern serious maternal reasons, so that a pregnant woman can be said to acting responsibly toward the fetus she carries, including where she refuses medical treatment, for instance, for religious reasons. In other much less likely cases, where a woman refuses treatment for non-existent or apparently insufficiently serious or trivial/inappropriate reasons, the State's *de facto* interest in protecting fetal life (or the health of the future child) may be expressed in the encouragement of responsible treatment decisions. In these ways human life is valued: the unborn child through the opportunity for discussion, counselling and (in limited circumstances) persuasion in the face of maternal refusals of treatment, which are thus not seen as entirely "insulated" choices, and the pregnant woman by allowing her always to make the final decision herself.

PART III

The Legal Arguments from Duty

Introduction

IN PART II I examined the maternal–fetal cases within the framework of the law relating to treatment refusal, intersecting this in chapter four with aspects of abortion law. This part explores the relevance of two additional areas of law to these cases, namely, tort and rescue law and begins with consideration of certain "technical" arguments from abortion law, some of which relate to "arguments from duty".

Chapter five explores the relevance of certain key points from US abortion law to our understanding of the maternal–fetal conflict. In particular, I try to understand whether abortion law mandates the imposition of affirmative legal obligations upon a pregnant woman, for instance an obligation to submit to delivery by caesarean section in order to save the life of the fetus. I also discuss the application of the principle that where "necessary", the State prioritises maternal over fetal life even after viability: by this principle, the State deems unlawful any attempt to enhance fetal welfare at the expense of the well-being of the pregnant woman. The complex application of this point to the cases of maternal–fetal conflict is explored. (Note that this chapter does not discuss the US Supreme Court's decision in *Stenberg* v. *Carhart*,[1] which struck down a "partial-birth" abortion ban in a Nebraskan statute, partly because it did not incorporate an exception for abortions which were necessary to preserve women's health. This case is not discussed here for three reasons: first, the chapter is concerned with those US abortion cases upon which the maternal-fetal conflict cases and literature have drawn; second, in senses relevant to this chapter, *Stenberg* applies *Roe* and *Planned Parenthood of Southeastern Pennsylvania* v. *Casey*; thus, third, to include a discussion of *Stenberg* would unnecessarily complicate rather than add to the arguments here and would thereby distract attention from the caesarean cases which are the real subject of discussion.) The Supreme Court's abortion decision which was first introduced in chapter four—*Casey*—will also be considered for its legal recognition of my "social context" argument, formulated in chapter two.

In chapter six I turn to consider the application of arguments from the law of tort to the maternal–fetal conflict. A brief consideration of the development of the law relating to third parties' tortious duties to avoid prenatal harm is followed by a survey of the use of such law in the very different scenario of maternal–fetal conflict. The stage is then set for a consideration of the legitimacy of the idea of a maternal

---

[1] 147 L Ed 2d 743 (2000). The basis of the decision was two-fold: first, that the statutory provision lacked an exception for abortion where necessary to protect the women's health; second, that due to the imprecision of the statutory language, such that doctors might fear prosecution, the provision was an "undue burden" on a women's right to abort. As a result of the decision, the "partial-birth" bans of many other states became invalid.

prenatal legal duty of care toward the fetus or future child. This idea is first, and principally, explored with regard to the situation of maternal refusal of medical treatment which is the main focus of the book. Yet the idea of such a duty in the general "lifestyle" context is also usefully considered in this chapter by way of contrast, as it sheds further light on aspects of the conflict in the medical treatment context. In general, consideration of this additional area also provides further confirmation of the "social context" argument first introduced in Part I.

The relevance of the law of rescue to that of maternal–fetal conflict in the medical context is discussed in chapter seven. The chapter raises important questions about our understanding both of the maternal–fetal conflict cases and of cases which consider the idea of compelled donation of organs or tissue in a way which relates to problems or tensions discussed morally in Part I and legally in Part II. An important focus of this chapter is upon the approach, within the law of rescue, to the idea of compelled bodily invasions to benefit another. Here I briefly discuss moral, legal and policy considerations pertaining to the idea of compelled bodily invasions, with particular reference to the maternal–fetal conflict in the treatment context. I also put forward several reasons against the idea of compelled interventions which are specific to the maternal–fetal context.

5

"Technical" Arguments from Abortion Law

I. INTRODUCTION

As we have seen in Part II, the early US maternal–fetal cases themselves drew on abortion law, notably *Roe* v. *Wade*, in order to assert a State interest in the fetus. I examined this point of connection in chapter four, where I explored the State's potential interest in the fetus, as it might bear on a pregnant woman's right to refuse treatment, particularly the responsible exercise thereof.

Apart from this point of connection, however, the law of abortion very clearly concerns a distinct issue from that at stake in the maternal–fetal conflict. There are two reasons, however, further to consider its impact upon and role in the context of the maternal–fetal conflict. First, this is the principal area of law which specifically addresses *the relationship between a woman and her fetus and the State's role in this*. In this sense, as we have already seen with regard to the relationship between a woman's right and her responsibilities (indeed, in some ways the justification of this right in terms of the idea of responsibility) in chapter four, certain aspects of abortion law may give some guidance as to the triangle of interests which are also at stake in the maternal–fetal conflict. This grounds the second reason for considering this area, which is that both the US maternal–fetal cases and literature draw on certain key points from abortion law either to defend or to disapprove of forced obstetric intervention. (By contrast, the English decisions have left to one side the law on abortion. The chapter does, however, make some reference to the English position.) These points are addressed in this chapter.

II. THE RELEVANCE OF FURTHER ASPECTS OF ABORTION LAW TO THE MATERNAL–FETAL CONFLICT

As should already be apparent, abortion law is large and complex and only a handful of key points have relevance to the maternal–fetal conflict. This chapter addresses four points or problems at the interface between the maternal–fetal conflict and treatment refusal law on the one hand and abortion law on the other. Some of these are intricately related to one another. Where this is the case, they are only distinguished as separate areas for the sake of conceptual clarity. The discussion touches on some of the decisions between *Roe* and *Casey* which generally concerned the legitimacy of various state abortion regulations under *Roe*.

In mentioning these cases, however, I refer only to points relevant to the maternal–fetal conflict. Finally, in the interests of going to the heart of the relevant points, there will inevitably be some simplification of the issues (from an abortion perspective). (The reader is also referred to the brief constitutional background to abortion law provided in chapter four.)

Section A, *"the waiver argument"*, is technically an argument pertaining to the maternal–fetal conflict which draws upon points from abortion law. In effect, the argument states that a woman who has not exercised her right to abort is thereafter under a duty not only to avoid harming the fetus in any way but also to promote fetal welfare. As a matter of inference then, she would be obliged to submit to medical treatment on its behalf.

Section B concerns the distinction between *positive* and *negative* obligations and, particularly, which obligations abortion law imposes upon a pregnant woman and when. The argument in this section is closely related to that in the first: a full discussion of the first necessitates exploring the arguments in the second; yet, because the second can be discussed independently of the first I have identified these points separately.

The third section, C, concerns the law's *prioritisation* of the woman over the fetus even after viability, since abortions are permissible in the last three months of pregnancy if continued pregnancy poses a threat to a woman's life or health. The question of abortion methods, notably their effect on maternal health or prospects for fetal survival, is also in issue. I address a difficulty in the application of this principle to the maternal–fetal conflict. In effect, the "no trade-offs" principle, which has generally been thought to bolster a woman's *right* to refuse medical treatment, is associated with the particular question of the post-viability abortion *method* and thus hinges upon a prior *medical* judgment that an abortion is "necessary" for the mother. In this section I focus upon the differing role played by doctors in the abortion and treatment refusal contexts after viability, when a woman no longer has the right to *abort*, but does—in some US states—have the right to *refuse medical treatment*.

The remaining two sections are relatively brief. Section D highlights the important issue of the State's duty to the pregnant woman in the abortion context after viability, when its interest in her life and health is even more compelling than its interest in that of the fetus. Whilst in some US states a woman now has the relatively clear legal right to refuse medical treatment, this duty (which is not merely the correlative of her right) should not be neglected.

Section E touches on the legal recognition of the *social context* of abortion, a point which I refine to apply to the situation of maternal–fetal conflict, with reference to my earlier argument in Part I.

A. The Waiver Argument—Introduction

In this section I consider the argument, notably employed in the context of the maternal–fetal conflict by John Robertson, that once a pregnant woman decides not to have an abortion she effectively waives the right to harm the fetus[1] and could be said to be under a legal duty to take all reasonable steps to promote its well-being.[2] He writes that *Roe* holds that once a woman has continued her pregnancy to viability, a legal duty to carry the fetus to term can be imposed which in turn provides "implicit" support for certain mandated intrusions on the fetus's behalf.[3] There are both moral and legal ideas in these observations and it is unclear whether Robertson is making discrete moral and legal points: for instance that before via-bility a woman who has decided to go to term is under a *moral* duty in relation to her fetus's welfare, which crystallises into a *legal* duty following viability under *Roe*. Another passage suggests that Robertson is committed to the view that where a woman has decided to carry to term, even when her fetus is not yet viable, she is—or perhaps should be—under a *legal* duty in relation to its welfare.[4] His argument is thus a complex web of the moral and the legal which I shall try both to disen-tangle and assess.

As a matter of law, a woman who has decided not to abort does not lose the legal right to do so until viability itself. From this time onwards, perhaps it might be said that a woman who has not aborted comes under a legal duty to carry the fetus to term, although neither *Roe* nor *Casey* expresses the point in this way. Of course, if the fetus poses a threat to her life or health she can still abort after viability. It is not correct to say that at this time she still has the *right* to abort, however, for the pos-sibility of a post-viability abortion is allowed for by virtue of the *State's interest* in her life and health. So far as the law of abortion is concerned, then, Robertson's argument that a woman might be under a duty toward the fetus pre-viability seems at best true in the *moral* sense that, if a woman chooses not to abort, she comes under a *moral* duty to carry the fetus to term. (It was noted in chapter two, how-ever, that some women may not be in a position truly to decide this. Further, as we saw in Part I, it is difficult to determine the boundaries of what having a moral duty to carry the fetus to term can be said to entail, a point I revisit below.) Thus, Robertson may actually be conflating two points: first, a woman's actions and her moral responsibility for these and second, the proscription of the legal right to abort (at viability) and the consequences that flow from this. Alternatively, he may be making a normative argument about what the law *should* be and is, in effect, argu-ing for a legal duty in the sense of, for instance, a tortious duty. The idea of a mater-nal tortious duty will be examined in the next chapter, but even if Robertson is *also* employing the notion of a legal duty from beyond the law of abortion, his waiver argument does make some use of the idea of duty from abortion law itself and it is important to clarify the legal and the moral positions in this regard. This is the sub-ject of the next section which further develops the waiver argument.

---

[1] Robertson characterises this as the "right to produce a dead or unhealthy baby". J Robertson, "The Right to Procreate and *in utero* Fetal Therapy", (1982) 3 *J Leg Med* 333, 360, footnote omitted.

[2] *Ibid.*, 353.

[3] J Robertson, *Children of Choice: Freedom and the New Reproductive Technologies* (Princeton, NJ: Princeton University Press, 1994) 188.

[4] J Robertson, "Procreative Liberty and the Control of Conception, Pregnancy, and Childbirth", (1983) 69 *Va L Rev* 405, 446.

B. Positive and Negative Obligations—Development of the Waiver Argument

Although the discussion in this section elaborates the implications of the waiver argument, it deserves a heading in its own right because it concerns a distinction which is important on its own terms and which need not be discussed solely in connection with the waiver argument.

1. The Moral Position

Let us focus on the moral and legal positions in more detail; first, the moral. In choosing not to abort an unplanned pregnancy, a woman is under a moral duty to carry the fetus to term. I suggested in chapter two that whilst the initial abortion decision can be construed as declining to render positive assistance, once a woman has chosen not to abort and "lets" the fetus keep on developing, abortion thereafter (except for "new" reasons relating to her life or health) no longer seems a failure to render positive aid so much (perhaps) as the breach of a negative duty in relation to it. It is only in this sense, I think, that we can make any sense of Robertson's point that, once a woman has foregone abortion, she loses the "right to harm" the fetus. In fact, however, a woman never has a "right to harm" the fetus; rather, she has rights to bodily integrity and self-determination which will in turn affect the extent of her positive duty to help the fetus, such as in the case of medical treatment. Yet if abortion were possible (as late abortions may well be) without harming the fetus, then she has no right to bring about its death.[5] In short, following her decision not to abort, a woman has the negative moral duty not to abort but also, as I have previously argued, a positive duty to assist it where she can, for instance, where she does not have serious reason (relating to her moral interests) not to do so.

Where Robertson and I differ, therefore, is in regard to the *extent* of a woman's positive duty to assist the fetus in the medical treatment context. In this regard, Robertson writes:[6]

> "To impose on the mother a duty to undergo surgical delivery where it is necessary to save the child's life or to prevent it from being injured is not unreasonable when she has chosen to *lend her body* to bring the child into the world."

I do not think, however, that a woman "lends her body" in the strong sense which Robertson's argument requires: pregnancy is part of her life for nine months, not

---

[5] For a contrary view, see C MacKenzie, "Abortion and Embodiment", (1992) 70(2) *Aust J of Phil* 136.

[6] J Robertson, "Procreative Liberty", 456, footnote omitted, my emphasis. The "loan" argument was rejected in the 1990 hearing of *Re AC*, in which the court held that "surely . . . a fetus cannot have rights in this respect superior to those of a person who has already been born." 573 A 2d 1235 (DC App 1990), 1244, *per* Terry, AJ. This was in the context of a discussion about whether or not courts compel one person to allow a significant intrusion upon his or her bodily integrity in order to benefit another's health, on which see ch. 7.

the entire focus of every moment, movement and choice. This takes us back to a number of points made in chapter two. For instance, we saw that pregnancy may entail risks which, whilst ordinary to pregnancy, are *extra*ordinary by comparison with the demands even of special relationships. In this regard, I drew attention to the complexity in the very determination of a duty to assist another *through* the body, a point that was most forcefully illustrated by the case of *Re AC*. While this case was exceptional, I suggested that the question of determining whether a woman was under a duty to submit, say, to a caesarean, must pay attention to the peculiarly intimate and physical nature of such assistance. Whilst it is true that a woman can decline these burdens and risks by aborting, my "social context" argument tried to show that it is untenable to expect that pregnant women, who have the biological role of bringing children into the world, must thereby be committed to doing anything on behalf of their fetus. If this has any validity (and we shall later see that it is endorsed in legal terms in a different way in *Casey*), by undertaking to carry to term, a woman is not undertaking to do *anything* the fetus might require. Thus, a woman who elects not to abort and thereby chooses to carry a fetus to term is not at the same time undertaking to do *whatever* is required to prevent harm to the fetus and ensure that it is live-born and in good health, notwithstanding her moral duties to do all she can.

2. *The Legal Position*

In the 1987 hearing of *Re AC* in which, it will be recalled, a caesarean was ordered against the apparent wishes of the dying Ms C, the court confidently asserted that "as a matter of law, the right of a woman to an abortion is different and distinct from her obligations to the fetus once she has decided not to timely terminate her pregnancy".[7] The meaning of this statement is far from clear, but it appears that the court is alluding to the idea a legal obligation which arises once a woman has decided to carry the fetus to term, notwithstanding her continued legal right to abort until viability. What does the relevant law say?

As we have seen, a woman's legal right to abort is proscribed at viability. This is based on a number of considerations: most importantly that at this time the State's interest in the fetus becomes compelling (as the fetus now has interests of its own and the capacity for meaningful life outside the womb); but also, given the increased danger to a woman in a post-viability abortion, because the State's interest in her health and life provides an additional ground for the proscription of abortion after this time. Conversely, if the woman is at risk after this time, the State makes an exception to the rule against abortion. Although the law is expressed in terms of State interests, rather than duties, we might say, as noted above, that after losing her right to abortion (at viability), by implication a woman has a legal duty to carry the fetus to term. That is, after viability, a woman has a legal duty *not to abort*. Further, in the light of her earlier opportunity to abort, when abortion could

---

[7] 533 A 2d 611, 614 (DC App 1987).

arguably have been defended as a choice not to render *positive* assistance via the body, the duty not to abort post-viability is now in many ways a *negative* obligation.

This obligation, which *Roe* and *Casey* implicitly impose upon a woman after viability, is the most that we can extract from the legal proscription of the abortion right at this time. As the joint opinion in *Casey* observes, "[i]n some broad sense it might be said that a woman who fails to act before viability has consented to the State's intervention on behalf of the developing child."[8] In this context, "intervention" means the proscription of the right to abort based, particularly, on the now compelling State interest in the fetus. Thus, coincident with viability, a woman loses the legal right to abort and comes under the *negative legal* duty not to do so.

These observations support the arguments of scholars to the effect that *abortion law* does not mandate imposing *positive*, or affirmative, obligations on women after viability, but only (subject to the exceptions) mandates the negative obligation not to abort after this time. For instance, Nancy Rhoden points to the "quantum leap in logic between prohibiting destruction and requiring preservation" which some courts and scholars have not appreciated.[9] Thus, subject to the exceptions, the State can now prevent a woman undergoing a certain procedure—abortion—which will result in harm to the fetus; but it does not now have authority actively to intervene on the fetus's behalf, for instance surgically.[10] This means that the court in a case such as *Jefferson* lacked authority to compel Mrs Jefferson to submit to a caesarean section. The court had held:[11]

> "The Court finds that the State has an interest in the life of this unborn, living human being. The Court finds that the intrusion involved in the life of Jessie Mae Jefferson and her husband, John W. Jefferson, is outweighed by the duty of the State to protect a living, unborn human being from meeting his or her death before being given the opportunity to live."

---

[8] 120 L Ed 2d at 710.

[9] N Rhoden, "Cesareans and Samaritans", (1987) 15 (Fall) *Law, Med & Health Care* 118, 119. See also e.g. B Steinbock, *Life Before Birth: the Moral and Legal Status of Embryos and Fetuses* (New York, NY: Oxford University Press, 1992) 152; L Nelson, B Buggy and C Weil, "Forced Medical Treatment of Pregnant Women: 'Compelling Each to Live as Seems Good to the Rest' ", (1986) 37 *Hastings LJ* 703, 745.

[10] This is not always appreciated. Consider the following passage: "According to [one] view, *Roe* v. *Wade* has already mandated that the state cannot impose any controls upon the mother that are designed to further the fetus' wellbeing before the 28th week of pregnancy, when she loses her constitutional right to choose abortion for nontherapeutic reasons. I disagree with this view because the state interest in the treatment of the fetus is greater when a woman is planning to give birth than when she proposes to abort." M Field, "Controlling the Woman to Protect the Fetus", (1989) 17 (Summer) *Law, Med & Health Care* 114, at 124 (footnote omitted). Field wrongly implies (and elaborates upon this in her notes) that the State has authority to impose controls such as surgical intervention upon a pregnant woman designed to enhance fetal health both before and after fetal viability. At most, however, the State's interest in potential life is a "passive interest" in encouraging responsible maternal decisions, either before or after viability, in the sense discussed under *Roe* and *Casey* in ch. 4.

[11] Ga 274 SE 2d 457 at 460, *per curiam*. The court referred to *Roe* in support at the end of its judgment. The separate judgments of Hill and Smith JJ also referred to *Roe*.

In this connection, another scholar draws attention to the extensive nature of the "active state participation" undertaken in *Jefferson*: not only was Mrs Jefferson to be subjected to a caesarean section against her will, but the court authorised the dispatch of the sheriff to take her to hospital.[12] He observes that the State's interest in the fetus, while compelling at viability, is not strong enough to mandate this kind of active intervention. The arguments in this section therefore support the conclusion that, despite its compelling interest in the fetus at viability, abortion law does not impose *positive legal* obligations upon women. The same point applies even more strongly *before* viability.[13] As we saw in discussing the decision of *Pemberton* in chapter four, the same kinds of judicial "mistakes" that were evident in *Jefferson* are still being made.

Despite the lack of attention to abortion law in the English context, these points are also highly relevant to the English legal situation. We saw in chapter three that the Court of Appeal in *Re MB* expressed concerns that it may be "illogical"[14] that the State proscribes abortion after viability on the one hand, but that it allows a pregnant woman the right to refuse medical treatment which may lead to fetal death or harm, including for irrational reasons, on the other. I touch upon the relevant English law a little later, but, addressing the *Re MB* court's concerns here, the point for present purposes is that, whilst the law prevents abortions after viability (except where necessary to protect the life or health of the woman) it does not mandate the imposition of affirmative legal obligations: the State does not have authority *actively* to intervene by administering non-consensual treatment to the pregnant woman on the fetus's behalf. Nor, for that matter, is the refusal of medical treatment resulting in fetal death or harm "intentional" in the way that abortions are.[15] The court's concern about illogicality might further be bolstered if we recall a point made in relation to the purely moral argument in chapter two to the effect that whilst a woman has many months during which she can abort prior to viability,[16] hence that proscribing the abortion right thereafter can be said to be fair and just, the need for a caesarean section will only arise unpredictably at the point of birth.

In the light of these conclusions regarding the lack of a positive legal obligation which can be derived from abortion law, note might be taken of the American

---

[12] EP Finamore, "*Jefferson v. Griffin Spalding County Hospital Authority*: Court-Ordered Surgery to Protect the Life of an Unborn Child", (1983) 9 *Am J L & Med* 83, 88.

[13] See e.g. *Taft* v. *Taft*, 446 NE 2d 395 (1983), in which the Supreme Judicial Court of Massachusetts vacated an order which required a woman in her fourth month of pregnancy to undergo a "purse-string" operation, on the ground that there were no compelling circumstances to justify overriding her religious objections and her constitutional right of privacy. The Probate and Family courts had entered orders that the woman submit to the surgery. Since the sparseness of the record was the main consideration in this case, however, it has little precedential value.

[14] [1997] 8 Med LR at 226, *per* Butler-Sloss LJ.

[15] This point is also noted by S Michalowski, "Court-Authorised Caesarean Sections—The End of a Trend?", (1999) 62 *MLR* 115, 125.

[16] In English law, abortion prior to viability is subject to the authorisation of doctors: see extracts from the Abortion Act 1967 as amended by the Human Fertilisation and Embryology Act 1990, *infra* these notes.

maternal–fetal conflict case of *Re Jamaica Hospital*.[17] The misguided decision in this case illustrates some of the conceptual muddles that the arguments in sections A and B have sought to unravel. In this case, the court ordered the transfusion of blood to a Jehovah's Witness who was 18 weeks pregnant and objected thereto on religious grounds, on the basis that the State's interest in the *pre-viable* fetus outweighed the patient's interests. To reach this conclusion the court had both to rely on *Roe*, in order to find a "significant interest in protecting the potential of human life represented by an unborn fetus, which increases throughout the course of pregnancy, becoming 'compelling' when the fetus has reached viability";[18] and to distinguish it, by saying that since this was not an abortion case, then the interest in the fetus could here be strong enough—presumably compelling enough—to outweigh the woman's interests, notwithstanding that without the blood transfusion there was a strong chance of fetal death, rather than harm to the future child. Rather, as was argued in the preceding chapter, the State's interest in the potential life of the fetus in the context of maternal–fetal conflict is at most an interest in encouraging educated, responsible decisions.

C. The Post-viability Exception of Allowing Abortion Where "Necessary": Application to the Caesarean Cases

We have seen that, post-viability, the State has a compelling interest in the fetus, but that even at this stage an abortion must be permitted, under *Roe* and now *Casey*, "where it is necessary, in appropriate medical judgment, for the preservation of the life or health of the mother".[19] Notwithstanding its strong, indeed compelling interest in fetal life at this time, the State expresses a preference for not only the life, but also the health of the mother over that of the fetus. Indeed, the same is true in English law, as I shall explore in due course. In this section I discuss an argument within the maternal–fetal conflict literature which derives from the above principle, known as "no trade-offs", a phrase that has been coined with regard to the particular question of the post-viability abortion *method*. Regarding the maternal–fetal conflict, the idea is drawn upon to argue, particularly, that compelled caesarean sections are incompatible with the law of abortion in the sense that under abortion law the State expresses its preference for the life and health of the woman over that of the fetus even after viability.[20] Thus, Nancy Rhoden argues that "abortion doctrine reflects the view that a woman should not be used without her consent as a means to fetal health".[21]

Yet we shall see that the application of this point to the maternal–fetal conflict is actually far more complex than may have been foreseen. In essence, this is

[17] 491 NYS 2d 898 (Sup Ct 1985).

[18] *Ibid.*, 1007–8.

[19] The joint opinion in *Casey* reaffirms this point (120 L Ed 2d at 716) quoting its exact expression from *Roe* itself, 35 L Ed 2d at 165.

[20] See e.g. N Rhoden, "The Judge in the Delivery Room: The Emergence of Court-Ordered Cesareans", (1986) 74 *Cal L Rev* 1951, 1989–94.

[21] *Ibid.*, 2003.

because the "no trade-offs" point to the effect that the State cannot impose any additional risks upon a pregnant woman in the abortion method, only comes into play when an exception to the rule against post-viability abortions has been made and this in turn hinges upon the judgment that an abortion is necessary to protect either the life or health of the mother. This could mean that the principle does not lend quite the clear-cut support to a woman's right to refuse medical treatment as may have been supposed. The difficulties to which I draw attention stem from the different contexts of treatment refusal and abortion law and arise in particular, because, regarding the maternal–fetal conflict, our concern is with a woman's *right* (to refuse medical treatment) whereas in the abortion context after viability the focus is upon the *State's interest* in the life and health of the pregnant woman. Nevertheless, the discussion tends to confirm that a woman should have the legal right to refuse medical treatment, whilst at the same time drawing attention to the State's duties toward her. Given that the "no trade-offs" point concerns principally the issue of physical risk, this section of the chapter thus complements discussion in chapter four, much of which went principally to the question of religious or other serious, perhaps value-based reasons (with the exception of *Re AC*) for refusing medical treatment.

1. *The Justification of a Post-viability Abortion*

According to the "no trade-offs" principle, "where necessary" (the question of the judgment of which will be considered in the next section) a woman's life or health is to take priority over that of the fetus.

The notion of health was broadly interpreted in the case of *United States* v. *Vuitch* to encompass both psychological and physical well-being.[22] Elaborating these concepts, the case of *Doe* v. *Bolton*[23] emphasised that "the medical judgment may be exercised in the light of all factors—physical, emotional, psychological, familial, and the woman's age—relevant to the well-being of the patient".[24] Moreover, it was stressed that this provided "room that operates for the *benefit, not the disadvantage*, of the pregnant woman".[25] Therefore, we can see that the State's interest in the fetus after viability is not so strong that it is prepared to trade off the mother's

---

[22] 28 L Ed 601 (1971), 609. Mr Justice Black, delivering the opinion of the Court, acknowledged that the legislative history of the relevant statute gave no guidance as to whether "health" extended beyond the physical domain; he pointed, however, to the case of *Doe* v. *General Hospital of the District of Columbia*, 313 F Supp 1170 (DC 1970), in which District Judge Waddy interpreted the statute to permit abortions "for mental health reasons whether or not the patient had a previous history of mental defects" (at 1174–5), a view adopted by a higher court in the same case (28 L Ed at 609). Mr Justice Black also suggested that such a construction was in accordance with the "general usage and modern understanding of the word 'health'" (*ibid.*). He also noted that doctors are "routinely" called upon to judge whether a particular operation is necessary both for a patient's physical and mental health (at 610).

[23] 35 L Ed 2d 201 (1973). (The companion case to *Roe*, in which the Court did not find unconstitutionally vague a statutory requirement that a physician determine on the basis of his "best clinical judgment" that an abortion is "necessary", at 191–2).

[24] *Ibid.*, 192, *per* Blackmun J, who delivered the opinion of the Court.

[25] *Ibid.*, my emphasis.

life or health where these are judged at risk. In *Roe*, the justification for this prioritisation lay in the conclusion that the fetus is not a person for the purposes of the Fourteenth Amendment[26] and therefore lacks a right to life. In *Casey*, Justice Stevens considered that the Court implicitly reaffirmed this point as underlying the State's obligation to protect the mother over the fetus.[27]

2. The Post-viability Abortion Method

Abortion methods after viability must also recognise the primacy of the woman's life and health. The abortion case most often cited in support of this point is that of the Supreme Court in *Colautti* v. *Franklin*.[28] (*Stenberg* v. *Carhart* is not discussed here for reasons noted in the Introduction to Part III). This case considered part of a statute which directed physicians to employ the abortion technique "which would provide the best opportunity for the fetus to be aborted alive so long as a different technique would not be necessary in order to preserve the life or health of the mother".[29] For the majority, Justice Blackmun observed that the word "necessary" suggested that a particular technique must be "indispensable" to the woman's life or health, rather than merely desirable and that the term "life or health of the mother" did not necessarily imply that the physician must consider all of the factors relevant to the woman, as *Vuitch* requires. In his judgment, therefore, it was uncertain whether the physician was to consider the woman to be his primary patient or whether he was required to make a "'trade-off' between the woman's health and additional percentage points of fetal survival".[30] Justice Blackmun continued:[31]

> "Serious ethical and constitutional difficulties, *that we do not address*, lurk behind this ambiguity. We hold only that where conflicting duties of this magnitude are involved, the State, at the least, must proceed with greater precision before it may subject a physician to possible criminal sanctions."

The relevant section of the statute was declared void for vagueness, in the light of which the Court could hardly explicitly denounce any purported principle that the statute sought to express. Thus, *Colautti* does not in fact appear to be the clear authority upon which scholars such as Nancy Rhoden have sought to rely for the "no trade-offs" point.[32]

Still, Justice Blackmun later observed that in *Colautti* the Supreme Court "recognized the undesirability" of trade-offs between the woman and the fetus. This was in *Thornburgh* v. *American College of Obstetricians and Gynecologists*, which clearly decided that statutes allowing for trade-offs between the mother and the fetus in

---

[26] 35 L Ed 2d at 180.
[27] 120 L Ed 2d at 738.
[28] 58 L Ed 2d 596 (1979). See e.g. N Rhoden, "The Judge in the Delivery Room", 1990.
[29] Pennsylvania Abortion Control Act, s. 5(a)(2).
[30] 58 L Ed 2d at 612.
[31] *Ibid.*, my emphasis.
[32] N Rhoden, "The Judge in the Delivery Room", 1990–1.

the abortion method were unconstitutional.[33] The statute in this case required physicians to use the abortion method which would provide the best opportunity for the fetus to be aborted alive unless, according to the physician, this would represent a "significantly greater medical risk to the life or health of the pregnant woman".[34] In support of the wording of this section, it had been argued that "significantly greater medical risk" did not mean imposing an additional risk, in which case unconstitutionality was conceded, but only a "meaningfully increased" one. The Supreme Court agreed with the lower court to the effect that this reading was consistent with neither the statutory language nor its legislative intent, that the adverb "significantly" was "patently not surplusage", as had been argued, but in fact *modified* the risks put upon the woman, and that the statutory language was "not susceptible to a construction that does not require the mother to bear an increased medical risk in order to save her viable fetus."[35] For these (and other) reasons the statute was declared facially invalid. *Thornburgh* is therefore authority for the proposition that a required method of a post-viability abortion must not impose any additional risk upon a woman.

a) *Application to the Maternal–Fetal Conflict*

The relevance of the arguments about the abortion method is most apparent, suggests Nancy Rhoden, when we reflect that methods of inducing labour merge with post-viability abortion methods.[36] George Annas observes that the "no trade-offs" point makes us focus on the additional risks posed to a woman by a caesarean section, the purpose of which is to protect the fetus.[37] To impose a caesarean on a woman is thus to subject her to extra risks, to which she would not be subject in "natural" delivery. (Of course, the "no trade-offs" point has no application where not just the fetus, but also the woman, is at risk without a caesarean section.) Now, it could be argued that, with regard to post-viability abortion, the question of an abortion method only arises where a judgment has already been made to the effect that the continued pregnancy is a threat to the woman's life or health; that is, that the justification, as it were, for the illegitimacy of trade-offs with regard to the abortion *method* comes, in some way, from this. By contrast, with regard to the refusal of a caesarean section, no prior judgment has been made to the effect that the woman's life or health is at risk, which, as it were, might cover any decision with respect to the refusal of a caesarean. Nevertheless, the law's preference with regard to abortion seems clear: in the event of a post-viability conflict of interest between a woman's life or health and that of the fetus, the woman's interests should prevail. Thus, applying this to the situation of refusal of medical treatment, so long as a woman's life or health would be put at risk by a method of treatment intended to

---

[33] 90 L Ed 2d 779 (1986). Blackmun J's reference to *Colautti* is at 799.
[34] S. 3210(b) of a revised version of the Pennsylvania Abortion Control Act.
[35] 737 F 2d at 300.
[36] N Rhoden, "The Judge in the Delivery Room", 1992.
[37] G Annas, "Forced Cesareans: the Most Unkindest Cut of All", (1982) 12 (June) *Hastings CR* 16, 17.

enhance or protect fetal well-being, she should not be compelled to have that treatment. The refusal of a caesarean section would be a case in point.

In this regard, we might recall the reasoning of the trial court in *Re AC*, in which it was considered that the caesarean section would not *significantly* affect Ms C's condition because she had, it was estimated, at most two days to live. Whilst the majority in the 1990 appeal hearing of the case did not address this point, Associate Justice Belson (dissenting in part) was unsure whether the no trade-offs principle applied to the case of a caesarean section. If we trace his references at this point to *Thornburgh* and an academic article, it is apparent that in fact his reasoning is likely in line with that of the dissenting Justice White in *Thornburgh*.[38]

Justice White argues that the majority view in *Thornburgh* is inconsistent with *Roe* in two ways.[39] First, he says that the idea that if attempting to save the fetus puts any additional risk on the woman then she is permitted to destroy it is incompatible with the State's compelling interest in the fetus. Second, he argues that the idea contradicts *Roe*'s holding that the State may forbid all post-viability abortions unless *necessary* to save the life/health of the woman. In other words, he seems to be saying that the "additional risks" argument which relates specifically to the abortion method, does not fit with the "necessity" point inherent in the exception to the proscription of post-viability abortions. To try to show the inconsistency of these two points, he suggests that the fact that the State can forbid a post-viability abortion itself imposes a trade-off in favour of the fetus, on the basis that in fact such abortions may be statistically safer than going to term. Whatever the factual truth of the latter, however, this is completely misconstrued, since the State grants a woman the right to abort for a total of six months prior to viability. Thus, although she no longer has the *right* to abort after this time, she has plenty of opportunity to do so before this, which is why it is fair to restrict the right thereafter. This means that a fetus which has been developing for six months will not "arbitrarily" be aborted, but only in exceptional cases, "where necessary" to protect the woman's life or health. The "where necessary" judgment *is* different from the judgment about "any additional risks": but in the first case, the judgment is used to activate an exception; in the second case, *once that authorisation has been given* (by doctors), since the State's interest in the woman is greater than its compelling interest in the fetus *in these circumstances* (where an abortion is authorised after viability), the abortion method itself cannot be used to subvert this preference by putting additional risks upon the woman.

However, although this line of reasoning would appear to defeat the objections of Justice White with regard to abortion, in the process I think that some difficulties may have been opened up about the application of these points to the situation of a caesarean. These do not appear to have been apparent to the court however, in the 1994 caesarean decision of *Baby Boy Doe*. There, the court held that "[f]ederal constitutional principles prohibiting the balancing of fetal rights against

---

[38] Thus, he cites A Noble-Allgire, "Court-ordered Cesarean Sections: a Judicial Standard for Resolving the Conflict Between Fetal Interests and Maternal Rights", (1989) 10 *J Leg Med* 211, 236.

[39] 90 L Ed 2d at 824, joined by Rehnquist J.

maternal rights further bolster a woman's right to refuse a caesarean section", cit-ing *Thornburgh*. In interpreting the latter case, the *Doe* court went on:[40]

> "The Supreme Court, finding the statute unconstitutional for requiring a 'trade-off' between the woman's health and fetal survival, stressed that the woman's health is always the paramount consideration; any degree of increased risk to the woman's health is unac-ceptable."

Reasoning that a caesarean section necessarily presents some additional risks to the woman's health when recommended solely for fetal benefit, the court held that a forced caesarean section in such circumstances was unconstitutional.

Yet if we turn to the section of *Thornburgh* to which *Doe* refers at this juncture, we are reminded that the discussion is entirely about the question of a post-viability abortion *method*. In other words, the discussion assumes that a judgment has already been made that an abortion is "necessary" to protect the life or health of the mother under *Roe* or, to put it another way, that a post-viability abortion has already been legitimised. This means that the debate in *Thornburgh* is about the unconstitutional-ity, in effect, of individual states seeking to subvert the State's prioritisation of the woman over the fetus *in these cases* by imposing a method of abortion which increases the fetus's chances of survival. Moreover, the *Doe* court's reference to the way in which *Thornburgh* stresses that the woman's health is "always the paramount consid-eration" is in fact a reference to Justice Blackmun's gloss on *Colautti*: as we saw ear-lier, while Justice Blackmun *says* that in *Colautti* the Supreme Court "recognized the undesirability" of trade-offs between the woman and the fetus, in fact Justice White is quite correct to say (in *Thornburgh*) that in that case the Court "does no such thing".[41] Indeed, we saw that in *Colautti* the Court observed that there were "[s]eri-ous ethical and constitutional difficulties, *that we do not address*".

Although this difficulty might be thought to be remedied by the fact that in *Thornburgh* Justice Blackmun effectively says what he thinks the law should be—that is, that the woman's health should be paramount—there is an additional and more pervasive difficulty, namely that, like *Thornburgh*, *Colautti* was about the ques-tion of the abortion *method*, not about the acceptability of a post-viability abortion as a matter of *principle*. In other words, since *Thornburgh* is explicating the law about the abortion method when a judgment that an abortion is "necessary for the woman's life or health" under *Roe* has already been made, *Baby Boy Doe*'s judgment that a compelled caesarean is unconstitutional under *Thornburgh* hinges on an ellip-sis. In short, with regard to the use made in the caesarean cases of abortion law, we have not yet passed the first hurdle, namely, whether the *avoidance* of the caesarean is "necessary to protect the woman's life or health" under *Roe* and *Casey*. How damaging is this to the caesarean cases?

---

[40]   632 NE 2d at 333.
[41]   "The Court seems to read its earlier opinion in *Colautti* . . . as incorporating a holding that trade-offs between the health of the pregnant woman and the survival of the fetus are constitutionally imper-missible under *Roe* v. *Wade*. Of course, *Colautti* held no such thing." 90 L Ed 2d at 824.

The difficulties that now emerge concern the complexity of the "necessity" judgment in the context of the caesarean cases, and the question of who makes this judgment. On the first point, Robertson has criticised the application of the necessity point under *Roe* on the grounds of its *vagueness*.[42] He notes, particularly, that the Supreme Court has never indicated how serious the threat to the mother's health must be. There may be two related reasons for this: first, that the Court does not wish to tie the clinical hands of doctors and second, because the Court trusts that doctors will make appropriately professional judgments. Indeed, so far as abortion is concerned, *doctors* judge when there are grounds for activating the exception to the post-viability proscription of abortion. In this sense, the "necessity" argument hinges upon the *medical judgment* that fetal needs (continued pregnancy in the case of abortion) jeopardise maternal health or life. Recognition of this aspect requires us to reflect upon who makes this judgment in the context of maternal refusal of treatment, given the rights context still prevalent there, but which has clearly ceased in the abortion context after viability.

i) The Role of Third Parties in the Law of Abortion and the Law of Treatment Refusal

As we have seen in Part II, a pregnant woman has the right in some US states, albeit limited to non-invasive treatment, either to accept or refuse medical treatment, based upon the question of whether the treatment conflicts with personal questions such as her religious faith and/or upon information she receives about that treatment and her own assessment of the acceptability or otherwise of the burdens and risks attaching to it. This is the case not only if she considers unacceptable what others might deem to be a relatively small burden or risk, but indeed—as stressed particularly in England—for *any* reason, serious or trivial. That her *doctor* (or a judge) may consider that the treatment is necessary for her life or health and/or for that of the fetus is irrelevant to her *rights* in this regard. Note that while the question of non-invasive treatment is left open in those cases which have considered the issue (for example *Baby Boy Doe* and *Re Fetus Brown*), since this discussion of treatment refusals post-viability is primarily concerned with the issue of caesareans, which the *Baby Boy Doe* case did address, the undecided aspects of, for instance, Illinois law, need not concern us.

It might be noted, in passing, that in principle this discussion might also be said to apply to the English situation: thus, as noted in the last chapter, the Abortion Act 1967 (as amended by the Human Fertilisation and Embryology Act 1990) allows the termination of pregnancies up to 24 weeks in certain defined circumstances, and after 24 weeks where necessary to prevent "grave permanent injury to the physical or mental health" of the pregnant woman, or where continued pregnancy would "involve risk to the life of the pregnant woman greater than if the pregnancy were terminated". (There is also the fetal disability ground.) I think the following discussion is of relevance to the English situation, however, without addressing the detail of these sections of the law (particularly the question of the interpretation of the

---

[42] J Robertson, "The Right to Procreate", 360.

relevant sections).[43] Of course, the operation of English abortion law prior to viability involves medical judgment to a significant degree, but this does not affect the question of the reconciliation of the law *after* viability with a pregnant woman's right to refuse medical treatment, the point of concern in *Re MB*. The remainder of the discussion focuses explicitly on US law.

In applying the "where necessary" argument from abortion to the law of treatment refusal, we thus come upon the difficulty, apparently unnoticed by other scholars seeking support for the idea of a woman's *right* to refuse treatment in the "no trade-offs" point, that the role of doctors is quite different in each context.

In the case of *abortion*, after viability a doctor plays a crucial role in the operation of the law by providing the judgment which justifies an abortion after this time. The doctor's judgment that continued pregnancy would threaten the woman's life or health is that which ensures the State is expressing and abiding by its interest in the woman's life or health. In this light, regarding the case of *Re AC*, we might note that although her fetus was at or near viability, Ms C could have aborted if it was considered that the fetus threatened her health. Importantly, however, it would have been a *doctor,* not AC herself, authorising this decision. George Annas, by contrast, writes that in this circumstance "*she* could have authorized her pregnancy to be terminated at any time before her death".[44] This is surely not the case. Although she could have requested such termination, without a doctor's authority in accordance with the principles under *Roe* it would have been illegal. By contrast, in the *treatment refusal context* of medical law, a doctor's clinical judgment is merely a *step on the way* (in terms of the provision of information about risks and consequences and so forth) to the patient exercising her right to accept or refuse treatment, playing no active part in the final choice that is made. (Note that I am here concerned, as emphasised, with a doctor's medical knowledge and advice, not with the role a doctor may have in discussion and counselling with regard to moral issues as outlined in chapter four. Indeed, there I suggested that ideally a third party such as a counsellor should be involved in that kind of discussion.)

Importantly, the point is that the idea of "necessity" inherent in the exception to the post-viability proscription of abortion is part of the *State's interest* in the woman's life and health and is a matter to be decided by doctors: it is not connected with a woman's *rights*. The idea of necessity, therefore, cannot bolster the idea of a woman's rights at this point.

Yet, despite having unravelled this difficulty, it may be that the "necessity" point can ultimately work to support a woman's *right* to refuse treatment. Thus, if we were to assume, for the sake of argument, that the context is *not* one of a woman's rights, then I think that doctors would in fact have great difficulty in making the

---

[43] I note, however, that the phrase "grave permanent injury" probably results in a more restrictive approach than in the United States after viability. Further, with regard to the phrase "risk to her life", the section only requires that the termination *reduces* the risk to her life. On the latter point, see I Kennedy and A Grubb, *Medical Law*, 3rd edn. (London: Butterworths, 2000) 1424.

[44] G Annas, "She's Going to Die: the Case of Angela C.", (1988) 18 (Feb./March) *Hastings CR* 23, 24.

judgment that, for instance, a caesarean section would jeopardise maternal life or heath and hence that its refusal is "necessary" to protect her life and health. The "necessity" point will therefore be seen to confirm the illegitimacy of compelled obstetric intervention after viability (such as a caesarean section), but in a different way than has hitherto been explored. In order to demonstrate this, the following discussion assumes, for the sake of argument, that a pregnant woman has only, say, a *prima facie* right to refuse medical treatment such as the caesarean.

ii) Abortion and Treatment Refusal: Medical versus Moral Questions for Doctors

The question now is how doctors can judge the necessity point given the issues which remain open in the treatment refusal scenario.

With regard to *abortion*, since after viability a woman no longer has the right to abort and has had the prior opportunity to do so, the underlying question of the *morality of abortion* is no longer in issue at this point. Rather, what *is* in issue for doctors is whether some or all of certain *pre-determined factors* have been fulfilled so as to justify an abortion in circumstances in which the law has decided would otherwise be illegal. In the light of the State's established interest in the woman's life or health, if doctors deem her to be at risk from the fetus, they must authorise a post-viability abortion. Yet the kinds of factors at stake even in the broadly defined issue of health at this point are likely to be acute, such as an emotional breakdown. This is because if a woman *generally* perceived continued pregnancy as a threat to her emotional health she would most likely have decided to abort *before* viability. Moreover, questions relating to a woman's interest in self-determination are *un*likely to be invoked in post-viability abortions. Therefore, with regard to the possibility of the judgment that an abortion is "necessary" to protect the life or health of the mother, the large moral and legal questions are no longer at stake; rather, in issue is the question of the physical and psychological reasons grounding an exception in a context in which the significant moral questions have already been determined.

By contrast, with regard to the *refusal of a caesarean section*, the need for which will only arise at or after viability, we have noted elsewhere that a woman neither knows in advance if this will be needed, nor has the opportunity to refuse it other than near or after viability. In this way, assuming for the sake of argument that she has only a *prima facie* right to refuse medical treatment including after viability, all the large moral and legal questions would remain "pending" at this time. In effect, to decide whether the refusal of a caesarean is necessary for the woman's life and health is *to decide whether she should or should not, for the sake of the fetus, submit to it*. Certainly the narrow question of the "no trade-offs" point from the question of the abortion method *is* readily applicable: on this basis, so long as medical advice was that the caesarean imposes greater risks than natural delivery, then a doctor could not recommend a caesarean. However, as already pointed out, the primary issue of the "necessity" of the refusal of the caesarean has not been decided, analogously, as it were, to the necessity point activating the post-viability exception to the proscription of abortion. In other words, the question of not imposing *additional* risks only comes into operation in the abortion context once an abortion has *already been deemed necessary*. Further, with regard to the much broader issue of health, how is a doctor to decide the emotional and/or religious impact upon a woman of operating without her consent? That is, how can a doctor judge whether the refusal of the caesarean is "necessary" to her health? To ask doctors to attempt this kind of judgment is to ask them to *balance the interests of the woman against those of the fetus*: they do not have to do this with regard to abortion for the reasons explained in the preceding paragraph, namely that in the abortion context they are working within and simply giving effect to a predetermined legal weighting of rights and interests.

Yet, if doctors cannot make the judgment that the refusal of a caesarean is necessary for a woman's life and health, in turn this tends to imply that the woman should indeed have the absolute right to refuse it. Ultimately, therefore, consideration of the "necessity" point therefore *supports* a woman's legal right to refuse medical treatment, though not in the way that had originally been supposed, as for instance in *Baby Boy Doe*'s discussion of *Thornburgh*, above. The discussion thus lends additional weight to my arguments supporting a woman's legal right in Part II by highlighting the difficulties of subjecting her treatment choice to any third-party assessment such as that inherent in the "no trade-offs" test of necessity.[45] Moreover, in Part II I suggested that, notwithstanding the relevance of certain arguments from areas such as the law of abortion, the maternal–fetal cases are best understood and ultimately belong within the framework of the law of treatment refusal. This means that it seems more justifiable that a pregnant woman should keep throughout pregnancy the right which other patients unquestionably have, to make the determination of the effects of certain treatment on her life and health, broadly defined, herself.

D. A Woman's Right to Refuse Treatment and the State's Intrinsic Duty to Let Her Do So

The preceding discussion invites us briefly to reflect upon the question of the justification and relative importance of a woman's right to refuse treatment on the one hand and the State's duty to let her do so on the other. The following questions seem to arise: does the State's compelling interest in a woman's life and health post-viability in fact support, or justify, her right to refuse treatment? Does the State's interest in her life and health also mean that it has a duty, not correlated to a right on her part, to let her refuse treatment? Is either more important than the other?

With regard to the first suggestion, namely that the State's interest in her life and health justifies her right to refuse treatment, I argued in Part II that the State's

---

[45] The exception, of course, would be where her reasons are clearly trivial. In such cases, other arguments, discussed in ch. 4 and the final ch. 7 are in point, in addition, that is, to the aspect discussed in this chapter that the State does not have authority through abortion law to *impose* a procedure for fetal benefit, rather than to *prevent* abortions after viability in English and US law (in both cases with exceptions) and before viability in English law unless certain conditions are satisfied.

interest in the lives of patients—the preservation of life interest—can be construed not as "giving way to" but instead as supporting the right of patients to refuse life-sustaining treatment. I took note of the State's original concern that the value of life might be threatened by a treatment refusal; I also showed that, as the right to refuse medical treatment has developed, so the State has often come to understand that allowing such a refusal is more consistent with upholding life's "sanctity" than overriding a patient's choice. Given that we have concluded that the maternal–fetal conflict has more in common with treatment refusal than abortion law, then we might indeed say that the State's interest in the woman's life and health supports a *right* on her part to refuse medical treatment. By contrast, we have seen that its interest in these matters in the abortion context does not grant a *right* to abort after viability; rather, the State's interest in a woman's life and health implies a *duty* to let her abort in certain circumstances. Yet the conclusion that a woman has the right to refuse treatment does not preclude the conclusion that the State *also* has a duty, independently of her right, to let her do so.

In turn, this may be another reason why it is not "illogical", as the *Re MB* court considered it might be, that the State proscribes abortions after viability but allows a pregnant woman to refuse medical treatment, including for irrational reasons: just as the State has a duty to the woman to let her abort "where necessary" after viability, so it has a duty to let her refuse treatment, "where necessary": since I have argued that the State cannot make the judgment as to necessity in the treatment scenario, it must therefore allow the woman to do so. Otherwise, it may not attend to its responsibilities not to harm her.

E. The Social Context of Pregnancy

Whilst acknowledging that abortion goes beyond the realm of belief to that of action, with consequences not only for the woman concerned but also for those involved in abortion and for the society in which it is practised, the Court in *Casey* said that abortion cannot be proscribed outright because the woman's freedom is considered at stake in an "utterly unique" way which the law must recognise. In one of its most striking passages, the joint opinion held:[46]

> "The mother who carries a child to full term is subject to constraints, to pain that only she must bear. *That these sacrifices have from the beginning of the human race been endured by the woman with a pride that ennobles her in the eyes of others and gives to the infant a bond of love cannot alone be grounds for the State to insist that she makes that sacrifice.* Her suffering is too intimate and personal for the State to insist, without more, upon its own vision of the woman's role, however dominant that vision has been in the course of our history and our culture. The destiny of the woman must be shaped to a large extent on her own conception of her spiritual imperatives and her place in society."

---

[46] 120 L Ed 2d at 698–9, my emphasis.

In this passage, the Court highlights not only the intimacy of the abortion decision and the value of bodily integrity, arguably aspects of the social context of pregnancy, but also the wider social context point that although women have always been the bearers of children, that is not a reason for the State—a third party—to impose those sacrifices upon women. As observed in chapter four, this line of argument was noted by the Appellate Court of Illinois in *Re Fetus Brown* (1997) in which it held that a pregnant woman could refuse not just a caesarean section, but also a blood transfusion.[47]

This reasoning is further supported and developed in Justice Blackmun's opinion in *Casey*.[48] He suggests that the Court's framework for the assessment of abortion regulations "responds to the *social context* of women facing these issues of reproductive choice".[49] In this way, he suggests, the Court "remains sensitive to the unique role of women in the decision-making process".[50] In discussing a woman's interest in bodily integrity which underlies, in part, her abortion right, he notes:[51]

> "[C]ompelled continuation of a pregnancy infringes upon a woman's right to bodily integrity by imposing substantial physical intrusions and significant risks of physical harm. During pregnancy, women experience dramatic physical changes and a wide range of health consequences. Labor and delivery pose additional health risks and physical demands. *In short, restrictive abortion laws force women to endure physical invasions far more substantial than those this Court has held to violate the constitutional principle of bodily integrity in other contexts.*"

Thus, the inherent risks of pregnancy are acknowledged to be greater than the State can lawfully impose beyond the situation of pregnancy. With reference to these inherent risks and sacrifices, Justice Blackmun criticises the State's assumption that women owe the duty to continue a pregnancy "as a matter of course", as though they "can simply be forced to accept the 'natural' status and incidents of motherhood".[52] He suggests that this assumption relies on a vision of the role of women which has invoked the protection of the Equal Protection Clause.[53] Thus, it may be that my "social context" argument is related to equality arguments, a point further considered in chapter seven.[54] Moreover, he notes that this vision invokes

---

[47] 294 Ill App 3d 159 (Ill App 1 Dist 1997), 171.

[48] Concurring in the judgment in part, and dissenting in part. As SF Kreimer notes, whilst the joint opinion "played [this theme] in an undertone", Blackmun J "explicitly adopted [it]". SF Kreimer, "Does Pro-Choice Mean Pro-Kevorkian? An essay on *Roe*, *Casey*, and the Right to Die", (1995) 44 *Am Univ L Rev* 803, 849, footnotes omitted.

[49] 120 L Ed 2d at 746, footnote omitted, my emphasis.

[50] *Ibid.*

[51] *Ibid.*, 747–8, my emphasis.

[52] *Ibid.*, 748.

[53] Blackmun J is the only justice to make reference to this clause, which was not part of the original decision in *Roe*, and refers to the recognition of this point by an increasing number of commentators. See e.g. L Tribe, *American Constitutional, Law*, 2nd edn. (Mineola, NY: Foundation Press, 1988) s. 1510, 1353–1359; CA MacKinnon, "Reflections on Sex Equality Under Law", (1991) 100 *Yale LJ* 1281, 1308–24. See further ch. 7.

[54] See also discussion in ch. 6.

assumptions about women's *social role* that the joint opinion recognises to be inconsistent with its "understanding of the family, the individual, or the Constitution".[55]

With regard to a pregnant woman's interests in refusing medical treatment, these ideas relate to an aspect of my argument towards the end of chapter two, where I noted that pregnancy is very much an ordinary state of affairs with usual or inherent but at the same time somewhat extraordinary risks and burdens which we cannot insist are a matter of duty, partly because of the place that pregnancy occupies in society. Pregnancy carries a range of inherent risks, some of which are more extreme than others, but many of which are likely extraordinary by comparison with the physical demands normally made of individuals; further, the need for the most extreme of these—caesarean delivery—may arise, unpredictably, at the last moment of pregnancy. How can we insist upon these burdens when, although society needs women to bear children in order that it continue, each time, each pregnancy, it is only the woman who must endure them? For these (and other) reasons, then, the woman should have the right to decide to abort (pre-viability) as *Casey* confirms or, having decided not to abort, the right to refuse treatment based on her own spiritual or physical imperatives.

III. CONCLUSIONS

In this chapter I have surveyed the relevance of various points from the context of abortion law to that of the maternal–fetal conflict. Some of these have been closely related to one another, others not. Regarding these points, I have concluded the following: that a woman who continues a pregnancy without aborting is, in particular, under a negative moral obligation not to abort which becomes a negative legal obligation not to do so at viability.[56] Abortion law, however, never mandates the imposition upon her of affirmative legal obligations and thus cannot be cited in support of compelled obstetric intervention on behalf of the fetus. Moreover, the application of the "where necessary" point (deriving from the "no trade-offs" principle) from abortion to maternal–fetal conflict law has been explored in detail, resulting in the conclusion that a woman must always be able to decide when a particular form of treatment needed by the fetus can be rejected in the interests of her health or life. Here we are saying that she has the right so to decide but also, and perhaps more significantly, that the State has a duty to let her do so, deriving from its own interests in her life and health. Finally, I have drawn attention to the legal recognition of the social context of pregnancy, adapting this to the "subcontext" of the maternal–fetal conflict.

---

[55] 120 L Ed 2d at 727.

[56] As noted in ch. 2, the intuition that a woman who decides not to terminate a pregnancy thereafter comes under a negative duty not to abort would require more argument than that for which I have space.

6

Arguments from Tort Law

I. INTRODUCTION

T HE CASES so far have revealed some judicial and public disquiet, one which might be captured by the question "would not the *reasonable* pregnant woman submit to the caesarean, or blood transfusion, if necessary for fetal life?". Beyond the treatment context, another question concerns the *reasonableness* of maternal conduct and the notion of a pregnant woman's duty generally to conduct her life so as not to cause prenatal harm. This chapter explores the current law by considering the idea of a pregnant woman's "duty to bring the child into the world as healthy as is reasonably possible".[1] Regarding the treatment context, the discussion seeks to encourage understanding and acceptance of the current legal position upholding a pregnant woman's rights by analysing the difficulties inherent in the idea of her legal duty, explored through the tort of negligence. Beyond the treatment context, the appropriateness of a maternal legal duty of care is considered.

If I have already concluded that a pregnant woman should have the right to refuse medical treatment, why do we need a chapter arguing against a maternal prenatal duty of care? As noted in chapter two in the discussion at the level of moral theory, the argument "from duty" is not just the inverse of the argument "from rights". So far as the legal analysis goes, whereas in chapter four I defended the idea of a pregnant woman's rights in the treatment context in terms of the values underlying the grant of such rights with reference to treatment refusal and abortion law, this chapter analyses the difficulties inherent in the idea of legal duties, by exploring relevant aspects of the tort of negligence. Thus, here I examine a completely different area of law upon which both the maternal–fetal cases and literature draw. In so doing, a pregnant woman's rights are defended in an interest-based way, rather than through exploration of underlying values. Further, the chapter pays attention to important policy considerations.

Logically, the first question in considering whether a pregnant woman should have a legal duty of care toward her unborn child is whether it is appropriate to impose a duty in the circumstances. In English law, following *Caparo Industries plc* v. *Dickman*,[2] this is now answered by reference to the three-stage test of foreseeability, proximity and "fairness, justice and reasonableness". The first two hurdles

---

[1] J Robertson, "Procreative Liberty and the Control of Conception, Pregnancy, and Childbirth", (1983) 69 *Va L Rev* 405, 438.
[2] [1990] 2 AC 605.

are clearly relatively easy to satisfy in the case of the pregnant woman, both within the treatment context and (albeit less clearly on occasion) beyond it. Thus, much will turn on the third hurdle, typically construed as policy. It is a little too easy, however, to dismiss the notion of a duty of care *solely* on policy grounds and the acceptability of this move will in any event depend on one's policy vision. In large (but not total) measure, therefore, this chapter adopts what might be seen as an approach of principle, in that a considerable portion of the argument explores the *conceptual difficulties* we would encounter in seeking to establish the *standard* of maternal prenatal care, at least within the treatment context. Beyond this context the problems are rather different and considerable attention is devoted to high-lighting these differences so as to make clear that the primary reasons why there should be no maternal duty of care in the treatment context are based on principle, whereas beyond the treatment context policy has a stronger (but not absolute) sway.

The tort of negligence is generally concerned with liability for acts, rather than omissions. As regards the "ordinary citizen", the notion of a duty of care is typic-ally expressed through the injunction to take care not physically to harm another as he goes about his daily life. Thus, it is a duty attaching to the "general conduct" in which the individual engages which might include, for instance, a duty not to injure the fetus within a pregnant woman by driving carelessly. This realm of *neg-ative* duties is the customary province of the tort of negligence. Not surprisingly, then, the law is relatively well equipped to address the question of a pregnant woman's general conduct and the way this might harm the developing fetus. For instance, if she drives or crosses the street negligently, smokes, drinks excessive alcohol, takes drugs or bungee-jumps (the latter is most unlikely but clearly pos-sible) it might be argued that she is breaching a moral duty not to harm the unborn child, thereby creating a *prima facie* case for legal liability within the framework of the law of tort.[3] (Note that although a woman will *choose* to smoke, drink alcohol, take drugs (subject to addiction problems touched on in due course) or engage in "risky" sports, so far as the fetus is concerned, if harm occurs this can appropriately be seen as negligent rather than intentional.[4]) In terms of her general conduct, I argue that the pregnant woman is *to some extent* in the same position as the detached third party who does not harm the fetus in ways which implicate very personal beliefs, choices or questions about himself, expressed, for instance, in his moral and

---

[3] This is not to suggest that legal duties of care are necessarily founded in morality, but clearly many are. On tort law as a system of personal responsibility for conduct, see P Cane, *The Anatomy of Tort Law* (Oxford: Hart Publishing, 1997).

[4] It has been suggested that "[m]ost pregnant women who use controlled substances wish to avoid harm to their future children". KA De Ville and LM Kopelman, "Fetal Protection in Wisconsin's Revised Child Abuse Law; Right Goal, Wrong Remedy", (1999) 27 *J of Law, Med and Ethics* 332, 338 (footnote citing M Rosenblaum and K Irwin, "Pregnancy, Drugs, and Harm Reduction", in CL Wetherington and AB Roman (eds.), *Drug Addiction Research and the Health of Women* (Rockville: National Institutes of Health, 1998) 309–18 omitted). Further, it has been noted that "[w]ith substance abuse during pregnancy, the woman directly harms herself and typically only in so doing does she indi-rectly harm the developing fetus". F Baylis, "Case Comment And Note: Dissenting With The Dissent: *Winnipeg Child And Family Services (Northwest Area) v. G(DF)*", (1998) 36 *Alberta L Rev* 785, 795.

legal interests in self-determination and bodily integrity. Thus *prima facie* her obligations might well be commensurate with those of the "detached" third party. The situation is more complex, however, and is discussed by way of counterpoint in the second half of the chapter, in order to strengthen the first.

It is harder, however, to analyse the idea of a pregnant woman's legal duty to submit to medical treatment for the fetus's sake, the first topic, within the framework of the law of tort. If a pregnant woman had such a (moral and) legal duty it would be a *positive* or affirmative duty. I argue that there are difficulties, however, in determining the *reasonableness*—and hence the existence and extent—of a positive duty to aid in the treatment context. As we have seen in earlier chapters, this is because such a duty would rub up against the pregnant woman's (moral and) legal interests and rights in self-determination and bodily integrity.

Located at the interface between rights and duties, a pregnant woman's relationship to the fetus within the treatment context can thus be analysed both in terms of her *rights* and her *duties*. Whilst in the first part of chapter two and in chapter four I explored this relationship by focusing on her rights, the notion of duties is here the vehicle for analysis. In essence, this chapter considers the issues, both of principle and policy, which should incline us either to support or to reject the idea of a maternal duty of care during pregnancy. To start, I briefly consider the background law with regard to prenatal injury and death regarding third-party liability, first in the United States and second in England.[5] I shall then turn to the issue of maternal liability for prenatal harm/death.

II. THIRD–PARTY LIABILITY FOR PRENATAL HARM

A. United States

Until 1946 there was no tortious liability for *injuries* to the fetus *in utero*: this rule was established in 1884 in *Dietrich* v. *City of Northampton*,[6] on the basis that the fetus was not considered a separate entity from its mother. This position changed dramatically in the 1946 case of *Bonbrest* v. *Kotz*,[7] which allowed recovery for prenatal injuries if the fetus was viable at the moment of injury and born alive. Following *Bonbrest*, recovery for prenatal injury was widely recognised. Moreover, while some jurisdictions continued to maintain a viability requirement, others abandoned it.[8] In these cases, it is important to note that it is the *born child* who has the right

---

[5] For a more broadly based discussion of the liability of third parties to the fetus, see J Seymour, *Childbirth and the Law* (Oxford: Oxford University Press, 2000) 156*ff*.

[6] 138 Mass 14 (1884).

[7] 65 F Supp 138 (DDC 1946). The court relied in part on the dissent of Judge Boggs in the 1900 case of *Allaire* v. *St Luke's Hospital*, 56 NE 638 (1900), who argued that although the mother may die as the result of injury, a fetus may be capable of survival if removed from her body.

[8] For instance, in the case of *Hornbuckle* v. *Plantation Pipe Line*, 93 SE 2d 727 (1956), the Georgia Supreme Court held that recovery for any injury suffered after conception should be allowed.

to sue the party who injured her/him prenatally, *not the fetus*. This is because the aim of prenatal injury actions is to compensate the live-born but injured *child*.[9]

Importantly, it is in this light that the decision in *Smith* v. *Brennan*[10] should be considered. There, the New Jersey Supreme Court held that a "*child* has the *legal right* to begin life with a sound mind and body".[11] The decision is often interpreted as giving rights to the *fetus*.[12] For instance, Robert Blank makes repeated reference to the "right of the unborn to be born with a sound mind and body"[13] and suggests that scholars are now increasingly inclined to the view that tort law recognises the fetus as a person. This view is mistaken: as others have noted, *Smith* actually recognises the rights of the live-born *child* to recover for prenatal injury.[14] The legal status of the fetus, then, is not in issue. This is partly because the duty of care that a third party owes prenatally is a duty to the *future child* (that is, to the child who will be but is not yet born).[15] In support of this interpretation, the *Smith* court observed that it "is immaterial whether before birth the child is considered a person in being".[16] Rather, what was important was whether there was "harm to the child when *born*".[17] I shall return to *Smith* when I consider the issue of maternal liability.

If a child could only recover for prenatal harm if born alive, there would be no recovery (on behalf of relatives) for a stillborn child to whom the prenatal injuries had resulted in death rather than injury. Redressing this somewhat anomalous position relatively early on, the 1949 case of *Verkennes* v. *Corniea*[18] was the first to permit recovery for the death of the fetus *in utero* under a wrongful death statute. In considering actions for prenatal *death*, it is important to note the purpose of wrongful death statutes. The English Fatal Accidents Act 1846 was the first example of such legislation and provided that where someone wrongfully or negligently causes the death of another in such a way that he could have sued if he survived, an action

---

[9] For endorsement of this view, see LH Glantz, "Is the Fetus a Person? A Lawyer's View", in *Abortion and the Status of the Fetus*, W Bondeson *et al* (eds.), (Dordrecht: D Reidl Publishing Co., 1983) 107: "The fact that courts permit live born infants to recover damages for prenatal injuries does not mean that courts view the unborn as 'persons'. Instead the courts are interested in protecting the interests of the damaged live born person." (At 114.)

[10] 157 A 2d 497 (1960).

[11] *Ibid.*, 503, *per* Proctor J, my emphases.

[12] See e.g. J Myers, "Abuse and Neglect of the Unborn: Can the State Intervene?", (1984) 23 *Duquesne L Rev* 1, 60; B Chernaik, "Recovery for Prenatal Injuries: The Right of a Child Against its Mother", (1976) 10 *Suffolk U L Rev* 582, 608.

[13] R Blank, "Emerging Notions of Women's Rights and Responsibilities During Gestation", (1986) 7 *J Leg Med* 441, 441. In general Blank *presumes* rights on the fetus's behalf. See e.g. 465, 468–9.

[14] 157 A 2d at 504: "We believe that a *surviving child* should have a right of action in tort for prenatal injuries for the plain reason that it would be unjust to deny it." *Per* Proctor J, my emphasis. But see *Becker* v. *Schwartz*, 386 NE 2d 807, 812, (1978), which refused to recognise any right of a child to begin life with a sound mind and body: "There is no precedent for recognition . . . of 'the fundamental right to be born as a whole, functional, human being' "; citing *Park* v. *Chessin*, 60 A 2d 80, 88, (1977).

[15] Another reason is that the future child is not within the body of the third party: see the discussion *infra* in s. III(B)(3).

[16] 157 A 2d at 503, *per* Proctor J.

[17] *Ibid.*, my emphasis.

[18] 38 NW 2d 838 (1949).

may be brought to compensate certain family members for losses arising from the death of this person: while the duty of care is owed to the *deceased*, the *purpose* of the statute is to compensate the *remaining relatives* and the degree of compensation is based upon their loss.[19] (The current English law is to be found in the Fatal Accidents Act 1976.) The current US position is that a majority of states recognise a cause of action for the wrongful death of a viable fetus,[20] although, in the light of the purpose of damages in such a case, there appears to be little reason in principle to limit recovery to the period after viability.

In these cases, since the fetus does not live to become a legal person and yet a right of action can be brought for its death, we must ask whether the *fetus* gains legal rights. This is particularly apposite given the definition of the fetus as a person for the purposes of wrongful death statutes. Although scholars have argued that the fetus does thereby acquire rights, the underlying purpose of wrongful death statutes—which itself is the justification for the definition of the fetus as a person in such statutes—would suggest otherwise. This point was emphasised in *Roe* v. *Wade*,[21] in which the Court found it necessary to address the question of the consistency of its finding on abortion with wrongful fetal death actions permitted in most states. Justice Blackmun carefully emphasised that the purpose of such actions "is to vindicate the *parents'* interest and is thus consistent with the view that the fetus, at most, represents only the potentiality of life", concluding that *fetuses* "have *never been recognized in the law as persons in the whole sense*".[22] Thus, the definition of fetuses as persons for the purposes of wrongful death actions simply reflects the fact that in all such actions the duty is owed to the deceased, not to the surviving relatives, on behalf of whom the action is brought; the benefit of the action, however, accrues to the relatives, who are compensated, in the case of fetal death, because a fetus who would (but for the injury) have been born was killed prenatally.

As we shall see in turning to the issue of potential maternal liability, however, the recognition of the fetus as a person for the purposes of wrongful death statutes has been interpreted as granting the fetus rights which conflict with those of the pregnant woman. The American legal scholar who was early alert to this development was Dawn Johnsen,[23] who warned that the idea of fetal rights could expand in ways which would conflict with women's interests and rights and drew attention to the important "conceptual move" in identifying the fetus, rather than the

---

[19] For a more detailed discussion, see B Steinbock, *Life Before Birth: the Moral and Legal Status of Embryos and Fetuses* (New York, NY: Oxford University Press, 1992) 101.

[20] L Nelson, B Buggy and C Weil, "Forced Medical Treatment of Pregnant Women: 'Compelling Each to Live as Seems Good to the Rest' ", (1986) 37 *Hastings LJ* 703, 737. For a list of the majority and minority states see nn. 150 and 151 respectively therein.

[21] 35 L Ed 2d 147 (1973).

[22] *Ibid.*, 182, my emphasis. The point was reiterated by Stevens J, in *Casey*, who concludes: "Thus, as a matter of federal constitutional law, a developing organism that is not yet a 'person' does not have what is sometimes described as a 'right to life'. This has been and, by the Court's holding today, remains a fundamental premise of our constitutional law governing reproductive autonomy." 120 L Ed 2d at 738–9, footnote omitted, my emphasis.

[23] D Johnsen, "The Creation of Fetal Rights: Conflicts with Women's Constitutional Rights to Liberty, Privacy, and Equal Protection", (1986) 95 *Yale LJ* 599, esp. 602–4.

woman, as the locus of rights.[24] Before considering the idea of maternal liability for prenatal harm, I outline the relevant English law regarding third-party liability.

B. England

So far as fetal death is concerned, wrongful death actions are not recognised in England, although damages have been awarded to a mother for a stillbirth which resulted from negligent treatment.[25]

As regards fetal injury the relevant law can be divided into that which applies to children born before and after 22 July 1976. After this date, the Congenital Disabilities (Civil Liability) Act 1976 applies. Section 1 of the Act gives a cause of action to a child born injured as the result of an occurrence affecting: either of its parents in his or her ability to have a normal healthy child; the mother during pregnancy; or the mother or the child in the birth process, causing the child to be born with disabilities which it would not otherwise have had. Such disabilities are to be regarded as damage resulting from the wrongful act of the relevant third party. With regard to the issue of duty (subject to certain other points), a person is answerable to the child if he owed a duty of care to the parent (although no injury need be suffered by the parent). Hence, the child's claim under the Act *derives* from the breach of duty to its parent.

The relevant law for a child born before 22 July 1976 is the common law, as established in the 1993 Court of Appeal cases of *Burton* v. *Islington Health Authority* and *De Martell* v. *Merton and Sutton Health Authority*,[26] both of which addressed the question whether a child who is born alive, but suffers from disabilities caused by the defendant's negligence whilst he/she was *in utero*, has a cause of action in negligence against the defendant.

Dillon LJ recognised that a fetus has no legal personality in English law, as established in the cases of *Paton* v. *BPAS*[27] and *Re F (in utero)*.[28] However, he drew attention to the "other contexts" in which the English courts have incorporated the civil law maxim "that an unborn child shall be deemed to be born whenever

---

[24] For examples of writers advocating the restriction of women's rights for the sake of the fetus see M Shaw, "Conditional Prospective Rights of the Fetus", (1984) 5 *J Leg Med* 63; J Parness and S Pritchard, "To Be or Not to Be: Protecting the Unborn's Potentiality of Life", (1982) 51 *U Cin L Rev* 257, in which, for instance, the authors support the decision in *Jefferson* (at 288 and 294); C Simon, "Parental Liability for Prenatal Injury", (1978) 14 *Colum J Law & Soc Probs* 47, in which the author concludes that "[t]he parents' rights to autonomy should be limited when they conflict with the *right of the child* to be born whole." (At 90, my emphasis.). See also J Myers, "Abuse and Neglect of the Unborn", 60: "[T]he unborn child may be said to possess a right to protection from tortious injury, abuse, and neglect. Put another way, the unborn child possesses a right to gestation undisturbed by wrongful injury, and a right to be born with a sound mind and body, free from parentally inflicted abuse or neglect." (Footnote citing *Smith* v. *Brennan* and other cases omitted.)

[25] *Bagley* v. *North Herts Health Authority* [1986] NLJ Rep 1014. Damages under the Fatal Accidents Act 1976 were not permitted on the basis that the child had died *in utero* as a result of the negligence.

[26] [1993] QB 204. Dillon, Balcombe and Leggatt, LJJ.

[27] [1979] QB 276.

[28] [1988] 2 All ER 193.

its interests require it".[29] It was on the basis of this maxim that the Canadian Supreme Court reached its decision in *Montreal Tramways* v. *Leville*, in which Lamont J stated: [30]

"To my mind it is but natural justice that a child, if born alive and viable, should be allowed to maintain an action in the courts for injuries wrongfully committed upon its person while in the womb of its mother."

Most influential in *Burton* and *De Martell* was the 1972 Australian case of *Watt* v. *Rama*,[31] a decision of the Supreme Court of Victoria. In Winneke CJ's judgment, the defendant owed a duty to the plaintiff child at the moment of its birth, at which point the breach occurred. Yet it was apparent to him that there were a number of difficulties with this approach and therefore he outlined several theoretical bases for the defendant's duty to the child plaintiff: that there was a continuing duty; that the duty could be projected into the future; or that the duty was breached by an act antecedent to the accrual of the cause of action. With each of these approaches, as Ian Kennedy has observed, there are a number of theoretical difficulties.[32] These also afflict the different approach of Gillard J, who reasoned that the cause of action in negligence only accrued when the damage complained of was suffered, at which time the plaintiff was a legal person and could therefore sue, his or her antecedent injury simply being evidence of the causation of the damage at birth. However, Gillard J's judgment was that preferred by Phillips J in *De Martell*, whose conclusions were adopted by the Court of Appeal.

Thus, where a child is born with injuries inflicted on him while in the womb, the injury is or is deemed to be sustained by him at the moment of his birth and not before, since prior to birth he had no legal personality. Indeed, since he could not have suffered damage before existing, he suffered this at birth, the time when he acquired a legal personality and "inherited" his damaged body. Hence, the defendant health authority could not escape liability on the basis that "the organism that they injured was not in law the plaintiff"[33] and also deny liability for the defects with which the plaintiff was born, on the basis that these were inflicted before birth. Finally, the pre-birth events were "mere links in the chain of causation"[34] between the defendant's alleged lack of skill and care and the consequential damage to the plaintiff.

The means by which the Court of Appeal and the Commonwealth authorities upon which it draws achieve Lamont J's "natural justice" for the child born with injuries suffered at the hands of another's negligence whilst in the womb are notoriously problematic. For instance, as Andrew Grubb has observed regarding another

---

[29] [1993] QB at 226.

[30] [1933] 4 DLR 337 at 345. Dillon LJ noted that the *Montreal* decision influenced the decision in the US case of *Bonbrest* v. *Kotz*, *supra*. n. 7, [1993] QB at 228.

[31] [1972] VR 353.

[32] I Kennedy, "Commentary: Prenatal Injury: *Burton* v. *Islington Health Authority* and *De Martell* v. *Merton and Sutton Health Authority*", (1993) 1 *Med L Rev* 103, 105.

[33] [1993] QB at 219.

[34] *Ibid*.

Commonwealth approach, the law of negligence is intended to compensate plaintiffs made *worse* by another's negligent conduct, yet in such cases "[t]he plaintiff, *as
a legal person* has never been injured".[35] These difficulties need not concern us,
however, in our overall concern with the idea of a maternal prenatal duty of care.

It is more to the point to observe the lengths to which the courts have gone in
trying to compensate the born, but damaged, child in respect of the negligence of
third parties. Importantly, in distinguishing the cases which deny legal personality
to the fetus (*Paton* v. *BPAS* and *Re F (in utero)*) we saw that Dillon LJ spoke of and
moved on to what he dubbed "other contexts". In noting the contextual differences between *Paton* and *Re F (in utero)* on the one hand and *De Martell* and *Burton*
on the other, he is implicitly drawing attention to the different parties and hence
the different legal purposes in these different contexts: in the former cases, the
fetus's interests are being compared with those of its mother; in the latter, by contrast, its interests—or rather those of the subsequently born child—are pitted
against those of a detached third party. As shall be apparent, in the latter cases
recognition of a cause of action accruing at birth for injuries suffered *in utero* is an
acceptable development because in general it does not conflict with a defendant's
rights.[36]

III. THE IDEA OF MATERNAL LIABILITY

I move now from the law of third-party liability for prenatal harm to the idea—
considered as a matter of principle and policy—of maternal liability for such harm.
Before addressing the question of whether a woman should owe her unborn child
a duty of care I shall first consider the few maternal–fetal cases which touch upon
such a duty.

A. Relevant Maternal–Fetal Conflict Cases

In the 1990 appeal hearing of *Re AC* (in which, you may recall, the District Court
of Columbia allowed an appeal against the court order of a caesarean upon a
woman dying of cancer) the (partly) dissenting Associate Judge Belson cited
Bonbrest v. *Kotz* as authority for the right of what he dubbed "a living child"[37] to

---

[35] A Grubb, "Commentary: Pre-Natal and Pre-Conception Injury: *X and Y* v. *Pal and Others*",
(1993) 1 *Med L Rev* 119, 119, my emphasis.

[36] It is thus not correct to assert, as one scholar has, that "[i]t is only through the endorsement of the
premise of abstract 'separation' that an embryo, from the moment of conception, can bear interests
which warrant protection". That is, whether the embryo or fetus can bear interests warranting protection depends crucially on whose interests it is being compared with and the nature of those interests.
Conversely, to the extent that the fetus may be legitimately protected from harm by what I have dubbed
the "detached" third party, who is necessarily separate from the fetus, there is some truth in the quoted
statement. S Noonan, "Theorizing Connection", (1992) 30 *Alberta L Rev* 719, 724.

[37] 573 A 2d at 1255.

recover for damage suffered when unborn but viable and observed that *Bonbrest* was followed in the District of Columbia case of *Greater Southeast Hospital* v. *Williams*.[38] That case decided: "having determined that a *viable fetus is a person under the common law*, it follows that injury to the fetus resulting in death is actionable under our wrongful death statutes."[39] Belson AJ in turn concluded that both these cases established "for purposes relevant to the current one"[40] that a viable fetus is a person at common law with protectable legal rights. As we saw above, however, although wrongful death statutes may define the fetus as a person, this is strictly so as to enable recovery on the part of the parents and should not be taken to mean, as Belson AJ considers and the reasoning in the *Greater Southeast Hospital* case implies, that the fetus is a person for other purposes within the law. The majority judgment in *Re AC* does not refer to these arguments.

In another case, *Re Unborn Baby Wilson*,[41] a Michigan trial court drew upon *Smith* v. *Brennan*'s conception of "a child's . . . right to begin life with a sound mind and body" to compel a diabetic woman to accept a range of medical treatment, including injections of insulin, which her doctor considered necessary for the fetus. In order to achieve this result, the court found that the fetus was a "child" within the meaning of the state's child abuse and neglect statute. In ordering that the mother accept treatment for the fetus's benefit, the court held such action to be "most compelled by the legal premise . . . that a child has a legal right to begin life with a sound mind and body".[42] As observed above, the right recognised in *Smith*, if it exists, is a right possessed by the born child, not the fetus; in order to circumvent this, the *Wilson* court defines a fetus as a child, and thereby purports to give to the fetus legal rights for which there is no precedent. Of course, the *Wilson* court does this because it is seeking to compel certain treatment prenatally and thereby *prevent* injury, whereas the primary focus of a case such as *Smith* is to compensate a born child for harm that has already occurred prenatally.

The court in *Jefferson* v. *Griffin Spalding County Hospital Authority*[43] (which, it may be recalled, ordered a caesarean delivery over a religious refusal) understood the case before it in terms of a conflict of rights, thus: "We weighed the rights of the mother to practise her religion and to refuse surgery on herself, against her *child's right to live*. We found in favour of the child's right to live."[44] Yet we have seen that the fetus, which lacks legal personality, has no such "right to life". Moreover, consideration of the fetus's position in the law of tort with regard to third parties has shown that there is no question of the fetus having a right to life; nor does the fetus have a right be born with a sound mind and body. This suggests that the analysis in *Jefferson* is misguided, as is Robert Blank's conclusion to the effect

[38] 482 A 2d 394 (DC 1984).
[39] *Ibid.*, 398, emphasis in original.
[40] 573 A 2d at 1255.
[41] No. 81–108 AV (Calhoun County P Ct Feb. 3, 1981) aff'd, No. 810–108 AV (Calhoun County P Ct Mar. 9, 1981), leave to appeal denied, No. 57436 (Mich Ct App July 28, 1981).
[42] *Ibid.*, slip-op at 9–10, citing *Womack* v. *Buckhorn*, 187 NW 2d 218 (1971).
[43] Ga 274 SE 2d. 457 (1981).
[44] *Ibid.*, 460, *per* Hill J, my emphasis.

that the case "is critical for defining the legal right of the unborn to equal protection of the law."[45] Rather, both the *Jefferson* court and Blank are simply *asserting* rights on the fetus's behalf.

A fourth case of relevance in this area is that of *Grodin* v. *Grodin*,[46] in which a son sued his mother and her doctor for damage to his teeth allegedly resulting from the use of tetracycline during the pregnancy. Although *Grodin* does not concern the refusal of medical treatment needed for the benefit of the fetus, it is relevant to the extent that it touches on the related situation of a woman's right to consent to or refuse treatment for her *own* benefit. As such, in common with the three preceding cases, it raises the question of the interrelation between an area normally protected by a right and the idea of a legally imposable duty. The Michigan Court of Appeals in *Grodin* noted that the doctrine of intrafamilial tort immunity had been overruled by the Michigan Supreme Court in the case of *Plumley* v. *Klein*,[47] which meant that there was no bar to considering the issue in principle. Further, the Court of Appeals noted the principle of *Smith* v. *Brennan* that "a child has a legal right to begin life with a sound mind and body" and observed that Michigan's own *Womack* v. *Buckhorn*[48] did not limit the class of people who may be considered liable for prenatal injury, on the basis that *Smith* referred only to the wrongful conduct of "another". Accordingly, the court concluded that the mother "would bear the same liability for injurious, negligent conduct as would a third person".[49] There were two exceptions to *Plumley*'s abrogation of intrafamilial tort immunity, one of which was considered relevant in the *Grodin* case, namely "where the alleged negligent act involves an exercise of reasonable parental discretion with respect to the provision of . . . medical and dental services."[50] The Court of Appeals of Michigan considered that the question was "whether the decision reached by a woman in a particular case was a 'reasonable exercise of parental discretion' ".[51] The answer would turn, the court considered, on the "utility of the defendant's conduct . . . viewed in relation to the magnitude of the risk thereby created".[52] Thereafter the court remanded the case for a determination of the reasonableness of the allegedly negligent conduct.[53]

Viewed in relation to our initial consideration of third-party liability for prenatal harm, we can see the weaknesses of the reasoning in these maternal–fetal cases. Specifically, the aspects of the cases to which I have drawn attention either misinterpret the legal precedents for third-party liability for prenatal harm, or fail to consider the implications of the application of such liability to the maternal–fetal

[45] R Blank, "Emerging Notions", 466.
[46] 301 NW 2d 869 (1980).
[47] 388 Mich 1 (1972).
[48] 187 NW 2d 218 (1971).
[49] 301 NW 2d 869 at 870, *per* Cavanagh PJ.
[50] 388 Mich at 8, footnote omitted.
[51] 301 NW 2d at 870–1, *per* Cavanagh PJ, citing *Plumley* at 8.
[52] *Ibid.*, 870, *per* Cavanagh PJ, citing *Moning* v. *Alfono* (no citation given).
[53] The summary judgment of the trial court, which was for the mother and against which the son had appealed, precluded evidence on the utility of tetracycline for the mother or the risk for her unborn son.

context, or both. For instance, the approaches taken in *Grodin* and by Associate Judge Belson in *Re AC* illustrate both of these faults: in remanding the case for a retrial, the *Grodin* court does not appear concerned with the issues of principle or policy underlying the imposition of a maternal duty of care, merely with what it sees as the practical question of whether in fact Mrs Grodin's actions were "negligent";[54] whilst Belson AJ fails to consider that in another context the law might operate rather differently.

A fifth case, the 1994 Illinois case of *Baby Boy Doe*[55] is also relevant, but does not share the faults of the above cases. In this case, as we saw in chapter three, the Appellate Court of Illinois, held that "a competent woman's choice to refuse medical treatment as invasive as a cesarean section during pregnancy must be honored, even in circumstances where the choice may be harmful to the fetus".[56] This case relied heavily upon the reasoning in the Illinois case of *Stallman* v. *Youngquist*.[57] Since the latter case forms an important part of my discussion of the idea of a maternal legal duty of care, I defer further reference to *Baby Boy Doe* until later.

Finally, two cases pertaining to a woman's general conduct and the way this may harm the fetus are instructive and will be touched upon at points during the substantive discussion which follows.

In the first, *Bonte* v. *Bonte*,[58] the Supreme Court of New Hampshire held that a child could sue its mother for failure to use reasonable care in crossing a street: she was hit by a car, with the result that her seven-month old fetus was born with brain damage. The case is principally of assistance to this discussion in the reinforcement it gives to the important distinction I draw between the determination of duty in the area of general conduct on the one hand as opposed to the specific context of medical law rights on the other, and thus between third-party and maternal liability for prenatal harm on the one hand and between maternal liability within and beyond the treatment context on the other. The dissent in the case also draws attention to the public policy issues arising in respect of the latter.

The second is the important Canadian case of *Winnipeg Child and Family Services (Northwest Area)* v. *DFG* (1996).[59] In the intermediate stages, the Court of Appeal for Manitoba allowed an appeal against the trial judge's order, on the basis of a pregnant woman's alleged mental illness, committing her to a place of safety and requiring her to refrain from the use of intoxicants for the remainder of her pregnancy. Her two existing children suffered from chemical addiction, were developmentally handicapped, and both were wards of the plaintiff agency. The trial judge's order was made on the basis of the mother's mental illness, though he

---

[54] See the strong criticism of the case in *Stallman* v. *Youngquist*, 531 NE 2d 355 (Ill 1988), 358. *Stallman* is discussed *infra*.

[55] 632 NE 2d 326 (Ill App 1 Dist 1994).

[56] *Ibid*., 326, *per* De Vito PJ.

[57] 531 NE 2d 355 (Ill 1988).

[58] 616 A 2d 464 (NH 1992).

[59] [1996] 10 WWR 111. See the discussion of the case by A Grubb, "Commentary: Medical Treatment (Competent Adult): Pregnant Woman and Unborn Child: *Winnipeg Child and Family Services (Northwest Area)* v. *DFG*", (1997) 5 *Med L Rev* 125.

doubted his authority to do so solely to protect the unborn child. The basis of the Court of Appeal's decision was fourfold: that there was no evidence that the mother lacked capacity to organise her affairs or consent to medical treatment; that the only basis for the order could be that it would benefit the mother, as the court has no authority to seek to protect the unborn child (*Re F (in utero)*); that since the fetus was not a legal person, there was no basis for restraining the allegedly tortious conduct of the mother; and, finally, the undesirability of creating fetal rights that would conflict with those of the mother. The court noted that this could produce resentment in the mother, which may have a more detrimental effect than that of the conduct the court sought to limit and may deter other pregnant women from seeking antenatal care. The decision was upheld by the Supreme Court of Canada in 1997[60] and aspects of the judgments in the higher court will be considered in the substantive discussion of the issues which follows. I will also examine the highly important Canadian Supreme Court decision of *Dobson* v. *Dobson*,[61] concerning maternal liability for negligent driving.

B. Maternal Refusal of Medical Treatment

The ensuing discussion seeks to strengthen and confirm a pregnant woman's legal rights in the treatment context by approaching the issue in terms of the idea of *legal duty*. In effect, it asks why a pregnant woman should not be held to have a legal duty to accept medical treatment for the fetus or future child which overrides her rights to self-determination and bodily integrity *by comparing the idea of maternal liability with that of third-party liability for prenatal harm or death*. As part of this process, I consider whether it should make any difference whether we are considering the interests not of the fetus, but of the future child; moreover, the possibility that the latter might sue its mother after birth is also addressed.

Consideration of the idea of maternal duties in the treatment context requires us to consider the interrelation between the respective ideas of third-party liability for prenatal injury, a woman's medical law rights and the legal status of the fetus.

1. The Rights at Stake—the Interface with the Idea of a Duty

Here I compare the situation of third-party liability for prenatal injury with the idea of a maternal prenatal duty of care to accept medical treatment by focusing on the different interests at stake in each context.

a) *Self-Determination*

i) Third-party Liability

In the case of third-party liability for prenatal injury or death, what is in issue is negligent *conduct* (acts or omissions) which harms the fetus, to which the idea of a

---
[60] [1997] 152 DLR (4th) 193.
[61] [1999] 2 Can SCR 753.

negative duty not to harm attaches. To the extent that a third party can be liable for his conduct (thereby breaching that negative duty), his behaviour is essentially limited by the harm principle. On the one hand, if consciousness of a duty to the future child causes the would-be tortfeasor to act differently, then his freedom to act in a certain way is being limited by the interests of the future child (or the fetus if death is in issue); on the other, if he acts negligently and this creates harm, then he will have to pay "after the event" in the form of compensation. Either way, society justifies restricting people's general conduct in the interests of others, here the future child (who will be but is not yet born) or the fetus who may be killed *in utero*. In that process of restriction, however, usually no particular interest underlying the third party's moral and legal *rights* will be implicated in the injunction not to harm others, as first explored in chapter two. Indeed, on my view (which appears consistent with aspects of Joseph Raz's thought)[62] the domain of general conduct invokes not these moral and legal interests but only a very general sense of autonomy which thus does not merit the protection of any particular right.[63] This line of thought reveals the weakness inherent in an aspect of the reasoning of the dissenting Canadian Supreme Court justices in the *Winnipeg* case. For instance, Major J stated that "[i]t is a fundamental precept of our society and justice system that society *can* restrict an individual's *right* to autonomy where the exercise of that right causes harm to others",[64] the implication of which was therefore that the State could restrict the choices of pregnant women in the interests of fetuses. Yet, whilst we do restrict autonomy in the sense of the individual's choices pertaining to his/her *general conduct*—the domain typically in issue as regards the tort of negligence—it is less likely that we do so where rights protecting important moral interests pertaining to the individual are at stake.[65]

ii) Maternal Liability

Such very particular and personal interests and rights are at stake on the *pregnant woman's* part in the treatment context, of which the right to self-determination is one. I shall consider now the interaction between these interests and rights and the idea of a maternal prenatal duty of care. As explored in earlier chapters, the kinds of issues at stake in the exercise of self-determination in the medical law context

---

[62] As seen in ch. 2, on Raz's argument autonomy is a value from which specific rights may be derived: on his view, there are "derivative rights" (*The Morality of Freedom* (Oxford: Oxford University Press, 1986) 247) which protect and advance aspects of the individual's autonomy and contribute to making autonomy possible ("Right-based Moralities", (1982) in J Waldron (ed.), *Theories of Rights* (Oxford: Oxford University Press, 1984) 182–200, 195). The implication, I think, is that one's general conduct is not protected by specific rights. This is because, by definition, specific rights protect quite particular interests and choices.

[63] Note also my rejection of Hart's Choice theory of rights, at least in this context, in ch. 1.

[64] [1997] 152 DLR (4th) at 240, first emphasis in original; second added. He was joined in his dissent by Sopinka J.

[65] With regard to this point, note a rather striking passage from the dissenting judgment of Maher J in *Toth* v. *Goree*, 237 NW 2d 297 (Mich Ct App 1975), 305: "We are not concerned with the right of a mother to freely terminate her pregnancy at a certain stage. Rather we have the case of a wrongful and unwanted termination. Certainly a tortfeasor cannot invoke the mother's privacy rights to defend his wrongdoing."

are personal and intimate in a way that the issue of the third party's conduct that might harm the unborn child is probably not. This explains in part why, so far as the woman is concerned, what is in issue is explicitly her *right* to self-determination, underlying which is her interest in making important personal choices. This is very different from the situation of third parties, regarding whom tort law does not explicitly speak of balancing a defendant's right to act in a certain way against the interests of others; the idea of the defendant's rights is not directly in issue.[66] In this connection, an important aspect of the majority judgment in the Supreme Court in the *Winnipeg* case concerned the impact that recognition of a cause of action against the mother would have upon a pregnant woman's interests and rights. McLachlin J took note of the Canadian Royal Commission's report on New Reproductive Technologies, entitled *Proceed with Care*,[67] citing the following passage:[68]

> "From the woman's perspective, . . . considering the interests of the fetus separately from her own has the potential to create adversary situations with negative consequences for her autonomy and bodily integrity . . . [and] ignores the basic components of women's fundamental human rights—the right to bodily integrity, and the right to equality, privacy and dignity."

Thus, the majority held that a cause of action for maternal prenatal injury would create considerable potential for intrusion into a "woman's right to make choices

---

[66] Legal recognition of my point can be found in the case of *Stallman* v. *Youngquist*, discussed *infra*.

[67] (Ottawa: Minister of Government Services, 1993) vol. 2 at 957–8. The approach of the Commission to the relationship between a pregnant woman and her fetus has been described as "holistic". S Martin and M Coleman, "Judicial Intervention in Pregnancy", (1995) 40 *McGill LJ* 947. The Commission's three recommendations on judicial intervention in pregnancy were as follows. "273. Judicial intervention in pregnancy and birth not be permissible. Specifically, the Commission recommends that a) medical treatment never be imposed upon a pregnant woman against her wishes; b) the criminal law, or any other law, never be used to confine or imprison a pregnant woman in the interests of her fetus; c) the conduct of a pregnant woman in relation to her fetus not be criminalized; d) child welfare or other legislation never be used to control a woman's behaviour during pregnancy or birth; and e) civil liability never be imposed upon a woman for harm done to her fetus during pregnancy. 274. Unwanted medical treatment and other interferences, or threatened interferences, with the physical autonomy of pregnant women be recognized explicitly under the Criminal Code as criminal assault. 275. All provinces/territories ensure that they have in place a) information and education programs directed to pregnant women so that they do not inadvertently put a fetus at risk; b) outreach and culturally appropriate support services for pregnant women and young women in potentially vulnerable groups; and c) counselling, rehabilitation, outreach, and support services designed specifically to meet the needs of pregnant women with drug/alcohol addictions." (At 964–5.) An important reason for adopting recommendation 273 was fully to recognise and protect the Charter rights of women. The Commission stated: "Like other women and men, pregnant women . . . have a constitutional right to refuse unwanted medical treatment or control that threatens their bodily integrity or interferes with their ability to make independent decisions about their medical care." (At 955.) Martin and Coleman describe the Royal Commission's approach as "a comprehensive policy which places fetal health in its larger context", noting that "[t]his approach also allows the complexity of the problems to be addressed, including consideration of discrimination, poverty, substance abuse, and violence." (At 983.) As these authors note, however, whilst this was the view of the majority, the dissent had other views. For a thorough discussion of other Canadian cases and literature see S Martin and M Coleman, "Judicial Intervention in Pregnancy".

[68] 152 DLR (4th) at 210. The justices joining in the majority judgment were Lamer CJ, La Forest, L'Heureux-Dubé, Gonthier, Cory, and Iacobucci JJ.

concerning herself".[69] As noted in chapter three, the reasoning of the majority in *Winnipeg* was approved by the Court of Appeal in the most recent English decision confirming a woman's right to refuse a caesarean, the *St George's* case;[70] at the same time, the reasoning of the dissenting justices in *Winnipeg* was specifically rejected. Both cases in their earlier stages concerned the illegitimate idea of detention and treatment of a pregnant woman under the mental health legislation for the sake of the fetus.

The fact that specific rights are not directly implicated with regard to third parties means that we can more easily define the standard of care of the duty which third parties owe to the fetus/future child. Recall that these are typically negative duties, such as taking care in the conduct of a car, the reasonableness of which are thus readily determinable. Regarding the pregnant woman, however, we now return to the problem first introduced, in a rather different form, in Part I. There I noted the individual's interests in self-determination and bodily integrity which underlie the right to refuse medical treatment; moreover, that in the light of such interests being implicated in treatment issues, an individual will likely have serious reason to make her own decision about such treatment. I also drew attention to the difficulties of judging "serious reasons" for doing so. In turn, in Part II we observed the *legal* recognition of these deeply personal interests in the treatment context (for instance in *Cruzan*); moreover, that because certain private, deeply meaningful areas are the subject of "reasonable disagreement", individuals are justly granted the right to make certain decisions themselves (*Casey*).

As regards the pregnant woman, then, the problem is that in order to fulfil the law of negligence's requirement that we determine a standard of care regarding a possible duty on her part towards her fetus, we would have to try to judge her reasons for refusing treatment. In effect, we would be trying to weigh the recognised values of self-determination and bodily integrity on the one hand, against the interests of the fetus on the other. Conversely, to determine the standard of care with regard to the third-party tortfeasor's conduct so far as it may impact upon the fetus/future child, usually we have only to weigh a very general interest in "doing as he pleases" against the interests of the latter.[71] The idea of adopting "a conventional tort analysis" with regard to maternal duties toward the fetus, as one scholar has suggested,[72] is therefore distinctly problematic. Further, reinforcing earlier conclusions, the implication

[69] *Ibid.*

[70] [1998] 3 All ER at 690.

[71] In this regard, consider the following statement of one scholar: "Liability will be imposed for conduct by a pregnant woman that is generally known to result in injury to the fetus if the *utility* of the mother's conduct is outweighed by the harm to the fetus." G Bambrick, "Developing Maternal Liability Standards for Prenatal Injuries", (1987) 61 *St John's L Rev* 592, at 604–5, footnotes omitted, my emphasis. The phrase "utility" obscures the important point that, unlike the broad idea of conduct that is in issue in negligence generally, with regard to a pregnant woman, important rights are at stake, underlying which are well-recognised interests and values.

[72] SR Weinburg, "A Maternal Duty to Protect Fetal Health?", (1983) 58 *Ind LJ* 531. However, this author appears sensitive to some of the underlying problems, as the article concludes that decisions must be on a case-by-case basis since any uniform rule would either ineffectively protect fetal health or effectively nullify the mother's right of privacy.

in these cases is not only that the woman does not have the *legal* duty to have the caesarean, but also that we cannot even clearly say, in the scenarios outlined above, that she has the *moral* duty to do so, given the difficulties of formulating the positive duty where this encroaches upon moral interests and rights.

Where a pregnant woman refuses treatment for religious reasons—precisely the kind of reason intended to be protected by her right to refuse medical treatment in this regard—perhaps in some sense a court could judge that the exercise of her right in this fashion is in some way "justifiable" for the purposes of the law of negligence, for instance in terms of the "utility" of religious belief.[73] (We might think here of the "negligence formula" of importance in determining the standard of care.[74]) But to hold that the exercise of the right for the religious reason is "justifiable" is in fact to say that the pregnant woman has the *right* (to refuse the treatment), not the *duty* (to submit to it).[75] In *Baby Boy Doe*, in which a woman was allowed to refuse a caesarean for religious reasons, in upholding Doe's right to religious liberty the court relied upon a case concerning an action in negligence in which it was held that "[f]or the court to determine whether defendants breached any duty owed to decedent would require a searching inquiry into Christian Science beliefs and the validity of such beliefs . . . [which is] . . . precluded by the first amendment".[76]

---

[73] In this connection I note A Whitfield's observation that what might prevent a negligence claim against a mother "would be evidence that she was exercising her autonomy on the basis of a personal interest which the court considered legitimate or reasonable." "Common Law Duties to Unborn Children", (1993) 1 *Med L Rev* 28, 52. In elaborating upon the idea of "personal interest", Whitfield gives the example of "religious or medical belief genuinely held". However, what he does not say here (though he may mean to imply it) is that of course such personal interests are recognised in law as being the kind that are likely to be implicated on such an occasion to the extent that they are given the protection of legal *rights*. Hence we could say that it is no "accident" that such interests may be thought at least "legitimate" from the perspective of the law of tort. The contrast to which I draw attention between areas explicitly protected by rights and general conduct is further brought out when Whitfield continues: "To drink in defiance of a doctor's orders would not be such an interest". *Ibid*. My argument tries to show the qualitative difference between general conduct of third parties or pregnant women and specifically implicated rights of pregnant women in determining the question of a maternal prenatal duty of care to accept medical treatment; when I turn to address the issue of maternal conduct generally, we will see that there additional considerations preclude the imposition of a maternal duty of care.

[74] For discussion of the relevant elements (probability of harm, likely magnitude of harm, the value of the activity being pursued and the cost of the precautions needed to avoid the harm) and of the function of the negligence formula, see P Cane, *Atiyah's Accidents, Compensation and the Law*, 6th edn. (London: Butterworths, 1999) 34–8.

[75] For an example of a scholar arguing that religious reasons do not merit special protection, see PR Glazebrook, "What Care Must be Taken of an Unborn Baby?", (1993) 52 *CLJ* 20, writing on the English case of *Re S* (1992) and concluding: "It may soon be the duty of twentieth-century judges to hold that religious or philosophical views (such as those held by Mrs S) will not excuse a mother's deliberate neglect of the medical assistance needed to save her unborn child from death or injury." (At 22.) Glazebrook states that the decision in *Re S* implies that Mrs S had a "duty of care" to her unborn child, and that her refusal of the caesarean was criminal (at 21). See further my discussion of religious reasons for refusing medical treatment in ch. 2. where I noted the importance of the interest in and right to bodily integrity which is at stake in the case of the pregnant woman, but not in the case of the parent and the born child.

[76] *Baumgartner* v. *First Church of Christ*, 490 NE 2d 1319 (Ill App 1 Dist 1986) at 1325. The case concerned physical harm, indeed death, as the result of Christian Science treatment. The case of *Prince* v. *Massachusetts* was distinguished on the basis that in that case "the wrongful conduct, although religiously motivated, could be analyzed without first evaluating the tenets of a particular religion". (At 1325.) In

As acknowledged previously, it is possible, however, that a pregnant woman might exercise her rights to self-determination and bodily integrity in the refusal of medical treatment in a way which can readily be judged *unreasonable*. Consider again the obviously trivial reason (in the case of the caesarean, a refusal in order to avoid an abdominal scar); or the non-existent reason (for instance where a woman declines without explanation to take a pill vital for fetal welfare but with no adverse side-effects for her). In such cases, a judge could well conclude that the interests (rather than the rights) of the fetus suggest that her *exercise* of her right is unjustified on these occasions. In such cases, I have suggested the idea of "reasonableness" might then have a limited role to play in terms of discussion, counselling and, in carefully restricted circumstances, persuasion, but that to override the unjustifiably exercised right is both unacceptable and unwise, as first discussed in chapter four.

Given the possibility of clearly inappropriate maternal reasons for refusal, the counter-argument of the appellant agency in *Winnipeg* that a woman should have a duty of care "to refrain from activities that have *no substantial value to a pregnant woman's well-being or right of self-determination* and that have the potential to cause grave and irreparable harm"[77] to the subsequently born child can be seen to have some force. The *Winnipeg* case was concerned with the "lifestyle" issue of solvent abuse (although there was also an allegation of mental illness), rather than with the refusal of medical care, yet the argument of the appellate agency touches, in essence, upon the important idea of the *unjustified* infliction of harm and this idea is equally relevant to the refusal of medical treatment (the subject of this section). In this regard, the majority admitted in the *Winnipeg* case that it "may be easy to determine that abusing solvents does not add substantial value to a pregnant woman's well-being and may not be the type of self-determination which deserves protection".[78] (In fact, the reason why the mother's right to sniff solvents may not seem of much importance is surely connected with the fact that there is, in fact, no such right.[79]) Not surprisingly, but surely quite rightly, the dissenting justices likewise noted the dubious value to a pregnant woman of solvent abuse.[80] The majority's principal concern that it would be harder to determine the question of value regarding other activities is touched upon when I discuss liability for maternal conduct.

Nevertheless, although we do value the right to make important and intimate decisions, we also reason that other important interests and rights can, on occasion, override this. For instance, regarding parental refusal of life-sustaining treatment for born children we might note that, in general, parental rights of autonomy do not

---

that case Rutledge J had notably observed "[p]arents may be free to become martyrs themselves. But it does not follow that they are free, in identical circumstances, to make martyrs of their children before they have reached the age of full and legal discretion when they can make that choice for themselves". 331 US 158 (1944) at 170.

[77] 152 DLR (4th) at 210, as phrased by McLachlin J, my emphasis.

[78] *Ibid.*, 211, *per* McLachlin J.

[79] *State* v. *Murphy*, 570 P 2d 1070 (1977) (no fundamental right to use psychoactive substances).

[80] 152 DLR (4th) at 238–9.

extend to refusing such treatment, as noted in chapters two and three.[81] Thus, if only a pregnant woman's right of self-determination were in issue, we may decide that there is reason at least to consider the imposition of a maternal legal prenatal duty of care, thereby overriding her right of self-determination in the refusal of medical treatment. Importantly however, the autonomy at stake in each case is different, as first discussed in chapter two. Parental autonomy differs from personal autonomy in that the former does not implicate the parent's *own* life: parental refusal of life-sustaining treatment for children is not, in the final analysis, about *self-*determination. By contrast, autonomy—or, better "self-determination"—for the pregnant woman is "about" *herself*, notwithstanding that it may also "affect" the fetus. This is because the fetus is *inside* the pregnant woman whereas a parent is separate from her born child. Here we arrive at a right not implicated with regard to parental autonomy and children, that of bodily integrity. In other words, the fact that a pregnant woman's right of self-determination is different from that of a parent's (limited) rights regarding decisions affecting a born child is in turn related to the fact that another right—that of bodily integrity—is also in issue in her case.[82]

It is the fact that *self*-determination *and* bodily integrity are in issue with regard to the pregnant woman—but not with regard to the parent and her separate born child—that distinguishes their respective situations, both morally and legally. I therefore disagree with Adrian Whitfield's observation, to the effect that:[83]

> "wholly unreasonable refusal to go into hospital despite clear medical advice that home delivery would present a danger to the unborn child would seem to be a dereliction of duty which is difficult to distinguish from an unreasonable refusal to take a living child to hospital."

[81]   As one court pronounced on the matter as long ago as 1962, "this right [of a parent to practise her religion] ends where somebody else's right begins". *In re Clark* (1962) 185 NE 2d 128 at 132. In such a case "somebody else's right"—that of the minor child—begins upon birth when it is deemed a moral (and legal) person. For a discussion of developments in this area of the law, see RA McCall Smith, "Is Anything Left of Parental Rights?", in A McCall Smith and E Sutherland (eds.), *Family Rights: Family Law and Medical Advance* (Edinburgh: Edinburgh University Press, 1990) 4–20, who notes the "gradual demotion" of parental rights and suggests that we can interpret this as a welcome end to the "outmoded autocracy of powerful adults over vulnerable children". (At 18.)

[82]   For an example of a writer plainly ignoring these differences, see AE Doudera, "Fetal Rights? It Depends", (1982) 18 *Trial* 38. Writing about the maternal–fetal case of *Jefferson*, he states: "it would seem reasonable to suggest that the expectant mother, and perhaps the father, may have *some duty* to protect and to act in the fetus' best interests, especially when it has achieved viability. For example, in a case which attracted much publicity and concerned the rights of *parents* to select an unorthodox medical treatment for their *child*, the Massachusetts Supreme Judicial Court stated that the '[p]arental right to control a child's nurture is not grounded in any "absolute property right" which can be enforced to the detriment of a child, but rather is akin to a trust subject to . . . a correlative duty to care for and protect the child.'" *Richards* v. *Forrest*, 180 NE 508, 511 (Mass 1932). (At 44, my emphases.) Note the vagueness in "some duty" and the elision between the idea of a pregnant woman's duties as opposed to parental duties to furnish children with appropriate medical care. On the failure again to distinguish between born and unborn children, see M Shaw, "Conditional Prospective Rights", whose article relies heavily on child abuse laws to suggest that parents should be under legal duties to avoid prenatal harm, with little or no discussion of the situation and status of the fetus within the body of the pregnant woman.

[83]   A Whitfield, "Common Law Duties to Unborn Children", 50, my emphasis. However, Whitfield's use of the term "*wholly* unreasonable" (my emphasis) would suggest refusal to go to hospital for an utterly trivial reason, at which point such a choice seems clearly morally unjustifiable.

For the majority in the *Winnipeg* case, these differences between the situation of a parent and a born child on the one hand and a mother and fetus on the other underlie the inappropriateness of extending the *parens patriae* jurisdiction to protect the fetus (as an alternative to the law of tort):[84]

> "The *parens patriae* power over born children permits the courts to override the liberty of the parents to make decisions on behalf of their children where a parental choice will result in harm to a child . . . . The only liberty interest affected is the parent's interest in making decisions for his or her child. By contrast, extension of the *parens patriae* jurisdiction of the court to unborn children has the potential to affect a much broader range of liberty interests. The court cannot make decisions for the unborn child without inevitably making decisions for the *mother herself*. The *intrusion is therefore far greater* than simply limiting the mother's choices concerning her child."

Aspects of the Canadian Charter of Rights and Freedoms, discussed below, were also important. I now consider the implications of a pregnant woman's right to bodily integrity for the idea of a maternal prenatal duty of care.

b) *Bodily Integrity*

i) Third-party Liability

So far as tort law in general is concerned, a duty of care is never imposed to aid another in a way that invokes one's bodily integrity, for instance by donating a kidney or bone marrow.[85] Indeed, as noted above, the issue of duty touches upon a person's conduct, whether by act or omission. Reflecting on why this is so, one realises that it is quite difficult for someone to harm others in a way that invokes his/her own bodily integrity: a suicide bomber who swallows or attaches to himself a timed exploding device and then mingles in a crowd is one example, but clearly a highly constructed, if not unheard of, one. This is an example of an act, moreover one that in fact fails to fall within the bounds of negligence because it is about intentional harm. More relevant to our purposes is the question of how one might *omit* to help another *through* one's body. Notwithstanding that the bodily integrity of tortfeasors is not implicated generally in their duty of care, including to unborn children, normatively speaking, should pregnant women be under a duty which invokes their bodily integrity as, for instance, Robertson argues?[86]

---

[84] 152 DLR (4th) at 218, my emphases, *per* McLachlin J.

[85] The leading case on point is *McFall* v. *Shimp* 10 Pa D & C 3d 90 (Allegheny County Ct, 1978). The case concerned the refusal by a competent adult to donate life-saving bone marrow to his cousin. Essentially, the court held that, whatever the moral duties the one cousin may have owed to the other, it was not prepared legally to compel any such duty. I discuss this in the next chapter. At its core, the law of rescue (of which *McFall* is an example) is not about the imposition of legal duties which are to be realised through the body since, when it comes to the area of physical invasions, the law enters the arena of exceptions to the rule. In other words, the law of rescue concerns coming to the assistance of another by means of one's conduct.

[86] Robertson argues that the law may impose upon a woman who will not be aborting "a duty to assure that the fetus is born as healthy as possible". "The Right to Procreate and *in utero* Fetal Therapy", (1982) 3 *J Leg Med* 333, 352, footnote omitted. He continues: "A mother, as anyone else, can be liable for causing a child to be born in a damaged state which could have been avoided by use of due care." (*Ibid.*, 352–3, footnote omitted.) Although he acknowledges that bodily invasions are "highly disfavored"

ii) Maternal Liability

First, let us consider the value we give to bodily integrity: we cannot read this from the points relating to the tortious duty of care that I have just considered precisely because the right of bodily integrity is never in issue in negligence generally. Yet medical law clearly recognises the value we give to the individual's bodily integrity, by allowing him or her to resist unwanted bodily intrusions. Indeed, as Andrew Grubb has expressed the point, the law "pays great respect to a patient's right of bodily integrity".[87]

Second, let us clarify just what this hypothetical duty would consist in and justify. We should distinguish here between two ideas: that of imposing treatment on a woman in fulfillment of her duty (an idea which does not in fact cohere with the structure of the law of negligence), and that of a born child seeking compensation for damage resulting from a woman's refusal to accept certain treatment. The discussion indicates that both these possibilities are problematic with regard to the issue of medical treatment. I address first the notion of imposing treatment on a woman in order to *prevent* prenatal harm.

Recall the four elements of the tort of negligence, namely: duty, breach, causation and damage. The point, so far as prenatal harm is concerned, is that the idea of a tortious duty of care really goes to the issue of a born child's action for harm that occurred prenatally, that is, in the past. In other words, the damage has already been done. In this regard, Robertson's notion of a "duty to bring the child into the world as healthy as reasonably possible" would seem to relate to the idea of a post-birth action for compensation. Yet he also discusses the possibility of "pre-birth seizures", in which a woman could be compelled to submit to certain medical treatment in order to prevent prenatal harm.[88] Just as no legal duty can be derived from the law of abortion to justify such compulsion,[89] so with regard to negligence, even if a tortious duty of care were held to exist to submit to certain treatment, there are no legal "powers", as it were, until after the breach of any such duty has resulted in damage.

In this light, let us return to the judgment of the (partly) dissenting Associate Justice Belson in *Re AC*. To recap, in effect he drew upon tortious cases regarding the liability of *third* parties for death or injury to the fetus to assert, as he put it, that "for purposes relevant to the current one", the common law recognises a viable fetus as a person with protectable legal rights. His phrase "for purposes relevant to

by the law, he goes on to cite what in ch. 7 I try to show to be spurious authorities in their favour (at 353–4). Thus, he endorses the idea of a duty which can be imposed through the body and proceeds to argue that the precedents he cites would support compelled medical treatment where the need to preserve fetal life or prevent great injury is in issue (at 354).

[87] A Grubb, "Commentary: Treatment without Consent: Adult: *Re S: (Adult: Refusal of Treatment)*", (1993) 1 *Med L Rev* 92, 94.

[88] J Robertson, *Children of Choice: Freedom and the New Reproductive Technologies*, (Princeton, NJ: Princeton University Press, 1994) 186–90. Although he concedes there are a number of problems with such "seizures", nevertheless he suggests they "may occasionally be acceptable . . . where the intrusion is minimal, the benefit to the offspring clear and substantial, and all lesser means of persuasion have failed." (At 189.)

[89] See ch. 5.

the current one" is obviously intended to imply that in a case such as *Re AC* the fetus has legal rights assertable against its *mother*. Indeed, he suggests that the "already recognized rights and interests mentioned above are sufficient to indicate the need for a *balancing process* in which the rights of the viable unborn child are assigned substantial weight".[90] Given that the case of *Re AC* was concerned with the issue of compelled medical treatment and the right of Ms C to refuse such treatment (the caesarean section), the "balancing exercise" to which Belson AJ here refers is of course the classic balancing exercise by which the US law of treatment refusal determines whether the State has any valid interests to be weighed against the (*prima facie*) right of the patient to refuse treatment. In other words, Associate Judge Belson is using the idea of third-party liability for prenatal harm that has already occurred to create the idea of a maternal duty of care on Ms C's part to submit to the caesarean section for the purpose of preventing harm to her fetus. Thus, he contemplates an *enforceable* tortious duty to *prevent* prenatal harm. Lest there be any doubt about his intentions in this regard, consider his statement (a few paragraphs later) to the effect that he could not agree "that in cases where a viable unborn child is in the picture, it would be extremely rare . . . to *require that the mother accede* to the vital needs of the unborn child".[91] Yet, given the four requirements of negligence, such an approach could not be contemplated by means of the tort.[92] As the majority expresses this in the *Winnipeg* case:[93]

> "The law of tort as it presently stands might permit an action for injury to the fetus to be brought in the child's name *after its birth*. But there is no power in the courts to entertain such an action before the child's birth."

Still, in order to put to rest perhaps Robertson's,[94] but certainly Belson AJ's, idea of compelled medical treatment being justified in terms of tort law, we might note the moral difficulties in enforcing such a duty: namely, that in order to prevent prenatal harm in the face of a maternal refusal of a caesarean, for instance, we would have to operate on the pregnant woman against her will. Even in the case of refusal for trivial/non-existent reasons, this is an unacceptable option: the enforcement of legal duties which are to be fulfilled "via the body" (which implies the State "laying hands" on the individual's body) is a prospect that liberal societies find inherently morally problematic. I discuss this explicitly in chapter seven. Such enforcement raises literal and symbolic questions about moral and physical harm to pregnant women.

---

[90] 573 A 2d at 1256, my emphasis.

[91] *Ibid.*, 1257, my emphasis.

[92] A similar mistake was made by the court in *Raleigh Fitkin* v. *Anderson*. Thus: "[I]n *Smith* v. *Brennan*, . . . we held that a child could sue for injuries negligently inflicted upon it prior to birth. We are satisfied that the unborn child is entitled to the law's protection and that an appropriate order should be made *to insure* blood transfusions to the mother in the event that they are necessary in the opinion of the physician in charge at the time." (201 A 2d 537, 538, *per curiam*, my emphasis.)

[93] 152 DLR (4th) at 203, *per* McLachlin J, emphasis in original.

[94] Most likely, he does not consider that a tortious duty could justify such action; but it is worth finally dismissing the point in order to dispel any notion that in some way we can override a woman's refusal on the basis of a legal duty of care.

One might then consider the alternative, rather than of preventing prenatal injury, of allowing a damaged child to sue its mother after birth. Yet this is problematic for the generally unrecognised reason that to hold that a woman has breached a duty of care toward the fetus, we still need to be able to determine the standard of care in pregnancy.[95] Thus, we would still face the difficulty of determining the reasonableness, in any given treatment refusal, of the woman's decision: people think it is reasonable to assume quite different levels of physical pain, burden and risk for themselves and hence it is extremely difficult to pass judgment as to what treatment the *reasonable* pregnant woman will accept, at least with regard to issues such as surgery, the kind of issue presented with regard to the right to bodily integrity. In other words, defining the "standard of care in pregnancy", which scholars such as Robert Blank and Carol Simon[96] propose, would be very difficult. Although Blank acknowledges that determining such a standard would be a novel task, he is not unduly concerned about the prospects of success, asserting: "Once a standard of care is established and one can judge what a *reasonable person* would do under similar circumstances, negligence can be determined."[97] But how can we say of a pregnant woman who refuses a caesarean in order to avoid eternal damnation (*Baby Boy Doe* or *Jefferson*), or because she "would rather die" than have such surgery again (*Rochdale (NHS) Trust* v. *C*),[98] or because she would prefer a peaceful death from her cancer (*Re AC*), or because it carries a risk of death four times higher than "natural" delivery increased in her case by her morbid obesity (the "Colorado case"),[99] that she is falling below the standard of care that a pregnant woman owes to her fetus? As the dissent in *Bonte* expresses this:[100]

---

[95] For an example of scholars not aware of this difficulty at the level of principle (but who reject the imposition of a legal duty of care for policy reasons) see JC Callahan and JW Knight, "Women, Fetuses, Medicine and the Law", in HB Holmes and L Purdy (eds.), *Feminist Perspectives in Medical Ethics*, (Indianapolis, IN: Indiana University Press, 1992) 224–39, 235.

[96] C Simon, "Parental Liability", advocates a "reasonably prudent expecting parent standard" under which "the parent would be held to a minimum standard of knowledge which would be based upon what was commonly known in the community." (At 85.) See also J Robertson, *Children of Choice*, who discusses the idea of a "community judgment, constitutive of our understandings of parenthood" in this regard. (At 192.)

[97] R Blank, "Emerging Notions", 443, my emphasis. See also R Beal, "'Can I Sue Mommy?' An Analysis of a Woman's Tort Liability for Prenatal Injuries to her Child Born Alive", (1984) 21 *San Diego L Rev* 325, who suggests that the relevant standard of care must be an "external and objective one" (at 364, footnote omitted). But such an approach ignores the difficulties adverted to in this paragraph. In any event, Beal's article, which primarily focuses on the demise of intrafamilial tort liability, never really answers the difficult questions inherent in the idea of a maternal legal duty of prenatal care. Thus, in the last sentence before the conclusion, the author states: "The issue that must be addressed is whether the child's 'right' to be well-born is important enough to severely compromise a woman's right to use her body as she pleases." (The question posed is not answered in the conclusion itself.)

[98] [1997] 1 FCR 274.

[99] An unreported decision, known simply as the case of the woman in Colorado. J Robertson, "Procreative Liberty and the Control of Conception, Pregnancy, and Childbirth", (1983) 69 *Va L Rev* 405, n. 165. The woman weighed more than 157.7kg.

[100] *Per* Brock CJ and Batchelder J, 616 A 2d at 468, my emphasis. By contrast, the justices seem to assume that it would be possible to determine the extent of a woman's *moral* duties: they thus fail to see the conceptual connections I have made between the difficulties of determining the extent of *either* the moral *or* the legal duty.

"The majority discounts the problems associated with legally recognizing a mother's duty to her fetus and assures, that by subjecting the relationship to an 'appropriate duty of care' and by allowing the fact-finder to make a determination of negligence, no significant rights will be deprived. This conclusion begs the question: What will be the judicially defined standard of conduct for a pregnant woman? Indeed, *is it possible* to subject a woman's judgment, action, and behaviour as they relate to the well-being of the fetus to a judicial determination of reasonableness in a manner that is consistent and free from arbitrary results? We have serious doubts."

On my argument (as the discussion in the latter half of the chapter will reinforce) this reasoning is particularly pertinent to situations in which a pregnant woman's rights are invoked, as in the case of medical treatment, rather than the factual issue of general conduct (street-crossing) actually at stake in the *Bonte* case. Indeed, the dissenting justices acknowledged that "the fetus may sustain injuries from the negligent acts of its mother that may not directly implicate the unique relationship between mother and fetus"[101] (but not, as perhaps they should, that the special character of this relationship was *not* implicated in the way Mrs Bonte crossed the street).

This problem of determining the standard of maternal prenatal care was also recognised in the case of *Stallman* v. *Youngquist*, considered below, in which Justice Cunningham queried "by what objective standard" could a jury decide that a pregnant woman had or had not been negligent.[102] Herein lies the difficulty for a *post*-birth action against the mother for failure to accept certain treatment.[103] In connection with this point, it might be noted that as medicine continues to refine its prenatal knowledge, so doctors would be likely to press for the standard of prenatal care to be raised.[104] In this regard, Robert Blank writes of advances in medical technology enabling us more easily to demonstrate causation and to determine the standard of care in pregnancy.[105] Yet while causation may become less problematic, medical possibility itself can play little role in determining a standard of care in pregnancy.[106] This means Blank is quite

---

[101] *Ibid.*, 468.

[102] 531 NE 2d at 360. Cunningham J also adverted to the possibility of prejudicial and stereotypical beliefs affecting jury determinations of liability. In jurisdictions where such issues are not determined by juries, similar concerns may yet be felt to apply to a predominantly male judiciary.

[103] The solution suggested by one scholar is that pregnant women should only be liable for "gross negligence, an almost conscious disregard for the welfare of the fetus." B Chernaik, "Recovery for Prenatal Injuries", 607. Her reasoning is that otherwise pregnant women "would thus be held to a higher degree of care than the general public with respect to activities in which individual discretion ordinarily governs. This would impose an unfair burden on her and significantly impair her personal freedom". Whilst such an approach is preferable to that adopted either by Blank or Simon, general policy considerations are against this. See generally the arguments in the rest of this chapter.

[104] Medical writers have already been prominent in this regard. See e.g. R Lieberman *et al*, "The Fetal Right to Live", (1979) 53 *Obst & Gyn* 515; M Shaw, "Conditional Prospective Rights", 63. Others, however, have insisted upon maternal consent in the area, for instance, of medical treatment: T Shriner, "Maternal versus Fetal Rights—a Clinical Dilemma", (1978) 52 *Obstet & Gyn* 518.

[105] R Blank, "Emerging Notions", 468.

[106] I note the observation of Cunningham J in *Stallman* v. *Youngquist*, considered *infra*, to the effect "that causation alone cannot result in the recognition of duty". 531 NE 2d at 360.

misguided to suggest that "courts might be *forced* to adopt very stringent standards of care for pregnant women".[107] Such an approach ignores the important and wholly appropriate role that the law plays in actively responding to, rather than being determined by, technological developments. Further, while grossly unjustified refusals of medical treatment may be thought clearly to fall below any relevant conception of the maternal prenatal standard of care (meaning that "unreasonableness" can here be judged), policy considerations suggest that even a post-birth action for compensation in such cases is inadvisable: as has been noted elsewhere, the prospect of legal liability for refusing certain treatment could discourage women from seeking antenatal care.[108]

3. The Legal Status of the Fetus

The final reason against imposing a legal duty to accept medical treatment on the pregnant woman is that the fetus is not a person, legal or otherwise, a point intrinsically related to the question of her right to bodily integrity. I noted earlier *Smith v. Brennan*'s observation that the issue of the legal status of the fetus is not presented in respect of a third party's prenatal duty not to injure. Focusing for the moment on the issue of *injury* rather than death, why do I consider the fetus's legal status relevant in the case of the pregnant woman, but not (as the *Smith* court holds) in the case of a third party?

a) *The Relevance of the Legal Status of the Fetus to the Idea of Maternal Liability*

In the case of the third party, the duty not to injure is to the future child who is not yet but who will be born; in the case of the pregnant woman, the duty might also be said to be to that child. Regarding the overall question of a maternal duty of care to accept medical treatment, however, potential harm to the "other" is harm to a being currently inside the pregnant woman. To the extent that the future child's interests conflict with her interest in and right to bodily integrity I have suggested, especially in chapter one, that it is the *current*, not the future status of the being to whom she owes a duty that matters: that being is a fetus, not a legal person. The fact that that other being lacks the legal status of a person is *conceptually connected* to the question of its location inside her body. For this reason, the legal status of the fetus is relevant when we consider the idea of a *maternal* duty not to injure the future child *via her body* in a way that it is *not* regarding the *third party's* liability for prenatal injury. Conversely, a *third party's bodily integrity is never in issue* so far as injury to the future child is concerned; for this reason, *neither is the legal status of the fetus*. The argument within the maternal–fetal literature—that giving the fetus legal rights protects its interests as a subsequently born child—simply ignores

---

[107] R Blank, "Emerging Notions", 469, my emphasis.
[108] This was a point of concern to the majority in *Winnipeg* in relation to liability for lifestyle related fetal damage, 152 DLR (4th) at 213, cited *infra* in my conclusion. For related points, see further ch. 7.

the problems surrounding its current location within the body of a pregnant woman:[109] these are highly relevant to the question of imposing a duty on that person—the woman—but not to the idea of imposing a duty on a third party whose bodily integrity is not implicated in the duty issue.[110]

Arguably then, the extension of third-party liability for fetal harm to the pregnant woman could not even be simply a matter of logic, contrary to assumptions made in different ways by both the majority and the dissent in the *Bonte* case. Thus, for the majority, Thayer J states: "[I]f a determination based upon public policy can be made denying a cause of action *logically* recognized by our case law, that determination should be made by the legislature."[111] Dissenting, Brock CJ and Batchelder J observe that the legitimacy of maternal liability "is not properly a question to be decided by a mechanical application of logic",[112] noting that this is a policy matter which must be decided in terms of fairness and justice. My point is that, *in addition to* the policy objections against maternal liability, there may well be logical or conceptual objections regarding the situation of the refusal of medical treatment because, as here argued, the fact that the fetus is not a legal person is relevant when we consider the idea of a maternal duty not to injure the fetus *via her body* in a way that it is *not* regarding the third party's liability for prenatal injury. This is not to deny that the fetus's lack of legal personhood may in itself partly be a policy consideration: thus, I am drawing attention to the logical implications, if you like, of a normative, policy, point.

The above thoughts have concentrated on the issue of injury to the future child. Where the *death* of the viable fetus is in issue as the result of a treatment refusal the

---

[109] See e.g. J Robertson, *Children of Choice*, 176, who, as noted in ch. 1, argues that "the real party in interest is not the fetus itself but the child that the fetus will become". In this connection, I note that Blank moves swiftly from the idea of parents owing legal duties to their children to that of a woman owing such duties to her fetus, without any consideration of the difference between a fetus and a born child. R Blank, "Emerging Notions", 442: "Parental discretion can be limited when it violates the best interests of the child, whether born or unborn." Of course, this is in accordance with his interpretation of *Smith*, to which I drew attention earlier. This is not to say that Blank does not recognise a woman's bodily integrity to be an issue. To the contrary, he frequently refers to the balancing of "fetal rights" against those of the woman. However, he never seriously attempts this balancing process, thus leaving the truly difficult questions unanswered.

[110] That there are reasons of "logic", rather than simply of "policy", for not imposing a duty of care on pregnant women in ways which impinge upon her rights shows, I think, the weaknesses in Simon's reasoning, as follows: "If children can sue their parents for negligent conduct and can sue third parties for negligence causing prenatal injury, it is logically inconsistent to deny the cause of action of a child prenatally injured by parental negligence. The discrepancy between the position of the child prenatally injured by his parents and that of the child similarly injured by others is unjust. Since the parents are in a position of being able to inflict at least as much, if not more, harm than any third party tortfeasor during pregnancy, the discrepancy is even more disturbing." "Parental Liability", 84, footnotes omitted. The fact that Simon is inclined to focus upon parental liability generally rather than that of pregnant women in particular in part accounts for her failure to recognise the importance of the right of bodily integrity and the logical connections between this and the legal status of the fetus so far as the *pregnant woman* is concerned. Notice also that Simon is at least inclined to recognise causation as a *prima facie* reason for the recognition of a legal duty. An unreflective argument from causation to duty is also made by M Shaw, in "Conditional Prospective Rights", 66ff. In this regard, we should recall the view of Cunningham J, in *Stallman* v. *Youngquist*, cited earlier in these notes.

[111] 616 A 2d at 466, my emphasis.

[112] *Ibid*.

duty of the woman is to the fetus (rather than the future child). In the case of third parties, as we have seen, the fetus is a person for the purposes of wrongful death statutes in the United States: if it were not a person, then the parents could not seek compensation for wrongful death. In the case of the woman, no wrongful death action will lie (since the woman who had caused the death would be the beneficiary of such an action). Hence there is no reason to depart from the position that the fetus is not a legal person, a position conceptually related to her right to bodily integrity, a right likely implicated in the treatment context.

b)   *Challenging the "Born-Alive" Rule: the* Winnipeg *dissent*

Given the above, what are we to make of the argument of the dissenting justices in *Winnipeg*, to the effect that the "born alive" rule is a legal anachronism which should be set aside, at least for the purposes of the appeal in issue in that case? With particular reference to an academic article which purports to trace the purpose of the rule,[113] the justices argued that the rule that the fetus only acquires legal rights upon live birth is an evidentiary presumption stemming from rudimentary medical knowledge rather than a substantive rule of law. That is, they held that the rule has its origins in the difficulties of determining whether an unborn child was alive prior to birth, a difficulty long since eradicated by developments in medical technology. In effect, they purport to show that the rule no longer has a legal purpose, stating "[o]nce the purpose of the rule is known, it becomes more apparent that it should not apply in this case".[114]

In effect, a review of the reasoning in this dissent reveals a disingenuous, if well-intentioned, approach to the legal status of the fetus. In favour of the rejection of the "born alive" rule, the judgment relies heavily upon legal authorities relating to the problem of establishing homicide of a fetus, with regard to which the question of evidence was clearly crucial.[115] Yet the merits of retaining or discarding the rule with regard to the issue of proving homicide are irrelevant to the question of whether the fetus should have legal rights. It is true that issues of proof have historically been pertinent to the determination of (third–party) liability for prenatal injury, and in this regard Major J justly draws upon an aspect of the judgment in *Montreal Tramways* (mentioned earlier), which notes that advances in medical science may increasingly solve what had previously been obstacles to the issue of legal proof. Yet his judgment fails to acknowledge that there was no question in the *Montreal Tramways* case of granting legal rights to the *fetus*. Rather, the legal rights are those of the *born child*. This is an important conceptual and legal difference which was stressed in the introductory sections of this chapter. As we saw earlier, in the *Montreal Tramways* case, Lamont J stated:[116]

[113] CD Forsythe, "Homicide of the Unborn Child: The Born Alive Rule and Other Legal Anachronisms", (1987) 21 *Val U L Rev* 563.

[114] 152 DLR (4th) at 232, *per* Major J.

[115] On this point the dissent cites a relevant passage from AS Taylor, *Medical Jurisprudence*, 7th edn. (1861) 411, and discusses US and Canadian cases concerning homicide such as *Hughes* v. *State of Oklahoma*, 868 P 2d 730 (1994), *Commonwealth* v. *Cass*, 467 NE 2d 1324 (1984) and *R* v. *Sullivan*, [1991] 1 SCR 489.

[116] The dissenting judges in *Winnipeg* do cite this passage, but only to emphasise the issue of justice *per se*. 152 DLR (4th) at 242.

"To my mind it is but natural justice that a child, if born alive and viable, should be allowed to maintain an action in the courts for injuries wrongfully committed upon its person while in the womb of its mother."

Indeed, there is no reason why the accrual of fetal legal rights should necessarily be consequent upon *knowledge* of life in the womb. As the majority in the *Winnipeg* case notes, the idea (implied in the approach of the dissent) that there is no defensible difference between the born and the unborn is a *biological*, not a *normative*, argument having nothing to do with the law.[117]

Recall here the judgment in *Smith* v. *Brennan*, in which the New Jersey Supreme Court recognised a (third-party) cause of action for prenatal injury, holding that a "child has the legal right to begin life with a sound mind and body". As noted, scholars and judges (Belson AJ in *Re AC*) have interpreted *Smith* as giving rights to the *fetus*. However, since *Smith* actually recognises the rights of the live-born *child* to recover for prenatal injury, the legal status of the fetus is not in issue: we saw that the *Smith* court observed that it "is immaterial whether before birth the child is considered a person in being". Indeed, it would be of no legal benefit to a born child in such a prenatal injury case that it acquired rights before rather than after birth, as the prospect of a born child being able to sue for injuries negligently inflicted upon it whilst *in utero* is intended to act as a deterrent to a would-be tortfeasor's infliction of injury. If injury nevertheless occurs, this is not because the fetus lacked legal rights; rather, it is because a third party negligently inflicted damage on the fetus *in utero*.

By contrast, of course, the dissenting justices' desire that the fetus should have legal rights and thus standing to sue in the *Winnipeg* case, is intended to ground injunctive relief against the woman for the purposes of *coercively preventing*, rather than deterring, the relevant injury. Indeed, the dissent's argument that the fetus should be a legal person in this case is critical to the potential legality of any intrusion into the pregnant woman's life. At this point, we see the way in which the *Winnipeg* dissent is linked with an argument that the law of tort be extended to recognise an injunctive remedy infringing upon important rights of the woman. The majority is repeatedly at pains to emphasise that this would represent a major change in the law suitable only for Parliament to make.[118] But the dissent ignores the magnitude of this change, asserting that "there must exist jurisdiction to order a pre-birth remedy preventing a mother from causing serious harm to her foetus"

[117] *Ibid.*, 206–7.
[118] *Ibid.*, 205, 206, 208, 213, 214. For a critique of this approach, see F DeCoste, "Case Comment and Note: *Winnipeg Child and Family Services (Northwest Area)* v. *DFG*: The Impossibility of Fetal Rights and the Obligations of Judicial Governance", (1998) 36 *Alberta L Rev* 725, who argues that the Supreme Court ought to have decided the case by "articulating the grounds of principle" which weigh against fetal rights. (At 727.) "When the majority . . . musters arguments about the consequences of changing the rule on the rights of women, its arguments lack the ring and force of principle, since they are designed, not to defend the law, but to allow the Court to abandon the law to politics." (At 738.) Thus, De Coste suggests that the court's arguments hinge not upon principle but upon the size of the change, but of course these points might well be connected.

in a passage that follows upon the reiteration of the injustice of the "born alive" rule.[119] In this way the dissent *subsumes* the issue of the extension of the law of tort into the issue of the legal status of the fetus. As indicated, its discussion of the latter issue is seriously flawed by its elision between matters of evidence and proof on the one hand and normative issues of rights on the other.[120] Whilst the first may be relevant to the success of a cause of action and in this regard it may indeed be a matter of "injustice" that a plaintiff's cause of action fails for lack of proof, this is a different aspect of justice from that related to the second and normative issue of rights.

In fact I have considerable sympathy with the dissent in *Winnipeg* in the light of the *unjustifiability* of the solvent abuse in issue in that case, given its indefensible value to the pregnant woman and the certain harm to the future child which would ensue. Indeed, nothing written here denies the dissenting justices' point that "where a woman has chosen to carry a foetus to term . . . [h]aving chosen to bring a life into this world, that woman must accept some responsibility for its well-being" (assuming, I add here, she has freely made that choice).[121] Yet although it is hard to deny that the result which obtained on the particular facts of *Winnipeg* has an element of injustice, arguments as to the injustice of this case will be flawed by issues relating to the woman's (lack of) control over her addiction, an aspect noted by the majority, once again perhaps reflecting the understanding that "ought follows can".[122] Indeed, the autonomy of women with serious addiction problems is likely to be seriously diminished, in part by their compulsive behaviour and in part by their personal history (for instance being the victim of severe violence or abuse) which may

---

[119] 152 DLR (4th) at 243, *per* Major J.

[120] For interesting thoughts on the misplaced reliance on science in Major J's judgment and his failure to integrate this reliance with a consideration of policy issues see T Caulfield and E Nelson, "Case Comment And Note: *Winnipeg Child And Family Services* v. *DFG*: A Commentary On The Law, Reproductive Autonomy And The Allure Of Technopolicy", (1998) 36 *Alberta L Rev* 799. The note "seeks . . . to dispel the allure of science as the driver of legal and social policy". (At 799.) "Science should inform social policy, not direct it". (At 800.)

[121] 152 DLR (4th) at 237, *per* Major J.

[122] The majority noted that some choices adversely affecting the fetus "may be the products of circumstance and illness rather than free choice capable of effective deterrence by the legal sanction of tort." *Ibid.*, 211, *per* McLachlin J. For a thoughtful article highlighting the use of language in *Winnipeg* see M Randall, "Pregnant Embodiment and Women's Autonomy Rights in Law: An Analysis of the Language and Politics of *Winnipeg Child and Family Services* v. *DFG*", (1999) 62 *Sask L Rev* 515, 533–534: "Pervasive in the dissenting judgment . . . is the language of 'choice', reflecting Major J.'s apparent opinion that the circumstances in which Ms. G. found herself were entirely of her own making. In describing Ms. G, Major J. observes that 'she chose to remain pregnant, deliver the child, and continue her substance abuse.' But the notion that Ms. G 'chose' to continue an addiction flies in the face of what is known about the debilitating physical and psychological effects of addiction and implies that to overcome its grasp is a mere matter of will power . . . At certain points in the dissenting judgment, Major J. speaks the language of lifestyle choice to describe Ms. G.'s circumstances. But can poverty really be described as a lifestyle choice? For that matter, can addiction be accurately or helpfully characterized in this way?" (Footnotes omitted.) She also notes that Ms G was aboriginal (at 539).

have undermined their ability to develop the conditions required for autonomy.[123] Indeed, as Justice McLachlin observed for the majority in *Winnipeg*:[124]

> "This is not a story of heroes and villains. It is the more prosaic but all too common story of people struggling to do their best in the face of inadequate facilities and the ravages of addiction."

With these points in mind, the *Winnipeg* case might well be seen as more tragic than unjust. Nevertheless, where a maternal choice which will inflict harm on the unborn child is voluntary and clearly unjustified, in Canada as in England it is for Parliament to decide if a different result should obtain in such cases. Hence, it is surely naïve of the dissenting *Winnipeg* justices to argue that the law should be changed for the purposes of achieving justice on the particular facts of the instant case for, as the judgment of McLachlin J reminds us:[125]

> "Having broken the time-honoured rule that legal rights accrue only upon live birth, the courts would find it difficult to limit application of the new principle to particular cases. By contrast, the legislature, should it choose to introduce a law permitting action to protect unborn children against substance abuse, could limit the law to that precise case."

In fact, broader policy considerations touched upon elsewhere in this chapter suggest that neither the interests of justice nor the health of (subsequently born) children would generally be well served by forcibly detaining and treating a woman in the manner sought by the appellate agency in the *Winnipeg* case, hence that legislative intervention would not be appropriate.[126]

4. Conclusions regarding the Idea of a Maternal Legal Duty to Submit to Medical Treatment

The normative question of whether a duty of care should be imposed upon the woman to accept medical treatment in the interests of the future child or to prevent fetal death, then, is resolved by a consideration of the nature and value of the rights implicated, particularly that of bodily integrity, the difficulties of determining a standard of care, particularly where a duty is to be realised through the body, and the question of the legal status of the fetus. I also touched on the moral

---

[123] C McLeod and S Sherwin, "Relational Autonomy, Self-Trust, and Health Care for Patients who are Oppressed", in C MacKenzie and N Stoljar (eds.), *Relational Autonomy: Feminist Perspectives on Autonomy, Agency and the Social Self* (New York, NY: Oxford University Press, 2000) 259, 271–2. The authors suggest that these forms of violence or abuse are instances of oppression because they are highly systemic and hence can be defined as social practices (at 272).

[124] 152 DLR (4th) at 200. She notes that the respondent in this case argued "that at an earlier stage of her pregnancy she had voluntarily sought treatment but had been turned away due to lack of facilities, that when asked to take treatment she agreed and only later refused because she had fallen into a state of intoxication, and that once taken to hospital, she remained until discharged, although the custodial order requiring her to remain had been stayed". (At 199–200.)

[125] *Ibid.*, 206.

[126] Note that the dissent held that "[t]he mother remains free to reject all suggested medical treatment". *Ibid.*, 239, *per* Major J, who noted that "[t]he confinement serves only to prevent her using toxins strong enough to cause serious and permanent damage to the foetus".

inappropriateness of an enforceable maternal duty of care to prevent prenatal harm, which could entail operating on a pregnant woman without her consent. Consideration of these arguments and points suggests that a woman should *not* be deemed to have a legal duty of care to accept beneficial medical treatment for the fetus or future child (or not to accept treatment meaningfully beneficial to herself which may cause prenatal harm or death).

Two further points should be noted. First, the purpose of allowing recovery against a third party should be recalled: not only is a damaged child being compensated, but also other potential tortfeasors are deterred from acting in ways which harm other future children, generally at little or no cost to themselves other than by following the injunction to take care. In the case of the woman who wishes to refuse medical treatment, however, the aim of deterrence is unlikely to have any impact when women refuse treatment for serious personal or religious reasons. If it were otherwise, then it is doubtful that we would recognise the areas of self-determination or, especially, of bodily integrity as deserving the protection of rights in the first place. Second, the standard tortfeasor's act or omission is not usually something which touches upon his or her own welfare, whereas in the case of pregnancy, the question of seeking maternal benefit (such as religious salvation in *Baby Boy Doe* or *Jefferson*, a peaceful death in the case of *Re AC* or, in Mrs Grodin's case, antibiotic treatment for an infection (assuming there was no suitable alternative antibiotic)) is very much in point. As for the wider policy considerations regarding the idea of a maternal duty of care, I shall review these following consideration, to which I now turn, of the idea of a maternal duty of care with regard to maternal conduct during pregnancy.

C. Maternal Conduct during Pregnancy

In its most obvious guises the idea of a maternal duty *generally* to act in a way which does not harm the fetus/future child typically invokes such negative injunctions as not smoking,[127] taking drugs[128] or drinking alcohol[129] (though the problems of

---

[127] As noted by J Seymour, cigarette smoking when pregnant "can retard fetal growth, result in low birth weight or premature birth, and increase the risk of *abruptio placentae*, *placenta praevia*, premature rupture of the membranes, bleeding during pregnancy, stillbirth, and neonatal death. It may also be associated with deficits in growth and emotional and intellectual development and with an increased incidence of childhood cancer." J Seymour, *Childbirth and the Law*, 223, citing recent literature relating to this and my next two notes.

[128] "Taking drugs such as heroin and cocaine during pregnancy often causes fetal harm, although much of this is a product of associated health, nutritional, and social problems. The most common complications caused by these drugs are premature labour, intra-uterine growth retardation, *abruptio placentae*, premature rupture of the membranes, and perinatal death. The neonate may experience narcotic withdrawal and long-term developmental retardation. In addition, cocaine use can result in children being born suffering from physical abnormalities (such as *atresias* and limb reductions, neurological and gastrointestinal abnormalities, and brain damage)." *Ibid.* In fact, both prescription and non-prescription drugs can also damage the fetus. C Simon, "Parental Liability", 73–4. Note that in 1989 it was estimated that each year some 375,000 newborns may be harmed by maternal substance abuse in the US. "Note: Rethinking (M)otherhood: Feminist Theory and State Regulation of Pregnancy", (1990) 103 *Harv L Rev* 1325, 1325.

[129] "[H]eavy drinking can result in the birth of a child with fetal alcohol syndrome, characterized by congenital malformations, growth and mental retardation, central nervous system impairment, and

proof of harm to the future child to which each of these are subject should be noted). Such negative injunctions might extend to the question of a pregnant woman's liability to her unborn child through her negligent driving, or other such conduct where she might also harm third parties. But there is also scope for the idea of positive obligations, for instance the injunctions to take beneficial exercise such as swimming during pregnancy, or to eat a healthy and balanced diet.[130]

Two points might be noted in introduction. First, once again if *injury* to the fetus is in issue, a woman's potential duty would be to the future child, which acquires legal rights upon birth. I have argued that this child's interests may be stronger where its mother's bodily integrity is not invoked, given the importance of its location *in utero* in the determination of the strength of its interests as compared with those of an already born child.[131] Importantly, its mother's bodily integrity is unlikely to be invoked regarding her general conduct, in which she is engaged in activities (or omissions to act). Indeed, here she may well harm the future child in ways akin to a detached third party. In turn, consistent with my earlier reasoning in relation to third parties, this means that the future child's current lack of legal status carries little weight. Nevertheless, other maternal rights situated particularly within the legal debate may in some jurisdictions be called into play, such as the legal right of privacy. Where maternal conduct threatens fetal *death*, a woman's duty is to a being who is not a legal person: in the United States no wrongful death action will lie since the woman would be a beneficiary; in England, we have seen that in any event no such action is recognised.

Second, with regard to the scenario of maternal conduct or lifestyle choices, once again we should distinguish between the prospect of preventing women from acting in certain ways and allowing post-birth actions for compensation. As we have seen, the law of tort cannot currently be used in the first way; hence this discussion concerns the issue of post-birth actions.

In order to focus what could otherwise be a very open-ended debate, the discussion of liability for maternal conduct is grounded in the key Canadian, American and Australian precedents concerning the issue of negligent driving.

---

proneness to learning and speech disabilites and severe behavioural problems." J Seymour, *Childbirth and the Law*, 223. For a moving account of a family's struggle to deal with the effects of fetal alcohol syndrome upon a born child, see M Dorris, *The Broken Cord* (New York, NY: Harper and Row, 1989). Note however that the "concrete level [at which] drinking or smoking causes harm remains much disputed". M Brazier, "Parental Responsibilities, Foetal Welfare and Children's Health", in C Bridge (ed.), *Family Law Towards the New Millennium: Essays for PM Bromley* (London: Butterworths, 1997) 263–93, 272. At present, fetal alchohol syndrome affects 0.29 to 0.48 per 1000 children born in the US (about 1200 children per annum). See SN Mattson and EP Riley, "A Review of the Neurobehavioral Deficits in Children with Fetal Alcohol Syndrome or Exposure or Prenatal Exposure to Alcohol", (1998) 22 *Alcoholism: Clinical and Experimental Research* 279, as cited in KA De Ville and LM Kopelman, "Fetal Protection in Wisconsin's Revised Child Abuse Law; Right Goal, Wrong Remedy", (1999) 336.

[130] Nutritional deficiencies may lead to low birth weight, causing a higher incidence of defects such as impairment to the brain and also mortality. C Simon, "Parental Liability", 73.

[131] See chs. 1 and 2.

1. Negligent Driving and Prenatal Harm

Following the *Winnipeg* case of 1997, in 1999 the Supreme Court of Canada made another highly significant contribution to its jurisprudence on the idea of maternal liability for prenatal harm in *Dobson* v. *Dobson*.[132] The case concerned a boy's suit against his mother for prenatal injuries sustained as a result of her negligent driving. The Supreme Court overturned the decision of the Court of Appeal for New Brunswick, holding—apparently on *policy* grounds—that no such action can lie. At the same time, however, the Court held that it may well be appropriate for the legislature to create an exception to maternal tort immunity in the context of negligent driving. Supposedly then, *policy* might also support a legislative initiative to allow such actions. There is some tension between these positions, not all of which is dissipated by the different legal methods embodied by the judiciary and the legislature, notably that as regards the latter's product of legislation, one cannot reason by analogy to other contexts.[133] Rather, this tension is fuelled by the majority's acceptance of the view that "policy" arguments stand against maternal tort liability in *any* context. Arguably, despite the Court's contrary view, there are some interesting distinctions between different kinds of maternal conduct which may cause prenatal harm. In turn this means that the policy arguments require closer examination.

Mrs Dobson was 27 weeks pregnant when her car collided with another. This resulted in prenatal injuries to her fetus which in turn necessitated a caesarean birth. These injuries caused permanent mental and physical disabilities to her child and he sued his mother alleging that her negligent driving had caused the accident. The trial judge, Miller J, noted that there was no common law bar to actions in tort by children against their parents and that Canadian courts have used the fiction of juridical personality of the fetus to protect its interests upon birth, as in *Montreal Tramways* v. *Leville*.[134] He found that the child had a cause of action against his mother, holding that:[135]

> "if an action can be sustained by a child against a parent, and if an action can be sustained against a stranger for injuries suffered by a child before birth, then it seems to me a *reasonable progression* to allow an action by a child against his mother for prenatal injuries caused by her negligence."

The implication is that it is a matter of logic that a pregnant woman might also be liable for prenatal injuries.[136] The judge did observe, however, that this "is a ques-

---

[132] [1999] 2 Can SCR 753.

[133] As Cory J notes, *ibid.*, 791, regarding the English Congenital Disabilities (Civil Liability Act) 1976, which allows a claim by a born child against its mother for prenatal injuries *exclusively* for injuries suffered as a result of negligent driving.

[134] [1933] 4 DLR 337.

[135] (1997) 143 DLR (4th) 189, 192, my emphasis.

[136] For a recent academic suggestion that this is a matter of logic, in authors against the idea of maternal legal duties, see S Fovargue and J Miola, "Policing Pregnancy: Implications of the *Attorney-General's Reference (No. 3 of 1994)*", (1998) 6 *Med L Rev* 265, 287–9, footnote omitted: "If the courts continue to personalise the foetus, thereby granting it the rights and interests of a legal person, then it is logical that the foetus must be protected from *all* harm, including that inflicted by the mother."

tion with obvious expanding implications and is one which must ultimately be determined by a higher court of the judicial structure".[137]

In the Court of Appeal Hoyt CJNB made a crucial distinction between what he saw as the "narrow" issue of a pregnant woman's negligent driving on the one hand and the issue of her lifestyle choices on the other.[138] He found support for this distinction in the decision in *Bonte* v. *Bonte*[139] in which, as we have seen, the Supreme Court of New Hampshire held that a child could sue its mother for failure to use reasonable care in crossing a street, and in the writings of JG Fleming.[140] He also drew upon the decision of the New South Wales Court of Appeal in *Lynch* v. *Lynch*,[141] in which Clarke JA had observed that the issue of lifestyle choices raises different policy questions from that of negligent driving.[142] Further, Hoyt CJNB took note of the exemption for maternal immunity from prenatal injury in the context of negligent driving provided by the English Congenital Disabilities (Civil Liability Act) 1976, which thereby distinguishes between a general duty to drive carefully and the lifestyle choices of the pregnant woman. Accordingly, he found that Mrs Dobson's duty did not inhere in parenthood, but was an instance of her general duty to drive carefully, a duty she owed both to other road-users and to her unborn child.[143] As we shall see, the majority of the Supreme Court rejected this distinction.

For the majority, Cory J set the agenda by defining the issue to be decided as whether a pregnant woman should be liable in tort for damage to her child arising from a prenatal negligent act.[144] In other words, the issue was not, as Major J was to hold for the dissent, the "narrower" one of whether a child born alive can sue its mother in tort for prenatal injuries sustained as a result of her negligent driving.[145] As will become apparent, this difference in the delineation of the issue goes some distance towards determining the outcome of the appeal.

Turning to the substantive arguments, in essence Cory J deemed that to impose a duty of care on a pregnant woman not to cause prenatal harm (his definition of the issue) would fall foul of the second stage of the test in *City of Kamloops* v. *Nielson*,[146] the Canadian decision which closely mirrors the pre-*Caparo* test

---

[137] 143 DLR (4th) at 192.

[138] (1997) 148 DLR (4th) 332, 336.

[139] 616 A 2d 464 (NH 1992). Mrs Bonte was hit by a car, with the result that her 7-month old fetus was born with brain damage.

[140] "A distinction is in order between the general duty to avoid injury which the defendant owes to all others and those peculiar to parenthood. An instance of the former is the duty to drive carefully, which even the mother at the wheel owes to her foetus. On the other hand, there is strong aversion against inquisition into alleged parental indiscretions during pregnancy, like excessive smoking, drinking or taking drugs." JG Fleming, *The Law of Torts*, 8th edn. (1992) at 168.

[141] [1992] 3 Med LR 62.

[142] *Ibid.*, 71. However, as noted *infra*, Clarke JA decided that public policy was in favour of maternal liability in the driving context.

[143] 148 DLR (4th) at 336.

[144] [1999] 2 Can SCR at 763. Joined by Lamer CJ, L'Heureux-Dubé, Gonthier, Iacobucci and Binnie JJ.

[145] *Ibid.*, 803. Joined by Bastarache J.

[146] [1984] 2 SCR 2.

formulated in *Anns* v. *Merton LBC*.[147] Thus, whilst he found that there was a sufficiently close relationship between "the parties"[148] (the first stage of the test), he
held that there were significant public policy considerations which should negative
this duty.[149] These consist in the impact that such a duty would have upon a pregnant woman's rights to bodily integrity, privacy and autonomy.[150] In other words,
the impact upon a pregnant woman's rights of a finding of a duty of care toward
the fetus/future child is cast as a *policy* issue. This is an interesting characterisation.
One could simply argue, for instance, that a pregnant woman cannot be said to
have the legal *duty* where she has legal *rights* grounded in certain of her legal interests (for instance those in bodily integrity and self-determination which are so
prominent in the treatment context). In a Dworkinian sense, the broad sense in
which principles describe rights rather than goals (which are described by policies),
this might be seen as an argument of *principle*.[151] But of course Cory J *has* to cast
the impact upon rights in terms of *policy* in order to fit the structure of the *Kamloops*
test: if there is sufficient proximity to give rise to a duty of care, then the only way
this can be negatived is by what are dubbed "policy" considerations. Hence the
bundling of rights into the policy basket.

As other judges before him had done, Cory J emphasised the "unique and special relationship"[152] between a pregnant woman and the fetus she carries, citing
such cases as *Re F (in utero)* and *Paton* v. *BPAS Trustees* and holding that it was the
special nature of the relationship which determined the outcome of the appeal: it
was the nature of the relationship which distinguished the idea of maternal liability from that of third-party liability.[153] Here he relied on aspects of the dissenting
judgments in *Bonte* v. *Bonte* and upon the judgment of Justice Cunningham in the
Supreme Court of Illinois case of *Stallman* v. *Youngquist*[154] (which likewise concerned the question of maternal liability for negligent driving) to the effect that a
fetus has no cause of action against its mother for injuries unintentionally
inflicted.[155]

---

[147] [1978] AC 728.
[148] [1999] 2 Can SCR at 767. Cory J both makes reference to the born alive child (in para. 18) and
to the fetus (in para. 19), but admits regarding the latter that it would be contrary to the decision in
Winnipeg to assume that the fetus and its mother can be treated as separate legal entities. Nevertheless
he suggests that it is "appropriate" (para. 19) to assume rather than decide this issue in this case.
[149] This was also important in the Supreme Court's reasoning in *Winnipeg*. See 152 DLR at 210, *per*
McLachlin J, at which point she cited the Royal Commission's Report *Proceed with Care*.
[150] [1999] 2 Can SCR at 768–9.
[151] On principles, for instance, Dworkin writes: "A 'principle' [is] a standard that is to be observed,
not because it will advance or secure an economic, political or social situation deemed desirable, but
because it is a requirement of justice or fairness or some other dimension of morality." On policies, he
says: "A 'policy' [is] that kind of standard that sets out a goal to be reached, generally an improvement
in some economic, political, or social feature of the community." *Taking Rights Seriously*, 2nd impression (corrected) with appendix (London: Duckworth, 1978) 22.
[152] [1999] 2 Can SCR at 769.
[153] *Ibid.*, 770–1.
[154] 531 NE 2d 355.
[155] *Ibid.*, 359.

The decision in *Stallman*, which hinges on two related points, is highly significant and has proved influential in related decisions, such as the *Baby Boy Doe* caesarean case. First, Justice Cunningham considered that a child's cause of action for prenatal injury against its mother would establish a legal duty on the woman's part "to effectuate the best prenatal environment possible".[156] In rejecting this idea, Cunningham J noted that to allow a fetus a right to begin life with a sound mind and body which could be asserted against its mother would be to create an unprecedented legal duty on one person to "guarantee" the health, both mental and physical, of another. This would amount to the imposition of an affirmative or positive legal duty of care toward the fetus. In such a way, a pregnant woman and her fetus would be "legal adversaries from the moment of conception until birth".[157] The second argument was that to hold a third party liable for prenatal injuries does not affect that party's *"right* to control his or her own life".[158] By contrast, imposing liability for prenatal injury on the pregnant woman would be "to subject to State scrutiny all the decisions a woman must make in attempting to carry a pregnancy to term, and *infringes on her right to privacy and bodily autonomy*".[159] Cunningham J is correct, I submit, to identify a crucial difference between third-party and maternal liability for prenatal harm as inhering in the impact that the latter, but not the former, would (tend to) have upon *rights*, as the first half of this chapter shows with respect to the treatment context. Thus, relying on *Stallman*, we saw in chapter three that the treatment refusal case of *Baby Boy Doe* drew attention to *Stallman's* "conceptual linking" of a woman's rights to privacy and bodily autonomy, as evidenced in the passage cited above. The question remains, however, whether this argument applies in the very different *driving* context.

a) *Driving, Duties and Rights*

As did Justice Cunningham, Justice Cory for the majority in *Dobson* assumes that a pregnant woman's rights—in bodily integrity, autonomy and privacy—are always called into play by the idea of a maternal duty not to cause prenatal harm. A pregnant woman's rights to bodily integrity, self-determination and privacy are often invoked in the medical treatment context, not one discussed in *Dobson*, whilst a legal right of privacy may arguably be invoked by many forms of potentially harmful maternal conduct such as smoking or drinking alcohol. But are rights of privacy and autonomy invoked in the driving context? Addressing for now the privacy point, we should distinguish between two senses of private: first, that which does not occur in public; second, that which reflects some degree of personal preference.

In the first sense, a car can obviously be driven *in private*, for instance on a privately owned estate. Here the right of privacy may be invoked in a highly constructed sense. As for the question of the relationship between the activity of driving on such an estate and other people, if there are no others present, the manner

---

[156] *Ibid.*
[157] *Ibid.*
[158] *Ibid.*, at 360, my emphasis.
[159] *Ibid.*, my emphasis.

of driving is irrelevant; but where there is the prospect of harm to others then it may be helpful to examine the activity in terms of the idea of *reason*: was the manner of driving unreasonable? In these terms, if the owner of the private estate were to drive in such a fashion as to injure a trespasser, I suggest that we would be unlikely to hesitate in imposing, nor to have difficulty in determining (upon suitable evidence) the breach of a legal duty.[160]

Second, it is not just that driving most often occurs on *public* roads, but also that it is arguably very much a means to an end (notwithstanding that some people very much enjoy the process). This brings us to the second sense of private. In this sense, arguably the choice, say, whether to smoke, drink alcohol, eat certain types of food or bungee-jump when pregnant is a matter of personal preference in a way that driving typically is not: consistent with *Lynch* and the Court of Appeal in *Dobson*, the former, but not the latter, are "lifestyle" issues.

Yet, implicitly at least, Cory J maintains that driving typically *can* invoke privacy interests (including when it occurs in public). Thus, critical to his judgment is the rejection of the infant respondent's argument (which was in line with the approach of Hoyt CJNB in the Court of Appeal) that there is an important distinction between the idea of general duties owed to others and duties peculiar to parenting. Rather, Justice Cory maintains that this distinction is "unworkable" and that "[d]riving is an integral part of parenting in a great many families", relying on several US authorities which reject a parental immunity exception in the context of negligent driving. The jurisprudence on parental immunity, its abrogations and exceptions is notoriously complex and there is only space for a brief comment here upon the use made by the Supreme Court of these cases. Essentially, its use of these cases is unsatisfactory for two reasons. First, in one of the cases cited—*Hartman by Hartman* v. *Hartman*[161]—the court criticised the finding (in an earlier case) that the doctrine of parental immunity was abrogated except in circumstances involving parental authority or discretion regarding care such as food, housing and medicine on grounds of vagueness, holding that courts have had to make "arbitrary distinctions" as to whether some particular parental conduct falls within one of the exceptions.[162] But how could negligent driving seriously be the subject of arbitrary judgments on these criteria, as Cory J needs if he is appropriately to rely on *Hartman* here?

Justice Cory also cites several US cases (but all from Illinois) in which driving was considered a family activity protected by the parental immunity doctrine. Of these, in *Hogan* v. *Hogan*[163] and *Eisele* v. *Temuta*,[164] the Appellate Court of Illinois did little more than recite the existence and purpose of the parental immunity rule. In neither case was the sense in which the driving relevantly constituted a family purpose explained; nor did the court consider how the policy underlying the doc-

---

[160] See e.g. *British Railways Board* v. *Herrington* [1972] 2 AC 877; Occupier's Liability Act 1984, s. 1.
[161] 821 SW 2d 852 (Mo 1991).
[162] *Ibid.*, 856.
[163] 435 NE 2d 770 (Ill App Ct 1982).
[164] 404 NE 2d 349 (Ill App Ct 1980).

trine was served in the cases under consideration. Both cases rejected a finding in *Schenk* v. *Schenk*,[165] in which a daughter's driving injured her father as pedestrian, that the family immunity doctrine was inapplicable. Here the court had judged that where there was a beach of duty owed to the general public, liability would not be disruptive to family harmony in the way that a duty primarily owed to the family would be: only the latter would bring into issue the "inner workings of the family".[166] As for the last case cited by Cory J, in *Johnson* v. *Myers*, the court baldly and somewhat incredibly held that despite the many pleadings of ordinary negligence relating to the driving in question, no facts had been pleaded which would show that the conduct arose outside the family relationship.[167] What additional facts could possibly have been pleaded here?

On a more promising note, however, regarding the parental immunity doctrine *Johnson* v. *Myers* appropriately notes that it is a rule based *not upon lack of duty* but upon immunity from liability.[168] Thus, at least this court would have recognised what I suggest is a problem with Justice Cory's view that "driving is integral to parenting": immunity from liability is not premised upon *rights* but on *policy*. This makes it very difficult for *driving to be protected by rights*, as Cory J needs within the overall structure of the judgment.

i) The Standard of Care

The point that driving invokes *rights* forms part of Justice Cory's argument formulating the difficulties of judging the standard of a maternal duty of care. As we have seen, this may well be a legitimate approach as regards, say, the idea of a maternal duty to accept medical treatment for the fetus, given the clear implication of the rights of bodily integrity and self-determination in that context. But it is uncertain to what extent it is appropriate as regards driving. This in turn raises the question of what is the real objection to liability in *Dobson* in Justice Cory's mind.

Indeed, given any driver's duty to drive carefully, how can the activity of driving invoke the *right* to self-determination, as Justice Cory's judgment requires? For instance, one could argue that a *right* to self-determination cannot be invoked by the manner in which one drives one's car, with the possible exception of driving on that privately owned estate upon which no others are present. Rather, driving might be seen as an instance of "general conduct", which must be gone about with a view to avoiding physical harm to others. That is, one has a negative moral duty—the reasonableness of which is thus readily definable—not to harm others in driving. Indeed, this is consistent with the way driving is treated by the law. In line with this approach, Justice Major urges in dissent that a pregnant woman's "freedom of action"[169] in driving is already restricted by her duty to other road-users. Put another way, she is already under a duty to drive carefully. So far as arguments

---

[165] (1968) 241 NE 2d 12.
[166] *Per* Jiganti J in *Eisele* 404 NE 2d at 351.
[167] 277 NE 2d 778 (Ill App Ct 1972), 779, my emphasis.
[168] *Ibid.*, 778–9.
[169] [1999] 2 Can SCR at 809.

against maternal liability are concerned, we can now begin to appreciate the difficulties of relying on the complexities of determining a standard of care in the driving context. Consider, for instance, the case of a woman whose negligent driving injures not only her unborn child, but *also* the driver in an oncoming car. That is, the *same act* of negligence has caused injury to both parties. This means that to the extent that this woman has breached a duty of care to the driver in the other car, so too has she breached a duty to her own unborn child, *assuming she owes such a duty*. This last is a critical point upon which, it may be thought, the differences between the majority and dissenting judgments turn.

ii) Duties—to Whom?

Can it be said that where a pregnant woman owes a general duty to others so too she can owe a duty to her fetus/future child, a view the majority in *Dobson* ascribes to the Court of Appeal? The argument of the majority is that there can be no such general duty owed to others: the duty is always owed by one to an actual other.[170] Yet, in the light of the rest of the majority judgment, this objection is something of a red herring. For the overreaching argument of the majority judgment is *not* that there is no *prima facie* case for the imposition of a maternal duty of care towards her unborn child, but rather that "policy" issues, namely the impact upon a pregnant woman's rights, preclude the imposition of such a duty under the second stage of *Kamloops*. In other words, Cory J has *already admitted* that there is a *prima facie* duty, but holds that this is negatived by the "policy" considerations of that duty's impact upon rights. In a parallel fashion, albeit one which reaches the opposite conclusion, the dissenting Justice Major's argument is that where a pregnant woman owes a duty of care to a third party (when she drives), the child's *prima facie* right—again, already established through the first stage of *Kamloops*—cannot be negatived under the second part of the *Kamloops* test by arguing that her freedom of action is thereby hampered:[171] hence, it is not that the coincidence of harm emanating from the same act or omission can itself decide the (*prima facie*) duty issue. In other words, both Cory and Major JJ hold that there is a *prima facie* duty, but they reach different conclusions on the policy issues under the second stage of *Kamloops*, influenced, in turn, by their original definition of the issue on appeal in broad and narrow terms respectively. This means that Justice McLachlin's criticism of Justice Major, to the effect that his judgment favouring maternal liability in the driving context "makes recovery conditional on the serendipitous coincidence that another person stood to be injured"[172] is somewhat misjudged.

At one level, then, Justice Cory is clearly saying that there is no maternal duty of care because of the impact such a duty would have upon a pregnant woman's rights (the second stage of *Kamloops*). His answer to the question of how driving can invoke privacy and autonomy rights is, it appears, that driving can be part of parenting. Yet the discussion has indicated that, to the extent that the same act of

---

[170] [1999] 2 Can SCR at 788.
[171] *Ibid.*, 811.
[172] *Ibid.*, 801.

negligent driving might harm both a third party and a woman's unborn child, then the crucial issue is whether a duty is owed to that unborn child. However, given the strictures of *Kamloops*, since proximity is apparently satisfied, then the only way to rebut duty is through the second-stage policy test regarding the impact that imposing a duty of care in driving would have upon *rights*. But then one immediately comes up against the contradiction that the *same conduct* can apparently be protected by rights (regarding injury to the unborn child) and not protected by rights (regarding injury to third parties, *including* a born child of the pregnant woman)[173] which is surely somewhat difficult to swallow.[174] In one sense this amounts, I think, to a serious flaw in the majority judgment. It is a flaw which is shielded, however, by the way in which the majority buries the issue of driving within the category of all maternal conduct, consistent with its argument about the impact of broad maternal tort liability upon a pregnant woman's rights. Importantly, underlying these points is, of course, the majority's definition of the issue in *Dobson* as maternal tort liability generally, rather than the narrower one of maternal tort liability for negligent driving. In turn, lying behind these differences are questions about the appropriateness of common law versus legislative action.

2. Policy and Precedent: Problems of Legal Method

In what ways, then, could Justice Cory have avoided, if desirable, the imposition of a maternal duty of care, at least as regards negligent driving? First, could he have denied proximity at the first stage of *Kamloops*? Probably not. Second, could he have admitted that the issue of driving does not invoke rights on the pregnant woman's part, but then pinned his judgment upon other reasons associated with her rights: for instance, that *judicially* to allow liability in the driving context would create a risky precedent as regards maternal conduct in other contexts? Arguably yes. In other words, as the supporting Justice McLachlin says, allowing maternal liability in the driving context:[175]

"carries the *potential* to bring the whole of the pregnant woman's conduct under the scrutiny of the law. This in turn has the *potential* to jeopardize the pregnant woman's fundamental right to control her body and make decisions in her own interest".

This statement is in the context of her concerns about applying common law liability for "negligence generally",[176] but what she seems to be saying is that if the Court were to allow liability in the driving context, this could have considerable

---

[173] As Hoyt CJNB noted in the Court of Appeal, "it is common ground that a child may sue its parent or parents in tort", 148 DLR 4th at 335, citing a host of Canadian authorities and observing that the position is the same in English law.

[174] Related to this point is Major J's observation which is, arguably at least, clearly legitimate in the *driving* context, that to the extent that there are policy considerations relating to intra-familial litigation, these must bar all actions by children rather than only those injured while *in utero*. [1999] 2 Can SCR at 814–15.

[175] *Ibid.*, 800, my emphases. McLachlin J refers to *Morgentaler* [1988] 1 SCR 30, *per* Wilson J. Cory J also notes this "potential" (at 772) discussing McLachlin J's judgment in *Winnipeg*.

[176] [1999] 2 Can SCR at 799.

ramifications across the board of maternal conduct. Indeed, whilst she appears implicitly to accept that the idea of liability in the driving context would *not* unacceptably infringe upon a pregnant woman's rights,[177] her "difficulty" is that she considers that the common law cannot secure this limited end. Those who wish to pursue this route, she says, must:[178]

> "cast themselves on the horns of a dilemma: either they must shape the common law in a way that has the potential to render pregnant women liable for a broad range of conduct and unjustifiably trammel liberty and rights to equal treatment; or they accept category-based restrictions antithetical to the common law method. Legislative action, the route chosen in England, can accomplish the limited goal of permitting children like the respondent to access motor vehicle liability insurance without these negative consequences. In these circumstances, the courts should not intervene."

Ultimately then, the problem is not one of legal principle, nor (so far as driving goes) of public policy, but rather of *legal method*. Importantly, this in turn explains the ways in which the majority and the dissent *define* the issue in *Dobson*. This point about legal method is made less forcefully in Justice Cory's judgment, notwithstanding his apparent endorsement of the idea of a legislatively crafted exception for damage caused to a child upon its birth as the result of its mother's negligent driving.[179] Taking note of the UK's Congenital Disabilities (Civil Liability) Act 1976, which (as noted previously) grants exemption from tort liability for prenatal harm to pregnant women *except* in the course of negligent driving, he suggests that it is inappropriate for a court to draw support from this for maternal liability in the driving context in the light of the highly sensitive public policy and insurance issues at stake.[180] Indeed, he notes that the UK exception was the "direct result"[181] of compulsory insurance and the policy that victims of road accidents should be compensated.

It is instructive to compare the approach of the New South Wales Court of Appeal in *Lynch* when faced with the same problem. The trial court judge, Grove J, queried on what basis the class to whom injury which was foreseeable could rationally exclude a pregnant woman's own unborn child but not that of another:[182]

> "As the test of liability for the consequence of negligent conduct includes foreseeing that injury might be caused to the unborn children of others I can see no reason for artificial exclusion of foreseeability of injury to one's own unborn. The definition of a class to

---

[177] "Those who urge intrusion of common law tort liability into the lives of pregnant women do not, in the main, contest the impermissibility of broad interference with the rights of women to make decisions about their bodies and lives. They seek rather to reduce the intrusion on the autonomy of the pregnant woman to the point where the infringement on her liberty and equality interests *is acceptable*." [1999] 2 Can SCR at 801, my emphasis.

[178] *Ibid.*, 802.

[179] *Ibid.*, 794.

[180] *Ibid.*, 791.

[181] *Ibid.*, 792.

[182] [1992] 3 Med LR at 66.

whom injury is foreseeable could not rationally specify only the unborn of others in distinction from the unborn of a woman's own."

In terms of principle, the discussion has indeed indicated that there does not seem to be an answer as regards the driving context. Thus, giving the judgment in the Court of Appeal, Clarke JA noted that given that a third party can be liable for injuries to an unborn child in the context of negligent driving (*Watt* v. *Rama* (1972))[183], then the concept of foreseeability cannot do the work of excluding a pregnant woman's liability, consistent with Grove J's point above.[184] (In this way, as John Seymour has noted, we can see that English, Australian and Canadian law rely heavily on the notion of foreseeability and associated concepts as compared with the US decisions considered earlier, which were strongly concerned with the status of the fetus.[185]) Rather, the answer lies in public policy and thus a careful examination of whether public policy is for or against maternal liability for prenatal harm. Up to this point, the judgment is broadly in line with both Justices Cory and Major in *Dobson*. The main reason which had been put forward against liability in *Lynch* was that it would be contrary to public policy. Turning to face the public policy issue, Clarke JA suggests that there are:[186]

"different policy considerations which arise in the context of a claim based on negligent driving and those which may arise, for instance, in a claim based on the mother's taking of unjustified risks of physical injury."

Regarding the former context, it was necessary to consider the social policy underlying the Motor Vehicles (Third Party Insurance) Act 1942 (as amended), which consists in the twin ideas of compensation (subject to contributory negligence) and compulsory insurance contributions. Given the policy of the Act, Clarke JA submits that it is hard to see how policy can be against maternal liability for negligent driving. Indeed, he observes that the arguments concerning natural sentiment and social acceptability which persuaded the English Law Commission not to allow a child *generally* to sue its mother for prenatal injuries are irrelevant in the context of negligent driving.[187] Further, and critically, he notes that to allow such a claim would not require the scrutiny of a mother's conduct during pregnancy. Rather, courts would only have to engage in the factual inquiry, to which they are well suited, of whether the mother drove negligently.

Is the "category-based restriction" crafted in *Lynch* so clearly "antithetical to the common law method" (*per* McLachlin J) when it is the legitimate consideration of

---

[183] (1972) VR 353.

[184] In the light of the way in which Lord Bridge in *Caparo* likens "proximity" to "neighbourhood", it is unlikely that proximity could be denied also on the *Caparo* test. Rather, a duty of care would most likely be denied on the basis that it would not be "fair, just and reasonable" to impose a duty on the pregnant woman. [1990] 2 AC 574 at 617–18.

[185] J Seymour, *Childbirth and the Law*, 164. This difference of approach has one important difference of result: the approach of some US courts permits an action for a stillbirth under a wrongful death Act, whereas the Canadian, English and Australian approach does not.

[186] [1992] 3 Med LR at 71.

[187] *Ibid.*, 72.

public policy which does the restricting? Not necessarily. After all, whilst the *Kamloops* test closely mirrors the two-stage formula laid down in *Anns*, with the decision in *Caparo* English law now gives "greater significance to the more traditional *categorisation* of distinct and recognisable situations as guides to the existence, the scope and the limits of the varied duties of care which the law imposes".[188] Thus, looking back to *Donoghue* v. *Stevenson*,[189] whether one prefers the approach of Lord Atkin (reflected in *Anns*) or Lord MacMillan (reflected in *Caparo*), both have had their defenders.

Hence one must press again the question why in *Dobson* the Supreme Court of Canada could not likewise have plumped for the option of saying that public policy is not against maternal liability in the driving context but is against liability in other areas, as Clarke JA clearly did. Given the difficulties explored earlier, it is submitted that if the Court had taken this approach its judgment would have been both clearer and stronger, making it less subject to Justice Major's stinging criticism that where public policy is held out as being against liability it must be "clear and compelling",[190] which arguably it was in the Court's decision in *Winnipeg*. But the Court seems to have been motivated by a real fear that the public policy arguments against a generalised maternal duty of care would *not* be made out in the future, notwithstanding that they clearly *could* be and *were* being made out also on behalf of the infant respondent in the case.[191] In many ways, Justice Major is thus right to allege that "slippery-slope and floodgate types of argument"[192] muddied the majority waters. Indeed, despite discussing both the English and NSW positions, the Court did not make clear that the NSW Court of Appeal in *Lynch* had faced the same kinds of dilemmas and yet clearly chosen the path of distinguishing the negligent driving context. It is thus somewhat misleading that Cory J notes in relation to *Lynch* that, given the insurance rationale, there was no need to decide whether a pregnant woman owed a duty of care to her "foetus or subsequently born child".[193] Rather, as we have seen, given Clarke JA's assessment of how easy it is to satisfy foreseeability as regards the pregnant woman's driving and the unborn child, the implication was that there must be a *prima facie* duty which is then subject to the policy issues discussed. Yet Clarke JA does not seem to have been concerned, as Cory J was, that a judicial finding of maternal tort liability in the driving context would require legislative amendment. Thus, somewhat unclearly, Cory J states:[194]

---

[188] [1990] 2 AC 605 at 618, *per* Lord Bridge, my emphasis. Lord Bridge cited Brennan J in *Sutherland Shire Council* v. *Heyman* (1985) 157 CLR 424 to the effect that the law of negligence should proceed "incrementally and by analogy with established categories".

[189] [1932] AC 562.

[190] [1999] 2 Can SCR at 813.

[191] Following the judgment, the infant respondent's counsel, Ann MacAulay, was reported as saying: "It was always our view . . . this could be restricted to the specific facts, like motor vehicle accidents. It was never the intention for this to bloom into the right to [*sic*] an unborn child to be able to sue its mother for various things that she had done while pregnant. We would not want that broader application to be allowed, because that would unduly restrict women's rights." *The Lawyer's Weekly*, 23 July 1999, 9.

[192] [1999] 2 Can SCR at 811.

[193] *Ibid.*, 795.

[194] *Ibid.*, 798–9, my emphases.

"If this approach were to be adopted, the provincial legislatures *would be required* to amend their legislative compensation schemes for motor vehicle accidents. Any such amendment *might well be required* to specify that it constituted an exception to the general rule of maternal tort immunity for prenatal negligence, and that the injured child could not recover damages above the limit established by the insurance scheme."

The unclear language suggests uncertainty as to whether or not legislative amendment would truly be necessary, rather than simply about the reasons for such amendment.

3. *The Role of Insurance*

Although the relationship between tort and insurance is extremely complex and cannot be pursued in detail here, it is worth reflecting briefly on the insurance point in its own right. Justice Cory emphasises that the law of tort "is not, and should not be, result-oriented in this manner", citing Canadian authority[195] and the House of Lords' 1957 authority of *Lister* v. *Romford Ice & Cold Storage*,[196] in which Viscount Simonds observed that the existence of insurance cannot be determinative of the rights of the parties. Is insurance determining the right of the born child to sue in *Lynch*? In one sense the answer is yes, but in another sense surely no: as we have seen, Clarke JA first concedes that there is a *prima facie* duty of care owed by the pregnant woman to the born alive child, but then holds that public policy—which includes but is not limited to the insurance issue (recall that he had observed that the issue of negligent driving raises different policy questions from that of lifestyle choices)—is not against the duty. In other words, it is not that insurance *per se* determines the existence of the duty. Thus, it is not clear that liability insurance is being used as what Jane Stapleton (critical of the reliance upon insurance in arguments concerning tortious liability) has dubbed an "independent factor" or the "make-weight factor" in the determination of whether there exists a duty of care.[197] Moreover, a narrow and clear-cut exception providing for maternal liability in the context of negligent driving, such as that developed in *Lynch*, clearly supervenes upon prior *legislative* initiatives regarding driving generally. In this way, maternal common law liability for negligent driving would not be akin to the naïve development of judicial intervention in the life of the pregnant glue-sniffer advocated by the dissenting justices in *Winnipeg* and criticised by Justice McLachlin therein.

In fact, the Court in *Dobson* is in the awkward position of both *relying* on public policy (to preclude liability) and *distancing* itself from it (by saying that it is for

---

[195] *Hamstra (Guardian ad litem of)* v. *British Columbia Rugby Union* [1997] 1 SCR 1092, 1108.

[196] [1957] 1 All ER 125, 133.

[197] J Stapleton, "Tort, Insurance and Ideology", (1995) 58 *MLR* 820, 827. She argues that we should be wary of arguments based upon the relevance of insurance or insurability in that, in addition to being indeterminate, they can suppress any corrective justice or deterrence goals of tort liability. In turn this can prompt the argument that tort is a surrogate for first-party insurance, which then highlights the need to retrench tort entitlements. (At 843.)

the legislature to fix liability in these circumstances if it deems fit). If the underlying worries about common law method are persuasive (which seems uncertain given decisions such as *Lynch*), such that a finding of liability could or would have constituted a risky precedent encouraging findings of maternal liability beyond the driving context, it is submitted that it would have been preferable, whilst denying the child's claim, openly to acknowledge that public policy is not against maternal liability in the driving context but hold, for reasons of legal method, that it was for Parliament to craft the solution. Instead, however, the Court has effectively put itself in the position of holding that public policy is both for and against liability, caught, as it was, between policy considerations it was obliged to consider under *Kamloops* on the one hand and concerns about the analogical workings of the common law on the other. In these ways, the decision represents a lesson to other courts and to legislatures in general. To be sure, given that Cory J (supported by McLachlin J) endorses the idea of the legislature allowing for maternal liability in this context, observing that "if it were carefully drafted, such legislation would not constitute an undue intrusion into the privacy and autonomy rights of pregnant women",[198] it is very difficult to reconcile this recommendation with his apparent stance that at the same time it would be contrary to public policy: thus, how does the endorsement of a legislative exception for maternal liability for driving fit with the idea of driving being integral to parenting? It is submitted that the nub of the problem thus lies in Justice Cory's, but especially Justice McLachlin's, identification of the "potential" of such liability to impinge on other areas of a woman's life in future cases. Hence the ultimate problem in *Dobson* is one of uncertainty about the use to which such a precedent would be put. This is the answer to the earlier question of what is the "real difficulty" about a finding of liability in Justice Cory's mind.

4. Moving beyond Driving

The discussion so far has not questioned the appropriateness of the judgment that, beyond the driving context, a maternal duty of prenatal care is unsuitable. Nevertheless, if this is so, then some reasons must be offered. One way to start would be further to reflect on *part* of the reason why liability is appropriate in the driving context, namely the insurance position. Even if the existence of insurance is *a* reason for imposing, or rather not *not* imposing liability in the driving context, this in turn makes us ponder why third-party insurance has become compulsory in the driving context. The legislative initiatives touched upon in this discussion have clearly been swayed by the need to compensate blameless victims. No doubt this in turn was motivated by certain characteristics of road-traffic accidents, including the likelihood and incidence of their occurrence and the serious nature of the injuries often sustained in them. Further, establishing causation is generally unproblematic in road-traffic accidents. By contrast, the English Law Commission con-

---

[198] [1999] 2 Can SCR at 794.

sidered that problems of proof were an issue counting against maternal liability for damage caused by such activities as smoking and the consumption of alcohol.[199]

a) *The Distinction between General Duties and Duties of Parenthood*

Let us return to consider the distinction between general duties and duties of parenthood accepted by the Court of Appeal in *Dobson* and relied upon by the infant respondent before the Supreme Court. Touching upon arguments put forward by Ian Kerr in response to the judgment of the Court of Appeal in *Dobson*,[200] Justice Cory points out that a general duty would impose tortious liability on mothers for prenatal injuries in any situation in which a general duty is owed to third parties. In this vein, Kerr had argued that the Court of Appeal's distinction between duties owed to the general public and duties pertaining to parenthood, far from narrowing the issue in *Dobson*, could allow a child to sue a pregnant woman for various lifestyle choices, such as:[201]

> "roller-blading, shopping in a crowded mall, spraying weedkiller on her crops, sailing, lighting fireworks for her children on Canada day, or any other activity where there is a risk of harm to the general public. There is nothing unique or narrow about the act of driving a car. It is just as much a lifestyle choice as any of the other activities just mentioned".

As for the last part of this quote, given that the purpose of driving (progression from A to B) is a constantly desired end and that driving is a very common choice of means to achieve that end, arguably there is at least *some* basis for distinguishing it from the activities of spraying weedkiller or sailing (in which some people will never engage throughout their lives). Although people sometimes drive just for pleasure, usually people are using their cars to proceed from A to B. But this is not my strongest point.

Rather, first I refer back to my earlier argument that we can clearly judge the standard of care as regards negligent driving. So too, as the large number of cases on point testifies, can we determine the appropriate standard of care as regards sailing accidents. The examples of roller-blading and shopping in a crowded mall are somewhat different. On the one hand roller-blading is relatively new, but not so new that the negligent roller-blader has yet to enter the law reports, as evidenced by a Canadian case in 1999 in which a roller-blading supermarket price-checker negligently ran over a customer's foot.[202] On the other hand it is not all that easy nor common to injure someone in a crowded shopping mall: that is, it might not be too difficult to knock someone over, but injury (legal damage) is unlikely unless,

---

[199] Law Commission Report No. 60 (1974), para. 55, s. 1, referring to the Bar Council's Memorandum. For discussion of related difficulties in the context of solvent abuse, see F Baylis, "Case Comment And Note: Dissenting With The Dissent: *Winnipeg Child And Family Services (Northwest Area) v. G (DF)*", 792–3: "[I]n many cases, clinical judgment about the likely harmful effects of exposure to human teratogens during pregnancy is subject to much uncertainty."

[200] I Kerr, "Pre-Natal Fictions and Post-Partum Actions", (1998) 20 *Dal LJ* 237.

[201] [1999] 2 Can SCR at 788. Kerr, "Pre-Natal Fictions", 270–1.

[202] *Blunt* v. *Westfair Foods Ltd* (1999) 88 ACWS (3d) 92.

say, the person is elderly (and, for example breaks a hip). In both cases, however, whilst notions of the standard of care may be a little hazy, they are not incapable of determination. Likewise with the negligent lighting of fireworks. And consider again, in somewhat different terms, the example of a hasty cyclist who knocks a small child into a river. If the cyclist had instead been a pregnant woman who fell off her bike in the collision, thereby causing injury to her unborn child in addition to the child she knocks into the river, there would be no problem about determining the legal standard of care. Perhaps this is because one does not have the *right* to engage in such conduct in a way which risks physical harm to others. If so, then it is unclear why it would be problematic, as Kerr clearly implies, for a pregnant woman *also* to be liable to her unborn child when she is already taking care to avoid injury to third parties. That is, it is not that her *rights* would thereby be infringed.

b) *The Social Context of Pregnancy*

Importantly, however, the situation is different if the pregnant woman is cycling, sailing or roller-blading *on her own* (clearly she cannot shop in a crowded mall on her own). Perhaps she is mountain-biking on deserted hills, sailing in an otherwise empty ocean or practising her roller-blading in a huge and miraculously empty carpark. The point now is that *she cannot do these things alone*: her unborn child is always with her. This is what we might identify as a further aspect of what I have previously dubbed the "social context" of pregnancy, the emphasis here being on the 24 hours-a-day, nine-months-long nature of gestation. This important aspect of pregnancy was highlighted by Justice Cunningham in the Supreme Court of Illinois case of *Stallman* v. *Youngquist* as standing against maternal liability for prenatal harm:[203]

> "As opposed to the third-party defendant, it is the mother's *every waking and sleeping moment* which, for better or worse, shapes the prenatal environment which forms the world for the developing fetus. That this is so is not a pregnant woman's fault: it is a fact of life. In practice, *the reproduction of our species is necessarily carried out by individual women who become pregnant*. No one lives but that he or she was at one time a fetus in the womb of its mother."

In this light, for a pregnant woman to be liable to her unborn child when she "solo" cycles, sails or skates (without third parties present) would be unjust because she can never be without her unborn child: pregnancy is a state of constant "duo". Further, given the place of pregnancy and reproduction within our social life—the fact that pregnancy is essential to the continuation of society—it is hard (we might say unjust) to defend the idea that women should be legally compelled to consider the impact of all of their actions upon their unborn child. Very interestingly the point is also taken up by Justice McLachlin in *Dobson* who observes:[204]

---

[203] 531 NE 2d at 360, my emphases.
[204] [1999] 2 Can SCR at 800, my emphases.

"In addition to the *usual duties of prudent conduct imposed on all* who engage in life's various activities, pregnant women would be subject to a host of *additional* restrictions. Any other individual can *avoid being a tortfeasor* by isolating himself or herself from other members of society. The pregnant woman has no such choice. She carries her foetus 24 hours a day, seven days a week."

As she notes, it does not answer the issue to say that women choose pregnancy.[205] This is consistent with pregnancy's "social context".[206]

These passages represent the crux of the matter as regards the current discussion: notice, first, that Justice McLachlin implies that we are all subject to duties of prudent conduct, presumably where our conduct carries a risk of harm to others; notice, second, the identification of the "additional restrictions" which would be imposed on pregnant women by virtue of the fact that they can never be "alone". Importantly, her reasoning in fact implies that there would be no injustice in a pregnant woman owing duties to her unborn child in those contexts where she *also* owes a duty to third parties: here she would be subject to the duties of prudent conduct to which we are all subject. This is consistent with aspects of the reasoning of the dissenting justices in *Bonte* v. *Bonte* noted earlier.[207] The problem as regards the unborn child is that the woman can never put herself in such a position as to avoid the risk of harm to "another". Thus, whereas a *non*-pregnant woman on her own is free to do whatever she wants (in senses relevant to the current discussion), if a pregnant woman were to owe a legal duty to her unborn child also through her conduct "on her own", this would intrude upon what Justice McLachlin identifies as her "liberty interest".[208] On the argument of the majority which she endorses it would also infringe a pregnant woman's legal right to privacy, discussed below.

Justice McLachlin, who stresses that the common law must reflect the Canadian Charter of Rights and Freedoms, also argues that maternal liability to the unborn child in such contexts would violate a woman's right to equal treatment, a line of reasoning somewhat surprisingly not addressed in *Winnipeg*.[209] In this way, her argument appears in line with the approach the Canadian Supreme Court has taken regarding equality matters. Thus in *Brooks* v. *Canada Safeway Ltd* Dickson CJ stated:[210]

"That those who bear children and benefit society as a whole thereby should not be economically or socially disadvantaged seems to bespeak the obvious. It is only women who

---

[205] By contrast, note the statement of the (partly) dissenting Belson AJ in *Re AC*, that "the expectant mother has placed herself in a *special class of persons* who are bringing another person into existence". 573 A 2d at 1256, my emphasis.

[206] Similarly, in *Winnipeg*, she observed that a pregnant woman's "liberty is intimately and inescapably bound to her unborn child". 152 DLR (4th) at 209. She also noted "the right of every person to live and move in freedom", "the most sacred sphere of personal liberty." *Ibid.*, 214.

[207] Brock CJ and Batchelder J, 616 A 2d at 468.

[208] [1999] 2 Can SCR at 799.

[209] For criticisms of this lack in *Winnipeg* see S Rodgers, "Case Comment And Note: *Winnipeg Child And Family Services v. DFG*: Juridical Interference with Pregnant Women in the Alleged Interest of the Fetus", (1998) 36 *Alberta L Rev* 711.

[210] [1989] SCR 1219, 1243–4.

bear children; no man can become pregnant . . . it is unfair to impose all the costs of pregnancy upon one half of the population. It is difficult to conceive that distinctions or discriminations based upon pregnancy could ever be regarded as other than discrimination based upon sex, or that restrictive statutory conditions applicable only to pregnant women did not discriminate against them as women."

Thus, the Court suggests that laws aimed specifically at pregnant women are likely to be discriminatory and, as noted in chapter five, it may be that my "social context" argument is related to equality issues. In *Dobson* Justice McLachlin notes that Canadians generally "enjoy the full right to decide what they will eat or drink, where they will work and other personal matters".[211] Clearly, these are matters which cannot cause physical harm to others in the absence of pregnancy. In other words, it seems that those "duties of prudent conduct imposed on all" do not invoke equality issues: only those things which matter (in the relevant sense) because a woman is pregnant (for instance, what not to eat and drink and so forth) can do so. Discussion of the social context of pregnancy has revealed that issues of equal treatment are also raised if a pregnant woman sails, skates or cycles (and so on) "on her own", but would not be if she were to engage in these activities in situations where others might get hurt.

My conclusion regarding the distinction between general duties and lifestyle choices, and I tentatively submit that it is not in fact inconsistent with Justice McLachlin's arguments when the implications of these are teased out, is that so far as general conduct which might or does harm third parties is concerned (because they are present), it would not intrude upon a pregnant woman's *rights* to hold her liable for the same conduct to her unborn child for prenatal injury. (This is not to say, however, that I think such liability would necessarily be a good thing, for instance if it would increase the stresses of pregnancy: see below.) Thus, if there is potential liability to others in a sailing accident caused by a pregnant woman, so might there be liability to a pregnant woman's unborn child. (It matters not whether others are actually injured: the point is that she is already taking care to avoid injury.) Before it is objected that this argument hinges upon the "serendipitous coincidence" that others "stood to be injured", it should be recalled that where others stand to be injured, there are no public policy reasons standing in the way of liability so as to negative an *already existing prima facie* maternal duty of care towards her unborn child. Importantly, the "social context" of pregnancy is not implicated in these examples.

Conversely, and critically, the "social context" point that a pregnant woman cannot avoid being a tortfeasor ultimately amounts to a strong argument of public policy against liability regarding conduct where no third parties were or might have been injured (because they were not present). Importantly, in relation to activities which a pregnant woman does on her own but which might harm others when others are present (for example, sailing, mountain-biking and so on), ultimately it is not so much that we could not judge the standard of care as regards any *one*

---

[211] [1999] 2 Can SCR at 800.

instance of the conduct as that the indications are (and I return to this) that it would be *unjust* to impose a duty from which the pregnant woman could not escape until the end of the pregnancy and of which she would to a great extent be mindful, perhaps more so than most of us in our "duties of prudent conduct" about the prospect of injury to third parties.

In practice, however, making distinctions in court between activities conducted with and without the presence of third parties would be prone to difficulty and hence *judicial* determination of these issues would be inappropriate. In this sense, the dissenting justices in *Bonte* v. *Bonte*, upon whom the majority in *Dobson* rely, were right to be concerned that efforts to distinguish between maternal acts which were common torts on the one hand and those invoking privacy interests on the other would "result in arbitrary line-drawing resulting in inconsistent verdicts."[212] Once again this highlights the connection between a clearly defined exception of maternal liability for negligent driving and previous legislative initiatives.

As an additional practical matter related to issues of social policy, there may or may not be insurance to call upon vis-à-vis, for instance, Ian Kerr's examples of weedkilling, shopping in a crowded mall or roller-blading: in the roller-blading case cited earlier, the price-checker was clearly acting in the course of his employment, since price-checkers wore roller-blades to increase efficiency in what was a very large store; hence there was never a question about the identity of the (insured) defendant, namely the store itself. The presence or absence of compulsory insurance is, I have suggested, related to the potential incidence and severity of certain kinds of accident. The absence of insurance in certain contexts may thus be quite *reasoned* in terms of public policy (very few accidents in crowded shopping malls) but *arbitrary* in terms of justice and hence unjust (a blameless victim goes without compensation).

5. Compensation—to Whom?

Returning to the driving context, although Cory J expresses concern about a pregnant woman being liable for her operation of her car when she is alone,[213] I submit that this is actually a case in which to know that she is insured when driving also as regards injury to her unborn child would actually *decrease* her anxiety (actually a benefit to fetal health)[214], as the English Law Commission apparently

---

[212] 616 A 2d at 468.

[213] [1999] 2 Can SCR at 780.

[214] One recent study found an association between maternal anxiety in pregnancy and increased uterine artery resistance index, suggesting a mechanism by which the mother's psychological state may affect the development of the fetus. "Although there are many contributors to fetal growth and birth weight, reduced blood flow through the uterine arteries could partially explain why women who are anxious during pregnancy tend to have smaller babies. It is also possible that this mechanism is related to some of the findings . . . which have linked low birth weight to a later predisposition to coronary heart disease." JMA Teixeira, NM Fisk and V Glover, "Association Between Maternal Anxiety in Pregnancy and Increased Uterine Artery Resistance Index: Cohort Based Study", (1999) 318 *BMJ* 153, 157 (footnotes citing literature on point omitted).

considered in relation to a pregnant woman's driving generally.[215] After all, it is not as if she would *want* to crash—alone or otherwise—or have any *interest* in doing so. Nor is it clear why she would have any desire to assert a right to privacy or equal treatment in this context. Indeed, might it not in *some* way be argued that a right to equal treatment implies that a pregnant woman should be protected when she harms her unborn child while driving and thereby from the situation in which her child goes without compensation? In turn, this would be consistent with the fact that, as Justice Cory notes, "in this particular case, the material interests of the mother and child are aligned, notwithstanding the fact that their legal relationship is adversarial".[216] Given the compulsory insurance in such cases, to allow a child to sue its mother would be to direct financial resources to, rather than away from, the family and hence there is no reason to think that such a claim would threaten family harmony. Not surprisingly, once again this distinguishes maternal from third-party liability for prenatal harm. What these reflections bring to the fore is that ultimately to *some* extent, given the physical, emotional and financial costs of caring for a disabled child, it is the (previously) pregnant woman who is being compensated here, such that in some sense ideas related to first-party insurance rumble confusingly beneath the surface.

In turn, however *unlikely* this may be, if in the future the issue of maternal lia-bility for prenatal injury beyond the driving context were to receive Canadian or other legislative attention, it might be appropriate to consider whether—apart from driving—there are any other contexts where pregnant women would be *reassured*, rather than threatened, by the knowledge that their unborn children could recover as a result of their negligence. The answer might well be in the negative, but at least an important issue would be identified and faced head-on. Whether public policy is ultimately for or against a pregnant woman's *prima facie* duty of care toward her unborn child must surely be related to this question. In turn, this will be connected at some point with the issue of insurance and the question of who is being insured.

To the extent that *at some level* compensation benefits the once-pregnant mother one cannot help but think that public policy could be against a child recovering for damage due to his mother's smoking (assuming this could be cast as negligence) subject perhaps to broad social and political but also recent medical[217] arguments about addiction. By contrast, if many pregnant women could only avoid prenatal

---

[215] [1999] 2 Can SCR at 792, as noted by Cory J.

[216] *Ibid.*, 795.

[217] A recent report published by the Tobacco Advisory Group of the Royal College of Physicians suggests a major change in attitude is required by doctors, other health professionals and society gener-ally toward smoking, highlighting the "need to acknowledge nicotine addiction as a major medical and social problem" on a par with addiction to particular hard drugs such as cocaine and heroin. Z Kmietowicz, "Doctors Told to Treat Nicotine Addiction as a Disease", (2000) 320 *BMJ* 397, 397. The *BMJ* editorial in the same issue ("Nicotine Addiction Should be Recognised as the Central Problem of Smoking", 391) observes: "The central theme of the report, . . . is that cigarette smoking should be understood first and foremost as a manifestation of nicotine addiction. Nicotine is as addictive as 'hard' drugs such as heroin. Smokers usually start the habit as children, are addicted to nicotine by the time they are adults, and thereafter the choice to stop becomes an illusion. Thus, although two thirds of smokers want to quit, and about a third try each year, only 2% succeed." *Ibid.*, 391.

injury by spending most of the day lying down (as sometimes occurs), would we not, given the likely difficulties of fulfilling this prescription, want to allow recovery and access to insurance? (Whether we could afford this is another matter.) As regards these examples, the implication is that compensation would be *in*appropriate where avoidance was (supposedly) possible and vice versa. Given that tort law may well find negligence in the first but not the second case (given the "utility" of not always lying down here), the issue of maternal liability for prenatal harm clearly calls for a very particular study of the purposes (if any) of liability on the one hand and the appropriate nature of insurance in this context on the other.

Here it is helpful to return again to the road-traffic context, which Jane Stapleton has noted is atypical of tort scenarios in two respects: first, given that both parties are keen not to be injured, the concept of "fault" has an artificial ring to it; second, people tend to think their chances of being injured by "carelessness" are not much different from their chances of causing injury, such that the pools of potential defendants and plaintiffs are almost identical. This means that although compulsory liability insurance is "technically" intended to cover situations where injury is negligently caused to *others*, it can seem tantamount to a system in which drivers actually contribute to cover the risk of *themselves* being injured. The result is that liability insurance can here seem equivalent to first-party cover against the risk of being injured, notwithstanding that compensation is fully restorative. In this light, she suggests, it could well be appropriate to replace the cumbersome and costly tort system in this context with a system of *actual* first-party insurance covering all road-traffic injuries rather than only those caused by fault.[218]

These thoughts are intriguing for my purposes for two reasons. First, given that at some level compensation for the disabled child aids the once-pregnant woman, it seems to highlight the sense in which compulsory liability insurance and the associated legal liability of the pregnant driver may protect *herself* when she injures the fetus through the negligent conduct of her car. Second, regarding the issue of prenatal harm *beyond* the driving context, although I submit, in the light of this discussion, that maternal legal liability is probably inappropriate, if the issue of maternally caused prenatal harm beyond the driving context were ever to become of sufficient concern, it may be that some form of quasi-first-party insurance for prenatal injury caused by a pregnant woman could be in the interests of both the pregnant woman and her unborn child. This is not to deny that insurance companies would clearly have their own views as to what risks (and hence what maternal conduct) they would be willing to insure against. (Given that such a development would mean recovery rather than no recovery for the pregnant woman and her family, arguably it is less subject to Peter Cane's valid criticism that Patrick Atiyah's proposal to substitute a system of first-party insurance for third-party insurance is "politically naïve and ethically problematic",[219] in that (apart

---

[218] J Stapleton, "Tort, Insurance and Ideology", 842.

[219] P Cane, *Atiyah's Accidents, Compensation and the Law*, 6th edn. (London: Butterworths, 1999) 423, discussing P Atiyah, *The Damages Lottery* (Oxford: Hart Publishing, 1997) ch. 8.

from the road-traffic context where Atiyah advocates compulsory cover) many people would be left without cover.)

6. Protecting Maternal Conduct through Privacy

I have accepted that if a pregnant woman were to owe a legal duty to her unborn child through her conduct *on her own* this would infringe upon her legal right to privacy as the majority, supported by Justice McLachlin, argues in *Dobson*.

It is striking to reflect upon the types of maternal choices which, whilst being protected by a privacy right, may or may not be thought justifiable in the light of possible fetal harm. For instance, it would be very hard to determine, morally or legally, that a woman who works at a highly stressful job during pregnancy (potentially thereby causing prenatal stress),[220] or is heavily engaged in caring for a family or some other meaningful activity is behaving *unreasonably* in terms of the language of negligence. But arguably we *can* make this judgment of the real woman who smokes or the hypothetical one who regularly solo bungee-jumps during this time. As with the pregnant woman who gets much pleasure from smoking, we might say of our imaginary passionate solo bungee-jumper that she has a misplaced sense of the importance of her activity compared with her child to be (although this would require more fleshing out than space allows), particularly given that here the woman can avoid the bungee-jumping, however frustrating that might be, for the duration of her pregnancy. In this sense, arguably "risky sports" are the farthest removed from any possible protection of the "social context" argument. Similarly, with some effort and medical help, women probably can—albeit with difficulty where heavily addicted—avoid cigarettes and alcohol during this time, thereby placing smoking and drinking within the shadowy penumbra of the social context point. But it is not clear that a pregnant woman *should* avoid working during pregnancy. In this case, ideally she will gain personal satisfaction in addition to financial remuneration; moreover, were she to give up work during this time, she could well have difficulties in re-entering the workforce later on. Thus, it does not seem that to work during pregnancy would be to have the misplaced sense of value which could plausibly be said to attach to bungee-jumping or smoking during the same period. These points may perhaps helpfully be related to Ronald Dworkin's distinction between experiential and critical interests,[221] with a woman's work

---

[220] On fetal harm through maternal work see the important US Supreme Court case of *Automobile Workers* v. *Johnson Controls* (1991) 113 L Ed 158, (concerning the illegality of an employer's gender-based fetal protection policy) and associated literature, e.g. M Thompson, "After *Re S*", (1994) 2 *Med L Rev* 127, 141 *ff*; E Phillips, "The Status of Sex-specific Fetal Protection Policies", (1992) 57 *Missouri L Rev* 979 and references therein.

[221] R Dworkin, *Life's Dominion: An Argument about Abortion and Euthanasia* (London: Harper Collins, 1993) 201–2. I cannot explore this in detail here, but Dworkin's distinction is between "experiential interests" in such things as "playing softball, perhaps, cooking or eating well, or watching football, or seeing *Casablanca* for the twelfth time, or walking in the woods in October, or listening to *The Marriage of Figaro*, or sailing fast just off the wind, or just working hard at something", "pleasures [which] are essential to a good life" on the one hand and, on the other, "interests that it does make [people's] life genuinely better to satisfy, interests that they would be mistaken, and genuinely worse off, if they did

falling within the latter category. The point is that working or caring for other family members may be reflective of a person's critical interests, whereas smoking and drinking, hang-gliding and bungee-jumping are highly experiential in character. (Nevertheless, although morally these latter activities may be hard to defend during pregnancy (thus we have a hold on "unreasonableness" here),[222] in England (in ways discussed below) and Canada, a legal right of privacy would possibly step in to protect them from the reach of law.) Here the maternal–fetal conflict would then become a question of the appropriateness or otherwise of enforcing moral obligations.[223] Note that although it would theoretically be possible to judge that positive obligations such as eating a healthy and balanced diet are reasonable— given that such a duty would not conflict with deeply personal beliefs and choices—the ability to fulfil such a duty will be related to income and education.[224] In this connection, Margaret Brazier suggests that as regards concern about the impact on women's lives of maternal liability, the greatest impact would likely be on the disadvantaged.[225] In conjunction with a discussion of the Congenital Disabilities (Civil Liability) Act 1976 Brazier also notes the impact that *paternal* smoking may have on the fetus, or that nicotine or other toxins may have on sperm pre-conceptually. With regard to the latter she suggests that arguments that either women or men have a duty to protect their reproductive health to ensure that they

---

not recognize". He continues: "Convictions about what helps to make a life good on the whole are convictions about those more important interests. They represent critical judgments rather than just experiential preferences."

[222] Note, however, the English Law Commission's doubts regarding the possibility of defining a standard of care in pregnancy. Law Commission Report No. 60 (1974). In para. 55, s. 1, the Commission cited the Bar Council's Memorandum: "From a practical standpoint, the difficulty and unseemliness of some possible allegations of negligence in the ante-natal regime are discouraging. Do smoking and gin-drinking count as negligence in a pregnant mother?" Contrast the approach of D Meyers, who apparently considers, as did Miller J in *Dobson*, that the issue can be approached in *logical* terms: "The fetus, once born, may . . . sue third parties for negligently causing personal injury . . . Given this precedent, an action imposing legal liability on the mother for prenatal injury proved to have resulted from poor maternal habits, or drug use, may only depend on clear proof of causation after birth." D Meyers, *The Human Body and the Law* (Edinburgh: Edinburgh University Press, 1990) 13, footnote omitted.

[223] But note that L Doswald-Beck "tentatively" suggests that the European Court of Human Rights might make use of the test that "before an interference with private life is found amounting to the violation of the Convention, the activity wished to be pursued must be something of a serious nature, the forbidding or regulation of which clearly has an adverse effect on the applicant's development of his personality or recognition thereof". L Doswald-Beck, "The Meaning of the 'Right to Respect for Private Life' under the European Convention on Human Rights", (1983) 4 *HRLJ* 283, 309.

[224] In this regard, H Draper has suggested that undue attention is paid to the issue of smoking during pregnancy in that, although harm occurs to the fetus through maternal smoking, the effects are much less than harms incurred through "general and grim deprivation and poverty". H Draper, "Women, Forced Caesareans and Antenatal Responsibilities", (1996) 22 *JME* 327, 331. She also suggests that the damage from passive smoking after birth may be greater than that incurred *in utero*. In relation to the latter the conduct of either parent or other members of society in public places may be implicated.

[225] M Brazier, "Parental Responsibilities, Foetal Welfare and Children's Health", in C Bridge (ed.), *Family Law Towards the New Millennium: Essays for PM Bromley* (London: Butterworths, 1997) 263–93, 274. Although the "reasonable" pregnant woman would not smoke, Brazier explores the possible difficulties in giving up nicotine: "A pregnant woman coping with other small children on a low income with a poor diet and subject to countless domestic stresses may have the desire, but lack the capacity to protect her next child from her own habit" (at 274.)

or their partner can bear healthy children "reduce women and men to breeding machines".[226]

As regards the English position, although until recently it was thought that English law would not recognise a right to privacy, we noted in chapter three that following the Court of Appeal's decision in *Douglas and others* v. *Hello! Ltd*[227] it can now be said that English law will recognise and protect a right of privacy, either derived from the equitable doctrine of breach of confidence or by virtue of the courts' obligations under the Human Rights Act 1998: by virtue of section 6, all courts will have to decide cases compatibly with the Convention (unless primary legislation prevents them from doing so or provisions under such legislation cannot be read compatibly with the Convention; moreover, on account of section 2 of the Act, courts considering a "question which has arisen in connection with a Convention right must take into account" Strasbourg jurisprudence insofar as the Court considers it "relevant to the proceedings" in question.

Article 8(1) of the Convention provides: "Everyone has the right to respect for his private and family life, his home and correspondence". The question of maternal–fetal conflict has not to date been addressed either by the Court (or the Commission when it existed). Yet, as discussed in chapter three, some insight into the relevance of this issue can be gained by considering the jurisprudence upon abortion. We saw earlier that in *Brüggemann and Scheuten* v. *Germany* (1978),[228] the Commission considered that the abortion decision invokes a woman's private life, but held that some regulation of pregnancy was nevertheless consistent with respect for private life, since pregnancy "cannot be said to pertain uniquely to the sphere of private life".[229] The implication is that abortion regulation does not need to be justified under Article 8(2).[230] Judgments about how the Strasbourg Court might respond to the situation of maternal–fetal conflict can only be speculative. Nevertheless, it is tentatively submitted that, unlike the issue of abortion, regulation of pregnancy which would impinge upon the domain of maternal conduct, including "lifestyle" choices, would be deemed to infringe upon private matters. Indeed, David Feldman has suggested that given that Article 8 requires respect for family as well as private life, "freedom of action and lifestyle" are within its scope, observing that the protection of people's putting into effect of private choices is increased by the State's positive obligation of respect.[231] Here it should be noted that the respect for private and family life (and home and correspondence) extends

---

[226] C Bridge (ed.), *Family Law Towards the New Millennium: Essays for PM Bromley* (London: Butterworths, 1997) 263–93, 276. For important work highlighting the impact of paternal conduct on the fetus's health, see C Daniels, *At Women's Expense* (Cambridge, MA: Harvard University Press, 1993).

[227] [2001] 2 All ER 289.

[228] (1981) 3 EHRR 244.

[229] *Ibid.*, para. 59.

[230] "There shall be no interference by a public authority with this right except such as is in accordance with the law and is necessary in a democratic society in the interests of national security, public safety or the economic well-being of the country, for the prevention of crime and disorder, for the protection of morals, or for the protection of the rights and freedoms of others."

[231] D Feldman, "The Developing Scope of Article 8 of the European Convention on Human Rights", [1997] 3 *EHRLR* 265, 267.

beyond the physical domain of the home, since the article has been interpreted so as to protect the aspects of these areas which are especially significant for human flourishing as regards various kinds of social activity (arguably, say, one's work).[232] (By implication, the refusal of medical treatment would come within the same category.[233])

But it is not clear that the "negative" choices under discussion here would be protected by a right to privacy, particularly in the United States. We saw in chapter four that, although much debated, arguably the US right to privacy protects a zone of procreative autonomy and thus a realm of deeply significant personal choices. It is not at all clear, however, that the *Roe* v. *Wade* protection of abortion could or should possibly extend to a pregnant woman's drug-taking, cigarette or alcohol abuse.[234] In the United States, then, other arguments, such as policy arguments touched on in this and the next chapter, might be relied on. Further, as John Seymour notes, once we appreciate what might be at stake in preventing the relevant harm—perhaps incarceration—then liberty and equality rights will be implicated.[235]

As noted in chapter four, some feminist academics, such as Carol Pateman,[236] have been strongly critical of the public/private divide associated with liberalism. Yet the maternal–fetal conflict shows that the existence of a zone of privacy can work very much to the benefit, rather than the detriment, of women. Further, as Nicola Lacey has observed, since the value of privacy is contextual it is possible to support the idea of privacy without thereby endorsing a private realm as that term is typically understood.[237] As Lacey notes, *Roe* v. *Wade* is a prime example of the law protecting an aspect of life of great importance to women. So too with the maternal–fetal conflict we can see the value in decisions about certain aspects of maternal conduct (in addition, of course, to medical treatment decisions) being considered private and thus the subject of protection, rather than interference, by the State.[238]

---

[232] D Feldman, "Privacy-related Rights and their Social Value", in P Birks (ed.), *Privacy and Loyalty* (Oxford: Oxford University Press, 1997) 15–50, 36. E.g. sexuality and marriage.

[233] For a recent discussion of Art. 8 in the medical law context, see H Nys, "Physician Involvement in a Patient's Death: a Continental European Perspective", (1999) 7 *Med L Rev* 208.

[234] For instance, J Seymour has suggested, surely rightly, that this would "trivialize *Roe* v. *Wade*". J Seymour, *Childbirth and the Law*, 224. Seymour cites the observation of one of the judges in *Whitner* v. *State* 492 SE 2d 777, 786 SC, 1997): "It strains belief for [her] to argue that using crack cocaine during pregnancy is encompassed within the constitutionally recognized right of privacy." *Whitner* is discussed *infra* these notes. See also *In the Matter of Unborn Child* (1998) 683 NYS 2d 366.

[235] J Seymour, *Childbirth and the Law*, 225.

[236] C Pateman, "Feminist Critiques of the Public/Private Dichotomy", in S Benn and G Gaus (eds.), *Public and Private in Social Life* (London: 1983); reprinted in C Pateman, *The Disorder of Women: Democracy, Feminism and Political Theory* (Stanford, CA: Stanford University Press, 1989).

[237] N Lacey, "Theory into Practice? Pornography and the Public/Private Dichotomy", in A Bottomley and J Conaghan (eds.), *Feminist Theory and Legal Strategy* (Oxford: Blackwell, 1993) 112.

[238] In this connection, one author has suggested that State intervention in pregnancy regarding medical treatment or maternal substance abuse "represents a selective focus on one aspect of parental behaviour potentially harmful to children", noting the "broad range of conduct, from passive neglect to physical abuse" regarding which the State may be slow to intervene, possibly arising from "respect for family integrity and autonomy" or the State's "traditional reluctance to intervene in the 'private' sphere", or due to a "lack of commitment to the welfare of children". The author suggests these policies "reinforce male power within the family". Note, "Rethinking (M)otherhood: Feminist Theory and State Regulation of Pregnancy", 1336–7.

7. *Postscript*—parens patriae?

Since the law of tort cannot in fact be used to prevent prenatal harm, we might finally reflect on those mechanisms which could. Here we might observe the threshold for State intervention under *parens patriae* advocated by the dissenting justices in the *Winnipeg* case, who argued that there would be a case for intervention, assuming the pregnant woman had decided to carry the fetus to term[239] (itself in fact a relatively complex issue)[240] to protect the fetus only in "extreme" cases where there was proof to the civil standard that the mother's choices and conduct would cause serious and irreparable harm to the born child.[241] In such cases, they considered that the State should intervene, choosing always the "least rights-diminishing option", with confinement being selected only where, again on proof to the civil standard, there was no other "workable or effective" solution.[242] Yet, even though the value to the pregnant woman of an activity such as solvent abuse is indefensible (in the light of the serious fetal harm), the problem with the idea of a maternal legal duty in this kind of context ultimately inheres in the undesirability of the law intruding, rather than in the question of determining the relevant standard of care of a legal duty. Indeed, the plausible objection that confinement should require proof to the criminal standard—since, as the majority notes, it is only under criminal or mental health law that the State has power to confine an individual against her will—points toward the undesirability, as a matter of policy, of legal intervention, including that subject to the "high threshold" test of the dissenting justices in *Winnipeg*.[243] Whilst the dissenting justices held that "the mother remains free to reject all suggested medical treatment",[244] as Justice McLachlin observed, to detain and not treat would have no purpose.[245] Indeed, as Andrew Grubb notes, it would be impossible to justify detention without treatment under human rights legislation.[246] According to the dissent, however, the purpose of confinement would at least be to prevent her using toxins harmful to the fetus.[247]

---

[239] 152 DLR (4th) at 237.

[240] For thoughts on the voluntariness or otherwise of the continuation of a pregnancy, see ch. 2, s. III(A)(1)(a) and L Shanner, "Case Comment And Note: Pregnancy Intervention And Models Of Maternal–Fetal Relationship: Philosophical Reflections On The *Winnipeg CFS* Dissent", (1998) 36 *Alberta L Rev* 751.

[241] F Baylis notes, however, that "even if a causal relationship could be demonstrated, the probability of harm as currently reported does not meet the standard set by Justice Major for judicial intervention. None of the available evidence shows, on a balance of probabilities, that the fetus will be seriously and irreparably harmed by solvent abuse." F Baylis, "Case Comment And Note: Dissenting With The Dissent: *Winnipeg Child And Family Services (Northwest Area) v. G (DF)*", 794.

[242] 152 DLR (4th) at 239, *per* Major J.

[243] *Ibid.*, 214.

[244] "In such cases as this any remedy of confinement must be for the purposes of treatment, and not punishment." *Ibid.*, 239, *per* Major J.

[245] "Without mandatory treatment, the order for detention would lack any foundation." *Ibid.*, 201.

[246] A Grubb, "Commentary: Detention and Treatment (Competent Adult): Pregnant Woman and Unborn Child: *Winnipeg Child and Family Services (Northwest Area) v. G (DF)*", (1999) 7 *Med L Rev* 88, 92.

[247] 152 DLR (4th) at 239.

The undesirability of such legal intrusion has been recognised in English law. The potentially enormous impact of trying to restrict the activities of a pregnant woman was noted in the Court of Appeal case of *Re F (in utero)*, introduced in chapter three. In that case, it may be recalled, a local authority sought to make a fetus a ward of court in the light of a pregnant woman's conduct. Denying the application, which would have amounted to what Robertson has dubbed "pre-birth seizure", Balcombe LJ recognised that the purpose of the application was to control the woman's actions in order to protect the fetus and pointed to academic concerns about a pregnant woman being ordered to stop smoking, drinking or any other activity capable of harming the unborn child.[248] Further, as we saw, the Supreme Court of Canada's decision in *Winnipeg* echoes the approach in *Stallman* and *Re F* in its rejection of legal intervention to protect the unborn, either through the mechanisms of tort or, as in *Re F*, wardship. Although the *Winnipeg* court suggested that it was for Parliament to extend the law in such a way if it saw fit (as Balcombe LJ had done in *Re F*), we have seen that in fact the decision in *Winnipeg* shows a sound awareness of the policy considerations which would weigh against such a development.[249] (It should be noted, however, that although legislative

---

[248] [1988] 2 All ER at 200. Compare the New Zealand case of *In the Matter of Baby P (An Unborn Child)* [1995] NZFLR 577, in which Inglis J, QC, granted the Director General of Social Welfare's (D-GSW's) application for a declaration that a pregnant 15-year-old girl, who was already under the D-GSW's custody, was in need of care and protection, in the interests of the unborn child: the baby's father, to whom the mother was still deeply attached, had previously attacked her and threatened to kid-nap and kill the baby. The legal question in point was whether the fetus (which was viable) was a "child" within the meaning of the Children, Young Persons and their Families Act 1989. In granting the dec-laration, the judge took note of the fetus's viability, coupled with the lack of any legislative intent to restrict the relevant legislation to born children. Taking note of overseas authority with regard to the lack of fetal legal personhood, he noted particularly that the question of the legal status of the fetus need not be conflated with the question of whether the fetus is a human being entitled to the law's protec-tion. In one sense, this is precisely the distinction drawn, for instance, in the United States, between the fetus's lack of legal personality on the one hand and the State's interest in its potential life on the other. Indeed, the law *does* protect the fetus, notwithstanding that it is not a legal person, in various ways that I have emphasised at different points in this book (and other ways beyond these). Thus, as Andrew Grubb notes, the judge in the *Baby P* case is correct "at one level". "Commentary: Unborn Children: 'Persons' and Maternal Conduct: *In the Matter of Baby P (An Unborn Child)*", (1997) 5 *Med L Rev* 143, 144. Yet, for the purposes of the relevant legislation in that case, the fetus's lack of legal personhood was critical and hence the judge was wrong to deem that the fetus could be protected in the manner sought. An additional factor influencing Inglis J, QC's reasoning was that in the instant case there was little, if any, conflict between the interests of the mother and the fetus. On the specific and unusual facts of the case, this appears to have been so. However, as Andrew Grubb notes, the difficulty with the case is that it "runs the risk of creating a conflict with the mother's own interests" (*ibid.*) in ways which are the sub-ject of discussion, for instance, in this chapter.

[249] Note might be made here of the key Canadian caesarean decision of *Re Baby R* (1988) 53 DLR (4th) 69. In this case, following a woman's refusal of a caesarean section, the Superintendent of Family and Child Services "apprehended" the fetus under the British Columbia Family and Child Service Act 1980, giving him the power to consent to medical treatment. On appeal, the British Columbia Supreme Court held that the fetus was not a "child" within the meaning of the Act and followed *Re F (in utero)* in its condemnation of the action under consideration here. Related cases of interest are *Re Dittrick Infant*, 263 NW 2d 37 (1977), in which the Court of Appeals of Michigan held that the Probate Court had wrongly applied a state juvenile code concerning child neglect to order custody of a fetus. The case concerned allegations of continuing physical and sexual abuse of the defendant's first child, for which criminal charges were pending; and *Re Steven S*, 126 Cal App 3d 23 (1981) (noted in ch. 3) in which

attempts in many US states have failed to set up fetal protection policies directed at a pregnant woman's use of drugs and alcohol during pregnancy, some US states have recently succeeded in enacting new child abuse legislation which permits judges to confine pregnant women who use drugs or alcohol for the duration of their pregnancies.[250])

For similar reasons, the criminal prosecution of women for taking drugs during pregnancy resulting in postnatal addiction,[251] or for failure to seek medical care resulting in fetal death or harm to the future child,[252] represents an unwise policy

the Court of Appeal of the 2nd District of California held that the fetus is not a "person" within the meaning of the statute conferring jurisdiction on the juvenile court to adjudge any "person under the age of 18 years" a dependent child of the court on certain specified grounds. Note that some courts have considered that the fetus is a person for the purposes of neglect and abuse statutes and hence that maternal conduct which harms the fetus may amount to neglect. See e.g. *Felicia B*, 543 NYS 2d (1989) 637, 638, recognising the "legal right of every human being to begin life unimpaired by physical, mental or emotional defects resulting from the neglectful acts of the parent". See also *Danielle Smith*, 128 Misc 2d (1985) 976, holding that "an unborn child is a 'person' and, thereby, entitled to the protection of" the relevant child abuse statute. (At 980, footnote omitted.)

[250] See Wis Stat ss. 48.01–.347 *et seq*. (1998) and "Child Abuse and Neglect and Child Abuse Services", 1997 Wisconsin Laws 292 (AB 463) (enacted 16 June 1998). For an excellent discussion of the ill-thought-out nature of these provisions and the potentially dramatic intrusion into the lives of pregnant women which they represent, see KA De Ville and LM Kopelman, "Fetal Protection in Wisconsin's Revised Child Abuse Law: Right Goal, Wrong Remedy". In particular, the authors note that the child abuse model, on which the Wisconsin legislation is modelled, "*by its very nature*" cannot take account of the liberty interests of people involuntarily confined, since the liberty interests of parents are not at stake in regular child abuse prevention measures. (At 335, emphasis in original.) The authors note that the US Supreme Court has described involuntary civil commitment as a "massive deprivation of liberty", requiring that the standards and procedures of confinement effect an appropriate balance between individual rights and state interests. (At 335, citing *Addington* v. *Texas*, 441 US 418 (1979).) The authors also emphasise the inadequacy of current empirical evidence to support intervention on the basis that the pregnant woman's conduct will result in serious fetal injury (at 336), as well as the generally low evidentiary standards (a judge can confine a woman for treatment if there is a "substantial risk" that the fetus's health is seriously threatened by "habitual and severe" substance use) and hence the inadequacy of the procedural safeguards of the woman's liberty (at 337). Here the authors also note the complexity of the notion of risk.

[251] See *Reyes* v. *Superior Court*, 75 Cal App 3d 214, (Cal Ct App 1977) in which the Court of Appeal of the 4th District of California had to consider whether s. 273(a)(1) of the California Penal Code was intended to refer to a fetus. The section (as it existed at the time) stated: "Any person who, under circumstances or conditions likely to produce great bodily harm or death, . . . having the care or custody of any child, . . . willfully causes or permits such child to be placed in such situation that its person or health is endangered, is punishable by imprisonment in the county jail not exceeding 1 year nor more than 10 years." The court concluded that the legislation was not meant to include the fetus, and that the legislature would have made a contrary intention clear; moreover, that the woman's prenatal conduct (of taking heroin and failing to seek prenatal care) did not constitute felonious child endangering within contemplation of the statute. By contrast, see *Whitner* v. *State of South Carolina* 492 SE 2d 777 (SC, 1997) in which the Supreme Court of South Carolina held that a woman who had taken cocaine when pregnant and who gave birth to a cocaine-affected child had rightly been charged under a child endangerment statute. Of course, legislation can also be drafted which specifically applies to the fetus, as in Minnesota, authorising intervention to prevent drug use during pregnancy (Minn Stat s. 626.5561 (1998)) or which specifically includes the fetus within child endangerment provisions, as in New Jersey (NJ Stat s. 30:4C-11 (1999)), as noted by J Seymour, *Childbirth and the Law*, 8–9. See also *supra* these notes regarding Wisconsin and South Dakota.

[252] *People* v. *Stewart*, No. M508097, slip op. (San Diego County, 1987). Ms Stewart's baby was delivered by emergency caesarean section, was born with severe brain damage and died a few months later. It was alleged that on the day of her delivery Ms Stewart stopped taking medication to delay the onset

development.[253] Indeed, in either of these cases to talk in narrow terms of a conflict between maternal and fetal rights may distract from the spectrum of conditions
affecting the problem, such as lack of available prenatal care and treatment programmes for pregnant addicts.[254] (It might be noted that it also appears unwise to
force women onto treatment programmes.[255]) Although the position in English

of labour (due to *placenta praevia*), engaged in sexual intercourse, both of which were against medical
advice, took amphetamines and refused to go to hospital when she began bleeding. She was charged
under a California child-support statute which had been amended to include the fetus so as to allow
pregnant women to collect for their prenatal care from the men by whom they had been made pregnant. The judge ruled that the statute in question was not intended to apply to a pregnant woman's conduct and the court dismissed the charges before addressing the issue of the constitutionality of
criminalising maternal prenatal conduct. For a discussion of this notorious case, see B Steinbock, *Life
Before Birth*, who reports Ms Stewart's version of events, notably her partial understanding of the medical situation and her need to care for her two other young children which made it difficult for her to
stay off her feet, as she had also been advised to do (at 137). See also, on drug-taking, the infamous
Johnson v. *State* No. 89–1765 (Fla Dist Ct App 1989), in which a Florida woman was sentenced to 15
years for unlawfully providing drugs to a minor. The prosecution argued that the wrongful delivery
occurred through the umbilical cord after the baby was born but prior to the cutting of the cord. See
also D Johnsen, "The Creation of Fetal Rights", (against the idea of such prosecutions); and J Robertson
and JD Schulman, "Pregnancy and Prenatal Harm to Offspring: The Case of Mothers with PKU",
(1987) 17 *Hastings CR* 23 (apparently in favour). After the *Stewart* case numerous prosecutions were
brought across the US for conduct allegedly harmful to the fetus, a development also influenced by the
US Supreme Court's decision in *Webster* v. *Reproductive Health Services*, 106 L Ed 2d 410 (1989) (discussed in chs. 4 and 5). Note, "Rethinking (M)otherhood: Feminist Theory and State Regulation of
Pregnancy", 1329 (citing an example). The US literature is vast.

[253] There is a considerable body of American literature devoted to the question of drug-taking during pregnancy. See e.g. S Balisy, "Maternal Substance Abuse: the Need to Provide Legal Protection for
the Fetus", (1987) 60 *Southern Calif L Rev* 1209 (in favour of criminal sanctions); DM McGinnis,
"Prosecution of Mothers of Drug Exposed Babies in Constitutional and Criminal Theory", (1990) 139
U Penn L Rev 505 (against); M McNulty, "Pregnancy Police: The Health Policy and Legal Implications
of Punishing Pregnant Women for Harm to their Fetuses", (1987–8) 16 *Rev Law and Social Change* 277
(against); CS Palmer, "The Risks of State Intervention in Preventing Prenatal Alcohol Abuse and the
Viability of an Inclusive Approach: Arguments for Limiting Punitive and Coercive Prenatal Alcohol
Abuse Legislation in Minnesota", (1999) 10 *Hastings Women's LJ* 287. Once again, the literature is vast.

[254] Note, "Rethinking (M)otherhood: Feminist Theory and State Regulation of Pregnancy", 1326.
This author has rightly noted that "[t]he argument that women are the appropriate decisionmakers with
respect to most issues surrounding pregnancy and birthing may be less compelling in the context of
substance abuse by pregnant women. By definition, addictive behaviour does not reflect the woman's
overt consideration of potential consequences for the fetus." As the author notes, however, effective
promotion of maternal and fetal health will depend on understanding the needs of pregnant addicts (at
1341). On the double vision of US drugs policy except where pregnant women are concerned, this
author notes: "Drug abusers are at once criminals and victims; drug abuse is at once a moral failing and
a disease. Consequently, the 'war on drugs' includes both prosecutions, premised on the assumption that
drug use represents a choice that may be influenced by the threat of sanctions, and treatment programs,
designed to aid the victim of addiction. In the context of drug abuse by pregnant women, however, this
dual vision is narrowed. Drug abusing mothers are considered criminal . . . The harm to the fetus does
not make the woman's addiction more criminal. Rather, it highlights the severity of her disease."
(At 1341–2.) The author cites Massing, "The Two William Bennetts", *NYRB*, 1 Mar. 1990, who
quotes a pregnant drug user: "I knew that every time I picked up that drug that I was taking a risk of
harming my baby. But the need for that drug was so great." This author's solution involves rejecting
a framework of conflicting rights in favour of a recognition of maternal–fetal dependence and hence
care and responsibility. On justice versus care and for further thoughts on this author's approach, see my
discussion and notes toward the end of ch. 4.

[255] "The general consensus in the field of addiction treatment is that many of the addict's beliefs and
attitudes must change if she is to modify her behavior, and this change will not occur in treatment if she

law is somewhat uncertain following the decision of the House of Lords in *Attorney-General's Reference (No. 3 of 1994)*,[256] it is submitted that criminal prosecutions are inherently unlikely given judicial awareness of the potential intrusions into a pregnant woman's life displayed in cases such as *Re F (in utero)*, *Re MB* and *St George's*. The question of the removal of a child from its mother following birth is more complex, given the likelihood of continued drug abuse by a mother, with the strong possibility of child neglect thereafter.[257]

is there unwillingly. Hence, whatever the ethical arguments are about coercion in such cases, there is a strong pragmatic case against coercing any addict into treatment." C McLeod and S Sherwin, "Relational Autonomy, Self-Trust, and Health Care for Patients who are Oppressed", in C MacKenzie and N Stoljar (eds.), *Relational Autonomy: Feminist Perspectives on Autonomy, Agency and the Social Self* (New York, NY: Oxford University Press, 2000) 259, 271, footnote citing supporting literature omitted. For recognition of this point see also KA De Ville and LM Kopelman, "Fetal Protection in Wisconsin's Revised Child Abuse Law": "[G]rowing evidence suggests that mandatory inpatient drug treatment programs for pregnant women may aggravate the problems they are trying to sovle [sic] because they encourage women to avoid prenatal medical care of any kind for fear of incarceration and/or the loss of their children. Such a course of action risks leading to higher levels of neonatal morbidity rather than lower levels, as the policy presumably intends." (At 338, footnote citing supporting literature omitted).

[256] [1997] 3 All ER 936 (discussed further in ch. 3). For a very helpful discussion of the uncertainties surrounding maternal liability following this case see M Brazier, "Parental Responsibilities, Foetal Welfare and Children's Health". Brazier suggests that "[t]he criminal liability of mothers . . . should be expressly clarified to rule out even the faint possibility of maternal liability for prenatal neglect". (At 293.)

[257] For *civil* cases involving a pregnant woman's drug-addiction see *Re Baby X*, 293 NW 2d 736 (1980), in which the Michigan Court of Appeals held that a newborn suffering from narcotic withdrawal because of the mother's heroin addiction during pregnancy was properly considered a neglected child within the jurisdiction of the Michigan probate court; and *Re Ruiz*, 500 NE 2d 935 (1986), in which the Court of Common Pleas, Wood County, held that a pregnant woman's heroin use was prohibited conduct within the scope of the state's child neglect laws, with the result that the newborn child was removed from its mother. See also the English case of *D v. Berkshire County Council* [1987] 1 All ER 20, in which a local authority obtained a place of safety order and a juvenile court made a care order under s. 1(2)(a) of the Children and Young Persons Act 1969 committing a child to the care and control of the local authority on the ground, *inter alia*, that because of the mother's abuse of her own bodily health (through heroin) during the pregnancy, the child's proper development was being avoidably prevented or neglected or its health was being avoidably impaired or neglected or it was being ill-treated. In upholding this order, the House of Lords held that, in deciding whether to make a care order under the section, a juvenile court was required to consider whether, at the point in time immediately before the process of protecting the child was put in motion, there was a continuing situation of impairment, neglect or ill-treatment and emphasised that the court had to look at both the present and the past, and that in respect of past events it was permissible, when considering whether a child's proper development "is being" avoidably impaired, for the juvenile court to have regard to events before the child was born which were having an adverse effect on the child's development or health (*per* Lord Brandon). But note the judgment of Lord Goff, who considered that the juvenile court was not entitled to conclude that a child's development "is being" avoidably prevented or its health "is being" avoidably impaired by the mere fact of a past avoidable prevention of development or impairment of health even if there are symptoms or effects which persist or manifest themselves later, since it cannot be said in such circumstances that at the relevant time the child's health "is being" avoidably impaired. Rather "all that can be said is that its health has been avoidably impaired in the past". (At 44.) He upheld the order, however, in the face of the likely *continuation* of the relevant prevention or impairment.

IV. CONCLUSIONS

To different degrees, in both the "medical" and "conduct" scenarios it would be unfeasible and inadvisable to impose a legal duty of care upon women toward their unborn children, with the exception of liability for negligent driving. While the medical scenario may seem to present the very real opportunity, on occasion, of saving fetal life, at the same time it more obviously presents issues of clear, though not necessarily justifiably asserted, legal rights on the woman's part, markedly distinguishing this context from the manner in which a third party might harm the fetus or a pregnant woman might do so outside the treatment context. Regarding the latter issue, however, it was apparent that applied to a pregnant woman, the generally acceptable idea from the law of negligence of limiting conduct in the interests of others could well stall, in her case, on the problems of seeking to impose legal duties throughout pregnancy, thereby ignoring its social context, and in her private life, thereby potentially conflicting with her legal right to privacy. In general, issues of causation and proof would also be problematic as regards maternal conduct. (Note here recent data which suggests that there has been an exaggeration of the effects of crack cocaine on the unborn child on account of the confusing effects of the poverty and physical and sexual abuse suffered by many minority women.[258]) Additionally, problems may arise regarding the commencement of the duty.[259]

The question of the standard of care was subject to different problems in these two areas. First, with regard to the refusal of medical treatment, I drew attention to the tension between ideas of reasonableness present at some level in the idea of duty and a cornerstone of the law of negligence on the one hand and the idea of rights (both legal and moral) to refuse medical treatment on the other. In my view, to attempt to limit a woman's right to refuse treatment by incorporating standards of reasonableness in the interests of the fetus is a doomed project. In other words, to try to formulate a definition of the "reasonable pregnant woman" in the medical treatment context is to seek to swim against the tide in the waters of deeply personal interests which are the subject of reasonable disagreement. The law of tort, with its deterrent and compensatory purview over harm to others occurring in the domain of general conduct, does not usually attempt any such thing. Thus, we do not seem to have any choice—in moral and legal terms—but to accept her own judgment and hence her right. In so doing, most often we will be recognising that she has serious reasons, based on her underlying interests in either self-determination or bodily integrity or both, hence that she is *justifiably* exercising her right. On other occasions, discussion, counselling and, in strictly defined circumstances, persuasion may be called for.

---

[258] DA Frank *et al.*, "Growth, Development, and Behavior in Early Childhood Following Prenatal Cocaine Exposure: A Systematic Review", (2001) 285 *JAMA* 1613.

[259] "Even if a duty of care only commences after conception, must she actually know she is pregnant, or will the duty start from the time the pregnancy should have been diagnosed by a reasonable woman?" S Martin and M Coleman, "Judicial Intervention in Pregnancy", 982–3.

Second, attempting to define the standard of care of maternal conduct may be a more feasible project and may appear a more legitimate process. Indeed, the obstacles to the determination of a standard of care as regards a legal duty to accept medical treatment for the fetus are not present regarding instances of maternal conduct which may harm the unborn child, such as negligent driving, smoking, alcohol consumption or drug abuse. In effect, the idea of a moral duty not to engage in these activities is an example of a negative duty not to harm the fetus or future child (perhaps particularly the latter regarding the last three activities) in relation to which the determination of unreasonableness would be relatively clear. In the light of the severe harm to the unborn child which may result from these activities on the one hand and the lack of value to the pregnant woman in engaging in such conduct on the other, the judgment can here be made that a pregnant woman is breaching a negative moral duty she owes to her unborn child. Hence there is a *prima facie* case for the imposition of a tortious duty not to engage in such conduct, in the same way that third parties can be liable for harm to the fetus/future child of a pregnant woman by their negligent conduct, the fetus's lack of legal status being of little moment where maternal bodily integrity is not in issue. Yet, whilst the discussion centred on *Dobson* has demonstrated that many forms of maternal conduct do not invoke rights in self-determination or bodily integrity (such as driving), it has also indicated that some forms may implicate its "social context" (such as cycling on one's own rather than in the company of others), whilst others may in some jurisdictions at least potentially invoke a right to privacy (such as the "choice" to smoke, consume alcohol or drugs during pregnancy). Further, not only would it be impossible for many women to fulfil a preconceived notion of a maternal standard of care, but the idea of a maternal prenatal duty may impose a role upon women which is inconsistent with and damaging to other legitimate roles in their lives. Thus, beyond such activities as smoking, drug or alcohol abuse on the one hand and negligent driving and similar activities on the other,[260] we would at some point encounter difficulties in the determination of a maternal standard of care, particularly regarding activities of value to the pregnant woman, such as her employment.

Special considerations apply to the particular problems of smoking, drinking and drug abuse. Here, in reality issues such as lack of voluntariness, especially with regard to drug addiction, would cloud the duty issue. Thus, broad policy considerations weigh against the imposition of maternal tortious duties for such conduct. The *Winnipeg* majority expresses the potentially counterproductive effects of changes to the law of tort as follows:[261]

---

[260] Whether negligent driving (and such like) will result in damage depends, for a start, on whether an accident occurs. But the activities of continued smoking, drinking (more than minimal amounts of alcohol) and drug-taking are likely to cause some harm in themselves.

[261] 152 DLR (4th) at 213, *per* McLachlin J. Two points should be noted about this conclusion. First, as the majority states in an earlier passage "[n]o clear consensus emerges from the debate on the question of whether ordering women into 'places of safety' and mandating medical treatment provide the best solution or, on the contrary, create additional problems" (at 212–13): that is, it should be recalled that the court is not equipped, as the legislature would be, to decide this issue. Second, although it might

"First, it may tend to drive the problems underground. Pregnant women suffering from alcohol or substance abuse addictions may not seek prenatal care for fear that their problems would be detected and they would be confined involuntarily and/or ordered to undergo mandatory treatment. As a result, there is a real possibility that those women most in need of proper prenatal care may be the ones who will go without and a judicial intervention designed to improve the health of the foetus and the mother may actually put both at serious health risk. Second, changing the law of tort as advocated by the agency might persuade women who would otherwise choose to continue their pregnancies to undergo an abortion."

Contrary to the *Winnipeg* dissent's view that the rejection of a maternal legal duty of prenatal care "entail[s] the state to stand idly by while a reckless and/or addicted mother inflicts serious and permanent harm onto a child",[262] the policy arguments which preclude such a duty even in the extreme cases raise much broader social, political and economic questions which should focus our attention upon the roots, rather than the harmful outcome, of activities such as drug and solvent abuse. (Note here the 2001 US Supreme Court decision of *Ferguson* v. *City of Charleston*.[263])

Overall, therefore, while there will be extreme cases in which maternal conduct seems clearly unjustifiable (such as the *Winnipeg* case in which solvent abuse was an important issue), the Supreme Court of Canada is broadly right to hold, in *Winnipeg*, that "[n]o bright lines emerge to distinguish tortious behaviour from non-tortious once the door is opened to suing a pregnant mother for lifestyle choices adversely affecting the foetus".[264] This is not to deny, as the dissenting justices claim, that in extreme cases we *could* make a judgment as to which sorts of conduct might in theory be actionable; or that in cases of *ordinary conduct*—such as the negligent street-crossing in *Bonte*, the negligent sailing, weed-killing or cycling, not to mention the driving in *Dobson*—judgments as to unreasonableness could be made.[265] Nevertheless, although in Canada there is clearly a case for Parliamentary

be argued that it is better that a fetus be aborted than that a child be born harmed, this is an argument which, rightly or wrongly, could well cause offence to many (notably the disabled). Further, the law would be hard-pressed to present abortion as a preferable outcome in such circumstances.

[262] *Ibid.*, 228, *per* Major J.

[263] 149 L Ed 2d 205 (2001). This note is added at proof stage hence is necessarily brief. Here the US Supreme Court held that the policy of a public hospital under which it conducted non-consensual and warrantless testing of pregnant women's urine and first communicated these results to the police and later (when the policy was amended) used the results and threat of criminal sanction to deter drug use, violated the Fourth Amendment's prohibition against official nonconsensual searches not authorised by a valid warrant. The Court held that the testing did not fall within the narrow category of special needs—apart from the normal need for law enforcement—which justifies warrantless searches. Stevens J, for the majority (Scalia J and Rehnquist CJ dissenting), stressed that the absence of consent to the testing breached the right to privacy which could be expected in the physician–patient relationship (at 216). Importantly, he held that "[w]hile the ultimate goal of the program may well have been to get the women in question into substance abuse treatment and off of [*sic*] drugs, the immediate objective of the searches was to generate evidence for law enforcement purposes in order to reach that goal" (at 219–20, footnote omitted).

[264] 152 DLR (4th) at 211, *per* McLachlin J. Here she referred to D Johnsen's "The Creation of Fetal Rights", 606–7.

[265] As P Cane notes in considering what "reasonable" means for the purposes of negligence, although in some contexts "some or all" of the questions about the ethnic origin, sex, age, religion or

consideration of maternal duties in driving (as exists by Parliamentary and judicial means in England and Australia respectively), beyond this such duties would only be acceptable where these would not impinge upon rights in self-determination, bodily integrity and privacy, would not run up against the "social context" of pregnancy and, *critically*, where pregnant women would be reassured rather than threatened by the prospect of legal liability (with attendant compensation).[266] Clearly this bill would be very difficult to fit, making the possibility of maternal liability beyond the driving context inherently unlikely. At the same time, some form of quasi-first-party insurance would perhaps be more appropriate.

Ultimately the purpose of tort law must be recalled. With regard to third-party liability for prenatal harm, the legitimate purposes of deterrence and compensation are effected by granting legal rights to the fetus, with regard to wrongful death, and by insisting that the tortfeasor's acts or omissions are limited by the legal rights of the born child, in the case of injury. As we have seen, these purposes have less and sometimes no legitimacy in the case of pregnant women themselves, a point noted by the majority in the Supreme Court of Canada in *Winnipeg*.[267] Further, as others have argued, imposing a legal duty on pregnant women may create a climate of fear and resentment among women, upon whom falls the social burden—at once physical and emotional—of carrying and giving birth to future generations. For these reasons, the law should generally continue to recognise the values and social goals at stake in different contexts,[268] protecting the unborn child against the harmful conduct of third parties, but not, for all the reasons of principle and policy discussed here, against their mothers, even at cost to future children.[269] The interests of pregnant women are too important to do otherwise.

---

degree of wealth may be relevant, "[p]erhaps none of these differences between people is relevant, for instance, to questions about how a reasonable person would drive a car". P Cane, *Atiyah's Accidents, Compensation and the Law*, 6th edn. (London: Butterworths, 1999) 29.

[266] Note that the Canadian Royal Commission's report on New Reproductive Technologies, *Proceed with Care*, concluded that women should not be civilly liable for harm done to their fetuses (at 964.) As regards the English Law Commission's consideration of the idea of maternal liability in its Report No. 60, Margaret Brazier observes that the Commission was concerned about the potential impact on the parent–child relationship and considered it likely that such claims would only be brought by a father seeking to use such an action "as a weapon in a pre-existing dispute with the mother." M Brazier, "Parental Responsibilities, Foetal Welfare and Children's Health", 267.

[267] "While the law may properly impose responsibility for the consequences of addictive behaviour, like drunkenness, the policy question remains of whether extending a duty of care in tort in this particular situation as the remedy for redressing problems which are caused by addiction is a wise option. Given the lack of control pregnant women have over many of these harmful behaviours, it is doubtful whether recognizing a duty to refrain from them will significantly affect their choices. As a result, the general deterrent value of the proposed new duty of care is questionable." *Ibid.*, 212, *per* McLachlin J.

[268] For another writer advocating this position see e.g. CH Baron, "'If You Prick Us, Do We Not Bleed?': Of Shylock, Fetuses, and the Concept of a Person in the Law", (1983) 11 *Law, Med & Healthcare* 52, 53–6. A recent exponent of a contextualised approach is John Seymour in his *Childbirth and the Law*. Thus: "This approach does not seek consistency. It acknowledges that lawmakers will respond differently to claims made on behalf of the fetus, depending on the context, the actors involved, their relationships, and the techniques and purposes embodied in the particular law invoked." (At 186.)

[269] The original exponent of this argument was D Johnsen, in her "The Creation of Fetal Rights", 611.

7

Arguments from Rescue Law

THIS CHAPTER addresses an aspect of the law of tort, namely that of rescue law. Its relevance to the maternal–fetal cases is that it concerns the question of whether individuals ever have a legal duty to come to another's aid and, if so, what this entails. Whereas chapter two was concerned with the question of whether or not we could say that a moral duty lies in a given case of maternal–fetal conflict, this chapter is concerned with the issue of the *enforcement* of a duty—that is, with the imposition of a legal duty—in the few cases of refusals in which we think we may be able to judge there to be a moral duty to accept medical treatment. Thus, it is centrally concerned with the notion of force and if and when this should be used. In this way, and coming at the end of the book, the chapter serves to elaborate and round off a number of arguments which have been touched on in relation to the idea of compelling the pregnant woman to have certain treatment for the fetus's sake.

To start, I very briefly outline the basic principles of rescue law, particularly as they apply to special relationships, in the course of which I note the absence of legal obligations upon parents to undertake physically risky rescues for their children. If parents are not legally compelled to submit to bodily intrusions for their children, it is arguable that likewise pregnant women should not be so compelled. We therefore need to consider what the objections may be to such compelled intrusions. In part I do this by turning to the leading case of *McFall* v. *Shimp*,[1] which concerns a competent adult's refusal to donate life-saving bone marrow to his cousin. Essentially, the court in this case held that, whatever the moral duties the one cousin may have owed to the other, it was not prepared legally to compel any such duty.

Before addressing the issues of principle and policy inherent in this decision, I discuss the way in which *McFall* raises the question of to what extent either cases like *McFall* or of maternal–fetal conflict can in any event be understood in terms of the law of rescue. I question to what extent a case of aid which by definition seriously implicates the body and its integrity can beneficially be encompassed within an area of the law primarily concerned with the *conduct* of individuals and riddled with exceptions when dealing with cases involving physical *invasion*. In other

---

[1] 10 Pa D & C 3d 90 (Allegheny County Ct 1978).

words, the determination of such a duty *per se* (moral or legal) may be inherently problematic, as first discussed in chapter two. Thus, the questions falling for consideration in this chapter will again bring to the fore the distinction I have made between an individual's general conduct and his/her moral and legal interests in self-determination and, especially, bodily integrity. The latter, as we have seen, are explicitly protected by rights. We have noted that this is not to say that such rights themselves necessarily provide the moral and legal solutions. So far as this chapter is concerned, however, the values exemplified by the accordance of certain rights may be at least one indication that compelled assistance by means of the body is inherently morally problematic.

In this regard, the discussion of the moral and policy considerations in the *McFall* decision briefly contrasts a deontological with a consequentialist approach and asks what stance is appropriate for a judge in such cases, with particular reference to the maternal–fetal conflict. The chapter also finalises the discussion as to what we should do in the face of apparently trivial maternal refusals, notably in the hypothetical case of the refusal of the beneficial pill. To some extent policy considerations attending to consequentialist arguments suggest the undesirability of compulsion in such a case. By itself, however, this line of thought is less than satisfactory. Accordingly, here I very briefly consider a number of context-sensitive reasons against coercion of various kinds, touching on the problems relating to compelling treatment of women who, whilst potentially legally competent, may lack autonomy skills (perhaps because of past abuse), as well as equality arguments relating to forced treatment, arguments in turn related to my social context theme. An unavoidable issue seems to be that of potentially creating symbolic meanings of women as vehicles to maternal health.

Finally, consideration of cases relating to incompetent adults highlights the lack of consideration accorded to pregnant women in cases such as *Jefferson*[2] and *Re AC*.[3]

II. THE LAW OF RESCUE

Common law systems are generally perceived to impose highly minimalist duties to rescue compared with the codified systems of many continental jurisdictions. Yet as for instance Alexander McCall Smith has shown, in fact this is only partly true, as both criminal and civil liability are imposed for omissions (hence giving rise to a potential duty to rescue) where certain conditions obtain.[4] Most notable amongst these, for criminal or civil purposes, is the existence of a relationship between the person in danger and the would-be rescuer. The justification for liability in such cases lies in notions of dependence and reliance and, as McCall Smith argues, must ultimately be understood in terms of moral claims upon the potential

[2] Ga 274 SE 2d 457 (1981).
[3] 573 A 2d 1235 (DC App 1990).
[4] A McCall Smith, "The Duty to Rescue and the Common Law", in M Menlowe, and A McCall Smith (eds.), *The Duty to Rescue: the Jurisprudence of Aid* (Aldershot: Dartmouth, 1993) 55–91.

rescuer.[5] In this light, it is possible to observe certain underlying principles in the state of the law. One class of special relationships concerns such occupations as that of firemen, who have contractually assumed a special responsibility (to fight fires and rescue people),[6] the fulfilment of which may necessitate undertaking rescues at risk to themselves. But the clearest example of relationships giving rise to duties to rescue most relevant to our concerns is that of parents and children: for instance, a parent's duty to ensure her child receives medical assistance can be described as a duty to rescue, and the widely recognised existence of such legal duties was noted in chapter three. In the case of parental duties to furnish children with the necessities of life, including medical care, the criminal law's customary concern with issues of harm and causation—which McCall Smith notes may play a significant role in limiting liability in cases where no special responsibilities have arisen[7]—do not arise. The relationship between parent and child, however, does not give rise to a legal duty to engage in a *risky* rescue.

I want to turn directly at this point to cases of parental rescue where a child's medical need is to draw upon, in some sense, his or her parent's body.

A. Special Relationships—Parents and Children

That even parents are not legally required to undertake risky rescues for their children can be seen by considering an American case regarding the issue of the donation of life-saving bodily tissue by a parent to a child, a case which is generally discussed under the heading of "rescue law".

In *Re George* (1982)[8] a 33-year-old adoptee sought access to his adoption records for the purpose of finding a suitable bone marrow donor. The natural mother was found incompatible and from the adoption records the judge traced the presumed natural father, who denied paternity and refused to be tested. This was as far as the court was prepared to go, declining to give the presumed father's name to the dying adult child. One scholar questions the strength of the indication afforded by the case by suggesting that it is explained partly on the basis of the father's denial of paternity and partly in the light of evidence that neither parent would be a satisfactory donor.[9] The significance of *Re George* may indeed be limited by its facts, leaving us with arguments for and against compulsory donation by parents.[10]

[5] *Ibid.*, 66.

[6] Note that one physician assumes that physicians have a contractual duty to rescue not just the pregnant woman but also the fetus, and that maternal refusal should not be an obstacle to this, suggesting that the pregnant woman is not the rescuer. J Phelan, "The Maternal Abdominal Wall: A Fortress Against Fetal Health Care?", (1991) 65 *S Cal L Rev* 461, 483. This claim would, in part, have to be evaluated in the context of the relevant health-care system.

[7] A McCall Smith, "The Duty to Rescue and the Common Law", 57.

[8] 630 SW 2d 614 (Mo Ct App).

[9] A Noble-Allgire, "Court-ordered Cesarean Sections: a Judicial Standard for Resolving the Conflict Between Fetal Interests and Maternal Rights", (1989) 10 *J Leg Med* 211, 234.

[10] A related decision is that of the Supreme Court of Iowa in *Head* v. *Colloton*, 331 NW 2d 870 (1983), discussed *infra*.

John Robertson is in favour of compulsory donation by parents to children, seeking to support this idea with arguments from analogous areas of existing law. Although he notes that bodily intrusions without consent are "highly disfavored", he suggests they are also "not unknown".[11] He points to a case involving quite different State interests, *Schmerber* v. *California*,[12] in which the US Supreme Court held that a compulsory blood test to determine alcohol content was not an unreasonable search and seizure since the test was not risky/painful and hence that the State interest could override the individual's interests. But the blood test example from the *Schmerber* case is hardly indicative of the legality of invasive intrusions and in this regard an immediate counter-example is the case of *Winston* v. *Lee*, in which the Supreme Court held that to remove surgically a bullet from a suspect's body against his will for use as evidence against him would violate his constitutional rights.[13] Most importantly, apart from the fact that Robertson's example can be met with counter-examples such as this, these cases hinge upon interests of the State which are not at stake in relation to parent and child or woman and fetus. This is also true of another of Robertson's examples, namely *Jacobson* v. *Massachusetts*. My previous discussion of this case in (the notes to) chapter three emphasised that compulsory vaccinations are justified in order to protect the public at large, not one specific individual.[14] Robertson also relies on *Georgetown*, the basis of which I criticised in the (notes to the) same chapter. It is upon

---

[11] J Robertson, "The Right to Procreate and *in utero* Fetal Therapy", (1982) 3 *J Leg Med* 333, 355, 353–4.

[12] 384 US 757 (1966).

[13] 105 S Ct 1611 (1985) aff'g 717 F 2d 888 (4th Cir 1983). The right not to be subjected to unwanted surgical intrusions is contained within the Fourth Amendment's "right . . . to be secure in their persons . . . against unreasonable searches and seizures". Illegitimate intrusions are ones "which are not justified in the circumstances, or which are made in an improper manner". A legitimate intrusion is one regarding which the State can show the reasonableness. In this case, relying on *Schmerber*, the Supreme Court supported a case-by-case approach in which the State's interests in performing the procedure are weighed against the individual's interests in privacy and security. Factors relevant to the reasonableness of the intrusion were "the extent to which the procedure may threaten the health or safety of the individual" and "the extent of intrusion upon the individual's dignitary interests in personal privacy and bodily integrity". Weighed against this was the "community's interest in fairly and accurately determining guilt or innocence". (At 761–2.) In the English context, reference might be made here to the Police and Criminal Evidence Act 1984, s. 55 of which permits intimate searches without a suspect's consent. This point is noted by J Herring in "Caesarean Sections and the Right to Autonomy", [1998] 57 *CLJ* 438, 440. Notably, Rhoden discusses these cases in the section "Interventions to Promote *Other* State Interests" of "The Judge in the Delivery Room: The Emergence of Court-Ordered Cesareans", (1986) 74 *Cal L Rev* 1951, 1982*ff* (my emphasis).

[14] The same point might be made of cases such as *Schmerber* and *Winston*. As SF Kreimer notes in this regard: "The authorities have not chosen the safety of any other individual as paramount to that of the suspect or patient; rather, they vindicate an impersonal aggregate interest. By contrast, [regarding] a compelled bone marrow transplant . . . the State has said, in effect, that it values one citizen more than the other." "Does Pro-Choice Mean Pro-Kevorkian? An essay on *Roe*, *Casey*, and the Right to Die", (1995) 44 *Amer Univ L Rev* 803, 848. J Herring makes a similar point in "Caesarean Sections and the Right to Autonomy", 440, observing that "if a fearful epidemic threatened a State's population, would it not be permissible to take by force a blood sample from a citizen who appeared to have developed an immunity to the disease?" Thus, "community values might in extreme cases outweigh an individual's autonomy". Herring suggests this is supported by the fact that "the values and structure of a society" affect the choices available to individuals, noting that these choices are at the heart of autonomy.

these cases that he seeks to ground compulsory treatment of a parent (particularly to save the child's life or prevent serious injury and where the extent of the intrusion and risks to the parent are deemed limited). In the light of my earlier discussion of these cases, I suggest that his argument is highly speculative.

Ultimately, Robertson suggests that a "community judgment, constitutive of our understandings of parenthood, could reasonably be made that parents must accept both prenatal and postnatal physical intrusions for the sake of offspring."[15] Yet by trying to show that compelled parental donation to children on the one hand is equivalent to compelled prenatal treatment such as caesarean sections on the other and that both are morally and legally defensible, he in fact highlights the controversial nature of the caesarean cases such as *Jefferson* and *Re AC*. As Nancy Rhoden writes, Robertson's argument shows "the degree to which a court-ordered Cesarean violates fundamental tenets of American law".[16] Logic requires, she states, that "if Cesareans can be required, American law concerning duties to rescue must be radically restructured".[17] Otherwise, she notes, given that compelled obstetric interventions are "unparalleled" in American law they would be unjustified under equal protection doctrine.[18] Indeed, it has been suggested that it is appropriate to see the issue of duty here from the perspective of equality, a point I develop later.[19] Taking note of Robertson's argument and effectively recognising the logic of Rhoden's approach, Terry AJ (for the majority) in *Re AC* (1990) states "surely, however, a fetus cannot have rights in this respect superior to those of a person who has already been born."[20] Or, as a Washington State judge put the point, "I would not have the right to require the woman to donate an organ to one of her other children, if that child were dying . . . I cannot require her to undergo that major surgical procedure for this child."[21] Thus, although Robertson favours compelling parents generally to submit to bodily invasions where this would save the lives of their children, the very idea of such compulsion would represent a significant departure from the law as it stands.[22] But such criticisms are ultimately

---

[15] J Robertson, *Children of Choice: Freedom and the New Reproductive Technologies* (Princeton, NJ: Princeton University Press, 1994) 192.

[16] N Rhoden, "The Judge in the Delivery Room", 1979.

[17] *Ibid.*

[18] *Ibid.*, 1969.

[19] S Martin and M Coleman, "Judicial Intervention in Pregnancy", (1995) 40 *McGill LJ* 947, 954.

[20] 573 A 2d at 1244.

[21] Cited in VEB Kolder, J Gallagher and MT Parsons, "Court-Ordered Obstetrical Interventions", (1987) 316 *New Eng J Med* 1192, 1194. Such reasoning has been described as attending to "equity concerns" by P King in "Should Mom be Constrained in the Best Interests of the Fetus?", (1989) 13 *Nova L Rev* 393.

[22] As M Warren notes, there is a tension between Robertson's treatment of these issues and the emphasis upon reproductive freedom which characterises his *Children of Choice* (and work generally): even if a pregnant woman's *reproductive* liberty is not infringed, a claim Warren probably rightly characterises, I think, as "debatable" (given that the medical treatment issues arise *in the course of* reproduction), involuntary medical invasions "arguably" infringe other moral and legal rights such as those to bodily integrity. M Warren, "Review of J Robertson, *Children of Choice*", in (1996) 10 *Bioethics* 161, 163. For another writer relying on the point that parents are not compelled to donate tissue or organs, see A Ouellette, "New Medical Technology: A Chance to Reexamine Court-Ordered Medical Procedures during Pregnancy", (1994) 57 *Alberta L Rev* 927, 952.

question-begging in the absence of arguments debating the appropriateness of the legal imposition of presumed moral duties to rescue. I now move to a consideration of this issue by turning to the decision in *McFall* v. *Shimp*.

B. The Leading Case on "Bodily Duties"

1. McFall *v.* Shimp

McFall was suffering from aplastic anaemia and sought to compel his cousin Shimp to donate bone marrow after initial tests had indicated that Shimp would be the most potentially compatible family member. At this point Shimp refused to undergo further tests.[23] The court in turn refused to order him to do so and scholars have noted the same crucial points from the judgment:[24] that although the court viewed Shimp's conduct as "morally indefensible",[25] it considered that compelling him to submit to further testing and ultimately to donate would contradict the very principles on which society was based. The court observed: "Our society, contrary to many others, has as its first principle, the respect for the individual, and that society and government exist to protect the individual from being invaded and hurt by another."[26] Further, in a passage which has lost little force despite the frequency of its citation, Flaherty J continued:[27]

> "For a society which respects the rights of *one* individual, to sink its teeth into the jugular vein or neck of one of its members and suck sustenance for *another* member, is revolting to our hard-wrought concepts of jurisprudence. Forceable extraction of living body tissue causes revulsion to the judicial mind. Such would raise the specter of the swastika and the Inquisition, reminiscent of the horrors this portends."

This line of reasoning was cited with approval in the latest English caesarean decision of *St George's*.[28] In this way, Judge LJ's defence of a pregnant woman's right to refuse medical treatment alludes to the horrors, only too apparent in the *St George's* case in particular and perhaps over-dramatically alluded to in this much-cited passage of the *McFall* case, of taking steps to compel a person to submit to an invasion of his body against his will. In chapter three we noted Judge LJ's reference to the need to avoid "even minor concessions" regarding freedom coupled with his reference to the possibility that medicine may develop such that a very minor procedure undergone by one person could save the life of another.

---

[23] 10 Pa D & C 3d at 90.

[24] See e.g. N Rhoden, "The Judge in the Delivery Room", 1977–8; B Steinbock, *Life Before Birth: the Moral and Legal Status of Embryos and Fetuses* (New York, NY: Oxford University Press, 1992) 127, 152–3; L Nelson, B Buggy and C Weil, "Forced Medical Treatment of Pregnant Women: 'Compelling Each to Live as Seems Good to the Rest' ", (1986) 37 *Hastings LJ* 703, 755.

[25] 10 Pa D & C 3d at 91.

[26] *Ibid.*, *per* Flaherty J, who noted that many societies take a "contrary view which has the individual existing to serve the society as a whole".

[27] *Ibid.*, 92, emphases in original.

[28] [1998] 3 All ER 673, 688–9.

While the court in *McFall* distinguished the idea of a moral duty on Shimp's part from that of the legal enforcement of such duty, the heart of the judgment clearly concerns the second point, namely the inappropriateness of legally enforcing a (presumed) moral duty on Shimp's part. Before turning to the latter issue, I would like briefly to touch upon the issue of a moral duty on Shimp's part, which effectively takes us to the interface between rights and duties both morally and at law.

2. The Interface between the Duty (Law of Rescue) and the Right (Law of Treatment Refusal)

It may be recalled that one of the ideas with which I have been concerned is the tension, as regards the existence of a moral or legal right, between the reasons theoretically justifying it on the one hand and the manner of its exercise on the other. The latter point concerns the moral quality of the decision to exercise a right, be it moral or legal, in any given circumstances. In this section I show the way this tension may be subliminally at work in two scholars' reflections upon *McFall*.

The discussion of *McFall* v. *Shimp* in the maternal–fetal literature is embodied within a consideration of the law of rescue. For instance, Rhoden argues that the *McFall* court correctly characterised the situation as falling under Samaritan or rescue law,[29] aspects, of course, of the law of tort. Nevertheless, whilst acknowledging in a footnote that McFall's physician described the risks to Shimp as "very acceptable", she goes on to observe: "Under the informed consent doctrine, however, risks cannot be deemed acceptable or unacceptable in the abstract. Rather, they must be considered acceptable by the person who will undergo them."[30] The idea of "abstract risks" reminds us of the abstract "reasonable man" so beloved of the law of negligence, a vehicle for the idea of *duty*. Rejecting this kind of "reasonableness", Rhoden can here be seen to defend Shimp's choice on the basis of principles relating to the *right* to refuse treatment, despite the fact that she effectively endorses the *McFall* court's assessment of the case as falling to be analysed under rescue law. Although Rhoden's legal defence of Shimp's choice is consistent with the fact that she chose to discuss the *McFall* case under the heading "Interventions to Protect Others", a sub-heading of "Refusal of Treatment Needed to Benefit Another", yet within that section she has aligned *McFall* with Samaritan law. Bonnie Steinbock discusses the case under the heading "*McFall* v. *Shimp* and the Duty to Rescue". She then observes, however, that the court rejected the traditional balancing of interests approach characteristic of treatment refusal cases, noting that on such an approach the court could well have considered that Shimp's interests in "avoiding pain and minimal risk" were outweighed by McFall's interest in life.[31] Thus, Steinbock implicitly suggests that Shimp has the legal *right* not to consent, suggesting that his assessment of the risks must have been different from

[29] N Rhoden, "The Judge in the Delivery Room", 1977.
[30] *Ibid.*, 1977, n. 152.
[31] B Steinbock, *Life Before Birth*, 152.

that of McFall's physician. The point I am trying to make is that these observations about the work of Rhoden and Steinbock reveal a subconscious tension as to the legal placement, the appropriate legal *family*, of a case such as *McFall* v. *Shimp*: is it a case about rights or duties? The answer, at least morally, is of course both.

Indeed, the rationale of the decision in *Head* v. *Colloton*[32] could lend support to the classification of a case such as *McFall* as a *treatment refusal* case. In *Head* a leukaemia victim sought to compel a hospital to disclose the identity of a potential *un*related bone marrow donor whose compatibility with the plaintiff was suggested by the hospital's record of tissue typing. In this case, the potential donor was contacted but indicated that she did not wish to donate to a non-relative. McCormick J in the Supreme Court held: first, the bone marrow registry was a public record; second, that a person who submitted to tissue typing tests for purposes of determining suitability as a donor was a "patient" and that the record procedure constituted confidential hospital records, exempted from the general public's disclosure rights under the public records statute. Of particular note is the court's argument that someone who submits to tissue typing as a potential donor becomes a *patient*. The question of whether this was so was described as "[t]he critical issue" by McCormick J, who later observed: "When a person submits to a hospital procedure, the hospital's duty should not depend on whether the procedure is for that person's benefit or the potential benefit of someone else."[33] Finally, he noted that "just as with patients generally, a potential donor has a valuable right of privacy."[34]

Notwithstanding such an approach, the classification of a case such as *McFall* is clearly a matter of debate and tension. Indeed, the points from *Head* v. *Colloton* noted above might simply be understood as relating to the hospital's duty to the potential donor as a patient, rather than as giving any indication about that donor's moral obligations to the donee. Further, given the close relationship between the spirit of *McFall* and the maternal–fetal cases, these observations confirm that, whilst the maternal–fetal cases belong to the law of treatment refusal, they are subject to questions from the law of tort and moral theory in a way which creates a difficult and uneasy tension, one that is complicated by the further question of the relationship between morality and law. By the same token, earlier analysis of the maternal–fetal conflict (in chapter two) helps us to understand the issues at stake in *McFall* and that *McFall* itself might well be classified as a treatment refusal case.

Thus, as regards the decision in *McFall* we might conclude first that, at least if he had serious reasons, Shimp was under no moral *duty* to rescue McFall: in effect, Shimp had a moral *right* to refuse "bodily invasion" for McFall's sake which his strong reasons justified him in exercising. (In reality, we do not know enough about this case, particularly Shimp's problems: for all we know, he may well have been quite callous towards his cousin; alternatively, abhorrence of needles may have been an issue.) Such an analysis might in turn be thought to justify the legal

---

[32] 331 NW 2d 870 (1983).
[33] *Ibid.*, 875 and 876 respectively.
[34] *Ibid.*

position acknowledging or granting him the legal right to refuse to donate (notwithstanding that the decision itself turned purely, as we have seen, on the separation of moral and legal duties).

Second, to approach the problem from a different but now familiar angle, we might reflect on the difficulties of judging the *extent* of Shimp's duty to assist his cousin by means of his own body. In turn, this would undermine the justification for imposing a legal duty to assist his cousin. In this connection, recall the argument from duty in chapter two to the effect that, when we compare duties involving *conduct* and duties involving the *body*, it may actually be very hard to determine whether or not there is a duty in the latter case, such as in the treatment context. Thus, I drew attention to the possible variance between a pregnant woman's and a third party's assessment (or indeed *different* third parties' assessments) of the degree of physical burden, pain and risk that it is reasonable to assume, which in turn undermines the very project of attempting to say whether a pregnant woman is obliged to submit to surgery such as a caesarean section on behalf of the fetus. This is a point that takes us beyond the question of special relationships to the general idea of determining moral duties which seriously invoke the body. In this regard, I observed in chapter two that, by using the Good Samaritan analogy to explore a woman's moral obligations to the fetus, Judith Jarvis Thomson may have failed to give due significance to the body. As I noted there, the story of the Good Samaritan is essentially a story about the *conduct*, not the *body*, of the Good Samaritan.

Following this reminder of the complexity inherent in the determination of a duty which seriously invokes bodily integrity (an issue not discussed in *McFall* itself), I now turn to the issue actually at the centre of the decision in *McFall*, namely the appropriateness or otherwise of the legal enforcement of *presumed* moral duties which seriously invoke bodily integrity.

III.   MORAL AND POLICY REASONS AGAINST THE COMPELLED CAESAREAN SECTION

The judgment in *McFall* v. *Shimp* suggests that liberal societies feel uncomfortable about imposing or enforcing (perhaps to different degrees) a duty upon one person to help another by means of his body. Flaherty J's judgment seems to indicate that the reason lies in the form that the State's involvement in such cases would take. Let us return to part of the passage cited earlier:[35]

> "For a society which respects the rights of *one* individual, to *sink its teeth* into the jugular vein or neck of one of its members and suck sustenance for *another* member, is revolting to our hard-wrought concepts of jurisprudence."

In this light, we can appreciate that the argument that since McFall and Shimp were only cousins, *McFall* does not tell us anything about parents or pregnant women,[36]

[35] 10 Pa D & C 3d at 92, *per* Flaherty J. First and third emphasis in original; second added.
[36] A Noble-Allgire, "Court-ordered Cesarean Sections", 233.

completely misses the force of the judgment to the effect that the law finds the idea of forcibly using one person as a life-support for another disturbing and distasteful. Indeed, we should note that the *McFall* court does not appear to have been preoccupied with the question of the *relationship* between the individuals: there is no indication that if McFall and Shimp had been brothers, the result would have been different. Instead, the court seriously questioned the appropriateness of imposing a legal duty upon one person to help another by means of his or her body.

Despite or perhaps because of the force of the above passage, the court did not elaborate upon the moral, legal or policy reasons which would weigh against such judicial compulsion. Let us tease some of these out, with particular reference to the case of the pregnant woman.

For the purposes of this discussion, I shall assume that we are concerned with cases of a clear moral duty to submit to treatment on the fetus's part, or, put another way, with cases of unjustified refusals. Two rather different hypothetical examples from earlier discussions come to mind. First, the case of the refusal of a caesarean section delivery for the clearly trivial reason (for example, to avoid the abdominal scar) and second, the case of the refusal, for no apparent reason, to take the pill highly beneficial to fetal welfare. The latter, you may recall, is an example of treatment which does not seriously invoke the issue of bodily integrity and is chosen here by way of contrast. Regardless of arguments from other areas of the law (for example, abortion law), what are the reasons discernible within *McFall* for or against compelled prenatal intervention/treatment?

With regard to the refusal of the caesarean, given that I have previously suggested that even persuasion (rather than discussion and counselling) is morally problematic in such cases, then it is unlikely that compelled caesareans will be morally acceptable under rescue law, but what would be the specific objections from rescue law as captured in *McFall*?

Flaherty J's judgment hinges upon the idea of a judicial refusal to use one person physically to benefit another. Reference to respecting the rights of individuals, coupled with the metaphors of "sinking teeth" and "sucking sustenance", seem naturally to oppose a deontological and a consequentialist approach to judging, apparently choosing the former over the latter. Justice Flaherty effectively touches upon a complex, sophisticated and as yet unresolved debate central to moral philosophy in the latter half of the twentieth century. As such, it would be well beyond my scope to discuss this in any depth. I therefore confine myself to a few points which may provide some indication of the moral difficulties of compelling one person very physically to benefit another, with particular reference to the context of a pregnant woman and her fetus.

Put very simply, the essence of a consequentialist approach is that actions are judged good or bad according to their outcome. By contrast, a deontological approach naturally evokes Kantian ideas about ends and means and the injunction not to treat people as means, but only ever as ends: "Act in such a way that you always treat humanity, whether in your own person or in the person of any other, never simply as a means, but always at the same time as an end."[37] Does a court certainly treat a pregnant woman refusing a caesarean as a means when it authorises doctors to operate without her consent to save the fetus? In such a case, in a very physical sense, the path to the rescue of the fetus is through the woman. But does this imply that she is being used as a means in the specific Kantian sense? Moreover, whether or not this is the case, is it clear that this is more morally problematic than declining to intervene to rescue the fetus?

Some discussions have suggested that the woman is here being used as a means in a way which a deontological approach to the issue would preclude. For instance, Nancy Rhoden[38] seeks to show this by drawing upon a famous example of Thomas Nagel's. Thus, Nagel considers the situation of someone seeking help following a car accident and whether that person can twist a little boy's arm in order to compel his grandmother to lend a car in order to rescue the badly injured people.[39] The degree of harm that will befall the little boy by having his arm twisted is very minor compared with the potential fate of the injured passengers if you do not twist the boy's arm. Nevertheless, Nagel reasons that you should not twist his arm. His complex discussion raises many questions beyond my concerns and thus seeks to explain the moral problems at stake in twisting the boy's arm in more ways than are directly relevant to my purpose. I shall therefore confine myself to a few points which appear especially pertinent to our case.

Essentially, Nagel focuses upon the relation between the agent and the outcome, so that "[d]eontological reasons have their full force against your *doing something*— not just against its happening".[40] He suggests that the problem lies in the "collision between subjective and objective viewpoints". In another passage, he writes:[41]

> "To see the matter in this light is to see both the appeal of agent-neutral, consequentialist ethics and the contrary force of agent-relative, deontological ethics. The detached, objective view takes in everything and provides a standpoint of choice from which all choosers can agree what should happen. But each of us is not only an objective self but a particular person with a particular perspective . . . So our choices are not merely choices of states of the world, but of actions. Every choice is two choices, and from the internal point of view, the pursuit of evil in twisting the child's arm looms large. The production of pain is the immediate aim, and the fact that from an external perspective you are choosing a balance of good over evil does not cover up the fact that this is the intrinsic character of your action."

With regard first to the latter point about "the infliction of pain [being] the immediate aim", it is important to note that *whoever* sought to compel the pregnant woman to submit to the caesarean, be it a court, her doctor or her partner, the

---

[37] I Kant, *Groundwork of the Metaphysic of Morals*, HJ Paton (trans.) in *The Moral Law* (London: Hutchinson, 1964) 96.

[38] N Rhoden, "The Judge in the Delivery Room", 1997.

[39] T Nagel, "Autonomy and Deontology", in his *The View from Nowhere* (New York, NY: Oxford University Press, 1986) 164–8. Reprinted in S Scheffler (ed.), *Consequentialism and its Critics* (Oxford: Oxford University Press, 1988) 142–72, at 156–7.

[40] *Ibid.*, 157, my emphasis.

[41] *Ibid.*, 165–6.

"production of pain" is never the immediate aim that courts have found, as a matter of fact, will thereby be suffered by the mother.[42] For this reason, the caesarean scenario is importantly different from the case of twisting the little boy's arm in order to make the grandmother lend the car. After all, the purpose of twisting the boy's arm is to make the grandmother react to the boy's pain in such a way that her response is to lend the car. Another moral difference is that the pregnant woman is obviously related to and morally responsible for the fetus in a way that the boy in Nagel's example is not as regards the injured passengers.

But there is a more striking difference between Nagel's concerns and those with which we are confronted when considering whether it is permissible for a judge to compel Shimp or a pregnant woman to submit to certain treatment. In effect, the perspective of the law—as represented in our cases by the judges who must make these decisions—is not analogous to the perspective of the person who must decide whether to twist the boy's arm in order to compel the grandmother to lend the car so that he can take the injured passengers to the hospital. On the contrary, we invest the law with the authority to judge, in theory at least, from the "objective viewpoint", so to speak: the law, supposedly, is imbued with an impartiality and a neutrality that the agent in Nagel's example can only have in *addition* to his subjective location. This observation might sound somewhat naïve. Importantly, I do not mean to deny the human form of the judge and the moral and political, as opposed to merely judicial, facets of judging. Indeed, there are various lines of thought which might be pursued here but for which I do not have the space. With regard to the notion of the ideally transcendent judge, one might note both feminist and non-feminist work criticising in different ways Archimedean models of moral justification which critique such models in the first instance in moral and political terms and, in the second, in terms suggesting that such models are simply mistaken.[43] There is a great divergence of approach to this issue even within feminist thought, however, and some feminists are actively pursuing rather than abandoning the issue of moral justification, but in ways which are, according to Alison Jaggar, "less covertly elitist and authoritarian and more transparent and democratic".[44] To sketch in some possible connections with the law here, a judge, of course, is openly authoritative (rather than authoritarian). Further, a good judge will offer solid, consistent and context-sensitive reasons for her decision and will act in a way which does not usurp the role of Parliament, a point touched on in different ways in various chapters.

Thus, to return to Nagel, a court is supposed only to occupy the "external perspective" in which, even if it were "aiming" at the woman's pain for the sake of fetal life, it could arguably be said to be choosing a balance of good (fetal welfare/life) over evil (increased physical discomfort, pain and so forth for the woman). The contrast between the subjectively and objectively situated practical agent and the ideally

[42] E.g. *Baby Boy Doe*, 632 NE 2d at 328.

[43] A Jaggar, "Feminism in Ethics: Moral Justification", in M Fricker and J Hornsby (eds.), *The Cambridge Companion to Feminism in Philosophy* (Cambridge: Cambridge University Press, 2000) 225–44, 240.

[44] *Ibid.*, 241.

objective position of a judge is highlighted again in the following passage, where Nagel is concerned solely with the perspective of the former. He writes:[45]

> "*[T]hings* will be better, what *happens* will be better, if I twist the child's arm than if I do not. But I will have done something worse. If considerations of what I may do, and the correlative claims of my victim against me, can outweigh the substantial impersonal value of what will happen, that can only be because the perspective of the agent has an importance in practical reasoning that resists domination by a conception of the world as a place where good and bad things happen whose value is perspective-free."

As I have suggested, however, a judge has neither the burden, nor, perhaps, the luxury of being concerned that the "correlative claims" of those against whom she judges may outweigh the "substantial impersonal value" of her decision. This is not to deny that at some point "doing justice" may be limited by concerns about doing harm. For instance, if it is not to import concerns too disparate from the current subject, capital punishment may be an example of a case about which we might judge that the State's agency in the act of execution is not "covered up", to use Nagel's phrase, by what some at least may see as a balance of good over evil. Indeed, it might well be considered that the practice of capital punishment does not comport with the virtue of justice.

Now in fact Nagel makes reference to and recognises the differing perspective of politics and the law, saying that these are "rightly more impersonal than the morality of private life".[46] Nevertheless, he suggests that notwithstanding this difference, "the acknowledgment of personal values and autonomy is essential even at the level that requires the greatest impersonality".[47] In this he is surely right. Moreover, that this *is* the case to some degree can be shown simply by pointing to the numerous rights of the individual recognised by the law in the form of legal rights. Indeed, as Ronald Dworkin has famously written, rights "trump" utilities.[48] So, as regards the maternal–fetal conflict, we are not dealing with a situation of non-existent rights; rather, the question has been whether the rights of the woman should not—in some circumstances at least (unjustified refusals)—give way to the interests of the fetus/future child in life and health. In effect, we are dealing with neither a fully consequentialist nor a fully deontological framework.[49] Thus, where a pregnant woman has serious reasons for refusing a caesarean, such as a religious reason, this is a case in which I have earlier argued that the law must acknowledge "personal values and autonomy", to use Nagel's phrase. By contrast, in those (unlikely) cases where a refusal of a caesarean is apparently groundless, so that a woman is unjustifiably asserting her right to refuse treatment, the question remains (from the perspective of the law of rescue) whether the court should authorise intervention in order to prevent fetal harm or death.

---

[45] T Nagel, "Autonomy and Deontology", 162, emphasis in original.
[46] *Ibid.*, 171.
[47] *Ibid.*
[48] R Dworkin, *Taking Rights Seriously*, 2nd impression (corrected) with appendix (London: Duckworth, 1978) xi.
[49] Note that it could be said that consequentialism is a system with one duty—that of benevolence.

I think the real moral stumbling block to compelled surgery even in the case of refusal for the clearly trivial or non-existent reason is, in various ways, the body. In drawing the moral line here, I am encouraged by the fact that in debates pitting consequentialist against deontological approaches to ethics, consequentialists also seem to distinguish between the *risk of physical harm* coming to someone as the result of the disregard of a deontological constraint on the one hand and *actual bodily invasions* (with attendant risks) on the other. Indeed, no doubt this accounts for some of the all too easy criticisms that have been levelled against consequentialist and/or utilitarian analyses. Consider, for instance, Laurence Tribe's oft-cited statement: "That one person's two good eyes, distributed to two blind neighbours, might yield a net increase in happiness on the theory that one blind person will experience less misery than two, cannot justify a governmental decision to compel the exchange."[50] More interesting, and from the other side of the debate, is Brian Barry's scathing and well-argued criticism of Charles Fried's excessively rights-driven rejection of consequentialism, in which Barry cautions:[51]

> "It is . . . limited imagination rather than superior insight into the 'nature of things' that leads Fried along with Nozick to regard the idea that being a kidney donor might be a matter of morality as so utterly absurd that it can be used as the cornerstone of a whole theory of negative rights. It may, indeed, well be that kidney donation will never become a social norm anywhere. For it has several distinctive features which make it relatively unsuited to being the subject of a norm. But, just for that reason, anybody who has clear intuitions that even the mildest form of social pressure toward being a kidney donor would be unjust should beware of being stampeded into the kind of reckless generalizations engaged in by Fried and Nozick.
>
> Suppose, however, that kidney donation did become a norm to the weak extent, for example, that being a blood donor in Britain might be thought of as a norm. Would that really be such a terrible assault on individual integrity?"

Let me take this passage in two stages: first, what it may reveal about moral duties to donate, for instance, a kidney, and second, about the compulsion of such duties.

It seems that academics are often tempted to overstate their case when they are in fact hesitant about an issue. If we follow up the footnote to Barry's sentence that kidney donation "has several distinctive features that make it relatively unsuited to being the subject of a norm", we find the following: "First, giving up a kidney involves a *serious operation* and some increased *risk of eventual renal failure*", (though he no doubt correctly notes that "the prospect of this would be much less grim if one could be sure of a ready supply of donors in case one's remaining kidney were

[50] L Tribe, *American Constitutional Law*, 1st edn. (1978), 918. It seems unimaginable, however, that any consequentialist/utilitarian would wish to claim Tribe's target as his or her own argument.

[51] B Barry, "And Who is my Neighbour?", Review of C Fried, *Right and Wrong* (Cambridge, MA: Harvard University Press, 1977) (1979) 88 *Yale LJ* 629, 658, footnotes omitted. For an analysis which distinguishes between the permissibility of imposing a risk of harm on the one hand and the idea of a physical incursion (indeed, in this case death) to benefit others (five, to be precise) see JJ Thomson, "The Trolley Problem", (1985) 94 *Yale LJ* 1395. Whilst Thomson emphasises the idea of "stringent rights" being violated in the latter case, I do not think we are forced to draw upon the idea of rights here to find the moral difference.

to fail").[52] In other words—independently of the further issue of compulsion—it appears that Barry may in fact be reluctant to assert that to donate a kidney is *clearly* a matter of moral duty, despite his apparent condemnation of Fried and Nozick for their rejection of such duties. This in turn would tend to support my argument, made at various stages, concerning the increased complexity inherent in our determination of a duty which entails serious physical incursions.[53]

Turning next to the issue of the compulsion of such (presumed) duties, despite the moral wisdom and vision in evidence in Barry's passage as quoted above, I think that the passage may not sufficiently bring out the distinction between the respective ideas of a moral duty to donate a kidney on the one hand and the idea of being compelled to do so on the other. Surely it is the idea of the *compelled* kidney donation and the compelled caesarean, not the moral duty which may or may not lie depending on the facts, which can fairly, if somewhat dramatically be called, "a terrible assault on individual integrity". Indeed, we might note Shelly Kagan's comment, in a piece which generally questions the intuition that consequentialism demands too much: "The immorality of *imposing* a sacrifice upon an individual is completely compatible with that individual's nonetheless being morally *required* to take the sacrifice upon himself."[54] (Recall that I am here discussing clearly *unjustified* refusals of caesareans, for instance the hypothetical case in which the reason offered is the desire not to have an abdominal scar.) In effect, therefore, I submit that Barry would draw the line as Flaherty J and I have done, namely at the legal *compulsion* of duties involving bodily incursions (with attendant physical risks).[55]

With regard to the case of the pregnant woman refusing the caesarean for the clearly trivial reason, therefore, I submit that the discussion so far elicits three related reasons why the court should not operate against her will: first, the increased discomfort, pain and delayed recovery time that a woman will endure following a caesarean rather than natural delivery, even though this is not an "evil" at which the court directly "aims"; second, the fact that it will be imposing an increased risk of death upon her; third, beyond the denial of her autonomy, which it must be said seems less valuable and less worthy of respect in the unlikely event that she lacks serious reasons for refusal, the simple fact of a serious non-consensual bodily incursion is a moral obstacle to the court's authorisation and the doctor's performance of a caesarean section in these circumstances. This is, I think, where the real moral problem lies. Thus, if we had to pinpoint the problem precisely, it is the fact that

---

[52] B Barry, "And Who is my Neighbour?", n. 98, my emphases.

[53] Donald Regan has argued that if a case were presented in order to determine whether a parent had a duty to donate a kidney or bone marrow to his/her born child, most likely no legal duty would be found. In the light of the tenor of the rest of this important article (to which I referred in ch. 2) I think that Regan would also agree that it may be hard to determine if there is a *moral* duty in such cases. D Regan, "Rewriting *Roe* v. *Wade*", (1979) 77 *Mich L Rev* 1569, 1586.

[54] S Kagan, "Does Consequentialism Demand Too Much? Recent Work on the Limits of Obligation", (1984) 13 *Phil & Pub Aff* 239, 243, emphasis in original.

[55] Another philosopher drawing this line is SH Kadish, in "Respecting Life and Regard for Rights in the Criminal Law", in O Temkin, WK Frankena and SH Kadish, *Respect for Life in Medicine, Philosophy, and the Law* (Baltimore, MD: John Hopkins University Press, 1977) 83, 93–4.

the woman's body must be cut open against her will that is the bar to the compelled caesarean.[56] Ultimately, the legal authorisation of such an action may be an example of those exceptional cases (such as that of capital punishment) in which the arm of justice would find its hands tainted by the very physical character of the action, despite the overall view to effecting good consequences. In the light of this conclusion, it is striking to reflect upon a statement from the judgment in the early maternal–fetal case of *Re Madyun*, in which Mrs Madyun's right to refuse a caesarean was overridden:[57]

> "All that stood between the . . . fetus and its independent existence, separate from its mother, was, put simply, a doctor's scalpel. In these circumstances, the life of the infant inside its mother's womb was entitled to protection."

The "simple" truth that the scalpel lies between the surgeon and the fetus is also the enormously important truth that what the scalpel must cut through is the body of a non-consenting person. Notably, one woman who was compelled to submit to a caesarean in England described how this made her feel as though there was no "humanity" or "care" in her treatment and that she was a "package to be processed". As she put it, "I was something for somebody to cut open and take a baby out of."[58]

Most importantly, whilst the relevant moral and legal language thus far has touched on the rather abstract notions of the individual's sanctity or integrity, recent work has looked more closely at what happens to people when their bodily integrity is disrespected. For instance E Goffman regards the body as one of the primary territories of the self, arguing that a sense of control over one's body is vital to the maintenance of a complete sense of self as well as to the capacity to interact with others.[59] If others fail to recognise one's autonomous control over one's bodily integrity, one's self-image may be severely battered, along with the security one needs to interact well with others and to express one's own needs and feelings. In similar vein, Axel Honneth has explored the sense of humiliation, loss of the sense of self and of a coherent sense of reality following upon the lack of recognition of one's bodily integrity by others.[60] And David Feldman has argued that non-

---

[56] As other scholars have noted, it is not in fact simply rhetorical to describe the procedure of a compelled caesarean, or compelled donation of an organ by a parent to a born child, in these terms: "We describe the implications . . . this way, not as an exercise in inflammatory rhetoric, but to make evident the very harsh implications for pregnant women or parents of accepting the view in question." JC Callahan and JW Knight, "Women, Fetuses, Medicine and the Law", in HB Holmes and L Purdy (eds.), *Feminist Perspectives in Medical Ethics* (Indianapolis, IN: Indiana University Press, 1992) 224–39, 233.

[57] 114 Daily Wash L Rptr 2233 (DC Super Ct July 26, 1986). Published as appendix to *Re AC*, 573 A 2d 1235 (DC App 1990) at 1262.

[58] Caroline Spears, interviewed in connection with the publicity surrounding the *St George's* case on BBC 1 *News* at 9pm, 7 May 1998.

[59] E Goffman, "Territories of the Self", in *Relations in Public: Microstudies of the Public Order* (London: Allen Lane, 1971) 38 as cited in JL Cohen, "Rethinking Privacy: Autonomy, Identity, and the Abortion Controversy", in J Weintraub and K Kumar (eds.), *Public and Private in Thought and Practice: Perspectives on a Grand Dichotomy* (Chicago, IL: The University of Chicago Press, 1997) 133–65, 159.

[60] A Honneth, "Integrity and Disrespect: Principles of a Conception of Morality Based on a Theory of Recognition", (1992) 20(2) *Political Theory* 190, as cited in JL Cohen, "Rethinking Privacy: Autonomy, Identity, and the Abortion Controversy", 159.

consensual, especially invasive, medical treatment "is calculated to threaten one's sense of one's own worth and the feeling of being valued by others."[61] I cannot further explore this here, but these points are connected with the idea that bodily integrity is so significant because one's body is central to oneself and sense of self, as first identified in chapter one.

IV. MORAL, POLICY AND LEGAL REASONS AGAINST COMPELLED INGESTION OF THE "BENEFICIAL PILL"

Yet where does this discussion leave my argument regarding the second hypothetical example of maternal refusal of treatment to which I referred at the beginning of this section, namely the situation of the woman refusing the beneficial pill without reason? As may be recalled from earlier chapters, this example—in which bodily integrity can barely be said to be invoked—is one of the refusal of treatment analogous to an instance of "general conduct". That is, to suggest that swallowing a pill seriously invokes a woman's interest in bodily integrity is at the same time to trivialise that interest; and where there is no reason to refuse the pill, no serious moral interest in self-determination is invoked. (Indeed, it is no mere coincidence that it is hard to imagine a *reason* for refusal in such a case and hence, as noted previously, the example is entirely hypothetical.) In such a case, why should there be any bar to compelled ingestion of the pill?

A. Consequentialist Arguments—"Maternal Flight"

One important answer in this case is, I think, consequentialist in nature. That is, if courts were to allow doctors to force women to take such pills (or similar) for the sake of their fetuses/future children, the side-effects of such an approach would be counterproductive. Indeed, women may be deterred from seeking antenatal care if they feel they will be forced to accept treatments against their will, a syndrome dubbed "maternal flight" in the literature. In this connection, the American Public Health Association has stated:[62]

> "Rather than protecting the health of women and children, court-ordered caesareans erode the element of trust that permits a pregnant woman to communicate to her physician—without fear of reprisal—all information relevant to her proper diagnosis and treatment. An even more serious consequence of court-ordered intervention is that it drives

---

[61] D Feldman, "Human Dignity as a Legal Value, Part II" [2000] *PL* 61, 67–8.

[62] Brief for *amicus curiae*, American Public Health Association, *Re AC*, 573 A 2d at 1248. In the light of this phenomenon, we can see that A McCall Smith's observation that it may be appropriate to widen obligations of legal rescue given that the law represents "a powerful means—perhaps now the only realistic means—of social denunciation of wrongful behaviour", which may well have application in a number of areas, would not, as a matter of policy, be applicable to the situation of maternal–fetal conflict where maternal choices/actions are clearly unjustifiable (not a situation he addresses). A McCall Smith, "The Duty to Rescue and the Common Law", 89.

women at high risk of complications during pregnancy and childbirth out of the health care system to avoid coerced treatment."

Likewise the American Medical Association has concluded that "while the health of a few infants may be preserved by overriding a pregnant woman's decision, the health of a great many more may be sacrificed".[63] In a similar fashion, recently an English obstetrician, Dr Susan Bewley, observed:[64]

> "we don't want the law allowing us to do things to pregnant women, because it will entirely destroy the doctor/patient relationship between obstetricians and pregnant women, and it will drive more people away from care and cause many more avoidable harms if instead of saying 'Please do this', with the moral pressure of the whole of society and her family around her . . . we say 'But if you don't agree I will force you'. That is not helpful to doctors."

(But recall my discussion in chapter four to the effect that attempts at persuasion and pressure must themselves be carefully monitored.) Perhaps unfairly for those of consequentialist persuasion, this line of thought may not be recognised for what it is, namely an important consequentialist objection to compelled maternal treatment. Of course, the same point applies equally, perhaps even more strongly, to the case of the compelled caesarean, confirming Nancy Rhoden's suggestion, in what should at some point be recognised as the leading article on the topic, that the judicial desire to prevent tragedies in individual cases has much wider social costs:

---

[63]   AMA Board of Trustees, "Legal Interventions During Pregnancy", (1990) 263 *JAMA* 2663, 2666. Several cases bear out the "flight" phenonemon. Of the known cases, the physical outcomes seem to have been positive. For instance, *Jefferson* is of course a prime example in which the woman went into hiding following the court order of a caesarean. In another case, cited by Gallagher, a court ordered the police to collect a pregnant woman and bring her to a hospital where physicians would perform whatever medical treatment was deemed necessary, including a caesarean. Since the woman went into hiding, the police could not seize her. Two weeks later she gave birth to a healthy child. J Gallagher, "Prenatal Invasions and Interventions: What's Wrong with Fetal Rights", (1987) 10 *Harv Women's LJ* 9, 47, citing B Flanigan, "Fleeing the Law: A Matter of Faith", *Det Free Press*, 29 June 1982 at 3A, 4A. Gallagher suggests that liability could "push ambivalent women toward abortion, frighten pregnant women away from prenatal care, and deter women from carrying a fetus to term and giving it up at birth for adoption" (at 45, footnotes omitted). It is clearly possible, however, that a woman could be driven into hiding and then suffer complications regarding which she would wish to have medical help. See also W Chavkin, MH Allen and M Oberman, "Drug Abuse and Pregnancy: Some Questions on Public Policy, Clinical Management, and Maternal and Fetal Rights", (1991) 18 *Birth* 107, 111, who note that after the filing of criminal charges against 18 women who were alleged to have taken illegal drugs during their pregnancy, healthcare providers in the state in question reported an increase in the number of women giving birth at home, in bathrooms and in taxis. It is unclear how the latter location is necessarily relevant here. As J Seymour notes, problems of confidentiality are also at stake: if a woman thinks certain information she might otherwise disclose could be used against her in judicial proceedings, then she may well withhold information from healthcare professionals in a way which could be detrimental both to her health and that of the fetus. J Seymour, *Childbirth and the Law* (Oxford: Oxford University Press, 2000) 234. See also M Randall, "Pregnant Embodiment and Women's Autonomy Rights in Law: An Analysis of the Language and Politics of *Winnipeg Child and Family Services* v. *DFG*", (1999) 62 *Sask L Rev* 515, 531: "[I]t is the women who are most vulnerable, most socially marginalized, and, therefore, most in need of health care and treatment services who will be most likely to fear legal scrutiny and regulation".

[64]   In debate following a talk by J Grace QC, "Should the Foetus Have Rights in Law?", (1999) 67(2) *Medico-Legal J* 57, 64.

"I, for one, believe it is far better for our society to choose the occasional tragedy and for judges to stay out of the delivery room."[65]

B. Further Arguments

Nevertheless, given the prospect of harm to the future child following the hypothetical trivial refusal of the beneficial pill, the consequentialist approach outlined above may not entirely convince. Nor can it assist simply to point to principles. For instance, while in *St George's* the compulsion of even a "very minor procedure" is rejected on the basis that "the principle of autonomy would be extinguished",[66] an important concern of this book has been to fill out the notion of autonomy and its associated treatment context rights in such a way as to make clear that "empty autonomy" or, put another way, the exercise of the right for reasons unrelated to its theoretical support cannot possibly justify prenatal harm. This is consistent with the idea that what liberalism values is not freedom of choice for its own sake, but rather for the sake of pursuing projects that are valued in themselves.[67] When so much work has been put into the important project of going behind the rights in question to explore the reasons for their exercise and the relationship between these reasons and the underlying moral and legal interests in self-determination (richly conceived) and bodily integrity, in some sense it might seem unsatisfactory not to contemplate forced treatment in the case at hand. Some further reasons are therefore required.

Overall, of course, I am endorsing a broadly liberal approach to the problem of maternal–fetal conflict and at the unjustified end of the refusal spectrum I face what Stephen Guest has identified as an "urgent practical occasion" in which liberalism is "particularly difficult to sell". As he notes, "[i]t involves the liberal in the seeming doublethink of feeling the importance of . . . individual freedom, and then appreciating but permitting its abuse".[68] As noted at other points I cannot discuss in detail the sophisticated and complex defences of liberalism such as those developed by Ronald Dworkin or Joseph Raz. It should be noted, however, that not only Dworkin and Raz but also other liberals in different ways hold that we cannot make a person's life go well by coercive paternalism.[69] As Will Kymlicka expresses this, a point touched on in chapter one, liberals believe that "no life goes better by being led from the outside according to values the person does not endorse". Thus, "[m]y own life goes better if I am leading it from the inside, according to my beliefs about value".[70]

---

[65] N Rhoden, "The Judge in the Delivery Room", 2030.

[66] [1998] 3 All ER at 688.

[67] W Kymlicka, *Contemporary Political Philosophy: An Introduction* (Oxford: Oxford University Press, 1990) 209.

[68] S Guest, *Ronald Dworkin*, 2nd edn. (Edinburgh: Edinburgh University Press, 1997) 236.

[69] Regarding Dworkin, see A Swift and S Mulhall, *Liberals and Communitarians*, 2nd edn. (Oxford: Blackwell, 1996) 301. Raz endorses coercion only where this would promote autonomy. J Raz, *The Morality of Freedom* (Oxford: Clarendon, 1986) 333.

[70] W Kymlicka, *Contemporary Political Philosophy*, 203–4.

But of course in the case of the refusal of the pill beneficial for the future child here we concerned not so much with the *woman's* life as with that of the future child who, notwithstanding its current location *in utero*, will be born and will then acquire rights. Although it is beyond my scope to bring to bear a complex liberal position on this point, I can offer some further reasons as to why compelled treatment is not a good idea. This involves focusing on the context at hand and thus recognising, along with Gerald Dworkin, that whilst much general theoretical work has been done on paternalism and associated notions, the best way to make further progress on these questions is by close analysis of particular areas where a given issue arises.[71] Some of the reasons I offer apply not only to the case of the refusal of the beneficial pill but also to the case of the forced caesarean, notwithstanding my contention that it is the cutting open of a person against her will which is the critical bar in the latter case. Overall, this discussion is directed towards the issue of coercion—for instance, threatening a woman with the possibility of a court order (despite the fact that this may or may not be possible)—and the use of force for the sake of the future child.

First, a narrow legal point to which I have generally accorded little weight in the substantive defence of a woman's right to refuse medical treatment is that the fetus is not a person. Recalling my definition of the future child as the being who will be but is not yet born, then nor is the future child a legal person. This means that there is no jurisdiction to intervene on its behalf. The future child's rights crystallise at birth—when it becomes the born child—and can then be asserted against third parties in ways explored in the previous chapter.

Second, one might speculate that forcing a woman to accept such treatment will decrease respect for pregnant women generally, although the rejoinder to this might be that allowing a woman to refuse treatment so trivially reduces respect for future life, so this does not seem very helpful, at least in itself.

1. *Fostering Autonomy—a* Healthy *Child is in the Interests of the Pregnant Woman*

A consideration of some note, I think, is the question of how sure we can be that the woman is refusing the pill for trivial reasons. I have stressed repeatedly that this example is hypothetical, serving the purpose of elucidating my argument. This is because it is very hard to imagine a woman carrying a child to term (not aborting) and refusing a pill, for instance a vitamin pill, which she is told will greatly benefit her future child. Indeed, it borders on the fantastical. Thus if we do find a woman refusing such therapy, it seems likely that various factors might account for this. Perhaps she has not understood what is being proposed or its significance: maybe the language of the medical centre she is attending is not hers or some condition of hers (perhaps ill-health) is impeding her ability to "take in" the relevant medical information. (Legally, this could raise competence issues.) Additionally, she may have had bad experiences of hospitals or people in authority generally, for

---

[71] G Dworkin, *The Theory and Practice of Autonomy* (New York, NY: Cambridge University Press, 1988) 162.

instance associated with her socio-economic or family background.[72] In this connection, the inbuilt power imbalance of health-care settings does not assist.[73] In certain cases, this could result in her distrusting and thereby refusing medically recommended therapy for her unborn child. Importantly, in terms of liberal thought, implicit in these suggestions is the notion that we may then have been *mistaken* about why she was refusing the pill. It is unlikely that such a woman could be said to be acting autonomously. Indeed, it is much more likely that she would have a poorly developed capacity for autonomy, confirming the truly hypothetical nature of the example of the refusal for "trivial reasons". But it seems hard to believe that the solution in this sort of case would simply be to compel the ingestion of the relevant pill. In moral and social terms, this seems a somewhat short-sighted answer given the reinforcement of possible feelings of powerlessness and oppression this may produce with the likelihood that the woman will become that much more wary of medical interventions or authority generally.[74] This may not just be a problem for her: when her child is born, it could mean that she is reluctant to seek medical help in ways which affect its well-being much more dramatically than the beneficial pill would have done *in utero*.[75] Of course this is somewhat speculative, but the phenomenon of individuals or groups who, for the reasons hinted at here, are wary of figures whom it is desirable that they should be able to trust is well recognised.[76]

If the solution is not to force treatment, nor is to throw up our hands and walk away. Indeed, to resist coercing or forcing treatment will not be enough (in terms

[72] Note C McLeod and S Sherwin, "Relational Autonomy, Self-Trust, and Health Care for Patients who are Oppressed", in C MacKenzie and N Stoljar (eds.), *Relational Autonomy: Feminist Perspectives on Autonomy, Agency and the Social Self* (New York, NY: Oxford University Press, 2000) 259–79, with particular reference to addicts: "Gaining the trust of patients requires that providers honestly display moral concern for their well-being and competence in addressing their health-care needs. Addicts who are members of oppressed groups may have good reasons to doubt that providers will have either of these qualities, reasons that may relate, for example, to the fact that various health-care professions have tended to ignore the health-care needs of members of oppressed groups". (At 274, footnote omitted.)

[73] *Ibid.*, 267.

[74] *Ibid.*, 274 on drug treatment programmes: "Forcing them into treatment that will probably be ineffective (since coerced treatment typically is ineffective) will have the likely consequence of further undermining their already limited autonomy. Imposing treatment will increase the powerlessness of these addicts because all that it achieves is a further reduction in their decision-making power." From a different angle, see also N Rhoden: "Although there are no studies . . . of the safety of nonconsensual Cesareans, given the increasing recognition of the impact of emotions on health, it would not be terribly surprising if women having surgery against their will experienced increased morbidity." "The Judge in the Delivery Room", 2003, n. 70. I cannot substantiate the latter claim, but see ch. 4, s. IV(D)(i) on the inconclusive evidence as to the psychological effects of caesareans generally.

[75] For a similar view see R Petchesky, *Abortion and Woman's Choice: The State, Sexuality and Reproductive Freedom* (New York, NY: Longman, 1984) 344–5: "If things can be done to my body and its processes over which I have no control, this undermines my sense of integrity as a responsible human being and my ability to act responsibly in regard to others."

[76] Note C McLeod and S Sherwin, "Relational Autonomy, Self-Trust, and Health Care for Patients who are Oppressed", with reference to addicts: "Providers [of health-care] should not expect or encourage addicts, in particular those with abusive histories, to trust them before the addicts have any evidence of their trustworthiness. The root of many female addicts' problems lie in having trusted someone whom they should have been able to trust but who instead betrayed them severely." (At 274, footnote omitted.)

of the woman herself, that is, and her relationship to her unborn child) when she may not have had the chance to learn to exercise autonomy responsibly.[77] Underlying this lack, it may be that she has not had occasion to cultivate the degree of self-trust requisite for her to acquire and use autonomy skills competently.[78] The absence of these opportunities may result from some kind of oppression, as touched on in chapter six with regard to the drugs context, which might generally have led to the internalisation of a sense of social worthlessness and incompetence which in turn results in a lack of self-trust or self-worth. The result may be that she is unable to act according to her own interests,[79] which would include (where abortion is not an issue) giving birth to a healthy child. In recognition of the reduction in autonomy which an oppressive background of some kind might have created, certain cases might thus call for more developed or sustained counselling aimed at helping a woman develop or strengthen trust in herself.[80] Indeed, in *Baby Boy Doe*, the court observed the medical profession's recommendation that a pregnant woman's autonomy be upheld in the following fashion:[81]

> "The American Medical Association's Board of Trustees cautions that the physician's duty is not to dictate the pregnant woman's decision, but to ensure that she is provided with the appropriate information to make an informed decision. If the woman rejects the doctor's recommendation, the appropriate response is not to attempt to force the recommended procedure upon her, but to urge her to seek consultation and counseling from a variety of sources."

Notably, these reflections again highlight our duty to consider her interests and treat her well. Here it might be noted that increases in maternal stress and anxiety can result in lowered self-esteem as well as poor identification with the idea of motherhood, indifference regarding and possible rejection of the fetus.[82] In this regard, we might recall the *St George's* case and the "moderate depression" from which the woman in that case was apparently suffering. Although it seems she had a belief in letting "nature take its course" it is not inconceivable that this attitude

---

[77] C McLeod and S Sherwin, "Relational Autonomy, Self-Trust, and Health Care for Patients who are Oppressed", 262, with reference to drug addicts.

[78] I cannot further develop this here. For extremely interesting discussion, particularly regarding oppressed groups, see *ibid*. The authors identify three types of self-trust: first, trust in one's capacity to choose effectively in order to be motivated to exercise one's choices; second, trust in one's ability to act on one's decisions; and third, trust in the judgments which underlie one's choices (a substantive demand on autonomy). (At 263–4.) These points are explored in detail.

[79] *Ibid*.

[80] *Ibid*.

[81] 632 NE 2d 326, 335 (Ill App 1 Dist 1994).

[82] C Hammerman et al, "Does Pregnancy Affect Medical Ethical Decision Making?", (1998) 24 *JME* 409, 409, citing psychological and medical literature on point. This study of pregnant and postpartum women, which involved the use of a questionnaire, revealed that the postpartum women had a more aggressive attitude toward the treatment of (hypothetically) disabled newborns. The authors speculate that this may be due to the effects of somatic and psychosocial stresses of pregnancy on ethical decision-making, combined with the new mother's tendency, once delivered of a healthy newborn, to relate to the questions posed in an abstract rather than personal way (at 413.) By contrast, the still-pregnant woman—for whom the possibility of a disabled child is still a possibility—could very well be much more concerned with the possible impact upon her and her family of such a development (at 412).

could have been connected with her then depressed state. This was a case in which sympathetic discussion and counselling, not compelled intervention, was required.

A further point concerns the seriousness of the harm. The refusal of the pill, such as some form of vitamin therapy, will often not result in serious harm to the future child. In this sense, there would fortunately be some sense of proportionality between the seemingly unjustified refusal and the harm that may come to the child. But this will not always be the case. Suppose, for instance, that at the start of her pregnancy it was established that a woman was deficient in folic acid and that she should therefore rapidly begin a course of this to avoid the risk of a child born with spina bifida, a clearly serious disability. In such a case, however, once again it is unthinkable that a woman would autonomously reject this when the issues were properly and sympathetically explained to her, unless, say, she was planning to abort. After all, a child with spina bifida will not be in her interests.

2. Equality Issues

Next, as touched on earlier in this chapter and in chapter five, compelled treatment of the pregnant woman raises equality issues, an issue about which there is only scope to make a handful of comments here. In the United States the relationship between equal protection doctrine under the Fourteenth Amendment (which declares that states cannot deny any person "equal protection of the laws") and pregnancy has been the subject of extended and heated debate, one which can barely be touched on here.

Catharine MacKinnon's work has been a cornerstone of the debate on the Equal Protection Clause and women. In a leading article[83] she traces the way in which the judicial approach to sex equality initially followed that of racial equality, the underlying principle being that like should be treated alike,[84] arguing that this Aristotelian model, whilst defective when applied to race, "is stunningly inappropriate" when applied to sex:[85]

> "Society defines women as such according to differences from men: hence the sex difference, as gender is customarily termed. Then equality law tells women that they are entitled to equal treatment mainly to the degree they are the same as men."

As Nicola Lacey summarises the feminist critique, "liberal notions of equality are fundamentally premised on the idea of sameness: equal treatment is due to all who are similarly situated to the full liberal subject".[86] Given that it is a requirement of equality claims that individuals or groups be "similarly situated" and given that men never need abortions (and are rarely sexually assaulted), laws governing reproduction, MacKinnon argues, have been perceived as the legitimate focus of sex equality concerns. MacKinnon suggests that a sex equality approach to the law of

---

[83] CA MacKinnon, "Reflections on Sex Equality Under Law", (1991) 100 *Yale LJ* 1281, 1308–24.
[84] *Ibid.*, 1288.
[85] *Ibid.*, 1290–1.
[86] N Lacey, *Unspeakable Subjects: Feminist Essays in Legal and Social Theory* (Oxford: Hart Publishing, 1998) 240.

reproductive control entails "situating pregnancy in the legal and social context of sex inequality and capturing the unique relationship between the pregnant woman and her fetus".[87] If the law relating to reproductive control was thus theorised as a problem of sex inequality, the starting point would be consideration of the way in which reproduction affects the status of the sexes. By this means we would see that "a narrow view of women's 'biological destiny' "[88] has shaped and constrained many women. It is beyond my current scope to review the vast debate on equality and pregnancy and the varying feminist approaches to the debate on equality and difference, but a few key points are relevant here.[89]

First, an important limitation on the application of the US Equal Protection Clause, as Aileen McColgan observes, is that it applies almost completely only to direct discrimination.[90] To have an intention to discriminate, the body imposing the rule must be aware of its disparate impact and must have "selected or reaffirmed a particular course of conduct at least in part 'because of', not merely 'in spite of', its adverse effects upon an identifiable group".[91] As McColgan notes, a Fourteenth Amendment violation will not be established even if an intention to discriminate formed one of the reasons for disparately impacting practice if the rule would still have been imposed, regardless of this reason. From the viewpoint of women, the difficulty of interpreting the Equal Protection Clause as applying to direct discrimination, as McColgan notes, is that "disadvantages women suffer *as women* . . . go unchecked".[92]

Returning directly to the reproduction context, how might we apply equality reasoning to the treatment refusal context under consideration? As Rhoden observes, there are two possible replies to the argument that compelled treatment raises equal protection concerns.[93] First, one might argue that there is no equal protection problem because there is no situation sufficiently similar and hence no

[87] CA MacKinnon, "Reflections on Sex Equality Under Law", 1309.

[88] *Ibid.*, 1311

[89] For a useful outline of the feminist debate see J Conaghan, "Pregnancy and the Workplace: A Question of Strategy?", in A Bottomley and J Conaghan (eds.), *Feminist Theory and Legal Strategy* (Oxford: Blackwell, 1993).

[90] A McColgan, *Women Under the Law: The False Promise of Human Rights* (Harlow: Longman, 2000) 36, citing *Washington* v. *Davies*, 426 US 229 (1976).

[91] *Massachusetts Personnel Administrator* v. *Feeney*, 442 US 256 (1979).

[92] A McColgan, *Women Under the Law*, 37, emphasis in original. She suggests that "the approach taken by the Supreme Court to the Equal Protection Clause and, in particular, to its application to sex . . . renders it unsuitable for challenge to anything but the most obvious and unjustifiable sex discrimination" (at 80). See also Note, "Developments in the Law—Medical Technology and the Law", (1990) 103 *Harv L Rev* 1519, 1571, citing *Washington* v. *Davis*, 426 US at 240, noting the "basic equal protection principle" that the "invidious quality of a law claimed to be . . . discriminatory must ultimately be traced to a . . . discriminatory intent".

[93] N Rhoden, "The Judge in the Delivery Room", 1987. See also Note, "Rethinking (M)otherhood: Feminist Theory and State Regulation of Pregnancy", (1990) 103 *Harv L Rev* 1325, 1336: "The extent to which the regulation of pregnancy reflects and reinforces gender hierarchy becomes apparent when these policies are compared with the regulation of other health care decisions and other forms of state intervention in the family." This writer also argues in social context equality terms, suggesting: "Policies that deny women's ability to make independent choices about their conduct during pregnancy, whether explicit choices about health care or less conscious decisions regarding physical conduct, subordinate women to their reproductive role." (At 1341.)

relevant comparison can be made. The difficulties with this approach have been noted above with regard to MacKinnon's observation that it is "stunningly inappropriate" when applied to sex. Second, one could argue that in fact we should compel parents generally to benefit others by means of their bodies, for instance to compel a father to donate a kidney to one of his offspring (John Robertson's approach). Yet, as Rhoden argues, to impose theoretically similar burdens on men would not result in substantive equality if those burdens were either hypothetical or very rare.[94] This highlights the distinction between formal and substantive equality.[95] An additional problem concerns the requirement of direct discrimination noted above by McColgan: in this regard, as one author has noted, court-ordered (or sanctioned) obstetric interventions are not intended to discriminate against pregnant women, but rather to protect or save the fetus.[96] In the light of these difficulties, it would seem that the solution is for us to apply equality reasoning in a way which attends to the social context of pregnancy as exemplified in various ways by the approach of MacKinnon and others, refining this to apply to the treatment refusal scenario. This has always been an important aspect of my approach. Further, it appears in line with D Majury's concern that "a lot of time and energy are spent talking and theorizing about equality [so] that 'equality' becomes vested with a life and meaning of its own, divorced from the particularized experiences of inequality it is intended to address".[97]

Can the law of reproduction respond in such a context-sensitive way? The absence of equality reasoning in *Roe* v. *Wade* has been noted in the legal literature, for instance by Cass Sunstein[98] and Ruth Bader Ginsburg. Ginsburg argues

[94] N Rhoden, "The Judge in the Delivery Room", 1988.

[95] *Ibid.*, 1989. For work related to this point, see M Minow, *Making all the Difference: Inclusion, Exclusion, and American Law* (Ithaca, NY: Cornell University Press, 1990) 41–3, arguing that the law's official neutrality treats women like men but allows women to bear the burdens created by differences. See also S Law, "Rethinking Sex and the Constitution", (1984) 132 *U Pa L Rev* 955, who argues that laws concerning reproductive biology "should be scrutinized by courts to ensure that (1) the law has no significant impact in perpetuating either the oppression of women or culturally imposed sex-role constraints on individual freedom or (2) if the law has this impact, it is justified as the best means of serving a compelling state purpose". (At 1008–9.) Thus, she proposes an impact analysis with regard to equal treatment. So, if a given set of legal arrangements has the effect described under the first limb, then the State must try to justify that impact under the second limb.

[96] Note, "Developments in the Law—Medical Technology and the Law", 1571–2.

[97] D Majury, "Strategizing in Equality", in MA Fineman and NS Thomadsen (eds.), *At the Boundaries of Law, Feminism and Legal Theory* (New York, NY: Routledge, 1991) 320, 331. Majury is concerned that both the equal treatment and limited recognition of women's difference perspectives can readily work against the interests of women.

[98] CR Sunstein, "Neutrality in Constitutional Law (With Special Reference to Abortion, Pornography and Surrogacy)", (1992) 92 *Colum L Rev* 1, 42: "An argument from sex equality seems preferable to one that posits a general or acontextual privacy right, and also to the view that restrictions on abortion simply do not raise constitutional questions. In particular, the equality argument has a large advantage over the 'prochoice' position in that it does not rest on privacy; freely acknowledges and, indeed, insists on the strength of the interest in protecting fetal life; and stresses rather than disregards the fact that women alone become pregnant and the existence of discrimination and coercion in the realm of reproduction." Regarding the interest in fetal life, Sunstein writes: "Even if the fetus has all of the status of human life, the bodies of women cannot, under current conditions, be conscripted in order to protect it." (At 40.)

that the lack of a constitutionally based sex-equality perspective weakened the decision:[99]

> "The conflict . . . is not simply one between a fetus' interests and a woman's interests, narrowly conceived, nor is the overriding issue state versus private control of a woman's body for a span of nine months. Also in the balance is a woman's autonomous charge of her full life's course . . . her ability to stand in relation to man, society, and the state as an independent, self-sustaining, equal citizen."

The influence of this line of thought can be seen in subsequent relevant law. For instance in chapter five, we saw that in *Casey* Justice Blackmun is critical of the State's assumption that women have a duty to continue a pregnancy "as a matter of course", as though they "can simply be forced to accept the 'natural' status and incidents of motherhood". This assumption, he suggests, depends upon a picture of the role of women which has invoked the protection of the Equal Protection Clause.[100] I explored this line of thought in connection with my "social context" argument and it would seem that equality concerns may well be related to that argument. This can be appreciated by reflecting on the judicial language on point, for instance Justice Blackmun's observation, partly cited above. Further, we saw that in *Casey* he explicitly suggested that the Court's framework for the assessment of abortion regulations "responds to the *social context* of women facing these issues of reproductive choice",[101] suggesting that the Court thereby "remains sensitive to the unique role of women in the decision-making process".[102]

Developing this approach here, recalling that I am at this point concerned with the question of whether or not we should compel treatment when the reason for refusal is trivial, on the one hand a review of my arguments in chapter two about the social context of treatment refusal during pregnancy suggests that the extent to

---

[99] RB Ginsburg, "Essay: Some Thoughts on Autonomy and Equality in Relation to *Roe* v. *Wade*", (1985) 63 *N Carolina L Rev* 375, 383, footnotes omitted.

[100] Justice Blackmun is the only justice to make reference to this clause, which I have noted was not part of the original decision in *Roe*, and refers to the recognition of this point by an increasing number of commentators, including e.g. L Tribe, *American Constitutional Law*, 2nd edn. (Mineola, NY: Foundation Press, 1988) s. 1510, 1353–9 and CA MacKinnon, "Reflections on Sex Equality Under Law", 1308–24. There are echoes here of the Canadian position noted in ch. 6, since in *Brooks* v. *Canada Safeway Ltd* the Supreme Court held that "[i]t is difficult to conceive that distinctions or discriminations based upon pregnancy could ever be regarded as other than discrimination based upon sex". [1989] SCR 1219, 1243–4. *Per* Dickson CJ.

[101] 120 L Ed 2d at 746, footnote omitted, my emphasis.

[102] *Ibid*. Similarly, as noted in ch. 6, in *Brooks*, Dickson CJ notes: "That those who bear children and benefit society as a whole thereby should not be economically or socially disadvantaged seems to bespeak the obvious. It is only women who bear children; no man can become pregnant . . . it is unfair to impose all the costs of pregnancy upon one half of the population." [1989] SCR 1219, 1243–4. See also the Canadian Royal Commission's Report, *Proceed with Care*, discussed in ch. 6: "A woman has the right to make her own choices, whether they are good or bad, because it is the woman whose body and health are affected, the woman who must live with her decision, and the woman who must bear the consequences of that decision for the rest of her life. In this respect, pregnant women are no different from any other responsible individual; to treat pregnant women differently from other women and men, or to impose a different standard of behaviour on them, is neither morally nor legally defensible." (At 956.) Of course, the fact that the woman must live with the consequences makes it very unlikely that she will genuinely willingly choose to refuse treatment for trivial or non-existent reasons.

which this line of reasoning helps with the refusal for "trivial" or "non-existent" reasons is not immediately apparent. (For instance, in chapter two I pointed out that the need, at least for a caesarean, may arise unforeseeably at the point of birth, such that where a woman has serious problems with such surgery, to deny her the right to refuse would be tantamount to implying that she should not reproduce.) On the other hand, it may be that a writer such as MacKinnon would at this juncture draw on the points I have discussed above relating to the likely vulnerability and powerlessness of women who might refuse treatment in these ways. I think this is important and is a point which could in turn form part of an argument related to the social context of pregnancy, recalling that this is an argument which recognises that the physical and emotional burdens of pregnancy are ones which essentially fall on women. Equality reasoning might thus be capable of defending the position of the woman "trivially" refusing the beneficial pill.

As for the State's interest in the fetus from abortion law which could certainly weigh in here in the US context, not only could this only become compelling at viability, but I have also argued (in chapters two and five) that there is no justification for it to become compelling in the treatment context even at this time. Conversely, where harm to the future child is in issue (rather than the fetus which will die *in utero*), it might be argued that it makes more sense for the State's interest to become compelling much earlier in pregnancy, but this is most unlikely and problematic in various ways, for instance in the potential for obstruction of the abortion right unless the contexts are clearly delineated.

Lastly on the issue of equality, the situation in England would be somewhat different in that the prohibition on discrimination in Article 14 of the European Convention on Human Rights under the Human Rights Act 1998, including on the grounds of sex, is not designed as a general guarantee of equal treatment. Rather, Article 14 only requires that access to other Convention rights be equal.[103] Regarding the question of whether Article 8 protects the right to refuse medical treatment when pregnant, protection by means of Article 14 would ensue if, following the decision in *Lithgow* v. *United Kingdom*, a woman can show that she has been treated differently from people "placed in analogous situations".[104] She would thus have to show that her situation is similar to those who have been treated differently.[105] As we have already seen, with regard to pregnancy this is problematic, as MacKinnon, Rhoden and others have shown in different ways. (It is beyond my scope to review the more favourable approach to sex equality under the Canadian Charter.[106])

---

[103] Art. 14 states: "The enjoyment of the rights and freedoms set forth in this Convention shall be secured without discrimination on any ground such as sex, race, colour, language, religion, political or other opinion, national or social origin, association with a national minority, property, birth or other status." See e.g. the discussion in J Wadham and H Mountfield, *Blackstone's Guide to the Human Rights Act 1998* (London: Blackstone, 1999) 111–13.

[104] (1986) 8 EHRR 329, para. 177.

[105] *Fredin* v. *Sweden* (1991) 13 EHRR 784, para. 60.

[106] For a review of the Canadian position under s. 15 of the Charter, see A McColgan, *Women Under the Law*, 45, who notes "at least in relation to distinctions drawn on the basis of sex, Canada's Supreme

Aileen McColgan (discussing the issue of abortion) outlines two approaches that might be taken under the Human Rights Act. First, English courts might adopt the approach of the European Court of Justice, under which a pregnant woman is compared with a non-pregnant man, such that restrictions on abortion clearly restrict the freedom of the former.[107] Given the way in which the courts have tended inadequately to grasp this approach, however, she suggests it is more likely that the approach of the European Court of Human Rights would prevail. In this regard, she suggests that, given its finding (in *Brüggeman*) that pregnancy does not lie completely within the private sphere, the ECHR might reject the comparison between a pregnant woman and a non-pregnant man on the basis that the two are not in analogous positions. In other words, the "placed in analogous situation" requirement of *Lithgow* would not be fulfilled. If a court were to find discrimination in relation to abortion, which McColgan suggests is unlikely, it would then of course proceed to consider the issue of justification. The court in *Lithgow* notes that Article 14 is only breached where the discrimination " 'has no objective and reasonable justification,' that is, if it does not pursue a 'legitimate aim' or if there is not a 'reasonable relationship of proportionality between the means employed and the aim sought to be realised' ".[108] McColgan suggests that since restrictions on abortion are not intended to discriminate against women and in the light of the (previously existing) Commission's position on pregnancy, the protection of the fetus would "likely" constitute such a justified aim.[109]

Indeed, reasoning about a woman's rights under the Human Rights Act requires that we acknowledge any countervailing rights of the fetus. The question of whether Article 2 of the ECHR under the Human Rights Act might be interpreted as granting the fetus a right to life by English courts, an issue left open by the Commission for instance in *Paton*, was touched on in earlier chapters. As noted in chapter three with regard to the abortion jurisprudence under the ECHR, P van Dijk and G van Hoof have observed with regard to the reasonable weighing of the rights and interests involved, "[a]s long as the question of whether Article 2 is applicable to the unborn life has not been answered in the negative, this reasonableness will have to be reviewed in each individual case".[110] It is an open question what might happen here, although in chapter three aspects of the judgments

---

Court does not suffer from the unduly formalistic approach which has beset the US Supreme Court". McColgan notes that in *Andrews* v. *Law Society of British Columbia* [1989] 1 SCR 143 the Court adopted a substantive rather than a formal model of discrimination in connection with a challenge to legislation which required Canadian citizenship in order to enter legal practice. In *Andrews*, she suggests, "[n]ot only did that court require that the impact of legislation, rather than its form, be considered, but it also sought to move beyond the sterile search for 'similarly situated' individuals that has bedevilled so much discrimination jurisprudence in the UK and the US." (At 42, footnote omitted.)

[107] A McColgan, *Women Under the Law*, 272.

[108] (1986) 8 EHRR 329, para. 177. Here the court cites for instance the *Rasmussen* judgment of 28 November 1984, Series A no. 87, para. 35 and para. 38. The court also considered the issue of the margin of appreciation which we have seen to be irrelevant under the Human Rights Act 1998.

[109] A McColgan, *Women Under the Law*, 272–3.

[110] P van Dijk and G van Hoof, *Theory and Practice of the European Convention on Human Rights*, 3rd edn. (The Hague: Kluwer, 1998) 301.

of the English Court of Appeal in *Re F (in utero)* and *Attorney-General's Reference (No. 3 of 1994)* were highlighted as revealing at least some judicial sensitivity to the complexities of granting legal rights to the unborn child.

Relevant to equality arguments would also be the consideration, first identified by Kolder and others, that force in relation to refused treatment or the use of criminal or child protection proceedings in relation to drug and alcohol abuse, have been invoked disproportionately against women from minority ethnic groups.[111] In this regard, one study found that, although traces of drugs were found just as often in the urine of black and white newborns, only black mothers were referred to the prosecution or child welfare authorities.[112] At the same time, however, as John Robertson notes, it may be relevant that evidence of marijuana was more likely to be found in white women and of cocaine in black women, and there is no evidence that prenatal use of the former is as harmful to future children as the latter.[113] (Recent evidence doubting the effects of the latter was, however, noted in chapter six.)

Scraping the barrel somewhat, a further line of reasoning which we might invoke in this context is privacy reasoning (discussed in earlier chapters). It was noted that this may not be the strongest argument, however, when we are considering trivial or non-meaningful or even non-authentic exercises of autonomy. Whilst with regard to the compelled caesarean one could also raise the issue of bodily integrity, as noted in chapters one and two the right to bodily integrity is invoked most trivially in the case of the ingestion of the beneficial pill. It is for this reason that I have concentrated here on damage to possibly already weak autonomy interests as well as equality concerns. Overall, in these cases in which we have been concerned that the values protected by the right might not seriously be at stake, cases which Dworkin might call "marginal",[114] what has emerged is that, although in the case of the seemingly trivial reason a deeply meaningful choice is not being protected, nevertheless values central to rights, namely the "vague but powerful idea of human dignity" and/or political equality are very much in issue.[115]

3. Allowing Coercion—Problems of Abuse

Despite the above thoughts, it may be objected that in fact it requires *courage* to intervene on behalf of the unborn child, that although there are concerns about vulnerable women whose background or upbringing has resulted in weak autonomy skills and poor self-esteem, physical harm to the unborn child is at stake and this must be prevented. Thus perhaps I, for one, lack that courage. One can have some considerable sympathy with this view, noting that this objector's answer to the problems which might arise in terms of the mother mistrusting or resisting medical interventions when the child is born will likewise be to compel treatment,

---

[111] VEB Kolder, J Gallagher and MT Parsons, "Court-Ordered Obstetrical Interventions", 1195.

[112] IJ Chasoff, "The Prevalence of Illicit Drug Use during Pregnancy and Discrepancies in Reporting in Pinellas County, Florida", (1990) 344 *New Eng J of Med* 1202, cited by J Robertson *Children of Choice*, 184.

[113] J Robertson *Children of Choice*, 184, n. 35.

[114] R Dworkin, *Taking Rights Seriously*, 200.

[115] *Ibid.*, 198, 199.

and that this is not nearly as problematic when this is in a child's best interests and does not impact on the self-determination or bodily integrity of the woman. Nevertheless, a problem with this approach, I think, is that it is open to abuse. This is a familiar argument. For instance Joseph Raz has suggested that a valid reason concerning the use of coercion is that often but not always it is liable to be abused.[116] Whilst such an argument is hard to make out in the absence of specific examples witnessing abuse, there is some point in noting these kinds of concerns here. If we allow doctors to force, say, the vitamin or other drug therapy on pregnant women when the reasons for refusal are apparently trivial or non-existent, it is hard not to have the feeling that the possibility of this option in this case may completely override the need to understand the woman's seemingly misplaced objections. Moreover, given the availability of the option in the one case, there will surely be a temptation to use it in another, for instance when a woman is refusing the therapy because of concerns about unpleasant side-effects on her (contrary to assumptions I made in earlier chapters for the sake of argument) or when she is refusing some other kind of intervention. I am not suggesting that the risk of abuse here would take us all the way down the slippery slope to the caesareans, but it does seem that a doctor's well-intentioned judgment about side-effects could easily mean that she viewed a refusal as trivial in a way which could be inappropriate.

4. Symbolic Meanings

Lastly, as Joseph Raz has noted, it can be easy to exaggerate the wrongs of coercion or, by implication, forced treatment, in comparison with the wrongs and misfortunes which befall people at various times or of course the future child in the context under discussion. Raz notes that the wrong of coercion often lies in its insulting or affronting nature rather than in the consequences in the particular case, which may not be serious.[117] He notes, however, that there is an important difference between coercion by an ideal liberal state (influenced by a public morality concerned with individual autonomy) which does not insult individual autonomy, and most other origins of coercion.[118] With regard to the latter he suggests that, whatever the consequences of coercion (and manipulation), they have acquired a strong "symbolic meaning expressing disregard or even contempt for the coerced or manipulated" because of the kind of treatment that they are (reducing options and distorting decision-making and preference formation).[119] The use of coercion, manipulation or force in the maternal treatment context likewise carries disturbing symbolic meanings of women being the *vehicles* to maternal health. These thoughts would clearly apply to doctors and other health professionals. As regards our judge, although earlier, of course, I suggested that to some extent we had to view her as representative of the ideal liberal state, I think that the symbolic meanings are here

---

[116] See e.g. J Raz, *The Morality of Freedom*, 421.
[117] *Ibid.*, 156.
[118] *Ibid.*
[119] *Ibid.*, 378.

so strong that they cannot be readily resisted, even by the judge. Given the difficulties inherent in the processes of gestation and birth which necessarily fall only on women, actions which reinforce or contribute to these meanings should be resisted.

These various answers as to why we should not compel prenatal treatment, be they reasons of morality, law or policy, are predominantly contextual. They require us to consider not only the unique position of women and the way their bodies are implicated with regard, in particular, to surgical options, but also the possible vulnerability of some women, which may be increased when pregnant. If the answer is thereby to turn to the realities of the context in question, rather than to arrive at a purely theoretical answer to the problem, this may in part be because, as Isaiah Berlin apparently considered, the moral life we find there is so rich and deep compared with the "empty vistas of moral theory".[120] Overall, as others have repeatedly argued, it appears that more energy and resources should, if possible, be devoted to protecting the fetus and the future child through enhanced support of pregnant women, an approach which Dawn Johnsen has characterised as "facilitative" rather than "adversarial".[121]

V. POSTSCRIPT: REFLECTIONS ON CASES CONCERNING INCOMPETENTS

This final section briefly considers aspects of cases concerning the compelled donation of organs/tissue from incompetents. In one sense such cases are clearly irrelevant to the maternal–fetal cases. Following a brief outline of the main considerations in the cases concerning incompetents, however, I shall suggest why reflection upon them is salutary to our understanding of the maternal–fetal conflict.

Jefferson is the first maternal–fetal case to draw on this area of the law, citing *Strunk* v. *Strunk* (1969).[122] In that case, the mother of a 27-year-old incompetent ward sought authority to proceed with a kidney transplant from the incompetent to her 28-year-old son who was suffering from a fatal kidney disease. In the Court of Appeals of Kentucky, Osborne J affirmed the order of the county court, which had employed the doctrine of "substituted judgment" to consider the well-being

---

[120] J Gray, *Isaiah Berlin* (London: Harper Collins, 1995) 64: After outlining a scenario creating a possible impasse between a consequentialist and a deontologist, he notes: "For Berlin, the phenomenology of moral life, which abounds in incommensurabilities and radical choices, merits primacy, if only because of the striking feebleness of the moral theories which seek to displace it. The fact is that we do not have a workable felicific calculus, or an account of a structure of compossible rights. We have no reason to abandon the richness and depth of moral life, with all of its undecidable dilemmas, for the empty vistas of moral theory."

[121] D Johnsen, "Shared Interests: Promoting Healthy Births Without Sacrificing Women's Liberty", 43 *Hastings LJ* (1992) 569, 596, my emphasis. As noted in the notes to ch. 3, this article promotes a "facilitative" rather than an "adversarial" approach to the maternal–fetal relationship which makes sound policy sense but tends to obscure the very real moral conflict that may well be presented in the medical treatment context as opposed, for instance, to broader social concerns about drug-addiction or the different issue of *access* to medical care.

[122] Ky 445 SW 2d 145. The case is cited without explanation as part of the *per curiam* opinion of the *Jefferson* court. Ga 274 SE 2d at 460.

of the incompetent brother, finding that the operation would be "beneficial" to the incompetent on the basis of his "emotional and psychological dependence on his older brother"; moreover that the incompetent's well-being would be "jeopardized more severely by the loss of his brother than by the removal of a kidney".[123] Thus, the transplant was justified on the basis that the older brother's death would be much more damaging to the incompetent's well-being than incurring the risks of the kidney donation.

Strunk should be contrasted, in particular, with the more recent case of *Curran* v. *Bosze*,[124] in which the Supreme Court of Illinois refused to order three-and-a-half-year-old twins to submit to a bone-marrow harvesting procedure for the benefit of their half-brother who had leukaemia, on the basis that the procedure was not in their best interests. Critical to the judgment of Calvo J was the lack of an existing close relationship between the potential donors and donee:[125]

> "If there is any benefit to a child who donates bone marrow to a sibling it will be psychological benefit. According to the evidence, the psychological benefit is not simply one of personal, individual altruism in an abstract sense, although that may be a factor. The psychological benefit is grounded firmly in the fact that donor and recipient are known to each other as family."

The absence of a psychological benefit to the donor was similarly important in the Illinois case of *Re Pescinski*.[126] Both these authorities were cited in the 1994 caesarean decision of *Baby Boy Doe*. By contrast, the presence of a close relationship between donor and donee was decisive in favour of the legal authorisation of the donation of bone-marrow in the English case of *Re Y*,[127] in which the family was particularly close. As Andrew Grubb notes, however, the evidence of a psychological benefit does not appear to have been as strong as in the American case of *Strunk*, in which, as I noted above, the donor brother was deemed emotionally and psychologically *dependent* on his brother.[128] The fact that the risks inherent in the bone-marrow harvesting procedure were minimal was an additional consideration justifying the order in the best interests of the potential donor.

Following this necessarily brief introduction to some of the factors critical to the leading cases on donation by incompetents, I now return to the maternal–fetal cases.

The differences between the cases involving incompetents on the one hand and the maternal–fetal cases on the other are readily apparent and several scholars have drawn attention to them. For instance, writing shortly after *Jefferson*, one scholar observes that the only similarity between that case and the case of *Strunk* is that each

---

[123] Ky 445 SW 2d at 146.
[124] 566 NE 2d 1319 (Ill 1990). (The decision was cited in the caesarean decision of *Baby Boy Doe* 632 NE 2d 326 (Ill App 1 Dist 1994).)
[125] *Ibid.*, 1343
[126] 226 NW 2d 180.
[127] [1996] 2 FLR 787.
[128] A Grubb, "Commentary: Adult Incompetent: Legality of Non-therapeutic Procedure: *Re Y*", (1996) 4 *Med L Rev* 204, 206.

concerned the imposition of surgery on one person for the benefit of another.[129] In fact, even this is not really true since in the *Jefferson* situation, of course, the "other" who will benefit (the fetus) is not a separate individual and hence not a legal person.[130] Yet, despite the radical differences between cases involving incompetents and those of the maternal–fetal conflict, the former are pertinent to our reflection upon those maternal–fetal cases, such as *Jefferson* and *Re S*, in which pregnant women have been denied the right to refuse caesareans.

First, we might reflect upon the idea of the *psychological benefit* to a pregnant woman from ordering (in the United States) or declaring lawful (in England) a caesarean where her fetus may otherwise be lost through the refusal of the same. The question of psychological benefit, for instance, was a relevant consideration in the English "needle phobia" cases of *Re MB* and *Re L*. But in such cases we have seen that the women were effectively prevented from consenting to surgery by their phobia, despite their "true desire" to submit to caesarean delivery. In such a case, therefore, the question of psychological benefit to the woman from the compelled anaesthesia (as a precursor to the surgery) is a legitimate concern of the court. By contrast, in the case of a truly competent refusal—where a woman refuses the caesarean for religious reasons or out of serious concerns about a caesarean section *per se*—provided the likely outcome has been discussed with her, there can be no place for a paternalistic justification of the rescue of the fetus.

Second, focusing upon the narrow issue of *medical benefit*, the courts in these caesarean cases may well have *seen* themselves (illegitimately) as looking out for the best interests of Mrs Jefferson, or Mrs S: the chances of Mrs Jefferson surviving vaginal delivery were put at "no better than 50%" and it was considered that a caesarean section was the only way to save Mrs S's life. The fact that the courts absorbed these risks and probabilities into their justifications may suggest that the women were in some sense being treated, paternalistically, as if they were incompetent.[131] Once again, however, where a woman's choice to refuse treatment such as a caesarean is truly autonomous, paternalistic concerns about saving her life are out of place.

A dimension of the cases concerning incompetents which gives pause for thought is the dissenting opinion in the American authority of *Strunk* of Steinfeld J. Regarding the kidney donation by the incompetent brother, he considered that it had not been "conclusively demonstrated that it will be of significant benefit to the incompetent".[132] In this he was supported by two other judges, making the split in the *Strunk* court a close four to three.[133] Thus, if one judge had decided differently, the incompetent's interests might well have been protected much more

---

[129] EP Finamore, "*Jefferson* v. *Griffin Spalding County Hospital Authority*: Court-Ordered Surgery to Protect the Life of an Unborn Child", (1983) 9 *Am JL & Med* 83, 91.

[130] J Lenow also makes this point in "The Fetus as a Patient: Emerging Rights as a Person?", (1984) 10 *Am JL & Med* 1, 20.

[131] This may well be a particularly apposite interpretation of *Re S*, since currently English law only employs a "best interests" test in relation to incompetents.

[132] Ky 445 SW 2d at 151. He suggested the evidence did "not rise to that pinnacle".

[133] Neikirk and Palmore, JJ concurred in Steinfeld J's dissent. Supporting Osborne J for the majority were Hill CJ, Milliken and Reed JJ.

stringently. In the light of Steinfeld J's concern about evidence of an *incompetent's* wishes, it is not a little shocking to reflect upon the failure in *Re AC* (1987) properly to obtain evidence of Ms C's wishes. Presumably, if she had lived, the District Court of Appeals would have sent the matter back to the trial judge for rehearing on this issue. When we consider the protection afforded to *incompetents*, we see that George Annas's notable (if somewhat dramatic) observation to the effect that the reasoning in *Re AC* "would, for example, permit the involuntary removal of vital organs prior to death when they were needed to 'save a life' "[134] is not far off the mark. Ms C was granted none of the protection accorded to the incompetent in *Strunk* or the other cases concerning incompetents; the court simply never decided whether she was competent or incompetent. Highly critical of the lower court's decision, the 1990 court in *Re AC* held that "courts do not compel one person to permit a significant intrusion upon his or her bodily integrity for the benefit of another's health."[135] *McFall* v. *Shimp* was cited in support.

Consideration of the cases of incompetents, notably the protection afforded to these individuals by the courts, therefore tends to highlight in what low esteem the interests of pregnant women were held in cases such as *Jefferson*, *Re S* and *Re AC*. Although, as has been acknowledged, the courts in *Jefferson* and *Re S* may have seen themselves as acting in the "best interests" of Mrs Jefferson or Mrs S, in reality they paid attention only to these women's "medical interests" and ignored their interests (and *prima facie* rights) in bodily integrity and self-determination and associated religious interests. But, however it is understood, "best interests" is a concept associated with incompetence, just as autonomy is linked with competence. In effect, these courts ignored the important sense in which to order or declare lawful a caesarean section was to deny the women's interests in religious autonomy and bodily integrity. Ultimately, it may be because women such as Mrs Jefferson or Mrs S were competent moral agents with supposed duties to their unborn children that they were accorded less protection than the incompetent adult who has no such duties (notwithstanding that the judicial reasoning in *Jefferson* was presented in terms of a State interest in the fetus and a conflict of rights between Mrs Jefferson and the fetus she carried). Yet, as I have argued here and earlier, it seems impossible to defend the proposition that either of these women—whose refusals of a caesarean were based upon serious (religious) reasons—had a moral duty, potentially enforceable in law, to come to the rescue of their fetuses by means of a caesarean section.

In conclusion to this reflection upon the relevance of cases of incompetent donations, I note Andrew Grubb's comment on the English case of *Re Y*, to the effect that a court might well look for the agreement (though clearly not the consent) of an incompetent to a donation; moreover, that it would be "unthinkable" for a

---

[134] G Annas, "She's Going to Die: Going to Die: the Case of Angela C.", (1988) 18 (Feb./Mar.) *Hastings CR* 23, 25. *Re AC* (1987) itself makes no reference to the area of law in issue, though the court did take note of literature on compulsory caesarean sections, some of which refers to the points now under discussion.

[135] 573 A 2d at 1243–4, *per* Terry AJ.

court to order a donation on the basis of "best interests" if there were any evidence of objection to the procedure on the incompetent's part.[136] By contrast, one of the reasons why this has been thinkable in the case of refusals by competent pregnant women has lain in the rejection by third parties of their reasons for refusal. At this point we should, I think, be reminded of the suggestion in Part II—in connection with the English caesarean case of *Re MB*—of moral infusions seeping into the determination of the critical issue of competence.

VI. CONCLUSIONS

In discussing the application of points from the law of rescue to the maternal–fetal conflict, this chapter has reached the following principal conclusions, some of which have drawn upon earlier sections of the book.

First, although a pregnant woman is specially related to her unborn child, the fact that she has voluntarily assumed a pregnancy and that pregnancy commonly carries what are extraordinary risks by comparison with the demands of other special relationships (such as that of parent and child) does not justify the imposition of moral duties to submit to a physically burdensome rescue on her part. Hence, there are no grounds for a legal duty in this regard, unless she has no apparent reason for refusing the rescue in question. In the latter case, attention must focus on the appropriateness of legal enforcement of a then presumed moral obligation.

Next, although both *McFall* v. *Shimp* and the maternal–fetal cases can be conceived as "rescue" cases, arguably the case of *McFall* can also be understood as a treatment refusal case while the maternal–fetal cases are best placed within this area. Since there are enormous difficulties in determining when it is reasonable or unreasonable to submit to a certain physical invasion (with attendant pain, burden and risk) in the treatment context, even one to benefit or rescue some other, determining a standard upon which we could build the idea of a legal duty is fraught with difficulty.

Having revisited this point with reference to *McFall*, a central discussion of this chapter focused on the inappropriateness of legally compelled physical invasions, an issue left open by the prospect of the unjustified refusal. A number of problems with compelled interventions have emerged. Given the unjustified (hence unprincipled) nature of such refusals, a consequentialist argument for or against interventions was a natural starting point here. In this regard, I observed that also consequentialists have good reason to stop at seeking to effect a balance of good over bad when doing so entails non-consensual bodily incursions. Despite the ideally objective stance that the law occupies, in some cases achieving justice may involve legitimising actions too morally objectionable in themselves. The case of the compelled caesarean section (which I considered in response to a clearly unjustified refusal) is just such a case.

---

[136] A Grubb, "Commentary: *Re Y*", 207.

Further, there are some good consequentialist objections to the compulsion of treatment (the beneficial pill) not seriously invoking a woman's interest in bodily integrity or self-determination, such as concerns over "maternal flight". The consequentialist answers had a somewhat unsatisfactory ring to them, however, albeit to a lesser extent than an argument from the principle of autonomy would have here. Taking my cue from Gerald Dworkin's suggestion that regarding issues such as coercion a close analysis of the particular area—rather than a general theoretical argument—is most helpful, I explored a number of reasons against compelled interventions in the case of non-invasive treatment (since I had concluded that the cutting open of a person against her will is the critical bar to interventions in the case of the apparently unjustified refusal of the caesarean). Here I touched on the idea that we could be mistaken about the nature or basis of a woman's refusal (through language and associated cultural issues) and noted the possibility of poorly developed autonomy skills possibly arising from an abused background, suggesting that increased efforts at discussion and counselling were required. I also reflected on the issue of equality, noting the difficulties of applying equality reasoning as traditionally conceived under the US Equal Protection Clause and under the European Convention on Human Rights (with their requirement that claimants be "similarly" or "analogously" situated). By contrast I observed the helpfulness of the approach of Catharine MacKinnon, Ruth Ginsberg and of Justice Blackmun in *Casey*. We saw that Justice Blackmun criticised the State's assumption that women have a duty to continue a pregnancy "as a matter of course", as though they "can simply be forced to accept the 'natural' status and incidents of motherhood", a line of thought which in chapter five I had related to my "social context" argument. Here I suggested that in the case of the seemingly unjustified refusal, issues pertaining to the vulnerability and powerlessness of women who might refuse treatment in these ways was important. Lastly, following Joseph Raz, I noted potential problems of abuse if we allow some compelled interventions and the point that when coercion is not conducted by an "ideal liberal state" it carries important symbolic meanings, in this context the notion of women as *vehicles* to fetal health. Coercion by doctors and other health professionals would clearly be in point; further, although the judge has to be seen as representative of the ideal liberal state, here the symbolic meanings seem too powerful even for her to resist. Overall, the context-sensitive nature of these thoughts on the issue of coercion was noted.[137]

Finally, the cases relating to incompetents revealed a concern with not harming the potential donor unfortunately lacking in cases such as *Jefferson*, *Re AC* and *Re S*.

---

[137] For further very recent thoughts on issues relevant to this chapter, see S Bewley, "Restricting the Freedom of Pregnant Women", in DL Dickenson (ed.), *Ethical Issues in Maternal–Fetal Medicine* (Cambridge: Cambridge University Press, 2002) 131–59. For instance, Bewley notes that "[t]here is no evidence that threat strategies prevent harm. What little work there is on substance abuse reporting laws show [*sic*] no change in substance abuse in subsequent pregnancies." (At 144, citing I Delke *et al*, "Effects of Substance Abuse Reporting Laws on Cocaine in Subsequent Pregnancies", (1993) 168 *Am J of Obstet & Gyn* 403. In the same volume, see also F Baylis and S Sherwin, "Judgements of Non-compliance in Pregnancy", 285–301, who are concerned with the multiplicity of possible reasons for refusing medical treatment or not following medical advice and with the importance of fostering autonomy.

Conclusions to Part III

IN THE main, Part III has been concerned with arguments from duty. So far as the law of abortion is concerned, we have seen that no positive legal duty can be derived from that context to that of maternal–fetal conflict in the treatment context. Further, examination of abortion law's prioritisation of the life and health of the pregnant woman even after fetal viability was explored and adapted to the situation of maternal–fetal conflict in a way which supports a pregnant woman's legal right to refuse medical treatment. Attention was also drawn to the State's duties to the pregnant woman, stemming from its important and continuing interest in her life and health.

From the law of tort, we have seen that the ideas of third-party and maternal liability for prenatal harm raise radically different questions, which in turn point toward the rejection of the proposition that a mother should owe a legal duty of care toward her fetus. Moreover, certainly no such duty currently exists at law. This chapter also rejected the idea of a maternal legal duty of prenatal care outside the treatment context. In reaching these conclusions, the chapter particularly demonstrated the difficulties inherent in the idea of a duty of care that would be owed to a being *inside* one from conception until birth, especially in terms of the idea of such a duty being owed *via* or *through* one's own body.

The moral and legal problems inherent in the idea of a legal duty which is to be fulfilled by means of the body was also a central issue in the final chapter on the law of rescue. Here the discussion sought briefly to confirm that the idea of a moral duty to be realised "via" the body may be problematic in itself, that is, regardless of the further question of legal enforcement thereof. In this connection I explored the sense in which the "rescue" cases such as *McFall* are not in fact satisfactorily encompassed within Samaritan law. I put forward the view that the moral problems inherent in the idea of compelled physical invasions may really lie in the law's agency with regard to such compulsion and touched upon the broader policy considerations which weigh against compelled prenatal interventions. I also put forward a number of context-sensitive reasons against compelled interventions particularly relating to the fostering of autonomy and to equality. Lastly, I took note of the law relating to incompetents in a way which gives us pause for thought regarding past—and future—cases of maternal refusals of medical treatment in pregnancy.

Concluding the Arguments

I HAVE EXAMINED, in ethical and legal terms, the question of a pregnant woman's refusal of medical treatment needed by the fetus she carries, occasionally contrasting this, by way of counterpoint, with the question of the effects that day-to-day maternal conduct may have, particularly, upon the child who will subsequently be born. While the primary issues have centred around medical treatment, since we have been concerned with the refusal of treatment needed by a developing human being, the topic has been seen to extend beyond the ethics and law relating to medical treatment and to raise questions pertinent—but by no means identical—to those arising in relation to abortion. In effect, neither maternal refusal of medical treatment needed by the developing fetus nor abortion (much more obviously) can simply be characterised as *medical* issues. Rather, these issues present important *moral* problems because of the harm that will befall a fetus in either case, raising questions on the one hand about the justification of such harm and on the other about when, if at all, the rights which permit it should be limited.

A central task, therefore, has been the understanding of some important points of connection between questions relating to medical treatment on the one hand and abortion on the other, as they come together in the scenario under consideration, coupled with the delineation of significant points of departure. In this process, it has been apparent that attempts to address the maternal–fetal conflict which concentrate too much upon the ethics and law of refusal of medical treatment on the one hand or abortion on the other will lack both depth and conviction. Indeed, a central fault of much of the literature has been a failure to recognise the quasi-hybrid nature of the maternal–fetal conflict as it occurs within the treatment context. Thus, either the reproductive process is highlighted, so that a woman's intention to carry the fetus to term, hence not abort, is in some way thought to negate her interests and rights as these may be called into play in medical treatment issues. Alternatively the treatment refusal rights of the pregnant woman are asserted without thought to the need for their justification, given the possibly fatal consequences for the fetus. The first tendency characterised the early maternal–fetal cases, whilst the latter may come to seem a weakness of the more recent cases as the scope for *in utero* interventions increases. In reality, a coherent and convincing account of the law and ethics of the maternal–fetal conflict must address and resolve these tensions, on the one hand drawing attention to the interests and values common to the ethics and law of treatment refusal and abortion, on the other successfully explaining the differences and the reasons for these.

A pregnant woman and the fetus she carries are physically related by the presence of the fetus in her womb. Whatever the emotional depth and extent of the relationship between born individuals, including parents and children, no other human relationship has such a peculiarly *physical* impact upon a person. Thus, notwithstanding that our concern is with the voluntarily pregnant woman, once a pregnancy is begun or accepted, nothing (in a normal pregnancy) will halt the increasing impact which the fetus makes upon the woman's body. A pregnancy, then, cannot be stopped and re-started at will. Further, at term the fetus simply must leave her body (whether this is by natural or caesarean delivery) and the birth itself will be an immensely physically (and emotionally) demanding experience. In a curious sense, then, despite the choice to have a child (or not to abort an unplanned one), the physical gestation of the fetus becomes something that "happens" to a pregnant woman. This is not to deny the active processes of psychological adjustment that will be necessary on the pregnant woman's part. Likewise, it does not mean that no maternal choices remain. Indeed, I have defended the view that when a pregnant woman wishes to decline medical treatment needed by the fetus (such as caesarean delivery) or, by implication, when she needs medical treatment herself which may impact adversely upon the fetus (such as cancer treatment), then, because of her continuing interests in bodily integrity and self-determination and the magnitude of these very personal interests, it is appropriate that she should have the moral and legal right to decide what treatment she takes for herself or, more particularly for the purposes of the cases under discussion, accepts or refuses for the fetus.

Hence the position established by the English Court of Appeal that a pregnant woman has the absolute right to refuse medical treatment needed by the fetus, thus can decline it "for religious reasons, other reasons, or for no reasons at all", is sound (*Re MB*). So also is the current position in some US states that a pregnant woman has the right to refuse treatment as invasive as a caesarean (*Baby Boy Doe*), or as a blood transfusion (*Re Fetus Brown*), despite the adverse consequences for the fetus. We have seen that the reasoning of the English decision hinges upon the fetus's lack of legal personhood, whilst the US decision of *Baby Boy Doe* goes beyond this to the nature and value of the treatment refusal rights of the pregnant woman. The latter approach is better suited to reflection upon the justification of such rights, through attention to a woman's underlying interests in bodily integrity and self-determination. Indeed, it may be no mere coincidence that it is in the English case of *Re MB*, rather than the American decision of *Baby Boy Doe*, that the leading judge is left pondering the "ethical dilemmas" residual upon the confirmation of a pregnant woman's legal right to refuse medical treatment, or that *Re Fetus Brown*— which, as with *Re MB*, places considerable emphasis upon the fetus's lack of legal personhood—similarly raises a query as to the "apparently disparate" nature of a pregnant woman's ethical and legal obligations. Moreover, the attribution of a woman's right to refuse medical treatment purely on the basis of the lack of legal personhood of the fetus is at its weakest in the event that, rather than the fetus dying *in utero*, a child—a legal person—is subsequently born harmed.

If the moral and legal justification of a pregnant woman's right to refuse medical treatment is properly based upon the moral recognition and legal protection of her interests in self-determination and bodily integrity, then the appropriateness or justifiability of her actual choice to exercise the right to refuse medical treatment will in turn depend upon whether her reasons for so doing are intrinsically related to these underlying interests. Given the impact of her choices upon the fetus, the merit of her decisions will be measured by the extent to which she has acknowledged and "can answer to" the moral claims of the fetus in relation to her own spiritual or physical imperatives. This is the cornerstone of a gradualist approach to the maternal–fetal relationship which I defended in chapter one, which rejects as question-begging and absolutist the denial of the fetus's rights (moral or legal) on the one hand or the assertion, without more, of a woman's rights (moral or legal) on the other and hinges upon a sense of *proportionality* between the growing moral claims of the fetus and the strength of maternal reasons for refusing medical treatment. This was an argument which I refined to apply to the future child who may in due course be born with damage suffered *in utero*, suggesting that a woman's reasons must relate particularly to the body in the latter case, given that the most important distinguishing feature between a born child and the future child (who will be but is not yet born) is that the latter is *in utero* until birth.

Recall to mind the obvious illustrations of this gradualist approach: the refusal of the caesarean delivery by the Born-Again Christian who believes she will go to hell if she submits to surgery, which particularly relates to a woman's interest in self-determination (*Jefferson, Re S*); or the refusal by the woman in the light of a previously physically and emotionally traumatic experience of a caesarean, which may relate particularly to her interest in bodily integrity (the *Rochdale* case); or the refusal by the woman dying of cancer with at best two remaining days of life, a case perhaps raising equally interests in self-determination and bodily integrity (*Re AC*). In these cases, the apparent seriousness of the reasons and concerns at stake *theoretically* justify the unintentional harm to the fetus even allowing for its heightened claims at the point of birth. In *practice*, however, given the peculiarly personal and physical nature of the arena in which these decisions are being made, we cannot accurately judge whether a serious reason for a refusal is sufficiently serious to justify fetal harm. In such cases, then, we must take its seriousness "on trust", a point which ultimately underscores the attribution of moral and legal rights in such a context. Thus, in each of these cases, we must conclude that the pregnant woman justifiably asserts her legal right to refuse medical treatment needed by the fetus. Further, the implication in these cases is not only that the woman does not have the *legal* duty to have the caesarean, but also that we cannot even clearly say—in the scenarios outlined above—that she has the *moral* duty to do so.

By contrast, in the hypothetical case of the woman refusing the caesarean on the cosmetic grounds of the scar, the exercise of the legal right to do so no longer retains the intrinsic connection with the underlying moral and legal interests which form the foundations of the right. Moreover, the triviality of the reason makes it relatively easy for us to agree that the reason for the refusal is not "appropriate" in the light of the enormity of the possible harm to the fetus. In such a case, a woman is clearly breaching her moral duties to the fetus, whilst retaining the legal right (unjustifiably asserted) to refuse the caesarean. The same is true of the woman (again hypothetical) who refuses the pill which would be highly beneficial for fetal welfare and would have no adverse effects upon herself. Indeed, whilst the pill "technically" belongs to the treatment context (being a form of medical treatment), its refusal by a pregnant woman would be much more akin to an instance of general conduct on her part, since her specific and very personal interests in self-determination and bodily integrity are not seriously invoked in relation to such treatment: correlatively, it is very hard to think of a reason, let alone a serious one, why she should refuse it.

The critical synthesis of these ethical and legal ideas regarding a pregnant woman's *rights* occurred in the examination of the interests and values underlying both the legal right (of the "ordinary" competent patient) to refuse medical treatment and the legal right to abort, primarily in US law, followed by the application of these ideas to the arguably "hybrid" nature of a pregnant woman's right to refuse treatment in chapter four.

In the first case, examination of early case law prior to the establishment of a near-absolute right to refuse even life-sustaining medical treatment revealed that the State, which weighed its interest in the preservation of life against the *prima facie* right of the patient, tended to allow individuals to refuse treatment where it was felt that they had "serious reasons" for so doing, consistent with the idea that the possession of life is a "good and valuable thing". Further, given the connection between these kinds of reasons and the patient's moral and legal interests in self-determination and bodily integrity, such reasons did not deny—but could instead be thought to respect—the value of human life: recall, for instance, the bedridden and painful state of Elizabeth Bouvia (a treatment withdrawal case), whose pitiful and permanent medical condition and lack of familial support meant that she felt she had no reason to continue living. In recognising that the values inherent in the preservation of life interest would not be upheld by forcing Miss Bouvia to continue to receive treatment, the State was effectively recognising that to grant the individual the right to refuse life-sustaining medical treatment need not necessarily be to cease to uphold public values about the worth of human life.

Second, examination of aspects of the law of abortion—through consideration of the State's interest in the potential life of the fetus as originally asserted by the US Supreme Court in *Roe* v. *Wade* and more recently re-articulated in *Planned Parenthood of Southeastern Pennsylvania* v. *Casey*—revealed a parallel concern that the abortion decision should not be taken lightly but should be serious and considered. In *Roe,* we find Justice Blackmun asserting that a woman is not "entitled to terminate her pregnancy at whatever time, in whatever way, and for whatever reason she alone chooses", in a passage which is targeted at the question of setting *limits* to the abortion right at viability. In *Casey* this becomes a concern, not with the limits to the right, but with the *way that right is exercised* before viability, resulting in the legitimisation of the establishment, by states, of a "reasonable framework" within which women could make a decision raising profound questions about the "meaning of procreation" and human "responsibility and respect" for it.

These ideas from the law of treatment refusal on the one hand and abortion on the other were then considered in relation to the maternal–fetal cases. Given that a pregnant woman's decision to refuse treatment has ramifications for the potential life of the fetus (that is, a life other than that of the right-holder), at some perhaps subliminal level her right and the manner of its exercise invoke aspects of both the State's interest in the preservation of life and in potential life, or rather some "hybrid" of the two, giving the State a limited "passive" interest (one that does not negate her right) in the moral quality of her choice. Through attention to and reflection upon the motivations for the exercise of a pregnant woman's right to refuse medical treatment affecting the life of the fetus or the health of the future child, it will generally be apparent—to recall a phrase from the important 1977 treatment refusal case of *Saikewicz*, which drew upon *Roe*—that a pregnant woman's exercise of her right does not in fact "cheapen the value which is placed in the concept of living". Thus, rather than being in conflict with or otherwise undermining her right to refuse medical treatment, the combined force of these State or public interests (in the preservation of life and in potential life) can actually be seen to vindicate it depending, in practice, upon the nature of her reasons for refusal.

To appreciate the proper location of the maternal–fetal cases within the law of treatment refusal and grant women the absolute right to refuse medical treatment, as the English cases of *Re MB* and *St George's* and the US cases of *Baby Boy Doe* and *Re Fetus Brown* (in the latter cases at least regarding treatment as invasive as caesareans or blood transfusions respectively) have done, can be understood, on the one hand, as recognising and protecting what the US Supreme Court described in *Cruzan* as the individual's "deeply personal interests" in the treatment context and, on the other, as appreciating, from the abortion context, that because certain highly personal, deeply meaningful areas are the subject of "reasonable disagreement" (*per Casey*), individuals are justly granted the right to make certain decisions fundamental to their liberty themselves. Although these "justifications" explicitly inhere in US rather than English law, so far as the law of treatment refusal in each jurisdiction is concerned, there are clear links between the two. At the same time, regarding the law of abortion, reflection upon the reasoning and values underlying the US law can assist in the evaluation and acceptance of the English law regarding treatment refusal during pregnancy.

Thus, the sense in which a pregnant woman's treatment decision is generally related to important considerations of value within her own life (analysed either in liberty or privacy terms) can be seen to answer to that aspect of *Casey* which is concerned with the moral quality of the decision to exercise a right affecting fetal life. At the same time, the unlikely possibility that such decisions are ill-considered or for trivial reasons opens up the possibility of third-party involvement in the exercise of the right. Reflection upon the construction of a framework in which such involvement can take place in either the American or English context at once provides a defined avenue for counselling and, in strictly limited cases, the persuasion which the English Court of Appeal legitimised, but did not delineate, in *Re MB*.

Without this, there is the very real chance in the English context, given the third "weighing" element in the test of competence in the English case of *Re C* (the balancing of risks and needs which may translate, effectively, as maternal risks versus fetal medical needs), that moral infusions may seep into the determination of a pregnant woman's competence, thus illegitimately negating her legal right to refuse medical treatment and raising serious concerns under the Human Rights Act 1998. (Recall here that the European Convention on Human Rights is meant to guarantee rights in practice, not just in theory.) That this may occur is particularly apparent in the light of Lady Justice Butler-Sloss's acknowledgment in *Re MB* that the decision raises many questions about the ethics of the conflict which the court could not answer. Meanwhile, regarding the currently open question surrounding *non-invasive* treatment in those US states which have considered the issue, the approach advocated here would support the extension of a pregnant woman's right to refuse any treatment, with the opportunity for the involvement of others where her reasons do not appear serious or considered, an unlikely but clearly possible scenario. The same approach would apply to those US states yet to address the issue in any fashion or those which may revisit early precedents (such as Georgia regarding *Jefferson*) overriding a pregnant woman's treatment refusal rights.

The implication of the position that a pregnant woman has the legal *right* to refuse medical treatment required by the fetus is that she does not have the legal *duty* to accept treatment on its behalf. Yet here the idea that she does not have such a duty has been the subject of a separate, if related, defence in the formulation of the argument from duty. This began with the attempt to define maternal moral duties toward the fetus and later moved on to the issue of legal duties through consideration of aspects of the law of abortion, tort (in particular) and rescue (an aspect of the law of tort).

The discussion of duty in chapter two highlighted a number of important distinctions, most of which came to light through reflection upon the point that (unintentional) physical harm to others customarily occurs in the course of general day-to-day conduct and pertains to a breach of an individual's negative duty not to harm others. In contrast, a pregnant woman's duty to accept treatment for the fetus (to avert physical harm to it) would be a duty positively to assist it. Within the philosophical discussion, exploration of the ideas of negative and positive duties suggested that in the case of the former, it is generally easier to determine the reasonableness of the duty, and hence to assess when a negative duty not to harm another has been breached. In the case of the positive duty to rescue another, by contrast, at some point questions about the abilities and nature, physical or psychological, of the would-be rescuer appear to become relevant in a way which eventually gives us pause for thought as to whether a duty to rescue actually lies. This line of thought was acutely accentuated when we turned from the issue of rescues in the domain of general conduct, which may at most carry physical risks, to the idea of rescuing another quite literally *through one's body*, as in the case of the pregnant woman who "rescues" the fetus by means of the caesarean, or the relative who "rescues" another by the donation of a bodily organ or tissue. That is, the determination of reasonableness—and hence, crucially, of the existence and extent of the duty—became more complex and uncertain in the latter cases. In turn these points threw into relief the limitations of attempts to analyse a pregnant woman's duties to the fetus in terms of Good Samaritan arguments, since the latter pertain to the domain of general day-to-day conduct. Similarly, the idea of a pregnant woman's duty to accept a caesarean for her fetus's sake is wrongly characterised as an instance of an ordinary neighbourly duty to help another, as by definition the latter duty does not invoke extraordinary bodily invasions.

Nevertheless, since the women who are the subject of the maternal–fetal cases are essentially voluntarily pregnant (or at least did not abort, though some important issues surrounding the availability of abortion were noted here) and always intended to carry their fetuses to term, they necessarily took on certain particular or special responsibilities toward their fetuses/future children. How, it might be objected, can this not include the duty to submit to a caesarean the moment before birth? The answer is that a woman who undertakes a pregnancy is not analogous, say, to the fireman with special and stringent positive duties to aid others. Beginning a pregnancy is not just the assumption of a social role with concomitant social duties but rather is a choice to reproduce—to create—another human being. Whilst individuals undertaking strict positive duties to aid others can always choose other ways of doing so (although their original roles will then need to be filled by others who do not have qualms about the burdens or risks involved), pregnant women (and their partners) cannot choose another way to have their child (subject to irrelevant exceptions). Given the acute personal importance to the woman (and partner) of reproduction, it is neither fair nor just to say that either a pregnant woman must accept any treatment required by the fetus, in particular the highly invasive and potentially religiously problematic caesarean section, or not reproduce. The possible objection that such a woman should adopt, rather than reproduce, is highly unsympathetic to the reality of a woman's (or couple's) emotional involvement in reproduction. By contrast, the fireman is unlikely to have a great interest in fighting fires in particular, rather than helping people in general, so that his "calling" can be satisfied, if desired, in other ways. Further, the really extraordinary nature of the physical invasiveness of surgery to benefit the fetus such as a caesarean, by comparison with demands customarily present in other human relationships, is belied by the very ordinary, indeed fundamental nature of pregnancy in human life. Indeed, it is this ordinariness which may incline people, incorrectly, to consider that the incidents and burdens of pregnancy, such as caesarean delivery, must surely be accepted "as a matter of course", to recall Justice Blackmun's phrase in *Casey*, in which he criticised this view, thereby giving legal expression to an argument which I dubbed the "social context" of pregnancy.

Indeed, not surprisingly, given my view that the problem of the maternal–fetal conflict within the medical treatment context is a problem lying at the interface between rights and duties, both moral and legal, the reasoning underpinning the argument from duty at the moral level was found to be highly pertinent to discussion of the idea of a pregnant woman's legal duties toward the fetus. I stressed that these conceptual links do not appear to have been recognised elsewhere, in the light of the tendency to emphasise solely the appropriateness of legally enforcing commonly supposed moral duties, which—of course—is not to deny that broader policy considerations are additionally relevant to the idea of imposing legal duties.

The primary conceptual link between the discussion of a pregnant woman's moral duties on the one hand and her legal duties on the other related to the difficulties in determining a standard of care for the purposes of the law of negligence discussed in chapter six, which arises because, at least in the medical treatment context, a pregnant woman's *rights* are called into play. In other words, to try to define the "reasonable pregnant woman" in the medical treatment context is to seek to swim against the tide in the waters of deeply personal interests about which we reasonably disagree. Tort law, with its deterrent and compensatory range over harm to others occurring in the arena of general conduct is not customarily in the business of attempting any such thing. Approaching the issue of a legal duty to submit to the caesarean in this light, the Appellate Court of Illinois in *Baby Boy Doe* considered that a pregnant woman does not have such a duty because of the extensive impact this would have upon her life, but especially her rights. Similarly, as courts such as the Supreme Court of Canada recognised in the *Winnipeg* case, the idea of imposing legal duties upon a pregnant woman could intrude upon a "woman's right to make choices concerning herself". Given that the factual issue in that case pertained to the domain of general conduct, it was argued that this line of reasoning is better and properly applied to the situation of maternal refusal of medical treatment, which will likely invoke a woman's valuable moral and legal interests in self-determination and/or bodily integrity. The same is true of the Court's reasoning in *Dobson*, in which it arguably unnecessarily rejected maternal liability for negligent driving.

Indeed, the obstacles to determining a standard of care as regards a legal duty to accept medical treatment for the fetus are not present regarding the question of possible instances of maternal conduct which may harm the fetus, such as smoking, alcohol consumption (which is more than minimal) or solvent abuse. In effect, the idea of a moral duty not to engage in these activities is an example of a negative duty not to harm the future child, in relation to which the determination of unreasonableness would be relatively clear: in the light of the severe harm to the future child which may result from these activities on the one hand and the lack of value to the pregnant woman in engaging in such conduct on the other—which is intrinsically connected to the fact that she does not have a specific right to do so— the judgment can here be made that a pregnant woman is breaching a negative moral duty she owes to her future child. This means that there is a *prima facie* case for the imposition of a tortious duty not to engage in such conduct, in the same way that third parties can be liable for harm to the fetus/future child of a pregnant woman by their negligent conduct. Social problems of addiction, however, would cloud the duty issue in relation to maternal use of drugs, smoking and alcohol. Further, as regards maternal conduct more generally, beyond such obviously harmful activities as smoking or solvent abuse, we would at some point encounter difficulties in determining a maternal standard of care, particularly in relation to activities of value to the pregnant woman, such as her work or family or other important commitments.

In reality, broad policy considerations were seen to weigh against the imposition of tortious duties as regards a woman's general conduct, including the idea that the imposition of a legal duty could intrude heavily into the privacy of a pregnant woman's life since she can never be "alone" during pregnancy, an argument perhaps especially relevant in Canada, and in England following the Human Rights Act 1998. As the Supreme Court of Illinois recognised in the case of *Stallman* v. *Youngquist*, unlike the third-party tortfeasor whose conduct may harm the fetus, it is a pregnant woman's "every waking and sleeping moment which, for better or worse, shapes the prenatal environment which forms the world for the developing fetus". Giving further legal expression to my social context argument, Justice Cunningham observed that this was not a "pregnant woman's fault" but "a fact of life". Indeed, to impose a tortious duty upon a pregnant woman would make the woman and her fetus "legal adversaries from the moment of conception until birth". For reasons much rehearsed in the literature, this would be an unwise policy choice which could well be detrimental rather than beneficial to prenatal health, by potentially discouraging women from seeking antenatal care, for fear, for instance, that their harmful habits become known.

Examination of the law of rescue in chapter seven, in particular the cases concerning the idea of compelled organ donation, resulted in further reflection upon the complexity inherent in the determination of the existence or extent of a duty to aid another through one's body, rather than by general conduct (with attendant physical risks). But the particular contribution of this brief study was to try to unravel why the law generally recoils, as clearly it always has outside the obstetric arena, from compelled bodily aid. That is, independently of the issue of whether a moral duty lies in a given case, in the end it is important to understand the objections within the law itself to the idea of forcing one individual to help another in this way—objections alarmingly absent, of course, in the original maternal–fetal cases.

In the leading case of *McFall* v. *Shimp*, Flaherty J insisted that "for a society which respects the rights of one individual, to sink its teeth into the jugular vein or neck of one of its members and suck sustenance for another member, is revolting to our hard-wrought concepts of jurisprudence". Taking this passage as a starting point, the discussion noted the opposition between deontological and consequentialist approaches which these words naturally highlight and proceeded to reflect upon the role of the law in such a way as to question whether, generally speaking, a judge has the luxury of being concerned, as a matter of deontological ethics, that the "correlative claims" of those against whom she judges may outweigh the "substantial impersonal value" of her decision. Thus, the judge does not have, as the ordinary practical agent arguably does, both a subjective and an objective place in the world, producing agent-relative and agent-neutral perspectives upon it. Rather, her proper place is the latter, from which she is meant, ideally at least, to be able to take an objective view. Nevertheless, despite the ideally objective stance of the law, at some point concerns about harming may limit the power of judicial sanction: in particular, that the very physical character of operating on a competent pregnant woman without her consent (or one relative to extract a kidney for another) would taint even the action of the State, despite the judicial desire to achieve justice (for instance in the case of the maternal refusal for the grossly inappropriate reason) and effect good consequences (especially a live pregnant woman and newborn child). In other words, the idea of compelled bodily incursions represents a moral line probably respected by both deontologists and consequentialists alike. In addition to the symbolic messages that such forced intervention would send to pregnant women, there is the further possibility that women would become reluctant to seek antenatal care. Thus, in an acute moral and also a broad policy sense, compelled obstetric (especially surgical) interventions, can be seen to be both indefensible and inadvisable. It is partly in policy terms attending to consequentialist considerations that compulsion of treatment such as the (largely hypothetical) pill beneficial for fetal welfare is unwise. But, more significantly, it was important to note a number of context-sensitive reasons against coercion of various kinds: in particular, the problems relating to forcing treatment on women who, whilst possibly legally competent, may nevertheless lack autonomy skills (perhaps because of past abuse), thereby confirming Justice McLachlin's thought from *Winnipeg* that we are not dealing with "heroes and villains", as well as equality arguments relating to compelled treatment. These arguments were in turn related to my social context theme. There was also the question of creating symbolic meanings of women as vehicles to maternal health. Once again these thoughts confirmed the importance of attending to context in our moral and legal reasoning about a very difficult problem.

Returning, in a sense, to where I began in these concluding thoughts, and particularly to the need to distinguish aspects of the law relating to a pregnant woman's refusal of medical treatment from aspects of the law of abortion, arguments in chapter five (which concentrated particularly on US law) took note of the lack of positive legal obligations which can be derived from abortion law, given that the latter's restriction of the abortion right after viability is tantamount to the imposition of a negative duty not to harm, in particular not abort, rather than a positive duty to benefit the fetus. Further, consideration of the American and English legal prioritisation of a pregnant woman over her fetus even after viability was explored in a way which confirmed a woman's right to refuse medical treatment, by highlighting the difficulties of third parties—doctors or judges—in judging upon the physical, psychological or spiritual questions that could arise in relation to treatment issues, in comparison with the purely medical issues arising in relation to the protection of the woman's life or the prevention of grave or permanent injury to her after viability in the abortion context. The latter, of course, are assessments which doctors are qualified to make regarding post-viability abortions. In such cases, they are working within a predetermined legal framework in which a woman's rights are no longer in issue.

Furthermore, with regard to the concern expressed in *Re MB* regarding the possible inconsistencies in the law of abortion after viability and the law of maternal treatment refusal before or at birth, it was suggested that, given that in England a pregnant woman effectively has opportunities to abort in the first two-thirds of pregnancy, increased restrictions upon access to abortion are appropriate after this time. Similarly in the United States the right to abort is justifiably limited following viability. In contrast, as part of the social context argument with regard to the idea of a woman's duties toward the fetus, it was noted that the need for treatment such as a caesarean arises unpredictably, if not necessarily completely unforeseeably, at the last moment of pregnancy, such that safe avoidance thereof could only be achieved by electing not to reproduce. In this way, for the law to hold the caesarean, or such like, to be a matter of legal duty would be both unsympathetic and unjust toward pregnant women.

Lastly, as noted earlier, the unique sense in which, physically at least, a pregnancy (once begun and not aborted) is something which, in a very real sense, "happens" to a pregnant woman, coupled with the fact that the reproduction of the species is always a task falling principally upon women, suggests that justice is broadly served by recognising how important it is for women to have as much control as possible over medical treatment issues in this process. Whilst I have analysed the problem in a way which allows for the involvement of others in treatment decisions where this is appropriate, ultimately the interests of society will be served, not simply by the possibility of having a limited role in discussion, counselling and—on rare and strictly defined occasions—persuasion in the treatment context, but also by the recognition of the value of a pregnant woman's right responsibly to decide treatment issues herself. In this way, pregnant women will receive the message that they are valued. Overall, this in turn will be in the best interests of unborn children.

Bibliography of Works Cited

Allen, A, *Uneasy Access: Privacy for Women in a Free Society* (Totowa, NJ: Rowman and Littlefield, 1988)

American College of Obstetricians and Gynecologists, "Patient Choice: Maternal-Foetal Conflict", Committee Opinion No. 55, October 1987

American Medical Association Board of Trustees, "Legal Interventions During Pregnancy: Court-Ordered Medical Treatments and Legal Penalties for Potentially Harmful Behavior by Pregnant Women", (1990) 263 *Journal of the American Medical Association* 2663

Annas, G, "Forced Cesareans: the Most Unkindest Cut of All", (1982) 12 (June) *Hastings Center Report* 16

——, "Pregnant Women as Fetal Containers", (1986) 16 (Dec.) *Hastings Center Report* 13

——, "The Impact of Medical Technology on the Pregnant Woman's Right to Privacy", (1987) *American Journal of Legal Medicine* 13

——, "Protecting the Liberty of Pregnant Patients", (1987) 316 *New England Journal of Medicine* 1213

——, "She's Going to Die: the Case of Angela C", (1988) 18 (Feb./Mar.) *Hastings Center Report* 23

——, "Foreclosing the Use of Force: *AC* Reversed", (1990) 20 (July/Aug.) *Hastings Center Report* 27

Annas, J, "Women and the Quality of Life: Two Norms or One?", in M Nussbaum and A Sen (eds.), *The Quality of Life* (Oxford: Clarendon Press, 1993) 279

Aristotle, *The Nicomachean Ethics*, trans. by D Ross, rev. by JL Ackrill and JO Urmson (Oxford: Oxford University Press, 1980)

Atiyah, P, *The Damages Lottery* (Oxford: Hart Publishing, 1997)

Atwood, M, *The Handmaid's Tale* (Boston: Houghton Mifflin, 1986)

Audi, R, "Intuitionism, Pluralism, and the Foundations of Ethics", in W Sinnot-Armstrong and M Timmons (eds.), *Moral Knowledge: New Readings in Moral Epistemology* (New York: Oxford University Press, 1996) 101

Baier, A, *Moral Prejudices* (Cambridge, Mass.: Harvard University Press, 1994)

Balisy, S "Maternal Substance Abuse: the Need to Provide Legal Protection for the Fetus", (1987) 60 *Southern California Law Review* 1209

Bambrick, G, "Developing Maternal Liability Standards for Prenatal Injuries", (1987) 61 *St John's Law Review* 592

Barclay, L, "Autonomy and the Social Self", in C MacKenzie and N Stoljar (eds.), *Relational Autonomy: Feminist Perspectives on Autonomy, Agency and the Social Self* (New York: Oxford University Press, 2000) 52

Barendt, E, "Privacy as a Constitutional Right and Value", in P Birks (ed.), *Privacy and Loyalty* (Oxford: Oxford University Press, 1997) 1

Baron, CH, "'If You Prick Us, Do We Not Bleed?': Of Shylock, Fetuses, and the Concept of a Person in the Law", (1983) 11 *Law, Medicine and Healthcare* 52

Barry, B, "And Who is my Neighbour?", Review of C Fried, *Right and Wrong* (Cambridge, Mass.: Harvard University Press, 1977) (1979) 88 *Yale Law Journal* 629

Baylis, F, "Case Comment And Note: Dissenting With the Dissent: *Winnipeg Child And Family Services (Northwest Area) v G (DF)*", (1998) 36 *Alberta Law Review* 785

Baylis, F and Sherwin, S, "Judgements of Non-compliance in Pregnancy", in DL Dickenson (ed.), *Ethical Issues in Maternal-Fetal Medicine* (Cambridge: Cambridge University Press, 2002) 285

Beal, R, "Can I Sue Mommy? An Analysis of a Woman's Tort Liability for Prenatal Injuries to her Child Born Alive", (1984) 21 *San Diego Law Review* 325

Beckwith, FJ and Peppin, JF, "Physician Value Neutrality: A Critique", (2000) 28 *The Journal of Law, Medicine and Ethics* 67

Benhabib, S, *Situating the Self: Gender, Community and Postmodernism in Contemporary Ethics* (New York: Routledge, 1992)

Benn, S, "Abortion, Infanticide and Respect for Persons", in J Feinberg (ed.), *The Problem of Abortion* (Belmont, Calif.: Wadsworth, 1973) 135

Berlin, I, "Two Concepts of Liberty", in his *Four Essays on Liberty* (Oxford: Oxford University Press, 1969) 156

——, *The Magus of the North: JG Hamann and the Origins of Modern Irrationalism* (London: Fontana, 1994)

Bewley, S, "Restricting the Freedom of Pregnant Women", in DL Dickenson (ed.), *Ethical Issues in Maternal-Fetal Medicine* (Cambridge: Cambridge University Press, 2002) 131

Blake, M, "Physician-assisted Suicide: A Criminal Offence or a Patient's Right?", (1997) 5 *Medical Law Review* 294

Blank, R, "Emerging Notions of Women's Rights and Responsibilities During Gestation", (1986) 7 *Journal of Legal Medicine* 441

——, "Maternal-Fetal Relationship: the Courts and Social Policy", (1993) 14 *Journal of Legal Medicine* 73

Bowes, WA and Selgestad, B, "Fetal v Maternal Rights: Medical and Legal Perspectives", (1981) 58 *American Journal of Obstetrics and Gynecology* 209

Brahams, D, "A Baby's Life or a Mother's Liberty: a United States Case", (1988) *The Lancet* 1006

Brazier, M, Guest Editorial, "Hard Cases Make Bad Law?", (1997) 23 *Journal of Medical Ethics* 341

——, "Parental Responsibilities, Foetal Welfare and Children's Health", in C Bridge (ed.), *Family Law Towards the New Millenium: Essays for PM Bromley* (London: Butterworths, 1997) 263

Brody, B, "The Morality of Abortion", from *Abortion and the Sanctity of Life: A Philosophical View* (Cambridge, Mass.: MIT Press, 1975); repr. in TL Beauchamp and L Walters, *Contemporary Issues in Bioethics*, 4th edn. (Belmont, Calif: Wadsworth, 1994) 292

Buchanan, A, Brock, D, Daniels, N and Wikler, D, *From Chance to Choice: Genetics and Justice* (Cambridge: Cambridge University Press, 2000)

Caird, GB, *The Pelican New Testament Commentaries: The Gospel of St Luke* (Harmondsworth: Penguin, 1963)

Callahan, D, *Abortion: Law, Choice and Morality* (New York: Macmillan, 1970)

——, "Minimalist Ethics", (1981) 11 (Oct.) *Hastings Center Report* 19

——, "Autonomy: A Moral Good, Not a Moral Obsession", (1984) 14 (Oct.) *Hastings Center Report* 40

Callahan, JC and Knight, JW, "Women, Fetuses, Medicine and the Law", in HB Holmes and L Purdy (eds.), *Feminist Perspectives in Medical Ethics* (Indianapolis, Ind.: Indiana University Press, 1992) 224

Callahan, S, *In Good Conscience: Reason and Emotion in Moral Decision-Making* (New York: Harper Collins, 1991)

Canadian Royal Commission, *Report on New Reproductive Technologies: Proceed with Care* (Ottawa: Minister of Government Services, 1993)

Cane, P, *The Anatomy of Tort Law* (Oxford: Hart Publishing, 1997)

——, *Atiyah's Accidents, Compensation and the Law*, 6th edn. (London: Butterworths, 1999)

Case Comment, "Constitutional Law—Transfusions Ordered for Dying Woman over Religious Objections", (1964) 113 *University of Pennsylvania Law Review* 290

Caspar, MJ, *The Making of the Unborn Patient* (New Brunswick, NJ: Rutgers University Press, 1998)

Caulfield, T and Nelson, E, "Case Comment And Note: *Winnipeg Child And Family Services* v *DFG*: A Commentary On The Law, Reproductive Autonomy And The Allure Of Technopolicy", (1998) 36 *Alberta Law Review* 799

Charlesworth, M, *Bioethics in a Liberal Society* (Cambridge: Cambridge University Press, 1993)

Chasoff, IJ, "The Prevalence of Illicit Drug Use during Pregnancy and Discrepancies in Reporting in Pinellas County, Florida", (1990) 344 *New England Journal of Medicine* 1202

Chavkin, W, Allen, MH and Oberman, M, "Drug Abuse and Pregnancy: Some Questions on Public Policy, Clinical Management, and Maternal and Fetal Rights", (1991) 18 *Birth* 107

Chernaik, B, "Recovery for Prenatal Injuries: The Right of a Child Against its Mother", (1976) 10 *Suffolk University Law Review* 582

Cherry, A, "Maternal-Fetal Conflicts, The Social Construction of Maternal Deviance, and Some Thoughts about Love and Justice", (1999) 8 *Texas Journal of Women and Law* 245

Chervenak, FC and McCullough, LB, "Perinatal Ethics: A Practical Method of Analysis of Obligations to Mother and Fetus", (1985) 66 *Obstetrics and Gynecology* 442

——, "Clinical Guides to Preventing Ethical Conflicts Between Pregnant Women and their Fetuses", (1990) 162 *American Journal of Obstetrics and Gynecology* 303

Churchill, H, *Caesarean Birth: Experience, Practice and History* (Hale: Books for Midwives Press, 1997)

Cohen, JL, "Rethinking Privacy: Autonomy, Identity, and the Abortion Controversy", in J Weintraub and K Kumar (eds.), *Public and Private in Thought and Practice: Perspectives on a Grand Dichotomy* (Chicago: The University of Chicago Press, 1997) 133

Conaghan, J, "Pregnancy and the Workplace: A Question of Strategy?", in A Bottomley and J Conaghan (eds.), *Feminist Theory and Legal Strategy* (Oxford: Blackwell, 1993) 71

Cox White, B, *Competence to Consent* (Washington, DC: Georgetown University Press, 1994)

Crisp, R, "Medical Negligence, Assault, Informed Consent, and Autonomy", (1990) 17 *Journal of Law and Society* 77

Crisp, R and Slote, M (eds.), *Virtue Ethics* (Oxford: Oxford University Press, 1997)

Daniels, C, *At Women's Expense* (Cambridge, Mass.: Harvard University Press, 1993)

——, "Between Fathers and Fetuses: the Social Construction of Male Reproduction and the Politics of Fetal Harm", in DL Dickenson (ed.), *Ethical Issues in Maternal-Fetal Medicine* (Cambridge: Cambridge University Press, 2002) 113

DeCoste, F, "Case Comment and Note: *Winnipeg Child and Family Services (Northwest Area)* v *DFG*: The Impossibility of Fetal Rights and the Obligations of Judicial Governance", (1998) 36 *Alberta Law Review* 725

Delke, I et al, "Effects of Substance Abuse Reporting Laws on Cocaine in Subsequent Pregnancies", (1993) 168 *American Journal of Obstetrics and Gynecology* 403

Dennis, B, "Care Study: Severe Needle Phobia", (1994) *Midwives Chronicle and Nursing Notes* 58

De Ville, KA and Kopelman, LM, "Fetal Protection in Wisconsin's Revised Child Abuse Law; Right Goal, Wrong Remedy", (1999) 27 *The Journal of Law, Medicine and Ethics* 332

Diamond, M, "Echoes from Darkness: The Case of Angela C", (1990) 51 *University of Pittsburgh Law Review* 1061

van Dijk, P and van Hoof, G, *Theory and Practice of the European Convention on Human Rights*, 3rd edn. (The Hague: Kluwer, 1998)

Dodds, S, "Choice and Control in Feminist Bioethics", in C MacKenzie and N Stoljar (eds.), *Relational Autonomy: Feminist Perspectives on Autonomy, Agency and the Social Self* (New York: Oxford University Press, 2000) 213

Dorris, M, *The Broken Cord* (New York: Harper and Row, 1989)

Doswald-Beck, L, "The Meaning of the 'Right to Respect for Private Life' under the European Convention on Human Rights", (1983) 4 *Human Rights Law Journal* 283

Doudera, AE, "Fetal Rights? It Depends", (1982) 18 *Trial* 38

Dougherty, CJ, "The Right to Begin Life with Sound Body and Mind: Fetal Patients and Conflicts with their Mothers", (1985) 63 *University of Detroit Law Review* 89

Draper, H, "Women, Forced Caesareans and Antenatal Responsibilities", (1996) 22 *Journal of Medical Ethics* 327

Douglas-Scott, S, Review of R Dworkin's *Life's Dominion: An Argument about Abortion and Euthanasia* (London: Harper Collins, 1993) (1994) 2 *Medical Law Review* 255

Dworkin, G, *The Theory and Practice of Autonomy* (New York: Cambridge University Press, 1988)

Dworkin, R (ed.), *The Philosophy of Law* (Oxford: Oxford University Press, 1977)

——, *Taking Rights Seriously*, 2nd impression (corrected) with appendix (London: Duckworth, 1978)

——, *A Matter of Principle* (Oxford: Oxford University Press, 1985)

——, *Law's Empire* (Cambridge, Mass.: Harvard University Press, 1986)

——, "Liberal Community", (1989) 77 *California Law Review* 479

——, "Unenumerated Rights: Whether and How *Roe* v *Wade* Should be Overruled", (1992) 59 *University of Chicago Law Review* 381

——, *Life's Dominion: An Argument about Abortion and Euthanasia* (London: Harper Collins, 1993)

——, "The Foundations of Liberal Equality", in S Darwall (ed.), *Equal Freedom* (Ann Arbor, Mich.: University of Michigan Press, 1996) 214

——, "Assisted Suicide: What the Court Really Said", *New York Review of Books* (25 Sep. 1997) 40

Elias, S and Annas, G, *Reproductive Genetics and the Law* (Chicago: Yearbook Medical Publishers, 1987)

Ely, J, "The Wages of Crying Wolf: Comment on *Roe* v *Wade*", (1973) 82 *Yale Law Journal* 920

English, J, "Abortion and the Concept of a Person", in J Feinberg (ed.), *The Problem of Abortion*, 2nd edn. (Belmont, Calif.: Wadsworth, 1984) 151

Ewing, KD, "The Human Rights Act and Parliamentary Democracy", (1999) 62 *Modern Law Review* 79

Feinberg, J, "Abortion", (1979) in his *Freedom and Fulfillment* (Princeton, NJ: Princeton University Press, 1992) 37

——, "The Nature and Value of Rights", in his *Rights, Justice and the Bounds of Liberty* (Princeton, NJ: Princeton University Press, 1980)

——, "The Moral and Legal Responsibility of the Bad Samaritan", (1984) in his *Freedom and Fulfillment* (Princeton, NJ: Princeton University Press, 1992) 175

Feinberg, J, *Harm to Others* (New York: Oxford University Press, 1984)
——, *Harm to Self* (New York: Oxford University Press, 1986)
Feitshans, I, "Legislating to Preserve Women's Autonomy during Pregnancy", (1995) 14 *Medicine and Law* 397
Feldman, D, "Secrecy, Dignity, or Autonomy? Views of Privacy as a Civil Liberty", (1994) 47 *Current Legal Problems* 41
——, "Privacy-related Rights and their Social Value", in P Birks (ed.), *Privacy and Loyalty* (Oxford: Oxford University Press, 1997) 15
——, "The Developing Scope of Article 8 of the European Convention on Human Rights", [1997] 3 *European Human Rights Law Review* 265
——, "Human Dignity as a Legal Value", Part II [2000] *Public Law* 61
Ferguson, JM, Taylor, CB and Wermuth, B, "A Rapid Behavioural Treatment for Needle Phobics", (1978) 166 *Journal of Nervous and Mental Disease* 294
Field, M, "Controlling the Woman to Protect the Fetus", (Summer 1989) 17 *Law, Medicine and Health Care* 114
Finamore, EP, "*Jefferson v Griffin Spalding County Hospital Authority*: Court-Ordered Surgery to Protect the Life of an Unborn Child", (1983) 9 *American Journal of Law and Medicine* 83
Finer, JJ, "Toward Guidelines for Compelling Cesarean Surgery: of Rights, Responsibilities and Decisional Authenticity", (1991) 77 *Missouri Law Review* 239
Finnis, J, "The Rights and Wrongs of Abortion: A Reply to Judith Thomson", (1973) 2 *Philosophy and Public Affairs* 117; repr. in R Dworkin (ed.), *The Philosophy of Law* (Oxford: Oxford University Press, 1977) 129
Fleischman, AR, "The Fetus is a Patient", in S Cohen and N Taub (eds.), *Reproductive Laws for the 1990s* (Clifton, NJ: Humana Press, 1989) 249
Fletcher, JC, "Healing Before Birth: an Ethical Dilemma", (1984) 87 *Technical Review* 27
——, "Drawing Moral Lines in Fetal Therapy", (1986) 19 *Clinical Obstetrics and Gynecology* 595
Foot, P, "The Problem of Abortion and the Doctrine of Double Effect", in B Steinbock (ed.), *Killing and Letting Die*, (Englewood Cliffs, NJ: Prentice-Hall, 1980) 156; repr. from the *Oxford Review*, No. 5 (1967)
Forsythe, CD, "Homicide of the Unborn Child: The Born Alive Rule and Other Legal Anachronisms", (1987) 21 *Valparaiso University Law Review* 563
Fortin, J, "Legal Protection for the Unborn Child", (1988) 51 *Modern Law Review* 54
Fovargue, S and Miola, J, "Policing Pregnancy: Implications of the *Attorney-General's Reference (No. 3 of 1994)*", (1998) 6 *Medical Law Review* 265
Frank, DA, Augustyn, M, Knight, WG, Pell, T and Zuckerman, B, "Growth, Development, and Behavior in Early Childhood Following Prenatal Cocaine Exposure: A Systematic Review", (2001) 285 *Journal of the American Medical Association* 1613
Fried, C, "Distributive Justice", (1983) 1/1 *Social Philosophy and Policy* 45
Friedman, M, "Autonomy, Social Disruption and Women", in C MacKenzie and N Stoljar (eds.), *Relational Autonomy: Feminist Perspectives on Autonomy, Agency and the Social Self* (New York: Oxford University Press, 2000) 35

——, "Feminism in Ethics: Conceptions of Autonomy", in M Fricker and J Hornsby (eds.), *The Cambridge Companion to Feminism in Philosophy* (Cambridge, Cambridge University Press, 2000) 205

Gallagher, J, "Prenatal Invasions and Interventions: What's Wrong with Fetal Rights?", (1987) 10 *Harvard Women's Law Journal* 9

——, "Fetus as Patient", in N Taub and S Cohen (eds.), *Reproductive Laws for the 1990s* (Clifton, NJ: Humana Press, 1989) 185

de Gama, K, "A Brave New World? Rights Discourse and the Politics of Reproductive Autonomy", in A Bottomley and J Conaghan (eds.), *Feminist Theory and Legal Strategy* (Oxford: Blackwell, 1993) 114

——, "Case Note on *Re S*", (1993) *Journal of Social Welfare and Family Law* 147

Gavison, R, "Privacy and the Limits of Law", (1980) 89 *Yale Law Journal* 421

Gewirtz, P, "Aeschylus' Law", (1988) 101 *Harvard Law Review* 1043

Gillett, G and Reid, MC, "The Case of Medea—a View of Maternal-Fetal Conflict", (1997) 23 *Journal of Medical Ethics* 19

Gilligan, C, *In a Different Voice* (Cambridge, Mass.: Harvard University Press, 1982)

Gilligan, C, Ward, J and Taylor, J (eds.), *Mapping the Moral Domain* (Cambridge, Mass.: Harvard University Press, 1988)

Gillon, R, "Pregnancy, Obstetrics, and the Moral Status of the Fetus", (1988) 14 *Journal of Medical Ethics* 3

——, "Editor's Reply", to C Strong and G Anderson, "The Moral Status of the Near-Term Fetus", (1989) 15 *Journal of Medical Ethics* 25

Ginsburg, RB, "Some Thoughts on Autonomy and Equality in relation to *Roe* v *Wade*", (1985) 63 *North Carolina Law Review* 375

Glantz, LH, "Is the Fetus a Person? A Lawyer's View", in W Bondeson, H Engelhardt, Jr, S Spickler and D Winship (eds.), *Abortion and the Status of the Fetus*, (Dordrecht: D Reidl Publishing Co, 1983) 107

Glazebrook, PR, "What Care Must be Taken of an Unborn Baby?", [1993] 52 *Cambridge Law Journal* 20

Glendon, MA, *Abortion and Divorce in Western Law* (Cambridge, Mass.: Harvard University Press, 1987)

——, *Rights Talk: The Impoverishment of Political Discourse* (New York: Free Press, 1991)

Glover, J, *Causing Death and Saving Lives* (Harmondsworth: Penguin, 1977)

Glover, V and Fisk, NM, "Fetal Pain: Implications for Research and Practice", (1999) 106 *British Journal of Obstetrics and Gynaecology* 881

Goffman, E, "Territories of the Self", in *Relations in Public: Microstudies of the Public Order* (London: Allen Lane, 1971)

Goldbeck-Wood, S, Editorial, "Women's Autonomy in Childbirth", (1997) 314 *British Medical Journal* 1143

Goldberg, S, "Medical Choices During Pregnancy: Whose Decision Is It Anyway?", (1989) 41 *Rutgers Law Review* 591

Grace, J, QC, "Should the Foetus Have Rights in Law?", (1999) 67 *Medico-Legal Journal* 2 57

Gray, J, *Berlin* (London: Fontana, 1995) 33

Greschner, D, "Abortion and Democracy for Women: A Critique of *Tremblay* v *Daigle*", (1990) 35 *McGill Law Journal* 633

Grisso, T and Applebaum, PS, *Assessing Competence to Consent to Treatment: A Guide for Physicians and Other Health Professionals* (New York: Oxford University Press, 1998)

Gross, H, "The Concept of Privacy", (1967) 42 *New York University Law Review* 34

Grubb, A, "Commentary: Treatment without Consent: Adult: *Re T (Adult: Refusal of Treatment)*", (1993) 1 *Medical Law Review* 83

——, "Commentary: Treatment without Consent: Adult: *Re S (Adult: Refusal of Treatment)*", (1993) 1 *Medical Law Review* 92

——, "Commentary: Pre-Natal and Pre-Conception Injury: *X and Y* v *Pal and Others*", (1993) 1 *Medical Law Review* 119

——, "Commentary: Treatment without Consent: Adult: *Re C (Refusal of Medical Treatment)*", (1994) 2 *Medical Law Review* 92

——, "Commentary, Unborn Child (Pre-Natal Injury): Homicide and Abortion: *A-G's Reference (No. 3 of 1994)*", (1995) 3 *Medical Law Review* 302

——, "Commentary: Medical Treatment (Competent Adult): Pregnant Woman and Unborn Child: *Winnipeg Child and Family Services (Northwest Area)* v *DFG*", (1997) 5 *Medical Law Review* 125

——, "Commentary: Unborn Children: 'Persons' and Maternal Conduct: *In the Matter of Baby P (An Unborn Child)*", (1997) 5 *Medical Law Review* 143

——, "Commentary: Detention and Treatment (Competent Adult): Pregnant Woman and Unborn Child: *Winnipeg Child and Family Services (Northwest Area)* v *G (DF)*", (1997) 7 *Medical Law Review* 88

——, "Commentary: Killing the Unborn Child: Abortion and Homicide: *Attorney General's Reference (No. 3 of 1994)*", (1998) 6 *Medical Law Review* 256

——, "Commentary: Incompetent Patient (Adult): *Bland* and the Human Rights Act 1998: *NHS Trust 'A' and 'M'; NHS Trust 'B' and 'H'* ", (2000) 8 *Medical Law Review* 342

Grubb, A and Pearl, D, "Protecting the Life of the Unborn Child", (1987) 10 *Law Quarterly Review* 340

Guest, S, *Ronald Dworkin*, 2nd edn. (Edinburgh: Edinburgh University Press, 1997)

Gunn, MJ, Wong, JG, Clare, ICH and Holland, AJ, "Decision-Making Capacity", (1999) 7 *Medical Law Review* 269

Halper, T, "Privacy and Autonomy: from Warren and Brandeis to *Roe* and *Cruzan*", (1996) 21 *Journal of Medicine and Philosophy* 124

Hammerman, C, Lavie, O, Kornbluth, E, Rabinson, J, Schimmel, MS and Eidelman, AI, "Does Pregnancy Affect Medical Ethical Decision Making?", (1998) 24 *Journal of Medical Ethics* 409

Hare, R, "When Does Potentiality Count? A Comment on Lockwood", in (1988) 2/3 *Bioethics* 214

Harris, J, *The Value of Life* (London: Routledge and Kagan Paul, 1985)

Hart, HLA, *Law, Liberty and Morality* (Oxford: Oxford University Press, 1963)

——, *Punishment and Responsibility* (Oxford: Oxford University Press, 1976)

——, "Between Utility and Rights", 79 *Columbia Law Review* (1979) 828

——, "Are There Any Natural Rights?", in J Waldron (ed.), *Theories of Rights* (Oxford, Oxford University Press, 1984)

Held, V, *Rights and Goods: Justifying Social Action* (New York: The Free Press, 1984)

——, "Feminism and Moral Theory", in E Kittay and D Meyers (eds.), *Women and Moral Theory* (Totowa, NJ: Rowman and Littlefield, 1987) 111

——, "Feminist Transformation of Moral Theory", 50 *Philosophy and Phenomenological Research* (Supplement, Autumn 1990) 321; extracts repr. in P Singer, (ed.), *Ethics* (Oxford: Oxford University Press, 1994) 166

Hendriks, A, "Commentary: *X v Commission of the European Communities* (Judgment of 5 October 1994)", (1995) 2 *European Journal of Health Law* 180

Herman, B, "Mutual Aid and Respect for Persons", (1984) 94 *Ethics* 577

Herring, J, "Caesarean Sections and the Right to Autonomy", [1998] 57 *Cambridge Law Journal* 438

Heyd, D, "Prenatal Diagnosis: Whose Right?", (1995) 21 *Journal of Medical Ethics* 292

Hohfeld, WN, *Fundamental Legal Conceptions as Applied in Judicial Reasoning* (New Haven, Conn.: Yale University Press, 1919)

Honneth, A, "Integrity and Disrespect: Principles of a Conception of Morality Based on a Theory of Recognition", (1992) 20/2 (May) *Political Theory* 190

House of Lords, *Report of the Select Committee on Medical Ethics* (Session 1993-1994) vol. 1

Hunt, M, "The 'Horizontal Effect' of the Human Rights Act", [1998] *Public Law* 423

Hursthouse, R, "Virtue Theory and Abortion", in R Crisp and M Slote (eds.), *Virtue Ethics* (Oxford: Oxford University Press, 1997) 217; repr. from (1991) 20 *Philosophy and Public Affairs* 223

Jacobs, FG and White, RCA, *The European Convention on Human Rights*, 2nd edn. (Oxford: Clarendon Press, 1996)

Jaggar, A, "Feminism in Ethics: Moral Justification", in M Fricker and J Hornsby (eds.), *The Cambridge Companion to Feminism in Philosophy* (Cambridge: Cambridge University Press, 2000) 225

Johnsen, D, "The Creation of Fetal Rights: Conflicts with Women's Constitutional Rights to Liberty, Privacy, and Equal Protection", (1986) 95 *Yale Law Journal* 599

——, "A New Threat to Pregnant Women's Autonomy", (1987) 17 (Aug.) *Hastings Center Report* 33

Johnsen, D, "Shared Interests: Promoting Healthy Births Without Sacrificing Women's Liberty", (1992) 43 *Hastings Law Journal* 569

Kadish, SH, "Respecting Life and Regard for Rights in the Criminal Law", in O Temkin, WK Frankena and SH Kadish (eds.), *Respect for Life in Medicine, Philosophy, and the Law* (Baltimore: John Hopkins University Press, 1977) 83

Kagan, S, "Does Consequentialism Demand Too Much? Recent Work on the Limits of Obligation", (1984) 13 *Philosophy and Public Affairs* 239

Kant, I, *Groundwork of the Metaphysic of Morals*, trans. by HJ Paton, in *The Moral Law* (London: Hutchinson, 1948)

Karpin, I, "Legislating the Female Body: Reproduction Technology and the Reconstructed Woman", (1992) 3 *Columbia Journal of Gender and Law* 325

Kennedy, I, "A Woman and her Unborn Child", in his *Treat Me Right* (Oxford: Oxford University Press, 1992) 364

——, "The Moral Status of the Embyro", in his *Treat Me Right* (Oxford: Oxford University Press, 1992) 119

——, "Commentary: Prenatal Injury: *Burton* v *Islington Health Authority* and *De Martell* v *Merton and Sutton Health Authority*", (1993) 1 *Medical Law Review* 103

——, "Commentary: Refusal of Treatment: Adult Prisoner: *Thor* v *Superior Court*", (1994) 2 *Medical Law Review* 220

——, "Commentary: Consent: Force-feeding of Prisoners: *Secretary of State for the Home Department* v *Robb*", (1995) 3 *Medical Law Review* 189

——, "Commentary: Refusal of Consent, Capacity: *Re MB (Medical Treatment)*", (1997) 5 *Medical Law Review* 317

Kennedy, I and Grubb, A, "Commentary: Withdrawal of Artificial Hydration and Nutrition: Incompetent Adult: *Airedale NHS Trust* v *Bland*", (1993) 1 *Medical Law Review* 359

—— and ——, *Medical Law: Text with Materials*, 2nd edn. (London: Butterworths, 1994)

—— and ——, *Principles of Medical Law* (Oxford: Oxford University Press, 1998)

—— and —— (eds.), *Principles of Medical Law* (3rd cumulative supplement) (Oxford: Oxford University Press, 2000)

—— and ——, *Medical Law*, 3rd edn. (London: Butterworths, 2000)

Kerr, I, "Pre-Natal Fictions and Post-Partum Actions", (1998) 20 *Dalhousie Law Journal* 237

King, PA, "The Juridical Status of the Fetus: a Proposal for Legal Protection of the Unborn", (1979) 77 *Michigan Law Review* 1647

——, "Should Mom be Constrained in the Best Interests of the Fetus?", (1989) 13 *Nova Law Review* 393

Kinlaw, K and Strong, C, "Commentary: Maternal Rights, Fetal Harms", (1991) 21 (May/June) *Hastings Center Report* 22

Kluge, E-HW, "When Cesarean Section Operations Imposed by Court are Justified", (1988) 14 *Journal of Medical Ethics* 206

Kmietowicz, Z, "Doctors Told to Treat Nicotine Addiction as a Disease", (2000) 320 *British Medical Journal* 397

Knopoff, K, "Can a Pregnant Woman Morally Refuse Fetal Surgery?", (1991) 79 *California Law Review* 499

Kolder, VEB, Gallagher J and Parsons, MT, "Court-Ordered Obstetrical Interventions", (1987) 316 *New England Journal of Medicine* 1192

Korsgaard, C, "The Reasons We Can Share: an Attack on the Distinction between Agent-Relative and Agent-Neutral Values", in her *Creating the Kingdom of Ends* (Cambridge: Cambridge University Press, 1996)

Krauss, DJ, "Regulating Women's Bodies: The Adverse Effects of Fetal Rights Theory on Childbirth Decisions and Women of Color", (1991) 26 *Harvard Civil Rights, Civil Liberties Law Review* 523

Kreimer, SF, "Does Pro-Choice Mean Pro-Kevorkian? An essay on *Roe*, *Casey*, and the Right to Die", (1995) 44 *The American University Law Review* 803

Kymlicka, W, *Contemporary Political Philosophy: An Introduction* (Oxford: Oxford University Press, 1990)

——, "Liberal Individualism and Liberal Neutrality", in S Avineri and A de-Shalit (eds.), *Communitarianism and Individualism* (Oxford: Oxford University Press, 1992) 165

Lacey, N, "Theory into Practice? Pornography and the Public/Private Dichotomy", in A Bottomley and J Conaghan (eds.), *Feminist Theory and Legal Strategy* (Oxford: Blackwell, 1993) 112

——, *Unspeakable Subjects: Feminist Essays in Legal and Social Theory* (Oxford: Hart Publishing, 1998)

Ladd, R, "Women in Labour: Some Issues about Informed Consent", (1990) 4/3 *Hypatia* 37; repr. in HB Holmes and L Purdy (eds.), *Feminist Perspectives in Medical Ethics* (Indianapolis, Ind.: Indiana University Press, 1992) 216

Lanham, D, "The Right to Choose to Die with Dignity", (1990) 14 *Criminal Law Journal* 401

Laurance, J, "Caesarean Decision Reduces Women to Walking Wombs", *The Times*, 15 October, 1992, 5

Law Commission, *Report on Injuries to Unborn Children*, No. 60 (1974)

——, *Report on Mental Incapacity*, No. 231 (1995)

Lenow, J, "The Fetus as a Patient: Emerging Rights as a Person?", (1984) 10 *American Journal of Law and Medicine* 1

Levy, JK, "Jehovah's Witnesses, Pregnancy, and Blood Transfusions: A Paradigm for the Autonomy Rights of All Pregnant Women", (1999) 27 *The Journal of Law, Medicine and Ethics* 171

Lewis, P, Law Notes, "*Tameside and Glossop Acute Services v. CH*", (Winter 1996) 7/1 *Dispatches* 4

Lieberman, JR, Mazor, M, Chaim, W and Cohen, A, "The Fetal Right to Live", (1979) 53 *Obstetrics and Gynecology* 515

Lloyd, G, *The Man of Reason: Male and Female in Western Philosophy* (London: Methuen, 1984)

——, Review of M Tooley's *Abortion and Infanticide,* (1986) 64 *Australasian Journal of Philosophy*, Supplement "Women and Philosophy", 144

Lockwood, M, "When Does A Life Begin?", in M Lockwood (ed.), *Moral Dilemmas in Moral Medicine* (Oxford: Oxford University Press, 1985) 9

Loucaides, LG, "Personality and Privacy under the European Convention on Human Rights", (1990) 61 *British Year Book of International Law* 175

Macedo, S, *Liberal Virtues: Citizenship, Virtue and Community in Liberal Constitutionalism* (Oxford: Clarendon Press, 1990)

MacKensie, TB, Nagel, TC and Rothman, BK, "When a Pregnant Woman Endangers Her Fetus", (1986) 16 (Feb.) *Hastings Center Report* 24

MacKenzie, C, "Abortion and Embodiment", (1992) 70/2 *Australasian Journal of Philosophy* 136

MacKenzie, C and Stoljar, N (eds.), *Relational Autonomy: Feminist Perspectives on Autonomy, Agency and the Social Self* (New York: Oxford University Press, 2000)

MacKinnon, CA, *Feminism Unmodified: Discourses on Life and Law* (Cambridge, Mass: Harvard University Press, 1989)

——, *Toward a Feminist Theory of the State* (Cambridge, Mass.: Harvard University Press, 1989) 215

——, "Reflections on Sex Equality Under Law", (1991) 100 *Yale Law Journal* 1281

Mahawold, M, "Beyond Abortion: Refusal of Cesarean Sections", (1989) 3/2 *Bioethics* 106

Majury, D, "Strategizing in Equality", in MA Fineman and NS Thomadsen (eds.), *At the Boundaries of Law, Feminism and Legal Theory* (New York: Routledge, 1991) 320

Martin, S and Coleman, M, "Judicial Intervention in Pregnancy", (1995) 40 *McGill Law Jounrnal* 947

Mason, JK and McCall Smith, RA, *Law and Medical Ethics*, 4th edn. (London: Butterworths, 1994)

—— and ——, RA, *Law and Medical Ethics*, 5th edn. (London: Butterworths, 1999)

Matthieu, D, *Preventing Prenatal Harm: Should the State Intervene?* (Dordrecht: Kluwer, 1991)

Mattingly, S, "The Maternal–Fetal Dyad: Exploring the Two–Patient Obstetric Model", (1992) 22 (Jan./Feb.) *Hastings Center Report* 13

Mattson, SN and Riley, EP, "A Review of the Neurobehavioral Deficits in Children with Fetal Alcohol Syndrome or Exposure or Prenatal Exposure to Alcohol", (1998) 22 *Alcoholism: Clinical and Experimental Research* 279

McCall Smith, RA, "Is Anything Left of Parental Rights?", in A McCall Smith and E Sutherland (eds.), *Family Rights: Family Law and Medical Advance* (Edinburgh: Edinburgh University Press, 1990) 4

——, "Beyond Autonomy", (1997) 14 *Journal of Contemporary Health Law and Policy* 23

McColgan, A, *Women Under the Law: The False Promise of Human Rights* (Harlow: Longman, 2000)

McGinnis, DM, "Prosecution of Mothers of Drug Exposed Babies in Constitutional and Criminal Theory", (1990) 139 *University of Pennsylvania Law Review* 505

McKnight, CJ, "Pluralism, Realism and Truth", in D Archard (ed.), *Philosophy and Pluralism* (Cambridge: Cambridge University Press, 1996) 87

McLachlin, B, "The Charter of Rights and Freedoms: a Judicial Perspective", (1988-89) *University of British Columbia Law Review* 579

McLean, S, "Women, Rights and Reproduction", in S McLean (ed.), *Legal Issues in Human Reproduction* (Aldershot: Gower Press, 1989) 219

McLeod, C and Sherwin, S, "Relational Autonomy, Self-Trust, and Health Care for Patients who are Oppressed", in C MacKenzie and N Stoljar (eds.), *Relational Autonomy: Feminist Perspectives on Autonomy, Agency and the Social Self* (New York: Oxford University Press, 2000) 259

McNulty, M, "Pregnancy Police: The Health Policy and Legal Implications of Punishing Pregnant Women for Harm to their Fetuses", (1987-88) 16 *Review of Law and Social Change* 277

Menlowe, M and McCall Smith, A (eds.), *The Duty to Rescue: the Jurisprudence of Aid* (Aldershot: Dartmouth, 1993)

Merleau-Ponty, M, *The Phenomenology of Perception* (1945), trans. by C Smith (London: Routledge and Kegan Paul, 1962)

Meyers, D, *The Human Body and the Law* (Edinburgh: Edinburgh University Press, 1990)

Michalowski, S, "Court-Authorised Caesarean Sections—The End of a Trend?", (1999) 62 *Modern Law Review* 115

Midgley, M, *Heart and Mind: The Varieties of Moral Experience* (London: Methuen, 1981) 96

Mill, JS, *On Liberty* (1859) in Mill, *Utilitarianism*, M Warnock (ed.), (London: Fontana, 1962)

Millar, D, *Social Justice* (Oxford: Clarendon Press, 1976)

Miller, L, "Two Patients or One? Problems of Consent in Obstetrics", [1993] 1 *Medical Law International* 97

Minow, M, "Interpreting Rights: An Essay for Robert Cover", (1987) 96 *Yale Law Journal* 1860

Mitchinson, W, "Agency, Diversity, and Constraints: Women and their Physicians, Canada, 1850-1950", in S Sherwin (coord.), *The Politics of Women's Health: Exploring Agency and Autonomy* (Philadelphia, Penn.: Temple University Press, 1998) 122

Munzer, SR, *A Theory of Property* (Cambridge: Cambridge University Press, 1990)

Muramoto, O, "Bioethics of the Refusal of Blood by Jehovah's Witnesses", (1998) 24 *Journal of Medical Ethics* 223

Murray, TH, "Moral Obligations to the Not-Yet-Born: The Fetus as Patient", (1987) 14 *Clinics in Perinatology* 329

Myers, J, "Abuse and Neglect of the Unborn: Can the State Intervene?", (1984) 23 *Duquesne Law Review* 1

Nagel, T, "Autonomy and Deontology", from his *The View from Nowhere* (New York: Oxford University Press, 1986) 164; repr. in S Scheffler (ed.), *Consequentialism and its Critics* (Oxford: Oxford University Press, 1988) 142

Neff, CL, "Woman, Womb and Bodily Integrity", (1991) 3 *Yale Journal of Law and Feminism* 327

Nelson, L, Buggy, B and Weil, C, "Forced Medical Treatment of Pregnant Women: 'Compelling Each to Live as Seems Good to the Rest'", (1986) 37 *Hastings Law Journal* 703

Nelson, L and Milliken, N, "Compelled Medical Treatment of Pregnant Women: Life, Liberty and Law in Conflict", (1988) 259 *Journal of the American Medical Association* 1060

Noble-Allgire, A, "Court-ordered Cesarean Sections: a Judicial Standard for Resolving the Conflict Between Fetal Interests and Maternal Rights", (1989) 10 *Journal of Legal Medicine* 211

Noddings, N, *Caring—A Feminine Approach to Ethics and Moral Education* (Berkeley: University of California Press, 1984)

Note, "Constitutional Limitations on State Intervention in Prenatal Care", (1981) 67 *Virginia Law Review* 1051

Note, "Developments in the Law: Medical Technology and the Law", (1990) 103 *Harvard Law Review* 1519

Note, "Rethinking (M)otherhood: Feminist Theory and State Regulation of Pregnancy", (1990) 103 *Harvard Law Review* 1325

Noonan, JT Jr, "An Almost Absolute Value in History", in JT Noonan Jr (ed.), *The Morality of Abortion: Legal and Historical Perspectives* (Cambridge, Mass.: Harvard University Press, 1970); repr. in J Arras and N Rhoden (eds.), *Ethical Issues in Modern Medicine*, 3rd edn. (Mountain View, Calif.: Mayfield Publishing Co, 1989) 261

Noonan, S, "Theorizing Connection", (1992) 30 *Alberta Law Review* 719

Nozick, R, *Anarchy, State and Utopia* (Oxford: Blackwell, 1974)

Nussbaum, M, "An Aristotelian Conception of Rationality", in her *Love's Knowledge: Essays on Philosophy and Literature* (New York: Oxford University Press, 1990) 54

——, "Non-Relative Virtues: An Aristotelian Approach", in M Nussbaum and A Sen (eds.), *The Quality of Life* (Oxford: Clarendon Press, 1993) 242

——, "Feminists and Philosophy", A Review of LM Anthony and C Witt (eds.), *A Mind of One's Own: Feminist Essays on Reason and Objectivity* (Boulder: Westview Press, 1993) *New York Review of Books* (20 Oct. 1994) 59

——, "The Sleep of Reason", *Times Higher Education Supplement* (Feb. 1996) 17

——, "Is Privacy Bad for Women? What the Indian Constitutional Tradition can Teach us about Sex Equality", (April/May 2000) 25 *Boston Review* 42

——, *The Fragility of Goodness: Luck and Ethics in Greek Tragedy and Philosophy*, updated edn. (Cambridge: Cambridge University Press, 2001)

——, *Upheavals of Thought: the Intelligence of Emotions* (Cambridge: Cambridge University Press, 2001)

Nys, H, "Physician Involvement in a Patient's Death: A Continental European Perspective", (1999) 7 *Medical Law Review* 209

Orentlicher, D, "The Influence of Professional Organization on Physician Behavior", (1994) 57 *Albany Law Review* 583

O'Neill, O, *Constructions of Reason: Exploring Kant's Practical Philosophy* (Cambridge: Cambridge University Press, 1989)

——, "Justice, Gender and International Boundaries", in M Nussbaum and A Sen (eds.), *The Quality of Life* (Oxford: Clarendon Press, 1993) 303

——, *Towards Justice and Virtue: A Constructive Account of Practical Reasoning* (Cambridge: Cambridge University Press, 1996)

Oberman, M, "Mother's and Doctors' Orders: Unmasking the Doctor's Fiduciary Role in Maternal-Fetal Conflicts", (2000) 94 *Northwestern University Law Review* 451

Osowski, BD, "The Need for Logic and Consistency in Fetal Rights", (1992) 68 *North Dakota Law Review* 171

Ouellette, A, "New Medical Technology: A Chance to Reexamine Court-Ordered Medical Procedures during Pregnancy", (1994) 57 *Albany Law Review* 927

Overall, C, *Human Reproduction: Principles, Practices, Policies* (Toronto: Oxford University Press, 1993)

Palmer, CS, "The Risks of State Intervention in Preventing Prenatal Alcohol Abuse and the Viability of an Inclusive Approach: Arguments for Limiting Punitive and Coercive Prenatal Alcohol Abuse Legislation in Minnesota", (1999) 10 *Hastings Women's Law Journal* 287

Parent, WA, "Recent Work on the Concept of Privacy", (1983) 20 *American Philosophical Quarterly* 341

Parness, J, "Social Commentary: Values and Legal Personhood", (1981) 83 *West Virginia Law Review* 487

——, "Duty to Prevent Handicaps: Laws Promoting the Prevention of Handicaps to Newborns", (1983) 5 *Western England Law Review* 431

Parness, J and Pritchard, S, "To Be or Not to Be: Protecting the Unborn's Potentiality of Life", (1982) 51 *University of Cincinnati Law Review* 257

Pateman, C, "Feminist Critiques of the Public/Private Dichotomy", in S Benn and G Gaus (eds.), *Public and Private in Social Life* (London: Croom Helm, 1983); repr. in C Pateman, *The Disorder of Women: Democracy, Feminism and Political Theory* (Stanford, Calif.: Stanford University Press, 1989)

Peart, NS, Campbell, AV, Manara, AR, Renowden, SA and Stirrat, GM, "Maintaining a Pregnancy Following a Loss of Capacity", (2000) 8 *Medical Law Review* 275

Petchesky, R, *Abortion and Woman's Choice: The State, Sexuality and Reproductive Freedom* (New York: Longman, 1984)

Phelan, J, "The Maternal Abdominal Wall: A Fortresss Against Fetal Health Care?", (1991) 65 *Southern California Law Review* 461

Phillips, A, *Endangering Democracy* (University Park: Pennsylvania State University Press, 1991)

Phillips, E, "The Status of Sex-specific Fetal Protection Policies", (1992) 57 *Missouri Law Review* 979

Phillips, M, "Maternal Rights v Fetal Rights: Court-ordered Caesareans", (1991) 56 *Missouri Law Review* 411

Plomer, A, Review of R Dworkin's *Life's Dominion: An Argument about Abortion and Euthanasia* (London: HarperCollins, 1993) (1996) 59 *Modern Law Review* 479

Purdy, L, "Are Women Foetal Containers?", (1990) 4/4 *Bioethics* 273

Quintero, RA, Reich, H, Puder, KS, Bardicef, M, Evans, MI, Cotton, DB and Romero, J, "Brief Report: Umbilical-Cord Ligation of an Acardiac Twin by Fetoscopy at 19 Weeks of Gestation", (1994) 330 *New England Journal of Medicine* 469

Raines, E, "Editorial Comment", to R Jurow and RH Paul, "Caesarean Delivery for Fetal Distress Without Maternal Consent", (1984) 63 *Obstetrics and Gynecology* 596

Randall, M, "Pregnant Embodiment and Women's Autonomy Rights in Law: An Analysis of the Language and Politics of *Winnipeg Child and Family Services* v *DFG*", (1999) 62 *Saskatchewan Law Review* 515

Rawls, J, *A Theory of Justice* (Cambridge, Mass.: Belknap Press of Harvard University Press, 1971)

——, "Kantian Constructivism in Moral Theory: The Dewey Lectures 1980", (1980) 77 *Journal of Philosophy* 515

——, "Justice as Fairness: Political not Metaphysical", in S Avineri and A de-Shalit (eds.), *Communitarianism and Individualism* (Oxford: Oxford University Press, 1992) 186

Raz, J, "Right-based Moralities", (1982) in J Waldron (ed.), *Theories of Rights* (Oxford: Oxford University Press, 1984) 182

——, *The Morality of Freedom*, (Oxford: Oxford University Press, 1986)

——, "Rights and Individual Well-Being", first published in (July 1992) 5 *Ratio Juris* 2; repr. in his *Ethics in the Public Domain: Essays in the Morality of Law and Politics* (Oxford: Oxford University Press, 1994) 44

——, "Liberating Duties", first published in (1989) VIII *Law and Philosophy* 3; repr. in his *Ethics in the Public Domain: Essays in the Morality of Law and Politics* (Oxford: Oxford University Press, 1994) 29

——, "Duties of Well-Being", in his *Ethics in the Public Domain: Essays in the Morality of Law and Politics* (Oxford: Oxford University Press, 1994) 3

Reece, E and Homko, C, "Embryoscopy, Fetal Therapy and Ethical Implications", (1994) 57 *Albany Law Review* 709

Regan, D, "Rewriting *Roe v Wade*", (1979) 77 *Michigan Law Review* 1569

Rhoden, N, "The Judge in the Delivery Room: The Emergence of Court-Ordered Cesareans", (1986) 74 *California Law Review* 1951

——, "Trimesters and Technology: Revamping *Roe* v *Wade*", (1986) 95 *Yale Law Journal* 639

——, "Cesareans and Samaritans", (Fall 1987) 15 *Law, Medicine and Health Care* 118

Ridley, D, "Jehovah's Witnesses' Refusal of Blood: Obedience to Scripture and Religious Conscience", (1999) 25 *Journal of Medical Ethics* 469

Robertson, J, "The Right to Procreate and *in utero* Fetal Therapy", (1982) 3 *Journal of Legal Medicine* 333

——, "Procreative Liberty and the Control of Conception, Pregnancy, and Childbirth", (1983) 69 *Virginia Law Review* 405

——, *Children of Choice: Freedom and the New Reproductive Technologies* (Princeton, NJ: Princeton University Press, 1994)

Robertson, J and Schulman, JD, "Pregnancy and Prenatal Harm to Offspring: The Case of Mothers with PKU", (1987) 17 (Aug.) *Hastings Center Report* 23

Rodgers, S, "Case Comment And Note: *Winnipeg Child And Family Services v DFG*: Juridical Interference With Pregnant Women In The Alleged Interest Of The Fetus", (1998) 36 *Alberta Law Review* 711

Rosenblaum, M and Irwin, K, "Pregnancy, Drugs, and Harm Reduction", in CL Wetherington and AB Roman (eds.), *Drug Addiction Research and the Health of Women* (Rockville: National Institutes of Health, 1998) 309

Rothman, BK, "Commentary: When a Pregnant Woman Endangers Her Fetus", (1986) 16 (Feb.) *Hastings Center Report* 25

Royal College of Obstetricians and Gynaecologists Guidelines, "A Consideration of the Law and Ethics in Relation to Court-Authorised Obstetric Intervention", No. 1, April (1994) 15

Ruddick, W and Wilcox, W, "Operating on the Fetus", (1982) 12 (Oct.) *Hastings Center Report* 10

Sachs, BP, Yeh, J, Acker, D, Driscoll, S, Brown, DA and Jewett, JF, "Cesarean Section-Related Maternal Mortality in Massachusetts 1954–1985", (1988) 71 *Obstetrics and Gynaecology* 385

Sandel M (ed.), *Liberalism and its Critics* (Oxford: Blackwell, 1984)

——, "Moral Argument and Liberal Toleration: Abortion and Homosexuality", 77 *California Law Review* (1989) 521

Savulescu, J, "Rational Desires and the Limitation of Life-Sustaining Treatment", (1994) 8/3 *Bioethics* 191

——, "Two Worlds Apart: Religion and Ethics", (1998) 24 *Journal of Medical Ethics* 382

——, "Liberalism, Harm to Others and Involuntary Medical Treatment in Pregnancy", (1997, unpublished, on file with author)

Savulescu J and Momeyer, RW, "Should Informed Consent be Based on Rational Beliefs?", (1997) 23 *Journal of Medical Ethics* 282

Sayre-McCord, G, "Coherent Epistemology and Moral Theory", in W Sinnot-Armstrong and M Timmons (eds.), *Moral Knowledge: New Readings in Moral Epistemology* (New York: Oxford University Press, 1996) 137

Schedler, G, "Women's Reproductive Rights: Is There a Conflict with a Child's Right to be Born Free from Defects?", (1986) 7 *Journal of Legal Medicine* 357

Schoeman, F, "Privacy: Philosophical Dimensions of the Literature", in F Schoeman (ed.), *Philosophical Dimensions of Privacy: An Anthology* (Cambridge: Cambridge University Press, 1984)

Scott, R, "Autonomy and Connectedness: A Re-evaluation of *Georgetown* and its Progeny", (2000) 28 *The Journal of Law, Medicine and Ethics* 55

Seymour, J, *Childbirth and the Law* (Oxford: Oxford University Press, 2000)

Shanner, L, "Case Comment And Note: Pregnancy Intervention And Models Of Maternal-Fetal Relationship: Philosophical Reflections On The *Winnipeg CFS* Dissent", (1998) 36 *Alberta Law Review* 751

Shaw, M, "Conditional Prospective Rights of the Fetus", (1984) 5 *Journal of Legal Medicine* 63

Sheldon, S, "Who is the Mother to Make the Judgment?: The Construction of Woman in English Abortion Law", (1993) 1 *Feminist Legal Studies* 3

——, "The Law of Abortion and the Politics of Medicalisation", in J Bridgman and S Millns (eds.), *Law and Body Politics: Regulating the Female Body* (Aldershot: Dartmouth, 1995) 105

Sherwin, S, "Feminist and Medical Ethics: Two Different Approaches to Contextual Ethics", in HB Holmes and L Purdy (eds.), *Feminist Perspectives in Medical Ethics* (Indianapolis, Ind.: Indiana University Press, 1992)

Shriner, T, "Maternal versus Fetal Rights—a Clinical Dilemma", (1978) 52 *Obstetrics and Gynaecology* 518

Siegal, R, "Reasoning from the Body: A Historical Perspective on Abortion Regulation and Questions of Equal Protection", (1992) 44 *Stanford Law Journal* 261

Simon, EC, "Parental Liability for Prenatal Injury", (1978) 14 *Columbia Journal of Law and Social Problems* 47

Singer, P (ed.), *Ethics* (Oxford: Oxford University Press, 1994)

Skegg, P, *Law, Ethics and Medicine* (Oxford: Clarendon Press, 1985)

Smith, H, "Fetal-Maternal Conflict", in A Buchanan and JL Coleman (eds.), *In Harm's Way: Essays in Honour of Joel Feinberg* (Cambridge, Mass.: Cambridge University Press, 1994) 324

Stapleton, J, "Tort, Insurance and Ideology", (1995) 58 *Modern Law Review* 820

Steinbock, B, *Life Before Birth: the Moral and Legal Status of Embryos and Fetuses* (New York: Oxford University Press, 1992)

Steinbock, B, Marquis, D and Kayata, S "Case Studies—Preterm Labor and Prenatal Harm", (1989) 19 *Hastings Center Report* 32

Steiner, H, *An Essay on Rights* (Oxford: Blackwell, 1994)

Stern, K, "Court-Ordered Caesarean Sections: in Whose Interests?", (1993) 56 *Modern Law Review* 238

Stocker, M, "Duty and Friendship: Toward a Synthesis of Gilligan's Contrastive Moral Concepts", in E Kittay and D Meyers (eds.), *Women and Moral Theory* (Totowa, NJ: Rowman and Littlefield, 1987) 56

Strong, C and Anderson, G, "The Moral Status of the Near-Term Fetus", (1989) 15 *Journal of Medical Ethics* 25

Such, S, "Lifesaving Medical Treatment for the Nonviable Fetus: Limitations on State Authority under *Roe* v *Wade*", (1986) 56 *Fordham Law Review* 961

Sunstein, CR, "Neutrality in Constitutional Law (With Special Reference to Abortion, Pornography and Surrogacy)", (1992) 92 *Columbia Law Review* 1

Swift, A, and Mulhall, S, *Liberals and Communitarians*, 2nd edn. (Oxford: Blackwell, 1996)

Taylor, C, "Atomism", in S Avineri and A de-Shalit (eds.), *Communitarianism and Individualism* (Oxford: Oxford University Press, 1992)

Teixeira, JMA, Fisk, NM and Glover, V, "Association Between Maternal Anxiety in Pregnancy and Increased Uterine Artery Resistance Index: Cohort Based Study", (1999) 318 *British Medical Journal* 153

Thomson, JJ, "A Defence of Abortion", (1971) 1 *Philosophy and Public Affairs* 1; repr. in P Singer (ed.), *Applied Ethics* (Oxford: Oxford University Press, 1986) 37

——, "The Trolley Problem", (1985) 94 *Yale Law Journal* 1395

——, *The Realm of Rights* (Cambridge: Cambridge University Press, 1990)

Thompson, M, "After *Re S*", (1994) 2 *Medical Law Review* 127

Thorpe, LJ, "The Caesarean Section Debate", [1997] *Family Law* 663

Tooley, M, "Abortion and Infanticide", (1972) in P Singer (ed.), *Applied Ethics* (Oxford: Oxford University Press, 1986) 57

Tribe, L, *American Constitutional Law*, 2nd edn. (Mineola, NY: Foundation Press, 1988)

Tushnet, M, "Legal Conventionalism in the US Constitutional Law of Privacy", in E Paul, F Miller Jr, and J Paul (eds.), *The Right to Privacy* (Cambridge: Cambridge University Press, 2000) 141

Veitch, S, *Moral Conflict and Legal Reasoning* (Oxford: Hart Publishing, 1999)

Verkerk, M, "A Care Perspective on Coercion and Autonomy", (1999) 13:3/4 *Bioethics* 358

Wacks, R, *Personal Information: Privacy and the Law* (Oxford: Clarendon Press, 1989)

Wadham, J and Mountfield, H, *Blackstone's Guide to the Human Rights Act 1998* (London: Blackstone, 1999)

Waldron, J (ed.), *Theories of Rights* (Oxford: Oxford University Press, 1984)

Walzer, M, *Interpretation and Social Criticism* (Cambridge, Mass.: Harvard University Press, 1987)

Warren, MA, "On the Moral and Legal Status of Abortion", (1973) 57 (1) *The Monist* 43; repr. in J Arras and N Rhoden (eds.), *Ethical Issues in Modern Medicine*, 3rd edn. (Mountain View, Calif.: Mayfield Publishing Co, 1989) 276

Warren, MA, "The Moral Significance of Birth", (1989) 4 *Hypatia* 3; repr. in HB Holmes and L Purdy (eds.), *Feminist Perspectives in Medical Ethics* (Indianapolis, Ind.: Indiana University Press, 1992) 198

——, Review of J Robertson, *Children of Choice: Freedom and the New Reproductive Technologies* (Princeton, NJ: Princeton University Press, 1994) (1996) 10 *Bioethics* 161

——, *Moral Status: Obligations to Persons and Other Living Things* (Oxford: Oxford University Press, 1997)

Weinburg, SR, "A Maternal Duty to Protect Fetal Health?", (1983) 58 *Indiana Law Journal* 531

Wells, C, "On the Outside Looking in: Perspectives on Enforced Caesareans", in S Sheldon and M Thomson (eds.), *Feminist Perspectives on Health Care Law* (London: Cavendish Publishing, 1998) 237

Wertheimer, R, "Understanding the Abortion Argument", (1971) 1 *Philosophy and Public Affairs* 67

West, R, "Jurisprudence and Gender", (1988) 55 *University of Chicago Law Review* 1

——, "Taking Freedom Seriously", (1990) 104 *Harvard Law Review* 43

Whitfield, A, "Common Law Duties to Unborn Children", (1993) 1 *Medical Law Review* 28

Williams, B, "A Critique of Utilitarianism", in JJC Smart and B Williams (eds.), *Utilitarianism: For and Against* (Cambridge: Cambridge University Press, 1973)

——, *Moral Luck: Philosophical Papers 1973–1980* (Cambridge: Cambridge University Press, 1981)

Williams, G, "The Fetus and the Right to Life", [1994] 53 *Cambridge Law Journal* 71

Wolf, S, *Freedom within Reason* (New York: Oxford University Press, 1994)

Wreen, MJ, "Autonomy, Religious Values and Refusal of Lifesaving Medical Treatment", (1991) 17 *Journal of Medical Ethics* 124

Young, I, *Justice and the Politics of Difference* (Princeton, NJ: Princeton University Press, 1990)

Index of Names

Subject Index